Paris '44

PARIS '44

The City of Light Redeemed

William Mortimer-Moore

CASEMATE
uk

Oxford & Philadelphia

Published in Great Britain and
the United States of America in 2015 by
CASEMATE PUBLISHERS
10 Hythe Bridge Street, Oxford OX1 2EW, UK
and
1950 Lawrence Road, Havertown, PA 19083, USA

Hardcover Edition: ISBN 978-1-61200-343-6
Digital Edition: ISBN 978-1-61200-344-3

A CIP record for this book is available from the British Library

Printed in the United Kingdom by Short Run Press, Exeter

For a complete list of Casemate titles, please contact:

CASEMATE PUBLISHERS (UK)
Telephone (01865) 241249
Fax (01865) 794449
Email: casemate-uk@casematepublishers.co.uk
www.casematepublishers.co.uk

CASEMATE PUBLISHERS (US)
Telephone (610) 853-9131
Fax (610) 853-9146
Email: casemate@casematepublishers.com
www.casematepublishers.com

For My Mother

Contents

Preface

A Mission of National Importance

GENERAL LECLERC HAD BEEN FOND OF PARTRIDGE SHOOTING since his boyhood in Picardy, and gladly pursued this sport again during off-duty hours in French Morocco during late 1943. His chief of staff, Colonel Jacques de Guillebon, or his young ADC, Lieutenant Christian Girard, usually accompanied him on these outings. Both men, like himself, had followed General de Gaulle and the small but splendid flag of "Free France" since the country fell to the Germans in June 1940. But on that first Sunday of December Leclerc was accompanied by Captain Alain de Boissieu.

While Leclerc had been in Africa since de Gaulle gave him his first mission in August 1940, Boissieu's route to the "Free French", as de Gaulle's followers were known, was more tortuous. Captured in 1940 following one of the last French cavalry charges, Boissieu was among a select group of officers who escaped from Germany to the Soviet Union only to be re-imprisoned. But when Hitler attacked the Soviet Union in June 1941, Sir Stafford Cripps, Great Britain's ambassador to Moscow, negotiated their release.

De Gaulle always favoured men who made strenuous efforts to join him, and from this group, known as "Russians", he selected Boissieu and Captain Pierre Billotte for his staff. Though Boissieu repeatedly begged to join Leclerc, de Gaulle preferred using him as a roving envoy to French colonies turning to Free France for leadership rather than Marshal Pétain's collaborationist government in Vichy. In late 1943, de Gaulle finally allowed Boissieu to join *La Colonne Leclerc* when its successful conquest of southern Libya was finished and Leclerc was forming a new armoured division around his original force.

But Leclerc was anxious, needing to know what he was aiming at. Which of the French Army's new American-equipped armoured divisions would go to England and join in the invasion of Europe? What could he tell his men? When would he finally receive all the equipment he had been promised? Only General de Gaulle could tell him and, knowing that de Gaulle liked the dark, studious-looking Boissieu, he was the obvious envoy to send. There were even inklings of romance between Boissieu and de Gaulle's pretty daughter Elizabeth.

While spaniels gathered fallen partridges, Leclerc briefed Boissieu. Uppermost in Leclerc's thoughts was that during September the Allies had informally agreed that a French division should join in the forthcoming invasion of northern France and "assure the liberation of Paris".[1]

On 6 December Boissieu boarded a Dakota transport aircraft for Algiers. Usually dour-faced, de Gaulle greeted Boissieu with a slight smile before reading Leclerc's letter. "You tell Leclerc that I attach great importance to what happens to his division which, if it becomes necessary, will have to take the artillery it is still lacking from another large unit," said de Gaulle firmly. "As for the Tank Destroyer regiment, maybe he will have to choose one from among those already formed. Your division, I very much hope, will be put at the disposal of the Allied command in Europe, but make it clear to Leclerc that if it happens that I need him for a mission of national importance then in such a case he must obey my instructions only. The situation among the Allies is not good, anything could happen. American politicians manoeuvre against me; in particular Roosevelt wants to impose AMGOT* in France, along with currency printed by the American treasury. All this is intolerable and at the first opportunity I will return to France

---

* AMGOT = Allied Military Government of Occupied Territories, an organisation for recreating basic government functions once any part of a Nazi-occupied country was liberated.

with or without the Allies' consent. You mustn't speak of this except with Leclerc who must keep it secret even from his closest associates. If the Allies knew any of this they would invent the slightest pretext not to take the 2e DB* to England. I will have to see Eisenhower on 24 December when everything will be decided. There is a difference between Roosevelt, who understands nothing of French affairs and who moreover doesn't like France—of which I am certain—and Eisenhower, who understands our political problems. In any case the conduct of French troops under General Juin has shown him what we can do. As regards the necessary, it is understood, we must try to find the self-propelled guns and three artillery regiments that you're lacking, but tell Leclerc not to worry himself unduly. If I can obtain the transport for one division it will be his that goes to Great Britain."[2]

De Gaulle wrote the gist of this as a handwritten note and passed it to Boissieu. But when Boissieu turned towards the secretary's door, de Gaulle shouted, "Where do you think you're going?"

"To Madame Aubert to get it typed up," replied Boissieu.

"I don't want a record of this," said de Gaulle. "If the Americans know that I intend to use the 2e DB to re-establish the French state in Paris, they won't transport you. Leclerc must keep this to himself."[3]

Boissieu stayed in Algiers to chase up the balance of the 2e DB's artillery, which had erroneously been sent to Anzio, even though equipment allocated to the French rearmament programme was marked with long *Tricolore* stripes before leaving the USA. But, when Boissieu returned to the 2e DB's HQ in Morocco, Leclerc grinned broadly at de Gaulle's note. Now Leclerc wanted Boissieu to visit de Gaulle again, *before* the meeting with Eisenhower planned for 24 December.

De Gaulle received Boissieu at Les Glycines on 15 December. Leclerc's second letter assured Free France's leader that the 2e DB would do what he expected, but they could not embark for England without the promised equipment and missing artillery regiments.

---

* *Deuxième Division Blindée*, Leclerc's famous Second Armoured Division, always called the *Deuxième DB* in French.

Recognising how much Leclerc wanted this plum mission, de Gaulle smiled and explained to Boissieu that while he wanted the 2e DB to liberate Paris, this goal was only notional to *les Anglo-Saxons.* Then, taking a piece of writing paper from his desk, de Gaulle wrote that he appointed General Leclerc "interim military governor" of Paris, while saying that the appointment was "interim" because General Koenig* would take over after the liberation. While Madame Aubert typed it up, de Gaulle insisted to Boissieu that this document was for Leclerc's eyes only.[4]

Immediately afterwards Boissieu telephoned General Leclerc, "Everything is going for the best." Back in Temara, Boissieu suffered a serious malarial attack and was hospitalised in Rabat.[5]

On 30 December 1943, General de Gaulle welcomed the Allied Supreme Commander, General Dwight D. Eisenhower, to Les Glycines to discuss the progress of the US-sponsored French rearmament programme. De Gaulle also obtained Eisenhower's verbal confirmation that Leclerc's division would join in "the northern operation" while General de Lattre de Tassigny's French First Army prepared for landings in Provence. In closing, de Gaulle asked Eisenhower to promise that the Allies would not enter Paris without French troops. Eisenhower replied, "You may be sure that I have no notion of entering Paris without your troops. People have given me the reputation of being abrupt. I have the feeling that you informed your opinion of me without having made enough allowance for the problems I was confronted with in performing my mission with regard to my government. At that time it seemed to me that you did not want to put your full weight behind me. As a government you had your own very difficult problems. But it seemed to me that the carrying out of operations had absolute priority. (At present) I admit that I was unjust to you and I had to tell you so."

---

* General Koenig commanded the First Free French Brigade whose stand at Bir Hakeim on the southern end of the Gazala Line in June 1942 was the first major action the French had fought against the Germans since the fall of France in 1940.

De Gaulle always regarded the French language as part of France's identity, always to be kept in the forefront. On this occasion he relented. "You are a man," he told Eisenhower in English, before assuring him that France would give him every assistance; especially "when confronted with the question of Paris in the field of action".

"I am prepared," continued Eisenhower, "to make a declaration stating the confidence I have derived from our contacts, acknowledging my injustice with regard to you, and adding that you have said that you are ready to help me in my mission. For the forthcoming French campaign I shall need your support, the assistance of your civil servants, and the backing of French public opinion. I do not yet know what theoretical position my government will require me to adopt in my relations with you. But apart from principles there are facts. I must tell you that, as far as facts are concerned I shall acknowledge no other authority in France other than yours."[6]

Eisenhower knew that President Roosevelt saw de Gaulle as something between a twentieth-century Joan of Arc and an unelected Franco-style dictator. Any undertakings given to de Gaulle regarding Paris were subject to whatever realities prevailed once the Allies landed in France. The US high command regarded the re-equipped French forces training in French North Africa, Leclerc's division included, as under their operational control, to be used as they saw fit. Every bullet the 2e DB fired on the training ranges was manufactured in the USA. But to keep France's end up, de Gaulle, in the name of the Committee for National Liberation, mentioned that if the Allies' use of French units did not "correspond to the national interest, our armies and our freedom of action", those units might be withdrawn. While Eisenhower's priorities were practical and military, de Gaulle's hopes of re-establishing the French state depended on Leclerc entering Paris as its Liberator.

Acronyms

2e DB = *Deuxième Divison Blindee*. French Second Armoured Division.

AMGOT = Allied Military Government of Occupied Territories.

CFLN = *Comité Français de Libération National*. The French National Liberation Committee which, under de Gaulle's leadership, evolved into a government in exile.

CGT = *Confédération générale du travail*. A French trade union.

CNR = *Conseil National de la Résistance*. The National Council of the Resistance created in 1943, of which Jean Moulin was the first president. Many of its members were involved in de Gaulle's preparations to reinstate the French Republic.

COMAC = *Comité Militaire d'Action*. – Military action committee consisting of three men, the three 'Vs,' who had the authority to order military operations to the resistance in France.

COSSAC = Chief of Staff Supreme Allied Commander and those under his authority.

CP = Command Post.

CPL = *Comité Parisien de Libération*. Paris Liberation Committee created in 1943 in parallel with other resistance committees; its role was preparation during the period before the insurrection but not actual fighting. Their role included the identification of *collabos*, hence the interrogators of Sacha Guitry in Cartier-Bresson's photograph are wearing CPL arm bands.

ERR = *Einsatzstab Reichsleiter Rosenberg.* A German art theft bureau.

FFI = *Forces Françaises de l'Intérieure.* French Forces of the Interior or, in other words, the Resistance, including all its factions, under the nominal leadership of General Marie-Pierre Koenig.

FTP = *Franc-Tireurs et Partisans.* The most disciplined and committed of the Communist inspired resistance groups, from which men like Henri Rol-Tanguy emerged.

GPRF = *Gouvernement Provisoire de la République Française.* – De Gaulle's provisional government which emerged from the CFLN.

GT = *Groupement Tactique.* Battle group.

LST = Landing Ship Tank.

LVF = *Légion des Volontaires Français.* French soldiers fighting voluntarily for the Wehrmacht in Russia.

OKW = *Oberkommando der Wehrmacht.* The German High Command.

OSS = Office of Strategic Services. US intelligence agency.

P1 = Resistance code for the Paris area.

PPF = *Parti Populaire Français.* French fascist party led by Jacques Doriot.

RBFM = *Régiment Blindée des Fusiliers Marins.* Leclerc's anti-tank regiment recruited from naval personnel.

RCA = *Régiment des Chasseurs d'Afrique.* A colonial hussar-style cavalry regiment.

RCC = *Régiment des Chars de Combat.* Tank regiment.

RMSM = *Régiment de Marche de Spahis Marocains.* Leclerc's reconnaissance regiment.

RMT = *Régiment de Marche du Tchad.* The Chad Regiment.

SD = *Sicherheitsdienst.* German security service within the SS.

SHAEF = Supreme Headquarters Allied Expeditionary Force.

SIPO = *Sicherheitspolizei.* Nazi security police.

STO = *Service de Travail Obligatoire.* German war work imposed on French populace.

TD = Tank Destroyer. A long-range 76mm anti-tank gun mounted in a light, fully turning turret on a Sherman hull.

Dramatis Personae of Key Characters

The "2e DB" (Deuxième Division Blindée—French Second Armoured Division)

Colonel Pierre Billotte—ADC to General de Gaulle from 1942 until 1944. When Leclerc needed a third battle group commander in July 1944, de Gaulle sent Billotte to replace Marcel Malaguti. Billotte later became a general and distinguished postwar politician.

Captain Alain de Boissieu—Acted as de Gaulle's roving emissary before joining Leclerc in 1943. By 1944 Boissieu was head of the 2e DB's HQ protection squadron.

Captain Jacques Branet—An experienced cavalry officer captured in 1940 who escaped to join de Gaulle. He trained an armoured squadron in England and later led the assault on the Hotel Meurice.

Colonel Louis Dio—One of Leclerc's old-timers from Chad who became a 2e DB battle group commander.

Captain Raymond Dronne—Journalist, lawyer, author and post-war politician. Also one of Leclerc's most experienced infantry officers from the Chad era, appointed to command the Chad Regiment's 9th Company, *La Nueve*, composed almost entirely of Spanish Republicans.

Lieutenant Philippe de Gaulle—Naval officer and son of General Charles de Gaulle, Philippe transferred to Raymond Maggiar's *Régiment*

Blindée des Fusiliers Marins (the 2e DB's anti-tank regiment) shortly after D-Day.

Lieutenant Christian Girard—Pre-war trainee diplomat from Paris. Leclerc's urbane and well-mannered ADC.

Commandant (Major) André Gribius—Also from Paris, Gribius joined the 2e DB as part of Langlade's 12e Chasseurs d'Afrique regiment, quickly becoming Leclerc's G3, head of operations planning.

Colonel Jacques de Guillebon—Another of Leclerc's old-timers from Chad days, subsequently the 2e DB's chief of staff.

Commandant (Major) Jean Fanneau de la Horie—Saint-Cyr classmate and old friend of Leclerc who remained loyal to Vichy until 1942. Leclerc claimed la Horie from du Vigier's 1e DB when forming his division. La Horie played a major role on Liberation Day.

Colonel Paul de Langlade—Loyal to Vichy until after Operation Torch. When Leclerc formed his division, Langlade brought in his 12e Chasseurs d'Afrique, comprising enough men for two armoured regiments on the US model. He subsequently became one of the 2e DB's three battle group commanders.

Major-General (*général de division*) Philippe *Leclerc* de Hauteclocque—A high flyer throughout his early military career, as soon as Leclerc presented himself to de Gaulle in July 1940 he was given important tasks in the Free French interest, culminating in command of the 2e DB.

Colonel Jacques Massu—Former camel soldier of *La Coloniale* and Free French old-timer from Chad, Massu commanded the Chad Regiment's second battalion. Subsequently a post-war paratroop general.

Colonel Paul Repiton-Préneuf—A pre-war oil executive who became the 2e DB's head of intelligence.

Colonel Joseph Putz—An experienced French officer with left-wing leanings who fought in the Spanish Civil War. He commanded the Chad Regiment's third battalion and was Dronne's immediate superior.

The Free French Establishment

General (*général de brigade*) Charles de Gaulle—The French Army's leading tank expert during the 1930s who founded 'Free France' after the 1940 armistice, enabling Frenchmen to continue the war beside the Allies. President of France, 1944–1946 and 1958–1970.

General Alphonse Juin—Saint-Cyr classmate of de Gaulle who commanded a division in the Italian campaign and became de Gaulle's chief of staff after the liberation of Rome in June 1944.

General Marie-Pierre Koenig—One of Free France's earliest supporters who led the 1942 defence of Bir Hakeim against Rommel. De Gaulle made Koenig nominal head of the *Forces Françaises de l'Interieure* – ie, the Resistance.

Charles Luizet—Saint-Cyr classmate of Leclerc who was based in French North Africa when France fell in 1940. He immediately became one of de Gaulle's agents. In August 1944 he was sent to Paris to replace Bussière as Prefect of Police.

Alexandre Parodi—A senior civil servant and experienced *clandestin* of the Resistance. He was head of de Gaulle's 'Delegation.'

Edgard Pisani—Law student and *résistant*, Pisani was sent to the Préfecture of Police to act as Luizet's deputy.

Germans

Otto Abetz—The Nazi ambassador to Occupied France based in Paris' Rue de Lille, from where he supervised the despoliation of France.

Lieutenant Dankwart Graf von Arnim—Arnim was Boineberg-Lengsfeld's ADC and subsequently performed the same role for General von Choltitz, his distant cousin.

Emil 'Bobby' Bender—A senior Abwehr (military intelligence) official with anti-Nazi sympathies.

Lieutenant-General Wilhelm von Boineberg-Lengsfeld—The penultimate German military governor of Paris and an anti-Hitler conspirator. One of the luckiest survivors of the failed 20 July coup.

General Dietrich von Choltitz—The last German military governor of Paris, appointed on the basis of his record on the Eastern Front. Unbeknown to General Burgdorf, who drew up the short list, von Choltitz was loosely connected to the 20 July conspirators.

Ernst Junger—German writer and intellectual based in Paris as part of the Occupation forces.

Field Marshal Hans von Kluge—German Commander of the Western Front who was involved in the 20 July coup and subsequently committed suicide upon learning of a summons to Berlin.

Field Marshal Walter Model—Experienced German general from the Eastern Front, where he earned the reputation of 'Hitler's Fireman', replaced von Kluge as German commander in the West.

SS Major Kurt Neifeind—Sadistic officer based in the Rue de Saussaies Gestapo HQ, involved in the Santé Prison incident, 20 July and the putative disarmament of the Paris Police.

SS General Karl Oberg—The SS chief in France. A porcine man, Oberg was believed to detest Nazi excesses and had a good working relationship with the penultimate German military governor of France, General Karl-Heinrich von Stulpnagel, based on old regimental ties.

Erich von Posch-Pastor—Anti-Nazi Austrian Catholic working for the German occupation authorities, recruited as an agent by the Resistance and as an associate of Raoul Nordling (see below).

General Hans Speidel—Chief of Staff of Army Group B and privy to the 20 July plot.

General Karl-Heinrich von Stulpnagel—The penultimate German military governor of France. Stulpnagel was a deeply conflicted man, capable of cooperating with anti-Jewish policies while plotting against Hitler.

General Otto von Stulpnagel—Cousin of the above and the first German military governor of France, appointed in the summer of 1940.

Sonderfuhrer Robert Wallraf—German officer and diarist based at the Hotel Crillon.

Collaborators

Jean Bassompierre—*Milice* (Vichy militia) officer. Undoubtedly brave, Bassompierre had fought in Russia. His performance at the Santé Prison uprising mitigated potential Nazi reprisals but contributed to his own indictment after the war.

General Brécard—A well known and popular cavalry general between the wars, Brécard was sucked into collaborationist politics by his loyalty to Pétain.

René Bouffet—Prefect of the Department of the Seine whose offices were situated at the Hotel de Ville.

Robert Brasilach—Collaborationist journalist arrested at the liberation.

Amédée Bussière—Last Vichy prefect of the Paris Police based at the Préfecture on the Ile de la Cité.

Joseph Darnand—Head of the *Milice*—the French pro-Nazi militia which fought both the Resistance and the Allies.

Pierre Drieu de la Rochelle—A talented writer and Vichy supporter.

Philippe Henriot—Vichy's head of propaganda who encouraged young Frenchmen into the *Milice*.

Max Knipping—Head of the *Milice* in northern France.

Pierre Laval—Vichy's Prime Minister based between Vichy and the traditional French premier's residence at the Hotel Matignon.

Jean Mansuy—*Milicien* and murderer of Georges Mandel.

Marshal Philippe Pétain—One of France's most successful generals in the First World War for defending Verdun and healing the French Army after the 1917 mutinies. However, in 1940, seeing France being overwhelmed, Pétain asked the Nazis for an armistice and created the collaborationist Vichy régime.

Pierre Taittinger—A member of the champagne family who previously had his own right-wing political party during the 1930s, the *Jeunesses Patriotes*. Also a member of the Paris Municipal Council for the Vendôme *quartier* and Head of the Municipal Council.

The Resistance (undercover names are in Italic)

Georges Bidault—Replaced Jean Moulin as chairman of the CNR (*Conseil National de la Résistance*) and became foreign minister in de Gaulle's post-liberation provisional government.

General DP Bloch *Dassault*—French general and *résistant*, later Chancellor of the Légion d'Honneur.

Jacques *Chaban*-Delmas—The youngest 'brigadier general' in the French Army after a political appointment, Chaban-Delmas was General de Gaulle's military delegate to the Paris Resistance.

Captain '*Gallois*' (Roger Cocteau)—A cousin of Jean Cocteau, *Gallois* joined the Resistance via *Ceux de la Résistance* and became a staff officer under *Rol*-Tanguy in 1944.

Roger Ginsberger (*Villon*)—One of COMAC's three 'Vs.' Son of a rabbi and a left-winger.

Leo Hamon—Lawyer and senior Resistance activist. On 20 August he was one of the architects of Nordling's truce.

Maurice Kriegel *Valrimont*—One of COMAC's three 'Vs.' A militant Communist and Resistance activist raised to COMAC in the spring of 1944.

Colonel *Lizé* (Jean Tessier de Marguerittes)—Formerly an artillery officer; though traditional, Lizé was prepared to march with men of the Left for the Liberation of France and headed the Resistance of the Department of the Seine in 1944.

André Malraux—French Resistance officer and well-known writer.

Raymond Massiet *Dufresne*—*Résistant* originating from *Ceux de la Résistance*, one of Colonel Lizé's officers.

Jean Moulin—Formerly Prefect of the Eure et Loir, Moulin created MUR (*Mouvements Unis de la Résistance*) the forerunner of the CNR (*Conseil National de la Résistance*) but was arrested on 21 June 1943 at Caluire (Lyons) in circumstances that remain controversial.

Doctor Robert Monod—Surgeon and Resistance member who played a key role in helping Roger Cocteau-*Gallois* reach the Allied lines.

Alexandre de Saint-Phalle—Banker and *résistant* who was the first intermediary between Raoul Nordling and the Resistance. Saint-Phalle's Rue Séguier home was used as a Resistance HQ during the insurrection.

Pierre Sonneville—Former naval officer and *résistant*, sent from London in early 1944 but who found himself sidelined by the Resistance's strong FTP element.

Roger Stéphane—FFI *Résistant* originating with *Combat*, who led the assault on the Hotel de Ville. Later a gay activist in post-war France.

Colonel Henri *Rol*-Tanguy—FTP *résistant* and former combatant in the Spanish Civil War, *Rol*-Tanguy graduated through trade union politics and industrial sabotage to become one of the most disciplined Resistance leaders in 'P1' – the Paris area, and a hero of the Liberation.

Charles Tillon—Founding member of left-wing resistance group *Francs Tireurs et Partisans,* or FTP.

Dr. Victor Veau—A distinguished and elderly surgeon.

Count Jean de Vogüé (*Vaillant*)—One of COMAC's three 'Vs.' a populist aristocrat and former naval officer, Vogüé joined the Resistance through *Ceux de la Résistance* and graduated to COMAC in spring 1944.

Other French, Parisian and non-aligned characters

Pastor Marc Boegner—Distinguished Protestant clergyman and diarist of the Nazi Occupation.

Colette—Famous writer of libidinous, semi-autobiographical novels and stories who also hid her Jewish husband throughout the Occupation.

Henri Culmann—French civil servant at the Ministry of Industrial Production.

Jean Galtier-Boissière—Journalist and former proprietor of the satirical journal *Le Crapouillot,* who gave up writing for the duration of the Occupation but nevertheless kept a detailed diary.

Françoise Gilot—Beautiful art student who became Picasso's mistress early in 1944.

Sacha Guitry—Well known playwright, actor and impresario based at the Théatre Madeleine, and unfairly accused of collaboration.

Georges Mandel—Distinguished Jewish-French politician from the inter-war era who opposed appeasement and advocated continuing the war in 1940. Handed over to the Germans by Vichy, Mandel was returned to France in 1944 simply so the *Milice* could murder him.

René Naville—Swiss consul involved in humanitarian missions in Nazi-occupied Paris.

Raoul Nordling—Swedish Consul General based at the Rue d'Anjou. Basically a Parisian despite the technicality of his Swedish nationality, Nordling's father had been Swedish consul before him.

Félix Pacaut—Butler to the Rothschild family at their Avenue de Marigny mansion.

Pablo Picasso—Famous Spanish-born modernist artist residing on the Avenue des Grands Augustins, Picasso had Resistance connections but was too well known for the Nazis to dare touch him.

Rose Valland—Doughty curator at the Musée de Jeu de Paume who catalogued German art theft.

British and Americans

General Raymond 'Tubby' Barton—Commander of the US 4th Infantry Division.

General Omar Bradley—Commander of the US 12th Army Group.

Colonel David Bruce—OSS officer and diplomat.

Alfred Duff-Cooper—Churchill's liaison to the Free French, first British ambassador to France after the liberation, diarist and commentator.

General Dwight D. Eisenhower—Supreme Commander Allied Expeditionary Force.

General Leonard Gerow—Commander US Vth Corps. Leclerc's corps commander for the liberation of Paris who advised caution regarding German forces north of the city.

Major General Sir Francis (Freddie) de Guingand—Montgomery's chief of staff, who first welcomed Leclerc to Montgomery's Tripoli HQ in January 1943.

General Wade Haislip—Commander US XVth Corps. Leclerc's corps commander for the Argentan-Falaise campaign, and again through the winter of 1944.

Ernest Hemingway—US novelist and war correspondent.

General Courtenay Hodges—Commander of the US First Army.

General Sir Hastings Ismay—Secretary to Churchill's War Cabinet.

Field Marshal Sir Bernard L. Montgomery—Commander of the British 21st Army Group.

Malcolm Muggeridge—British Intelligence officer.

General George S. Patton—Commander of the US Third Army.

Maps

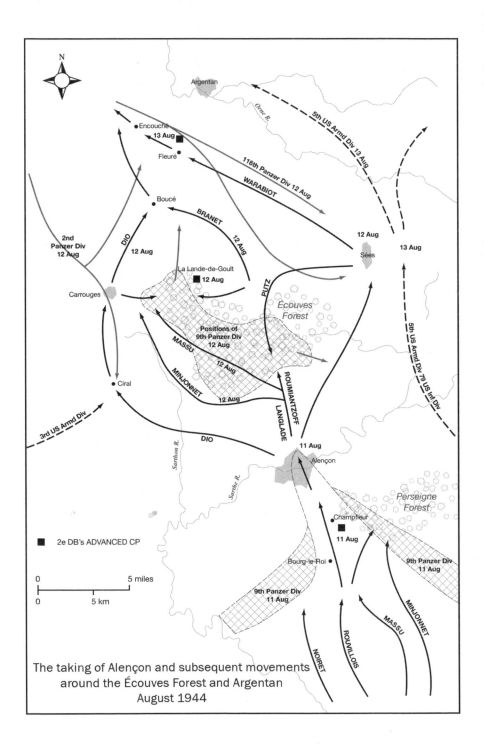

The taking of Alençon and subsequent movements
around the Écouves Forest and Argentan
August 1944

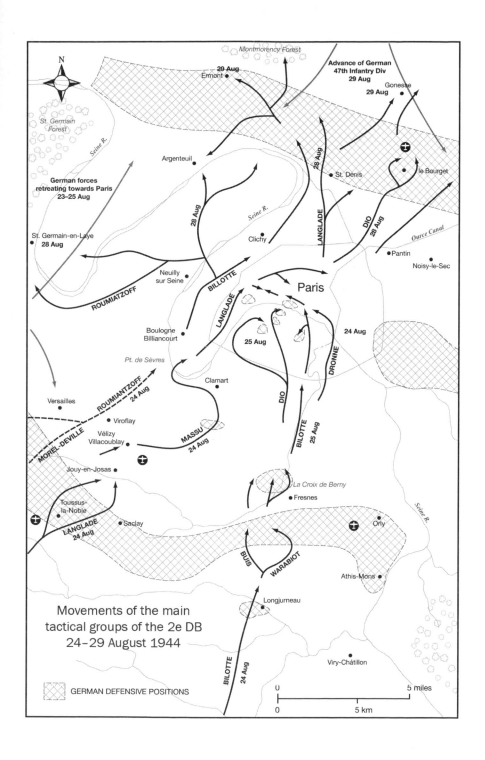

N

Montmorency Forest

**Advance of German
47th Infantry Div
29 Aug**

29 Aug
Ermont ●

●───── 29 Aug
Gonesse ●

St. Germain
Forest

Seine R.

Argenteuil ●

28 Aug

St. Dénis ●

le Bourget ●

**German forces
retreating towards Paris
23–25 Aug**

LANGLADE

DIO
28 Aug

Ource Canal

Clichy ●

St. Germain-en-Laye ●
28 Aug

Seine R.

Pantin ●

Noisy-le-Sec ●

Neuilly
sur Seine ●

BILLOTTE

Paris

ROUMIATZOFF

LANGLADE

24 Aug

Boulogne
Billiancourt ●

25 Aug

Pt. de Sèvres

DRONNE

ROUMIANTZOFF
24 Aug

Clamart ●

DIO

Versailles ●

BILLOTTE
25 Aug

Viroflay ●

MOREL-DEVILLE

Vélizy
Villacoublay ●

MASSU
24 Aug

Jouy-en-Josas ●

La Croix de Berny

Fresnes ●

Toussus-
la-Noble ●

Saclay ●

LANGLADE
24 Aug

Orly ●

BUIS

WARABIOT

Athis-Mons ●

Movements of the main
tactical groups of the 2e DB
24–29 August 1944

Longjurneau ●

Seine R.

BILLOTTE
24 Aug

Viry-Châtillon ●

GERMAN DEFENSIVE POSITIONS

0   5 miles

0   5 km

Paris at the height of the Insurrection showing barricades most numerous in the working-class and left-wing areas and marking significant headquarters

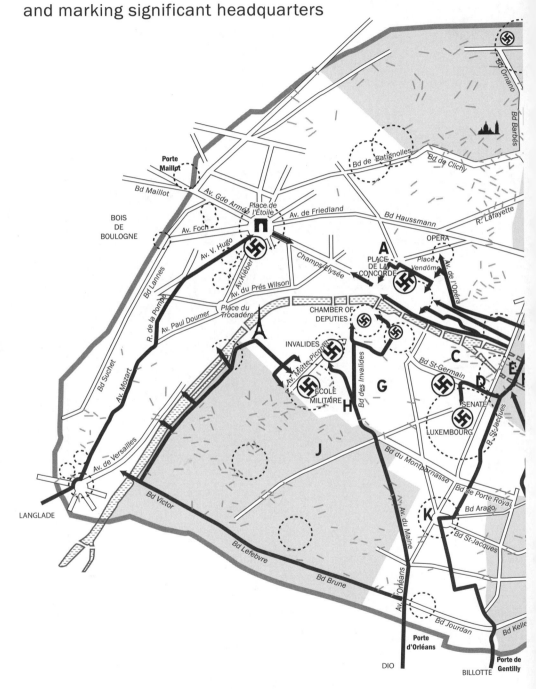

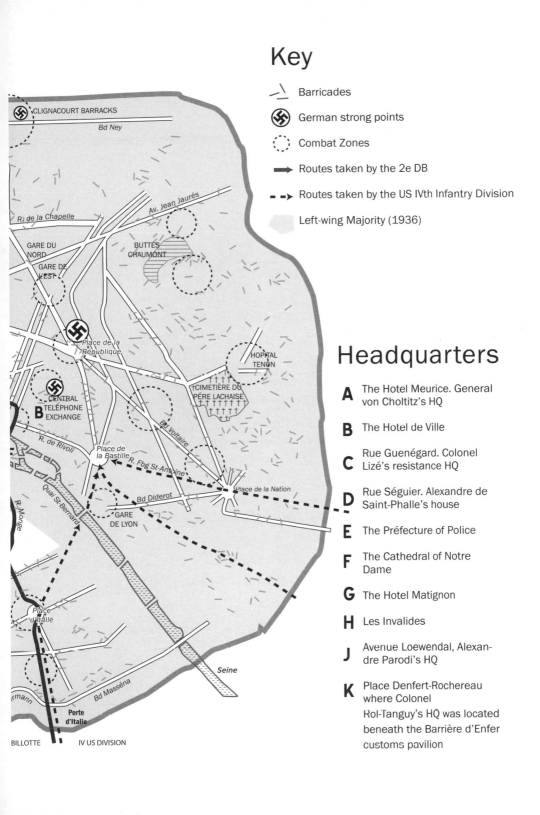

Key

↘ Barricades

☸ German strong points

⬭ Combat Zones

➡ Routes taken by the 2e DB

▪▪➤ Routes taken by the US IVth Infantry Division

Left-wing Majority (1936)

Headquarters

A The Hotel Meurice. General von Choltitz's HQ

B The Hotel de Ville

C Rue Guenégard. Colonel Lizé's resistance HQ

D Rue Séguier. Alexandre de Saint-Phalle's house

E The Préfecture of Police

F The Cathedral of Notre Dame

G The Hotel Matignon

H Les Invalides

J Avenue Loewendal, Alexandre Parodi's HQ

K Place Denfert-Rochereau where Colonel Rol-Tanguy's HQ was located beneath the Barrière d'Enfer customs pavilion

CLIGNACOURT BARRACKS

Bd Ney

Av. Jean Jaurès

R. de la Chapelle

GARE DU NORD

BUTTES CHAUMONT

GARE DE L'EST

Place de la République

HOPITAL TENON

CENTRAL TELEPHONE EXCHANGE

B

CIMETIÈRE DU PÈRE LACHAISE

R. de Rivoli

Bd Voltaire

Place de la Bastille

R. Fbg St-Antoine

Place de la Nation

Quai St-Bernard

Bd Diderot

GARE DE LYON

R. Monge

Place d'Italie

Seine

Bd Masséna

Porte d'Italie

BILLOTTE   IV US DIVISION

Chapter 1

De Gaulle, the French, and the Occupation, 1940–1944

June 1940

IN 1940 COLONEL CHARLES DE GAULLE was one of the French Army's foremost thinkers and an authority on armoured warfare. After a brave, moderately distinguished record in the First World War,[*] his intellectual bent was noted by Marshal Philippe Pétain who, as Colonel Pétain, first welcomed newly commissioned 2nd Lieutenant de Gaulle to the 33rd Infantry Regiment in 1913. During the 1920s de Gaulle ghostwrote a book for Pétain to publish as his own, but the Marshal's high-handedness over this extra-hierarchical matter led to them falling out. De Gaulle subsequently declared, "Marshal Pétain was a great man who died in 1925."

During the 1930s de Gaulle published several books on military theory, most notably *Vers l'Armée du Métier* (published in English as *The Army of the Future*), arguing that France should re-arm herself with tanks and aircraft. These were views he developed with the lively retired Colonel Émile Mayer over lunches at the Brasserie

---

[*] De Gaulle was wounded three times. The last time was at Verdun when his regiment was attacked and decimated. Cornered in a shell-hole, de Gaulle was bayoneted in the thigh and captured. He made five unsuccessful escape attempts, but his period of captivity was more notable for the magisterial lectures on warfare that he gave to his fellow prisoners.

Dumesnil opposite the Gare Montparnasse. Book-writing turned de Gaulle into a high-flyer nicknamed "Colonel Motors" for lobbying French politicians for the introduction of armoured divisions. While Germany's expanding Wehrmacht enthusiastically embraced these ideas, they met with little enthusiasm in France. Visionary officers like Colonel du Vigier, Commandant of Saumur's Cavalry School, agreed with de Gaulle, but most cavalry officers hated the idea of tanks replacing cavalry as the "fast arm" capable of transforming battlefields at a stroke.

Money was another problem. Under Admiral Darlan and naval minister Georges Leygues, France gave herself a large modern navy during the interwar years, regarding it as an imperial necessity. While on land the fact that France held back the Germans with trenchlines and static defences for most of the "Great War" made senior army officers predict that future land wars would also be static, a view supported by War Minister André Maginot. Millions of francs were spent on the vast "Maginot Line" fortifications, leaving little for other things the army desperately needed. New armoured vehicles appeared as awkward designs, under-armed, lacking radios, assembled in incoherent formations that were neither infantry nor armoured divisions. The French Air Force made similar mistakes.

The Second World War's first nine months passed uneventfully for France. The winter of 1939–1940 was a cold one, the enforced inactivity having a catastrophic effect on French Army morale. In the spring, the Germans began their campaign by seizing Denmark and Norway. On 10 May 1940 they launched their western offensive, crossing the Meuse at Sedan and sending a massive tank attack to punch through and corner the British Expeditionary Force and the French First Army against the sea around Dunkirk. A British armoured counterattack at Arras, intended to break the encirclement, was held back by German anti-tank artillery, while at Stonne another armoured counterattack led by Captain Pierre Billotte, son of French general Gaston Billotte, was repulsed.

Bouleversé by the ferocity of Germany's attack, much of northern France's population fled their homes, becoming road-clogging refugees. Having virtually broken down, French commander in chief General Gamelin was replaced by General Maxime Weygand, formerly Marshal Foch's adjutant in 1918. No sooner had Weygand organised a new defensive line than the Germans broke through it. A local success at Moncornet by Colonel de Gaulle's tank force finally persuaded French premier Paul Reynaud to listen to him, promoting him *général de brigade* (brigadier general). Dashing into Paris to meet Reynaud and collect his new uniform, de Gaulle entered tailors Petitdemange a colonel and emerged a general.[1] He then led a larger counterattack at Abbeville, for which General Weygand kissed him on both cheeks.

Reynaud first offered de Gaulle a political appointment at the Abbeville briefing. De Gaulle accepted in principle, but was more interested in creating armoured formations capable of protecting Paris.[2] But it was too late for that. The British were evacuating from Dunkirk. Furthermore, population deficiencies caused by the First World War combined with losses sustained since 10 May meant that France's army was outnumbered by three to one.

When the Germans crossed the lower Seine, Reynaud summoned under-secretary of state de Gaulle from the Hôtel Lutetia in the small hours. "Who could defend Paris and how?" Reynaud wondered. De Gaulle suggested Jean de Lattre de Tassigny, whose division was performing well. But Reynaud feared that more senior generals might resent a mere *divisionnaire* (divisional commander) directing the capital's defence, even though Gamelin and Weygand were clearly overwhelmed. Ignoring de Gaulle's advice to circumvent normal hierarchies, Reynaud appointed the dour General Henri Dentz instead.[3]

The French government evacuated to Bordeaux. Sickened, de Gaulle drafted a letter of resignation which he showed to Georges Mandel. The tough-minded Jew advised de Gaulle against this; there would be no one left in Reynaud's government with any guts.[4] With defeatism hanging heavily in the air, Weygand, Pétain and Admiral Darlan prepared to sue for peace and dismantle French democracy as soon as they could. To veteran British liaison officer Major-General Sir Edward

Spears, only de Gaulle possessed the drive to continue fighting, while among the civilians, only Mandel impressed him.

Arriving at the Château de Muguet for the Briare conference, de Gaulle met Pétain for the first time in two years. Pétain congratulated de Gaulle on his promotion before remarking sourly, "But what use is rank in a defeat?"

"But Marshal," replied de Gaulle, "it was during the retreat of 1914 that you yourself were given your first stars."

"*Aucun rapport!*"—"No comparison!" replied Pétain.[5]

Discussions with the British deteriorated when Pétain complained that, whereas he brought forty divisions to relieve General Gough during the "*Kaiserschlacht*" of 1918, the British now seemed unwilling to return the favour. Nor, thanks to Air Marshal Dowding's insistence, was Churchill prepared to commit more fighter aircraft. When Churchill asked the French to hold out for a few months Weygand replied that France needed help immediately to avoid seeking terms. Particularly disappointing for Churchill was that Reynaud's fighting spirit was consistently undermined by his self-centred mistress, Countess Hélène de Portes, who encouraged him to appoint defeatists in important positions. Reynaud saw no hope without massive American intervention. To compound the disaster, Italy joined the war on Germany's side on 10 June and the British 51st Highland Division surrendered at Saint-Valéry. With a quarter of her population now refugees, France also faced a massive displacement crisis.

Walking in the gardens, Churchill asked Spears' opinion of de Gaulle. "Completely staunch," replied Spears.[6] After further disappointing discussions, seeing de Gaulle standing taciturnly beside his ADC, Captain Courcel, Churchill muttered, "*L'homme du destin*," in his inimitable Franglais.[7]

Shortly afterwards de Gaulle warned Spears that Paul Baudouin was spreading stories that Churchill would understand if France negotiated a separate peace. Furious, Spears drove after Churchill, who had already departed for the airfield. Churchill categorically assured Spears that he *never* consented to France making a separate peace.[8]

DE GAULLE'S SUSPICIONS WERE CORRECT. Earlier that day General Émile Barazer de Lannurien arrived from General Héring requesting clear instructions regarding the defence of Paris. After walking in the garden with Weygand, Lannurien had his answer. Although the capital had escaped with only sporadic bombardment from the Kaiser's "Paris gun" during the previous war, Weygand decided that 1940 was different and that Paris should be declared an "open city." Pétain and Reynaud—also in the garden awaiting Churchill's arrival—agreed without demur. Hence both Churchill and de Gaulle attended the Briare conference unaware that General Lannurien was already returning to Paris to give Héring and Dentz their orders.[9] Yet Spears later acknowledged that defending Paris "would have been a stupendous undertaking even with the full and enthusiastic backing of Pétain and Weygand".[10]

When General Dentz realised he had only been appointed military governor of Paris to conduct its surrender, he wrote to Weygand protesting vehemently. Weygand telephoned his reply, "My decision is final; you must stay in Paris." The following day Paris was declared an open city. Fighting within her boundaries was banned. French troops were ordered to retreat around rather than through Paris. General Héring, who commanded the Army of Paris, withdrew his men on 12 June, bidding Dentz *adieu* at Les Invalides. Dentz wrote forlornly in his diary, "As to having the people of Paris take up arms—what arms? To resist tank divisions which had just chopped up French armies—such talk would only have led to a massacre."[11]

The city's Prefect of Police, Roger Langeron, now faced thousands of deserters fleeing southwards into Paris along with the possibility of the militant working class taking the city's defence into their own hands. Many Paris policemen wanted to leave and join the armies still fighting. But Langeron ordered them to remain at their posts to "preserve security and order". Some left anyway, but most did not. Recognising the depth of feeling, Langeron called a meeting in the Préfecture, the Paris police's imposing nineteenth-century headquarters on the Ile de la Cité's south quay between the Palais de Justice and the treasured cathedral of Notre Dame. Langeron reminded them their duty was to Paris, to protect Parisians, even from themselves, and to prevent looting and anything that might provoke reprisals. Those with young children, especially daughters, or previously involved in intelligence cases, Langeron permitted to leave. The rest shouted "*Vive la France!*"[12]

"Thousands of people of all nationalities, French, Canadian, English, Belgian, Romanian and even Italian are turning to us in despair for advice and comfort. The fact that I am here is a strong element in preventing a fatal panic," US Ambassador William C. Bullitt wrote to President Roosevelt.[13] A tradition began during the French Revolution that, whoever else fled the city, the American Ambassador would not.

The following day General Dentz requested Bullitt's help. Once posters proclaiming Paris an open city appeared, Bullitt telephoned America's ambassador in Switzerland asking him to relay this information to Berlin. Although consoling himself that his duty was merely to keep order rather than negotiate the city's surrender, Dentz would not escape that role. At 5pm the Germans asked the French to send them a truce party. Dentz took a call from Weygand who was reassured that the atmosphere in Paris was calm. The Germans, however, angered that their negotiators were fired upon from the French lines, now insisted that unless a French truce party reached them by 5am the following morning, their attack on Paris would begin. Dentz sent Major André Devouges to General Erich Marcks' HQ at Ecouen. In a manor house's candlelit dining room, Devouges heard the German terms: Paris was to be surrendered in full working order, including utilities and broadcasting stations; security and safety services must remain in place; the population must remain indoors for forty-eight hours after German troops entered the city. There was some haggling over this last item, which Devouges believed was unenforceable. Then a German orderly announced, "Paris has surrendered!"[14]

The city was stunned; its great boulevards were free of automobile traffic so that German staff officer General Walter Warlimont, flying overhead in a Fieseler Storch, asked his pilot to land on the Champs Élysées. Having witnessed Germany's defeat in 1918, this was the most exhilarating moment of his life.[15] The Wehrmacht's joyride into Paris began.

AS FRANCE FELL, CHURCHILL CAST AROUND for ways of propping her up. "As things now stand," de Gaulle said, "you must neglect nothing that can support France and maintain our alliance." After several hours discussing how to prevent defeatists from taking power, Churchill suggested a Franco-British union; the idea had come from Jean Monnet a few days earlier. This was gesture politics, but it seemed worth a try. Churchill telephoned Reynaud, "*Il faut tenir*"—"You must hold on." During these days de Gaulle established himself in Churchill's eyes as a future great Frenchman: "Here is the Constable of France." Even so Churchill refused to send any more aircraft or troops across the Channel. De Gaulle himself ordered a French cargo ship carrying American munitions to divert to a British port. Nevertheless, using an RAF aircraft, de Gaulle took Churchill's union suggestion to Paul Reynaud. Landing at Bordeaux, de Gaulle learned that Reynaud had resigned. Eighty-four-year-old Marshal Pétain had formed a government and would undoubtedly seek an armistice. Pétain dismissed Churchill's proposed Franco-British union as "fusion with a corpse. We do not want to be a British dominion!"[16]

De Gaulle thought Reynaud "gave the impression of a man who had reached the limits of hope".[17] But, ever a patriotic Frenchman, in his last act as premier, Reynaud ordered a hundred thousand gold francs to be delivered to de Gaulle's hotel.* De Gaulle then sent Roland de Margerie to his family at Carantec in Brittany, advising them to leave for England.[18]

The following morning de Gaulle returned to the airfield with Lieutenant de Courcel. On the way they visited the French Army's emergency HQ on Bordeaux's Rue Vital-Carles. According to Jean Mistler, "De Gaulle sat down at General Lafont's desk. I can still see

---

* According to Philippe de Gaulle's book, *De Gaulle, Mon Père*, vol. 1, p. 117, the exchange at the time was 167Fr to £1. Jean Laurent delivered the money.

him with his arms raised, saying dispassionately, calmly, as though it was obvious: 'The Germans have lost the war. They are lost and France must keep on fighting.'"[19] These were delusional utterances unless he believed American intervention was certain.

With German forces closing in, chaos reigned at Merignac's airfield. The pilot of the RAF Dragon Rapide raised no objection to carrying three passengers—Spears accompanied them—but insisted their luggage was tied up when stowed. Leaving France as an obscure brigadier-general, de Gaulle later wrote, "The departure took place without romanticism or difficulty."[20] Flying northwards along France's west coast, he saw ships burning in the ports of La Rochelle and Rochefort, smoke from burning munitions and, somewhere down there, at Paimpont, was his bed-ridden mother. According to Courcel, "The General, lost in his thoughts, seemed scarcely to be concerned with the immediate present, but rather with what was awaiting him over there." Of the emotional storm churning inside him, de Gaulle later admitted to André Malraux, "It was appalling."[21]

They landed on Jersey, which was still in British hands, to refuel. Spears offered de Gaulle coffee from his Thermos. "I handed it to him, whereupon taking a sip, he said that this was tea. It was his first introduction to the tepid liquid which, in England, passes for either one or the other. It was the beginning of his martyrdom," wrote Spears.

They landed at Hendon around noon, almost simultaneously with Pétain's ceasefire broadcast. Over a million French soldiers entered German prison camps for several years. Pétain's decision undoubtedly saved lives and spared France much destruction, but France was diminished and humiliated by the defeat and, as de Gaulle later wrote, "France cannot be France without greatness."

After dropping their luggage at a hastily arranged flat, Spears took de Gaulle and Courcel for lunch at the RAC Club. At 3pm Churchill received them in the garden of 10 Downing Street. No one should imagine that Churchill's generous welcome ever turned de Gaulle into an Anglophile. He was a proud Frenchman, programmed by history to distrust the British. He simply wanted British sponsorship, for no longer than was absolutely necessary, to liberate his country, after which he would wave the British, and subsequently the Americans, good-bye. De Gaulle also believed that, unless France did everything possible to liberate herself, the sense of shame would last for generations. That evening, after dining with Jean Monnet and reading a transcript of what he regarded as Pétain's "treasonous" ceasefire order, de Gaulle drafted his famous *Appel*.[22]

Churchill agreed immediately that de Gaulle should make a broadcast. But, within twenty-four hours of his departure, the Bordeaux government declared de Gaulle *persona non grata* for rejecting Pétain's authority. Lord Halifax particularly advised against anything that might nettle Pétain. "It was undesirable that General de Gaulle, as *persona non grata* to the present French government, should broadcast at the present time, so long as it was still possible that the French government would act in any way comfortable to the interests of the alliance."[23] Warned of this development by Alfred Duff Cooper, Churchill's Francophile Minister of Information, Spears pleaded with Churchill as he napped following his "Finest Hour" speech. Churchill advised Spears to lobby the cabinet individually, and de Gaulle was authorised to speak to France via the BBC that evening.[24]

Accompanied by Courcel and chain-smoking, de Gaulle was welcomed to Broadcasting House by Stephen Tallents, the head of news. After a voice trial an announcement was made at 8.30pm that he would speak at 10pm on 18 June; becoming '*l'homme du 18e juin*.'* When the moment came, de Gaulle stepped forward to the microphone and into history:

> The leaders who have been at the head of the French armies for many years have formed a government. This government, alleging the defeat of our armies, has entered into communication with the enemy to stop the fighting. To be sure we have been submerged, we are submerged, by the enemies' mechanised forces on land and in the air. It is the Germans' tanks, planes and tactics that have made us fall back, infinitely more than their numbers. It is the Germans'

---

* De Gaulle is sometimes called '*l'homme du 18e juin*,'—'the man of 18 June' because of the *Appel*.

tanks, planes and tactics that have so taken our leaders by surprise as to bring them to the point they have reached today. But has the last word been said? Must hope vanish? Is the defeat final? No!

Believe me, for I know what I am talking about and I tell you that nothing is lost for France. For France is not alone. She is not alone! She is not alone! She has an immense empire behind her. She can unite with the British Empire which commands the sea and which is carrying on the struggle. Like England she can make use of the vast industries of the United States. This war is not confined to the unhappy territory of our country. This war has not been decided by the Battle of France. This is a worldwide war. All the faults, all the delays, all the sufferings do not do away with the fact that in the world there are the means for one day crushing our enemies. Today we are struck down by mechanised force; in the future we can conquer by greater mechanised force. The fate of the world lies there.

I, General de Gaulle, now in London, call upon the French officers and soldiers who are on British soil or who may come onto it, with their arms or without them, I call upon the engineers and the specialised workers in the armaments industry who are or who may arrive on British soil, to get in contact with me. Whatever happens, the flame of French resistance must not and shall not go out.

Tomorrow, as I have done today, I shall speak again from London.

MOST FRENCHMEN SIMPLY WANTED to recover a sense of normality, even of the grey kind. Young Pascale Moisson, who fled Montmartre to find her family home at Dole near Dijon, found those weeks unbelievably miserable. When two lads offered to share their large bakelite radio she accepted enthusiastically and, together with these future *résistants*, Pascale listened to de Gaulle. "Then what joy, what hope seized our hearts! It was the famous *Appel* of 18 June. From that day and during the four long years that followed, we never lost hope, even in the darkest moments."[25]

On 19 June, Alain de Boissieu was trudging with a column of prisoners through the Belgian village of Beauraing. "A brave Belgian woman approached us offering bread. She informed us that the previous evening, on the radio from London, she heard the message of a French general saying that all was not lost for France and he was continuing the fight. The news spread along the column. Among the more determined it was a light of hope. While the more submissive shrugged their shoulders. I will never forget that day. For many young men of my generation it had the effect of being the first landmark on a long road leading to revenge and rebirth."[26] Reaching Oflag IID, Boissieu met Jacques Branet, another cavalry officer captured on horseback. They became firm friends and escaped together in an adventure worthy of a film.[27]

Having escaped via Dunkirk and then returned to France, André Gribius was still fighting south of the Loire when the Armistice was announced. "As for the *Appel* of 18 June," he wrote, "it was not heard by combatants, only by troops overseas or isolated groups who, regardless of what was going on around them, or unable to fight through either being cut-off, prisoners or wounded, had the opportunity to hear via the air-waves the message of hope from 'the unknown' called Charles de Gaulle. We were a long way from being able to imagine, four years later, the reconquest of our country, the popular enthusiasm and the marvellous faculty of being able to bury things under an armband or a *Tricolore* flag."[28] Through ties of regiment, loyalty and tradition, Gribius accepted Pétain's authority until 1942.

Of those "troops overseas" in the far-flung outposts of France's empire, it was often individualistic members of *La Coloniale*, France's former "naval" troops, whose badge was the anchor, who provided de Gaulle's early pool of manpower, especially in colonies surrendered by Germany in 1919 which did not relish being handed back.[29] Another useful source was Republican Spaniards; the 13th "Demi-Brigade" of the Foreign Legion largely consisted of such men. This unit was resting in Great Britain after withdrawing from Narvik. The arrival of all the young men of military age from the Breton Isle of Sein was also encouraging. So too was the arrival of the submarine *Rubis* whose officers allowed their crewmen to vote between Pétain and de Gaulle. Yet in 1940 most French servicemen remained loyal to Pétain. De Gaulle's early supporters were regarded as "men with nothing to lose". Spanish Republicans were easily marked down as desperadoes, while *La Coloniale* was never "smart" compared to the *metropolitan* French Army.

But no one could call Captain Philippe de Hauteclocque a man with nothing to lose. The second son of a Papal count, descended from centuries of northeast French nobility, Hauteclocque was personally wealthy. He married a social equal immediately after graduating from Saumur, rapidly producing a large family raised on a country estate given to him as a wedding present. He was also charming, accomplished, and a high-flyer. Having won his first Croix de Guerre in Morocco during the summer holidays while a cavalry instructor at Saint-Cyr, Hauteclocque attended the École Supérieur de Guerre, France's staff college. He was serving as operations officer of General Musse's 4th Infantry Division when the war began. Shortly after the German attack on 10 May, being part of Blanchard's First Army, Musse's 4th ID was forced into the Lille pocket in which capitulation was the obvious outcome. Not relishing becoming a prisoner, Hauteclocque asked permission to take his chance. "*Entendu*," replied Musse. Making his way through the German corridor, Hauteclocque was briefly captured but persuaded his interrogator he was merely a *poilu* (ordinary soldier) looking for his family. Disgusted by Hauteclocque's apparent lack of patriotism, his interrogator had him thrown into the street. After rejoining the main French Army, Hauteclocque was appointed to an armoured brigade and directed one of the last Char B tank attacks on foot with a walking stick due to the lack of radios. While recuperating from a head wound in hospital at Avalon, Hauteclocque heard that France had fallen. Bandaged, he sought news of his family in Paris, watching the humiliated city familiarise itself with life *sous la botte nazi*. On learning that his wife and children had gone south, Hauteclocque made his way to his sister's château near Grugé l'Hopital in northern Anjou. It was there, after dinner on 26 June, that Hauteclocque heard a repeat broadcast of de Gaulle's *Appel* and decided to join him. First he needed to find his family who were beyond the new demarcation line, in the unoccupied "Free Zone". It was on hastily concocted papers enabling him to cross this line that Philippe de Hauteclocque first used the name by which he became famous: Leclerc. Weeping with joy to find Thérèse at the family's holiday home, Leclerc told her his plan. In the French of "Old France" patricians, using *vous* not *tu*, Thérèse told her husband to go where he believed his duty called him and said that she would look after the children. In the meantime she would return to their home in Picardy and carry on as normal. If that proved impossible she would sell up and get their children to Canada where she had relations. At dawn on 4 July, after a quick breakfast, Leclerc said, "Courage, Thérèse, our parting may be long." Then he cycled towards Bayonne and took a train across Spain and Portugal to Lisbon where he boarded a ship for England. On 25 July Leclerc presented himself at de Gaulle's London offices.

IN A STROKE OF GENIUS, Hitler allowed France to retain a modest army and the whole of her navy. Distrust of German promises combined with Admiral Darlan's political unreliability so concerned Winston Churchill that he subsequently ordered all French ships in British ports to be seized. Then a Royal Navy task force was sent to issue a degrading ultimatum to Admiral Gensoul, who commanded France's West Mediterranean squadron at Mers el Kebir in French North Africa. Like many government ministries quitting Paris for the new makeshift capital at Vichy, the French admiralty was in disarray. Darlan's deputy, Admiral Le Luc, handled Gensoul's referrals for advice, rejecting various options suggested by the British and ordering that reinforcements set off from Toulon and Algiers. When the British Admiral James Somerville got wind of this he ordered his ships to open fire on the moored French squadron, causing nearly fourteen hundred casualties and frosting relations between Great Britain and Pétain's Vichy régime for the next thirty months. On the one hand Churchill's action demonstrated to the world, especially the Americans, that Great Britain would fight the Axis ruthlessly, even striking a fallen ally. But French North Africa's garrison had largely been sympathetic to de Gaulle, and Somerville's attack rekindled Anglophobia in a country which had not fought the British since Waterloo.

De Gaulle found Mers el Kebir deeply depressing and even considered resigning his new role and emigrating to Quebec. Instead he put his dourly brave face on the situation, even though Free French recruitment slowed to a trickle. For two years Great Britain had to fight Petain's France concurrently with fighting Hitler. Being sponsored by Great Britain, de Gaulle was forced to fight his fellow countrymen, turning Britain's last war with France into a French civil war as well. While Leclerc uncompromisingly regarded the French Navy and the garrison of French North Africa as "playing Germany's game", many Frenchmen took a more complex, embittered view.

BELIEVING THAT THE FACE OF EUROPE would be German-dominated for the foreseeable future, Marshal Pétain wanted to demonstrate that, despite their military defeat, the French were men of parts. He insisted that Paris return to normal; shops and places of entertainment were to be re-opened. But the city's senior *boulevardier*, playwright and impresario, Sacha Guitry, was skulking in the southwest and considering exile in Spain. The expatriate community disintegrated. Hemingway was in America. Literary lesbians Gertrude Stein and Alice B. Toklas hibernated in *la France profonde*. Sylvia Beach, proprietor of the bookshop Shakespeare and Co., was one of very few who remained to uphold the city's expat intellectual tradition.

"*Rentrez à Paris et collaborez*"—"Return to Paris and collaborate" Petain yelled down the telephone to Sacha Guitry in his Dax hotel. Guitry obliged, but maintained his faith in an ultimate Allied victory by keeping his reserves of sterling.[30] Meanwhile the exchange rate of twenty francs to the Reichsmark so favoured the Germans that the world-class shops and emporiums of central Paris were soon empty. France's economy was so paralysed by ever-tightening German demands that restocking became impossible.

Paris still had to be governed. Aged fifty-three, Mayor Pierre Taittinger, in customary French practice, held several elected offices: he represented Paris in the Chamber of Deputies alongside being President of the Municipal Council at the Hôtel de Ville, where he represented the exclusive Quartier Vendôme. Amid personal grief at losing a son at the height of the fighting, Taittinger returned to his office. While Taittinger was undoubtedly a key Parisian collaborator, the Occupation turned his family's politics many shades of grey. His surviving sons served de Gaulle.[31]

The incoming German authorities had little option but to use hotels as offices. Except for German servicemen on leave, tourism ceased throughout the Occupation. The Hôtels Majestic and Raphael on Avenue Kléber were taken over. So too were central hotels like the Crillon and the Meurice on the Rue de Rivoli and others around the Place Vendôme and Avenue de Marigny. Although the costs of the Occupation were charged to the French treasury, the Germans paid for those hotels, whose owners rarely lost out. Meanwhile many ministerial and embassy buildings were mothballed.

The Wehrmacht quickly recognised the city's potential for pomp and pageantry, draping their dramatic swastika flags wherever possible. Every day a company of German infantry marched down the Champs Elysées to the sound of a band complete with glockenspiels; an immense wound to Gallic pride.

Inevitably Wehrmacht personnel had liaisons with French women. Today thousands of French citizens are descended from these relationships. Many women, actress Arletty explained afterwards, are "colour blind" when it comes to uniforms.[32] The couturier and designer Coco Chanel also romanced a German officer during the Occupation. Neither Arletty nor Chanel were young women in 1940.

The French still believed themselves culturally more advanced than the Germans. However, Parisian high society, culture and economic life could not have survived the Occupation without significant *collaboration*. Friendships between Parisians and their German occupiers had the same inevitability that affected social choices before the war: wealth, social class, political and moral values. The German staff officer Ernst Junger, already an established writer, entered *salon* society with little difficulty. Hans von Luck, an energetic Panzer officer, found friends of an equivalent upper-class background.

As stocks dwindled in the shops, the Occupation's grey sullenness began to bite, often regarded as an illness to be endured. The Germans were often simply ignored, many French preferring *attentisme*—to wait and see.

ACTIVE RESISTANCE MEANT RISKING what bearable normality there was. It was only on 11 November 1940, when Great War remembrance ceremonies became anti-German demonstrations, that the flame of resistance first flickered in Paris. The German authorities reacted quickly. Of one hundred and twenty-three arrests, over a hundred were school-children and students. In London, the Free French cheered this development but little could be made from a spontaneous outbreak of raw patriotism with no recognisable faction behind it.[33]

The first Parisian to be executed for anti-German activities was an engineer named Jacques Bonsergent, and his offence was merely to witness a trivial scuffle involving Frenchmen and Wehrmacht personnel. The only one arrested after the incident, tragically Bonsergent pleaded guilty, perhaps believing other pleas were pointless and that the incident was trivial. But he was sentenced to death. Despite appeals, German military governor General Otto von Stulpnagel wanted to make an example; Bonsergent was shot at Vincennes on 23 December 1940. Posters announcing the execution so enraged Parisians that many became shrines decorated with *Tricolores* and Union Jacks.[34]

Now that blood had been spilt, the London French had an incident to build on. The BBC French Service asked Parisians to stay indoors on New Year's Day between 3pm and 4pm, an act of passive resistance widely heeded in Paris despite German offers to distribute free potatoes during that hour.[35] Although a miners' strike crippled northeastern France, there was little direct anti-German activity in Paris during early 1941. The Germans were, however, watchful and in February uncovered an escape line for Allied servicemen run by ethnologist Boris Vilde from the Musée de l'Homme. Its leaders were shot at Mont Valérien.

While communists later became the most committed and disciplined *résistants*, during the Occupation's first year they were split between those who saw Germany as the Soviet Union's ally following the Ribbentrop-Molotov pact and others who thought that position ludicrous. The latter included the FTP's Henri Rol-Tanguy.* After two years in the International Brigades fighting for a doomed cause in Spain, and involvement in trade union politics, Rol-Tanguy tapped into working-class resentment at French industry being sucked into Germany's war effort. Knowing to avoid buildings, Rol-Tanguy's recruitment meetings usually occurred in parks, either the Bois de Vincennes or Bois de Boulogne.[36]

A big police *rafle* (round-up) against left-wing activists during October 1940 forced Rol-Tanguy to live apart from his wife, Cécile, who was pregnant for a second time. During her confinement the following May a health visitor asked where her husband was. "Oh, he comes and he goes," Cécile replied. After 1945 she learnt that, had the health services known about her circumstances, she could have been helped more. But distrust towards Occupation officialdom was so great that she dared not take the risk.[37]

1940–1941

DURING LATE 1940, FREE FRANCE'S WAR WITH VICHY preoccupied de Gaulle more than fledgling resistance in Metropolitan France. Although the failure at Dakar, where his men were repulsed by Vichy forces, was among the saddest episodes of de Gaulle's life, Leclerc had meantime established Free France's stake in Africa by taking the Cameroons and Gabon. Four months after escaping from France, former trainee diplomat Christian Girard arrived in the Cameroons

---

* FTP = *Franc Tireurs et Partisan*, a Communist inspired resistance grouping which became one of the best organised, committed and disciplined.

to witness a smart parade by colonial infantry commanded by Leclerc. "Once more I felt we were in France," wrote Girard.

Leclerc's success kept de Gaulle in the game. Whereas at first the Free French appeared lacking in realism—Major General Sir Edward Spear's wife called de Gaulle's early followers "sweet, silly boys"—now they had fought and killed their fellow countrymen. They hardened and became uncompromising. Previously Vichy loyalists captured in French Equatorial Africa who refused to join de Gaulle were courteously returned to France. Once home several of these officers reported Leclerc to Vichy authorities as none other than Philippe de Hauteclocque, former cavalry instructor at Saint-Cyr. But once de Gaulle's officers were being tried for treason *in absentia* and death sentences handed down, to be carried out upon their capture, it became necessary to retain captured Vichy personnel as potential hostages. While no more an Anglophile than de Gaulle, Leclerc was shocked by Vichy's pro-Fascist attitude when he perused captured papers in Gabon.[38]

Apart from inflicting a few casualties at Dakar and a weak air-raid against Gibraltar, Vichy usually suffered most in its skirmishes with the British and de Gaulle's Free French; a pattern that would continue. When, during late October, Vichy diplomat Louis Rougier arrived in London pleading for quarter so that French merchantmen could ply the Mediterranean with foodstuffs from French North Africa without Royal Navy interference, he was met with open ears. After Churchill initially told him that Britain would "bombard" Vichy, an informal agreement was made. The Free French and Vichy would accept the existing status quo in the colonies and de Gaulle would turn his attention elsewhere. Attacks on Pétain in the international media would cease and Vichy would undertake not to hand over any French imperial bases to the Axis. Given the agreement's informal nature, Churchill could not sign it himself, though he penned some terse remarks in the margin—one directed at General Weygand, exhorting him to bring French North Africa over to the Allies, and another aimed at Laval and Darlan, threatening to bring down Vichy if they made further concessions to the Axis. The Rougier-Strang agreement instilled some restraint into the tense situation between London, the Free French and Vichy until the Syrian affair the following summer. Meanwhile de Gaulle directed Leclerc to carry the war to the Italians.

Owing to the foresight of Chad's colonial governor, Felix Éboué, de Gaulle's Cross of Lorraine soon flew over Fort Lamy, thereby forestalling potential Italian demands for the Sarra Triangle. Shortly after Leclerc arrived in Chad, Major Ralph Bagnold of the British Long Range Desert Group (LRDG) visited Fort Lamy seeking Free French assistance in attacking Italy's south Libyan bases Kufra and Murzuk. Leclerc was impressed by LRDG methods and their stripped-down Chevrolet trucks bristling with machine-guns, but he also prefered not to waste the traditions of the Corps Méhariste—the "Camel Corps"—founded by Henri Laperrine. So Leclerc used camels to build up depots on roads not yet robust enough to take mechanised traffic. Next Leclerc souped up the LRDG concept to something resembling the Foreign Legion's marching columns. For the Murzuk raid Leclerc sent officers Colonna d'Ornano* and Jacques Massu to sample LRDG methods, while for Kufra he furiously gathered intelligence, including aerial photographs, and organised a mechanised column supported by light artillery. Kufra was Free France's first land victory against the Axis. Inside the Italian colonial fort of El Tag, Leclerc made his men swear never to lay down their arms until the *Tricolore* flew again over Strasbourg Cathedral. This became known as "the Oath at Kufra".

Leclerc's main strategic aim, however, was to link-up with the British forces fighting the Italians in Libya and Egypt. But the arrival that February of Rommel's Afrika Korps, who recovered everything lost by the Italians during the winter of 1940–1941, delayed this plan for twenty months. In the meantime Leclerc's force guarded the Allies' southern flank in Africa and the valuable air route from Takoradi to Cairo.

---

* Colonel Colonna d'Ornano was killed on the Murzuk raid and buried along with a New Zealand sergeant on the return trip in a ceremony movingly reminiscent of the burial of Sir John Moore after Corunna.

ON 22 JUNE 1941 THE WEHRMACHT INVADED the Soviet Union. That same day in Paris the Germans seized the Soviet Legation along with everyone inside at the time, particularly the reading room, a second home for many French communists. Among these was François Le Bihan, Cécile Tanguy's father, who later died in Auschwitz.[39]

The communist resistance group *Francs Tireurs et Partisans*—FTP—now took up arms against the common foe, provoking a spate of arrests against communist activists. Henri Rol-Tanguy was forced to hide while Cécile found yet another home for herself and their newborn daughter in an attic apartment at 10 Rue de l'Ouest. Comradeship in working-class Paris ensured that activists like Rol-Tanguy were hidden and fed.

An FTP speciality was train derailments, such as occurred at Épinay sur Seine on the night of 17–18 July 1941. By August FTP's activities had graduated to assaults on German personnel; a German soldier was murdered outside a brothel near the Porte d'Orléans. On other occasions German personnel were followed, but the *résistants'* nerve failed at the thought of killing and reprisals. On 21 August, however, Spanish Civil War veteran Pierre Georges pumped two pistol shots into German naval lieutenant Alphonse Moser at Barbes-Rocheouart Metro station in Montmartre.

Next, in an extraordinary, unlinked incident, when Pierre Laval and Marcel Déat attended a Versailles parade ground to wave off the *Légion des Volontaires Français* to fight alongside the Wehrmacht against the Soviet Union, one of the volunteers, Paul Collette, produced a small pistol from inside his new German uniform and fired five shots at Laval and Déat, gravely injuring both of them.[40]

When Pierre Georges sent Gilbert Brustlein—his accomplice at Barbes-Rocheouart—to Nantes to assassinate the local Feldkommandant, Lieutenant Colonel Karl Hotz, the FTP committed a serious "own goal". General Otto von Stulpnagel insisted that fifty Nantais hostages should be shot as a reprisal. While in Paris, although the assassination attempt on Laval was a Vichy matter, Stulpnagel insisted that one hundred Frenchmen should be executed in reprisal for Barbes-Rocheouart. The final victims included Honoré d'Estienne d'Orves, one of de Gaulle's early envoys to Paris, who was captured in January, and Dutchman Jan Doormik. After a memorial service for these victims in London's Westminster Cathedral, de Gaulle announced that he and he alone would give orders for resistance operations.[41]

FOR THE FTP, DE GAULLE WAS TOO FAR AWAY to be relevant to their lives. They saw him merely as an officer who wanted to rebuild the French Army as a fighting force. But while they could not accept his advice against killing German personnel and provoking reprisals, they respected his refusal to accept defeat and encouragement in obstructing "the pillage of France". Since most Parisian workers had families to feed, very few could take part.

There were also limits to how many fugitives the clandestine networks could protect. Early FTP industrial sabotage missions were organised by Polish emigré Joseph Epstein.

Having been a weapons expert during his national service, Henri Rol-Tanguy devised time bombs for industrial sabotage. When L'Air Liquide's depot at Saint-Ouen was targeted, Rol-Tanguy went to instruct workers on planting his devices. Taking Cécile and baby Hélène with him, Rol-Tanguy instructed the saboteurs outside the factory in broad daylight while Cécile played with Hélène on the grass nearby; a typical summer lunchtime scene.[42]

To counter the Resistance, the Gestapo and German security police became increasingly efficient, forcing *résistants* to become more watchful. Compared to the Germans the French police could be *blasé*, but it depended hugely on who was in charge. FTP members usually avoided venturing out unnecessarily. Metro stations were particularly dangerous if the police had set up a checkpoint thirty metres from the bend of a long connecting corridor between platforms. Usually the police were content to see an old military ID card; perhaps an individual policeman's patriotism could be appealed to. But over the months the police accumulated considerable intelligence about the Resistance, and some senior police officers were determined to be respected professionally in German eyes.[43]

Rol-Tanguy got around by bicycle wearing a civil defence uniform when going to meetings. His contacts among taxi drivers, who often worked as waiters once petrol shortages kicked in, enabled Rol-Tanguy to hide his bicycle at numerous bistros before continuing on foot, using his extensive knowledge of Parisian alleys and rat-runs. On one occasion, hearing unfamiliar footsteps outside the mansard bedsit he was renting away from Cécile, Rol-Tanguy clambered down the lift cable which exited outside his window. It was indeed the police. On another occasion, no sooner had a gypsy read his palm at a streetside café, promising him a long life, than Rol-Tanguy felt a twinge of danger. An unfamiliar man in blue workers' overalls appeared unusually interested in him. Walking away, Rol-Tanguy realised he was being followed. Again his superior knowledge of backstreet Paris protected him.

After warning his group that they were *fliqués*—under surveillance—Rol-Tanguy moved to a bedsit in Malakoff. The police found him there as well, but luckily the concièrge warned him that enquiries were being made and he moved on. Perhaps the police wanted him warned. In any case Rol-Tanguy was determined never to be taken alive and always carried two small pistols in good working order. He quarantined himself for his comrades' safety, not having any contact with anyone for ten days. By August 1942 Rol-Tanguy was back in contact with Cécile, who was forced to give up her secretarial job with a cosmetics firm once the police seemed suspicious.[44]

1942

IN AUGUST 1942, HAND-GRENADES were thrown among off-duty Luftwaffe personnel at a Paris sports stadium, leading to more hostage-taking and executions. But this did not stop the FTP. As British weapons became available it fell to men like Henri Rol-Tanguy to distribute pistols and ammunition. He always avoided using adventurous language when talking about this work because security demanded meticulousness over mundane things, and until August 1944 he never met FTP leaders such as Charles Tillon. Such was clandestine life.[45]

Like all armies, however, the Resistance had to learn from its mistakes. Rol-Tanguy was sufficiently experienced to veto a poster threatening that "for each patriot [shot] six German officers will pay" because it was "unrealistic and uselessly provocative". But events in the Rue de Buci on 31 May 1942 demonstrated that even civil protests where fatalities were not expected could escalate lethally. A communist activist, Madeleine Marzin, and three FTP heavies barged into a grocer's shop known to serve German soldiers and began giving jars of preserves and sugar to hard-pressed housewives. Chaos ensued, and when the police arrived the FTP men began firing pistols. Two policemen were killed and several wounded before Marzin and the FTP men were overpowered and arrested. The men were guillotined while Madeleine Marzin was imprisoned in Rennes.[46]

Rol-Tanguy concluded that such operations required precise planning and must be executed sufficiently quickly that neither the police nor the Germans could react. Another "*action*" was planned for 1 August on the junction of the Avenue d'Orléans[*] and the Rue Daguerre in south Montparnasse. Starting at 4pm, communists marched into a shop and began giving food to housewives. Firing began and one policeman and a German were wounded before the housewives dispersed and the FTP withdrew without loss. Both British and Russian radio celebrated this outbreak of lawlessness which demonstrated, if only briefly, that someone other than the Germans ran the streets of Paris. The FTP leadership recognised, however, that things needed to cool down, and Rol-Tanguy was sent to lie low in the Free Zone.[47]

ANTI-JEWISH LAWS ENACTED during the Occupation's early months were now enforced, with the French police fulfilling German deportation quotas—usually to certain death in camps like Auschwitz.

---

[*] Now called the Avenue du général Leclerc.

From January 1941 an SS officer was placed in the Préfecture de Police in Paris. When the Germans advertised for supplementary staff to fulfill the anti-Jewish policy, six thousand responded in the Paris area alone to fill two thousand vacancies.[48]

The first round-up of Parisian Jews happened in May 1941; almost four thousand were sent via the Gare Austerlitz to fetid Vichy transit camps. But in July 1942 Operation Spring Breeze—called in French *la grande rafle* (the big round-up)—gathered over thirteen thousand Jews including four thousand children at the Vélodrome d'Hiver, the winter cycling stadium where Parisians watched a favourite French sport.

Although the Paris police arrested fewer Jews than the Germans wanted, over thirteen thousand people were held for five days in a stadium designed for seventeen thousand, whose visit would normally have lasted up to three hours. The six lavatories quickly became blocked. Food and sanitation were desperately inadequate for the incarceration of so many people. Dysentery broke out. Some, sensing the merciless logic of their situation, tried to kill themselves with varying degrees of success, placing extra burdens on overstretched medical staff. Next stop was transit camps like Pithiviers or Beaune La Rolande, or, if their departure to the death camps was sooner, to Drancy, an unfinished modern housing estate outside Paris.

During 1942 alone over forty thousand Jews resident in France, mainly foreign but including many French citizens, were deported via Vichy's transit system. Only a few lucky ones were released. Henriette Petrocochino, an elderly Dutch Jewess and widow of a Greek diplomat, was arrested but her British relations secured her release via the Red Cross. Returning home to the Boulevard de Beausejour, she found that Wehrmacht officers had used her apartment during her enforced absence; only a radio was missing.[49] If she had not been released, all her possessions would have vanished. Her flat contained superb ornaments, such as Sèvres porcelain, and, being the daughter of Dutch artist David Bles, she owned good paintings. Billeting officers in the homes of arrested Jews was a usual phase. Once the German authorities knew their owners would not return, their possessions were processed.

There are moving examples of faithful servants hiding family treasures from grasping Nazi hands, like Baron de Rothschild's superb butler, Félix Pacaut, sealing off part of the cellar in their Avenue de Marigny mansion.[50] But German pillage of Jewish assets was highly organised. Installing itself at the Musée de Jeu de Paume shortly after *la Chute*, the *Einsatzstab Reichsleiter Rosenberg* (ERR), an *ad hoc* organisation within the SS, was charged with the confiscation of Jewish art collections. When she realised what her beloved Jeu de Paume would be used for, the unassuming yet tough curator Rose Valland asked Jacques Jaujard, the director of the Louvre, what she should do. Jaujard told her to remain at her post *"coute que coute"*, and keep him informed. Barred to the public throughout the Occupation under the ERR, the Jeu de Paume became a clearinghouse for art theft, as old masters, Impressionists and modern work by men like Matisse, Braque and Picasso were shipped to Germany. From the Occupation's first winter Rose Valland inventoried as much as she could in the brief, descriptive language of auction house catalogues. After Operation Spring Breeze the pace in Rose's *carnets* intensifies.[51]

PERHAPS PIERRE LAVAL ADVISED FRENCH OFFICIALS to make collaboration over the Jewish question as ineffective as possible. But his biographer Fred Kupferman emphasises that during 1942 Laval swapped one rabidly anti-Semitic commissioner for Jewish Affairs, Xavier Vallat, for the more sinister Darquier de Pellepoix, at Otto Abetz's behest.[52] Besides, on the first anniversary of Operation Barbarossa, Laval declared publicly, "Germany is fighting Communism. Great battles are taking place in the east, from Petsamo to the Caucasus. I wish for a German victory, for without it, Bolshevism will take over everywhere in Europe." Pétain was furious.[53]

Since Nazi Germany's conquests reached their zenith during mid-1942, at no other time did it make more sense for Vichy France to knuckle under. As Leclerc's men in Chad prepared to join forces with the British Eighth Army's autumn offensive, they faced unprecedented hostility from their compatriots in Vichy-controlled Niger, whereas during 1940–1941 this area saw tacit co-operation between the two Frances. Leclerc's men blamed this on Laval.

De Gaulle was experiencing the worst phase in Free French history since Dakar. During the spring of 1942 the British cut him out of the operation to seize Madagascar, France's island colony in the Indian Ocean.* If Laval had joined France into a full alliance with Germany, de Gaulle's position in London would have become farcical and his men merely volunteers of conscience.

When, on 8 November 1942, the British and Americans landed in French North Africa in Operation Torch, they faced stiff resistance from the Vichy French. De Gaulle's then ADC, Captain Pierre Billotte, was warned by General Sir Hastings Ismay three hours before the operation began.[54] Contemplating the enormity of what was happening but deciding against disturbing de Gaulle with news of the latest high-handed behaviour by *les Anglo-Saxons*, Billotte spent the night at his desk drafting speeches before waking the Free French leader at 7am. De Gaulle stood speechless in his dressing gown while Billotte spoke.

"*Eh, bien,*" said the Constable. "I hope the Vichy people throw them back in the sea. You don't get into France *par effraction*—'by breaking and entering'!"[55]

But the Allies required complete control of North Africa's shoreline. It was too important to forewarn anyone by first "asking nicely". The Vichy French fought for three days, until it was clear the Anglo-American forces meant serious business. Despite suffering three thousand casualties, the *Armée d'Afrique* and the French Navy went over to the Allies. The French Navy lost most in terms of men and equipment resisting Torch. The *Armée d'Afrique* and the French Air Force found that, compared to American equipment, all the tanks and

---

* Under Vichy control, Madagascar's intricate shoreline provided hideouts for Japanese submarines that sank British supplies *en route* to Egypt for the Eighth Army; an intolerable situation for the Allies.

aircraft that Marshal Weygand spirited to French North Africa, away from the prying eyes of the Armistice Commission, were obsolete.

PARISIAN REACTION TO "TORCH" was mixed. Right-wingers like Jacques Doriot and Joseph Darnand were appalled, but many Frenchmen were thrilled that the Americans were involved at last. Liberation looked to be a serious possibility.

In Vichy the German Consul, Krug von Nidda, handed Prime Minister Laval a letter from Hitler offering France an immediate alliance *"durch dick und dunn"*—"through thick and thin". But Pétain refused. Recognising the danger, Hitler ordered his troops to invade southern France. Vichy's modest army was ordered not to resist. One divisional commander, the same General Jean de Lattre de Tassigny recommended by de Gaulle to defend Paris in 1940, made a token resistance to satisfy French honour, and was arrested for his pains. Thereafter he decided that de Gaulle was more deserving of his allegiance.

At Toulon, France's Mediterranean naval base west of the Riviera, Admiral Jean de Laborde—who, with eighty vessels, controlled much of the French Navy—dithered catastrophically. Admiral Auphan's orders to either keep the Germans outside the naval base or scuttle the ships did not help. The third option was the open sea. But the paintings of naval battles with *les Anglais* in Toulon's museum spoke louder to Laborde's Anglophobic soul than General Blaskowitz's panzer divisions devouring the *Midi*'s main roads. When Laborde realised he had neither the means to protect Toulon's naval base from tanks, nor time to make steam and put to sea, he gave the shameful order, *"Sabordez la flotte!"*—"Scuttle the fleet!" With tear-filled eyes his loyal *matelots* primed explosives and opened scuttling cocks, consigning superb ships to the shallow bed of the inner *Rade.*[*] Their heart-breaking

---

[*] The scuttling's prsctical results were first that the water in and around Toulon's port was polluted for two years; second that the naval base was unusable until around 1950 when the last of the scuttled vessels was raised and scrapped.

task completed, the *matelots* marched through Toulon town shouting, "Have them! Have them!" to Blaskowitz's panzer crews.[56]

In Paris, among several poignant indications of national despair, that great toyshop, Au Nain Bleu, set the *Tricolore* at half-mast on model battleships in their window. After losing both French North Africa and the fleet, Vichy was naked. Pétain's wiser aides advised winding up his relationship with Germany and flying to French North Africa. He refused this option too.

Admiral Darlan, who was in French North Africa to visit his sick son at the time of Operation Torch, negotiated the ceasefire with US General Mark Clark, much to Allied relief. But his weathercock politics had angered too many Frenchmen, and a group of Gaullist *résistants*, helped by the British, drew straws for who would kill him. In an incident pregnant with controversy, Darlan was gunned down by a royalist *résistant* called Bonnier de la Chapelle, who was subsequently executed by firing squad on Boxing Day 1942.[57]

Old-fashioned imperialists living in the *Haussmanien* apartment blocks of central Paris recognised that Torch presaged Germany's defeat. Those who had over-committed to fascism and *collaboration* now had nowhere to go, becoming die-hards. Allied air attacks on railways and industrial complexes around Paris ensured the hostility of this minority to both *les Anglo-Saxons* and de Gaulle. For pie-eyed gentleman writer Alphonse de Châteaubriant, owner of the *collabo* newspaper *La Gerbe*, and Joseph Darnand, head of the re-organised fascist militia, the *Milice*, Allied bombing provided a pretext for Nazi-style rallies at venues like the Vélodrome d'Hiver where, glistening with sweat, Jacques Doriot harangued the *collabo* right.[58]

1943

AS MONTGOMERY PUSHED THE AFRIKA KORPS westwards along the North African littoral following his victory at El Alamein, the time had come for Leclerc's long awaited link-up with the

British Eighth Army. Through Christmas 1942 his ragtag force drove northwards. Although Leclerc's men needed British material assistance, they were determined to maintain a sense of French independence. Advancing through southern Libya, rolling up outposts of Italy's empire, the Free French installed new governors and raised the *Tricolore*. By late January 1943, when Leclerc presented himself to Montgomery outside Tripoli, his force controlled two-thirds of Libya, which remained a French mandate until the 1950s.

With de Gaulle's permission, Leclerc now joined Montgomery; his men were issued British battledress and their equipment was beefed up with anti-tank guns and armoured cars. *La Colonne Leclerc* now became the British Eighth Army's 'Force L' entrusted with guarding their inland flank, a role they performed admirably. Following the final Axis collapse in May, a handful of Force L's least battered trucks tacked themselves onto the tail end of Eighth Army for the Tunis victory parade. Everyone cheered.

For Frenchmen, Leclerc's African achievements made him a greater hero than Lawrence of Arabia. Meanwhile, General de Gaulle was establishing his political ascendancy over the man the Americans wanted to replace him, General Henri Giraud. It seems strange that President Roosevelt chose Giraud as an alternative French leader. But he was handsome and undoubtedly brave so his name went in the hat as soon as he escaped from Schloss Koenigstein.[59]

De Gaulle had not endeared himself to Churchill and Roosevelt. As his role grew, so too did his sense of self-importance. In 1947, his eyes sparkling with irony, de Gaulle told Claude Guy, "Once he realised that I really was France, he [Churchill] fought me!"[60] But it was not really like that. Churchill was a public school educated aristocrat; Roosevelt and de Gaulle were their countries' equivalents. But Churchill and Roosevelt were their countries' elected chief executives which de Gaulle was not. De Gaulle's vainglorious notion that he *was* France provoked Churchill into saying, "He thinks he's Joan of Arc, we're looking for some bishops to burn him." Typical British schoolboy humour that Roosevelt would have winked at. There was also the problem that the

Free French were widely regarded by the *Armée d'Afrique* and the French Navy as traitors, making a *rapprochement* more difficult. Roosevelt wanted as many French servicemen supporting the Allied war effort as possible, thereby saving American lives. The US government was happy to re-equip French forces provided they were united.

Politically General Giraud was no match for de Gaulle. Whereas Giraud delayed dismantling Vichy's North African punishment camps, de Gaulle closed them instead. Giraud also had insurmountable authority problems with those who had followed de Gaulle since June 1940 who now claimed a moral ascendancy over their formerly Vichyite compatriots. During the 1930s Leclerc regarded Giraud as a soldier's soldier. But in 1943 Leclerc tersely advised Giraud to emulate General Catroux who, while outranking de Gaulle, recognised de Gaulle's political pre-eminence and consented to serve *under* him. Giraud's riposte was that Gaullists were too pure, unrealistically disregarding the shades of grey required to negotiate with Germany after 1940. He even accused Leclerc of wanting to erect a guillotine in every village square; Emmanuel d'Astier de la Vigerie made impassioned demands for the heads of *collabos* (he was filmed doing it) but Leclerc never did.

The antagonism between Leclerc and Giraud finally boiled over at a dinner given by Montgomery in early April. Sitting around a U-shaped dining table, using Leclerc's ADC Christian Girard as an interpreter, Giraud regaled Montgomery with the story of his escape from Schloss Koenigstein and subsequent negotiations with the Germans after he returned to Vichy. For these proud *Gaullistes de la première heure*, the sight of a French general describing his imprisonment and Vichy's compromised shenanigans to a British general looking radiant with victory was profoundly embarrassing. "Meanwhile," Leclerc interjected irritably, "we have been here fighting these last three years!"[61]

"I cannot understand him, the little Hauteclocque. Why should he be like this?" asked Giraud afterwards. "After all, it was I who gave him his *Légion d'Honneur* in Morocco!"[62]

General Giraud's greatest service to French interests was negotiating the American re-armament programme. During 13–24 January 1943, under what became known as the Anfa agreement, the Americans undertook to provide the French with sufficient equipment for three armoured divisions, nine motorised infantry divisions, and a thousand aircraft of which two hundred and fifty were modern fighters, as many again were bombers, and the rest much-needed transport aircraft. The Americans were less forthcoming over re-arming the French Navy. Important vessels like the battleship *Richelieu* and the cruiser *Georges Leygues* were reconditioned, but French naval tonnage would not resume 1939 levels for quite some time. Surplus French *matelots* were absorbed into the French Army by creating regiments of *Fusiliers Marins*, or marines. Small arms and replacement uniforms were also provided, meaning that, but for French insignia, French personnel appeared indistinguishable from their American allies.[63] Liberty ships delivered new equipment to French North Africa through 1943, the first convoy's arrival being watched from the Moroccan coast by Giraud himself.

THE ATMOSPHERE BETWEEN GAULLISTS and the larger *Armée d'Afrique* remained fractious. For Leclerc, the fight-back began with de Gaulle's *Appel* of 18 June 1940. General Giraud, however, insisted that French recovery began when he negotiated the Anfa agreement, challenging Gaullist orthodoxy by discounting the achievements of Generals Koenig and Leclerc. The controversy over whether de Gaulle was right all along or whether following Pétain was the correct path caused fistfights in the bars of Casablanca and Algiers. Christian Girard remarked in his diary that Giraud was creating "a basket of crabs".

To reduce tension, the original Free French brigades were ordered to leave French North Africa for Sabratha in northwest Libya. At first Leclerc refused to go, but General Sir Brian Horrocks threatened to cut off his supplies unless he complied. This, however, did not end the problems between the two Frances. Young men escaping from France via Spain to join the Allies in French North Africa came for de Gaulle, hoping to join Free French units. There were also numerous incidents of soldiers already serving with the *Armée d'Afrique* who simply transferred themselves to Leclerc. While not quite desertion, this practice became known as "*spontanément muté*"—"spontaneous self-transferral". Their behaviour mirrored the sea-change across French North Africa, where thirty months of loyalty to Pétain were swept away by de Gaulle.

The command of one of France's new armoured divisions was allocated to Leclerc, who took his promotion to *divisionnaire* modestly, telling Girard, "De Gaulle has no one else", which was probably true. Several French armoured warfare experts from the 1930s, like Jean Touzet du Vigier and Roger Leyer, had remained loyal to Pétain, but now saw plentiful American equipment as a splendid opportunity to remould France's tank arm. Under Leyer's supervision du Vigier formed the new First Armoured Division, or *Première Division Blindée*, Leclerc the *Deuxième Division Blindée* and, just to confuse matters, General Saint-Didier the Fifth or *Cinquième Division Blindée*.

Even with enthusiastic recruits choosing him, Leclerc had under four thousand men, while an American armoured division required sixteen thousand. In addition, much of Leclerc's original force consisted of black colonial troops and it was unheard of for coloured personnel to form part of an armoured division in any Western army. Leclerc was ordered to transfer his coloured soldiers to the First Free French Infantry Division, much to the sadness of career colonial officers such as Jacques Massu who truly loved these faithful soldiers of France. After deducting coloured troops in the obligatory *blanchiment* (whitening) process, the Chad veterans became the new division's motorised infantry regiment, but they were insufficient to provide a battalion for each of the new division's three battle groups. Regarding armoured regiments, formations that had served under the British Eighth Army, the *1e Régiment de Marche des Spahis Marocains* (1st RMSM) became the 2e DB's reconnaissance regiment, swapping their Marmon Herrington armoured cars for new American M8s. The *1e Régiment des Chars de Combat,* which had also served with the Eighth Army, along with supplementary personnel sent out from

Great Britain, became the 501e RCC, retaining its Crusader tanks for training purposes until Shermans arrived. But Leclerc still needed men to form two more tank regiments, a tank-destroyer regiment, three artillery regiments, engineers, more infantry, military police, medics and a handful of pilots (an American armoured division had six Piper Cub spotter aircraft).

Allowed back into French North Africa to begin his new task, Leclerc set up his divisional HQ on Algiers' Rue de Constantine. The Americans, who replaced the British as Free France's bankers and quartermasters, were everywhere: booking out the best hotels, forcing up restaurant prices, bringing largesse and can-do spirit to everything they touched. Heavy-hearted and reluctantly recognising that he needed to go cap in hand to the *Armée d'Afrique* for most of the men he needed to create the 2e DB, Leclerc took himself out for dinner to a popular restaurant outside Algiers. While enjoying his food, he noticed another French officer standing smartly beside him. Around a decade older than Leclerc, Colonel Paul de Langlade commanded the *12e Régiment Chasseurs d'Afrique* (12e RCA), a smart colonial cavalry regiment which converted to tanks during the late 1930s. Over brandy Langlade described his men's soul-destroying inactivity from 1940 until the Torch landings which, thanks to being quartered too far east, they had not opposed. Leclerc invited Langlade to bring his men into the 2e DB.[64] The 12e RCA had enough men for two tank regiments on the US model, so half became the 12e Cuirassiers to acknowledge Metropolitan cavalry regiments in suspended animation since *la Chute*.

Compared to individual "self-authorised transfers" this was a *spontanément muté* of an entire regiment. General Leyer was not pleased. But since Leclerc's division would necessarily include followers from both Free France and Vichy, General Giraud decided that it should include formed regiments whose colonels had proper authority wherever possible. Langlade's *grenouillage* (leap-frogging) was forgiven. "So are we Gaullists now?" asked Commandant Furst, one of the 12e RCA's least *Vichyste* officers, when their transfer to Leclerc was confirmed.[65]

In the interests of unity, Leclerc gave important divisional appointments to men who joined the 2e DB with Paul de Langlade. Captain André Gribius became the division's G3, or operations officer. Though detesting Vichy, Leclerc had to moderate his views of Pétain's former followers if he was to rebuild bridges with old friends like Jean Fanneau de la Horie. When Leclerc visited brother *divisionnaire* Jean Touzet du Vigier, his former instructor, to ask for La Horie, du Vigier emphasised that after *la Chute* Leclerc had the freedom of choices while du Vigier had a regiment to consider, but now it was necessary for France and her empire to work together.[66] Leclerc agreed, but privately, and not always particularly in private, his staunch Gaullist viewpoint remained unchanged.

AN UNAVOIDABLE REALITY OF CLANDESTINE WARFARE is that it is most successfully prosecuted by the working class. De Gaulle's early attempts to send agents into Occupied France often met with tragedy. In the meantime resistance groups grew from the bottom up, glued together by proletarian disciplines: unobtrusiveness, appearing unassuming, knowing how things work, manual practicality and lack of sentimentality. Since the proletariat is more numerous, a *résistant* had more people to hide among following acts of sabotage or assassination. But the tragedy of large-scale hostage shootings after FTP operations made de Gaulle determined to bring the *résistance interieure* under centralised command. When senior civil servant Jean Moulin arrived in London, de Gaulle thought he had the perfect candidate to unite the *résistance interieure*.[67]

Now codenamed *Max*, Moulin's first trip back to France on de Gaulle's orders went well; he joined three groups under the authority of MUR—*Mouvements Unis de la Résistance*. These were Henri Frenay's *Combat*, Emmanuel d'Astier de la Vigerie's *Libération* and, most importantly, Jean-Paul Lévy's *Francs Tireurs*, thereby demonstrating a working-class resistance group's willingness to accept centralised command. Returning to London, Moulin was accompanied by sixty-four-year-old General Charles Delestraint, who commanded an armoured unit during 1940. Already linked to Frenay, when de Gaulle decided to merge *Combat*, *Libération* and *Francs Tireurs** into the *Armée Secrète*, he appointed Delestraint its commander to avoid unfairly favouring one of the three group leaders over another, despite Delestraint's lack of clandestine experience.[68]

Other working-class *résistants* also turned to de Gaulle for central leadership. Prompted by Moscow, Fernand Grenier arrived in London offering to place the FTP under de Gaulle's authority. After the horrific losses inflicted by the German invasion, Stalin favoured anything that diverted Nazi pressure from the Soviet Union; French unity under de Gaulle served his interests. He was also grateful to de Gaulle for sending fighter pilots to serve with the Red Air Force, and had little wish to undermine him. But de Gaulle distrusted the communist FTP while the FTP regarded the London connection as a useful source of weapons while they continued operating as before.[69] Moulin's formation of the *Conseil National de la Résistance* (CNR) was useful progress for de Gaulle. But the FTP regarded hierarchies as alien to the essentially fluid nature of clandestine warfare.

In mid-1943 a set of tragedies befell the Resistance that echo to this day. Arriving back in France in March 1943, General Delestraint soon had authority problems; the FTP regarded his belief in fixed base units as tantamount to creating sitting ducks for SD[†]s detection units and a waste of the armaments now available from England. Graciously, the traditional Delestraint accepted their viewpoint. However, the FTP's underlying realism was grimly justified when Delestraint, a proud, distinguished-looking man, not given to camouflaging himself, and his adjutant, both smartly dressed, were arrested at the 16th Arrondissement's La Muette Metro Station. From SIPO's mugshots of Delestraint taken after his arrest, the only thing missing was a bowler hat.[70] They were followed all the way from Dijon. After

---

* Not to be confused with the communist group, *Franc Tireurs et Partisans* (FTP).
† SD = *SicherheitsDienst*—the 'Security Service' which came under the authority of the SS.

a two-day interrogation, Delestraint was imprisoned in Fresnes before being sent to Dachau.[*]

Compounding the tragedy, when Jean Moulin called a meeting at Doctor Dugoujon's house in Lyons' Caluire suburb to decide Delestraint's replacement, the Gestapo captured all of them. There are several theories over who betrayed him: whether it was René Hardy, who had been arrested, interrogated and released shortly before Moulin's arrest; or simply that there was an atmosphere of jealousy, squabbling and betrayal among the Resistance anyway.[†] Nevertheless, basic precautions were ignored. Several present at the Caluire meeting were already known to the Gestapo and, as marked men, should have quarantined themselves for weeks rather than days. Interrogated brutally by the notorious Klaus Barbie, Moulin died a couple of weeks later on a train to Germany.[71] The Caluire arrests inflicted a massive setback on de Gaulle's efforts to bring the disparate resistance groups under central control.

De Gaulle never found anyone in Moulin's league to head up the CNR. Georges Bidault, a left-wing Catholic was decent enough, but nowhere near as effective. FTP leader Charles Tillon later wrote that de Gaulle, the Free French and the Allies were reactionaries and *attentistes* who simply wanted to control the Resistance for their own ends, imposing bankrupt tactics of doing nothing. Bemused that de Gaulle should appoint former Legion officer Marie Pierre Koenig to command the FFI—*Forces Françaises de l'Intérieure*—the FTP believed the best way to save French lives was to hit the enemy by every possible

---

[*] Even in Dachau Delestraint was attended by his ADC. Delestraint was executed a few days before the German surrender.

[†] An interesting footnote on p. 255 of Charles Tillon's book, *FTP*, suggests that the Gestapo were able to unravel Delestraint's connections, and thereby Moulin's as well, because one Paul Lieu was not only a member of *Combat* but also belonged to a réseau called *Alliance* set up by former Cagoulard Georges Loustaunau-Lacau. Loustaunau-Lacau's loyalties wavered during the early Occupation between Vichy, where he was linked to anti-Semite Xavier Vallat, then veering towards the *maquis* and then being betrayed. Untidy loyalties left trails.

means, cutting railways, immobilising locomotives and sabotaging factories. They thought it criminally stupid to place themselves under foreign military command and, while tugging a forelock to de Gaulle in return for weapons, they thought submission to that portion of the French Army he controlled—mainly *la Coloniale*—was little better.[72]

De Gaulle fell back on a system of military delegates to maintain his authority in mainland France. Though sixteen years younger than Moulin, it was no coincidence that his chief delegate, Jacques Chaban-Delmas, also hailed from France's *grandes écoles*. This time, recognising Chaban's ability (Chaban was a *nom de guerre*) de Gaulle bounced him up from reserve captain to *général de brigade*. Furthermore, having been a *résistant* since 1940, Chaban understood clandestine life and, like Rol-Tanguy, developed a sixth sense for when something felt wrong. Though good-looking, Chaban was of medium height with no eccentricities of dress or physique to distinguish him. As a keen three quarters rugby player, Chaban was also a fast runner; a talent that had saved his life.[73]

To de Gaulle's chagrin Chaban had little authority over military matters in the *Conseil Nationale de la Résistance*. The FTP dominated the *résistance interieure* and, while they regarded the London link as essential, they formed COMAC (*Comité Militaire d'Action*), a three-man committee to decide on military action, standing separately from the hierarchy Moulin created. COMAC regarded Chaban's role as advisory and to provide weapons.

Between COMAC's leaders—"the three Vs", so-called because all their *noms de guerre* began with a V—the Left, and Jews, predominated. Roger Ginsberger, the son of a rabbi, architect and trade unionist, was *Villon*. Maurice Kriegel, a young radical Jewish lawyer with syndicalist connections, was *Valrimont*. The third man, in a perverse linking of social opposites, was Count Jean de Vogüé—*Vaillant*—an aristocratic naval officer. Vogüé had made the pilgrimage to London but had not got on with de Gaulle. Torn in several directions by the Occupation, Vogüé's populist leanings won through and he returned to France to fight, going under cover and eschewing all contact with family and friends. Vogüé was "my exact antithesis", wrote Kriegel-*Valrimont*, "the typical class enemy. My first meeting with him was not friendly. But on getting to know him, I was astonished. He wanted the same thing I wanted; to fight for freedom giving no quarter. We recognised our differences, certainly, but apart from that, he was a rebel in himself, an absolute hero." Kriegel-*Valrimont* considered himself in good company on COMAC.[74]

WITHIN PARIS ITSELF YET ANOTHER COMMITTEE was created during late August 1943, providing yet another parallel command chain, the *Comité Parisien de Libération*—the Paris Liberation Committee, or CPL. As veteran French historian Christine Levisse-Touzé writes, "It held executive power over deliberating assemblies, both national and Parisian, and over a clandestine army, the FFIs, from 1 February 1944."[75]

On the CPL, once again, left-wingers abounded. Under the authority of André Tollet, a CGT union official, the CPL included André-Max Hoschiller to manage liaison between the police and FFI, George Marrane of the French Communist Party; Marie-Helene Lefaucheux, the wife of a *résistant* industrialist, from the *Organisation Civile et Militaire*, one of the earliest resistance groups; Leo Hamon from *Ceux de la Résistance*; Robert Deniau, secretary of the CGT union, also representing resistance group *Libération Nord*; and Jacques Bingen,* a Jewish engineer related to the Citroen family, to act as consultant for the CFLN (*Comité Français de Libération Nationale*).[76]

Reflecting French enthusiasm for bureaucracy, the CPL's role was defined by two separate texts: first in the *Statuts des Comités Départmentaux de Libération* of 23 March 1944, and secondly the *Ordonnance* of 21 April. During the remaining months of the *période clandestine* the CPL's task was to "co-ordinate immediate action against the enemy and his accomplices, prepare the national

---

* In May 1944 Jacques Bingen was arrested in Clermont Ferrand following betrayal by an Abwehr double agent, but managed to take his cyanide pill.

insurrection and the allocation of powers for the day of liberation".
Next, during the *période insurrectionelle*, the CPL was to "organise and
co-ordinate the actions of patriots in order to dislocate the German
forces and eliminate enemy agents; to facilitate the establishment
of new public offices, notably representing centralised power". On
liberation the CPL's role would become "to act as the provisional
representatives of the population in the department until the [arrival
of] designated authorities of the central power and to assist them
in their task".[77]

Before the insurrection, or rather before the shooting began, the
CPL's administrative tasks were preparing posters, organising protests,
helping those evading the hated STO (*Service Travial Obligatoire*),
encouraging strikes and other forms of collective action. The phrase
"*milice patriotique*" (as distinct from Darnand's *collabo* paramilitary
Milice) was used to describe rank and file *résistants* from all groups.
The CPL's advice was that *résistants* should be organised along the lines
of an infantry section of six to eight people. The envisaged actions
were intended to dissipate German efforts to create an organised
defence. The CPL also intervened in everyday issues to control the
cost of living, maintain bread quality and denounce suppliers of
stale meat.[78]

From September 1943 its media officers devised wall posters to
correct the lies put out by German propaganda, like the *Deutsche
Wochenschau*, by reproducing information from the BBC World
Service. It aimed to create an atmosphere of upheaval to shake Parisians
into activity, a goal that was only partially achieved. Beginning in
November 1943 the CPL's newspaper, *Le Patriote Parisien*, encouraged
strikes in factories supporting the Nazi war effort. During the *période
clandestine*, however, the CPL advised against attacking German
personnel directly. Sabotage, such as derailments, was permissible but
military violence came under COMAC's authority.[79]

Short of direct military action the CPL performed initial measures
of the process which became *épuration* (the purge)—identification
of traitors and *collabos* so they could be brought to justice. Since the

Third Republic, Paris had developed exceptional municipal institutions. The elected Municipal Council administered all aspects of life falling outside the political control of the Prefect of the Department of the Seine (which shared offices at the Hôtel de Ville) or the Prefect of Police based at the Préfecture. Being tainted by Vichy, prefects René Bouffet and Amedée Bussière, loyal, dutiful Parisians though they were, would have to be replaced.[80]

But the left-wingers dominating the Resistance deluded themselves if they thought liberation provided a springboard for revolution. Basically conservative, de Gaulle was not such a fool as to remove Vichy officials without having his own replacements waiting in the wings. Well before D-Day he chose Marcel Flouret as Prefect of the Department of the Seine and Charles Luizet as Prefect of the Paris Police. The Constable never intended to allow Paris to fall to the Left at the liberation.[81]

Alexandre Parodi, de Gaulle's political delegate in France, bore two *noms de guerre*: *Quartus* and *Cerat*. Tasked with uniting the Resistance around Paris, Parodi was assisted by two secretaries: Felix Gaillard, who negotiated the labyrinthine layers of governance that bedevilled Occupied France, and Michel de Boissieu,[*] who advised on political matters. They were supported in their turn by regional adjutants Jacques Maillet (*Mirabeau*) for the south of the country, and Roland Pré (*Daru*) for the north, who had recently been parachuted in from London. This "Delegation" included various committees covering areas such as intelligence appraisal, finance, press, radio and social matters. These organs accomplished important groundwork enabling the new régime to hit the ground running once France was liberated, avoiding the need for AMGOT. Though quietly spoken, Parodi demanded absolute discipline. With the Gestapo and their *collabo* henchmen becoming more experienced, Parodi prioritised security just as much as Henri Rol-Tanguy.[82]

---

[*] A cousin of Alain de Boissieu, who commanded Leclerc's HQ protection squadron.

1944

FOR THE MUNICIPAL COUNCIL the bombing of railways and factories clearly indicated that the invasion was imminent. It also made the feeding and fuelling of Paris far more difficult. A useful corrollary of this problem was that the Municipal Council could claim fit young men and women as essential workers who might otherwise have been sent to Germany under the hated STO. Though not directed by the London French, Taittinger insisted this form of resistance deserved respect.[83]

Since Paris had been declared an open city in 1940, Taittinger hoped for a similar arrangement as liberation approached. Both the United States Army Air Force and the Royal Air Force were asked not to bomb central Paris.[84] The Municipal Council struggled to ensure that as few factories as possible made Paris a legitimate military target. After an SKF ball-bearing factory was destroyed in the *banlieues,* its Swedish proprietors suggested rebuilding it at the Parc des Expositions. But when another of their factories was destroyed near the Porte de Versailles, SKF relented and considered Dugny-Le Bourget instead.[85]

Metro workers warned the council that an abandoned line was being used as a German munitions factory. Emissaries protested to Vichy, insisting that if Paris was bombed Germans would be endangered as well as French; an obviously frail argument when German cities were suffering much worse.[86] Similar protests were made when German anti-aircraft guns were sited on the esplanade of Les Invalides. After weeks of negotiation, Taittinger got them removed. He found that Germans who had served in Russia were least sympathetic, whereas those stationed in Paris the longest were much kinder.[87]

Yet, whatever privations they caused, Allied bomber crews were grudgingly respected by Parisians. When an RAF bomber came down on the Rue St Honoré after desperately attempting to ditch in the Seine, Taittinger described the crew's deaths as *"glorieuse".*[88]

Nor did efforts to de-militarise Paris stop with the Municipal Council. Taittinger was also supported by Cardinal Emmanuel Suhard, the Archbishop of Paris. Although, like many Catholic clergymen in occupied Europe, Suhard trod the confused moral line between alleviating suffering while detesting communism, he perfectly understood Taittinger's aims. So too did senior Protestant pastor Marc Boegner, a friend to many senior *collabos*.[89]

Having done well from the Aryanisation of Jewish property, Taittinger was anxious to build credit with the Gaullist establishment in Algiers by pleading for captured *résistants*, though Gaullists more often than communists. "Are all your friends like this?" sneered General von Boineburg-Lengsfeld, the Military Governor of Paris, albeit amenable to a champagne magnate's pleas.[90]

Boineburg-Lengsfeld's immediate superior, General Karl-Heinrich von Stulpnagel, who replaced his cousin General Otto von Stulpnagel as Military Governor of France, was also morally conflicted by the matter of prisoners, whether Jews or *résistants*. Long aware that Hitler would lead Germany to disaster, Karl-Heinrich von Stulpnagel nevertheless served him competently. During the opening six months of the Russian campaign Stulpnagel's attitude toward massacring Jews was contradictory, to say the least. Sometimes he facilitated *Einsatzgruppen* activities, on other occasions he asked their commanders not to shoot Jews in front of his soldiers. Transferred to Paris, Stulpnagel had a good working relationship with SS Chief Karl Oberg, based on former regimental ties. Both detested hostage killings but abetted the Nazis' Jewish policy. Under Stulpnagel's auspices the German military HQ in Paris became a hotbed of anti-Nazi resistance. "He is tired though," Ernst Junger wrote of Stulpnagel. "His face betrays sorrow."[91]

As a Francophile German Ambassador, Otto Abetz became deeply depressed at how the war was going. Four years of helping the Third Reich exploit his wife's fellow countrymen and endless pleas for prisoners had taken their toll. These negotiations now went both ways. Once de Gaulle controlled French North Africa and political trials of *collabos* captured after the Axis collapse began, Abetz could not help but reflect on the possible fate of his French friends when they fell into Gaullist hands.[92]

SWEDISH CONSUL-GENERAL RAOUL NORDLING had an untroubled conscience. A large, affable, wealthy man, corpulent from good living, whose blue eyes twinkled with sophistication and kindness, Nordling had only briefly worn uniform for national service. His weapons were his open face, his soft pleading voice, his humanity and Sweden's neutrality.

Born in 1881 of a Swedish father and French mother, Nordling was twenty-three when appointed Vice-Consul, to act as his father's deputy. His first experience of wartime diplomacy came in 1914, when Frenchmen anguished over captured relations or with family behind the German lines in eastern France would call at the Rue d'Anjou Consulate. The Nordlings also helped France maintain commercial links with Sweden, preventing Germany from becoming Sweden's sole trading partner. Raoul Nordling was as much a Parisian mandarin as Taittinger but, cloaked in Swedish neutrality, more doors were open to him.[93]

Nordling's memoirs make fascinating reading. During late 1942 he was approached by the elderly Italian journalist and anti-fascist refugee, Domenico Russo, who wanted to discuss a possible peace treaty negotiated through the Vatican. Many Italians detested Mussolini's alliance with Hitler, believing they would be occupied once the African war was lost. Once that happened, Russo believed the Papacy would be powerless to mediate, leaving only Sweden's King Gustav V capable of doing so. Nordling admitted, "I was sceptical but, in a way, I was also seduced." The fact that Russo had Swiss support lent credibility but, realistically speaking, Nordling knew there was little he could do. Nevertheless, by early 1944 Russo had involved Pierre Laval who, while publicly bullish about Germany's victory prospects, privately disabused himself that Germany could still win the war. At a large reception at the German Embassy, Laval led Nordling towards a quiet corner.

"We ought to stop this war," said Laval.

Surprised at Laval's frankness, Nordling was evasive.

"But you know King Gustav, *Monsieur le Consul General*," Laval insisted.

Nordling reminded Laval of the promise he gave the German authorities in 1940 not to involve himself in politics.

"If I had a free hand, I would broach the matter with [Anthony] Eden and the Americans. I now have better relations with the Anglo-Saxons," said Laval, in willful denial of the effect of his actions since 1940. "But it would be preferable if such negotiations could be made through Stockholm."

Abetz's deputy, Consul-General Schleier, was listening from a discreet distance.

"It would be best, Monsieur Nordling," said Schleier, "that you have a conversation with Ambassador Abetz."

A few days later Abetz invited Nordling back to the Rue de Lille. "What sort of man is he [Russo]?" asked Abetz. Nordling explained how Russo was introduced by the Hungarian Consul-General in 1942, distancing himself by explaining that German diplomats knew more about Hungary than a Swede.*

"There are in Germany various factions who would seize power, and it is not always easy to tell which are important," said Abetz sternly. "In your place, Monsieur Nordling, I would be prudent. One does not want it said that it is Germany who is seeking peace."

Visiting the Swedish legation in Vichy, Nordling discovered more about Laval's overtures. Much to everyone's embarrassment, the story reached a London-based Swedish journalist, leading to a small article being released via Reuters. On 20 March Nordling telephoned Abetz to mitigate the damage.

---

* By March 1944 Hitler was exasperated by Hungarian Regent Admiral Horthy's slowness in fulfilling the de-Jewification programme, the Hungarian Army's poor showing in Russia, and Prime Minister Miklos Kallay's peace feelers to the Allies.

"We have become objects of interest to the world's press, Monsieur Nordling," said Abetz. "They are absolutely furious in Berlin, because it's Germany who appears to have asked for peace."

Later, at the German Embassy, Abetz accused Nordling of indiscretion. Nordling categorically denied this, or that any indiscretion came from Stockholm. A few days later, "during a restrained press conference", Abetz claimed the Allies were seeking peace, quipping that "the Swedish Consul General has been short-listed for the Nobel Peace Prize".

"I thought I heard you say recently that you suspected me of putting my candidature forward for a Nobel prize," replied Nordling. "Wasn't that linked to these mediation feelers, Monsieur Ambassador?"

Abetz shrugged, "It's possible that my tongue is too long."

Next, in a priceless indiscretion, one of Abetz's deputies informed Russo that the German Foreign Ministry might negotiate if Germany was promised a free hand in the Ukraine. Again Abetz was furious, railing that Russo was "a notorious agent in the pay of England". Russo was arrested for a few days, after which he lay low. Nordling reported personally to Stockholm, but before leaving he visited Abetz, who tried to push Nordling into a corner of his *salon*.

"Is there a microphone?" asked Nordling.

"Certainly not," said Abetz, who seemed verging on despair. "Himmler has his police and so does Ribbentrop. There's no security anywhere."

Nordling recognised the fear behind this remark.

"Sweden is the only country in the world through which we could seek a peace," Abetz remarked solemnly. "I beg you not to do anything that could close this avenue."

But the Nazis would never agree to anything remotely resembling the "unconditional surrender" the Allies had required since Casablanca, and Nordling's only reward for this affair was that several of Abetz's staff nicknamed him "the Gentleman of Paris".[94]

MOST PARISIANS WERE OBLIVIOUS of these negotiations, distracting themselves from the Occupation's greyness as best they could. Some remained in bed whenever possible. Despite reduced electricity supply, cinemas flourished. Eighty-one directors made films during the Occupation; around a quarter were first-time filmmakers.[95] Stars like Ginette Leclerc, Arletty, Michele Morgan, Maurice Chevalier and Jean Gabin continued working. Some were subsequently accused of collaboration, but most Frenchmen recognised that entertainment was necessary during hard times.

Just as French directors produced films whose subject-matter marginalised the war, so did the Germans. UFA Studio's *Baron Munchausen*, starring Hans Albers, provided pure fun and fantasy of which the Hungarian Korda brothers, then working in England, would have been proud. With Venetian gondola scenes, topless black women and wonderful special effects, it opened in February 1944 at the Champs Élysées' Normandie Cinema to such crowds that the Paris police had to intervene.[96]

Sacha Guitry worked throughout the war. The German authorities approved his film *Ceux de chez nous*, which innocuously celebrated French artists of sculpture, literature, theatre and painting including Rodin, Monet, Degas, Anatole France, Edmond Rostand and Sarah Bernhardt, to whose house his father Lucien took him as a child instead of church.[97] During this period Guitry finished another marriage and pleaded for various Jews including his friend, Henri Bergson. Wantonly denounced by bottle-blond actress Françoise Rosay, who was stranded in French North Africa after Torch and where, among other trivialities, she tried flirting with General Leclerc,[98] Guitry would have trouble at the liberation simply because his Théatre Madeleine was popular among German officers.

Shortages meant that Parisians arrived at theatres and cinemas by bicycle. Plentiful French forestry meant wood was used far more than usual; charcoal-powered gazogene converted engines on cars, wooden-soled shoes became commonplace, and clogs reappeared. Even with paper rationing, French publishing produced more titles during the Occupation than Great Britain and America combined. Moral compromises and endless permutations of the *double jeu*—double game—were inevitable and limitless. Jean-Paul Sartre's play *No Exit* opened at the Vieux Colombier Theatre that summer. Sartre's words also filled Resistance pamphlets. But *collabo* writers like Châteaubriant, Céline, Maurras and Drieu la Rochelle would have much to fear when the liberation came, as would critics whose articles supported Nazi values, such as Robert Brasillach. Once a bright young man writing for *Action Française*, Brasillach switched to the new *Je suis partout* which disintegrated into a *collabo* rag after 1940. Notably, however, Brasillach recognised the bizarre avoidance of contemporary events in French drama, though Anouilh's *Becket* was full of allusions.

Of those writers who retained their pre-war beliefs, bean-pole tall, satirical journalist and Great War veteran Jean Galtier-Boissière closed down his journal *Crapouillot* (slang for "trench mortar") rather than submit to *collabo* censorship, eking out a slender living selling secondhand books in the university area instead. Jean Guehenno felt similarly and became a teacher.[99]

Colette, the famous author of libidinous semi-autobiographical novels, was in her late sixties when the Occupation began. Surprisingly, she wrote for *collabo* publications including Châteaubriant's *La Gerbe*. Meanwhile, she hid her third husband, the Jewish jeweller turned writer Maurice Goudeket, in her Palais Royal apartment. Seventeen years her junior, Goudeket was captured in 1940. He escaped back to Paris only to be placed under protective house arrest by his wife. Since she nicknamed him "Mr. Goodcock" his incarceration may have had reasons beyond his safety.[100]

SO WHEN PABLO PICASSO LED the beautiful young art student Françoise Gilot up into the *forêt** above his *atelier* and said, "There's one thing I'd like very much, and that is if you would stay there,

---

* In French *forêt* does not only mean 'forest' but also a heavily timber-beamed attic.

beginning right now, up in the *forêt*; just disappear completely so that no one would ever know you were there. I'd bring you food twice a day. You could work up there in tranquillity, and I'd have a secret in my life that no one could take away from me," it seems less weird than it might today.[101] Considering that Gilot had recently been chucked by the young man she hoped would deflower her, quarrelled with her father over wanting to become a painter, and was living with her kindly grandmother while teaching rich children to ride in the Bois de Boulogne to make ends meet, Picasso's offer, irrespective of his age, was inevitably attractive.

Being blacklisted as "degenerate" and banned from exhibiting only increased Picasso's cachet. After Céline called him a "Jew", Picasso recognised some caution was necessary but mainly continued as before. If he had run-ins with the authorities he complained as high as he could. Besides, he had Hitler's favourite sculptor Arno Breker to protect him. Picasso displayed moments of moral cowardice, like when he refused to sign a petition for the release of Max Jacob in February 1944, and moments of bravery as well.[102] Early in their relationship Picasso introduced Françoise to André Malraux, whose books she admired. After Malraux left, Picasso said, "I hope you appreciate the gift I made you, letting you talk to Malraux. After all no one should have seen him here. It's too dangerous. He just slipped in from the *maquis*."

"I told him I did not know whether I was grateful or not," she later wrote.[103]

Picasso could have emigrated in 1940, like other anti-fascist Spaniards. Instead inertia overwhelmed him, keeping him in Paris mixing with bohemians, several of whom were *résistants*. Throughout the Occupation, *Guernica*, his great abstract protest at the bombing of a defenceless Basque town, remained in his *atelier* where several Germans saw it. When one asked, "Did you do this?" Picasso replied superbly, "No. You did!" Picasso embellished this anecdote with each retelling until the German became Otto Abetz himself.[104]

Though in many ways an appalling man, Abetz loved art. Following Hitler's directive of 30 June 1940, Abetz confiscated fifteen of the most important Jewish private art collections in Paris.[105] He then took what he wanted; his apartment at the German Embassy contained seven Picassos, fourteen Braques and four by Fernand Léger.[106] Yet, of the paintings passing through the *Einsatzstab Reichsleiter Rosenberg's* Jeu de Paume showroom, several Picassos were inventoried as *"prévu pour la destruction"*—to be destroyed—for "degeneracy".[107]

AFTER FRANCO'S VICTORY IN THE SPANISH CIVIL WAR, many Spanish Republicans crossed the Pyrenees into France to be interned in fetid camps dotted around *la France profonde*. Many were absorbed into French society while others emigrated to French North Africa, only to find themselves badly caught out in 1940 when the colony came under Vichy rule. Men of military age were offered service in the Foreign Legion, but usually refused the invitation to join Vichy's portion of that famous corps. Around thirty thousand Spanish Republican *refuseniks* were incarcerated in sadistic prison camps, such as Hadjerat M'Guil, and sent to work on the Mediterranean-Niger railway in grim conditions. When de Gaulle closed these camps in 1943, their worst commandants were sentenced to the firing squad with the words, "You have disgraced France."[108]

After such treatment one might imagine that fighting for France was the last thing these Spaniards would do. But for de Gaulle, they did. The *Corps Franc d'Afrique* was formed from miscellaneous Frenchmen, Spaniards, Jews and other oddballs, becoming an effective unit which performed well during the Tunisian campaign. Afterwards they were absorbed into the *Regiment de Marche du Tchad*, Leclerc's motorised infantry regiment, to bring it up to strength after transfering its African personnel. "A toff like me commanding a bunch of reds!" sighed Leclerc when he heard what he had received.[109]

EVEN WITH EISENHOWER'S GOODWILL, de Gaulle still lacked President Roosevelt's support; Roosevelt disliked the idea of unelected generals assuming power. Churchill shared these misgivings and was dismayed by the show trials of *collabos* in French North Africa, particularly that of Pierre Pucheu, calling the Algiers government, "De Gaulle and his vindictive crowd".[110] A senior *collabo* who tried to change sides, Pucheu was initially protected by General Giraud, but Gaullists demanded Pucheu's arrest. The trial descended into farce: insubstantial evidence, judges falling asleep, and then, after the charges were redrafted on the hoof, a predictable death sentence.

Even Leclerc's officers became concerned over what kind of France they were fighting for. "The trial of Pucheu has made a deplorable impression," wrote Christian Girard. "It's not so much the verdict that has given rise to reproaches, but that the conduct of the trial appears to be a parody of justice. Little proof in the form of documents or facts, almost nothing but a few witness declarations. If circumstances require, as I suspect, the condemnation of Pucheu, it would be better to do it in a way that does not give rise to such an outcry."[111]

Disregarding pleas for clemency, de Gaulle spent a sleepless night before confirming Pucheu's death sentence, saying, "I owe this to France."[112] While CFLN Commissioner Emmanuel d'Astier de la Vigerie thought sparing Pucheu would be a slap in the face to the Resistance, Churchill's ambassador to the Algiers government, Alfred Duff-Cooper, was appalled. "Pucheu was shot this morning. He met his death apparently with great courage, shaking hands with the firing squad and giving the order to fire himself. I am very glad that they allowed him to do this and did not bind him."[113]

Nevertheless, despite the foreseeable ugliness of French liberation politics, senior COSSAC* planner General Morgan deemed it essential that the D-Day landings had CFLN support. Eisenhower preferred to wait and see what local conditions made practicable, but British Foreign Secretary Anthony Eden protested that only a uniform decision would avoid chaos. The only alternative to dealing with the CFLN was negotiating with Vichy, which as René Massigli pointed out, would not do.[114]

---

* COSSAC = *Chief of Staff Supreme Allied Command*, ie General Frederick Morgan but also the considerable staff under him who were responsible for planning.

Since January de Gaulle had been lobbying Duff Cooper over the transportation to England of the 2e DB. Noting that General Leclerc "is said to be the most popular man in France after de Gaulle", Duff Cooper advised de Gaulle to mention the 2e DB before raising matters like the Syrian affair and AMGOT, since AMGOT particularly was the most contentious.[115]

Despite Churchill's misgivings over de Gaulle personally, the British vocally promoted the idea of a French division joining the northern campaign rather than leaving all the newly equipped French divisions with de Lattre's First Army. This was confirmed by SHAEF* on 12 January 1944. Considering the pressures an armoured division placed on ship space, it was also noted that, if Leclerc's division was included, an American armoured division would be held back.[116] Transporting the 2e DB required twenty-four LSTs (Landing Ship Tanks), which could only be done using vessels returning from supplying the Italian front. The same day that Pierre Pucheu was sentenced to death, Duff Cooper received a telegram from Churchill: "He [Churchill] tells me that he is much in favour of the Division fighting with the main invasion forces from England, that Eisenhower agrees with him, and that he is, therefore, doing all in his power to overcome the difficulties of transportation. I am glad to have this information to give de Gaulle, which ought to cheer him up."[117]

On 29 March Leclerc boarded an RAF aircraft for Algiers. Seeing him off, Girard watched fascinated as the crew saluted Leclerc with discreet deference. In Algiers Leclerc met his wife's cousin, Canadian Major-General Georges Vanier, and Duff Cooper, whose diary reads, "I went out to see Vanier during the afternoon in order to meet General Leclerc, a dapper little soldier exactly like an English officer, quiet and giving one the impression of competence. I told Leclerc and Vanier that it was almost certain that his division would go to England to take part in the invasion. He was naturally delighted to hear it."[118]

---

* SHAEF = *Supreme Headquarters Allied Expeditionary Force.*

Awaiting his commander's return beside Temara's airstrip, Girard fell asleep in the Ford.

"Ambassadors, no less, have been concerning themselves with the 2e DB," said Leclerc as he got in the car. "We're the *political* division!"

Major General and Madame Vanier's arrival from Algiers accompanied by Leclerc's brother, Guy de Hauteclocque, indicated that the 2e DB was becoming the renascent French Army's pre-eminent division. Girard found it strange walking among comrades who remained unaware of SHAEF's decision; "I had to suppress the desire to shout the news from the rooftops," he wrote.[119]

On 7 April General de Gaulle arrived in his personal Lockheed Hudson. First he inspected the tank regiments at Rabat, walking along rows of parked Shermans, Stuarts and M8 armoured cars, shaking hands as he passed. Colonel Louis Dio, one of Leclerc's closest associates since 1940, paraded the Chad Regiment at Skhrirat. Bayonets fixed, they presented arms in an enormous phalanx, as de Gaulle walked slowly through their ranks. Though supplemented by Spaniards and other nationalities from the *Corps Franc d'Afrique*, many of these men had been Gaullists for four years. They would get their reward. That evening, in Temara's casino, de Gaulle told Leclerc's officers that the 2e DB would soon depart for England. They cheered. The letter appointing Leclerc "interim governor" of Paris was no empty gesture. They were going.

AMAZINGLY, DURING EARLY 1944 Marshal Pétain's popularity lifted. On 25 April the Prefect of the Seine, René Bouffet, summoned Pierre Taittinger and the Prefect of Police Amedée Bussière to his office at the Hôtel de Ville. Pétain would visit Paris the following morning for the first time since 1940 to show Parisians his solidarity with their hardships and the uncertainty that lay ahead. He would attend a requiem mass at Notre Dame for those killed by the bombing in the 18th Arrondissement on 20 April and do a walkabout. But there should be no announcements and no publicity.

"The Marshal must come without any visible police escort," insisted Louis-Dominique Girard, an emissary from Vichy. "There must be no exaggerated protective measures and certainly no German uniforms at any price. If Paris is left to the Parisian population and if the Marshal can communicate directly with them then there shouldn't be any incidents to worry about."

Paving the way, Girard visited arch-collaborator Fernand de Brinon, Vichy's ambassador in Paris, to impress upon him that Pétain refused to meet any Germans, *collabos* or *Milice* leaders—a measure clearly intended to dissociate the Marshal from reprisals and excesses committed against the Resistance. To Cardinal Suhard, Girard also insisted that visiting dignitaries enter Notre Dame discreetly through the Rue du Cloitre Notre Dame side entrance. After the service a lunch reception would be held at the Hôtel de Ville.[120]

On 26 April, with no prior warning, those gathered on the *Parvis* of Notre Dame de Paris began cheering when Pétain arrived, sitting in the back of an open topped limousine between Prefects Bouffet and Bussière, all in smart uniforms. Even Gaullist sympathiser Claude Mauriac was moved to see Pétain in his khaki greatcoat and gold braided képi bathed in spring sunshine. During the service, news spread that the Marshal was in Paris and crowds gathered between Notre Dame and the Hôtel de Ville, waving *Tricolores* for the first time since June 1940. Infant children who had never seen France's flag were made to look at it by their mothers.

During the luncheon the crowd thickened on Place de l'Hôtel de Ville.

"The acclamations are for the Victor of Verdun, to the uniform that you wear; saluting in you the army of another time in the hope of having a new army tomorrow. You are the incarnation of *la Patrie* and not of a government. One should not seek to find a political argument in the cheers they are giving you," Taittinger told Pétain.[121]

After luncheon in the Salon Jean-Paul Laurens, Pétain was asked several times if he was returning to Paris permanently.

"I have returned as a stranger," he replied. Then, almost as if he saw himself as Christ, believing in the kitsch busts of himself decorating every *mairie*, he announced, "On our soil we can no longer make our laws. *I will come among you again* when, as in the past, we are able to be among ourselves."

Outside, Pétain mounted the plush draped scaffold to be engulfed by cheering. The famous blue eyes welled up. Trying to prevent himself from choking, he spoke hoarsely. "I have come at a time of great unhappiness to lift from you the ills which hang over Paris. It is the first visit that I have made to you. I hope that I will be able to return before long *without being obliged to warn my guardians*. Today is not a formal arrival in Paris; it is a little reconnaissance visit. I think of you always. When I return we will have a lot to say to each other. That, then, will be an official visit. *À bientôt*, I hope." The crowd cheered, but the new relay equipment malfunctioned. Only a few strongly ennunciated phrases, such as "my hope to find myself once again among the people of Paris who had been so tested", were audible.[122]

The Germans left the Marshal's visit uninterrupted, expecting him to denounce Allied air raids; Pétain did not even mention them. The crowds were simply immensely moved to see him because, as Taittinger said, he symbolised a more glorious France. As Pétain's motorcade toured bomb-damaged areas it "was hailed by cheering Parisians without any hints of discord, no wolf-whistles, not a single hostile shout". Throughout the hardest hit arrondissements the reception was the same. "Particularly in the Quartier des Épinettes and in the 18th, a notoriously revolutionary arrondissement, which was particularly welcoming."[123]

At the Hôpital Bichat, Petain's party was welcomed by a well-built matron. "One doesn't need to see that old monkey," she muttered as Pétain toured the hospital, exchanging greetings. Outside, another crowd gathered, shouting "*Vive Pétain*." After comforting the injured, Pétain was driven through the bomb-damaged streets where people rummaged through their ruined homes. He ordered his chauffeur to stop. Breaking through the police cordon, the crowd soon surrounded him.[124]

Lastly Pétain visited the grace and favour apartment on the Square de la Tour-Maubourg allocated to him after the 1919 Armistice, where he greeted his cook Adele for the first time since 1940. In that most military neighbourhood the crowd was ecstatic. "You see, Monsieur," a lady explained to Taittinger, "*Le Maréchal est du quartier!*"[125] Of General de Gaulle, once Petain's subaltern, there was no mention. It was Petain's day; his last parade.

OVER EASTER THE 2e DB DISMANTLED their Moroccan encampments. Some were still on leave, especially artillerymen owing to the late arrival of their Sherman-based self-propelled guns. Leclerc had also finally received his anti-tank regiment, the *Régiment Blindée des Fusiliers Marins* (RBFM), recruited from French Navy personnel who lost their ships fruitlessly resisting the Torch landings and who were re-equipped with US-built Tank Destroyers. Since they had come from the most Vichyite of the French armed forces, Leclerc's attitude towards these sailors was contemptuous. Their leader, Captain Raymond Maggiar, a school contemporary of Leclerc, was the 2e DB's only regimental commander to have been imprisoned by the British after being sunk off Madagascar in 1942. After their heroic defence of Dixmude in 1914, *Fusiliers Marins* wore red lanyards around their left shoulders. After leaving the RBFM in no doubt that de Gaulle had foisted them upon him, Leclerc made them remove these lanyards, not to be replaced until they had been earned afresh. Finally Leclerc said, "If you can't get on with the rest of the division I shall leave you behind in England."

The 2e DB would be shipped to Great Britain in two halves; first the tanks and tracked vehicles under Colonel de Langlade, followed a few weeks later by the rest under Colonel Dio. Langlade supervised the Casablanca embarcations from a cabin on the damaged battleship *Jean Bart*. Further along the dockside, huge US-built LSTs lined up, their prows facing the quay, bow doors open, ramps down, ready to load the 2e DB's vehicles. Different regiments' equipment were deliberately mixed and distributed equally between the LSTs, so that if a ship was lost no regiment lost more than another. It also meant that personnel from different units got to know each other during the voyage.

The 2e DB's staff flew to England in a converted Liberator bomber on 18 April. By lunchtime the next day, Leclerc was back at 4 Carlton Gardens where he had first reported to de Gaulle on 25 July 1940. Pulling open empty drawers, Leclerc exclaimed, "What do these people do all day?" His adjutant, Weil, and Girard shrugged.[126] Since 1943 de Gaulle's staff had mostly transfered to Algiers.

On 23 April Langlade's convoy was met at Swansea docks by Leclerc and Girard. Acclimatising to the British home front, the 2e DB soon learnt who was helpful and who otherwise. Once disembarked they travelled north to battle schools around Hull and Beverley in Yorkshire. Insufficient trains meant most tanks had to be driven there and the British Quakers—the division's stretcher-bearers—doubled as traffic policemen. Leclerc was allocated Dalton Hall, the home of the Hotham family, as his HQ, and for three months the 2e DB shared training grounds with the British Guards Armoured Division and the Polish 1st Armoured Division.

If Leclerc and Langlade were good examples of France's traditional officer type, Joseph Putz was definitely not. An oddball inherited by Leclerc along with the *Corps Franc d'Afrique*, Putz had a French mother and a German father who refused to acknowledge him. His experiences as an ordinary *poilu* during the First World War made him deeply compassionate towards ordinary soldiers, subsequently turning him into both an excellent officer and a left-winger. During the Spanish Civil War Putz became a colonel in General Walter's 14th International Brigade and was wounded several times. Some believe that Ernest Hemingway based Robert Jordan, his hero in *For Whom The Bell Tolls,* on Putz. After 1940, Putz supervised labour groups on the Mediterranean-Niger railway for a while. But, after witnessing Vichy's despicable treatment of Spanish Republicans, Putz dissociated himself and turned towards resistance activities. When French North Africa went over to the Allies, Putz helped form the *Corps Francs d'Afrique*'s third battalion, mainly Spaniards, who subsequently transfered into the 2e DB's Chad Regiment.[127]

The Chad Regiment's 9th Company, *La Nueve,* included "*têtes difficiles*"—tough, difficult men who had experienced a lot but still had much to give. Captain Raymond Dronne, a *Gaulliste de la première heure* and one of Leclerc's best and toughest officers in Africa, was the obvious choice as their commander, not only because he spoke Spanish, but also because he was intelligent enough to handle them.[128] They affectionately dubbed him "*El Kapitan*". They possibly preferred serving under Frenchmen like Putz and Dronne than Spaniards they knew too well. Some of Leclerc's Spaniards were undoubtedly communists, but mostly they were anti-Franco and hoped for a rematch once Hitler was defeated.[129] In the uniquely cosmopolitan 2e DB, personality clashes were inevitable until everyone got used to each other. Leclerc's clear leadership style ensured that the combination worked. *La Nueve* were among the 2e DB's proudest members; it was no accident that Leclerc chose them for special missions in the months ahead.

Arriving in Yorkshire, Jacques Massu's 2/RMT* were encamped at Fimber Station, adjacent to "an immense prairie cut in two by the road to Wetwang. On our arrival, an Irish Guards tank regiment was encamped to the west of this great space and bonds were forged quickly, full of jollity and mutual respect. Drink followed drink signifying a brotherly welcome and, helped by whisky, the *Entente Cordiale* was re-established."[130]

3 June 1944

WAITING BESIDE A COUPLE OF AVRO YORKS at Algiers' airfield, Alfred Duff Cooper was relieved when Gaston Palewski confirmed that de Gaulle would visit Great Britain for consultations

---

* RMT = *Régiment de Marche du Tchad,* ie the Chad Regiment. 2/RMT = 2nd Battalion the Chad Regiment.

with Churchill. The Constable's indignation over AMGOT had become extreme.[131] When they arrived at Northolt the following morning. Duff Cooper was "surprised to see a large Air Force band and a Guard of Honour of at least fifty men. The band played the *Marseillaise* extremely well." The Englishman hoped this would soothe de Gaulle's injured patriotism.[132]

For D-Day, Churchill's personal train was parked at Droyford, which significantly lacked the War Cabinet's London facilities. Nevertheless it was to this inconvenient lair that Churchill welcomed de Gaulle, whose entourage now included the GPRF's[*] London ambassador, Pierre Viénot, General Koenig, the commander of the FFI, and de Gaulle's ADC, Colonel Pierre Billotte.[133] The British were represented by Ernest Bevin, Anthony Eden and, to Duff Cooper's surprise, the South African Field Marshal Jan Smuts, who had once declared publicly that France would never be great again.[134]

At luncheon the conversation was businesslike. Whereas Great Britain and America were the invasion's key players, France's unfortunate role was to provide the battlefield while trying to retain her sovereignty. The idea that one of America's great military forts housed political officers preparing to govern France through AMGOT infuriated de Gaulle. Anglo-Saxon high-handedness risked making a nonsense of his efforts to prepare a new political class to govern France after liberation.[135] Hence, when Churchill suggested "talking politics", de Gaulle's party was apprehensive.

"Politics? Why?" asked de Gaulle.[136]

After lunch, everyone but Churchill and de Gaulle repaired to the carriage's tight corridor.[137] Churchill told Gaulle he should visit Roosevelt and submit to AMGOT. The old chestnut again; the Constable was unelected and neither Churchill nor Roosevelt approved of that.

---

* GPRF = *Gouvernement Provisoire de la République Française*, ie de Gaulle's provisional government.

"Why do you seem to think that I am required to put myself up to Roosevelt as a candidate for power in France?" de Gaulle protested. "The French government exists. I have nothing to ask of the United States of America, any more than I have of Great Britain. That being understood, it is important for all the Allies that relations between the French administration and the military command be set in order. We have been proposing this for the last nine months. Since the armies are going to land tomorrow, I quite see that you are in a hurry to have this question settled. We ourselves are ready. But for this settlement where is the American representative? Furthermore, I observe that the Washington and London governments have taken measures to dispense with any agreements with us. The troops who are preparing to land have been furnished with 'so called' French money which is absolutely unrecognised by the government of the Republic. Tomorrow General Eisenhower, in agreement with you, [will proclaim] that he is taking France under his authority. How do you expect us to negotiate on this basis?"[138]

Churchill breathed deeply before telling de Gaulle the realities of his special relationship with Roosevelt. "And what about you? How do you expect us, the British, to adopt a position separate from that of the United States? We are going to liberate Europe, but it is because the Americans are with us to do so. For get this quite clear, every time we have to choose between Europe and the open sea, it is always '*le grand large*'—the open sea that we shall choose. Every time I have to choose between you and Roosevelt, I shall always choose Roosevelt."

Witnessed from the corridor, this exchange is rightly remembered. Eyeing the Frenchman he had supported since 1940, Churchill raised his glass.

"To de Gaulle, who never accepted defeat," he said.

"To Britain, to victory, to Europe," de Gaulle replied.[139]

Churchill then took the French group to Eisenhower's HQ. Eisenhower was deeply concerned that bad weather could delay the invasion.

"What do you think?" he asked de Gaulle.

"If I were in your place," de Gaulle replied, "bearing in mind the disadvantages of a delay of many weeks, which would prolong the psychological tension of the attacking forces and endanger secrecy, I should not put it off." As it turned out, Eisenhower's meteorologists advised him that he only needed to postpone the invasion for one day.

Then Eisenhower showed de Gaulle a draft of the announcement he intended to read via the BBC declaring that, once Allied troops landed, France was taken under his authority. De Gaulle was appalled. "It was a summons to obey a foreign general," wrote Jean Lacouture.[140] It negated the sacrifices de Gaulle had asked of his compatriots.

"I am ready to change it according to your remarks," said Eisenhower.

Deeply angry, de Gaulle repaired to the Connaught Hotel to draft his own appeal to the French. When a British official informed him that he was scheduled to broadcast on the afternoon of the 6th, *after* the monarchs of Norway, Belgium and the Netherlands, he flatly refused.[141]

5 June 1944

AFTER DE GAULLE'S SO-CALLED "POSTURING", it was left to Free France's London ambassador, Pierre Viénot, to smooth things over with the Allies. Viénot explained the depth of French feeling to Churchill and Eden but, as had so often happened since the Americans entered the war, Churchill threw accusations of "treason at the height of battle".

"You have said untrue and violent things that you will regret," replied the exhausted, sick Viénot. "What I wish to say to you on this historic night is that in spite of everything, France thanks you."[142]

That evening de Gaulle's son Philippe, a young naval officer, dined with him at his Seymour Place apartment. De Gaulle had not seen Philippe for eighteen months. From a small table they observed the hired valet moving with such apparent familiarity that de Gaulle remarked in French, "Doubtless a member of the [British] Intelligence

Service." While dining on English wartime fare—soup followed by beef casseroled in beer and milk pudding—de Gaulle told Philippe about his mother and sisters. His male cousins of military age had joined "Fighting France". His uncles had escaped to Switzerland, but—more worryingly—various relations had been deported by the Nazis.

With so much news to exchange they were still eating at 11pm, though de Gaulle rarely took much time over dinner. More unusually, de Gaulle took tea afterwards, gulping anxiously while telling Philippe how General Juin had led his French Expeditionary Corps into Rome beside the Americans. Philippe watched the clock's hands junction at midnight.

"That's it!" said de Gaulle suddenly.

"What do you mean?" asked Philippe.

"The landings," replied de Gaulle. "At this very moment our second parachute regiment are in the air heading for Vannes. Hundreds of thousands of *maquis* are already in place, the French will be the first to land in France. Leading elements of the British and American armies, including our marine commandos, are about to attack Normandy."

De Gaulle was choked with emotion, his face immobile, his hands clenched in enormous fists. "*Voila*, our *raison d'être* for the last four years has finally arrived." Then he told Philippe, "Now you're free to leave if you want. But you must not say anything to anyone before 6am."

At the end of that unforgettable evening, Philippe embraced his father.[143]

The following day Philippe presented himself at Ribbesford Hall, Free France's Saint-Cyr in Worcestershire. Since 1940 Philippe de Gaulle had commanded Motor Torpedo Boats, but now his father wanted him to serve under Leclerc. Before joining Raymond Maggiar's RBFM, he had to take a three-week conversion course to learn the ways of the French Army.[144]

Chapter 2

D-Day—"It's Happened!"

6 June 1944

PEDALLING FURIOUSLY ALONG THE RUE BUFFON, already late for his neurology lecture, Parisian medical student Bernard Pierquin passed the Jardin des Plantes where he heard a young woman shout to her husband, "It's happened! They've landed!" At Picrquin's teaching hospital everyone knew. "Once the *Anglo-Americains* get their hands on an important port the Germans will be done for," a bright spark speculated.[1]

Préfecture official Yves Cazaux remembered that everyone was trying to behave normally, maintaining their composure until the news was officially confirmed at noon. When a secretary put the BBC's French Service on loudspeaker, Cazaux's office erupted with joy.[2]

Prefect of Police Amedée Bussière telephoned Pierre Taittinger.

"This time it's serious," said Bussière. "It's the real thing. It's succeeding. It'll hold."

"The news spread around Paris, giving the capital, under the worried eyes of the Germans, an air of secret celebration," wrote Pierre Taittinger. Their spirits lifted, and an exquisite smile appeared on Parisian faces. They greeted each other with renewed joy. *La bonne humeur* was everywhere. *Parisiennes* in summer dresses peddled bicycles with spirited rhythm. "The last act would be played. The conclusion of this dreadful four-year drama was now visible for us."

Though practically unable to avoid collaboration, Taittinger was contemptuous of a manifesto signed by Déat, de Brinon and Darnand demanding Laval's dismissal for playing "the double game", and insisting that France should ally herself with Germany.[3] With the moment of truth upon them, many arch-*collabos* went into denial. "The landings have been totally stopped. The news is always good. The landings have been halted in Normandy," wrote Marcel Déat. "Throwing the invasion forces back into the sea is just a formality," wrote Victor Barthelémy, Doriot's No. 2 at the Parti Populaire Français (PPF).[4]

ALMOST FOUR YEARS AFTER THE *APPEL* OF 18 JUNE 1940, Charles de Gaulle spoke via the BBC's French Service:

> The supreme battle has begun. It is the battle in France and it is the battle of France. France is going to fight this battle furiously. She is going to conduct it in due order. The clear, the sacred duty of the sons of France, wherever they are and whoever they are, is to fight the enemy with all the means at their disposal.
>
> The orders given by the French government and by the French leaders it has named for that purpose must be obeyed exactly. The actions we carry out in the enemy's rear must be co-ordinated as closely as possible with those carried out by the Allied and French armies. Let none of those capable of action, either by arms, or by destruction, or by giving intelligence, or by refusing to do work useful to the enemy, or allow themselves to be made prisoner and remove themselves beforehand from being seized and from being deported.
>
> The battle of France has begun. In the nation, the empire and the armies of France there is no longer anything but one single hope, the same for all. Behind the terribly heavy cloud of our blood and our tears, here is the sun of our grandeur shining out once again.

Listening from the cabinet room, Winston Churchill felt tears running down his cheeks, while General Sir Hastings Ismay, a discreet supporter of Free France's interests since 1940, sat apparently unmoved.

"You great tub of lard," said Churchill. "Have you no emotion?"

After witnessing the bizarre role played by General Patton as head of the fake US 1st Army Group, Leclerc was interested that the landings happened in Normandy rather than the Pas de Calais. "The battle of France has started," he wrote to Pauline Vanier. "I have no illusions that we will rediscover France somewhat damaged, but anything is preferable to Nazi slavery. Regarding my family I have complete trust in Providence. I would be so proud to see my eldest son take part in the fight. Perhaps he is already in the *Maquis*."[5]

But the 2e DB complained at not being included in the first wave, even though this was planned months before. News of hold-ups and delays cheered them because it meant the war would still be going on when they got there.

FROM HIS LAIR IN SOUTHERN PARIS, Henri Rol-Tanguy recognised that everything had changed. On 2 June de Gaulle's *Comité Français de la Libération National* had became the *Gouvernement Provisoire de la République Française*. Now he had called France to arms via the BBC. "It was normal for the commander in chief of invading forces to demand the execution of longstanding plans to obstruct enemy movements, spreading insecurity and harrying his reinforcements on the roads," Rol-Tanguy told his biographer, Roger Bourderon. "But the order to carry out these plans at once, everywhere, did not take into account the exceedingly diverse situations facing different resistance groups."[6]

Following Pierre Lefaucheux's arrest a few days earlier, Rol-Tanguy was promoted another grade within P1, the FFI's Paris department. If de Gaulle wanted the FFI to perform larger operations, then his military delegates needed to supply more weapons. While many FFIs— mostly FTP—were very experienced at sabotage, firearms remained so scarce that, when Rol-Tanguy gave his first post-D-Day order on 8 June to sabotage Wehrmacht supply routes, he ordered his officers to keep unarmed *résistants* out of built-up areas, lest they encounter well-armed Germans.[7]

Much of what de Gaulle asked of the Resistance on 6 June was impracticable. In the departments nearest the Normandy bridgehead, risks were justified to destroy bridges and railway lines used for

Wehrmacht logistics. The Resistance operation in Brittany involving ten thousand *résistants* supported by a regiment of French paratroops was of huge benefit. On the other hand, taking over country towns when relief by Allied regular forces was weeks away would lead to tragedy. In Ussel, Guéret and Tulle, German reaction was swift and brutal, resistance ringleaders being hung from the lampposts of Tulle watched by female SS auxiliaries sipping coffee outside a café. Then came Oradour-sur-Glane.

Several resistance groups in *la France profonde* were ordered to harass the 2nd SS Panzer Division *Das Reich* as it journeyed northwards to the Normandy front. In retaliation, one of *Das Reich*'s infantry battalions entered Oradour-sur-Glane at lunchtime on 10 June. They herded the women and children into the church and set it alight with petrol and hand-grenades while the menfolk were shot in garages and barns. The village was then torched. With 642 fatalities, Oradour became one of the most infamous Nazi atrocities. The village is now a memorial. *Lieu de supplice* (place of execution) signs mark where the men were shot. Rusting car hulks remain *in situ*. Pedal-frame sewing machines lean against roofless kitchen walls to this day.

After Oradour, General Koenig ordered all resistance groups: "Put maximum check on guerrilla activity. Impossible at present to supply you with enough arms and ammunition. As far as possible break off contact everywhere to allow reorganisation. Avoid concentration of large numbers. Set up small isolated groups."[8] What became known as "the Koenig Pause" was usually communicated in good time, though in some cases, like the Vercors, tragically late. When de Gaulle's military delegate, Jacques Chaban-Delmas, joined a COMAC meeting on 12 June, none of the three Vs knew about it. Since only around two hundred and seventy resistance operatives had direct radio contact with London, this was unsurprising. COMAC's attitude, however, was so combative, demanding universal action everywhere, that Chaban thought there was little point in passing on Koenig's directive.[9] Meanwhile Rol-Tanguy complained that he needed more cash, thereby giving Chaban a useful thread by which to draw COMAC and P1 into de Gaulle's command chain; he recommended that further requests should be made through himself.[10]

A couple of days later, judging COMAC's mood to be calmer, Chaban-Delmas showed them Koenig's telegram calling for cessation of action. They exploded, repeating their habitual viewpoint that the London French "understood nothing and risked nothing". Koenig's order was unanimously rejected. With a heavy heart, explaining the combative attitude of Resistance leaders in Paris, Chaban asked for Koenig's order to be modified. So Koenig sent a fresh order to the Paris Resistance saying they should maintain "elusive" attacks on the enemy's lines of communication.[11]

"WE ARE NOT IN THIS WAR," insisted Pierre Laval in a national radio address. "You should not take part in any combat; if you don't keep this rule, if you fall prey to indiscipline, you will provoke reprisals the magnitude of which the government will not be able to mitigate. You will suffer personally and materially and you will worsen the situation facing our country. You should refuse to listen to these insidious appeals addressed to you. Those who ask you to stop work and incite you to revolt are the enemies of your country."

Milice leader Joseph Darnand made the same point with equal ferocity, and the German military governor of *Gross-Paris*, General von Boineburg-Lengsfeld, warned of draconian measures in new announcements—*affiches*—printed on yellow paper:

Parisians, the enemy is making new attempts to bring the war to French soil.

For the bringing of supplies into the capital to be assured it is essential that order and calm are maintained. To this end, the governing bodies of the State and the city, the Police and the public services must continue their functions. Industrial and business concerns, banks and shops must remain open.

The duty of everyone is to carry on their business as usual.

No evacuations are allowed unless ordered by the military.

Curfew remains fixed at 9pm.

Public assemblies, the distribution of tracts, strikes and lock-outs, and any Germano-phobic behaviour will be subject to severe punishment.

Acts of violence or sabotages of any kind will be severely punished.

The supplying of information to the enemy will be regarded as spying. All orders from the military authorities will be carried out without exception. All hostile actions will be punishable by death."

The Commandant of *Gross-Paris*.

Boineburg-Lengsfeld even accompanied his yellow *affiche* with a red one known as a *Bekanntmachung* ordering Parisians to avoid public highways reserved for Wehrmacht use. Theatres and cinemas would close but restaurants could stay open. Doors to private houses had to be left unlocked. Windows were to be closed at night and occupants were to stay away from both doors and windows. Then, extraordinarily, Boineburg-Lengsfeld scrubbed both these *affiches*, announcing instead that the German authorities would not impose more restrictions on Parisians provided order was maintained, though restrictions on coal would remain in force. Two days later the curfew was extended to 1am so Parisians could enjoy late-night cinema shows. However, the German authorities also asked Parisians to turn in any carrier pigeons they might find, offering substantial rewards for pigeons complete with message clasp, the message clasp without the pigeon, but less for just the pigeon—which presumably ended up in a pie.[12]

French ancillary workers at the Hôtel Meurice kept Rol-Tanguy informed about these "hesitations" among the city's German governors, even supplying P1's *2e bureau* with copies of Boineburg's rejected *affiches*. "It seemed that the Germans really didn't know what attitude to adopt regarding the Paris population; first because they seemed to be an immense enigma, second because they had to take into account such considerations as their own available manpower," Rol-Tanguy told Bourderon. "It is why they avoided any provocative measures which could have lit the touch paper and pointlessly aggravated their own situation while Paris remained well outside the combat zone."[13]

German journalist Robert Strobel knew that D-Day presaged *Götterdämmerung*. Sonderführer Robert Wallraf had long expected the landings. In his office, Wallraf and his friends predicted the landings would happen in Normandy; the Pas de Calais was too obvious. Even with Germany's defeat imminent, they seemed curiously satisfied; such was their loathing of the Nazi régime. Diehard Nazis said, "The poor Americans, none will escape alive!" Pessimists said, "Pack your suitcases. They will be here in a fortnight." And those who knew French history warned, "Just wait, there will be something extraordinary in Paris; riots, possibly revolution. Not a single German will be able to walk the streets. You will see a city in uprising. They will throw rocks from the rooftops if they haven't got weapons."[14]

SINCE 1943 THE ORATORY OF VICHY IMFORMATION MINISTER Philippe Henriot had persuaded many naïve young Frenchmen to join Joseph Darnand's *Milice*. When Germany's power was at its zenith little could be done about Henriot; he enjoyed support from all classes. Now retired and devoutly *Vichyste*, General Le Barazer de Lannurien said, "The tempers raised against Monsieur Philippe Henriot are the best indicator of the good he has done and the bad that he has stopped."[15]

The Resistance felt differently, especially after Henriot crowed over the airwaves at the Glières tragedy.* Evaluating the impact of his diatribes, COMAC decided Henriot was more dangerous than Pétain or Laval. *L'Humanité*'s underground journalists reckoned that for every Frenchman sent to Germany for STO, Henriot received a hundred francs. Moscow-based writer Jean-Richard Bloch called Henriot a "master *provocateur*" with a "treacherously melodramatic voice", who denounced patriots to the Gestapo.[16]

---

* During early 1944 the Resistance in the Haute Savoie, commanded by *Chasseurs Alpins* officers, set up a strong point on the Glières plateau. A combined force of *Milice*, French police and Wehrmacht surrounded them and hunted them down inflicting around 140 resistance fatalities. Glières was a tragically premature uprising.

Since Vichy power rested on German force of arms, counter-arguments were ineffective against Henriot. He had to be silenced before more naive youngsters joined the *Milice*. Initially the Resistance intended to capture Henriot and fly him to Algiers. A team was shortlisted for the operation but one of them was arrested by the Gestapo before anything happened. A new assassin was needed. In the southwest, young colonial administration student Charles Gonard, codename *Morlot*, impressed COMAC by eliminating a German double agent, so Maurice Kriegel—*Valrimont*—summoned *Morlot* to Paris to deal with Henriot.

Initially *Morlot* planned to kidnap Henriot, but *Valrimont* advised, "Rather than risk the operation it would be better to kill him." This then became, "Don't complicate life; the order is to kill him." Intelligence reports indicated that, when in Paris, Henriot used a first floor apartment at 10 Rue de Solferino which, until 1940, housed a civil service union. The concièrge, a Resistance sympathiser, still lived there. To "execute" Henriot inside his apartment *Morlot*'s team needed to seize temporary control of the building and escape afterwards. He required sixteen armed men. Security precautions meant using men from different regions. The weapons came from the Haut-Jura while the assassins came from Paris and Toulouse. By D-Day, *Morlot*'s team was ready, only waiting for Philippe Henriot.[17]

THE SAME DAY THAT THE SS *DAS REICH* DIVISION MASSACRED the inhabitants of Oradour sur Glane, General Leclerc and his ADC, Christian Girard, drove to England's south coast for a staff meeting. Leclerc was in high spirits. The 2e DB's training was going well and relations with their English hosts were excellent. A conversation with the Polish 1st Armoured Division's General Maczek made Leclerc recognise that, compared to the Poles, his men had much to smile about. "You, General Leclerc," said Maczek bleakly, "you are lucky. You know where you're going. Perhaps you will find your country in ruins but you will be able to rebuild it. But for us, there's no hope. What can we expect? Whether our country is occupied by the Germans or the Russians, we will be just as oppressed."[18]

As the olive drab Buick sped them southwards, Leclerc told Girard they were visiting Major-General Freddie de Guingand, who had welcomed them to Montgomery's Tripoli HQ in January 1943. Greeted by Guingand's US liaison officer they entered a medium-sized country house where Captain Johnny Henderson, one of Montgomery's ADCs whom Leclerc and Girard remembered from Tripoli, offered sherry and canapés. When de Guingand arrived, exclaiming "*Mon cher Leclerc*," Girard wrote that Leclerc shrivelled as he did sometimes when the British were painfully confident; something 1940 did to him.[19]

After lunch de Guingand ushered them into a drawing room where, opposite the fireplace, a wall-sized map of northern France showed the day's positions. De Guingand explained events since D-Day in fluent French, enumerating losses, ground gained and the destruction inflicted on French territory. "He didn't bat an eyelid and neither did we," wrote Girard. "But what next?"[20]

Knowing that Leclerc wanted to speak with de Guingand alone, Girard arranged a little manoeuvre between the salon and the corridor whereby Leclerc could corner de Guingand. While Leclerc visited the bathroom, Girard engaged de Guingand's aides in time-serving conversation while excluding de Guingand—who outranked him considerably. A few minutes later, Leclerc reappeared and approached de Guingand, who listened to him intently. Girard later learnt that Leclerc requested the 2e DB should serve under British command.[21]

For an entirely US equipped division to operate under British command would have created a logistics nightmare that Montgomery would never have allowed. There is only one reason why Leclerc made this request: the Allied positions from D+1 to D+4 would have suggested that the British positions were a better springboard for the 2e DB to make its lunge for Paris.

14 June 1944

DE GAULLE SPENT SEVERAL DAYS PREPARING for his first step on liberated French soil. The previous evening, dining at the British Foreign Office, Anthony Eden passed him a letter from Churchill lifting Montgomery's practical objections. The Free French frigate *Combattante** was waiting at Portsmouth. The Constable would be accompanied by Pierre Viénot, Admiral Thierry d'Argenlieu, Generals Koenig and Béthouart, Gaston Palewski, Colonel Billotte, and longstanding retainers such as Geoffroy Chaudron de Courcel, his ADC in 1940.[22]

Combattante dropped anchor near the Norman coastal village of Courseulles, and de Gaulle's party chugged ashore in a DUKW, while François Coulet sat atop a trunk containing twenty-five million francs. They were welcomed by popular beachmaster Commander Colin Maud, along with a tam-o-shanter wearing Canadian major and Montgomery's French liaison party under Commandant Chandon.[23]

Visiting Montgomery's HQ, de Gaulle was amused to see Rommel's portrait hanging in Monty's caravan. Robert Aron's version of this meeting emphasises Montgomery's thick shoe soles and his adoring little dog. As a matter of etiquette, de Gaulle addressed 21st Army Group's staff.[24] While de Gaulle confered with Montgomery, Admiral d'Argenlieu, General Koenig, Gaston Palewski and Colonel de Boislambert, in full uniform, had effectively canvassed Bayeux, creating a storm of excitement. Being a priest alongside his naval career, the extraordinary Thierry d'Argenlieu knocked up the local bishop, Monsignor Picaud, chief of the abbey where d'Argenlieu was once a novice monk. "Do I call you Père or Admiral?" the bishop asked. "Admiral, of course," replied d'Argenlieu.[25]

Next, led by General Koenig clutching a bunch of peonies, d'Argenlieu, Palewski, de Boislambert and the war correspondent

---

* The *Combattante* was a British built Hunter-class frigate.

Jeannerat marched towards the Place du Château while two local electricians drove around the town with loudspeakers, proclaiming de Gaulle's imminent arrival.[26]

De Gaulle had an eventful drive into Bayeux. First, outside Courselles, the local priest rode after him proclaiming that after hearing the *Appel* of 18 June 1940 he became a *résistant*. "I do not shake your hand, I embrace you," said de Gaulle.[27] Next, seeing two policemen cycling from Bayeux, de Gaulle hailed them. Noticing his general's képi, the policemen stopped and saluted. When de Gaulle introduced himself they were so awestruck they let their bicycles fall over.

"My friends," said de Gaulle. "I am going to ask you to do me a service. I'm on my way to Bayeux; would you be kind enough to go back there and tell them I am coming, so that I take no one unawares. We shall not move from here for a quarter of an hour."[28]

When de Gaulle entered Bayeux he found the streets deserted since everyone was congregating in the Place du Château.* "A type of stupor had seized the inhabitants which immediately burst into *vivats* and tears of joy," he wrote. "Coming out of their houses, they made a procession around me amid extraordinary emotion. Children surrounded me. Women smiled and sobbed. The men offered me their hands. And so we went, all together, overwhelmed and fraternal, feeling both joy and pride that our nation's hopes were rising out of the shadows, to the sub-prefecture in whose salon, merely an hour before, the portrait of Marshal Pétain had hung."[29]

In truth much was happening under the surface; incumbent sub-prefect Rochat was grilled about food supplies and French currency usage. Only when they were satisfied, and Pétain's official portrait was removed, did de Gaulle's party return outside where the crowd was

---

* De Gaulle's original nominee as Commissioner in Normandy, Bordeau de Fontenay, had been unable to get out of Rouen, which was still in German hands. But de Gaulle was relieved to find that Coulet had liaised with the local mayor, Monsieur Dodeman, and was waiting to receive him with the entire Bayeux town council.

thickening. Immensely moved, the Constable could only say "How are you?" as mothers offered children to be kissed.[30]

De Gaulle had known since 1943 that he was the most popular man in France and had already experienced his compatriots' adulation in French North Africa. But this was the first time he was fêted on French soil. Against a backdrop of Allied flags, he gave a speech. "We are all moved to find ourselves together again in one of the first Metropolitan French towns to be liberated; but it is no moment to talk of emotion. What the country expects of you, here behind the front, is to continue the fight today as you have never ceased from fighting since the beginning of the war and since June 1940. Our cry now, as always, is a war-cry, because the path of war is also the road to liberty and of honour. This is the voice of *la Patrie*. I promise you to continue to fight till sovereignty is re-established over every inch of our soil. No one shall prevent our doing that.

"We shall fight beside the Allies, with the Allies, as an ally. And the victory we shall win will be the victory of liberty and the victory of France. I am going to ask you to sing with me our national anthem, the *Marseillaise*."

To sing the *Marseillaise* with the once obscure general who now represented the voice of France moved Bayeux's citizens to tears. They crowded around de Gaulle's party, preventing their departure until British military police arrived.[31]

Next the French convoy entered the battered village of Isigny. Soon people emerged from damaged buildings waving *Tricolores* and cheering, apparently oblivious to streams of British half-tracks and artillery limbers trying to pass through. Since Isigny was in a combat area, de Gaulle's walkabout was getting in the way, and this was soon reported to Montgomery. Again, de Gaulle asked the people to sing the *Marseillaise* with him. Returning to Courseulles, de Gaulle visited the fishing village of Grandcamp, which had prepared for his arrival. The ritual was repeated a third time: an effusive welcome at the *mairie*, a road-blocking crowd, and another rendition of the *Marseillaise*.[32]

Following his visit, de Gaulle's HQ at 4 Carlton Gardens estimated that he shook hands with around three thousand French citizens. De Gaulle's latest British biographer, Jonathan Fenby, wrote, "As in Africa, de Gaulle had shown that, whatever distance he maintained in personal relationships, he could work a crowd to perfection. The popular reaction would be used to give the lie to Roosevelt's insistence that he was not a representative figure." But Montgomery was less than pleased to find his troop movements interupted by de Gaulle's PR campaign, even ordering that de Gaulle should return to England, under arrest if necessary. De Gaulle never forgave Montgomery.[33]

21 June 1944

DURING OCTOBER 1943 LECLERC ADDRESSED HIS OFFICERS in the casino at Temara, impressing upon them that France was in dire straights and their task was to retrieve her former glory. But at that time Leclerc's division was half-formed. Now, reassured by Patton that they would soon arrive in Normandy, Leclerc called *all* the 2e DB's officers to Dalton Hall's great lawn where loudspeakers were set up and he delivered this address:.

> I have brought you together to tell you why we are here. Last summer when General de Gaulle told me to form the 2e DB he asked me if I thought it was possible to form a solid unit from elements of such diverse origins. My reply to him was, "Yes, since our goal these last four years has always been to see the maximum number of Frenchmen return to the war behind him. From the moment a man retakes his arms after the *Appel*, we would be be in agreement." The General completely agreed with this conception of "Fighting France".
>
> Once the decision to open a second front was taken, General de Gaulle demanded that the French Army was represented, especially by our unit. We had less equipment than the others. We are, perhaps, less well trained. But in his eyes that was of small importance. He has succeeded. We were the first designated to take part in the campaign of liberation. For each of us this is the greatest honour of our career. Since Africa until now, obviously I have not been able to speak to all of you. We must rise to this moment, especially

in our attitude to combat. Where bravery and guts are concerned, I am not worried. As soon as Frenchmen are properly equipped and armed they fight well. You have already shown that. Our comrades in Italy have confirmed it. Nevertheless you must be aware that the task ahead will be hard.

Because the armoured force has become the rapid force, the difficult force. One of our generals wrote during the last century "the cavalry will not tolerate mediocrity". Otherwise we will be charging into a hop field, like at Reichshoffen!* This is even more true today for armoured forces.

You will be thrown into battle without adjustment. You will not have the time to familiarise yourself with the terrain nor with your adversary. You will have to take rapid decisions. You must prepare yourselves for a brutal entry onto the battlefield. I say this particularly to unit chiefs. But be in no doubt that the battle awaiting you will not tolerate mediocrity and that leaders, whether of a troop or a single tank, will be weighed in the balance.

The fight will be particularly difficult because because we are so few, being French in the midst of large foreign formations, which creates its own problems. Reflect on your responsibilities as officers and don't lose a minute in improving the quality of the men entrusted to you.

I would also draw your attention to a second point. I ask you to be of the highest conduct out of combat and afterwards. Tomorrow, both during the campaign of liberation and afterwards, we have to find out whether or not France can be a great nation again. Having been invaded, bloodied and diminished, she runs the risk of never being able to become a great power again. She has not been in such danger for centuries. This is not a gratuitous remark; this is sadly a fact.

The French are always optimistic. It is so easy to fall back on grand phrases: "Eternal France", "The Educator of the Human Race". For fifty years we have known what this has cost us. Therefore it is wiser to look reality in the face and understand how France has got into such danger.

It is because our leadership classes, our élites, have failed. Before 1939 this élite led France to the chasm into which she has fallen. Since 1940 another class has lacked the will to mitigate the situation from the Empire, preferring either directly or indirectly to assist Germany. When you meet a *notable* tomorrow,

---

* A battle during the Franco-Prussian War of 1870 where a French cavalry force sacrificed itself in conditions similar to the Charge of the Light Brigade against a Prussian force three times greater.

you will be able to ask him whether he was an incompetent before 1940 or a coward afterwards. Obviously there will be numerous exceptions, but most of our governing classes cannot escape from this dilemma.

This moral crisis is already materialising presently with the Resistance. I have met several of them recently. One of them, taking an example, who came from the *maquis* where he had been playing an admirable part, while bearing witness to the faith and idealism of his comrades, told me how worried he was by the lack of leaders. A few days afterward I met another who came from a group made up of old soldiers who deplored the lack of rank and file *résistants*. So "the *maquis* has men but no leaders and the *Résistance* has leaders but no men". In other words, under the German threat, while recognising the task and knowing the importance, these Frenchmen have not yet refound their unity.

Considering the moral difficulties and the material destruction, and the enormous setback that France has suffered compared to other nations who are already preparing for peace-time, and you will have some idea of the formidable tasks awaiting you. Why have I deemed it useful to raise these problems with you? Normally, before sending men into battle, one avoids discouraging them by enumerating the difficulties. It is because of the officers' *galons* that you wear, and here, it is especially to the young that I am speaking. You are officers. You do not have the right to be ignorant of these problems. It is your duty to enlighten your subordinates.

How will France get out of such a situation? The ideal would be to do what Russia has done for several years and isolate herself completely from the rest of the world while rebuilding herself. Sadly this is not possible for France owing to the situation she already has in the world. I think, in the first place, it is necessary to be ardently patriotic, and in saying this to officers, it is because at the moment, there is a definite tendency, even in the army, to regard patriotism as something narrow and retrograde. It should now be seen as "progressive". Taking other nations' example and reading their newspapers, never is patriotism less than an honour in Russia, in England and even in the United States.

I believe it is also necessary to have strong authority, and in this we are very lucky to have General de Gaulle. For those of you who don't know him well, I would point out some of his character traits. He is above all a man of irreproachable character from the moral viewpoint. It would be impossible to find, either before 1940 or since, a single flaw. He is the best type of French officer, in every meaning of the term, against whom it would be impossible to find any weakness.

He is also a man very susceptible to the patriotic viewpoint. I have born witness to this for the last three years. The difficulties concerning our dealings with London prove that to you. And I can tell you that, without General de Gaulle, the unity of the French Empire would today be little more than a memory.

In short we can be sure that such a man would never put his personal interest above the national interest. That is the most precious of guarantees. In the chaos facing our country, such authority needs solid foundations, a real lifeline; the Division, or whatever remains of it after the battle, must constitute a healthy organism.

Voila Messieurs! That's what I wanted to say to you. My language may have surprised you since I departed from day-to-day subjects, but you must see that one does not succeed unless one is obsessed by an ideal. In fact you must be obsessed by your return to the battlefield. From the moment that you set your feet back on the soil of France, be obsessed by the fact that you will not free her just by words and promises. We must make a gigantic effort. It is your duty to make your men understand. Show that you really are officers.[34]

The implication for the 2e DB's officers was clear, "If I'm incapable of evicting *les Boches*, then I must be a *Vichyste*!" For those RBFM officers who once revered Admiral Darlan as the father of the modern French Navy, this was a hard pill to swallow. But then Leclerc began handing out the divisional badges; these silvery white metal and blue enamel shields had only just arrived, all numbered on the back. "No. 1 is for Captain Divry who has already departed for France," Leclerc announced. "No. 2 is for General de Gaulle. No. 3 is for me. No. 4 goes to Lieutenant Girard who has saved me from starving ..."

In single file each officer received his badge from Leclerc, saluting smartly and having it placed in his hand. As for the Normandy campaign they would soon join, they knew little beyond what was reported via the BBC and British newspapers. "While reading the papers," wrote Girard, "the joy of liberation was put in the shade by the sight of villages in ruins. This evening I saw a picture of a delightful eighteenth-century château with a gracious frontage of balustrades and balconies, columns and central pediment, typical of France. Looking closer, beyond its elegant façade, I noticed the higher windows through which one could see the sky. Please God, don't let this become the face of France!"[35]

27 June 1944

"HENRIOT IS STAYING AT RUE SOLFERINO TONIGHT," announced *Morlot's* contact. The team assembled; like *Morlot* himself, they were young, tough and experienced.

"I will be killed," Vichy Information Minister Philippe Henriot had told Sacha Guitry mere months before. Yet Henriot remained surprisingly naïve over security, travelling with just one bodyguard, albeit a tough LVF veteran. Henriot spent the day seeing off his son, then serving as a Wehrmacht traffic policeman in Italy. Afterwards, accompanied by his wife and minder, he visited a cinema on the Champs Élysées before returning to the Rue Solferino apartment. "Go and rest," he told his bodyguard. "I don't need you any more today." After drafting another of his infamous speeches, he walked along the cracking parquet floor to a bedroom decorated with butterfly-patterned wallpaper to join his wife. During the early morning they were woken by two telephone calls five minutes apart. Hearing no answer, Madame Henriot became suspicious. They had little protection except the policemen on the nearby Rue de Lille, whose principal task was guarding Abetz's German Embassy. Henriot reassured his wife.

Shortly after 5am, three cars took up position at the junction of Rue de Las-Cases and Rue de Bellechasse. *Morlot's résistants** began patrolling the Rue Solferino and Rue de Lille on foot, checking that the police and sentries outside the German Embassy remained where they should be. Annoyingly two policemen were ambling along Rue de Lille near the Rue Solferino turning. One of *Morlot's* men, *Michel*, accosted them. "*Résistance*," *Michel* announced, opening his jacket to reveal two pistols tucked into his trouser top. "Don't put your hands

---

* Some versions of this incident say *Morlot's* men wore *Milice* uniforms.

up, just give me your weapons and follow." The policemen obeyed while the German Embassy's sentries, a hundred metres away, remained unaware. These *Gardiens* later claimed they were confronted by six *résistants*, while their senior officer insisted that everything happened too quickly for the German Embassy sentries to notice.

At Rue Solferino's south junction with the Boulevard Saint-Germain, three policemen stood talking outside the large police station when a Resistance car drew up.

"*Messieurs*, a word if you please," said a *résistant*.

The policemen approached unwarily, but were soon bracketed by a second car and facing Sten-wielding *résistants* who disarmed them. Meanwhile *Michel* tried the door of 10 Rue Solferino.

"Who's there?" asked the concierge.

"It's the Minister's guard," replied *Michel*.

The door opened.

"But I've never seen you before," lied the concierge, who clearly recognised *Morlot* from his reconnaissance visits.

Toting Stens and revolvers, *Morlot*'s men rushed past. The captured policemen were pushed into the concierge's lodging and guarded by five *résistants*. *Michel*'s group took control of the building and disabled the switchboard while *Morlot* and two others went upstairs. Reaching Henriot's floor, *Morlot* was surprised that no one was on guard and returned downstairs to ask why. The concierge insisted the apartment was Henriot's and explained that Henriot's bodyguard, Pantalucci, had the night off. *Morlot* returned upstairs and knocked on Henriot's door.

"Who's there?" Henriot's replied.

"*Milice, Brigade Spéciale*," said *Morlot*. "Terrorists want to kidnap *Monsieur le Ministre*. He must come down so that he can be protected."

"Don't open the door," shouted Madame Henriot, "They're assassins!"

"But how? What do you know?" said Henriot to his wife.

Morlot slid a *Milice* ID card under the door and Henriot opened up, to face *Morlot*'s armed men. In white pyjamas, with his frightened wife in a dressing gown, Henriot looked harmless.

"You lot!" said Henriot, seeing raincoated *résistants* pointing Sten guns. "I see."

"No harm is intended to you, *Madame*," said *Morlot*. "It isn't you that we want."

Henriot tried to grab the *résistants'* Sten guns by the barrel but was pushed back. *Morlot* ordered, "Fire!" Short bursts of 9mm bullets poured into Henriot, while his wife cowered silently in a corner. *Morlot* lent over Henriot who still seemed to be breathing. He fired another burst. It was over.[36]

The whole incident lasted thirteen minutes, after which the five policemen were released and *Morlot's* team scattered into the countryside. Following visits by the 7th Arrondissment's Commissioner Didier and a doctor, Henriot was confirmed dead by 7am. There was no sensible explanation other than a resistance operation. The five policemen briefly incarcerated by *Morlot's* men were exonerated of any professional shortcomings.

Laval and Pétain were informed first. The rest of France heard when Radio Paris announced, "You await, like every day, the voice of Philippe Henriot. You won't hear him again. He was assassinated this morning at the Ministry of Information, shot even before the eyes of his wife. This great voice of France, passionate and eloquent, was known to all. It was either loved or dreaded. Without the means to reply to Henriot, they shut him up. Unable to shut his mouth, they closed his eyes." His death released a geyser of grief across all *collabo* media, who recognised perhaps that this was their last hurrah. A large *affiche* appeared showing Henriot's photograph over the words, "He told the truth and they killed him."[37]

Fernand de Brinon and Joseph Darnand wanted Henriot's body laid out at the Hôtel de Ville for Parisians to pay their respects. Vetoing this idea, Pierre Taittinger and Victor Constant said there was no precedent. The *Milice* immediately accused the Municipal Council of *Gaullisme*. De Brinon and SS chief Karl Oberg protested to Laval, but the Hôtel de Ville remained instransigent. "We prefer to stay out of it," declared Taittinger and Constant jointly, further upsetting diehard *collabos*. As a conciliatory offer, Laval suggested a memorial in the middle of the Place de l'Hôtel de Ville; a small thing created by a bespoke mason, which could easily be removed. Taittinger and Constant won this round of their battle to distance themselves from France's occupiers.[38]

While the Hôtel de Ville successfully sidestepped involvement in the Henriot affair, Cardinal Emmanuel Suhard, the Archbishop of Paris, and senior priest of Notre Dame, was not so lucky. "Such contempt for a human being derives from contempt for life," wrote Suhard in his journal. But four years of Occupation had turned him into a troubled, self-questioning man. Mere hours before Henriot's death, Suhard prayed over the body of Père Cloarec, a Franciscan priest with Resistance connections, shot by the Gestapo. Furthermore, Suhard lacked his two closest advisers, Père Le Sourd and Père d'Ouince, who were on retreat at Conflans, leaving Cardinal Suhard with only Monsignor Beaussart to discuss whether Henriot's funeral should be held in Notre Dame once the request was made. Beaussart, though not a *collabo*, inclined towards Vichy.[39]

However, once Vichy decided that Henriot merited a state funeral, Suhard was always going to have difficulty preventing it from happening in Notre Dame. French state funerals *always* happened there. But where Cardinal Suhard made his mistake, certainly in de Gaulle's eyes, was by maintaining the principal that a priest should officiate in his own church. Sadly Suhard made this decision before Père le Sourd could persuade him that such a contentious service should be performed by Notre Dame's Archdeacon, Monsignor Brot. Yet, there remained certain matters over which Suhard refused to be manipulated. When Laval asked him to condemn Henriot's assassins in his address, Suhard refused. Next, making the mistake of pricking a moderately willing horse, Dr. Klassen, a German Embassy official, told Suhard intimidatingly, "We won't *control* your discourse before or after, but you must speak!" One does not use words like "control" to a cardinal-archbishop; Suhard abruptly terminated the interview. Thereafter he did the absolute minimum, leaving Monsignor Brot to welcome Henriot's body into Notre Dame, only performing the absolution of Henriot's sins himself; just as he would do for a criminal. Next, while the service continued, Suhard silently returned to the Sacristy, disrobed and left Notre Dame by the side door. The *collabo* press denounced his silence. But for de Gaulle, Suhard had not gone nearly far enough.[40]

2 July 1944

FOR THE AMERICANS TO SET ASIDE AMGOT while remaining the Allies' bankers required that de Gaulle do some things the way they wanted. French liaison officers with passable English were belatedly allocated to British and American divisions in Normandy. The fact that the GPRF in Algiers was hardly a "government" as London or Washington understood the word, was deftly circumvented by de Gaulle's ambassador in Washington, the charming Henri Hoppenot. Thirdly, there arose a political consideration; the US Constitution has no mechanism for self-suspension during wartime. Roosevelt needed to seek re-election the following November to secure a fourth presidential term and finish the war. The Democratic vote came from ordinary Americans; those least likely to favour their president supporting a self-appointed military dictator.[41]

In this regard de Gaulle could have helped himself more. A simple declaration that his role was an emergency one and that free elections would be held when practically possible might have sufficed. But de Gaulle rejected the notion that "France" should explain herself to other nations irrespective of her *faiblesse* since 1940, even if France required their blood and treasure to liberate herself. Hence President Roosevelt regarded de Gaulle as "a fool", prophesying that he "would become a very little figure" in the fullness of time.[42]

There was also a feeling among the American press that while American boys gave their lives for French freedom, de Gaulle haggled over the finer points of Gallic dignity. When the billions of US dollars financing French military resurrection—the sight of the battered French battleship *Richelieu* being towed under Manhattan Bridge on her way to be refitted was a memorable spectacle—were added to the balance, it was high time the French Mahommed visited the American mountain. "I should look upon this journey as a tribute paid by France at war to the President himself, as well as to the American people and the American armies which have made and which are making such efforts and such sacrifices for the liberation of Europe and Asia," de Gaulle wrote to Hoppenot.[43]

During the thirty-hour flight de Gaulle spoke at length with French journalist Hervé Alphand. Like Roosevelt, Alphand worried that de Gaulle might appoint himself dictator, given that his family were once typical *Action Française* readers. "The General was clear sighted," wrote Alphand. "He did not want to have anything to do with that France based on Maurras' ideas, xenophobic and closed in upon itself. Not at all, he wished above all to restore France to its place, to provide the French with the mystique of reconstruction and unite them without tyrannising over them."[44]

It was a warm summer's day in Washington, but the American greeting—merely a seventeen-gun salute rather than twenty-one guns—was clearly designed to remind de Gaulle that he was not France's head of state.[45] De Gaulle gave an elegant, short speech in English. "I am happy to be on American soil to meet President Roosevelt," he began. "I salute and pay tribute to all those American men and women who at home are relentlessly working for the war and, also, those brave American boys, sailors, soldiers and airmen who abroad are fighting our common enemies. The whole French people is thinking of you and salutes you Americans, our friends."[46]

Welcomed to the White House, de Gaulle bowed, in the words of Jean Lacouture, "like a well-bred albatross". "*Si content de vous voir*"— "So pleased to see you," said Roosevelt, offering a wizened hand from his wheelchair.[47] Roosevelt's staff tactfully refrained from questioning de Gaulle's legitimacy. After three long conversations, de Gaulle decided that Roosevelt was a class act; "a patrician", he told Gaston Palewski.[48] But for all that, Roosevelt entered politics as a Democrat and de Gaulle's *hauteur* would always arouse the contrarian in him even though he called de Gaulle a "friend" on the portrait photograph he signed for him. Privately, however, Roosevelt remained dismissive of de Gaulle, calling him "President of some French committee or other", when not simply calling him "an egotist".[49]

The visit certainly had its moments. At tea time Roosevelt remarked to his chief of staff Admiral Leahy that Vichy water would have suited him better.[50] For his part, de Gaulle certainly tried. His staff did their homework on Roosevelt, noting his naval interests. De Gaulle gave Roosevelt a beautiful working model of a submarine created in Bizerta's naval arsenal, which Roosevelt subsequently gave to his grandson. When Eleanor Roosevelt protested at him giving away de Gaulle's gift, the president replied, "He is not a foreign head of state, he is merely the head of a committee."[51]

When Roosevelt remarked that over-frequent French elections made it difficult for him to remember the name of France's president, de Gaulle recognised that he was being put in his place. "For the moment you are here," said Roosevelt archly, "and you have seen the consideration with which my country has welcomed you. But will you still be in the same place at the end of this tragedy?"[52] Afterwards de Gaulle wrote magnanimously of America's leaders: Morgenthau was "a friend to our cause", General Marshal was "a bold organiser", Admiral King was "fervent and imaginative", and Admiral Leahy, who was slowness itself in recognising the extent of Vichy's grovelling to Germany, was "taken aback by events that defied his conformism, astonished at seeing me there but making the best of it". Unconvinced by Roosevelt's famous urbanity, de Gaulle wrote that the president's "idealism clothed the will for power".[53] Privately Roosevelt wrote that de Gaulle "is very touchy where the honour of France is concerned, but I think he is essentially selfish".[54] Raoul Aglion, a Free French representative in Washington, described the visit as "devoid of trust on both sides".[55]

Despite Roosevelt's groundless fears that de Gaulle wanted to become another military dictator, he had to acknowledge de Gaulle's usefulness in rallying Frenchmen to the Allied cause.[56] Henry Stimson advised Roosevelt to recognise de Gaulle's provisional government. Cleaving to his lifelong democratic beliefs, Roosevelt felt unable to do this. The most he could concede was to grant the GPRF "temporary *de facto* authority for the civil administration of France", which effectively ended the AMGOT row.[57]

De Gaulle learnt of this victory once he returned across the Atlantic. Interestingly Churchill and Eden greeted the news more cynically; Roosevelt's antipathy to de Gaulle created the problem in the first place. Should he be thanked for lifting his own impediment?[58]

3 July 1944

SINCE DE GAULLE WAS STILL IN WASHINGTON, it fell to the hero of Bir Hakeim and head of the FFI, General Marie-Pierre Koenig, to review the 2e DB's big parade before embarking for France. His Piper Cub landed on Dalton Hall's front drive later than expected, allowing the grassy parkland more drying time after the morning's rain. Nor had Koenig finished dressing; he passed his medal bar to Christian Girard, to pin onto his British battle-dress tunic.

"The parade was splendid," wrote Girard. "The regiments were impeccably arranged around the parkland's great lawn, bordered by magnificent trees. They could be told apart by their head-dress; the black berets of the tanks, the red caps of the Spahis, sky blue of the Chasseurs, navy blue with red piping of the RMT, navy blue with white piping of the cuirassiers. The whole *ensemble* had a character of striking elegance. Before standards held horizontal on their staffs, Koenig—more martial than ever, his profile tight and erect—addressed the men with brevity, appropriateness and clarity."[59]

As regimental colours were presented to the 2e DB's senior chaplain, Père Houchet, to be blessed, Girard could not help smiling, watching Houchet's characteristic small paces. Afterwards Houchet replaced his head-dress, turned smartly to the left and walked away. "It's the liturgical about-turn," Houchet told Girard afterwards. Although certainly not parade-ground soldiers, Girard wrote that the 2e DB "had a stiff pride which projected itself towards the guests in an almost tangible manner. Watching the march past by the Spahis, the tanks, and the Régiment de Marche du Tchad certainly brought a lump to my throat."[60]

Though deeply upset when Leclerc's black soldiers tranfered to other units, Jacques Massu smiled to see a few left in the artillery and support units. A fifth of his 2/RMT were North Africans; hardly black, but definitely not white.[61]

A superb buffet *à la Française* was laid before visiting dignitaries, some of whom, like medical corps General Sicé, had followed Free France since 1940. "Friends of the Free French" who paid for the 2e DB's regimental colours to be made by the same firms that serve the British Army also attended, along with the kind local lord who gave the wine.

Several British dignitaries attended, including Dalton Hall's owner, Lord Hotham. But when asked why few Americans were present, Girard had no answer. Patton, by then earmarked to command the soon to be activated US Third Army, had higher priorities, while corps commander General Gilbert Cook sent his ADC, Captain Garretson. "Your officers told me a lot," Garretson told Girard. "They think they will not be used. They are wrong. They will be used and perhaps a great deal more than they think. We only want one thing, to be behind you when you return to Paris. You will be the first to go in, we promise."[62]

Afterwards Girard wandered into Dalton Hall's great drawing room where Jacques de Guillebon sat silently, staring out over the sunken rose garden towards the big lawn. Two years earlier Girard had asked Guillebon for a role befitting his diplomat's training. But when Guillebon recommended him to be Leclerc's ADC, Girard protested. "Don't be stupid," said Guillebon. Now Leclerc was rarely without the well-mannered Girard.

"I have complete trust in this division," said Guillebon quietly. They were on the last leg of a journey that began in French Equatorial Africa four years earlier.[63]

7 July 1944

HENRIOT'S ASSASSINATION WAS QUICKLY FOLLOWED by a second blow to the *collabo* community. On 30 June Colonel Magnien, who commanded a regiment of French phalangists against the Allies during the Tunisian campaign, was sentenced to death in Algiers. *Collabos*, especially the *Milice*, wanted blood. After Henriot's funeral, Abetz advised Laval that several pre-war French politicians, including Georges Mandel, could be returned to Vichy authority to act as hostages in case other *collabos* or Vichy servants were executed. Talented and experienced, through the 1930s Mandel had held several government posts. He was also unapologetically Jewish, informing friend and foe alike, "Remember, I'm a Jew." His scholarly demeanour aside, Mandel combatively opposed appeasing the Nazis during 1937–1939. When France fell in 1940, surveying defeated French faces for those with some fight left in them, General Sir Edward Spears saw not only de Gaulle but also Mandel. But Mandel felt that London needed a soldier, not a politician. When, on 16 June 1940, Spears pressed Mandel to leave France, Mandel replied, "You're only worried for me because I am a Jew. It is precisely because I am a Jew that I will not leave with you tomorrow. People will think I am just saving myself; that I gave in to panic. In three days' time I might consider it."[64] Mandel subsequently fled with other politicians to French North Africa aboard the *Masilia*. Next came his arrest and repatriation for a Vichy show trial at Riom; then four years in Buchenwald where his health stood up surprisingly well.[65]

Abetz first suggested using pre-war French politicians as hostages after Pucheu's execution.[66] When, at Henriot's wake, Abetz said Mandel could be executed as a reprisal,* Laval replied, "That's not the sort of

---

* It is easy to assume that the murder of Jean Zay by the *Milice* on 20 June was part of this vengeance cycle, but Henriot's assassination was planned too early to suuport this idea. As with the murders of Victor and Hélène Basch, such incidents merely demonstrated the *Milice*'s criminality.

present to give me." Laval subsequently warned Algiers of the danger to Georges Mandel if they executed Colonel Magnien but, once Magnien was dead, Paris *Milice* chief Max Knipping began negotiating Mandel's return to France.

Arriving in Paris on 4 July, Mandel was first held at SD safehouse 3 *bis* Square du Bois de Boulogne. In the meantime Knipping's *Miliciens* decided that, to make Mandel's execution appear a wholly French affair, he should go to his death from a French prison, the Santé.[67]

Director of Prisons André Baillet* protested at having such an "important man" foisted on a penitentiary used for the capital's common criminals. Arriving around 2pm on 7 July, Mandel protested on similar grounds and refused to take part in the induction process or give fingerprints, believing such proceedings *infra dignitatem*. When Mandel asked if his old Parisian doctor and dentist might visit him, Baillet told him such requests needed higher authorisation.

"Thank you for your good offices," Mandel told Baillet, before remarking realistically, "While I remain within your walls, I doubt that anyone will kill me. But I don't think they will leave me very long under your protection."

Mandel only stayed three hours at the Santé. Bertrand Favreau, Mandel's biographer, writes that Baillet telephoned the prison's senior governor confirming Mandel's arrival, expecting him to be transferred to the *Milice*'s Château des Brosses prison near Vichy.[68]

Around 5pm three cars left the *Milice*'s Rue le Peletier HQ. The lead car, a Citroen 11CV traction, was driven by *Milicien* Jean Mansuy. With five criminal convictions behind him, Mansuy embraced the *Milice*'s blend of camaraderie and cruelty gleefully. Beside Mansuy sat the equally nasty Pierre Boéro. In the back sat Georges Néroni, a barman at La Potinière, a popular *collabo* nightclub. The second, more

---

* In January 1944 the prison service came under the authority of Joseph Darnand, head of the *Milice*. Baillet was a *collabo* nominee, whom Mandel seems to have trusted during his final hours, doubtless unaware of Baillet's *Milice* membership and involvement in the murder of Jean Zay. Baillet was executed after the war.

powerful Citroen was driven by Paul Fréchoux, head of Vichy security in northern France. He was accompanied by SS Obersturmführer Dr. Schmidt wearing civilian clothing, and two *Miliciens*. In the third car came Max Knipping with his driver. With empty roads they quickly reached the Santé.[69]

With few illusions over the fate awaiting him, Mandel was unsurprised when Baillet revisited his cell. "It is nothing to die," Mandel told Baillet. "But what is sad is to die before seeing the liberation of our country and the restoration of the Republic."

"Received the here named Mandel Jeraboam at 5pm Paris, 7 July," wrote Knipping in the ledger. Then, as a sick joke, he wrote underneath, "'*Liberated*', 7 July. Max Knipping."

After placing Mandel in Mansuy's Citroen, the three-car convoy left the Santé. Knipping returned to Rue le Peletier while the other two cars exited Paris via the Porte d'Italie.[70]

During the journey Mandel tried to relax by engaging Néroni in conversation about Buchenwald, his family and his relief at being back in France. Neroni also remembered Mandel saying, "I will make you see that a Frenchman knows how to die." Perhaps, like many intelligent hostages, Mandel hoped to create some kind of rapport with these *Miliciens*. Reaching the Forest of Fontainebleau, they turned towards Nemours at the Obelisk. A little further on, Mansuy turned along a B road and halted, claiming the Citroen had broken down.

Boéro got out of the car and fiddled with the engine for a few moments before saying it might take a while to fix and they should stretch their legs. Saying nothing, Mandel got out. Néroni told him they were near Mont Morillon. Then, totally without warning, Mansuy unceremoniously fired a burst into Georges Mandel's back from a submachine-gun. Mandel fell backwards, shaking convulsively. Mansuy fired again, into Mandel's neck and temple, finally killing him. The second Citroen carrying Fréchoux and SS Dr. Schmidt now arrived.

"You are mad," Boéro told Mansuy.

"Both sides were in agreement," said Mansuy. "It isn't you who's in command."

"I had orders," said Fréchoux, taking charge. "Put Mandel back in the car and take him to the morgue at Versailles."[71]

The cover-up began; they would blame a Resistance ambush. Mansuy fired a few bullets into his Citroen, perforating the roof and trunk, carefully avoiding essential working parts. The Versailles Intendant de Police, Anquetin, a known *collabo*, co-operatively allowed Mandel's body into the morgue. The death certificate claimed the cars were ambushed not at Fontainebleau but Rambouillet. Unfortunately for the murderers, Intendant Anquetin was not particularly influential. His subordinate, police commissioner Brimborgne, noticing that Mansuy's Citroen was only shot through the roof and trunk, rejected the *Milice* story.[72]

While Fréchoux and SS Dr. Schmidt reported their mission's successful completion to Max Knipping and SS Colonel Knochen, Versailles' forensic surgeon, Doctor Paul, began his autopsy. Leaning over his dissection table, Paul recognised Mandel from 1930s newspaper photographs, and immediately telephoned Mandel's pre-war secretary, Joseph Besselère, who informed Mandel's family and friends.[73]

The following morning Joseph Darnand telephoned Laval with news of Mandel's death. Believing Mandel was still in Germany but remembering Abetz's extraordinary offer, Laval questioned Darnand. Visibly shaken, nervously smoking a cigarette, Laval arrived at Vichy's Hôtel du Parc at 9am. "They've killed Mandel," he told his cabinet secretaries. Almost weeping, Laval explained how, although he sometimes disagreed with Mandel, they had respected each other and Mandel never deserved such a fate. Laval telephoned de Brinon in Paris who, at that very moment, had Max Knipping in his office explaining his version of what happened.

"The SS in Paris are very pleased with the death of Mandel," Brinon told Laval. "They think it will have a very good effect. Their only regret is that Mandel was not formally executed by the French government."

"Then I protest with utmost indignation," said Laval.

Would Brinon and Abetz now have former Premier Leon Blum returned to France to face a similar fate? Laval persuaded Abetz that such murders could only further complicate the situation in France.[74] Towards the end of the afternoon, Laval screamed angrily at Jean Tracou and Charles Rochat, "I've had enough. I can't do this anymore. I can't cover up these horrors any longer!"[75]

AFTER HIS THREE-WEEK COURSE at Ribbesford Hall, Philippe de Gaulle headed for Yorkshire, to join the *Régiment Blindée des Fusiliers Marins*. With his Tank Destroyers lined up in the undulating fields of Tatton Park, Capitaine de Vaisseau Raymond Maggiar, wearing British battledress with the shoulder flash "France", gave Philippe a glacial welcome.

"It's less than forty-eight hours since we were warned of your arrival," said Maggiar coldly. "We were not asked how we felt about it. In fact, we don't need you, we don't know what to do with you and we're already at full strength."

His first dinner among Maggiar's officers was unfriendly; resentments among "Darlan's boys" clearly ran deep. Afterwards Christian Chavane de Dalmassy, three years Philippe's senior, was more welcoming. But Dalmassy was rare. Most of Philippe's fellow officers had fought the British or Americans until Torch. Some had been imprisoned with Germans. But, opening up to Philippe, several admitted that both their sense of duty and their superb modern ships were wasted by Vichy. Now, wearing US uniform with French naval insignia, they just wanted to liberate *la Patrie*.[76]

The RBFM comprised around six hundred men, mostly sailors, a smattering of north-African soldiers to bring them up to strength, and traditional French naval officers. Their main asset was their technical professionalism. Compared to ships, Tank Destroyers were easier to manage. Based on a Sherman chassis, the M10 Tank Destroyer was armed with a three-inch gun which was both heavier and more powerful than an ordinary mid-war Sherman. To maintain the vehicle's speed, the gun was mounted in a lighter, open turret. When introduced to the M10 Tank Destroyer in Morocco, French sailors augmented its basic gun sight with naval range finders, giving them a useful edge during training competitions in England and afterwards in action. After witnessing the RBFM's gunnery skills, General Patton said they were among the best he had seen.

The RBFM were the last of the 2e DB's regiments to receive their colours. At the ceremony Leclerc was angered that an older petty officer, Renou, wore the red lanyard earnt by their predecessors at Dixmude in 1914, until Captain Maggiar told him that Renou actually fought at Dixmude. When his old friend, Jean Fanneau de la Horie, reminded him how well the RBFM were doing in training, Leclerc stopped treating them as "Darlan's Boys".

EVEN MORE FASCINATED BY FRENCH SOLDIERS than Americans, local women congregated around the 2e DB's Yorkshire encampments offering "free love". Over lunch in Dalton Hall's dining room, Leclerc, whose asceticism was, according to Christian Girard, "*effectivement terrible*", complained about this to Colonel Bernard. "*Mon Général*," said Père Fouquet, one of the chaplains, "leave Bernard to get on with his work, no one's going to change anything."[77]

More seriously, Leclerc had a major disagreement with battlegroup commander Colonel Michel Malaguti. Malaguti had been severely affected by seeing his tank regiment destroyed by the Germans in 1940 but learnt much from the defeat, becoming a firm advocate of massed tanks operating like massed cavalry. Yet, between 1940 and 1944, further tactical developments occurred both in Russia and North Africa. Just as the notion of tanks supporting infantry was superseded, so too was the idea of massed tank attacks. American thinking now favoured fast-moving battlegroups, three to an armoured division; with tanks supported by motorised infantry and artillery to deliver the punch. An American army corps usually consisted of two infantry divisions and an armoured division. If a corps faced a big operation it might need two armoured divisions.

The French rearmament programme was conceived on the basis that France's new divisions conform to the American tactical model. Everything Leclerc's men did in their training was measured and marked according to this framework. Therefore, when Malaguti's criticisms reached a climax, Leclerc found himself in a delicate position. But for Leclerc's achievements in Africa, the popular Michel Malaguti would have been senior, so Leclerc had to consider very carefully how to handle him. Dreading the prospect of trying to liberate Paris at the head of a divided unit, Leclerc visited London, where he bought a shotgun for his eldest son in Holland & Holland. Returning to Yorkshire, Leclerc finally recognised that there was no room in the 2e DB for both himself and Malaguti. General Koenig pleaded with Leclerc for mercy, but Malaguti had written letters demonstrating his jealousy of Leclerc; he had to go.[78]

So, merely days before the 2e DB landed in France as "the political division", Leclerc lacked a third battlegroup commander. He appointed Warabiot, formerly of the *12e Chasseurs d'Afrique*, which had already provided several divisional staff officers. But during July resentments between original Free French and formerly Vichy controlled regiments still rattled around, and Malaguti did not help. Replacing him with ex-*Vichyste* Warabiot as head of a battlegroup whose tank regiment was the Gaullist 501e RCC was unwelcome.

14 July 1944

AS SHORTAGES CAUSED BY THE BREAKDOWN of the transport system closed ninety percent of food outlets, forcing up prices, the Parisian working class felt as desperate as they had in 1789 and took to the streets. On 7 July, the *Comité Parisien de la Libération* considered a mass evacuation, then decided that was impractical. Instead they advocated protests supported by violence and sabotage, though some, including the Socialist Daniel Mayer, thought this would merely provoke costly reprisals when France needed her manpower for the final liberation battle.[79]

Hundreds protested in working class *banlieues*, raising the banned *Tricolore* and singing the *Marseillaise*, while others reiterated revolutionary calls of "Bread! Bread!" There were demonstrations around the Étoile and the Latin Quarter. Brandishing anything coloured red, white and blue, the protesters provoked no larger German reaction than a few shots in the air and some arrests. The Paris police, the *Gardiens de la Paix*, began demonstrating their pro-liberation sentiments, singing the *Marseillaise* and warning the crowds of approaching German security troops or *Milice*. The only French Police unit to support the Occupiers were the *Brigades Spéciales*, special anti-resistance groups, whose pro-Vichy members had most to lose when liberation came. In Belleville they shot trade union leader Yves Toudic.[80]

In Choisy-Le-Roi, demonstrators gathered around the statue of Rouget de Lisle, composer of the *Marseillaise*. Unwisely the *résistants* leading the demonstration sported a captured German MG42 machine-gun on their car, provoking German soldiers into opening fire and arresting several workers. From this point the gathering descended into chaos as demonstrators fled through private houses and gardens. Over the next few days there would be frantic negotiations to get the arrested workers released.[81]

THE SANTÉ PRISON WAS BURSTING AT THE SEAMS. Of 4,634 prisoners held during July 1944, 2,510 were men held for ordinary crimes, 404 were "politicals", while the remaining 1,720 were remanded prisoners either awaiting trial or appeal, altogether crowding four prisoners into each of its 1,072 cells. Of the Santé's 207 guards, around twenty-eight were on duty at any given time; twenty-two inside the prison and another six in ancillary areas. The prison arsenal contained merely ten revolvers and twenty rifles, all old, and a little ammunition. The outer security picket, eighteen members of the *Garde de Paris*, had more modern weapons. On Bastille Day 1944 they were reinforced.[82]

After D-Day several *talauds* (convicts) developed unrealistic hopes that, if they could escape and reach the Allied lines, they could start their lives afresh. Every new arrival, every visiting lawyer, every visitor bringing news from Normandy raised these hopes, and talk of breaking out became more frequent. Experienced convicts knew such thoughts were pie in the sky. Nevertheless, among a few conspirators, the plan became known as the "*Secret de Polichinelle*"—"the Secret of Punchinello", or "Punch's Secret"—after the ubiquitous puppet character.

Resistance prisoners inside the Santé felt particularly vulnerable. In the spring a *Milice* squad visited the prison, held a drumhead trial of several Resistance prisoners, and shot them outside. Henriot's assassination and the retaliation murders of Georges Mandel and Jean Zay increased these fears. On 20 June the Regional Director of Penitentiaries, Roger Poirier, reported the boiling atmosphere in Parisian prisons. In the meantime the Santé's governor, Jean Farge, merely mentioned isolated incidents consistent with the atmosphere in Paris generally. "I can't envisage anything that could make one think there would be trouble in the near future." As a precaution he ordered extra watchfulness over the prisoners during the evening when conversation in and between the cells was at its height.[83]

The situation was further inflamed when Marcel Bucard, head of the *Françiste* party, one of several extreme right parties originating in the 1930s, linked to the *Milice*, was imprisoned at the Santé after a shoot-out with police when he and two others were looting the apartment of a deported Jewish family. Following a car chase, Bucard shot two policemen dead; crimes which normally merited the death penalty. Laval insisted that Bucard* face the law's process. Desperate to re-ingratiate himself, Bucard strove to avoid the guillotine by playing the snitch.[84]

Fingers were first pointed at Raymond Peuvion in Cell 117 and Jules Aubertin in Cell 127. They were joined by three newly arrested Parisian gangsters, including a police informer. From these men's "information" the Santé's directors discovered a plot involving the overpowering of guards, disabling alarms and releasing fellow prisoners—especially "politicals" and those condemned to hard labour. Jean Farge put these

---

* In 1946 Bucard was convicted of treason and executed by firing squad.

men in solitary confinement. But on 14 July the guards discovered a note saying, "Right, boys! It's tonight!" By late afternoon security was increased.[85]

Shortly after 10pm two whistle blasts roused the prisoners on the second and third floors of divisions 9 and 12, who rammed their bedsteads into their outward opening doors. Diverse objects rained down upon the guards. Reacting swiftly, the guards secured a handful of prisoners in central strong rooms while retreating from the affected floors. Alerted by André Baillet, Amedée Bussière, the Paris Prefect of Police, and Edmond Hennequin, Director of the Municipal Police, soon arrived along with sixty Paris policemen and a hundred *Gardes de Paris*. They were supplemented by the fire brigade and representatives of the main utilities (should it be necessary to cut off supplies), and officials from the Paris drain network; the main prison drain accessed a sizeable manhole on the Boulevard Arago. For good measure the Préfecture also sent a tear gas van which parked outside the Santé.[86]

From outside, the Santé was sealed off. Inside, prisoners were on the rampage; getting into the basements, they smashed the telephone and alarm systems. They also wrecked cells, broke door hinges, smashed locks and seized anything that could serve as a weapon or do damage. The perpetrators were mostly Parisian criminals. The "political" prisoners remained in their cells, listening anxiously as the mutineers roamed along steel staircases and corridors. When fires began in the library, infirmary and radio room, many "politicals" feared being burnt alive or dying of smoke asphyxiation. While several "politicals" knew about the "*Secret de Polichinelle*", they usually tried to dissuade the mutineers from their crazy initiative.[87]

An initial burst of machine-gun fire felled sixteen prisoners, but the police alone were not strong enough to restore order. A company of SS was put on standby. Around midnight, under the command of SS Major Neifeind and Lieutenant Hagon, the SS entered the prison courtyard. Four senior *Milice* officers also arrived, anxious lest the SS assume a task their own force should perform. Neifeind wanted to suppress the uprising by force immediately. The *Milice* officers, however, wanted Neifeind to await the arrival of two hundred *Miliciens* under Jean Bassompierre, a nobly born, right-wing eccentric who won the Iron Cross serving with the LVF in Russia.

The Prefect of Police, Amedée Bussière, faced a quandary. The SS might go further than the situation required, whereas the French could only suppress this uprising by using the *Milice*. Using his son to interpret, Bussière told Neifeind that the Santé uprising was a French affair and that he believed the prisoners were "having a blow", as often happened in France during the summer. He expected they would calm down and the situation would be reviewed at dawn when the matter could be dealt with by the *Milice* and the police if necessary.

"But you should chastise them," protested Neifeind. "You ought to shoot at least four hundred prisoners."

"Stay out of this," replied Max Knipping. "Leave it to our own French authorities to decide what punishments to hand out."

"We'll see in the morning," Neifeind said sceptically.[88]

Dawn was chilly. The smoke from fires in the library and sanatorium had died down. Shortly after 6am *Miliciens* arrived in the Santé's courtyard.

"Anyone who does not return to his cell will be shot," said Jean Bassompierre through a loudspeaker.

"Then what?" shouted some of the prisoners.

Miliciens fired warning shots. The prisoners fell back. Over the next few hours the Santé returned to normality; which was mentioned at Bassompierre's 1948 trial. "At 6AM Bassompierre took up sensible positions, precisely and energetically, which permitted him to re-establish order within two hours without a single victim; the prisoners were back in their cells and the political detainees were safe. By 10AM, his mission accomplished, Bassompierre left the Santé."[89]

A doctor arrived to write death certificates for the six prisoners killed during the night and tend those who were wounded. But when Dr. Delabre requested the transfer of wounded prisoners to the hospital at Fresnes, SS Major Neifeind blocked their transfer, demanding again that four hundred prisoners should be shot.

"That's too many," replied Knipping.

"Order can only be restored by violence," Neifeind insisted.

Milice officers Bassompierre and Gallet helped Knipping calm Neifeind down.

"I want to enter cells red with blood," insisted Neifeind.

The *Milice* officers managed to haggle Neifeind's demands down to a hundred executions. But, mistrusting the French, Neifeind insisted fifty prisoners should be shot immediately or else his men would shoot a hundred before they left. While Knipping took a call from Edmond Hennequin, Bassompierre and Gallet argued with Neifeind. "Couldn't Major Neifeind content himself with fifty ringleaders of the uprising being shot?" the Frenchmen asked. Neifeind insisted on a hundred executions.[90]

How were the victims to be chosen? When the *Milice* asked prison officer Delpont for names, he refused to give any, professing to be more interested in tidying his office. But the names of a hundred of the revolt's ringleaders and keenest followers were obtained by *Miliciens* wandering around the cells. "How many in this cell?"—"Who is the leader?"—"What's your name?"—Thereby selecting dimwits who fancied themselves leaders.

"I am glad you're back," Bassompierre told Knipping. "We're going to shoot a hundred mutineers."

"Not unless I say so," said Knipping. "Whose order is this?"

"Neifeind," replied Bassompierre. "He told me that he will retract his demand to shoot four hundred on the condition that the *Milice* executes *one* hundred."

"You don't carry out German orders," said Knipping. "You'll do nothing unless I tell you to."

Neifeind had returned to his office on the Rue de Saussaies when Knipping caught up with him to make further protest.

"I've forbidden the shooting of a hundred prisoners," said Knipping. "Only a court martial can condemn the guilty," he insisted, displaying scruples he never entertained toward Georges Mandel.

"Only on two conditions," said Neifeind. "That the court condemns at least fifty and that they are executed the same day."

"The number will be decided by the judges," insisted Knipping. "I can't entertain any other viewpoint."

"If the court does not condemn fifty," insisted Neifeind, "I will shoot the balance."[91]

By telephone from Vichy, Darnand gave Knipping the go-ahead to convene a "field court martial" to try fifty common law prisoners with civil offences. Twenty-seven-year-old *Milice* officer Pierre Gallet presided. Gallet was legally qualified, but service in 1940 followed by early involvement in *collabo* politics had prevented him from practising. He thoroughly enjoyed the opportunities provided by the Occupation. Through the afternoon Gallet's "court" handed down twenty-eight death sentences, mostly to working-class youths.* They were taken to the execution site on the Boulevard Saint-Jacques to be presented in batches before a firing squad of reluctant *Gardes Mobiles* who deliberately missed, obliging their commander to kill the lads with his *coup de grace.* One lad, aged only twenty, had been arrested four days earlier for a disrespectful utterance towards Vichy; neither a crime nor an act of resistance.[92]

AFTER ROGER LANGERON ORDERED THEM TO REMAIN AT THEIR POSTS when Paris fell in 1940, the "*fonctionnaires d'autorité par excellence*" of the Paris police pursued *résistants* for four years, often passing those they arrested to the Gestapo and thus a probable death. After the Armistice, maintaining order to benefit both the French population and the Germans was one way the French could retain a sense of autonomy. While at first the German authorities had been "correct", once their demands became more inhumane the consciences of French policemen became increasingly troubled. Most joined the police to uphold the law, and found it galling to round up Jews, or witness men they respected face execution for loving the same

---

* At his post-war trial, Pierre Gallet's defence claimed that Gallet's actions prevented a greater loss of life if SS Major Neifeind had had his way. Gallet was condemned to death in 1948 but reprieved and released in 1953.

freedoms they loved themselves, condemned by the French judiciary's "special sections". So the flame of resistance within the Paris police took hold.[93]

In 1944 the Paris police comprised 21,067 men, consisting of about two hundred officers, two thousand six hundred sergeants or *brigadiers*, seventeen thousand ordinary policemen, and an investigative branch of around eleven hundred. This last portion included the *Brigades Spéciales*, whose role was to hunt *résistants*. In this struggle the Gestapo was also supported by "police auxiliaries", numbering about thirty thousand across France; effectively the grudge-informer class which any society would produce under such circumstances. "This *Gestapo Française*," wrote Philippe Aziz, "was a splinter in the flesh of France. Without them, the German security forces would have been deaf and dumb. This indigenous Gestapo enabled the Germans to inflict their most murderous and effective blows."[94]

To the communists and FTP, the Paris police were simply continuing Langeron's 1940 policy, to uncover clandestine communist networks in the Seine area. A "big house" attitude to both communists and the Left had pervaded the senior ranks of the Paris police since the politically turbulent 1930s. In December 1943 Himmler himself remarked, "The French Police is useful to a certain extent in the struggle against Communism. However one cannot be so sure of them against French Nationalists."[95] Communist *résistants* were more likely to be handed over to the Gestapo than their Gaullist counterparts. During Bussière's tenure there were over sixteen thousand arrests for anti-German propaganda (i.e. leaflets and *affiches*) alone. Bussière subsequently wrote, "This audacious and patriotic attitude was the same throughout my time at the Boulevard du Palais."[96]

For many Paris policemen the turning point was the big round-up of Jews during the summer of 1942. Even the dullest soul on the Préfecture's payroll recognised that without French support the anti-Jewish programme would have been rudderless.[97] By 1944 many *Gardiens de la Paix* in Paris were turning towards the Resistance. Gratifying though this was, Serge Lefranc, a leader within the resistance group *Front National de la Police,* wrote cynically that out of nearly twenty-two thousand policemen, "At the maximum one could only have counted between six hundred and eight hundred patriots." The rest, said Lefranc, "were largely *attentiste* chickens along with a lot of cowards and traitors who had previously arrested a lot of patriots".[98]

During July 1944, *collabo* Commissioner Rottée wrote, "Until now the presence in the capital of Occupation troops and relatively important Police forces has enforced upon the communists a certain prudence. But they are resolved to unleash an insurrection of considerable scope in the event of the Germans departing or if, on the arrival of the Anglo-Americans, military authority is not imposed immediately." Irrespective of his trial and execution after the liberation, Lucien Rottée perceptively believed that many ordinary Parisians secretly supported communist resistance groups like the FTP even if they were not communists themselves. He also recognised that, at a suitable opportunity, the Resistance would seize factories, power stations, *mairies* and the machinery of government.[99]

The Occupation deprived the Paris police of its traditonal expressions of pride and patriotism like band music; small wonder that the first resistance organisation to take root at the Préfecture was among band members. From 1943 they produced a secret magazine, *La Voix de la France*, which they distributed throughout the Paris region. One of them, Georges Prévot, until his arrest, maintained links with London and hid Allied airmen in his home. Another early resistance group within the Paris police was the *réseau*, founded in October 1940 by Brigadier (Sergeant) Arsène Poncey to forge ration cards and ID documents for French soldiers who evaded capture during *la Chute*. This group developed into *Valmy Armée Volontaire.* But Poncey was arrested after a civilian *résistant* betrayed him to Gestapo interrogators during February 1943. Poncey and his liaison agent Vannier were deported to Mauthausen where both died. Their successor, Edmond Dubent, was arrested in December, but meanwhile *Valmy Armée Volontaire* evolved into *L'Honneur de la Police*, which, confounding Lefranc's cynicism, developed into a remarkable organisation of fifteen hundred men under sub-prefect Yves Bayet, assisted by Brigadier Fournet. By 1944 they were carrying out their own operations; on 13 July they struck a *Feldgendarmerie* arsenal in Neuilly, acquiring three light machine-guns, thirty-two submachine-guns, seventy-five pistols, a hundred rifles and copious ammunition.[100]

The second largest resistance group within the Paris police, numbering around a thousand men, was the *Front National de la Police* founded by Léon Pierre. Originally called *Les bons volontés des Policiers Patriotes*, this group was basically Gaullist. In early 1942 they were contacted by Arthur Airaud, a CGT syndicalist and pre-war member of the Communist Party who, with surprising ease persuaded them to become *La Front National de la Police*. As with many early resistance groups a certain contempt existed towards later joiners, which possibly explains Lefranc's cynicism towards his fellow policemen. Following Airaud's arrest Serge Lefranc and Clément Roycourt (codenames *Gérard* and *Rivière* respectively) joined the group's controlling committee. But they had not heard the last of Arthur Airaud; he escaped in time to join resistance operations during August 1944.[101]

Thirdly came the movement *Police et Patrie*, consisting of around two hundred members recruited by Brigadier Charles Lamboley. They specialised in technical resistance, like conveniently timed power-cuts to the Préfecture's switchboard when arrests were planned, saving Resistance lives. Lamboley's group was connected to *Liberation Nord*.[102]

By late July 1944 active *résistants* in the Paris police numbered around 2,700 out of a total force of 21,067 (12.81%). According to French historian Pierre Bourget, "It would certainly be fair and honourable to say that the Resistance recruited mainly among the ordinary policemen and the lower grades than among the senior ranks who controlled their actions and left most policemen under the authority of officers who faithfully carried out the orders of Vichy." Hence characters like Captain Louis Renault in *Casablanca* were rare. There were more *résistants* (36.36%) among officers of the French "Armistice" Army before Torch. It should also be noted that the Paris police co-operated with the Nazis' Jewish policy virtually to the end;

on 30 June they supervised the entrainment of 1,150 Jews (transport No. 76) to Auschwitz and conducted their last round-up of five hundred Jews a month later. Hence, in the weeks that followed, it was a comparatively small proportion of *résistants* within the Paris police that steered their comrades towards a total strike and open combat against the Germans.[103]

19 July 1944

ANDRÉ GRIBIUS STRUGGLED TO HOLD BACK TEARS when he brought Leclerc the American order to move to England's south coast.

"You're emotional, Gribius," said Leclerc.[104]

Leclerc called senior divisional officers to Dalton Hall.[105] Entering the great drawing room, Paul de Langlade "found gathered all the battlegroup commanders, along with chiefs of services and different arms. Shortly after we were all together in the great *salon* which we were using as an assembly hall, we saw Leclerc enter. Everything in his manner forewarned us to expect an announcement of capital importance. We perceived in him, as he reached the large bureau facing us, an inner joy, mastered, yes, but striking to each of us individually.

"The room went silent and we listened, almost in shock, to his strong, clear voice. The division had to be ready to move to the English ports by the 20th, not even forty-eight hours, and our embarkation for France should follow after a brief delay. Precise orders were given to us that same evening."[106]

Leclerc gave each officer a prepared Order of the Day to read to his men.

> The division is in the final stage of its journey on foreign soil; our next stage will be France. The long awaited hour will strike at last.
>
> Tomorrow we will be entering the battle alongside our allies, and we will have the honour of being among the first units of the French Army fighting

on the national soil. Equally we will be the first to offer the hand of help to the heroic forces of the Resistance.

We owe this honour to General de Gaulle and his government.

To liberate the national soil, accepting that this may require the supreme sacrifice, is our first aim.

To restore France's greatness, that is our second aim.

To lead us in this second task, the heaviest and most difficult, one man commands our trust and that of all Frenchmen, the man who, for four years, despite everything, has held high the honour of France, General de Gaulle.

It is around him that all Frenchmen should unite.

The symbol of this reunion will, for us, be the insignia of the division. This insignia, we will wear tomorrow, to liberate the *Patrie*, and after the victory, to remake France.[107]

Leclerc advised his officers not to read it to their men, but to see that they saw it. Christian Girard watched logistics expert Colonel Adolph Vézinet receive his copy, glowing with joy. Leclerc wanted to unite the division behind a single aim, despite previous conflicts between original Gaullists and former Pétainists. "I said some bad things," Leclerc admitted to Girard, smiling sincerely.[108]

The US high command tightened its grip around the 2e DB. "It was an extraordinary sensation of being stripped of any rights one had," wrote Langlade. "Like being a cog wheel, taking its place in the assembly of an engine. It's admirable but practically speaking intolerable to the French temperament!"[109]

20 July 1944

AT 10AM, AT THE HÔTEL MAJESTIC, Colonel Eberhard Finckh took a telephone call from Berlin. "*Übung!*"—"Exercise!"—the signal that Colonel Claus von Stauffenberg was flying to Rastenburg in East Prussia, carrying a bomb in his briefcase, intending to assassinate

Hitler. Meanwhile life at the Majestic continued as usual, although Walter von Bargatzky ordered a wall of sandbags to be erected in the courtyard of the École Militaire—for the firing squad.

At 12.30pm, while General von Stulpnagel took lunch in the Hôtel Raphael's famous blue dining room, Stauffenberg's bomb exploded in Hitler's map room, killing several officers but only lightly injuring Hitler.

Around 2pm, Colonel Finckh received a second single-word message, "*Abgelaufen!*"—"Done!"

At 3.45pm, after a telephone conversation with Stauffenberg, Luftwaffe reserve Colonel Casar von Hofacker erroneously informed Stulpnagel of the assassination's success. Immediately Stulpnagel invited General von Boineburg-Lengsfeld up from the Hôtel Meurice. Within fifteen minutes Boineburg arrived accompanied by Colonel von Unger.

"A coup has taken place in Berlin," said Stulpnagel. "The chiefs of the SS and SD in Paris must be arrested immediately. If they resist, shoot them."

By 4.30pm Boineburg-Lengsfeld was back at the Meurice drafting orders to arrest Nazi officials across Paris. As far as Boineburg-Lengsfeld was concerned the dice was thrown; he received his orders in good faith and had to carry them out. Despite Boineburg's difficulty in contacting Lieutenant Colonel Baron von Kraewel, commanding the 1st Security Regiment, the alert sounded at the Clignancourt Barracks and two of the 1st Security Regiment's battalions swung into action, sealing off central Paris from the Étoile eastwards.[110]

To Parisians these clean, fresh troops looked like reinforcements destined for Normandy. Their lorries rolled along Avenue Foch, halting outside numbers 72–88, the SS and SD offices. The 1st Security Regiment's second battalion sealed off the front while the first took the ancillary streets behind to seal off rear entrances. By 8pm, Kraewel's men were in place with sufficient transport to evacuate prisoners. The operation could have commenced at 8.30pm but Boineburg postponed it until 10pm when fewer Parisians could witness the occupying power's internecine embarrassment. At 10.30pm, two SS sentries were curtly ordered: "Lay down your weapons or you will be shot out of hand." Kraewel entered 72 Avenue Foch.

"What do you want?" asked a service officer who had drawn his pistol.

"I have orders to arrest all the SD," said Kraewel. "Give me your pistol."

Kraewel then made the service officer man the switchboard and call each room, ordering everyone downstairs. Within forty-five minutes the city's SD personnel were gathered in the foyer ready to be herded onto waiting lorries. Finding that SD chief, Standartenführer Dr. Helmut Knocken, was dining at a nearby restaurant, Kraewel sent his adjutant, Lieutenant David and an SD officer to find Knocken, who meekly surrendered his pistol. Concerned for the growing numbers of prisoners in his charge, Kraewel had the other ranks transfered to prisons while the officers waited. Kraewel's statement says all this happened calmly, though some SS protested that Boineburg-Lengsfeld had got his facts wrong.[111]

While Kraewel's lorries deposited their prisoners at Fresnes and the Fort de l'Est, other arrests occurred on the Rue de Saussaies; Neifeind refused to come quietly. Two Luftwaffe generals who heard the radio while dining had told Neifeind that Hitler had survived the assassination attempt unharmed.

Since, in the Wehrmacht, a general could only be arrested by another general, Boineberg sent his adjutant, General Walter Brehmer and an armed escort, to arrest SS chief Karl Oberg at 57 Boulevard Lannes.

"I arrest you," declared Brehmer.

"Why?" asked Oberg.

"Superior orders," said Brehmer.

Oberg seemed puzzled and reflective.

"I am going to telephone Field Marshal Kluge at Saint-Germain," said Oberg.

"Not allowed," said Brehmer. "Follow me."

Driving to the Hotel Continental, Oberg behaved with almost feminine docility, saying little to the Wehrmacht major escorting him.

Watching from the street corner, Boineburg was pleased that everything was running smoothly; the SS were almost totally under arrest and the Wehrmacht was in control.[112]

However, since Hitler was alive, Stauffenberg's coup began unravelling from late afternoon. At 6pm Stulpnagel was telephoned by General Beck announcing the prearranged codeword, *Valkyrie*, supposedly confirming that Hitler was dead. This was followed at 6.15pm by a call from General Speidel summoning Stulpnagel to Field Marshal von Kluge's HQ at Saint-Germain. Kluge knew about the conspiracy, but refused to commit himself until others completed the dirty work. When news of Hitler's survival arrived, Kluge backpedalled fast. Despite growing evidence that Stauffenberg had failed, Stulpnagel and Hofacker desperately tried to persuade Kluge to join the conspiracy and open negotiations with the Allies. Kluge refused. When Stulpnagel told him the SS and SD were being arrested right across Paris, Kluge replied, "Release them immediately."

"Too late," said Stulpnagel.

Shaking his head, Kluge told Stulpnagel, "You're relieved of your duties."

With those words Stulpnagel and Hofacker became condemned men. But Kluge's chief of staff, General Gunther Blumentritt, whispered to Kluge, "You've got to help them," thereby demonstrating that something of their former comradeship remained. Kluge escorted Stulpnagel down the château's front steps to his car.

"Find some civilian clothes and disappear," said Kluge in a friendlier voice.

Crestfallen, Stulpnagel and Hofacker returned to Paris. They had been absent for five hours.[113]

Despite Kraewel's cordon around Avenue Foch, some SS personnel managed to contact members of General Kurt Meyer's *Hitlerjugend* Panzer Division who were on leave in Paris. Some *Hitlerjugend* personnel began threatening Kraewel's men. Luftwaffe General Hanesse meanwhile tried to deflate the situation with judicious telephone calls. But the best informed senior German officer in Paris, now determined to suppress the conspiracy, was Admiral Theodor Krancke, the Kriegsmarine's chief in the West whose office on the leafy Boulevard Suchet was close to Oberg's. Krancke received an official teleprint message from his chief Admiral Donitz denouncing "an infamous attempt to assassinate the Führer" who "had been miraculously spared". Donitz ordered the Kriegsmarine to close ranks "more tightly than ever around its Führer". When Krancke telephoned the Kriegsmarine's Potsdam command centre, Donitz said, "Only accept orders from me and the Führer. All other information and instructions must be regarded as suspect."[114]

Once the flow of orders from Stauffenberg's clique inside Berlin's Bendler block fell silent, Admiral Krancke recognised what had been happening. At Kluge's HQ General Blumentritt agreed that no credence should be given to the Bendlerstrasse's orders. But when Dontiz advised Krancke to place himself under the SS in Paris, Krancke faced an *impasse*; the SS had been arrested by Kraewel's 1st Security Regiment. Krancke's chief of staff, Admiral Hoffman, caught up with Kraewel by telephone, demanding to know who ordered the arrest of the SS and SD. Kraewel confirmed that his orders came from Generals von Stulpnagel and Boineburg-Lengsfeld. Next Kraewel took a call from the *Hitlerjugend* Division's General Kurt Meyer, ordering him to withdraw and reassemble his men in the Bois de Boulogne.

"I cannot accept your orders," replied Kraewel. "I take my instructions from General von Boineburg-Lengsfeld and I will only obey him."[115]

Following his disastrous exchange with Field Marshal von Kluge, Stulpnagel went into denial. When Kraewel arrived at the Hôtel Raphael to confirm his instructions from General Meyer, Stulpnagel said nothing of what had happened at La Roche-Guyon. Further bad news arrived from the fragile Colonel von Linstow, one of the last to speak to Stauffenberg before his arrest in Berlin. It was all over. When Boineburg reported the successful arrest of SS and SD personnel, Stulpnagel managed a feeble smile. Boineburg asked what Kluge had said.

"The Field Marshal has asked for time to think it over until 9 this morning," lied Stulpnagel. On hearing this Kraewel decided to go to bed; it had been a long evening and there was nothing more he could do.[116]

At 1am German time, Hitler spoke over German radio, excoriating the "small clique of ambitious officers" around Colonel von Stauffenberg. Stulpnagel stirred from the brief, catatonic spell into which intense sadness had thrust him. Would he allow Kraewel's men to be drawn into street fighting with Krancke's sailors after Krancke insisted that, if the SS and SD were not released, his men would act? For his part Kraewel, called on at his lodgings by his adjutant, was unfazed by Krancke's sailors, dismissing them as office boys, but he told Lieutenant David, "We don't want fighting between German soldiers in Paris."

Returning to the Raphael they saw Colonel von Linstow. "Be patient a little longer," he said.

"I am thinking the worst," replied Kraewel. "We need a decision immediately."

Seeing Linstow seized with nerves, Kraewel returned to Avenue Foch with Lieutenant David.[117] Stulpnagel, while doubtless recognising that his fate was sealed, slowly began the process of damage limitation and ordered Boineburg to release Oberg and everyone taken prisoner during the evening.[118]

"Boineburg, are you completely mad?" Oberg asked angrily when Boineburg entered the Hotel Continental. "What's this all about?"

"Ask my boss, General von Stulpnagel," Boineberg replied phlegmatically. "He has asked me to take you to him. My car is waiting."[119]

Watched by night-shift cleaners, Oberg followed von Boineburg-Lengsfeld across the Continental's vast foyer. It was 2am. In Berlin the conspiracy's ringleaders already lay dead. At the Avenue Foch's SD HQ, Kraewel took a call from Colonel von Unger ordering him to release everyone his men had arrested four hours earlier. Addressing his prisoners, Kraewel told them their arrest was suspended and their sidearms would be returned before his men departed. The ORs were returned from Fresnes and the Fort de l'Est in the same lorries as before. Returning to the Raphael, Kraewel saw Karl Oberg being led out.

"What have you been up to, Kraewel?" asked Oberg.

"I was simply obeying orders," answered the young colonel.

"I have been on the telephone to the Führer," said Oberg. "He asked me how many Wehrmacht *Schweinehunde* I had shot. I told him 'none'. Consider yourself fortunate that I said this to him because, without that, I would have had you shot. But now it's too late. The moment has past. You've been lucky, Kraewel."

Before Kraewel left the Raphael, Boineburg ordered him to reassemble his regiment in the Clignancourt Barracks' courtyard at 8.30am. Seeing Otto Abetz and General Blumentritt arriving at the Raphael, Kraewel refrained from asking questions.[120]

Having lunched with Stulpnagel a few days previously, Abetz knew of Stulpnagel's deep misgivings about Nazi policy and inevitably suspected that he was involved. Perhaps Abetz also wanted to control the failed conspiracy's fallout. Closeted with Stulpnagel, Linstow, Knocken and Oberg, Abetz made a show of accepting Stulpnagel's story that he sincerely believed Himmler was seizing power in Berlin and acted accordingly. Oberg did not believe a word of it, but Abetz's intervention helped cool tempers while he persuaded everyone that the evening's events were merely an exercise, carried off with Germanic efficiency. They drank to "comradeship" with champagne.[121] Few, however, were fooled; not the SD who noticed the vehemence with which Kraewel's men treated them, and certainly not Oberg or Knochen. Apparently as a courtesy, but in fact to cover his back, Boineburg showed Blumentritt and Oberg the draft of a speech he intended to make to Kraewel's men.

Eschewing the need for sleep, Stulpnagel went to his private apartment and began destroying incriminating papers. By 8am he was sitting at his desk in the Majestic. On the way there he met his friend Dr. Hans Buwert, whom he previously hoped might open negotiations with Allied diplomats in Lisbon. "Fate was against us," said Stulpnagel. "We all did what we did for the best. You get to a place of safety as soon as you can." Shortly afterwards Stulpnagel was called to Berlin; he knew what that meant.[122]

At 8.30am Colonel von Kraewel paraded his men on the courtyard of Clignacourt Barracks. General von Boineburg-Lengsfeld, one of the luckiest men in the 20 July story, addressed them.

"Soldiers, what you did last night was an exercise in order to check whether you will carry out your orders whatever the situation. This test has shown that you have been well trained. I congratulate you."[123]

21 July 1944

HEARING OF THE FAILED COUP, Pétain remarked to General Neubronn, "So there are stirrings among you." Later that day the old marshal drafted a letter commiserating with Hitler, but thoughts of Oradour-sur-Glane prevented him from sending it. Instead he allowed his aide, General Blasselle, to register his disapproval to Cecil von Renthe-Fink.[124]

While residents of the 16th Arrondissement noticed the comings and goings from Avenue Foch, it took someone in Pierre Taittinger's position to discover that the German authorities ordered seventy-five coffins from various Paris undertakers after 20 July. Taittinger was concerned for his "Alsatian" informant, an SD officer who helped Taittinger save several *résistants* who were former members of his *Jeunesses Patriotes*. The "Alsatian" had warned Taittinger about the SD's private execution chambers equipped with blocks and axes for decapitation. Now Taittinger feared that his friend had been secretly done away with.[125]

De Gaulle virtually ignores 20 July in his memoirs, even though Free France and the 20 July conspiracy attracted similar personalities. The sudden death that day of his London ambassador Pierre Viénot preoccupied him far more. Leclerc and Stauffenberg had much in common, but they never met each other and now they never would. Christian Girard wrote,

There is talk of trouble in Germany; of clashes between the SS and the regular army. One must not supplant realities with desires and it would not be the first time, without adequate intelligence, that a collapse seemed imminent in the enemy camp. If such an event did happen, we here would be appallingly disappointed to arrive too late. I struggle with this embarrassing possibility, knowing that our joy would not be without mixed feelings in such an eventuality. Alas this disappointment has been spared us.

In any case, the development in Germany of an anti-Nazi movement presents other dangers. If they did change régime, either tomorrow or the day after, they would expect all the sympathy of our American allies. They would treat with them and the English just as the Weimar Republic did in 1918. Fate now decreed that this would not happen. Already, over the last four years, many British and Americans have drawn a distinction between Germany and the Nazi regime. This tendency would not be left unexploited and the Germans would know how to use it to fool the Allies once again and we would have let them.

Common sense should tell the Germans not to fight among themselves. That is how it must be. The defeat of Germany on her own soil is necessary for the peace of Europe. It may be terrible to write, but this necessary result is worth the lives it will cost. Through sparing them in 1918, Foch has cost us more lives than he saved. Today it is not our interests that count but those of future generations.[126]

IF 20 July HAD SUCCEEDED, Karl-Heinrich von Stulpnagel might have taken the uniformed intellectual Ernst Junger into the Raphael's blue dining room and told him the war was all but over. Instead Stulpnagel told Countess von Podewils to send Junger his regrets. Carrying his briefcase and a vacuum flask of coffee, Stulpnagel left the Hôtel Majestic, the Avenue Kléber sentries presenting arms to him for the last time.[127]

Junger had only heard Stauffenberg mentioned a few times by Hofacker. The plethora of titled officers involved merely confirmed Junger's view that when things were at their worst the aristocracy gets involved. But many officers expected terrible reprisals. Knowing several Paris conspirators personally, Junger struggled to prevent himself from hitting one officer who called the *Attentat* (assassinatin attempt) "incredible muck". Now the problem for Junger's friends was "to keep the python in the bag and let them get away". Such men tend to face the music, or become too depressed to do anything, like Colonel von Linstow who wandered the Raphael's corridors "like a soul in pain". Extraordinarily, Junger's diary entry closes by declaring that Field Marshal Rommel's injury on 17 July, "threw away the only pillar on which such an enterprise could have rested". Then, almost mirroring Christian Girard's words, Junger wrote, "Even if the operation had succeeded, we would today have twelve boils to lance instead of one, with court martials in every village, every road, every house. We are moving towards a crisis which is both deep and necessary, and such machinery does not work in reverse."[128]

By late afternoon Stulpnagel's car reached the First World War battlefields. Once across the Meuse, Stulpnagel, with the map on his knee, gave his driver surprising directions, not towards Metz and the German border, but to Verdun where he had served in 1916. With a view of once bloodily disputed features, Stulpnagel told Sergeant Schauf to stop, then he walked to the banks of the Meuse, drew his pistol and shot himself in the temple. Rendered unconscious by the injury he fell into the river where his driver found him. The bullet blinded Stulpnagel but he was still breathing. In hindsight it might have been kinder if Schauf had allowed Stulpnagel to drown. But Schauf assumed that Stulpnagel had been shot by the Resistance and drove him to a military hospital.[129]

Of the other key players of 20 July in Paris—General von Boineburg-Lengsfeld, General Brehmer and Colonel Baron von Kraewel—all three escaped the Gestapo dragnet that followed. Brehmer went to the Eastern Front. Kraewel took his regiment to Normandy. Boineburg remained in Paris for several weeks before being posted to the Swiss border. Why did these officers survive while others, like poor Colonel von Linstow, did not?

"If we were not pursued or even questioned by a board of inquiry," Boineburg later wrote, "then it is to Oberg that we owe this. He had several motives for not attacking us; not least of which was the fact that the night of 20 July was hardly glorious for him. He behaved like a girl. What would his chief, Himmler, have said had he known of the docile manner in which the head of the SS in France submitted to his arrest? Also I believe that Oberg, partly through military comradeship, did not want to 'know too much'. Stulpnagel was going to pay; he was the leader of the conspiracy in Paris; that was enough. Why enlarge a matter in which Hitler could have found him culpable? Finally, in late July 1944, the military situation had become so dreadful that Oberg probably hesitated to do anything decisive. It was better to maintain unity between German forces. Lastly, given that there was no one to say anything else left in Paris, Oberg was happy to accept what we told him; we were simply carrying out orders."[130]

The 20 July plot was not well planned and, even if Hitler had been killed, the outcome for Europe would have remained deeply uncertain. But it certainly influenced subsequent events in Paris, by causing Hitler to appoint a new military governor. Despite the arrests of SS and SD on 20 July, the deportation of Jews from Drancy to Nazi extermination camps continued unfalteringly. On 21 July SS Hauptsturmführer Alois Brunner, finding himself a few hundred souls short of his target quota, raided Jewish orphanages to find the last two hundred and fifty of a thirteen hundred person shipment to Auschwitz. Barely one sixth returned.[131]

WHILE HIGH-MINDED GERMANS FAILED to wrest their country from its despoiler, the 2e DB prepared to leave Yorkshire. Compared to the damage suffered by other British country houses, the present Lord Hotham remembers the French as "user friendly".[132]

A letter arrived from Commandant Divry, whom Leclerc sent on a recruiting drive around liberated Normandy. Divry said morale among recruits was very high, but the atmosphere in France was *avachi*—"milked" or "drained" of joy and pride. "Truly France needs a blast of fresh air, plenty of young men and some not bad enthusiasm," Divry finished.[133]

On 21 July, amid summer drizzle, two olive green Buicks waited under Dalton Hall's portico. "No one remained," wrote Girard, "no guard, no sentries; nothing but the cows on the grass to observe the great entrance, its gates open towards the park. Then the sound of a cane tapping on the floor of the lobby, a few noises of doors closing, the cars rolling away on the compressed gravel, a last look back to the great façade, now sad in that grey early morning."[134]

It took several days for the 2e DB to leave Yorkshire and reassemble near the south coast. Using railways saved wear and tear on England's battered roads. As Hull's inhabitants watched, Leclerc's officers supervised the loading of equipment. Those moving south by road had a harder journey, not always welcomed by the towns and villages they passed through. "The French Army can only offer regret and best wishes," said one communiqué.[135] War-weary England hailed and saluted them on their way, observed Rochambelle Suzanne Torres.[136]

Paul de Langlade made a night stop at Burford's Bull Inn, a traditional coaching inn which reminded him of Dickens' *Pickwick Papers*.[137] Philippe de Gaulle, being more junior, shared his men's discomforts. "At each stage's end, we slept in our bedrolls on camp beds and ate from our mess tins in great tents prepared the length of the journey. We were served as we went along according to which unit arrived first, all filing through, irrespective of rank or station, black Americans appearing disconnected and blasé handing out lukewarm meat and beans, known as 'X' rations, washed down with either a cup of coffee or water. So would we be nourished every meal, in an identical manner, doubtless so that we could then absorb the individual 'K' rations every day for the next eight months."[138]

THROUGHOUT JULY THE FFIs' CAMPAIGN against the Wehrmacht's communications gathered pace, mostly involving the removal of railway track; sabotage which merely required tools and knowledgeable saboteurs rather than weapons or explosives. Two bridges were brought down on the lines Beauvais-Clermont and Creil-Compiègne. A railway engine was sent thundering into the big workshop at Argenteuil, wrecking itself and five others, and brake cables were cut liberally on wagons, causing havoc among rolling stock and marshalling yards.[139]

Some of this sabotage was quickly repairable but serious destruction would only be repaired after the liberation. The Germans retaliated where possible, hence *réseaux* that repeatedly hit targets in the same area placed themselves in greatest danger. The network of railways immediately north of Paris, linking Belgium and Germany to Normandy, was frequently targeted. Creil, Beauvais, Compiègne and Crépy-en-Valois were often hit several times a day, rendering connected railway networks useless for up to twelve hours a day.[140]

At four railway centres around Paris; Argenteuil to the northwest, Gagny on the east, Villeneuve-Saint-Georges to the south and Plaisir to the southwest, FFI sabotage was so effective that German reinforcements were carried in lorries via secondary routes never designed for heavy haulage.

Road traffic was hit as well; on 18 July six Wehrmacht tanker lorries were blown up in Paris. The following day another lorry was attacked, killing one man and wounding another. Nor, with the French capital's main arteries clogged by retreating Wehrmacht vehicles, did it take much to cause a serious traffic jam. P1's July report mentions a dozen deliberate punctures. Once vehicles became stationary they could be attacked, rendering captured weapons and other supplies to the Paris FFI. Just as sabotaging signal equipment caused railway chaos, so the removal or obliterating of signposts inconvenienced the Wehrmacht on the roads.[141]

When Montgomery's British 21st Army Group established a foothold east of the Orne River and the Americans built up for their big breakout and right hook, P1's *2e Bureau* knew by 24 July. By logging which German units went to Normandy and in what condition they returned, P1 gleaned an accurate picture of how the Wehrmacht was ground down. "All this information was, for my staff, of the utmost importance," Rol-Tanguy told Bourderon. "It signified that, unless there were massive transfers from other fronts, especially the East, German manpower was going to collapse. Also the arrival of reinforcements from the Russian front was unlikely since it would have been militarily suicidal."[142]

Yet, as Rol-Tanguy admitted, "The German war machine held." Even so, it became inevitable that there would be a big German fallback to the sort of lines held during the First World War. In more general terms P1's report notes the destruction of ports in Brittany and along the Mediterranean coast, developments like the first flying bombs, and the first stirrings of evacuation of German support personnel—German railway workers withdrawing from Brittany, the Organisation Todt leaving Saint-Nazaire, German postal facilities slimmed down at Paris-Montparnasse, ancillary supplies leaving the Hôtel Majestic, and vehicle spares evacuated to Belfort. From such details, Rol-Tanguy concluded that the Germans would soon pull out. But what damage would they leave when they went?[143]

27 July 1944

LA MUETTE METRO STATION in the 16th Arrondissement was lucky for the Gestapo. It was there, during 1943, that they had arrested General Delestraint and his ADC. On 27 July they were lucky again, capturing André Rondenay (codename *Jarry*)* the Military Delegate for northern France's Resistance regions P2 and P3. Rondenay's deputy, Alain de Beaufort, tried to escape but was shot in the leg and captured. Being only one rank below Jacques Chaban-Delmas, Rondenay's arrest was a triumph for the Gestapo. Previously that day Rondenay had met with Pierre Sonneville to discuss cutting off gas and electricity in Paris; they discarded such action as more likely to inconvenience Parisians than harm Germans. After Sonneville, Rondenay visited Maurice Bourges-Manoury, an experienced *résistant*

---

* André Rondenay had escaped from Oflag IVC, Colditz Castle, a couple of years earlier. Along with four comrades, he was shot by the SS at a well-used killing site in the woods near Domont in mid-August.

who smoothed Chaban-Delmas' promotion. It was while travelling between Bourges-Manoury and Chaban that Rondenay and Beaufort were arrested.[144]

This happened amid a spate of betrayals. A resistance leader in the Seine et Marne, named Renard, after beginning well, started to embezzle resistance funds to impress his mistress. When sanctioned, Renard threatened to denounce *résistants* to the Gestapo, a threat he probably carried out, leading to the betrayal of an arms cache in the monastery at La Brosse-Montceaux and over ninety deaths.[145]

There was also friction between different resistance groups. The FTP were pressing for the promotion of Henri Rol-Tanguy to command all active combatants in P1. Effectively this meant handing the practical management of the FFI around Paris to the FTP, something Chaban-Delmas was unlikely to welcome. COMAC's three Vs, with their populist outlook, supported Rol-Tanguy's candidacy. Even Count Jean de Vogüé prioritised an ability to integrate with ordinary FFIs, something that prevented him from previously supporting Rondenay. When news of Rondenay's arrest reached COMAC on 31 July, Paul Ély suggested Pierre Sonneville instead. But Sonneville was involved with damage limitation missions from which he had not returned, leaving Chaban-Delmas with no alternative but to confirm Rol-Tanguy's appointment while insisting that Rol-Tanguy's remit was "strictly technical".[146] Once again the arrest of a Gaullist *résistant* meant promotion for Rol-Tanguy.

Now that the FTP dominated the Resistance in the Department of the Seine, Chaban-Delmas recognised that it would be harder to stop them launching an insurrection when it suited them. Gratifyingly, the number of *résistants* in the Paris area had doubled since December 1943. But weapons were in desperately short supply and setbacks like La Brosse-Montceaux made things worse. Sixty thousand willing *résistants* there may have been, but P1 possessed only 1,750 firearms; a gun for one man in thirty-five.[147]

28–31 July 1944

EVEN AFTER FOUR YEARS no one suspected that Rose Valland was supplying detailed information to the Resistance. Dr. Walter Borchers, a Nazi art expert who occasionally expressed his distaste for the *Einsatzstab Reichleiter Rosenberg*'s methods, was amazed that canvasses by Braque and Picasso were still coming in. Then, after Borchers was posted to the Normandy front, came the contents of the Weil-Picard apartment: Fragonards, Boldinis, several lesser works in their style, and Impressionists including two Dégas and a Renoir.[148] Cataloguing the Weil-Picard collection took around a fortnight; sorting, hanging the best items in the *Salles des Martyrs*—as Rose Valland called the ERR's show rooms—and then dispersing the Weil-Picard family's possessions to depositories in Germany.

Next, on 21 June, the ERR cleared the Esders' apartment at 48 Rue du Villejuste. The Esders' possessions included several superb Ancien Régime portraits and Louis Quinze furniture. Wherever possible French treasures disappeared to Germany. On 7 July the ERR's Dr. Bruno Lohse, a friend of Goering who kept himself away from the front with skiing injuries and kidney complaints, arrived grinning at the Jeu de Paume with a lorry-load of thirty-six carpets. Valland writes that while these were mostly second-rate, Dr. Lohse's haul sadly also included three Gobelin tapestries. The Nazis' greedy eyes also appreciated small bronze statues, so often held in private collections during the nineteenth century. Whether they were busts of Voltaire, reproductions of classical gods or derived from sculptors like Rodin, into the Nazi maw they went. But with the Allies approaching, the ERR's activities became less disciplined. Rose Valland writes irritably that the ERR's Herr Rochlitz "has packed up all the goods, furniture, and pictures from the Grassier household and sent them to Switzerland. Has he obtained the proper authorisations? A package has been sent by young Rudolph Scholz, the ERR photographer, to the following address, 'Frau Rochlitz Hohenschwangau bei Fussen, Gipsmuhle'."

Given that Rochlitz had a dealership in Paris before the war, Rose was rightly suspicious.[149]

Towards the end of July Dr. Bruno Lohse received orders sending him to the front. The ERR put on a farewell party for him at the Jeu de Paume where he stood resplendent in uniform, exclaiming his Siegfried-like enthusiasm for the fight ahead. He returned to Paris on 28 July, driving a little *camionette* loaded with stolen poultry, butter and a whole lamb. While German troops suffered in Normandy Lohse held a banquet at his Avenue d'Iena lodgings attended by the ERR's Paris director, Baron von Behr.[150]

The art requisitions of June and July were now being sorted into one of the ERR's biggest-ever train shipments. But four years spent witnessing systematic theft, cowardice and sickening venality, made Rose Valland realise that this was a train she should stop.

AS THE 2e DB ASSEMBLED ON ENGLAND'S SOUTH COAST, the Malaguti affair played out its final coda. To General Koenig's final pleas for mercy to Marcel Malaguti, Leclerc replied, "If General de Gaulle wishes, when the hour of battle is upon us, to dismiss me from the command of this division which I have formed and built up into the magnificent weapon it is now, then I will carry out his orders. As for re-employing Malaguti under my command again, that is not something I will do at any price. The loyalty and trust required on this level cannot suffer reserve."[151] When news of Leclerc's intransigence reached de Gaulle, he appointed Colonel Pierre Billotte as the division's third battle-group commander "in the general interest", as he put it.[152]

Leclerc was relieved to reach Southampton. "After parking our vehicles on the roads, we gathered in a camp; long rows of enormous green covered tents," wrote Girard. Watching his men pass through a cafeteria-style mess, being served roast chicken, vegetables, cheese and hot coffee, Paul de Langlade was impressed by America's talent for mass provisioning.

That evening Leclerc suffered a malarial attack. He usually managed his symptoms by lying down with a handkerchief over his eyes to block the light. This time was worse than usual, compounded by fever and nightmares. Girard sent for Dr. Richet. "He arrived after ten minutes, which seemed an age, but was reassuring," Girard writes. "Such malarial attacks are usual among men who live so much on their nerves. This incident left a profound impression on me. I worried for him and for all of us."

Through the night the 2e DB's vehicles arrived at the quayside to be loaded aboard LSTs. By dawn, however, much of the division was still parked up along the streets of Southampton; their crews milling around waiting, chatting to locals fascinated by Frenchmen in US uniforms. "I walked along the quays," Girard continues. "The atmosphere! The funnels of tugboats, the masts of trawlers, the smell of iodine, reminded me of my old port of Dieppe. In one corner Dupont's company had formed a choir and the men were banging out songs amid great applause."

It was 4am before Leclerc's staff embarked. When their LST commander knew Leclerc was aboard he had his sail-maker create a pennant—blue and white diagonals surmounted by the Cross of Lorraine and the two stars of a *général de brigade*—and run it up the mast.* Recognising that another phase of his Gaullist odyssey had ended, Girard contemplated the previous four years. "Surely it was incredible to see, on the bridge of an American boat, a pennant fluttering which bore the Cross of Lorraine of those terrible *Free French*?"[153]

---

* Leclerc remained self-effacingly slow to upgrade his insignia to that of a *divisionnaire*.

Chapter 3

The 2e DB Lands in France

1 August 1944

WOKEN BY A FANFARE ON THE SHIP'S TANNOY, Christian Girard rose from his bunk, saw the French coast through the porthole, and smiled. Leclerc had a good night with no recurring malaria. Guy de Schompré and Paul Répiton-Préneuf were already ashore hooking up with US Army officialdom on Utah Beach. At 11am a launch tied up alongside the LST, rocking on choppy waves. Dressed in a raincoat and forage cap, sporting merely the two stars of a *général de brigade*, Leclerc led his staff down the stairs and jumped into the bobbing motor boat, quickly followed by Reption-Préneuf, Schompré, Girard, Gribius, Colonel Bernard, Robert Quillichini and Jacques de Guillebon.[1] As the launch pulled away, past Liberty ships swaying at anchor, towards the rose-pink sand of La Madeleine, Girard found himself dumbstruck by the depth of his feelings. Eventually the launch reached a prefabricated metal jetty. Leclerc and his staff climbed up and stomped along the jetty's walkway towards the beach.

"A strange impression," Leclerc remarked perkily.

"Awfully pleasing," replied Girard, matching his boss's mood.

Nearing the beach they encountered photographers; only two at first, but this quickly became twenty, jostling for the best photograph or cine-footage of France's most famous combat general coming home. Next, a short American general, smiling broadly, pushed past the photographers, introduced himself as General Walton Walker, the XX Corps commander, and shook Leclerc by the hand.

"Could you shake hands again, please?" asked a photographer.

Would General Leclerc return to the jetty and repeat his landing in France, a cine-photographer asked.

"*Non*," he replied firmly. "We're here to fight a war. Leave me alone."[2]

La Madeleine became a scene of furious activity as LSTs opened their bow doors and lowered ramps. Shermans, Tank-Destroyers and self-propelled artillery—emblazoned with the blue and white map of France superimposed by the Cross of Lorraine—rolled ashore. "But we were a little embarrassed," wrote Paul de Langlade. "A little shy, as if kissing in public after five years of separation, the woman one loved."[3] Soon they were driving inland to assemble at Area B near Saint-Germain de Varreville. "Everywhere there was an unforgettable magma flow of American troops and equipment," Langlade continues. "Great rows of trucks and tanks were disgorged, disembarking every day from the holds of ship convoys that arrived and left, also delivering great containers of petrol and supplies."[4]

After a fitful night, Ensign Philippe de Gaulle surveyed the French coast with binoculars and was delighted that Varreville's church spire remained intact. Watching his Tank Destroyers disembark, he noticed the emotion rising in every man; not just anticipating combat but returning home. Those who could dismount their TDs easily grabbed handfuls of damp sand, squeezing it through their fingers "*avec délectation*".[5] Here and there white tape cordoned off uncleared minefields. Everywhere Philippe witnessed the destruction of war: wrecked houses, shell craters, shattered trees, ruined farms and the sickly sweet, retch-making smell of corpses, either human or livestock. Suddenly, aircraft swooped down like a tornado. In an increasingly rare occurrence, four Focke-Wulf 190 fighter-bombers had penetrated Allied air cover. Next, a flight of USAAF Thunderbolts screamed after them. The Focke-Wulfs dropped their bombs among a battery of 2e DB artillery, inflicting casualties and damage to equipment. With their vehicles so closely parked, Philippe remembered how the flower of French chivalry, including one of his ancestors, had perished at Agincourt, in a disaster caused by the crowd as much as by English longbow men.[6]

Rochambelle* Édith Vézy watched with horror as German bombs destroyed several ambulances and crippled a fellow Rochambelle for life. Thenceforward, she always parked her beloved ambulance *Gargamelle* under cover rather than leaving her in the open. "Our homecoming had been so happy and here was the terrible reality," Édith wrote. The Rochambelles quickly began gathering the 2e DB's wounded.[7]

Unfazed by the destruction, Jacques Massu confessed to an overwhelming sense of well-being and optimism that sustained him throughout the liberation campaign, and which "helped me accomplish my tasks in the best conditions for success", he later wrote. "If the Germans had turned our lines in 1940, it was quite simply their turn to have the same thing done back to them to repay them for the years of waiting and the anxiety they caused. It therefore followed that they should be conducted with the least possible delay back towards the Rhine; a direction we all knew. We were trained and equipped to carry out this task and that is what we were going to do."[8]

Amid all this, Normandy's stoic peasants were uncomplaining. Most were thrilled to see a smart, modern, well-equipped French division. Hidden caches of cider and calvados were offered and, in several instances, they gave the 2e DB their most precious gift, their sons. Hundreds of Normans now joined Leclerc and were trained on the march.[9]

Initially it appeared the 2e DB would join Walker's XX Corps, although this was far from certain. General George Patton's US Third Army had only been activated that very day. Bradley now commanded the new 12th Army Group, comprising both his former command, the US

---

* The 2e DB's ambulance drivers were mostly provided by the *Groupe Rochambeau* named after the French general who served in the American War of Independence. The women serving in the *Groupe Rochambeau* were hence called 'Rochambelles.' Other 2e DB ambulance drivers were *Marinettes* from the French Navy and British Quakers.

First Army, and the new Third Army. With Third Army's activation came several new corps, including General Wade Haislip's XV Corps which so far consisted of the US 79th and 90th Infantry Divisions and the US 5th Armored. XV Corps' role was to push southeastwards around the German Seventh Army's unguarded southern flank. It was questionable whether only one armoured division was sufficient for such a task.

FOUR YEARS AND SIX WEEKS after General Walter Warlimont overflew Paris in his Storch spotter plane and landed on the Champs Élysées, it fell to him to deliver Hitler's orders for a counterattack to Field Marshal von Kluge. Operation Cobra—the Allied breakthrough operation, which had begun on 25 July—was turning into a roaring torrent which would force a German rout unless it was stopped. Withdrawal from France would deprive Germany of her land-link to Spain and Portugal's neutral ports, as well as France's Atlantic ports.[10]

Having been on the periphery of the 20 July conspiracy, Field Marshal von Kluge was a troubled man. His sense of honour prevented him from joining the plot but also made it impossible for him to inform on brother officers. Now Warlimont's task was to stiffen the wavering Kluge. Hitler wanted Sepp Dietrich's 1 SS Panzer Corps withdrawn from its positions facing the British at Caen and sent west, supported by other Panzer units, to attack the east flank of the American corridor through Mortain and cut it off on the coast at Avranches. Kluge greeted this plan with dismay, believing that withdrawing Dietrich's corps from its positions would simply allow a British breakthrough on top of an American one. Furthermore, while the plan was similar in concept to both the Arras counterattack in 1940 and Manstein's operation against Zhukov's push along the Black Sea coast in 1943, such operations only succeed with troops who are reasonably fresh and well-supplied rather than exhausted units.

Panzer Group West's General Eberbach thought Hitler's plan was utterly unsupportable, dreamt up by someone in serious denial. Most divisions were well below strength. SS General Sepp Dietrich, utterly loyal to Hitler since the early days, thought the Mortain plan was nonsense, while paratroop General Eugen Meindl looked at Warlimont as though he had fallen from a box of toy soldiers. German ground forces no longer had Luftwaffe support, while Allied fighter-bombers roamed at will.[11]

THE ALLIED ACQUISITION OF BRITTANY deprived Kluge of three divisions holed up in Brest. When the US 4th Armored Division was diverted to reduce the German garrison at Rennes, its commander, General John S. Wood, complained, "We're winning this war the wrong way, we ought to be going towards Paris."[12] Wood sincerely believed that he could have led 4th Armored to Chartres within two days, and pre-empted Kluge's coming counterattack. Previously Patton might have backed Wood, but Patton still had to regain both Eisenhower's and Bradley's confidence after his gaffes in Sicily the previous year. Besides, "Ham" Haislip's XV Corps was incomplete; it had been allocated two armoured divisions to accomplish its onerous tasks and Leclerc's 2e DB was not yet fully disembarked.

At Utah beach the weather prevented the unloading of anything except an LST which could drop its ramp. Dronne's Spaniards, who often associated beaches with miserable internment camps hastily erected in 1939 for Republican refugees on France's Mediterranean coast, began singing *La Cucaracha*, an old Spanish favourite about soldiers' boredom, dating from Napoleon III's Mexican adventure. Even more frustrating was that most of Joseph Putz's third battalion were among the first ashore.[13]

The weather cleared overnight, enabling *la Nueve* to begin disembarkation at 8am on 4 August. The lifting operation that loaded their half-tracks onto the ships in Southampton docks was repeated in reverse, this time into landing craft, each half-track looking like a giant beetle as it swung through the air. Eventually the first landing craft chugged towards the coast, followed by a second and so on through the morning. It was 1.30pm when Dronne finally stepped onto French soil, his heart almost missing a beat, his eyes moistening. He touched the ground with his fingertips. It was there. That was enough.[14]

With *la Nueve* ashore, Putz's battalion was complete. They camped that night in a ruined village. As Dronne's men set about camouflaging their vehicles they were visited by de-housed villagers sleep-walking through their astonishment and distress. But news that Patton's US Third Army had broken out of the bridgehead and the 2e DB would be part of his "right hook" energised the men.[15]

5 August 1944

NEEDING AUTHORITATIVE INSIGHT into Allied intentions towards Paris, Jacques Chaban-Delmas decided to visit London. After a broken train journey due to railway sabotage, Chaban reached Lyon. Maurice Bourgès-Maunoury had told him of a bistro whose owner would connect him to the Lyon resistance. Chaban presented himself there, inserting several *résistants'* codenames into the conversation until, eventually, the manager trusted him enough to take him through to the back to meet the region's head of air operations. Forty-eight hours later Chaban was hiding in a farmhouse awaiting a British aircraft. Once the BBC's French Service gave the signal "*Notre Printemps, c'est d'être ensemble*", Chaban knew he was going to London.

At 1.00am a Glen Martin bomber landed on a remote, grassy airstrip. By dawn Chaban was in London being welcomed to Carlton Gardens' Free French HQ by Colonel Henri Ziegler. Chaban savoured being able to walk unwarily around London until evening when General Marie-Pierre Koenig took him to dinner at the Army and Navy Club. Watched with slight curiosity by British officers, Chaban tucked into London's best wartime fare while explaining to Koenig his concerns that the over-eager Paris Resistance might attack the Germans prematurely, risking disaster. He needed to know when the Allies would reach Paris.

The man most able to give Chaban that answer was General Eisenhower. Nevertheless Koenig arranged an appointment for him to see Winston Churchill at 10 Downing Street on 7 August. When Chaban arrived, however, Churchill was taking his siesta and it fell to the Secretary of the War Cabinet, General Sir Hastings Ismay, to take the interview. Ismay hailed from a solid colonial family that had produced several soldiers and administrators. Marriage to an Anglo-American heiress had also made him exceedingly well-to-do; added to which his experience in military diplomacy ensured his promotion to high rank.

Chaban got straight to the point. The number of *résistants* in Paris was between twelve and fifteen thousand men who, while enthusiastic, lacked training and sufficient weapons—barely a rifle or Sten gun for one man in ten. On the German side the Paris garrison appeared to be about sixteen thousand men, who could probably be supplemented by troops in transit through the city, along with artillery and tanks. Above all, Chaban impressed upon General Ismay that, after four years of humiliation, the Paris Resistance was desperate to show what it could do. In this eventuality, Chaban told Ismay, Paris needed to be liberated sooner rather than later.

Ismay coolly impressed upon Chaban that, according to his information on Allied plans and target dates, the Allied Expeditionary Forces were unlikely to reach Paris before D+90; that is, ninety days after the landings, or early September. Disappointed, Chaban told Ismay it would be impossible to restrain the Paris Resistance for that long. Unless Allied plans were reconsidered, Chaban said, Paris could become another Warsaw.

Ismay was well aware of what was happening in Warsaw that summer. It must also be noted that, since 1940, Ismay had performed many undersung deeds to support Free France; Chaban could not have found a more sympathetic listener. As Chaban took his leave, Ismay emphasised how much he loved France and would hate to see Paris suffer Warsaw's fate. Ismay finished by assuring Chaban that his arguments would be faithfully reported to Churchill.

It is hard to see how much more Ismay could have offered. Yet Chaban regarded his trip to London as "six wasted days". After debriefing by General Koenig, Chaban needed to return to Paris as fast as possible. A lot had happened during his absence; Patton's breakout was transforming the Normandy campaign. In the meantime Koenig heard from Algiers: "No popular insurrection in Paris without my orders", a message from de Gaulle.[16]

6–7 August 1944

WHILE GENERAL ERICH VON DEM BACH-ZELEWSKI tore Warsaw apart and his hanging judge "Raving" Roland Friesler condemned the 20 July conspirators to the gallows of Plotzensee, Hitler needed a new, unconditionally obedient general as military governor of Paris. The involvement of several Paris officers in the plot necessitated new appointments. After his suicide attempt at Verdun only blinded him, General Karl-Heinrich von Stulpnagel was taken to the Gestapo cells underneath Berlin's Prinz Albrecht Strasse where, during a restless night, he shouted, "Rommel, Rommel!"—outbursts that sealed Rommel's fate. While Stulpnagel awaited trial, the newly promoted General Wilhelm Burgdorf shortlisted personal dossiers from which new military governors for France and Paris would be chosen.

Burgdorff alighted on the file of General der Infanterie Dietrich von Choltitz. On the face of it von Choltitz was a Prussian stiffneck with an unblemished record. "By disposition and ability an able soldier and officer" began a 1942 report. "Has a good tactical grasp and can make rapid decisions. Gets to the heart of a problem with few words. In battle leads his regiment with a sure, strong hand. When he puts his mind to it can be a personal example. Many successes can be credited to his personal initiative. Adept at socialising. Unfortunately, owing to the war, suffers from a stomach complaint. The increased nervousness makes him irritable at times and he then becomes very excitable as a consequence."[17] This assessment undoubtedly attracted Burgdorf, but if he sought a *ganzharter*—a whole hearted Nazi—willing to execute Hitler's wishes, however distasteful, Burgdorf's ignorance of Germany's aristocratic *milieu* meant that he had shortlisted the wrong man for what Hitler intended. Unknown to Burgdorf, von Choltitz was socially connected with several 20 July conspirators, including Carl Goerdeler and Claus von Stauffenberg. But having only been on the sidelines, von Choltitz escaped investigation.

Born of Silesian landed gentry, von Choltitz once served as a pageboy to the Saxon court. He fought competently during the First World War as an infantry lieutenant and, after the Treaty of Versailles, he was retained by the hundred-thousand-strong Reichwehr. Promotion, marriage and children followed and, when the Nazis expanded the army, von Choltitz was appointed colonel of the "air-portable" 16th Infantry Regiment. In this capacity he seized the smoking ruins of Rotterdam when Germany's *Blitzkrieg* in the West kicked off on 10 May 1940.

During 1942 von Choltitz took part in General Erich von Manstein's push along the Black Sea coast into the Crimea where, despite over 90% casualties, von Choltitz's regiment took Sebastopol. It was in the Crimea that von Choltitz was drawn into anti-Jewish *aktions* in support of Dr. Otto Ohlendorf's Einsatzgruppe D, which was attached to Manstein's Army.

Although von Choltitz himself has not attracted a serious biography, Field Marshal Erich von Manstein has attracted several* which, to varying degrees, recognise Manstein's powers of denial during post-war tribunals. Senior British Germanist Richard J. Evans confirms that questions about Manstein's involvement in Nazi atrocities remain "largely unanswered".[18] Yet Manstein's Chief of Staff, Colonel (later General) Hans Wohler, acknowledged Einsatzgruppe D's activities in 11th Army's sector, while Colonel Friedrich Hauck confirms that 11th Army gave Ohlendorff's men both logistical support and supplementary manpower to carry out mass shootings of Jews.[19] As Michael Burleigh writes, "There is no way that their commander, Manstein, did not know what his [Ohlendorf's] officers and men were doing."[20] By April 1942, Einsatzgruppe D had murdered ninety

---

* Three of the most recent biographies are by General Mungo Melvin, Benoit Le May and Marcel Stein.

thousand Crimean Jews,[21] deaths which haunted von Choltitz, although his personal role remains unclear.

Dronne describes von Choltitz as a general who never hesitated to destroy anything he was ordered to, proudly carrying a picture of "Karl", the massive siege mortar used at Sebastopol, in his wallet.[22] Conversely, in his memoirs, von Choltitz claims that while commanding rear guard actions during 1943, the year Germany suffered great reverses in Russia, he was never ordered to commit wanton destruction, nor would he have obeyed such orders.[23] However, this conflicts with threats he made to Pierre Taittinger and Raoul Nordling during the following weeks; incidents they both mention in subsequent writings.

From the periphery of 20 July, it was with a mourner's regret that von Choltitz wrote in his memoirs, "The 20 July put an end to our last hopes of changing the politics of our country. Similarly, that day was the point at which the Wehrmacht began to disintegrate. Seven hundred officers, including twenty-six generals, paid with their lives for the too long deferred attempt to rid ourselves of Hitler."[24]

Following Burgdorf's summons, von Choltitz reached Rastenburg on the morning of 7 August, knowing that many of his friends were facing execution. The effects of Stauffenberg's botched assassination attempt were everywhere; the wrecked map room, heightened security and the air of distrust between Wehrmacht officers and their SS counterparts.[25] After briefly explaining the Paris appointment, Burgdorf walked von Choltitz across to Hitler's bunker. As they entered, both General Guderian, the famous tank commander, and Admiral Karl Donitz, the head of the Kriegsmarine, were leaving a conference. Entering the bunker, von Choltitz noticed that Burgdorf was looking jerkily around in an obviously agitated state. After removing his cap, belt and pistol in the ante-room von Choltitz was led into the Führer's presence.

Von Choltitz thought Hitler appeared run down and had gained weight since he last saw him at a conference near Posen. Eighteen days after the assassination attempt, Hitler remained badly shaken. His hearing was damaged and his raw, sore-looking hands twitched uncontrollably. Warned by Burgdorf to be careful when shaking Hitler's hand, von Choltitz moderated his usual firm soldier's grip. A slight, welcoming smile lightened Hitler's pallid features.

"Does the General know what it's about?" Hitler asked.

"Yes, my Führer," replied Burgdorff.[26]

Then Hitler began a habitual harangue, telling von Choltitz how he took the German people in hand in 1933 and gave them purpose through the Nazi Party.

"A people who do not surrender can never be defeated," said Hitler. "Such a thing has never happened in history ..."

"Was he deluded?" von Choltitz wondered, listening while Hitler "trotted out all the old nonsense, so that I actually had to bite my tongue hard three times, to stop myself from bursting out."[27] Eventually Hitler calmed down sufficiently to discuss Normandy, which emboldened von Choltitz to interject, "My Führer, I am the general commanding the 84th Corps in Normandy, I have come ..."

But Hitler gestured von Choltitz to be silent.

"Yes, I am perfectly aware," said Hitler, talking down von Choltitz in a tone of astonishing self-assurance, vaunting the counterattack (the Mortain operation was happening at the time) which would drive the Allies back into the sea.

Having come from Normandy, where he witnessed German soldiers facing insuperable odds, von Choltitz was horrified. Moving on to the assassination attempt, von Choltitz saw Hitler's hideous glee at unmasking everyone who opposed him. With his mouth frothing, arms shaking, and fists banging on the table, Hitler told von Choltitz in grim detail how the People's Court was condemning dozens of officers to the gallows at Plotzensee where they were hung with piano wire, "high and short", suffering a slow, agonising end, rather than the long drop that would dispatch them quickly.[28]

"You needn't be alarmed," said Hitler, "It is not as though only the Army had taken part in this attempt by a few generals to usurp power. The whole people, with its opposition, slight though it is, whether it comes from middle class, Social Democrat or Communist circles, took part in it."[29]

Watching Hitler's eyes gleaming vindictively, von Choltitz realised he was mad.[30]

"Those usurpers wanted to surrender German soil," Hitler rambled on. "I will not yield a single yard of German soil."

Von Choltitz stiffened himself and said, "My Führer, the 84th Corps has been practically wiped out in defensive battle."[31]

"General, you are going to Paris," said Hitler, changing the subject and appearing to calm down. "You will keep order in this city which is an important staging post for our troops. Cooperate with Oberg. You will receive every assistance from here. I am nominating you general commanding all Wehrmacht troops in the city. You have all the absolute powers that a general can be given. You have the powers of a general commanding anywhere that is under siege."

When the interview finished Hitler offered his hand again, accompanied by a ferocious stare full of "suspicion and utter cruelty". Outside, von Choltitz found Burgdorf. Gripping the younger general's arm, von Choltitz said, "Burgdorf, this is crazy!"

"What would you have me do?" Burgdorf shrugged.

Breathing deeply, von Choltitz waited in an ante-room while the written order was produced. It read as follows:

> 1. The troops on the Western Front who, with exemplary valour, are fighting a superior enemy can expect, from any German finding himself in France, that he will do everything possible to assist them. From now onwards no German able to bear arms may be present in the rear areas unless his presence serves the immediate interests of the troops fighting at the front. This particularly refers to the area of Gross Paris.

> 2. With immediate effect, I nominate Major-General von Choltitz "*Befehlshaber*" of all German troops in Gross Paris." He is responsible to me for the following matters.

>> i) Paris must, as quickly as possible, shed its character as a place of leave with its *unhealthy symptoms*. The city must not become a reservoir of refugees and cowards, but a place of fear for anyone who is not an honest auxiliary or who is not supporting the troops fighting at the front.

ii) All unneccessary German administrators and, in particular, all those who do not have to be there, must leave as soon as possible. Men capable of fighting should go to the front line. Any unjustified entry must be rigourously forbidden. There will be no withdrawal of military command services or any other important service without my permission.

iii) The area of Gross Paris must be protected from all acts of rebellion, subversion or sabotage.

3. To accomplish this task the general commanding Wehrmacht troops in Gross Paris is empowered to give orders to all ranks of the Wehrmacht and Waffen SS, to detachments and organisations outside the Wehrmacht, to National Socialist Party and civilian services. In the event that orders derived from the Wehrmacht or any other high command of the Reich might conflict with the mission of the General commanding Gross Paris, I must be informed by *Oberkommando der Werhmacht* (OKW).

4. The General commanding Gross Paris is placed under the orders of the military commander in France. Where the military protection of Gross Paris is concerned, and the use of personnel made available for combat at the front, he will take his instructions from the High Command of the Western Front. The General commanding Gross Paris will retain the staff of the preceeding commander.

5. Following instructions from the Chief of OKW, he will receive the jurisdictional powers of any commander of a city under siege.

On the face of it, these orders made perfect military sense. But as von Choltitz re-read the document, mindful of Hitler's recent tirade, it became clear that this order was *carte blanche* to wreck Paris. Consoling himself with a stiff drink, von Choltitz shared a mess table with a senior SS officer whose name goes unmentioned in his memoirs but who turned out to be Robert Ley.[32]

Von Choltitz met Ley again later that evening on the train, advancing down the carriage corridor towards him, resplendent in his black uniform, copiously decorated with silver braid knots around the epaulettes and collar. Ley had also seen Hitler that day. As a result of 20 July, Hitler told him that new laws were being prepared whereby the families of anyone who committed treason were subject to reprisals. The concept of *Sippenhaft*—that traitors possess bad blood which runs in their family—was not entirely new in Nazi Germany, but it took 20 July to crystallise it into a law. In his memoirs von Choltitz claims it was the first time he heard about *Sippenhaft* and he was profoundly disturbed to learn that the families of Stauffenberg, von Tresckow and others were being dismantled; adults sent to concentration camps and children farmed out to foster parents. Railway couchettes are uncomfortable places to sleep, but Ley's news caused von Choltitz an utterly sleepless night *en route* to the most fateful weeks of his life.[33]

FOR SEVERAL DAYS PATTON'S US THIRD ARMY pushed southwards "like a great torrent flooding through a breach in a dam". The 2e DB was part of that torrent, rolling through country towns like Coutances, Gavray, La Haye-Pesnel and Avranches. Heading for the north bank of the Selune, southeast of Ducey, Dronne's Spaniards found the road lined with French country folk cheering *Les Leclercs*. "We've been waiting for you," said a 1914–1918 veteran. "You've been a long time coming. Well, here you are."[34] Guided by Eugene Bosquet, a young soldier whose family lived nearby, Putz's battalion continued until dusk. On reaching the Selune the 2e DB began camouflaging its vehicles for the night. Old desert hands knew the importance of this. If air cover was scarce camouflage could be a vehicle's only protection.[35]

As part of Hitler's counterattack, the Luftwaffe was active that night. Of course Hitler never expected the thrust to be halted at Mortain, the attractive Norman town after which it was named. But a gutsy holding action by the US 1st and 30th Infantry Divisions on Hill 314 meant Mortain was as far as Hitler's reckless counterattack got. From the 2e DB, only GT Langlade* became involved; sending a mixed force which took some prisoners. But the decisive factor was Allied air supremacy,

---

* GT = *Groupement Tactique*, ie a 'battle group.' The 2e DB had three 'battle groups' on the US armoured division model.

with British rocket-carrying Typhoons being directed onto the Panzer formations strung out along country lanes.[36]

Despite crippling losses, Hitler wanted Kluge to continue, even though the assault was clearly ineffective. The attack by Canadian First Army (Operation Totalize) towards Falaise, a little over twenty-four hours after the Mortain operation, presaged encirclement of all German forces in Normandy, pushing Kluge to the brink of despair. On the Allied side, the German failure at Mortain created splendid opportunities for exploitation. But it all came at dreadful cost as Dodge ambulances queued for about half a mile to access overloaded field hospitals. Mortain, like many pretty Norman towns, was wrecked.[37]

9 August 1944

PIERRE LAVAL SPENT 8 AUGUST ON THE ROAD, only arriving in Paris during the small hours of the 9th along with his wife and daughter, Countess de Chambrun. He then went straight into a hectic programme of negotiations, calling on the Municipal Council, headed by Pierre Taittinger, along with the Council of the Department of the Seine, headed by Victor Constant, to maintain governmental continuity until the liberation in the "general interest". Therefore Marshal Pétain should be brought to Paris from Vichy.[38]

At first Laval was gratified to discover that not only die-hard *collabos* accepted his idea, but also politicians who remained relatively uncompromised by Vichy. These included a few who remained in contact with Roosevelt's former ambassador to Vichy, Admiral Leahy, such as Anatole de Monzie, Georges Bonnet and Camille Chautemps.[39] But even if national bodies could be assembled and Pétain brought to Paris, Monzie thought it was too late and frankly informed Laval that he was too unpopular to reconvene anything on his personal initiative. Pétain might possibly retain enough personal prestige to perform that role, but not Laval. In any case, by Monzie's estimation, such efforts were pointless since the National Assembly would reconvene automatically at the liberation.[40] Laval listened calmly, then charmingly declared that he merely wished to install a transitional government to continue the duties of the state. Monzie thought Laval seemed like "*Pierrot* of the good old days" before 1940.[41]

But Monzie's view was correct. Probably the only person Laval spoke to that day, whose position in post-war France remained untainted by *collaboration* was "the Gentleman of Paris", Raoul Nordling, who visited the Matignon pleading for the release of French political prisoners before the inevitable German departure. Even on this pressing issue, so dear to Gaullist hearts, no one was going to approach Laval except through a neutral intermediary.[42]

DIETRICH VON CHOLTITZ ARRIVED IN PARIS that evening. According to his memoirs, the forces available to carry out Hitler's nihilistic orders totalled a mere six thousand on the day he took command, but even then several anti-aircraft batteries—whose equipment was versatile enough to be used against ground forces—were already pulling out. The only tanks available to him were mainly French Hotchkiss and Somua models taken into German service in 1940 and given Wehrmacht designations. Since these were unsuitable for frontline service they were used for internal security work. But those six thousand men were, to use a phrase popular among French historians, *intra muros*—within the walls, or old boundaries—of the city of Paris. Von Choltitz's motives for massaging down the available manpower in his memoirs are probably suspect; in post-war Germany many of his contemporaries regarded him as a disloyal officer. In any case, his forces also included around three thousand administrative and security personnel, including die-hard prison guards still running holding camps around the city, and another eight thousand outside the city boundary.[43] To this might be added an uncertain number of French personnel: *Milice* and members of similar *collabo* organisations; those shameless enough to remain.

Meanwhile, the Wehrmacht's three service HQs were pulling out. Stulpnagel's replacement, Luftwaffe General Karl Kitzinger, was ordered to prepare fallback positions similar to the 1914–1918 Western Front along the rivers Somme, Aisne, Marne and Saone. To man this new line, Army Group B needed to extricate as many forces as possible from the Normandy débacle.[44] But time was against them; nor did the lower reaches of the Seine represent a natural defence line. The Allies soon took several easy crossing points.[45]

Immediately under him, von Choltitz had General Hubertus von Aulock, a tough Silesian soldier whose brother, Andreas, had made the Americans pay dearly for Saint Malo. Taking position south and southwest of the city, von Aulock's makeshift corps comprised battlegroups from the 48th and 338th Infantry Divisions and a shock battalion sent from the First Army, but little in the way of heavy equipment beyond anti-aircraft guns (88mm) which were a mixed blessing without heavy tractors to pull them, and less effective with inexperienced crews. There were around sixty aircraft based at Le Bourget, but these rarely flew unless Allied aircraft were firmly committed elsewhere. Von Choltitz's only hope of reinforcements was that Army Group B would divert units retreating from Normandy. While such limited personnel and light arsenals were insufficient to defend the city in open battle, skilfully placed they could be used to fight prolonged rearguard actions, inflicting severe losses on the Allies and causing much destruction. After Normandy, the Allies did not underestimate the fighting qualities of the German soldier in defence.[46]

Of those staff officers who knew Paris well, several were recalled to Berlin for questioning over 20 July, especially associates of General von Stulpnagel. However, von Choltitz already knew his departing predecessor, Boineburg-Lengsfeld, and asked him to stay on in whatever capacity could be devised.

"No, I have nothing more to do here," Boineburg-Lengsfeld replied.

Over dinner at the Maison Coty, von Choltitz discussed Hitler's orders.

"I beg you," said a horrified Boineburg-Lengsfeld, "avoid anything that could bring such destruction to this city. You would never be able to justify such madness."

"You've got to watch out for that Führer!" said von Choltitz wryly. "That old corporal hates all us other generals. It's us and only us who are responsible for the success of the Allied landings!"[47]

Installing himself at the Hôtel Meurice and inheriting most of Boineberg-Lengsfeld's staff, von Choltitz felt he was joining a Prussian aristocrats' house party. Lieutenant Dankwart von Arnim, Boineburg's ADC whom von Choltitz took over, was a distant relation. Colonel Hans Jay was an old friend, while Adolf von Carlowitz, a reserve officer, was another cousin who always called him *"Dietz"*.[48]

Had he the inclination, von Choltitz could have done immense damage with the means available. Many Parisian buildings have significant timber structure which burns easily. Water supplies could be cut off; gas supplies were sufficient to boost conflagrations. The principal reason used to avoid this was that the city's main thoroughfares and glorious bridges were routes which the Germans needed kept open as long as possible so that forces escaping from Normandy could make their retreat.[49] Yet only around 10% of the German forces evacuating France went through Paris.[50]

During the early days of his appointment von Choltitz certainly *appeared* to take Hitler's orders seriously. But the results do not bear this out. It fell to Sonderführer Robert Wallraf to welcome the officers of a demolition battalion to their temporary lodgings in the Chamber of Deputies. "They were young, tough, suntanned men who seemed well-used to whatever the war offered them," wrote Wallraf. "With the contemptuous air of soldiers having recently arrived from the Eastern Front, they seemed well pleased with their new abode."

The stocky, taciturn engineer colonel particularly interested Wallraf. "If you've got to blow up forty-two bridges, it's not going to be easy," Wallraf remarked.

"Easy?" replied the engineer colonel mockingly. "I'm not interested in whether it's easy or difficult. The essential thing is that I get it done."

"When you start work on the bridges the Resistance may well shoot at you from windows and rooftops," warned Wallraf.

"Oh we're used to that sort of thing," replied the unfazed colonel. "We got out of Stalingrad with Russians sniping at us from all sides. We've blown up mines in Kharkov behind Russian lines. Even with the Russians in full advance we got it done. In Kiev we were prisoners for a night, but were liberated the following day. This is a jolly one, a few dozen bridges! It's nothing to men like us."

"How are you proposing to do it?" asked Wallraf.

"Aircraft bombs," replied the colonel. "We'll pack a few bombs under the span of each bridge and blow it up. We ought to do thirty or forty in a day."

"Do you honestly think they will let you do that?" asked Wallraf, appalled.

"At each bridge we'll have a machine-gun post and if that isn't enough, maybe a tank," replied the sapper colonel. "You've no idea how people respect machine-guns and tanks."

Although these grimly practical sappers were under his command, von Choltitz avoided discussing their task with anyone. The following day Wallraf witnessed an extraordinary conversation.

"Have you *got* explosives?" asked von Choltitz as though addressing a child.

"No Sir," replied the engineer colonel. "I have not."

"But what are you going to do without explosives?" asked von Choltitz.

"Sir, I've been ordered to use either aircraft bombs or torpedo heads."

"Have you lorries to carry them?" asked von Choltitz.

"No Sir."

"Well, then," replied von Choltitz. "We'll have to consider tomorrow how you're going to proceed. I haven't the time at the moment. We must also consider the best way to blow up the bridges in one go. If you would think about that and report back to me tomorrow."

Thus von Choltitz's obfuscations deferred the blowing of the city's bridges.[51]

"THERE IS CONSIDERABLE CONFUSION," General Omar Bradley later wrote, "as to whose 'historic' idea it was to turn US forces north and encircle the Germans" in what would become "the Falaise pocket". "Let me put it plainly. It was my idea."[52] However, given the opportunity that presented itself, the idea was sufficiently obvious for Bradley to remark to his ADC, Chet Hansen on 8 August, "The German is either crazy or he doesn't know what's going on. I think he is too smart to do what he is doing. He can't know what is going on in our sector. Surely the professional generals must know the jig is up."

"Hitler is your greatest ally, Sir," replied Chet Hansen.

"Yes," replied Bradley, ponderingly. "Perhaps he is."[53]

The following day Bradley outlined his plan to US Treasury Secretary Henry Morgenthau: "This is an opportunity that comes to a commander not more than once in a century. We're about to destroy an entire hostile army. If the other fellow will only press his attack here at Mortain for another forty-eight hours, he'll give us time to close at Argentan and there completely destroy him. He'll have nothing left with which to oppose us. We'll go all the way from here to the German border."[54]

On briefing Montgomery, the Americans were pleased to find him more flexible than usual, even boasting that Crerar's Canadian First Army would reach the notional meeting point at Argentan before Patton. Bradley, however, doubted that Canadian First Army would perform that well. General Simonds' Canadian II Corps was tasked with leading the southward attack but his Canadian 4th Armoured Division and Polish 1st Armoured Division, while undoubtedly brave, were inexperienced, frequently making the error of not bypassing enemy strongpoints.[55]

Leclerc recognised such errors as a risk when leading the 2e DB to their first "rude entry" on the battlefield. Fairly or unfairly, however, Bradley had acquired the impression that Leclerc was "notoriously undisciplined" and only interested in liberating Paris. Had Bradley known that Leclerc's wallet contained his appointment as "Interim

Military Governor" of Paris, he might have shown the mettlesome Frenchman more understanding.[56]

Leclerc met Patton on 8 August, requesting a combat mission as soon as possible. Paul de Langlade wrote that Leclerc knew that most of the 2e DB had barely rested for three days while marching south from Vesly. But uppermost in Leclerc's mind was their burning desire to experience their first battle. Besides, it seemed pointless, "having forged this magnificent tool (*cet outil magnifique*)", not to let them take their chance against the enemy.[57]

The 2e DB's transfer to General Wade Haislip's XV Corps was confirmed later that day and Girard drove Leclerc and Alain de Boissieu over to Haislip's HQ. After explaining that XV Corps would drive south to Le Mans, Haislip outlined the details for the subsequent thrust north on the axis Alençon-Argentan. On discovering that the US 5th Armored Division would advance on the 2e DB's *east* flank, therefore closer to Paris, Leclerc protested. "But the jovial General Haislip," Boissieu later wrote, "not yet being familiar with Leclerc, refused to change orders already issued by his staff and which he had already signed."[58]

As a countryman Leclerc instinctively understood the ground they were operating in. He knew the roads and how fast a modern army could proceed along them. Seeing the route north to Alençon and beyond, he knew what it would be like going there, how the Germans would defend it, and he was already considering how to keep the *bilan des pertes*—his losses—to a minimum.

Since his family was involved in forestry, Leclerc also eyed apprehensively the sprawling Forêt d'Écouves north of Alençon. If it was a working forest, and it would be, it would offer defending troops plentiful cover. There would be tracks, clearings and ditches intersecting the planted areas and running alongside the roads, where men could hide with rifles, machine-guns and *panzerfausts*. In its clearings would be brilliant sunshine while, even in daylight, its thickets would be dark as night.

Haislip had given Leclerc a mission where the 2e DB stood an excellent chance of being chewed up. The US 5th Armored may have had the Forêt de Perseigne across its northward route to close the pocket, but it was smaller than the Forêt d'Écouves, straddled fewer main roads and offered the enemy less cover. Leclerc wanted to please the charming, francophile Wade Haislip, but also to get the 2e DB through Alençon and north of the Forêt d'Écouves as cost-effectively as possible.

Nothing reinforced de Gaulle's agenda more forcefully in Leclerc's mind than the arrival of Colonel Pierre Billotte to command the division's third battlegroup. For Billotte it was something of a reunion; he knew Jacques Branet and Alain de Boissieu from Russia. Furthermore, in 1940, as Captain de Hauteclocque, operations officer of General Buisson's 3rd Division Cuirassé, Leclerc had given Billotte his final orders before the fateful engagement where he was captured after his Char B was knocked out.[59]

After explaining the Alençon operation, Leclerc led Billotte into the mess tent. De Gaulle, Leclerc explained as they ate, had consigned the 2e DB to American command for operational purposes only and on the express condition that it should be in a fit state to liberate Paris when the time came. But Leclerc reserved the right to withdraw it from operations if it was misused, as he regarded himself as accountable foremost to de Gaulle's provisional government. Billotte wrote: "The Americans understand nothing of important dispositions in the matter of sovereignty and the French political plan, which is a little complex for them. This can only result in difficulties." The two Frenchmen concluded that they faced potentially irreconcilable difficulties with the Americans, but that if they had to choose between obeying the Allies or de Gaulle, they would obey de Gaulle. "Easier said than done for a soldier in the line of fire," wrote Billotte.[60]

Billotte set off to find GT V's HQ where he informed Colonel Warabiot that he was taking over and that Warabiot would command the 501e RCC. Sadly, this perpetuated the command problems in that battlegroup. The 501e RCC was the 2e DB's only tank regiment composed of *Gaullistes de la première heure*, a source of immense pride, whereas Warabiot had been *Vichyste* until 1942. All four company commanders, Buis, Branet, Gavardie and Witasse, confronted Warabiot, politely declaring that it was inappropriate for him to lead them. Although Billotte understood the deep comradeship among early Free Frenchmen, he regarded their revolt as insubordination and Warabiot remained in command. Otherwise Billotte's battlegroup contained a surprising mix; his operations officer was Leclerc's Saint-Cyr *petit-co*—classmate—and former *Vichyste* cavalry officer Jean Fanneau de la Horie. Contrastingly, his infantry battalion consisted of Joseph Putz's mainly Spanish 3/RMT.[61]

ACTING ON BEHALF OF A POLITICAL DETAINEE, Nordling was driven in his car through the German Embassy's Rue de Lille gates. The guards saluted him but, on this occasion, a German military policeman brusquely gestured Nordling's car to one side. An impressive Wehrmacht staff car had arrived shortly before, from which alighted a German general. "How very *Prussian*," Nordling thought, noticing the German's pursed lips and deliberate movements.

"Who's that?" asked Nordling.

"That's General von Choltitz," the *Feldgendarme* replied. "The new commander of *Gross-Paris*."[62]

At that stage, however, the fate of Paris had not become Nordling's concern. He reckoned that over ten thousand political prisoners remained in the city's jails and holding centres around *les environs*. The Swede also knew that, when the Allies approached Caen, the Germans had shot around ninety prisoners in the town's jail irrespective of their gender, age or alleged offences.[63]

Around Paris hundreds of prisoners were held at Pantin and Compiègne awaiting transport to concentration camps. In the protracted negotiations he needed to undertake, Nordling needed every friendly face he could find. The Viennese aristocrat Erich von Posch-Pastor, despite his youth, was well-established in Paris. An intelligent man who also spoke a few languages, Posch-Pastor was, like Robert

Wallraf, a Sonderführer—a "special" or project leader—which gave him great flexibility, meaning that Nordling could call him whenever he liked. Though uninterested in politics, Posch-Pastor was an anti-Nazi, albeit uninvolved in 20 July.[64]

The previous spring, when one of Nordling's French friends was arrested, Posch-Pastor helped enthusiastically without needing to be begged or bribed. It later became clear to Nordling that Posch-Pastor had an equally anti-Nazi, kind and helpful senior called Major Émil 'Bobby' Bender. Initially Nordling described Bender as one of those "innumerable and mysterious personages who gathered around the Occupation authorities". Unsure whether Bender was German or another disaffected Austrian, or which ministry paid his salary, Nordling accepted Bender as part of the Nazis' Paris administration, even though he always wore civilian clothing. Of elegant physique, Bender was about fifty, silver haired with well-chiselled features and a youthful countenance. He spoke good, slightly accented French and his conversation was usually pleasant, as though he was a private individual who happened to have a little influence.[65]

In fact Bender was a businessman and reserve officer of the Abwehr's counter-espionage office based at the Hôtel Lutetia on the Boulevard de Raspail. His papers gave him sufficient authority to brush off unwelcome Gestapo involvement; Nordling even believed that Bender ran multiple identities like several shadier Germans operating in the half-light of Parisian espionage.[66]

During the winter of 1943–1944, while still dominating mainland Europe, the Germans were more merciful. Now, with so much going against them, they brutally brushed aside anyone making the slightest intercession from humanitarian motives. As the Allies advanced into France's interior, and *collabos* packed their bags, the Teutonic conquerors of 1940 "seemed less and less sure of themselves". But Nordling knew that the time had arrived when "I must place my cards on the table, and if one spoke frankly and directly with the Germans it should certainly be possible—I was deeply convinced of this—to save the lives of five to ten thousand innocents."[67]

LECLERC PIVOTED THE 2e DB AT LA-CHAPELLE-SAINT-AUBIN north of Le Mans, ready to turn northeast towards Alençon. As usual the locals were thrilled to see French troops in their village. First Leclerc was offered a chair to sit on; next a table and a vase of flowers was placed beside it. So another villager suggested that he might as well sit outside the village café. But Leclerc graciously pointed out that he was not on holiday; a reality the villagers grasped once his Shermans rumbled along the narrow road, each slowing a track to turn, coating charming dwellings in fine dust.[68] General Haislip arrived to watch progress, all smiles and *bonhomie*, only suggesting that the 2e DB should pull out their red aerial recognition panels to prevent Allied fighter bombers from attacking them.[69]

Both the 2e DB and the US 5th Armored Division were converging on the village of Tulagne, the junction of four roads never designed to take a single armoured division. Under such circumstances it was hard to prevent the 2e DB's battlegroups and sub-groups from getting muddled up, let alone having their vehicles stuck in US 5th Armored's bottlenecks. Eventually everything was sorted out and Sub-group Massu advanced through Souligné along similar routes to Normandy's *bocage* country; tight lanes with high-banked hedges covered with summer foliage. Around 2pm the inevitable happened: one of Massu's Stuarts was destroyed by a German flamethrower at a crossroads. Soon afterwards, four Shermans were destroyed, occasioning the deaths of popular lieutenants Zagrodski and d'Arcangue.[70] When Captain Langlois de Bazillac's 6e Compagnie met strong German resistance near the bridge of La Saunerie, a brutal exchange followed with a counterattack by German Panzer-Grenadiers being beaten off. The 2e DB was facing elements of the 9th Panzer Division, an Austrian cavalry formation and the 116th Panzer Division, known as the "greyhounds". They were guarding the German Seventh Army's southern flank.

Leclerc's philosophy since desert raiding days was that tough opposition should be bypassed, isolated and then suppressed by artillery. Irritated at so many battlegroups getting held up, Leclerc let rip at Alain de Boissieu: "Understand this, Boissieu, this division is the biggest disillusion of my life. In Morocco and England I thought I had in my hands a wonderful unit and *eh bien*! I haven't. It's just wind and currents of air."[71]

The only mid-rank officer performing as Leclerc wished that afternoon was the 12e Cuirassiers' Captain de Laittre. In textbook manoeuvres his Stuarts found gaps in the enemy line and forged through while Laittre passed coordinates of enemy strongpoints to the artillery. Sadly de Laittre was killed that same afternoon, bringing the 12e Cuirassiers to a virtual standstill.[72]

Leclerc's disappointment was mollified by a visit from the 5th Armored Division's chief of staff who confirmed that his own division was facing similar difficulties; the *bocage*-style countryside favoured defence and made it difficult to move. Even so, Leclerc told both Langlade and Dio that their battlegroups needed to get a move on. Being held in reserve, Billotte's group avoided *le Patron*'s criticism but, as a fellow "Russian", Boissieu was sent to explain Leclerc's viewpoint.

After their first real day of armoured warfare, Girard ambled down to the riverbank and plunged his head into the cool water. Refreshed, he sat up, looking at a meadow whose grass appeared vivid emerald in the fading light. Then a few divisional water tankers drove up to the river's edge to replenish, ending his brief reverie.[73]

AS THE ALLIED FOOTHOLD IN NORTHERN FRANCE grew ever larger, lorry loads of fresh German troops drove through Paris to the front, while ambulances of wounded and exhausted soldiers travelled the other way. Did any one dare to think that the once proud Wehrmacht that had marched from the Arc de Triomphe down the Champs Élysées every day for four years and two months was being reduced to a shadow of its former self? As tensions and liberation hopes rose, shortages in the shops were becoming acute.

In this atmosphere, Nordling strove to impress upon Otto Abetz that something should be done about political prisoners and the appalling conditions in the transit camps where they were held pending transport.

Abetz passed Nordling to a junior official called Hoffman who treated Nordling amiably enough. But Nordling's descriptions of how these prsioners were herded onto cattle trucks left young Hoffman serenely unmoved.

"Given the actual state of things," Nordling remarked urbanely, "every abuse of power by the German authorities can only worsen their situation. Equally, every gesture of humanity on their part will be to their credit."[74]

But Hoffman had no authority to agree to anything. Meanwhile, at the Hôtel Matignon, Abetz confered with Pierre Laval who now treated him with the disdain of a disappointed schoolmaster.

"My dear Ambassador," said Laval. "The Americans will soon be in Paris. Is your army going to make a fight of it? Have they the means? Are they mad enough to transform Paris into a battlefield?"

"No, Monsieur President," replied Abetz. "Given the state of its forces, the Wehrmacht is not capable of defending Paris."

"In that case," said Laval, "don't uselessly turn our capital into a landscape of ruins. Declare Paris an 'open city' like we did in June 1940."

"For that, I would have to refer to Berlin," replied Abetz.

"Refer, refer, dear Abetz," said Laval. "Don't think in terms of this only being a military problem, but also a political problem. Who is going to take power in Paris once the Americans get here? Have you thought? General de Gaulle and his provisional government? The interior resistance which is dominated by Communists?" Laval stood back, gauging Abetz's reactions to what he was saying. "Or a legal government, with the agreement of the British and Americans, to succeed my own government?"

"For my part the third eventuality looks like the least worst option," said Abetz.

"I was sure, dear Abetz, of your perspicacity," replied Laval. "In my opinion you need firstly to declare Paris and Versailles an 'open city'; secondly you should allow me to reconvene the National Assembly at Versailles—and for that I have absolute need of Edouard Herriot whom you are holding under house arrest near Nancy. Thirdly, you should allow Marshal Pétain to come to Paris. What do you think?"

"I must consult Berlin," replied Abetz.

"Do so quickly," said Laval. "It's essential to have a decision within twenty-four hours. It's necessary to avoid civil war and other mess. Later, both the French and the Germans will thank you."

Abetz promised to report back the following day. For his part, Laval thought he could congratulate himself.[75]

NORDLING HAD MAINTAINED CONNECTIONS with the French Resistance since 1943, when the international lawyer, Maitre Mettetal, introduced him to Parisian financier Alexandre de Saint-Phalle. Hence, it was to Saint-Phalle that Nordling referred his concerns over political prisoners awaiting deportation. De Gaulle's provisional government in Algiers was anxious that these prisoners were the very people post-war France would need.

Would it be acceptable to the provisional government, Nordling wondered, for these prisoners to be handed over to a neutral power like the Red Cross to be transported to more comfortable internment in Switzerland for the remainder of the war? German guards could remain until French ones could replace them, and the arrangement would then fall within the guidelines of the Hague Convention. Matters were becoming increasingly urgent. Saint-Phalle was bicycling across central Paris bringing Nordling news of further arrests.[76]

After consulting the Resistance and Swiss Consul René Naville, Nordling sent another note to the German Embassy drawing attention to Germany's sinking reputation over human rights, hoping that someone working under Abetz might be concerned for his country's image in the post-Hitlerian world. Encountering Hoffman again, Nordling was told emphatically that Abetz was virtually powerless in Paris and that he should direct his pleas to SS General Carl Oberg and then to Himmler.

"Then it will be too late to do what needs to be done," sighed Nordling.

"Do you really think things are moving so fast?" Hoffman replied, appearing anxious.[77]

Nordling also managed to see Laval, who was preoccupied with reconvening the National Assembly and saving Vichy's image before retribution arrived. Aside from Laval's last desperate efforts, Nordling found the atmosphere inside the Hôtel Matignon highly optimistic, as though liberation might not entail a bloodbath for *collabos* after all.[78]

11 August 1944

ON 11 AUGUST NORDLING WAS VISITED by the distraught wife of the principal of the École Normale Supérieure, whose husband had been arrested by the Gestapo for refusing to denounce *résistants* among his students. Although this was just another incident, Nordling decided it justified a call to Otto Abetz, to whom he had not spoken for twenty-four hours.

"That's not urgent," declared Abetz dismissively. "During the last twenty-four hours the military situation has changed radically. The German position is brilliant. We can discuss the prisoners later."[79]

Nordling's chest heaved with exasperation. Anyone knew that German hopes of victory were clutching at straws. Struggling to remain calm, Nordling pleaded for the principal of the ENS.

"That school," Abetz replied in a hostile tone, "is a den of murderers. It ought to be burnt down. The Gestapo is much too lenient towards such people. I've heard from the Gestapo about this teacher and he won't be released."

"Well, I hope there won't be a repetition of what happened at Caen,"[80] replied Nordling. "[Your people] shot a hundred Frenchmen without trial!"

"Put your self in the place of the prison governor," replied Abetz. "Ask yourself what you would do if you had over a thousand bandits to evacuate? ... No evacuation could have happened with the required security. There was no alternative but to shoot them."

As Abetz explained the brutal logic of Nazi thinking, Nordling breathed heavily. Moments later Abetz became more agreeable and consented to meet Nordling the following day.[81]

After further disappointment from Laval, Nordling approached Cardinal Suhard. Like many priests Suhard possessed a naive goodness which led him to make errors which tougher souls like Toulouse's Archbishop Saliege or Adam Sapieha, the Polish Archbishop of Cracow, might have avoided; Henriot's funeral being a good example. However, Nordling believed that Suhard had "great influence" over the Vichy government whereas Suhard probably reckoned his influence counted for very little. Nevertheless, wearing a black robe with red piping and a red skull cap, Suhard welcomed Nordling to 30 Rue Barbet-de-Jouy.* As Nordling catalogued the political prisoners sufferings and expounded his worries, the sixty-seven-year-old Suhard shook his white-haired head. "We agree on all these points," said Suhard, taking Nordling's hand. "Make use of me."[82]

AROUND DAWN, AS GIRARD DROVE LECLERC to GT Dio's positions at Meurcé, they came across a junior officer semi-catatonic after seeing comrades killed in action the previous day.

"You're only thinking about burying your dead," said Leclerc, before telling the young officer to pull himself together.

Leclerc was also deeply affected by seeing his men die, but such was the price of liberation. Nor was he concerned for his own safety; when a German soldier bolted across the road in front of them, Girard pressed on the accelerator, Maurois fired his Thompson into the bushes, but Leclerc merely laughed.[83]

German units around Alençon often consisted of "supply troops, maintenance platoons and tanks under repair"—well-worn Mk IVs from the Panzer *Lehr* Divison. Albeit exhausted along with their crews, their 75mm PAK guns outgunned most Allied tanks. Even though

* In 1905 the French state deprived the Archbishop of Paris of his traditional residence at the Hôtel de Chatelet.

collapse stared them in the face, the Wehrmacht's stern *Feldgendarmerie* threatened dishevelled soldiers with summary execution if they did not stand and fight. Field Marshal von Kluge, recognising the danger developing on his southern flank, ordered that *panzerfausts* should be issued to any soldier capable of using one.[84]

Near Dio's PC several stationary vehicles were halted at a crossroads. "Why aren't they moving?" asked Leclerc impatiently, tapping his cane on the ground. The rush of incoming shells and men ducking in ditches gave him his answer. The shellfire came from the 2e DB's own artillery to the south. They had reached the limit of their artillery cover; meaning they were moving fast.

As the Germans fell back northwards into La Hutte, Captain Savelli's reconnaissance detachment encountered a fresh roadblock. However, with the division advancing on every thoroughfare available, such obstacles were quickly circumvented. For Leclerc, however, the 2e DB's progress still seemed too slow as bottlenecks developed along narrow sunken lanes. On the other hand, advancing over open ground was risky. The 12e Cuirassiers lost several Shermans between La Hutte and Fye. For mostly unblooded crews, seeing their tanks turned literally upside down, as happened to the Sherman *Paimpol*, was quite unnerving.

When the inhabitants of Fye imprudently rang their church bells to signal their liberation, German shells rained on the village, killing a twenty-one-year-old girl in the château park. Liberation meant more than throwing flowers at *les Leclercs*. The villagers gently removed every dead crewman from the 12e Cuirassiers' destroyed Shermans, and gave them dignified funerals and burial in their own churchyard.[85]

Leclerc decided to lead GT Dio's advance towards Champfleur from his command tank, *Tailly*. "Towards mid-day," wrote Pierre Krebs, "we saw the general arrive, and the general did not look happy. He wasn't discouraged, that was not his style; rather he looked exasperated seeing that the men around appeared both discouraged and cowed. There had been losses around Fye and Rouessé-Fontaine, where two squadrons of my regiment had been engaged. At this moment the general created what he called 'sub-group Rouvillois'." *Chef d'escadrons* (cavalry major), Rouvillois was a *petit-co* of Leclerc's from Saint-Cyr. Leclerc's steadying influence brought a good result, and soon villagers delightedly peeked out of their homes, offering cider and calvados. Leclerc nodded that his men could drink cider but not calvados.[86]

Alençon, the 2e DB's first significant objective, remained ten kilometers to the north and, although the US 5th Armored Division made similar progress, Leclerc was anxious that his men were both seen in action and also remaining fit to march on Paris.

IN RESPONSE TO PIERRE LAVAL'S PROPOSALS, Abetz reported that Berlin would permit Edouard Herriot's return to Paris to reconvene the National Assembly. Laval hoped this would reassure the eighty-seven mayors of the Department of the Seine. A sizeable proportion were left-wingers elected before 1939 who were nevertheless grateful to Pétain for the 1940 armistice. During the Occupation, they mostly acquitted themselves honourably: maintaining stability, ensuring food supplies and resisting unreasonable German demands. But several now feared being thought of as *collabos*, particularly those representing industrial areas with a hard left electorate. As strikes increased, they worried that escalating incidents might bring German reprisals, so news of Herriot's impending release brought a sense of relief. Laval was back among them, just like the good old days, charming, reassuring, vulnerable, only wanting to maintain the republic's institutions, to keep the peace and avoid civil war. Clapping and cheering, they avowed their confidence in him.[87]

12 August 1944

AT AROUND 2AM CHRISTIAN GIRARD was woken by an enemy shell whistling past and he kicked off his sleeping bag. The next shell set a half-track alight, illuminating other vehicles parked nearby, a gift for a German artillery observer. Other shells followed, indicating that a German mortar crew had targeted their position. Once shaken awake, Leclerc quickly deduced that they were that near the German frontline, a small advance would punch through it.

"Gachet," Leclerc called. "Go and see what Colonel Noiret is up to."[88]

Noiret's sub-group had halted for the night at Saint-Gilles, merely three kilometres from Alençon. Given the proximity of the mortar crew that shelled them, Leclerc decided it was time to seize the initiative. Despite Boissieu's advice to take the Scout Car, Leclerc jumped into Gachet's Jeep and set off for Noiret's position escorted by Sammarcelli's M8s.[89]

The 12e Cuirassiers' Captain Gaudet had halted his squadron after his men destroyed a formidable German artillery emplacement. They were exhausted; Gaudet himself crashed out in a dreamless slumber. Suddenly he was being shaken awake by his North African batman.

"*Mon Cap'taine*," said Ait Abbat. "The General, he's here."

Leclerc looked down at him.

"Get going," said Leclerc, smiling slightly. "Back on the road! We're going to Alençon!"

"Everyone back in their tanks," said Gaudet. "We're leaving immediately."[90]

Not for the last time that August, Leclerc found a young *résistant* offering his services as a guide. Nineteen-year-old Raymond Ciroux left Alençon the previous day. His two years as a *clandestin* included arrest by the Gestapo, but he escaped before being shot. Since Alençon and the forests to its north represented the southern "shoulder" of the pocket enveloping the German forces, one might have expected stronger defences. But Ciroux* confirmed Leclerc's suspicions that German defences were patchy and that little stood between themselves and Alençon's central Pont Neuf, which the Germans left unmined. Once his Chad infantry invested the area, Leclerc walked onto the bridge and held a conference with Crépin, Repiton-Préneuf and Guillebon,

---

*   Ciroux joined the 12e Cuirassiers that day and stayed with the regiment for the remainder of the war.

guarded by "Small"—the diminutive HQ bodyguard—with rifle and bayonet fixed.[91]

"Seal off all roads into Alençon," Leclerc ordered.

From his new map room overlooked by a large portrait photograph of Pétain, Leclerc planned the 2e DB's next attack, which, he feared, might upset his American superiors. Remnants of the 9th Panzer Division sheltering in the Forêt d'Écouves could only be an obstacle to XV Corps' advance. The Americans' planned air strike on the Forêt de Perseigne, east of Leclerc's axis, suggests that neither the Americans nor Leclerc believed US 5th Armored Division would reach the pretty market town of Sées, east of the Forêt d'Écouves, as fast as they did. Leclerc, meanwhile, decided to envelope the Forêt d'Écouves from both sides. But elements of 5th Armored bypassing the Forêt de Perseigne met only light resistance, then advanced into Sées with sinking fuel gauges. Without proper liaison between the two armoured divisions an enormous traffic jam was inevitable. Leclerc, however, continued with his plan, giving Pierre Billotte his first combat orders since 1940.

"You've waited four years. Here's your chance to avenge what the Germans did to you," said Leclerc. Billotte's battlegroup would pass through Sées and then north of the Forêt d'Écouves to cut the Nationale 24.[92]

Jacques Branet's squadron was parked along roadsides south of Alençon when the order came. Heading northwards into the town they passed several 12e Cuirassiers Shermans, burnt out from the previous night's fighting, calcinated bodies still in their hulls; a sickening reminder of the grim end awaiting unfortunate tank soldiers. Passing through Alençon, Branet saluted Leclerc at the bridge before turning northeast. They passed a burning German tank on the east side of the Forêt d'Écouves and in the distance a convoy of German vehicles rolled eastwards between unenclosed fields. Branet's squadron fired, setting lorries and half-tracks alight. Soon Germans were surrendering and being passed to the rear.

Reaching Sées, with its attractive sandstone houses, elegant *mairie* and double-spired abbey, the 501e RCC was engulfed in an inter-divisional traffic jam with General Lunsford Oliver's 5th Armored Division. Ecstatic townsfolk served cider as the carousel of olive green vehicles descended into chaos. Recognising the danger should the Germans counterattack, Branet was relieved to be ordered northwest towards Argentan. Even so, the crowd obstructed his departure. The Americans attributed the Sées traffic jam to Leclerc's inexperience. GT Billotte has been accused of preventing 5th Armored from reaching Argentan before the 116th Panzer Division could prepare defences.[93] Conversely, if Leclerc had kept his division west of the Forêt d'Écouves, there is nothing to say that 9th Panzer Division might not have attacked US 5th Armored's west flank.

Leaving Sées, Branet recognised that 9th Panzer Division's shellfire was too dangerous to be ignored. With tanks tail to tail along the road to Argentan, German anti-tank guns sited in the Forêt d'Écouves would have a field day unless dealt with. Led by Spahi armoured cars, Putz's sub-group bounded into the forest's north side, firing at any position capable of sheltering Germans until they reached the central Croix de Medavi. Soon Leclerc arrived in his command tank *Tailly*.

"Putz," said Leclerc, "Infiltrate further south. Try to link up with Langlade. If you can't, then relieve any pressures he's facing." Then he turned to Branet, "Branet, pursue only your original mission. Head for Écouché via Le Cercueil, La Bellière and Francheville. If darkness suspends your mission, hole up in a village, but tell me. Do your best."

Branet returned to his squadron to give the order to turn about.[94]

Led by Elias' platoon, *la Nueve* headed northwest towards Saint-Christophe-le-Jajolet, several kilometres north of the Forêt d'Écouves. A small show of German resistance obstructing their path was scattered by a burst from the lead half-track's .50-cal machine-gun. Two Germans were killed while another six surrendered. In the village itself Elias' men captured vehicles carrying exhausted German infantry who gladly surrendered. For another hour Dronne and Buis carried all before them until meeting resistance at the hamlet of Vieux-Bourg. After pausing to evacuate prisoners and wounded, they found by 3pm that they were five kilometres south of Argentan.[95]

German resistance became tougher, inflicting several losses on Commandant Buis' Shermans. Dronne's Spaniards dismounted their half-tracks to guide Buis' remaining tanks down winding lanes. By nightfall Dronne and Buis were on the outskirts of Écouché, surveying gentle slopes of wheat fields and sumptuous green meadows. A few hundred metres northeast a long traffic jam of German vehicles, bumper to bumper, was fleeing the closing Allied pincers. Forming up in a line, Dronne's Spaniards in their half-tracks and Buis' Shermans advanced, firing all the way. "It was the most incredible butchery that I had ever seen," remembered José Cortés. "German vehicles were thrown in the air like dismembered toys. Those who were further away, on seeing that they didn't stand a chance stopped immediately and put their hands up." But a large German armoured car rushed towards them firing furiously. Keeping steady, Dronne's Spaniards turned their heavy machine-guns on the advancing *Panzerspähwagen*, putting it out of action, killing two of its crew and capturing the rest.[96]

On reaching Tanville, Branet re-organised his column. He had, in his own words, "the best mission a cavalry officer could ever be given". He placed Vézy's armoured cars up front; he himself would follow in a Jeep followed by Christen's troop of Shermans, the *Hartsmann-Willerkopf, Yser, Grand-Couronné, Mort-Homme* and *Douaumont*. Lieutenant Davreux's troop of Stuarts followed behind. The first enemy they encountered was a horse-drawn battalion bath unit which surrendered without fuss. "What does one do with them?" Branet wondered. They were disarmed and waved to the rear.[97]

Two kilometres further on Branet came upon a German ambulance convoy carrying three hundred. He left a Stuart light tank to shepherd these prisoners behind barbed wire. Passing the northwest corner of the Forêt d'Écouves they found a troop of German armoured cars endeavouring to sit out the battle under camouflage. They surrendered quickly. After destroying their tyres with a Thompson, Branet ordered these prisoners to the rear. "Run," yelled Branet, pointing southeast.[98]

Approaching the village of Francheville they spotted a heavy German column to their west. Instinctively, without needing an order, every machine-gun and cannon turned towards them and fired. The murderous action only lasted a few seconds. Getting down from *Hartsmann-Willerkopf*, Christen was joined by sergeants Bernard from the *Mort-Homme* and Bizien from the *Douaumont*. Walking jubilantly along the shot-up German column, they found four abandoned Panther tanks.[99]

AMERICAN HISTORIAN MARTIN BLUMENSON thought that Leclerc's sending Billotte's battlegroup east of the Forêt d'Écouves was possibly motivated by *"je m'en foutisme"*—a don't give a damn attitude—and competitiveness towards his allies even if it meant scuppering an operation. Yet Leclerc's history since 1940 supports the contrary argument that he was parsimonious with his men's lives and, like everyone else, wanted to get home.[100]

In any case, Blumenson also concedes that XV Corps' lunge northwards was risky enough. Its exposed west flank was vulnerable to any German general with the means to strike at it. XV Corps advanced beyond the notional halt line, and Haislip was uncertain what kind of German strength he would face in Argentan.[101]

British and Canadian troops fighting southwards towards Falaise faced the German Seventh Army's front rather than its softer rear; consequently they made slower progress. Many units in Montgomery's 21st Army Group had already had a long war. Furthermore, his flamboyant manner aside, Montgomery's command style was more that of a diligent planner than a *beau sabreur*. The "British effort seems to have [bogged] itself in timidity and succumbed to the legendary Montgomery vice of over-caution," wrote Bradley's ADC, Chet Hansen.

Both Bradley and Eisenhower knew what was going on with Haislip's XV Corps on 12 August. "I made no major move without consulting him [Eisenhower]," Bradley later wrote. "On the afternoon of 12 August, as Haislip's forces closed on the 'boundary' near Argentan, Ike came to my CP to monitor Haislip's progress, and he remained through dinner."[102]

That evening, Haislip reported to Patton that he was reasonably confident of possessing Argentan by mid-day on 13 August. Aware that SHAEF wished ground forces to avoid crossing bomb-lines, Haislip also asked Patton whether an advance north of Argentan was authorised. If this was the case, Haislip would have gladly continued, but he also reminded Patton that XV Corps was becoming too thinly spread to resist German forces determined to avoid encirclement.[103]

The idea of two armoured divisions, one French, advancing to close the gap undoubtedly appealed to Patton's sense of *l'audace*. He ordered Haislip to continue advancing towards Argentan before updating Bradley on the situation. "We have troops in Argentan," Patton told Bradley. This was not true, though Patton soon expected it to be. Bradley, having learnt from an Ultra decrypt that the encircled Germans were preparing an eastward surge to avoid being trapped, replied, "Nothing doing."

While Patton listened dumbfounded, Bradley explained his fears of friendly fire casualties as the Americans met up with the British and Canadians—something that never bothered the Russians when they encircled Stalingrad. "To have driven pell-mell into Montgomery's line of advance could easily have resulted in a disastrous error of recognition. In halting Patton at Argentan, however, I did not consult Montgomery. The decision to stop Patton was mine alone; it never went beyond my CP," Bradley later wrote.[104] At 10.40pm Patton gave Haislip the order to halt where he was and consolidate his existing positions to face the threat from his left flank.

AT 4AM LAVAL LEFT THE MATIGNON accompanied by a Gestapo escort commanded by Roland Noseck. After briefly stopping at Nancy, where he informed Prefect Jean Faure what he was doing, Laval arrived at the hospital in Maréville shortly before noon.

"I have come to liberate you," Laval told a stunned Edouard Herriot.

Laval did not tell the former President of the Chamber of Deputies everything that was going on, preferring to test the water before explaining his ideas for installing a transition government to greet the Allies. Herriot distrusted Laval. But since Laval's efforts had freed him, he showed Laval some warmth. Restoring France's constitutional government was important to Herriot, but he would never allow Laval to slip him into the Matignon as Vichy's creature. "I am not going back to Paris except as President of the Chamber of Deputies and I will stay *chez moi* at the Hôtel de la Presidence."

"Until the Germans leave, that'll be a few days," replied Laval.

While lunching in Nancy, Herriot told Laval, "You'll need to find Jeanneney, enrobed as President of the Senate to convoke the National Assembly."

"When he knows that I'm on the way out, he'll arrive at the gallop," replied Laval, smiling bleakly. Then he told Herriot it was also essential to bring Pétain to Paris.

Herriot agreed.

"In any case I shall not shake his hand," he said.[105]

Since Allied fighter-bombers were unlikely to attack after dusk, they returned to Paris after dark; the Herriots in one car and Laval accompanied by André Enfière in another, escorted by German police, along roads crowded with retreating Wehrmacht troops.[106]

Looking out of his apartment windows over the Place de l'Hôtel de Ville the following morning, René Bouffet saw six dark cars parked outside and plainclothes Gestapo getting out. "I'm done for," he murmured, assuming they were coming to arrest him. But the maid called out, "It's Monsieur le President Laval." Bouffet's wife nervously telephoned the switchboard for information. Then, leaving their apartment, she found herself facing Laval, Edouard and Madame Herriot, André Enfière and SS Haupsturmführer Roland Noseck, who was out of uniform. Madame Bouffet reassured her husband.

"You see the atmosphere we live in," Laval remarked to Herriot, as Noseck looked on unmoved.[107]

APPROACHING FRANCHEVILLE AFTER DARK, Branet's men had little choice but to recce the village on foot. The only thing Branet knew about Francheville was that a pre-war army friend owned the château. Otherwise, in the *chiaroscuro* light of burning vehicles, the village appeared deserted. Some stunned Germans stumbled towards them with raised hands. They informed Branet that a dozen Panthers were sheltering in woods nearby, which explained the distant rumbling noise. This was confirmed by the only villager to open her door, a brave teenage girl. Calling at the château at sunrise, Branet found his friend, the racehorse trainer Count Pierre de Montesson, looking healthy and well-fed, riding a fine horse that had been spared German requisition. Montesson agreed to take charge of Branet's prisoners. Preferring the protection of a French officer *chez lui* than the Resistance, the prisoners co-operated.

Moving on to Boucé, Branet's force encountered a troop of German armoured cars travelling from Carrouges towards Argentan. His Shermans and Vézy's armoured cars opened fire, capturing six men before dispersing along Boucé's main arteries, shooting up any German vehicles they found or any German who failed to raise his hands.

All Branet's tanks were carrying pink air-recognition panels behind their turrets but this did not prevent USAAF Thunderbolts from strafing his force, tragically killing a Frenchwoman instead. Otherwise the signs of German collapse were all around. South of Fleuré two abandoned Panthers had run out of petrol. Apart from bursts of machine-gun fire, little prevented Branet from entering Écouché. His men had accounted for fifteen tanks and forty other vehicles excluding ambulances. He could not count the prisoners they had taken. "We acquired a sense of superiority," Branet wrote.[108]

In Écouché the French were amazed to see a priest picking his way serenely through wrecked German vehicles administering the last rites to dying Germans. This was the well respected Abbé Berger. As Captain Buis dismounted his Sherman, Berger approached him.

"Thank you for liberating us," said Berger in English, assuming Buis was American.

"Thank General de Gaulle," Buis replied in French.[109]

Even *la Nueve*'s atheistic left-wingers were impressed by Berger's humanity. Cannonfire and Allied fighter bombers had left many of

Écouché's buildings roofless, including Berger's church where the statue of Sacré Coeur was blown off its plinth. Dronne's Spaniards organised a whip-round to replace it. Touched by such a gesture from non-believers, Berger organised a Mass for *la Nueve* which they all attended.

"Why?" asked Dronne.

"If we had priests like that in Spain, things might have been different," came the reply.[110]

13 August 1944

THOUGH NOW WELL SOUTH OF THE 2e DB'S FRONT LINE, the Forêt d'Écouves remained a dangerous place. The Sherman *Ourcq* from the 501e RCC's 3 squadron was damaged near Le Cercueil by an 88mm gun firing from the forest's north side. *Ourcq*'s driver succeeded in steering it into the cover of some scrub but, just as the crew dismounted the stricken tank, a second shell struck, killing its commander, Sergeant Bouclet, and its gunner, Trooper Cardiot. Both were young and had undertaken considerable odyssies to join the 2e DB. Bouclet escaped Occupied France by stowing away on a goods train passing through Spain, joining Leclerc when still only sixteen. Cadiot had journeyed from Peru.[111]

Leclerc now sited his CP north of Fleuré, six kilometres from Argentan, where Roumiantzoff's Spahis were already staking the 2e DB's claim. The famous lace-making town with its Benedictine Abbey, chosen as XV Corps' target by American generals who had never been there, was visible north of the Baize River. Leclerc's orders were not to advance north of the Orne since it represented a clearly visible line from the air, south of which Allied bomber crews knew not to release their payloads.

The road east from Argentan leads to Paris; hence Leclerc wanted to recce the town's southern approaches himself. Mounting his command tank *Tailly*, and escorted by two Stuarts from Lieutenant de la Fouchardière's troop, Leclerc set off towards Argentan while Girard shook his head. Roumiantzoff had already pushed his armoured cars as close as he dared before machine-gun fire chased him off. Given that *Tailly*'s cannon was a fake (*en zinc*) and that Boissieu's protection squad had not been prewarned, Leclerc's jaunt seemed foolhardy at best.

With the fraught Boissieu following in a Jeep, *Tailly* rolled down the road, hidden from view by embankments and tall hedges. After half a kilometre Leclerc flicked the diverter switch on his headset to direct his driver, inadvertently placing himself *incommunicado* just as radio reports arrived saying the area was dangerous. Using binoculars, La Fouchardière saw partially camouflaged German tanks guarding southern Argentan.

"*Mon Dieu!*" Boissieu said to La Fouchardière, fearing that Leclerc might become another charred corpse in a wrecked Sherman along with de Gaulle's handwritten note. *Tailly* rolled on until a Spahi officer waved it down. Leclerc opened his turret hatch. Captain Gerberon told him that the main German strength appeared to be on the southeast approach. Leclerc turned right. Boissieu and La Fouchardière found the tension intolerable. A German tank's cannon could be seen turning towards Leclerc. Suddenly *Argentanais* appeared in their Sunday best clothes, gesticulating that there were Germans nearby. Seeing the words on their lips through his periscope, Girard told Leclerc they should pull back. Another *Argentanais* opened a shutter and pointed to a Panther, camouflaged in enfilade, and Leclerc decided to withdraw. Invisible to Boissieu and La Fouchardière, *Tailly* backtracked, cleaving to all the available cover for fifteen minutes.

"For a quarter of an hour that seemed like an eternity," Boissieu later wrote, "I thought I had lost General Leclerc." He found Leclerc in a nearby farmstead, watching Rouminantzoff's Spahis through binoculars. Seeing the relief on Boissieu's face, Leclerc smiled serenely and accepted the crock of cider offered by the farmer. "I wanted to see when they would be evacuating Argentan," said the General.

Back at Fleuré, Guillebon took Boissieu aside.

"When you have the honour," Guillebon said tersely, "of being given command of the unit charged with protecting General Leclerc, you don't let him wander off alone in his tank."[112]

THE FIRST PAUL DE LANGLADE HEARD of the 2e DB being transferred from Haislip's US XV Corps to the newly activated Vth Corps was around 7am that morning, when a white Scout Car bearing two stars arrived at his CP.

"I am General Gerow, commander of the US Army corps in which your division is included," said an American with a Virginia accent. "Perhaps, since you command one of his combat groups, you might know where in Hell one might find General Leclerc at this moment?"

Langlade replied that he was not *au courant* with Leclerc's movements.

"Hear this," said Gerow tetchily. "I haven't the time to continue this wild goose chase. I have found you here. You are one of his group commanders. You find him." Gerow fixed Langlade with a hard, cold stare. "It is an order," said Gerow. "I repeat, it is an order. You go as fast as you can to the General, carrying the express order from me to halt his combat groups wherever they are engaged on routes they were not authorised to use, and to retake the axes of advance that they were given and to do it immediately. I hold you responsible for passing on this order."

From Gerow's tone Langlade understood that Leclerc's American superiors were displeased, and he sent Commandant Verdier to find *le Patron*.

"*Mon Colonel*," replied Verdier. "I am sorry but I can't take such a message to General Leclerc. Believe me, I know him well enough to know that he will not change decisions already taken and which he is seeing through to a conclusion ... I simply haven't the courage to bear the inevitable reaction from carrying such a message. Truly, *mon Colonel*, don't ask me to carry out this impossible mission. Get someone else."

Langlade then hit on Captain Arnaud. Bearing the responsibility and smiling like a martyr, he set off to find Leclerc who was supervising the mopping up of the last resistance in the Forêt d'Écouves. Arnaud returned to Langlade's CP a few hours later.

"The General replied," said Arnaud, blushing visibly, "tell Langlade that if this American is a c*** then that's no reason for him to be one too."[113]

By the afternoon of 13 August the 2e DB held a triangular position from Carrouges, on the northwest of the Forêt d'Écouves, to Sées on the northeast corner, stretching to a north pinnacle on the southern outskirts of Argentan. The line from Carrouges to Argentan via Écouché was most important since it faced the flow of retreating German traffic. While the US 79th and 90th Infantry Divisions gathered up exhausted remnants of the 9th Panzer Division, the 2e DB strengthened its positions and suppressed remaining pockets of resistance. This area, amounting to 260 square kilometres, contained fifteen thousand French inhabitants as well as thirty thousand Germans in broken, disorganised units. Luckily these mostly scattered infantry were happy to surrender after a few shots. Panzer troops or SS, however, required more persuasion before putting their hands up.

Whatever Gerow said, the 2e DB were not content to wait for orders if advantageous opportunities presented themselves. Leaving Écouché from the north, supported by *la Nueve*, Captain Buis' company of the 501e RCC reached the ridge overlooking the Orne's south bank where an enormous traffic jam of German vehicles converged on the bridge at Montgaroult.

The Spaniards and Lieutenant Galley's troop of Shermans opened fire, inflicting destruction, panic and flight. Compos' platoon dismounted their half-tracks and sealed off the bridge, albeit with a few casualties, while US Thunderbolts finished off the German columns. Now that he controlled a bridge over the Orne, west of Argentan, Leclerc ordered Buis to halt.[114]

Though the Orne valley's scenery was a painter's paradise, its high hedges and undulating countryside gave plenty of cover for experienced tank commanders wanting to creep up on their enemies. No sooner had Dronne's most experienced lieutenant, the forty-five-year-old Amado Granell, cried out with delight at finding a smart sports car among the rows of abandoned German vehicles, than it took a direct hit from a Panzer's cannon.[115]

During their first week in action *la Nueve* had destroyed or captured hundreds of German vehicles and killed or wounded countless enemy. Among their own ranks, these outcasts of Franco's Spain suffered two dead and two wounded in the fighting since Alençon. Notwithstanding their anti-clericalism, Écouché's Abbé Berger allowed *la Nueve* to lay out their dead in his church, and it was there that Miguel Sanchez paid his respects to the body of his cousin, clenching his fist over his chest: "I will avenge you, I promise."[116]

14 August 1944

IN ONE OF THE MATIGNON'S HUGE, ornate audience chambers Laval lent forward to shake Raoul Nordling's hand and then very pointedly stood back, body language intended to impress upon Nordling that there were other things concerning him besides Resistance prisoners. To further deflect the conversation from this matter, Laval subjected Nordling to his *esprit*—the sneering, sometimes inelegant wit intended to discomfort adversaries—for which he was well-known.

"Your mother originated in the Auvergne, *Monsieur* Nordling," said Laval, almost out of the blue. "And it was your father who was Swedish," Laval continued like Proust's Baron de Charlus. "The cross-breeding of a Swede and an *Auvergnatte* has produced excellent results. If I owned a bitch who, on her maternal line, came from the Auvergne, and on her father's side came from Spitzbergen, there couldn't exist a better creature."

Since this nonsense was intended to derail his humanitarian mission, Nordling struggled to remain affable.

"You mean Sweden, not Spitzberg," was Nordling's reply.

"Same difference," said Laval, giving Nordling a playful stare. "They're both up north."

Geography was not Laval's strong suit; a footnote in Nordling's memoirs explains the locations of Sweden and Spitzberg while omitting that a "Spitzbergen" is a sub-breed of sledge dog.[117]

Nevertheless Laval assured Nordling that he was taking his pleas regarding political prisoners "to heart", and needed twenty-four hours to talk with Abetz.[118]

WHEREAS MADAME HERRIOT could come and go as she pleased, Herriot himself was forbidden to leave the building or receive visitors. His German protectors were always there, watching him like hawks. That afternoon Laval told him that the former residence of the president of the Chamber of Deputies would become available in three days. But how was he to put in place France's transitional government? (Which was the very reason Laval had collected him from Maréville.) How could the National Assembly be recalled without access to the Palais Bourbon and Palais Luxembourg, which housed the Chamber of Deputies and the Senate? The buildings were now being turned into German strongpoints. How could Herriot plan a new France if Jeanneney, President of the Senate, was unavailable?[119]

For their part, the Resistance were horrified that Laval had taken possession of Edouard Herriot and installed him at the Hôtel de Ville under the supervision of Vichy prefect René Bouffet. They concluded correctly that Laval intended to install a transitional government to greet the Americans, thereby cutting out both wings of the Resistance— the FTP and the equally uncompromising followers of General de Gaulle. They could hardly negotiate with Herriot if he was under Vichy or German protection. A *résistante* on the Hôtel de Ville's domestic staff kept them *au courant* over Herriot's welfare.[120]

FROM PATTON'S VIEWPOINT, Leclerc's division was quite dangerously placed. If the Germans widened the pocket's southern jaw, the 2e DB would bear the brunt of the assault, since Collins VII

Corps was unable to reinforce Haislip sufficiently. Montgomery was having a tough time pushing southwards to Falaise. Bradley's planned encirclement was not working out as planned and Patton now believed that the 2e DB along with the 79th and 90th Infantry Divisions should hold the southern line while a new close-off point developed further east. This would mean sending Walker's XX Corps eastwards to Dreux and XII Corps to Chartres.[121]

Chastened by his own difficulties, Montgomery suggested something similar, writing to Bradley, "I think your movement should be northeast towards Dreux. Also any further stuff you can move round to Le Mans should go northeast. We want to head off the Germans and stop them breaking out to the southeast." But Bradley still believed that Falaise should remain the close-off point, albeit with Hodges First Army having the honour.[122] He described 14 August as "a long, tedious day during which many vital decisions had been discussed at the very highest levels". One result was Patton flying to see Haislip with news that XV Corps would be split and that he would be taking Oliver's 5th Armored and an infantry division towards Dreux, leaving Leclerc at Argentan. Haislip was thrilled by these developments but then he was not French; nor did his wallet contain the same things as General Leclerc's.[123]

The 2e DB's place in the line at Argentan was vital. Early on 14 August Hitler personally ordered Panzer Group Eberbach to attack south towards Argentan. Hans Eberbach was beside himself with frustration at Hitler's failing grip on reality as famous panzer divisions were reduced to fragments. The 1st SS Panzer, the vaunted *Liebstandarte Adolf Hitler*, had merely thirty remaining tanks, 2nd Panzer only twenty-five, and 116th Panzer only fifteen serviceable runners. Only a company of Panzergrenadiers remained from 9th Panzer Division after their showdown with the 2e DB in the Forêt d'Écouves.[124]

Hitler's counterattack did not materialise. German morale was collapsing with tanks being abandoned even before they ran out of petrol, and soldiers often preferring to surrender than to continue fighting in a useless cause. The *Feldgendarmerie* established "catch lines" to gather up Hitler's dishevelled soldiery and reform them into usable formations. Pushing into the "pocket", 2e DB patrols often encountered small battle units consisting of Luftwaffe, Wehrmacht and SS personnel.[125] Two British officers who drove through the pocket in a Jeep told Langlade that they saw the insignia of up to twenty German divisions on abandoned vehicles. These divisions included the Atlantic Wall's non-élite personnel who were hopelessly outclassed when facing the Allied onslaught.[126]

For Spahi Commandant Roumiantzoff, the sight of US artillery shells exploding in Argentan's southern *banlieues*, which straddled several main roads essential to the Germans' retreat before sheltering in the Forêt de Gouffern to the east, fired his lust for action. Born a White Russian, Roumiantzoff was fiercely patriotic for his adopted country. When he called for volunteers for a raiding party, enough men came forward to crew three M8 armoured cars. They penetrated Argentan via the railway bridge, quickly coming upon German troops. Firing their machine-guns at any target that presented itself, the Germans were too surprised to fire back. On the Spahis drove, firing at everything, sewing panic until they reached the town centre. Even there, among the massive clutter of a routed army, no one fired back. They stopped outside the *mairie*, climbed the tower and hoisted the *Tricolore*. The Germans reacted by sending Panthers into central Argentan. But the Panther crews could not engage the Spahi M8s without endangering more German soldiers.[127]

At noon Leclerc's CP was inundated with urgent messages that a battlegroup from 116th Panzer Division under Hauptmann Jess was hiding in the Bois de la Perdrière northwest of the Forêt d'Écouves. Consisting of at least four tanks, half a dozen Hanomags and armoured cars, Jess's force ventured out from its woody lair like a conger eel to keep the Nationale 808 open for German troops struggling to escape the pocket. For over twenty-four hours Jess was a demon in GT Langlade's rear, harassing every sub-group until eventually he ran out of petrol. Deciding to die like Napoleon's Old Guard, Jess formed his vehicles into a square which was obliterated by artillery.[128]

Around Écouché, GT Billotte faced remnants of the 2nd Panzer Division feeling their way to the pocket's opening, trying to avoid trouble. Though moving quietly, they ran straight into a sector held by Granell's platoon of *la Nueve*. Dronne ordered Montoya's platoon to reinforce Granell, supported by a troop of Spahi M8s and a troop of 501e RCC Shermans. Once within range the German column came under murderous fire. When the action ended Dronne interrogated the injured commander of a Panzer Mk IV. "This defeated and dying fanatic was the symbol of what we were fighting," wrote Dronne. "To veteran Republicans of the war in Spain, veterans of Free France and French youngsters, recently recruited, he represented the true enemy. We could only hate such fanaticism. But at the same time we could not help feeling a grudging respect for his courage."[129]

For Dronne, waiting at Argentan seemed extraordinary. "The High Command lacked audacity," he wrote in his *carnets*. "The Americans were very cautious and very slow. Their only top soldier who truly had the dash and mentality for using armoured forces was Patton."[130]

But neither Bradley nor Montgomery believed their forces were strong enough to close the gap. Whichever divisions performed that deed risked getting chewed up; the last thing Leclerc wanted to happen to the 2e DB.

15 August 1944

CHURCHILL SAW NO REASON FOR IT, but Eisenhower insisted that Operation Dragoon should go ahead. When the inhabitants of France's Cote d'Azur awoke on the Feast of the Assumption they saw an invasion fleet bobbing at anchor in the August morning sunshine, carrier-based Hellcats whizzing overhead, and grey landing craft disgorging troops along Fréjus' expansive beaches. General Jacob Devers' US 6th Army Group was coming ashore. It consisted of General Alexander Patch's US Seventh Army and General Jean de Lattre de Tassigny's French First Army—the old *Armée d'Afrique*—including the

1e and 5e DBs which, like Leclerc's 2e DB, were entirely equipped by the US rearmament programme.

While the Normandy front sucked most German troops northwards, Devers Army Group landed mostly unopposed. Recently installed heavy-duty defences, like those commanding the salt-flats at Hyères, were quickly circumvented. Some landing places were peaceful enough for hoteliers to offer drinks as the troops came ashore, resulting in Operation Dragoon sometimes being called "the Champagne Campaign". Inland the sun-drenched village squares of *la France profonde* found another reason to ring their church bells aside from the ancient Christian festival and processions led by statues of the Madonna.

NORTH OF THE FORÊT D'ÉCOUVES, throughout the previous night, prisoners kept coming in. For Raymond Dronne their eclectic provenance, "confirmed that the greatest confusion reigned in the Germans' ranks, that every unit had become mixed up and suffered enormous losses, that Allied aircraft attacked them incessantly".[131]

German theatre commander Field Marshal von Kluge spent the night at a small château with Sepp Dietrich's I SS Panzer Corps HQ. "Most unpleasant," said Kluge, describing the worsening German position. That morning he drove into the pocket to evaluate the situation for himself; and lost contact with OKW for most of the day.[132] His radio messages to OKW, begging to withdraw to the Argentan-Falaise line, were picked up by Ultra and sent to General Bradley, who now doubted his decision to close the pocket further east. In fact Bradley worried more than he needed; Allied intelligence consistently over-rated German strength.[133]

Somehow German signals intelligence heard Allied radio traffic asking after von Kluge's whereabouts; intercepts which convinced Hitler that Kluge was trying to contact the Allies. According to Kluge's son in law, Dr. Udo Esche, Kluge considered surrendering on 15 August and "went to the front lines but was unable to get in touch with the Allied commanders". Since Montgomery's intelligence chief warned that some kind of offer might come from Kluge, Hitler's suspicions were realistic.[134]

Meanwhile, in a field outside Montmerrei, among camouflaged vehicles, the 2e DB's senior chaplain Père Houchet set up a makeshift altar to celebrate Assumption Day. Leclerc's staff stood in the front row. With the Normandy campaign almost over and news of the Provence landings on everyone's lips, Leclerc's men speculated about Paris.

"Are we going to let the Americans go into Paris before us?"[135]

Leclerc pursed his lips. At his Fleuré CP an American broadcast unit caught up with him.

"How does it feel to be back in France?"

"How can we explain our feelings after stepping onto the soil of *la Patrie* a few days ago?" Leclerc replied, "This soil that we left four years ago, leaving France under the boot of the enemy, with all that this means to each and every one of us. We have returned as combatants after struggling for four years under General de Gaulle. We are rediscovering the faces of our fellow countrymen who salute us enthusiastically from the midst of their ruins. We can only guess what they have suffered. In the name of my officers, my non-commissioned officers and my men, my first duty is to salute those French who never despaired, who helped our allies, facilitating our victory. I admire them and congratulate them. For ourselves, the end is in sight as we come at last to take part beside them in the great fight for our liberation. *Vive la France!*"[136]

Two hundred kilometres east, at Warlus in the Department of the Somme, *Madame la comtesse* Thérèse de Hauteclocque[137] and her children were approaching the village square, intending to decorate the church for the evening's big Assumption service, when she was hailed by the proprietress of a small restaurant. Leclerc's broadcast was on the radio. The fact that Thérèse's husband had become the famous General Leclerc was a longstanding open secret. Despite intermittent threats of eviction from the Vichy authorities, nothing happened beyond some ugly incidents. Although she had a sporadic correspondence with her husband while he was in Africa, this was the first time she had heard his voice since he left her to join de Gaulle in 1940.[138]

Unaware that among the millions of French citizens hearing his broadcast was his beloved wife, Leclerc returned to division business. After General Haislip arrived to update Leclerc on Patton's latest decisions, General Gerow's premature visit to Langlade's CP made sense. The 2e DB and the US 90th Infantry Division were to stay where they were. Girard watched the effect of this news upon Leclerc. Though Haislip remained a friend to Leclerc for months to come, nevertheless, "The General is furious," wrote Girard.[139]

"I have a mission to accomplish for you," Leclerc told Haislip, "but I have another in my pocket."[140]

Leclerc drafted a letter to General Patton: "I wish to make clear the following to you. My officers and my men were persuaded by the Allied command that, after going to such pains to transport us from Africa to England and then to France, after we have been placed under your orders, you could not possibly refuse us the great recompense for us French, of being the first into Paris. We are ready to do whatever you ask of us, but to see other comrades return in our place into our capital city would, for my officers and men, be the greatest disappointment you could possibly impose upon us. We don't want anything else and don't want more than twenty-four hours, because both before and after we wish to fight under your orders. If this honour is refused us, I would ask of you that I am relieved of my command."[141]

Then Leclerc ordered one of his division's Piper Cub aircraft to take him to Patton's HQ where Bradley was conferring with Patton over the situation developing around Argentan. Fulminating, Leclerc gave Patton his letter.

"Stop conducting yourself like a child, General!" said Patton. "I do not accept that divisional commanders tell me where they want to fight. In any case, apart from anything else, I've left you in the most dangerous place."

Patton also pointed out that other armoured division commanders were equally frustrated.

"You see Wood?" said Patton in French, referring to the commander of US 4th Armored Division. "He's even more fed up than you are."

Witnessed by Bradley, Patton reassured Leclerc that the 2e DB was earmarked to go into Paris, the question being when.[142]

Patton later wrote that he told Leclerc "in my best French that he was a baby!" However, Patton also wrote, "We parted as friends."[143]

The southern shoulder of the pocket was a ringside seat for watching the German rout. "Above all," wrote Paul Repiton-Préneuf, the 2e DB's chief intelligence officer, "there was the surge coming from the west, this flood of units *en sauve qui peut*, ignorant of their situation, who came crashing into our positions. Some of them pulled themselves together, gathered up their equipment and mounted attacks; Carrouges, Boucé and Écouché were hit hard. We stopped them, then we ceased firing for the pleasure of going forward and gathering up prisoners. We saw there remnants of seven or eight divisions, including Waffen SS personnel."[144]

At Carrouges, Leclerc's longest serving battle-group commander, Louis Dio, had a whole German battalion parade past him into captivity.

"I hope we'll soon be going to Paris," remarked young Wallerand de Hauteclocque while dining at his uncle's CP.

"*Mais, moi aussi!*" replied Leclerc, smiling. "I would like to go there too!"[145]

FROM 15 AUGUST THE PARIS POLICE WENT ON STRIKE. Two days previously the Germans disarmed the *Gardiens de la Paix* in the Asnières and Saint-Denis regions. When news of this reached Paris the three police resistance groups, *Front National de Police*, *Police et Patrie* and *Honneur de la Police*, met at a house in the 3rd Arrondissement's Rue Chapon to discuss their predicament; if the police were on strike, keeping their weapons with them, then the Germans could hardly disarm them. Several senior non-police *résistants* were also present, including André Carrel and Roger Prou-Valjean from the CPL and Colonel Henri Rol-Tanguy who was invited by

Serge Lefranc.[146] All parties supported the strike but were nevertheless concerned that such action might enable the *Milice* to supplant the police. When the SD disarmed the police of Clermont-Ferrand, *Milice* leader Joseph Darnand advised them to submit to German demands. In Paris there was little sign that senior police officers would resist. Edmond Hennequin, *collabo* director general of the Municipal Police, ordered the *Gardiens de la Paix* of Paris to continue as usual while offering reassurance that the German measure only applied to units like the *Gendarmerie* and the *Garde Mobile* who had automatic weapons. "You can calm your men," SS Major Neifeind told Amédée Bussière. "They will neither be disarmed nor arrested."[147]

After the grim events involving the *Milice* at the Santé prison during July, and noticing that the Gestapo and other German security organisations were preparing to leave, Police *résistants* were unconvinced. When Hennequin drew up an order to be read out in all police stations at evening assembly, appealing to their sense of duty just as Langeron had done in 1940, but finishing with "No defiance will be tolerated", his words fell on deaf ears. The police were *collabos* no longer.[148]

"This decision was very important and satisfied me unreservedly," Rol-Tanguy later told Roger Bourderon. "It placed the Paris Police alongside the FFI and lifted the worry of an eventual conflict between them. I understood perfectly the objections of some of my comrades like André Tollet and André Carrel regarding the Police, but I did not share it because I reckoned that in the decisive hours that lay ahead we had to do everything to be on the same side. In any case they had already shown some willingness; despite orders they did nothing to intervene against the demonstrations on 14 July. That was an encouraging sign."[149]

Emboldened by this development, Rol-Tanguy called upon all law enforcement organisations, including the prison service, to stand beside the Resistance and refuse all German orders. The strike order was drawn up and distributed. It announced that "Those Policemen who do not obey this strike order will be regarded as traitors and collaborators."

Further down it also said, "On no account should our comrades allow themselves to be disarmed."[150]

An open statement was issued simultaneously to the people of Paris. "We know the mistrust of the people of Paris for the Paris police. We patriotic policemen have also greatly suffered from this situation. The proof now exists that the people of Paris have no reason to doubt that their police can be found today at the vanguard of combat for the liberation. The only word of greeting is 'Action'. A general strike is now in force among the Paris police until the liberation."[151]

Amédée Bussière faced a *fait accompli*. "I was beset by all sorts of worries," he wrote. "The Germans are there, never too late to intervene. But with what? The SS commander telephoned me. The exchange was very lively but he [Neifeind] seemed to have other preoccupations; he was constantly being interrupted by officers asking for instructions about evacuating their offices in the Rue de Saussaies. 'It's a bad business for you,' said Neifeind. 'The Military Governor of Paris is going to call you. You should give him an explanation. He will appreciate it.'"[152]

At the Hôtel Meurice, Bussière was greeted coolly and correctly. General von Choltitz recognised the situation's seriousness, however much Bussière minimised it, and threatened "to take the most rigourous measures". Bussière replied ineffectually that he would find a way to stop the strike spreading and have meetings in the six areas most affected. Von Choltitz seemed satisfied. But although the striking policemen gave Bussière a warm welcome, worn-out arguments about service and patriotism made no impression on men sickened by performing tasks that benefited the Germans.[153]

By late afternoon the *Milice* were stirring. A squad of *Miliciens* was sent from their temporary barracks at the Lycée Saint-Louis to take over the 5th Arrondissement's central station near the Pantheon. After locking up a few strikers they appointed themselves as the locality's new police force. Only a call from Bussière himself got the striking policemen released.[154] By mid-evening on 15 August, the strike was in force across the whole city.

That same day Pierre Laval's machinations to form a transitional government around Edouard Herriot became enmeshed with the police resistance group *L'Honneur de la Police*, who plotted to "rescue" Herriot and bring him under their protection. Alexandre Parodi and Georges Bidault agreed that police *résistants* were the perfect choice to perform this operation. Yves Bayet prepared plans and ordered a team under Sergeant Fournet to stand by. But after finalising the operation's details with Alexandre Parodi and Georges Bidault at a café on the Place de Breteuil, Sergeant Fournet felt troubled. What if Herriot refused to co-operate? "We kill him," suggested a colleague of Fournet's who also attended the meeting. But, preferring to avoid endorsing a political killing comparable with the murder of Jean Jaurez on the eve of liberation, Bidault and Parodi vetoed the operation.[155] This resulted in Sergeant Fournet impatiently hanging around for instructions; frustrating moments which influenced his decision making four days later.

With family loyalties split across every facet of French politics at this time, someone, somehow alerted André Enfière, Laval's *confidant* (and supposed contact with OSS*), of the operation, and Laval placed extra security around Herriot. Thereafter the only way the Resistance could contact Herriot was through his old *chef de cabinet* who could still get into the Hôtel de Ville; he told Herriot that the Resistance could access parliamentary records and so knew which deputies and senators supported Pétain in 1940.[156]

As previously arranged, Nordling visited the Matignon around 5pm. Laval appeared tired and drawn while openly continuing a telephone conversation regarding Pétain's destiny. When Pétain refused to come to Paris, Laval advised him to lose himself in *la France profonde*. But since the *maquis* controlled much of central France that option was unviable. "Tell the guards to hold on for twenty-four hours," said Laval. "I will send my cabinet secretary with a car. It will be followed by two other cars carrying armed guards as well as my own luggage and my

---

* OSS = *Office of Strategic Services*, the forerunner of the CIA.

dog." Putting down the receiver Laval turned to Nordling. Although he had been unable to speak to Abetz about the "politicals"' Abetz was due at the Matignon later that evening.

"I suggest that you be there too," said Laval. "Then we will be able to discuss this matter between the three of us."[157]

THE AMERICAN AIRCRAFT RETURNING JACQUES CHABAN-DELMAS to France touched down on a prefabricated metal runway near Saint-Lo. If de Gaulle's national military delegate remained doubtful that General Ismay's advice that the Paris insurrection should not begin before mid-September was anything but wise, he only needed to survey the damage eight weeks of modern warfare had inflicted on northern France.

Immediately after Rennes was liberated, one of de Gaulle's nominees, the experienced colonial administrator Bernard Cornut-Gentille, installed himself as the department's new *préfet*. De Gaulle requested Eisenhower's permission to visit Rennes, but Chaban-Delmas arrived first; Cornut-Gentille welcomed him handsomely. Once Le Mans was liberated another Gaullist *préfet* in waiting, Jean-Louis Costa, took office.

With the opposing front lines so fluid, Chaban decided to cross the German lines disguised as a foppish young man bicycling between summer tennis parties carrying a tennis racket and a couple of unplucked chickens. Chaban left Rennes in a US Army Jeep, carrying his bicycle in the back. On reaching Le Mans, Prefect Costa arranged the next phase of Chaban's return to Paris. As a fit young rugby player Chaban was undaunted by a two-hundred-kilometre bicycle ride provided he could avoid the Germans. Dropped off at a quiet section of the front by American liaison officers, Chaban donned tennis attire and began pedalling through Beauce's pleasant countryside and picturesque villages, all worryingly silent as he neared the German lines. His wariness was justified by a burst of machine-gun fire which miraculously left him untouched. Passing through unliberated villages, Chaban saw pro-Vichy posters bemoaning Allied bombing raids: "*Les anglais, eux. Toujours eux.*"—"The English, them. Always them."[158]

Nearing Chartres, Chaban heard an aircraft engine above him; his white tennis clothes had been spotted, an Allied fighter-bomber flew low enough to machine-gun him but veered away. Approaching Brou, Chaban met trouble not, as he feared, from the Germans but local *résistants*. These local toughs merely laughed when Chaban announced, "I am the National Military Delegate of General Koenig, the commander of the French Forces of the Interior. I am returning from a mission in London. I have important and urgent information to give the Resistance in Paris. Let me pass. Help me get back." Though initially sceptical, these young *résistants* decided to take Chaban to their local chief, a former gunsmith. Despite listening to Chaban's story, he remained unconvinced.

"If you've got a car," said Chaban, "why not send someone to Le Mans to see the *préfet de la libération*, Jean-Louis Costa. Ask him. He will confirm to you that I really am the National Military Delegate; that I have come from London and must reach Paris as soon as possible. And, just so that your people know, the Americans are at Connerré. Between Connerré and Brou I didn't come across any Germans, but there might be some stragglers."

While awaiting confirmation of Chaban's identity the gunsmith gave him a room for the night.[159] Once his story checked out, the gunsmith's men woke him somewhat penitently at around 6am. After breakfast, Chaban retook the road, pedalling ever eastwards until inevitably he was stopped at a German checkpoint where he gave his prepared story; a young husband who had merely bicycled out of underfed Paris seeking food for his family. When asked if he had encountered any Americans, Chaban replied, "Not a single one."

The weather had been fine all day, but nearing Christ de Saclay rain began falling, drenching Chaban's tennis whites. Nevertheless he reached Villacoublay by 5pm. From there the rain intensified into a bucketing deluge, making Chaban more conspicuous as he crossed the deserted Pont de Sevres. From there he headed for the 16th Arrondissement's Stade Jean-Bouin where he knew the caretaker, Monsieur Martin, was certain to take him in.

"Why? Monsieur Delmas!" said Martin. "You look like a drowned cat."

Without asking questions, Martin's wife gave Chaban a hot drink while he telephoned a friend for a change of clothes. Leaving Martin's home by the back door, Chaban ran fleetly across the empty stadium to the opposite stand's exit which placed him beyond the big Saint-Cloud checkpoint. From there he went to a secret lair on the Rue Claude-Lorrain.

AT 9PM RAOUL NORDLING'S FIRST ENCOUNTER with Alexandre Parodi began warily outside the Gare Montparnasse. Used to clandestine discipline, Parodi worried that Nordling might have been followed, but his concerns were unfounded. Nordling needed clarification that he was no longer just another neutral consul in occupied Paris; that henceforward he was negotiating on behalf of de Gaulle's provisional government.[160]

Once this issue was settled, Nordling drove to the Matignon for another audience with Pierre Laval. With Parisian utility workers also on strike, Paris seemed as ghostly as during June 1940. Passiing through the Matignon's gates at around 9.30pm Nordling was impressed by the encroaching darkness as caretakers wandered candle-lit corridors. Nordling took out the small pocket torch he had recently acquired. Laval, carrying a similar device, met Nordling in an antechamber and led him into the premier's study where an oil lamp burned brightly. While awaiting Otto Abetz they discussed the political situation; it seemed inevitable that Pétain would be deposed, but Laval's hopes for a transitional government, which required both Herriot's and Jeanneney's co-operation, were falling apart. Laval recognised that soon he too would have to leave Paris.[161]

Abetz also arrived carrying a small hand-torch. When Nordling explained the political prisoners' urgent situation, Abetz fobbed him off, painting a dishonestly rosy picture of their conditions; claiming Oberg informed him personally that cattle wagons did not carry one hundred and twenty prisoners, but merely eighty (which was bad enough). Furthermore Abetz informed Nordling that the Red Cross would feed the prisoners before their departure—another lie. But Nordling was not interested in comparatives, he wanted the deportation trains stopped altogether and prisons where "politicals" were held transfered to the authority of the Red Cross. To reassure Abetz, Nordling offered to allow German guards to remain and then be given safe conduct to rejoin other German forces when they withdrew.

"And with whom would you like me to sign a convention concerning political prisoners?" asked Abetz wryly.

"One would imagine a convention between yourself and the Gaullist government in Algiers," replied Nordling.

"So where is the Algiers government?" asked Abetz.

"I am taking on this role in the name of the French government," said Nordling.

"What are you talking about?" scoffed Laval. "If you'll excuse me, Monsieur le Consul, until the new order comes in, I am the one who represents the French government."[162]

Nordling replied that he was representing de Gaulle's provisional government in Algiers. At this revelation Abetz refused to continue negotiations. Supported by Laval, Abetz told Nordling he should leave. Abetz also reminded the envoy that political prisoners came under Oberg's authority.

Nordling politely drew Abetz's attention to Germany's increasingly desperate military situation, suggesting that the German authorities should not dismiss an opportunity to leave some good will behind.

"So you think Germany has lost the war?" said Abetz sarcastically.

"I think, in any case, that things are going very badly for your armies, *Monsieur l'ambassadeur*," replied Nordling.[163]

Nordling recognised that he had made as much progress as he could. That same day a train of cattle wagons left Pantin carrying 2,453 political prisoners to an uncertain future inside the Third Reich.[164]

16 August 1944

AFTER LYING IN A DITCH ALL DAY, Field Marshal von Kluge arrived at the HQ of Sepp Dietrich's 1st SS Panzer Corps late in the evening of 15 August. Meanwhile his chief of staff, General Gunther Blumentritt, had frantically complained to General Jodl about the state of German forces withdrawing from Argentan, and asked for a new army commander. SS Panzer General Paul Hausser was considered as an emergency replacement. When Kluge explained that his absence was spent taking cover after RAF Typhoons shot up his convoy, Hitler was unconvinced and decided Kluge should go. Before that happened, Kluge recommended the immediate withdrawal of all German forces from the Falaise-Argentan gap. The message was sent to OKW at around 2am in the small hours of 16 August.[165]

Recognising that he had insufficient troops to hold France, Hitler finally agreed not only to evacuate "the pocket" but to establish a new line further east, behind the Orne and Dives rivers; more than the frayed von Kluge originally asked for.[166] The stress of those weeks, witnessing once proud divisions being destroyed, combined with his profound inner turmoil over 20 July, had turned Hans-Gunther von Kluge into a broken reed. Even if it was unfair to blame Kluge for the failure at Mortain, Hitler realistically recognised that Kluge was of no further use to him and needed to be replaced by Field Marshal Walter Model. Unlike many high-ranking Germans, Model did not belong to the old aristocracy, which was thoroughly represented in the 20 July conspiracy; he was middle class, immensely good at his job and a thorough-going Nazi. Having sorted out several dangerous situations on the Eastern front, Model became known as Hitler's "fireman". The same day as his appointment to go to France, Hitler awarded Model the diamond clasp upgrade to his Knight's Cross. "Were it not for you, your heroic efforts and your wise leadership of brave troops," said Hitler effusively, "the Russians might have been in East Prussia today, or even the gates of Berlin." These words indicated that Hitler recognised that the war was no longer going his way.[167]

AFTER VISITING GENERAL WALKER'S US XX CORPS at Chartres, and Haislip's XV near Mantes, Patton returned to his Third Army HQ around 6.30pm. It was then that he took a call from Bradley ordering him to use Leclerc's 2e DB and the US 90th and 80th Infantry Divisions to advance on Trun "to meet the Canadians and close the Argentan-Falaise pocket". General Gerow would command these divisions as the reconstituted V Corps.[168]

16 August was also the day on which operational secrecy around the Falaise battles was lifted. The press corps visited the front, immediately making Patton enough of a star to efface his gaffe-prone past.[169] Towards the end of the afternoon reporters arrived at Fleuré where Leclerc's staff updated them on the 2e DB's achievements. Since Africa, Christian Girard had tried strenuously to make Leclerc more press-friendly, and gladly noted in his diary that his general "received them graciously", sitting on the ground in the middle of a meadow. Later that evening, after an excellent supper cooked by Fleuré's schoolteacher, Leclerc received an urgent message from Patton ordering him to a staff meeting at Valframbert.[170]

Prompted by intelligence warnings from Bradley's HQ that a German counterattack might materialise around Argentan, Leonard Gerow had driven through an unpleasantly wet night to Alençon where an impromptu HQ was set up at the Hôtel de France. Confusingly, Patton had sent Major General Hugh Gaffey to temporarily assume command of V Corps and lead the operation to link up with the British at Trun. The two American major generals agreed between them that Gaffey would lead the attack but Gerow would take over as corps commander the following evening.[171]

At around 11pm, accompanied by Girard and a bodyguard, Leclerc arrived at V Corps' new HQ. Gaffey explained to the Frenchmen that he was ordered to mount an attack for the morning of 17 August. They were to advance on Trun to finally close the pocket, thereby preventing any more German forces from escaping eastwards. Politely, Gaffey asked Leclerc for his viewpoint. Girard watched intently. Spotlights directed onto the maps lit up the faces of the officers perusing them, leaving all else pitch black. North of Argentan was the Forêt de Gouffern. Between the 2e DB's starting position at Fleuré and Gaffey's objective at Trun were the town of Argentan itself, the forest and then a network of country roads and villages; territory which could be doughtily defended by a desperate opponent.

Between the dillemma of wanting his division to take part in worthwhile actions and also keeping it strong enough to make its dash for Paris, Leclerc's heart must have sank. Girard writes that Leclerc looked irritated as he looked at the map before saying in French, "The terrain is utterly unfavourable to an armoured division" and "the operation ought to be an infantry matter". Then, through Girard, Leclerc asked Gaffey what sort of support he was offering the 2e DB.

"A regiment of three battalions," Gaffey replied.

Leclerc pursed his lips. At Alençon and the Forêt d'Écouves the 2e DB executed a large envelopement but not against an enemy they had watched dig in for five days. Such an operation could not help but be costly for the 2e DB's infantry, his valued veterans.

"I have orders to attack tomorrow morning," said Gaffey. "I will attack tomorrow morning."

"It's terrible!" Girard wrote in his journal. For the next hour the discussion swung to and fro as he translated Leclerc's argument that such an attack would write off two divisions as effective units. Nor did the timescale offer Leclerc's G3, André Gribius, nor his intelligence officer, Paul Repiton-Préneuf, time to prepare anything.

"Nothing is prepared," ran Leclerc's protest. "There aren't enough men. There hasn't been any reconnaissance, no fresh information, no reserves, no one beside us, no possibility of exploitation."

Gaffey had not expected this.

"I am in command," said Gaffey imperiously. "And I have given you an order."

"It is not executable," came the French reply. "There isn't a third of what's needed."

"Are you refusing to obey orders?" asked Gaffey before turning to an orderly and saying something that sounded to Girard like an instruction to take notes. Leclerc asked if the matter could be referred back to Patton. Gaffey replied that he would indeed refer back to Patton but only once the attack was ready to start; that he certainly would not telephone Patton in the middle of the night. "We felt like we were caught in a trap," wrote Girard.

Driving in darkness back to Fleuré, Leclerc was fuming, fearing that his division would be wrecked the following day.[172]

Pierre Billotte was waiting to see him.

"They wanted me to set off tomorrow morning at dawn and advance virtually alone from south to north towards Falaise," said Leclerc, shaking his head. "I refused. What do you think?"

"I think you were quite right," replied Billotte. "You've done what was asked of us since the 8 August. Since Montgomery has not succeeded from north to south with a whole army group, how does Bradley's chief of staff imagine that we can accomplish this with one division? It's flattering, but it isn't exactly realistic. And if by some miracle we got there, what state would we be in? We would certainly be incapable, should the moment arise, of liberating Paris, which remains our essential objective as determined by de Gaulle. So I can only support you. Perhaps you should expect some severe reactions from the Americans, but they will probably cool down."[173]

Unknown to Leclerc that night, his fears for the 2e DB were unfounded. Bradley had telephoned Patton at 11.30pm delaying Gaffey's attack.[174]

THAT SAME WEDNESDAY, Madame Herriot inspected what she believed would become her new home, the Hôtel de la Présidence de la Chambres des Deputés. The Germans had left it filthy, yet in spite of everything the Herriots decided to move in. It was not to be. At 10.15pm, SS Hauptsturmführer Noseck arrived at the Hôtel de

Ville in full black SS uniform and informed Herriot that the German government had decided to reintern him. Incandescent with rage, Herriot yelled, "You don't play with a man's dignity like this. It's certainly true that this is not the first time that Germany has broken its word and it won't be the last. I've always known you were pigs. You have no honour."

Noseck was unmoved. Laval's last gamble had failed.[175]

"This is that pig de Brinon!" Laval yelled.

In fact this development was the handywork of those extreme *collabos*, Déat and Darnand, who, like the Germans, found Laval's uncertain loyalties infuriating. They found Otto Abetz's efforts at humanity pretty infuriating too. So Déat and de Brinon turned to the SS, meeting Karl Oberg's adjutant, Colonel Knochen, that afternoon to warn him that Laval intended to change camp, to do a "Badoglio."* They also warned Knocken that a new government led by Herriot would join Pétain's and de Gaulle's supporters in an uprising of all Frenchmen against the Germans. Knochen referred to Oberg. Oberg had always despised Laval, believing that a palindromic surname could only belong to a two-faced person. Himmler was informed and the order to re-arrest Edouard Herriot arrived an hour later.[176]

RAOUL NORDLING NEVER HAD TO BEHAVE *AU CLANDESTIN*. Yet his second meeting with Alexandre Parodi began with a singular dance of walking to and fro across theatre land's Boulevard des Capucines before they finally acknowledged each other outside the Café de la Paix. Deciding that that famous restaurant was too conspicuous, they repaired to a small bar on the pokey Rue Boudreau behind the Opera. Parodi was accompanied by senior Gaullist linkman, Count Alexandre de Saint-Phalle; both were inconspicuously dressed.[177]

---

* In September 1943 the Italian Prime Minister General Pietro Badoglio pulled Italy out of its alliance with Germany with little warning and the following month declared war on Germany.

After Nordling described his meeting at the Matignon the previous evening, Parodi confirmed that the GPRF would allow German prison guards safe conduct out of Paris if the prisons could be placed under the authority of the Red Cross. In Algiers the GPRF considered ordering raids on the prisons and transit camps but rejected this idea because the guards were invariably well armed. It had even been reported that Fresnes was equipped with gas supplies to use on inmates if the prison was stormed. While the last ingredient was undoubtedly untrue, in view of these factors Nordling's negotiations seemed the wiser option, if only the Germans would listen. Parodi told Nordling that Algiers wanted him to continue the good work. Many important resistance prisoners were held at Fresnes; though since 14 August the German authorities had begun sending them to Germany.[178]

That evening yet another train left Pantin, feeding another twenty-four hundred *résistants* into Germany's concentration camps. With a heavy heart Nordling telephoned Erich von Posch-Pastor, who immediately agreed to contact Colonel Garthe at the Hôtel Lutetia and call Nordling back in the morning. As soon as Nordling put the phone down it rang again. The Marquis de Mun, head of the French Red Cross, had encouraging news. The evening's prison train to Germany was stopped at Nanteuil-sur-Marne. It was not yet certain whether this was due to mechanical failure or resistance sabotage, but the latter seemed more likely. But rescuing twenty-four hundred prisoners was a lot to expect from one of P1's small sabotage teams, and Mun's information was that a replacement train was on its way to transfer the prisoners and continue to Germany the following morning.[179]

FOR THE TRAIN THAT ROSE VALLAND WAS DETERMINED TO STOP, the endgame began in early August. A shipment of 148 cases—much of the Rosenberg collection, Weil-Picard's and choice objects belonging to dispossessed Parisian Jews—filling five railway wagons, was waiting to leave from Aubervilliers. In order to streamline their final thefts, *M-Aktion*—Baron von Behr's second plunder organisation devoted to stealing general antiques—would join another forty-six wagons to the train. The demands of the front meant that shipments were continually delayed so that by 7 August, Train 40044 remained in the Paris area. Rose consulted Jacques Jaujard, who agreed that the Resistance should stop the train. Everyone knew the Allies would soon arrive; why let the Germans steal any more?[180]

For striking Left-wing *cheminots*, obstructing a train filled with beautiful artefacts created by French hands was their pleasure. Rose felt quietly satisfied that the ERR's staff were finally leaving, with men like the ghastly Dr. Bruno Lohse recalled by the Wehrmacht a second time. It also meant good-bye to the less unpleasant Dr. Walter Borchers. Before he left, Borchers kept a promise he made to Rose, ensuring that statues taken from Edouard Rothschild's collection did not leave the Louvre complex. More personally he offered Rose his book collection, but she turned this final act of conqueror's patronage back on him, saying that if he did not take them with him they would be regarded as spoils of war. Outside, the SS guards were replaced by Georgians, turncoat Soviet prisoners from the Russian front.[181]

On 9 August Rose wrote chillingly, "Von Behr and Lohse have departed, saying that they will be back in a few days. It would be preferable that these two *personnages* were not here for the last acts of the Occupation. They would have the temptation to erase, not only evidence of their actions, but also their witnesses." After four years cataloguing Nazi theft, Rose desperately hoped that France's stolen heritage could be recovered. But where artefacts were offered as gifts the ownership question was harder to reverse. On 11 August five paintings and a tapestry left the Jeu de Paume "as presents no doubt", Rose writes. Then, "A Foujita, representing a reclining nude woman, with contrasting shades of black and white, was offered to the Japanese ambassador who had the good taste to refuse."[182]

On 12 August the *Einsatzstab Reichsleiter Rosenberg*'s Paris operation ended; but the *cheminots* prevented Baron von Behr's last train from going anywhere. When, on 16 August, the guards finally left the Jeu de Paume, Rose's diary entry ends expressively, "*Ouf!*" Until the Allies arrived she would guard her beloved museum herself.[183]

MID-AUGUST SAW THE LAST GREAT SINGLE TRAGEDY to befall the Resistance in Paris. While most *résistants* who bore arms in the ensuing weeks were already under orders, there were youngsters linked to both the OCM (*Organisation Civile et Militaire*) and JCC (*Jeunesses Chrétienne Combattante*), bursting with enthusiasm, hoping to be given weapons so they could harass the departing Germans before they left France. Their leaders, Jacques Schlosser, Guy Hémery and others were in their twenties and had Resistance experience. Unfortunately they became vulnerable to infiltration and denunciation once they contacted a businessman called Wigen Nercessian. While his surname suggests Armenian ancestry, Nercessian was a White Russian from the bourgeois-aristocratic expat community that escaped to France after the Russian Revolution.

Nercessian himself was an honest *resistant*, but he was compromised from early 1944 when he arrived in Marseilles to work with an escape line helping Russian prisoners reach Spain. After this group was denounced and several members captured, Nercessian felt around like a blind man for new resistance contacts and fell in with one Madame Rousselin, the English wife of a French naval officer. She introduced Nercessian to Charles Porel, who claimed to be both an Austrian Jew and a British agent empowered to provide funds. Nercessian was thrilled to receive fifteen thousand francs which enabled him to return to Meudon where his parents lived.[184]

Unaware who Porel was really working for, Nercessian continued his clandestine work and became friends with Abbé Borme, president of the Society of Saint Vincent de Paul for the 13th Arrondissement. Seeing that Nercessian appeared well funded, Abbé Borme advised Guy Hémery to ask him for weapons. On account of his connection to Porel, Nercessian replied, "It's possible." Porel told Nercessian that weapons were not his department and referred him to "Captain Jack".[185]

Captain Jack, who presented himself as a classic Englishman complete with Oxford accent, questioned Nercessian about his resistance contacts. Their second meeting was planned for 11 August at the Régence Café on Place du Théatre Français. Nercessian was accompanied by Guy Hémery and Jean Favé. "'Captain Jack' led the discussion, while Porel remained virtually mute," Nercessian wrote. "The *résistants* would provide the men and the lorries while British Intelligence would provide the weapons and, as a precaution, further lorries. 'Captain Jack' wanted to know the size of the *résistants*' lorries in order to gauge whether they could pass through a depot's entrance, whose whereabouts he was not yet prepared to say." A rendezvous was arranged for mid-August.[186]

As with the arrest of Jean Moulin, an incident occurred which should have warned anyone used to clandestine life that things were not quite right. Jean Guerin, a young *résistant* involved in arranging the early meetings, was arrested on 7 August. But it appeared an isolated event, as it was doubtless meant to. When young *résistante* Michelle Boursier—codenamed *Diane*—a senior member of the *Jeunesse Chrétienne Combattante*, lunched with her immediate superiors at a restaurant in the Latin Quarter on 15 August to finalise details, she believed their command chain went via Abbé Borme to the true Resistance, totally trusting her comrades and their connections.[187]

As arranged, at 10am on 16 August, *Diane*'s group arrived on the Rue Drouot where they learnt their lorry had broken down near the Gare de l'Est. "So, all on bicycles we pedalled off to the Porte Maillot where we arrived around 11.30," *Diane* later wrote. "Guy Hémery was there, near the Metro entrance. Not far away from the Avenue de la Grande Armée and Boulevard Pereire, stood 'Captain Jack' along with three lorries provided by him parked by Luna Park. He told us to help ourselves to one and Bellenger agreed. As we climbed up into this lorry our own lorry, which someone had managed to get going, finally arrived with four *résistants* armed with machine-guns on board."[188]

When Bellenger suggested they now use their own lorry, Captain Jack firmly insisted that they should use his. He also told the four armed *résistants* to give him their weapons so that, supposing they were stopped by the Germans none of them would arouse suspicion by being armed. Bowing to his apparent Britishness and seniority, they consented. Captain Jack now had fifteen unarmed young *résistants* aboard his lorry. "There will be two stops," he said. "At the first, no one is to move. At the second we will be at our destination, in a garage where we should obtain weapons."[189]

Diane's misgivings began when the tarpaulin flap fell back down, plunging the young *résistants* into half-light. She had never seen that driver before. No one sat beside him. No one was checking the route on a bicycle. The lorry pulled away and, mere minutes later, stopped. Looking through the flap a *résistant* saw German vehicles surrounding them.

"*Voici les Fridolins*,"* he said.

Amid banging on the sides of the lorries, machine-gun bursts into the tops of the lorry canopies and shouts of "*Raus*", the youngsters were ordered out. A few, who possessed revolvers, considered fighting, but soon recognised their situation was hopeless and jumped down from the lorry. *Diane* was third out, injuring her legs as she landed. Surprised to find a girl, the intimidating machine-gun bursts briefly stopped, then continued until all of them were standing in the road—probably the Avenue de Salonique—with their hands up. Their captors were twenty SS, two Gestapo and a *Milicien* in civilian clothes, all armed. For a few moments the Germans kicked them around, paying particular attention to *Diane*. Then they were ordered back onto the lorries and driven to the Gestapo HQ in the Rue de Saussaies.[190]

Their betrayer, Charles Porel, was really Karl Rehbein, an experienced German agent who had previously uncovered many *résistants* across southern France. His controller was SS Hauptsturmführer Alfred Wenzel, based at 11 Boulevard Flandrin, an annex of the SS offices on Avenue Foch. Captain Jack was Guy de Marcheret d'Eu, the elegant twenty-eight-year-old son of a White Russian and an aristocratic French lady, sophisticated and multi-lingual, but of uncertain politics and loyalties. Pretentious and vain, working for the SD appealed to Marcheret's love of role-playing.[191] Porel told French interrogators

---

* *Fridolin* was a name given to German soldiers and Occupation officials in France during WW2.

in 1946 that, "Being an Anglophile, Nercessian could always be persuaded to work for the Allied services, and he was very happy. He never imagined that he was working for the Wehrmacht and believed everything I told him. Perhaps he was negligent in not checking a few things out."[192]

On reaching the courtyard of the notorious Gestapo building the youngsters were ordered out of the lorries and made to stand against a wall, guarded by two *Miliciens*. After a while a German officer took an ID parade. Afterwards *Diane* and the young men, bloody, bruised and desperately frightened, remained standing with their hands above their heads for several hours. Around early evening *Diane* was moved to a single cell and, after another hour, was called to an office where her personal belongings were returned and, surprisingly, she was released. The courtyard where she last saw her comrades was empty except for a German soldier hosing it down. What became known as "*la grande fuite des Fritzs*", the German withdrawal from Paris, was under way.

Captain Jack had other victims that day. The groupe Sicard, connected to Hémery, were also lured to a fake rendezvous. Captain Jack met them on Place Saint-Ferdinand where, guided insouciantly by Wigen Nercessian, they arrived on Place Victor Hugo. Their next stop was 14 Rue Leroux, a building controlled by the Kriegsmarine. Following three ambushes, fronted unwittingly by Nercessian but masterminded by Porel and Captain Jack, the SD captured thirty-four *résistants*. That night they were taken to the bank of the *Cascade* (the waterfall) in the Bois de Boulogne. One by one they were taken down from the back of the lorry and shot by SS men, and their corpses left where they fell.[193]

At dawn the following day, on his way to work, Monsieur Lefebvre—the chief caretaker at the nearby École des Cadres de Bagatelle—saw the slaughtered *résistants* lying grotesquely beside the waterfall. Thirty-four became thirty-five because resistance Doctor Blanchet was shot by SS Captain Friedrich Berger at the SD's Rue de la Pompe annex and his body dumped beside the others. With the police on strike, the Bois de Boulogne *gardes* managed as best they could, taking the victims to their depot on the Rue Chardon-Lagache (16th Arrondissement) along with seven more victims from Avenue Foch. "In all my career, I have never seen such a massacre," forensic Dr. Paul told a post-war court of enquiry.[194]

Told of her comrades' deaths, *Diane* was invited to identify them, but recognised only nine, including Guy Hémery. The Red Cross identified the rest. With the Germans still in control, giving them family funerals was impossible, but Abbé Borme visited the Rue Chardon-Lagache to give the last rites to those young men he had unwittingly fed to the enemy.

Together Abbé Borme, Nercessian and the *résistante Jeanne* (Sabine Zlatin) worked out Charles Porel's role; Nercessian was distraught at having given Porel the addresses of Russian agents in Berlin. On 20 August Sabine Zlatin met Porel's mistress Lydia Tscherwinska but, although tainted with *collaboration*, Tscherwinska was merely an innocent accoutrement of Porel's undercover lifestyle. As for Porel himself, aka German intelligence officer Karl Rehbein, he had left Paris.

General von Choltitz was not responsible for this massacre. He had virtually no control over SS and Gestapo activities in Paris; a fact confirmed by another incident. Informed by a senior SS official, possibly Oberg, that an abandoned SS lock-up still held the wives of well-to-do Frenchmen, von Choltitz immediately visited the prison to find Swiss consul René Naville already there. Von Choltitz was horrified that four of these elegant, well-connected women had been raped and murdered, their naked corpses left lying in a cell. Von Choltitz apologised to the other thirty women and released them. Describing the incident to fellow prisoners at Trent Park, von Choltitz said, "They just felt like it. Those swine made off at night without telling me, they left their quarters open, full of arms and a cellar filled with explosives and a picture of Hitler as its only guardian! They simply drove off."[195]

Chapter 4

Laval, Taittinger and Nordling

17 August 1944

AT 7AM, WITH *"LA GRANDE FUITE DES FRITZS"*—"the Great Flight of the Fritzes"—getting under way, Raoul Nordling and his French nephew Édouard Fiévet drew up outside the Grand Hôtel, from where the "Taxis of the Marne" had departed for the front in 1914. In Erich von Posch-Pastor's office they met Count de Rohan-Chabot, a director of the French Red Cross. Next, Bobby Bender arrived. Rather than go through all the proper authorities, banging their heads against brick walls, Bender advised that they issue themselves with drafted orders from lower down the chain of command, which middle-ranking German officers—the grades commanding jails and railway stations— were unlikely to question, and go directly to the prisons and camps holding political prisoners.[1]

They first visited Fresnes, south of Paris. A prison built in the 1890s and designed to be humane and innovative, Fresnes became notorious during the Occupation for imprisoning *résistants*. Only five days earlier, Jewish aid worker Suzanne Spaak had been shot in the execution yard. Things seemed perfectly calm when Nordling arrived at the gate, but the wide roads southwards were recognised by the Germans as potential routes for liberating armies. One of General von Aulock's valuable 88mm guns was allocated to defend the jail's approaches and give defilading fire if any Allied vehicle crossed the main junction a few hundred metres away.

In the governor's office, Bender asked if the governor was disposed to release prisoners in line with "new policy".

"That is my greatest wish," he replied. "If I get the order, I shall release all the prisoners immediately."[2]

Even as the Allies closed in, Nazi officialdom was more robust than they hoped. They returned to Paris and called at the Hôtel Meurice where defences were being prepared. The west section of the Rue de Rivoli was being cordonned off, while inside the hotel machine-gun positions were being created on the main staircase and at windows with the best view over the surrounding area. Sandbags were being passed between helmeted soldiers, and the atmosphere was tense. Nordling and Fiévet waited in the lobby while Bender and Posch-Pastor went to find von Choltitz. While Nordling waited, SS Standartenführer Karl Oberg arrived. Nordling registered Oberg's bull-like demeanour and monocle screwed into his left eye socket. Ten minutes later Oberg majestically descended the stairs and left the building, Then Bender reappeared, saying von Choltitz wanted to see them. As they went upstairs Bender explained: Oberg had only come to say his good-byes before leaving Paris. When Choltitz asked whether Oberg objected to the release of non-military prisoners, Oberg replied, "I don't care."[3]

At the first of several historic meetings, von Choltitz asked Nordling how he saw the situation.

"It is of the greatest importance that a massacre of prisoners is avoided," said Nordling. "The responsibility for such a catastrophe would rest on the whole German Army."

Although painfully aware of SS excesses, von Choltitz had to keep his position.

"For me, as an officer," said Choltitz, "there's no such thing as civil prisoners. I only know about prisoners of war. Any civilians who fire on my troops will be regarded as *Francs Tireurs* and shot where we find them. This is not a matter of *Francs Tireurs* and so I see no reason to detain civil prisoners."

Von Choltitz explained that, while he was entitled to make decisions, many officers who had signed existing orders or whose authorisation

Nordling needed were already leaving Paris, including his services officer, Major Huhm. "Hurry," said Choltitz, "Huhm is leaving Paris at noon today." Huhm's office was at the Hôtel Majestic on Avenue Kléber.[4]

Nordling found the Champs Élysées and the Étoile deserted, but barriers were being erected around the Avenue Kléber as well. Outside the Majestic, as lorries came and went, smoke wafted from paper incinerators stoked by soot-smeared clerks. Major Huhm received Nordling immediately.

"General von Choltitz has just told me that he is disposed to allocate to myself the security of the political prisoners," Nordling told Huhm. "In so far as this matter concerns your office, I hope that you will not be difficult."[5]

Since Nordling carried no papers, Huhm had a junior officer telephone the Meurice for confirmation of what Nordling told him. Once Huhm received this confirmation, negotiations with Nordling began. Sadly, Huhm was quite a Nazi and, strictly speaking, more under General Kitzinger's orders than von Choltitz's; a pretext for being difficult.

"We ought to establish a convention," said Major Huhm. "If we liberate French prisoners then surely we ought to get back twenty-five German prisoners of war for every French civilian we're holding."

"I don't have any German prisoners," said Nordling. "And I have no reason to capture any."

But Huhm was intransigent, saying he saw no reason to make any agreement that did not benefit Germany. Although utterly powerless to make concessions, Nordling offered Huhm five Germans for each French detainee. Huhm went to find von Choltitz at the Hôtel Meurice while Nordling conferred with the advocate Maitre Mettetal and *résistants* linked to Algiers. Nordling also contacted his Swiss opposite number, René Naville, believing Naville's support would be more effective than involving the Swedish Foreign Ministry in Stockholm.

With undertakings he hoped would satisfy Huhm—even if the release of five Germans for each detainee was impossible to implement—Nordling returned to Huhm's office. The next obstacle the malign Huhm threw at Nordling was that the rubber stamps necessary for the order to become official were packed for the journey eastwards. Luckily a clerk remembered which packing case contained the stamps and pulled them out. According to Maitre Mettetal's "convention", all political detainees "whether in Paris or its environs" and "all trains of evacuation without exception were to be placed under the authority of the Consul-General of Sweden, Monsieur Raoul Nordling, and left under the supervision of the French Red Cross." It also stipulated that the German authorities relinquished control of these prisoners to the Swedish Consul-General and the French Red Cross. The final document comprised two pages of legalistic French. Surprisingly Major Huhm congratulated himself on this agreement, adding in his own hand, "The military command has no objection to the above accord." Following Huhm's signature, the document was stamped.[6]

Now Nordling needed SS agreement to ensure the prisoners were handed over. After visiting von Choltitz again, Nordling and Bender arrived at Oberg's HQ on Boulevard Lannes. Bender entered Oberg's office bearing the convention now signed by General von Choltitz and Major Huhm. Oberg wrote on the convention, "There are no political detainees in Paris, or in the environs, since the order to evacuate them was given on 15 August."

Nordling was unsure what to make of this; he saw prisoners peering from the windows of Fresnes that morning. And what about other prisons: Cherche-Midi, Santé, Villeneuve-Saint-Georges, Saint Denis, La Pitié, Val-de-Grace, and the camps at Compiegne, Drancy and Romainville? Nordling and Bender went swiftly to the Cherche-Midi jail, the mid-nineteenth-century military establishment which replaced the old Abbaye Prison at the junction of the Rue du Cherche-Midi and the Boulevard Raspail. Nordling found the gates shut and locked. When Count de Rohan-Chabot arrived they looked over the wall. The prison was abandoned. "Oberg was right," wrote Nordling. "Was Huhm's convention simply a comedy?"

At Fresnes, however, little had changed since their morning visit. Immediately after seeing the convention, Fresnes' German governor telephoned the Hôtel Meurice to obtain confirmation from General von Choltitz. Choltitz said that it only refered to the sick. But among underfed and demoralised prisoners, Nordling realised that von Choltitz's phrase could be interpreted very widely. The governor co-operated. Rohan-Chabot, who was imprisoned there earlier in the Occupation, savoured the moment. "The roles have changed," he murmured to Nordling. "Now it's us taking charge of things." Hearing the remark, the German governor took it in good humour and went to find the prisoner list. Meanwhile a barrister appeared demanding the release of seven clients who had been acquitted.

"It's no longer me in charge here," said the governor. "Fresnes is now under the orders of Consul General Nordling."

The barrister recognised Nordling from a previous occasion.

"What's this comedy?" the barrister asked. "Have you suddenly become a prison governor?"

Once Nordling explained the situation and authorised the release of the seven acquittals and others besides, the barrister was delighted. Next Nordling ordered the Red Cross flag to be raised over the prison. The women and sick were released first. Ambulances were called to take the sickest to hospitals. The male detainees would have to wait for their release until the following day.[7]

The five hundred dishevelled female prisoners suddenly released had no money for food or to book themselves into modest hotels for the night, forcing Nordling to offer four hundred thousand francs from consulate funds, though he knew the French Red Cross would reimburse him. One woman was too frightened to leave her cell. She was one of twenty-five condemned to death and was convinced she would be taken to the execution yard. When female warders tried to pull her out, she fought them off, only agreeing to leave when an interpreter explained Nordling's convention.[8]

Next on Nordling's list was a trainload of prisoners about to leave the Gare de l'Est. Nordling and Fiévet arrived around 5.30pm and showed the convention to SD and Gestapo officials. Far from finding a repeat of the co-operation experienced at Fresnes, Nordling was told that if he or his companions approached the train they would be shot. Nordling consoled himself with the possibility that the Resistance might stop the train east of Paris, and moved on to the Prison des Tourelles. There the warders were French and co-operated immediately.

The Fort de Romainville at Les Lilas held around sixty women, some quite young, who had the status of hostages. Among them were Madame Krug, a member of the champagne family, and Madame Peyerimhoff. Romainville was guarded by SS Captain Achenbach and a company of Georgians, who understood little German and no French. When Nordling arrived at Romainville's buff brick gatehouse, he found the Georgian guards drunk. When he finally got one of them to fetch Achenbach, Nordling was told they would only obey orders from the SS HQ at Compiègne. For the time being Nordling had to accept defeat. However, he did manage to persuade Achenbach to allow two French Red Cross nurses to enter the fort and care for the sickest prisoners. Noticing the appreciative glances these nurses received from the Georgians, Nordling extracted an undertaking from Achenbach that the nurses would not be "violated".[9]

By early evening Nordling reached Drancy, the wretched transit camp created from unfinished blocks of flats, from which Jews were transported to concentration camps. It was not known as "the antechamber of death" for nothing. Bender drove his car through the gate first. While Nordling and Fiévet waited they noticed a black German staff car leaving the camp carrying the sadistic SS Captain Alois Brunner, a major German player in the Holocaust. Having deported ninety thousand Austrian and Greek Jews to their deaths, Brunner arrived in France where he was directly involved in deporting twenty-five thousand Jews. As one of Himmler's élite, Brunner was recalled and would soon assist in liquidating Slovakia's last Jews. As Brunner passed through the gates, Nordling gained entry. On the face of it, for a warm summer evening, conditions were not too bad. Young Jews were wearing shorts and summer dresses, albeit scruffy. Some inmates sat on grass lawns. But the guards' control was obviously loosening. Although Brunner sent fifty-one Jews to Buchenwald that morning, the rest were released to Nordling. In one fell swoop "the Gentleman of Paris" liberated 1,482 Jews; but it was impracticable for them to leave Drancy without identity cards, money and food, which were organised for the following day.[10]

After Drancy, Nordling's convoy returned briefly to Paris before driving out to Compiègne where the transit camp of Royallieu held twenty-four hundred Jews. Doubtless intending to grease the wheels of Nordling's efforts, the Marquis de Mun had telegraphed the French Red Cross's representatives at Compiègne that the inmates of Royallieu would soon be released. *Messieurs* Grammont and de Laguiche, in their turn, approached the Commandant, SS Haupsturmführer Heinrich Illers, who smugly claimed to know nothing of the convention signed by Major Huhm, and that the last prisoners would soon leave for Germany. Then one of the two Red Cross representatives foolishly suggested that force might be used if Illers did not comply; and if that failed the Resistance could simply stop the train. Furious, Illers telephoned Oberg who scoffed back down the telephone. About that moment, Bender arrived and, being an intelligence officer, began to parley with Illers. Illers accused Bender of treason and threatened to have him summarily executed. Bender angrily replied that he had orders from General von Choltitz, and that it would be Illers himself facing Wehrmacht discipline. Illers' riposte was that both the Gestapo and the *Feldgendarmerie* had orders to arrest Bender. "You won't get far," sneered Illers.[11]

At this point Nordling arrived, accompanied by Erich von Posch-Pastor and the Mayor of Compiègne, delighted to be liberating Royallieu. But Bender said negotiation was pointless, that they should dim their headlights and follow him away from the camp. "I think you'll have to go your own way," Posch-Pastor said quietly to Nordling. "One has to think about security."

Without using headlights, Bender tried to navigate back to Paris by moonlight just as an air-raid began on the *banlieues'* remaining industry. Suddenly they found themselves on the edge of a Luftwaffe airfield, where they halted until the raid ended. Continuing on their way, Count de Rohan-Chabot, who was driving Nordling, fell asleep at the wheel, causing a small collision with a Wehrmacht lorry. Back in Paris, both Bender and Posch-Pastor decided to remain inside Wehrmacht controlled buildings while Oberg remained in the city.[12]

"*LA GRANDE FUITE DES FRITZS*" applied to *collabos* as well, notably Darnand's *Miliciens*. By 1944 Joseph Darnand knew he had made the wrong choice, though he attempted to persuade himself and others that he had acted on principle. He had lost great friends to the Resistance. Nor was he too stupid to recognise that the Resistance was now larger and better equipped than the *Milice* ever was. Informing Pétain that the *Milice* had suffered eighteen hundred killed and wounded, with another eight hundred missing, did not prevent Pétain being disgusted with him. On 10 August Darnand advised all *Miliciens* in the Ile de France to prepare to leave for Nancy, where they would regroup under the Waffen SS. Laval released eighty million francs for expenses, which was supplemented by another sixty million from the Germans (following recommendations from Abetz) which reached *Milice* coffers by 17 August. Minus their dependants, they assembled at the Lycée Saint-Louis. From there, on buses seized from the police by Jean Bassompierre, they left for Nancy.[13]

A fellow traveller now going eastwards was young right-wing journalist Christian de la Mazière, the future lover of Juliette Greco and Dalida, who was interviewed for Marcel Ophuls' documentary film *The Sorrow and the Pity*. Brought up on *Action Française*, throughout his youth La Mazière regarded the Left as a threat to the "Old France" values he held dear. After *la Chute* he was retained by Vichy's hundred thousand man French Army until 1942 before becoming a *collabo* writer on Pierre Clementi's right-wing magazine, *Le Pays Libre*. When D-Day became imminent, Roger Pingeault, another journalist on Clementi's journal advised La Mazière to switch to de Gaulle.

"Wake up, old fellow," Pingeault told him. "Hitler is finished. It's time to give up."

"Have you forgotten the men from all over Europe who are fighting on the Eastern Front?" La Mazière replied.

"Rest assured they'll be quickly forgotten when the war is over," said Pingeault.

And the fact that his girlfriend's outwardly *collabo* mother was also hiding Allied airmen made little difference. Alain Ballot, a *résistant* working on escape lines, told La Mazière, "You've been acting stupidly long enough, now you've got to listen to me." But, sharing Rhett Butler's taste for lost causes, La Mazière reported to the Kriegsmarine building in France's former Navy Ministry on the Place de la Concorde where *Miliciens* and *Francs-Gardes* were assembling. After an interview with Max Knipping, La Mazière received SS induction papers from an office at the Hôtel Majestic. Unlike ordinary *Miliciens*, La Mazière did not travel to Nancy in Bassompierre's buses but in his own smart little car.[14]

Many *collabos* and *Miliciens* departing eastwards honestly believed that Germany's setbacks were only temporary and that they could soon return. The previous week the PPF's Jacques Doriot and Victor Barthelémy had planned a new cabinet over dinner. And on 16 August, dining with Jean Lecan on the Boulevard Saint-Germain, everyone believed the golden years of *collaboration* would continue, until Radio Paris' *collabo* anchorman Jean-Herold Pacquis arrived to inform them that all significant *collabos* were advised to leave France. At once Barthelémy went to the PPF offices on the Rue des Pyramides and went through the PPF accounts; the millions of francs they had gathered from *collabo* businessmen. In lorries seized from Les Halles by pretending to be *résistants*, the PPF left Paris, leaving roads lined with astonished faces.[15]

Other *collabos* were prevented from joining the exodus to Germany by inertia and denial. *Collabo* journalist Robert Brasillach wrote, "They say the Germans will leave today and that the Americans will come. I ate at Solange's bistro, everyone was talking about it. It's idiotic because the Americans still have the Germans right in front of them and the Germans too will have to go somewhere. When I look at Paris I try to take its pulse, not from people's faces, but from the avenues and intersections. What kinds of faces are the houses making tonight? The ones at the corner of the Gobelins don't look like they are expecting anything important to happen."[16]

If Brasillach was living in a fool's paradise, Vichy Jew-baiter Louis Darquier de Pellepoix's conduct that summer was even more extraordinary. An *énergumène* (oddball) who could only have achieved power under a crackpot régime like Vichy, Darquier de Pellepoix and his slavishly loyal Australian wife Myrtle became rich on the proceeds of expropriated Jewish property and selling Aryanisation certificates. This enabled them to live swankily in the Rue du Faubourg-Saint-Honoré's Hôtel Bristol, where he remained undisturbed throughout August while smaller *collabos* were arrested and degraded.[17]

ON THAT SAME DAY, FIELD MARSHAL MODEL took over from von Kluge. With Normandy gone and Allied landings on the Riviera, OKW ordered a general evacuation of France. Model's task was to uphold dicipline and ensure the retreat did not become a rout. Shortly after arriving at Saint-Germain en Laye, Model had a Wehrmacht medical officer shot for drunkenness. At the Hôtel Meurice, Lieutenant Dankwart von Arnim was reprimanded for not wearing a helmet. When Model arrived in von Choltitz's office, announcing that he was replacing von Kluge, von Choltitz, who was unaware of Kluge's suicide, asked if Kluge knew he was being replaced. Model nodded gravely, leaving von Choltitz under the impression that Kluge would be joining others at Plotzensee.[18]

Without indicating his distaste for Hitler's orders, von Choltitz explained the situation in Paris and the measures so far taken. He also showed Model a CPL *affiche* calling Parisians to arms. "But," wrote von Choltitz, "I made no mention to the field marshal of the orders I had received to blow up the bridges. He [Model] had come straight from the Eastern Front; hence he was in a totally different mindset to that which reigned in Paris. Besides, this general, frequently wounded, was so exhausted by the dreadful thirty-six-hour journey that it did not seem the appropriate moment to discuss such complex issues with him. After a frugal dinner in the mess, he departed for his HQ. I did not see him again."[19] An officer like Model would hardly have regarded destroying bridges as too complex, however tired he was.

THE 2e DB HELD ITS TRIANGULAR POSITIONS south of Argentan for four days. But General Gaffey still wanted Leclerc's division to join in an attack northwards. A visit from Jacques de Guillebon resulted in Gaffey agreeing that the 2e DB should not weaken its present positions. If absolutely necessary Leclerc decided only to commit GT Langlade, giving Langlade strict instructions only to take up positions supporting the 90th Infantry Division but not to attack without Leclerc's orders. Leclerc also decided to send his senior US liaison officer, Major Robert Loumiansky, to the 90th Infantry's HQ to explain his viewpoint that it was a bad operation; "Badly prepared, misconceived and badly organised," said Leclerc, smiling at Loumiansky.[20]

Along with deciding which attacks should proceed, the matter of who would command V Corps remained atop Patton's agenda that morning. He needed to fly to Eagletac to see Bradley, but the previous night's bad weather had become quite a storm. It would be noon before Patton could take off. Before leaving, Patton prewarned Hap Gay that if he wanted Gerow to replace Gaffey he would simply radio "Change horses".[21] Bradley had not slept well, concerned that he was over-relying on Ultra, while allowing Patton to advance to the Seine meant there might be insufficient forces at Argentan to close the gap. Leclerc, whom Bradley regarded as undisciplined, said as much to Gaffey.[22] A combination of bad weather and command indecision gave Model a breathing space.

SHORTLY BEFORE NOON, OTTO ABETZ visited Édouard Herriot at the Hôtel de Ville to inform him that Germany's decision to prevent Laval from forming a transitional government was final. Abetz then offered Herriot and his wife the choice between internment in Germany or exile in Switzerland.

"I love Switzerland, the country of freedom," Herriot said indignantly to Abetz. "But I cannot go there due to lack of money. I am poor and I will go with the poor to Germany. Furthermore, if I go to Switzerland I would owe you something, and I don't want to owe you anything. I have been made and will remain your prisoner. But I promise you that you will be cursed by all peoples as a nation without honour that does not keep its word."[23]

Before lunch at the Matignon, Abetz told Laval that he and his ministers would be taken to Belfort in eastern France. Then, with their wives and Count and Countess de Chambrun, they entered the Matignon's dining room for an excellent lunch served by liveried servants.[24]

Rain gave way to brilliant sunshine, and the dining room's windows were open, looking across the beautiful garden. As they ate, Herriot reminisced about his appeasement efforts before the war, using the previous few days' experience to illustrate how pointless appeasement was. He also declared his intention to dissociate himself from both Laval and Vichy, and insisted upon returning to Maréville separately.[25]

Madame Laval normally stood back from her husband's business, but given the finality of these moments, she addressed Abetz. "Mr. Ambassador, this departure, under these conditions, is an outrage. See for yourself the painful situation it puts us all in."

"Please listen to her, Mr. Ambassador, listen; this is France talking to you," Herriot said morosely, after knocking back wine.

"These two men, of course, have not always been in agreement in the past," continued Madame Laval. "That was politics. France was happy then. But in the face of a great danger, now they come together. You can not condone an action that would make it appear as if my husband had instigated unscrupulous tactics resulting in Monsieur Herriot being forced to undergo the same fate as ours under duress."

Countess de Chambrun observed Abetz's expression, almost dying of shame, then offering to make things as comfortable as possible for the Frenchmen. Briefly the talk turned to lightweight anecdotes about the Duke of Windsor and Anthony Eden, but not for long.[26]

Herriot started on Laval. "For you, Laval, it's different. You will be able to explain. But, shake Pétain's hand? Never! He is the enemy of the Republic. I have no more confidence in him than in de Gaulle. They are ambitious. I wanted them kept apart from one another, that was why I came to Paris. They brought me by force. I can't do anything here other than submit."

Outside, unknown to the diners, SS troops had surrounded the Matignon. As the awkward luncheon ended, Laval and Herriot morosely congratulated themselves for having tried.

THAT PARIS SHOULD SURVIVE UNDAMAGED was Pierre Taittinger's most abiding concern as he presented himself at the Hôtel Meurice about the same time that Laval ate his final lunch at the Matignon. Although presumably, like most traditional German officers, General von Choltitz was well educated, Taittinger had with him the Hôtel de Ville interpreter, Madame Fontenille, to ensure he was understood.

Taittinger was sad to see the Meurice's foyer looking so shabby compared to the 1930s when he entertained the Spanish Ambassador there. Feeling as though he had the fate of Paris on his shoulders, visibly nervous, Taittinger entered von Choltitz's office. Von Choltitz sat in the centre of what would previously have been an important first floor bedroom, behind a large, flat-topped, ormolu-mounted bureau. On his right sat Doktor Eckelmann, while on his left stood various other officers, including Major von Gunther, whom Taittinger already knew. The windows were open to the balcony and a view of the Tuileries gardens on the far side of the Rue de Rivoli.

Von Choltitz began by reiterating to Taittinger in a carefully modulated tone the uncompromising content of the announcement that appeared in the press that morning, "... obliged to respect the

Wehrmacht which controls Paris," came the general's words, now in Madame Fontenille's French. "I have to tell you that I have decided to apply collective sanctions [which implied the shooting of hostages] for any acts committed against the representatives of the German Army."

Von Choltitz then asked an ADC to lay an enormous multi-panelled, broadsheet map over the bureau.

"If there are shootings," explained von Choltitz. "The reaction will be immediate in coming. My position is clear. Look, come and see for yourself. Imagine there's a shot at one of my soldiers from a building, situated for example on the uneven numbered side of the Rue de l'Opéra, between the Rue Gomboust and the Rue des Pyramides. I would burn down all these buildings and shoot everyone who lives there." The general glared at Taittinger as his fingers drummed purposefully on the map. "I have available to me twenty-two thousand troops, of which some are Waffen SS, a hundred heavy tanks and ninety pieces of artillery."

As Madame Fontenille finished repeating back von Choltitz's words, Taittinger, chilled to his spine, was trying not to choke. Von Choltitz's staff stood utterly motionless. For a moment there was silence, broken only when von Choltitz rescrewed his monocle into his eye socket and retook his chair.

"If it should happen that there are more serious actions than an isolated sniper shot," elaborated von Choltitz, toying with a pencil, "I will enlarge the punishment zone. In the event of an uprising or a riot, I will call in the Luftwaffe and suppress the area with incendiary bombs. You see, it's simple."

As Taittinger's face whitened, von Choltitz rose from his bureau again and took a few steps towards him.

"You are the representative of this capital city," said von Choltitz, looking into Taittinger's moistening eyes. "You have the authority. Use it. If the population won't move, I won't move them and we will both see how things turn out without too much misery." Von Choltitz turned to the map and made a crayon line along the bank of the Seine. "You are an officer, Monsieur Taittinger, and you can not be insensible to the security measures that I have to take regarding the troops I am responsible for. I am speaking to you as a soldier, do you understand?" Then muttering, "The bridges, the power stations, the railways ..."

After the blasé way von Choltitz handled the sapper officer sent to blow the Seine bridges, it may be that he was testing Taittinger's reaction. But from Taittinger's viewpoint, von Choltitz seemed to have already decided what he was going to do. "And, what then?" thought Taittinger, his imagination racing. With whole blocks wrecked, there would be broken water mains. Communications would break down even more than they had already. Parisians would not just be hungry but starving. They would try to drink any water they could find, which would then set off a cholera outbreak. And all this would happen just as the war in France was coming to an end. How could Germany gain from such a thing? What on earth was the point?

"In the matter of food supplies," said von Choltitz, "I can make things easier for you. I will help you, as has Doktor Eckelmann already on several occasions, busying ourselves with your transport problems and lending you, if it helps, some Wehrmacht lorries."

Taittinger felt the interview drawing to a close and his chance to plead for Paris slipping away. If he spoke frankly to the German, might he make things worse? Or could he make a difference? Clearing his throat, he was determined to have his say.

"We have at the present time," began Taittinger, "in the Paris region, half a million nervous and worried people. That's three hundred and fifty thousand in the districts and a hundred and fifty thousand in the city itself, who are waiting for nothing else but an uprising. If a fire breaks out somewhere in Paris, or there is gunfire, does it therefore follow automatically that the German Army will inflict a 'Paris Vespers', to rival the Sicilian Vespers in the history books? It's possible, General, even certain. And every German soldier would be marked down and killed as soon as the opportunity presented itself to a revolutionary or patriot, of which this city has plenty. Do you really want to run such an enormous risk, which could so easily become inevitable?"

This time it was von Choltitz who looked uncomfortable as Taittinger painted a tableau of what happened during the Paris Commune, including the final bloody showdown among the tombstones of Père Lachaise. "So," continued Taittinger, "in the purely military sense, if it turned out that there was a furious street fight in the capital, a real struggle between two bodies of men, then one could only persevere in the way that you suggest. If, on the other hand, one wanted to avoid such extreme situations, prevent needless killings and criminal destruction, then one should retain one's calm and *sang-froid*, and that goes for your side as well as ours."

Taittinger claims to have told von Choltitz at this stage that Parisians were valuable as historic witnesses. "My country," he continued, "due to the fact of this war and occupation, has suffered a lot, in its spirit and in its heart. If you want a flood of hate to worsen the river of tears and blood that already separates our two countries, go ahead. On the other hand, if you wish to prepare for better times, allow Paris to remember the better man inside you."

Von Choltitz's expression became less dour as Taittinger reminded him of the thousands of children, elderly and refugees in Paris, before expressing his love of beautiful architecture irrespective of nationality. "For my part," said Taittinger, "I felt it deeply that Westminster Cathedral[27] was savagely bombarded, and I deplored that Cologne Cathedral should have been engulfed by flames. Paris is one of those rare great cities in Europe that remains intact. You should help save it."

Von Choltitz approached the balcony and surveyed the summer afternoon scene of young families enjoying the Tuileries gardens. "I like the view from this window, watching the world go by."

At this point in his memoirs Taittinger remarks on the mystery of the German character, on the one hand intelligent and romantic, yet also the incarnation of barbarism, destroying without mercy. Suddenly von Choltitz asked a surprise question.

"How would you get on with General de Gaulle? What would he do with you?"

To this Taittinger says he replied that saving Paris was his sole aim, and for that purpose he needed General von Choltitz more than General de Gaulle.

"Well, the Allies," said von Choltitz, "are prepared to keep existing authorities in place, but only where there aren't any 'Free French'. That lot fully intend to take their places as soon as possible."

Next von Choltitz asked Taittinger for his thoughts on Amedée Bussière and the striking Paris police.

"I expect that the *Gardiens de la Paix* are hampered by the means left at their disposal, and that Amedée Bussière, like a good Frenchman, is doing what he can to prevent the worst," Taittinger assured von Choltitz.

Taittinger explained the difficulties of keeping Paris fed during the Occupation, emphasising that small children needed milk every day, piling on emotive issues in the expectation that his words, helped by the view of the Tuileries gardens, would soften von Choltitz.

"You see," said Taittinger, giving the speech of his life, translated in phrases by Madame Fontenille, "generals are rarely given the power to build, so much more often it is to destroy. Supposing you had, just once at the tip of your fingers, the power of God allowing you to preserve and protect—or to destroy—all of this. Imagine that one day, because I reckon the dice are already thrown, and the war is ending anyway, you came back to the Hôtel Meurice as a tourist, and that you came once again to this balcony. You look out at Perraud's colonade on the left, with our magnificent Louvre Palace; on the right the Palais de Gabriel and our Place de la Concorde and between these monuments so many houses full of history. See above all their witness to our joys, our sufferings and our anger, and your power to be able to say, 'It was me, General von Choltitz who could have, for one day, destroyed all this, but I protected it as a gift to humanity.' There, General, isn't that worth the glory of a conqueror? To preserve what centuries of civilisation and art have built, isn't that more, isn't that nobility?"

Seeing von Choltitz becoming quite emotional as he listened to Madame Fontenille's German translation of his words, Taittinger believed he was gaining ground.

"There is one thing that is of utmost importance to me," replied von Choltitz. "That is what happens, regardless of attacks, to five places that I have to hold militarily—my command post at the Hôtel Meurice, the Avenue Foch, the Place de l'Opéra, the Palais du Luxembourg and the barracks in the Place de la République. Otherwise I am prepared to shut my eyes to individual acts, I say *individual* and I will rely on the good sense of the Parisian population."

Taittinger realised that he had won an enormous concession. However, this was not enough. Even limited damage could trigger problems with food distribution; broken drains might cause epidemics. At last von Choltitz agreed that there would be no destruction or shooting of hostages, and he ratified these undertakings through his staff. He was prepared to shut his eyes to the settling of accounts among the French but the five places held by his troops were off limits.

Finally Taittinger pleaded that von Choltitz avoid violence, saying that it was entirely in his hands, which was not true.

"*Sehr schön*," replied von Choltitz. Returning behind his desk, he removed his monocle and briefly closed his eyes. After a short silence that seemed to last a century, he said, "You are a good ambassador for Paris, Monsieur Taittinger. You do your duty very well. I do my duty as a German general. In those areas where I am able, I will respond to your appeal where it concerns the historic fabric of Paris and the hostages. We will arrange to live with each other as well as we can for the last few days that we are together. We are going to evacuate Paris anyway. In a few days there will only be three or four thousand men remaining in place until the arrival of the Allies."

Taittinger sensed victory. Von Choltitz smiled sadly. Catching sight of a clock, Taittinger realised that they had been speaking for two whole hours. An hour later von Choltitz's undertakings were backed by written confirmation. He had won. How was it, he wondered, that this German general could feel compassion for Paris while so many other cities, towns and villages across Europe were obliterated? Had it only been his own eloquence? Or had the charm of Paris weaved its magic? Taittinger left the Hôtel Meurice radiant with joy. Looking at his fellow Parisians, he wondered if they knew what he had just done for them. And von Choltitz—had he done it for them or for his own soul? He feared for von Choltitz's family. Later that evening the German Ambassador, Otto Abetz, telephoned Taittinger to confirm General von Choltitz's decision.[28]

AFTER LAVAL'S LUNCH GUESTS LEFT THE MATIGNON, his family thronged around him. Madame Laval promised to accompany him to Belfort, though obviously this was just a stop on the way to Germany. His daughter, Josée de Chambrun, offered to accompany them, along with her husband, but one of Laval's withering looks squelched this idea. "*Alors,*" she said. "I'll stay in Paris."

Countess Clara de Chambrun, who visited despite the SS cordon, thought Madame Laval seemed remarkably self-possessed in the circumstances. They knew there would be Resistance retribution when the opportunity arose; yet Madame Laval still dreamt of fleeing to *la France Profonde* to live a simple peasant life unrecognised by anyone. Instinctively the older countess knew she would never see Laval again.[29]

After emptying his bureau by candlelight, Laval took his last bath in the superb marble tub. Then he dressed in his usual white shirt and white tie to receive the farewells of those Vichy minsters still in Paris: Bichelonne, Bonnard and Gabolde. At 9pm, Abetz returned to confirm that his government insisted that all of Laval's cabinet depart for Belfort, under force if necessary.[30]

Finally Laval left orders for René Bouffet and Amedée Bussière to keep Paris in good order ready to receive the Allies. When Pierre Taittinger arrived at 10pm, Laval asked him to withdraw the guards and liberate any political prisoners held in prisons under French authority: the Santé, La Roquette and Les Tournelles. Bussière immediately put a call through to Hennequin. In the courtyard outside Abetz muttered defiantly to Taittinger, "Don't rejoice too soon or too quickly. In three months we'll be back in Paris. It's impossible for us to lose this war. We've discovered unbeatable weapons, understand; unbeatable. The Führer hesitates to use them in case it's the beginning of the end of the world."[31]

Shortly afterwards, with SS watching, cane in hand, Laval walked down the steps of the Matignon saying his *adieux* to those who had served him. Turning to Lieutenant Henri Chevalier, commanding the *Groupe Spécial de Protection*, who had Resistance connections, Laval said quietly, "You are free. I know what you're going to do and I envy you." After seating himself in the black ministerial Hotchkiss, Laval saw Josée breaking down. Suddenly Laval was out of the car. "*Toi, encore une fois*," he said, embracing his daughter one last time before returning to the Hotchkiss. The SS opened the high, arched gates and Laval departed into darkness and the road eastwards.[32]

Back at the Hôtel de Ville, as Herriot prepared for his journey, Count de Chambrun arrived bringing books and cigars. Then, with René Bouffet's agreement, Chambrun offered to put Édouard and Madame Herriot in touch with the Army Resistance Organisation so that they could escape via the Hôtel de Ville's subterranean passages to an apartment owned by American friends of his. Knowing that dignified suffering was more his style, Herriot told Chambrun, "I must follow my fate." That evening the Germans returned him to Maréville.[33]

SEEING THE GERMANS BEGINNING TO LEAVE gave new impetus to *résistants* planning insurrection. Laval's final acts of political chicanery merely aroused their contempt, and seeing widespread strikes bring Paris to her knees with public workers gathering on the Place Hôtel de la Ville screaming "Bread!" and singing the *Marseillaise*, they saw their opportunities ripening. In such an atmosphere rebellious incidents proliferated; a *Tricolore* appeared over the *mairie* at Saint-Mandé, while, on the corner of the Rue Saint-Denis and the Rue de la Lune, a café was set alight along with a disused tyre shop.[34]

Chaired by Alexandre Parodi, the Delegation and COMAC debriefed Chaban-Delmas following his return from London. General

Hary, whose role was to assume command of all police, security and fire services, was concerned that COMAC intended the insurrection to begin as soon as possible, and Chaban-Delmas' advice, that the Paris FFI (P1) should avoid acting prematurely, was exactly what Hary wanted to hear. Furthermore, when Chaban-Delmas met General Gaffey, then Patton's deputy, on 13 August near Le Mans, before bicycling to Paris, Gaffey told him the Allies would not reach Paris for another fortnight. COMAC wanted their uprising, while the GPRF's representatives advised them to wait.[35]

Although Jean de Vogüé now inclined to Chaban's viewpoint, COMAC's other two leaders protested: "If you wait too long you will let the opportunity pass us by."

"If you go too soon you will compromise everyone and expose the city's population to the risk of a massacre," said the Delegation.

Furthermore the number of available weapons had barely improved since July. Rol-Tanguy liked to think they had over two thousand three hundred armed men out of twenty thousand willing *résistants,* while Colonel Lizé, the chief of the FFI's Seine Department, put the figure more conservatively at no more than two thousand, which meant a weapon for one man in ten. Arming the rest required enough weapons for an infantry division; which could hardly be wrested from the enemy.[36]

"The military delegates who pretend to command Paris in the name of Koenig's petulant staff in London know that we only have four heavy machinguns," FTP leader Charles Tillon said angrily. "Of the seventy-seven thousand appalling little sub-machinguns, those cheaply produced Stens, sent by SOE in London, only a hundred and fourteen have reached us here."[37]

Commandant Dufresne (Raymond Massiet), representing the Department of the Seine, gave a more detailed resumé of the weapons situation. Of the four heavy machine-guns, one was an old Hotchkiss with limited ammunition. Of the so-called machine-guns, around twenty were either British Brens or the equivalent French MAT 29. There were only 562 rifles, of which many were only hunting calibres, and a lot of pistols.[38] This meant that the only armed force in Paris of any size was the Police. Even then, initiating an insurrection without the Allies being considerably closer would be a grave error. Parodi preached caution.[39]

When COMAC, the CPL and CNR reconvened elsewhere for further discussions, André Tollet offered the text of a proposed *affiche* calling Parisians to arms, but Leo Hamon insisted this was premature without more weapons. Colonel Ély, representing Parodi, continued to recommend prudence. COMAC, however, remained committed to an armed insurrection aimed at hampering the Wehrmacht's retreat. While Parodi continued to advise prudence, Georges Bidault recognised that COMAC could not be held back and that it would be impossible to separate the rest of the Resistance—or Parisians generally—from these hotheads if they went ahead.[40]

18 August 1944

ON THE FOLLOWING MORNING, COMAC, THE CPL AND CNR met again in a modest apartment in Vanves. For the FTP and communists, it was imperative to launch an insurrection as soon as possible. Much of the Parisian Left consisted of the city's ancillary and industrial workers. For several days they had witnessed the Germans departing with everything they could carry. Supposing that German looting became demolition not only of fine buildings but water and sewage works, gas and electricity stations, meant that then, as always, the working class would suffer most. If the Germans were forced to leave Paris "*avec l'épée dans les reins*"—"with the sword at their kidneys"—they would have fewer opportunities to demolish the place. In Rol-Tanguy's view, lack of weapons was insufficient reason for failing to act; Allied weapons supply should have been more generous. He had been asking them for long enough.[41]

"The time has come to launch the insurrection," said Rol-Tanguy. "If you won't join us, we'll go it alone."

"But what about weapons?" came the predictable question from Leo Hamon, who remained a moderating influence.

"We've got six hundred," replied Rol-Tanguy, smiling slightly.

"That seems to me a bit weak for launching any word of an order for insurrection," replied Hamon.[42]

Even then André Tollet thought Rol-Tanguy overestimated how many weapons he had. "He wasn't even sure himself," Tollet later told Francis Crémieux.

"Weapons? One would simply have to find them. One could take them from the enemy; once the start-time for the insurrection was decided, the enemy would be on his back foot."[43]

Rol-Tanguy had already drafted and printed a general mobilisation order, ready to paste up around Paris. Other *affiches*, produced by the CGT and CFTC, calling for a general strike, were also appearing. According to André Tollet, paralysing industrial action was more what the CPL had in mind than an armed insurrection. Pierre Bourget writes that armed insurrection was never agreed with the CPL. So had the "extremists" among the Resistance forced the hand of others?[44]

Long regarded as the hot-head responsible for the Paris insurrection, Henri Rol-Tanguy is often quoted as saying, "Paris is worth two or three hundred thousand dead!" as though he would gladly have provoked a blood-bath. After the war, however, Rol-Tanguy protested vehemently that he never said such a thing.* His biographer Roger Bourderon emphasises that Rol-Tanguy, who maintained connections to both the Americans and Resistance groups elsewhere, fully understood the risks they might be running and did his best to mitigate them. Two days previously Lieutenant Mallet, an FFI officer from Brittany, arrived at Rol-Tanguy's Malakoff hideout to establish a link with Paris. Such initiatives were not unusual even among left-wing *résistants*.[45] That same day, Rol-Tanguy ordered

---

* Rol-Tanguy told Francis Crémieux that this story originated with the book *Is Paris Burning?* by Larry Collins and Dominique Lapierre, which came out in the 1960s.

Commandant de Varreux (*nom de guerre*: Brécy) to reach the Allied lines. As an FFI intelligence officer, de Varreux was well qualified to update the Americans on events in Paris and how they could support the insurrection when it began. Tragically Brécy never reached the Allies; nearing Étampes his vehicle was shot up by an Allied aircraft. Unfortunately Rol-Tanguy and his staff did not find out for some time. Brécy took several hours to die but, before he did, he told some *résistants* to send a message to London requesting that a radio liaison team be sent to Paris.[46] Hence Rol-Tanguy's decision-making before unleashing the insurrection was perhaps more responsible than has previously been recognised.

Rol-Tanguy's lair in Malakoff was inadequate for the forthcoming days of action, so new premises were found at 66 Rue de Meaux in the 19th Arrondissement, an elegant street dominated by the usual Parisian seven-storey terrace buildings comprising apartments over shops and businesses. It was not quite central but the communications were good enough. Other resistance offices were also concealed there.[47]

DE GAULLE'S ORDER FOR INSURRECTION in all large cities had reached the Delegation. So too had Charles Luizet, who arrived in Paris the previous day. A dark, bespectacled man in his early forties, Luizet's role was to replace Amedée Bussière as Prefect of Police. Luizet had been at Saint-Cyr with Leclerc but subsequently turned towards the diplomatic and admininstrative side of soldiering, finding himself an attaché in Tangier when France fell in 1940. Hit by the same "gut refusal" as other early Free Frenchmen, Luizet immediately placed himself unconditionally at de Gaulle's disposal. His first instructions were to remain at his post to assure liaison with Frenchmen arriving as refugees in French North Africa. Next he created an intelligence *réseau* running agents on General Charles Nogues' staff, thereby providing the London French with useful intelligence.[48] After the Torch landings Luizet became de Gaulle's new Prefect of the Tiaret region. Next, Luizet's burgeoning track record ensured his appointment as Prefect to newly liberated Corsica.[49]

Luizet took off from Croydon on 2 August expecting to land at a secret airstrip in the Ain. But though the RAF pilot searched for landing lights, none were visible, so the flight continued to Corsica while a possible betrayal of the Ain Maquis was investigated. From Corsica, Luizet went to Algiers, then Italy. Hence Luizet only arrived in Paris on 17 August, sharing a lorry with Francis-Louis Closon, de Gaulle's new Regional Commissioner for the North. While being shaved in a barber's shop, Luizet learnt that the police were on strike. Meeting Parodi, Luizet aired de Gaulle's concerns that either Laval's machinations might outwit the Resistance or the FTP and COMAC might frustrate the GPRF's efforts to reinstate the Republic. Luizet and Parodi agreed that, until Leclerc arrived in Paris, they should secure as many government buildings as possible. In the meantime a split in the Resistance had to be avoided. Concerns that the FTP and COMAC might act prematurely were superseded now that de Gaulle had given his own insurrection orders; they could not be held back much longer.[50]

Jacques Chaban-Delmas sent a message to General Koenig in London. "In Paris all the preparatory conditions for insurrection exist. Local incidents are on the rise, whether they are provoked by the enemy or even by impatient Resistance groups who've had enough of their troubles along with bloody reprisals on which the Germans seem able to decide and carry out. The disappearance of the Police due to their strike can only facilitate the unleashing of the insurrection. In consequence, if the military situation permits, it is necessary that you should intervene with the Allies to demand the rapid occupation of Paris. If this is impossible it is urgent in the first place to warn us by cable so that we can act accordingly; in the second place to warn the population officially via the BBC in order to avoid another Warsaw. *Quartus* (Parodi) and *Algebre* (General Ély) are in agreement with me on all these points. Respects. Signed *Arc* (Chaban-Delmas)."[51]

At de Gaulle's request Allied aircraft dropped leaflets over Paris. Entitled *Tous les Fronts* (All Fronts), the first page read, "Here is the news. The French authorities in Algiers communicate to the French population the following instructions: In Brittany all Frenchmen must co-operate with the FFI in destroying any enemy groups and isolated garrisons who try to rejoin those ports still in enemy hands or to disengage towards the east. Government employees should take their orders from those authorities trusted by the Resistance and who are the representatives of the Provisional Government of the French Republic. Special instructions will be given for Paris and the Paris area. Join the FFI, follow the advice of their officers: the national uprising is the prelude to the Liberation."

On the second page of this leaflet there was a photograph captioned "*Un vrai de vrai—Leclerc!*" ("The real thing—Leclerc!"), showing the 2e DB commander with his men, "who are actually fighting west of the Seine".[52]

THAT AFTERNOON, WHILE BEING DRIVEN along the Rue le Sueur past that flamboyant cul de sac, the Place Avenue du Bois, Nordling saw SS armoured cars escorting a smart open topped coupé in which sat Karl Oberg accompanied by a buxom German woman whom Nordling assumed was his cook. The car was loaded with provisions and two SS rode shotgun. Nordling found it a repulsive spectacle.[53]

Nordling spent those last twenty-four hours before the Insurrection negotiating with prison directors. Soon Fresnes' only inmates were German soldiers on disciplinary charges. At Romainville, however, things remained problematic; the uncooperative Major Achenbach saying he could not obey General von Choltitz since he was linked to 20 July. Although this accusation was probably based on SS gossip, it was also true.[54]

In all, however, 3,363 prisoners had been released. Of these, 963 were released by Amédée Bussière on orders from Laval shortly before he left the Matignon. The rest owed their freedom to Raoul Nordling and the supporting efforts of Swiss Consul René Naville. To these totals must be added eight hundred and fifty inmates of a prison train halted at Péronne whose commander accepted the Nordling-Huhm convention without demur. Many of these *résistants* would fight again in the coming days.[55]

But Nordling had not given up on Romainville. Early on 19 August von Choltitz sent staff Colonel Heigen to confront Achenbach. Heigen's authority immediately secured Nordling's entry to the main compound where the prisoners seemed reasonably healthy. Once again, however, the Georgian SS guards appeared drunk and unpredictable, exacerbating Nordling's concern for the women and children. Like many Hôtel Meurice staff, Heigen was no Nazi and sufficiently unimpressed by Achenbach and his Georgians to threaten them with transfer to the Eastern Front. Heigen also reminded Achenbach that, following Oberg's departure, he came under General von Choltitz's authority. Even then Achenbach insisted on seeing an order signed by Choltitz himself. Nordling and Heigen immediately visited the Hôtel Meurice where von Choltitz signed the order they needed. They returned to Romainville followed by ambulances. The Georgians, clearly nettled by Heigen's threat, fired warning shots, but Nordling was undeterred and soon controlled the jail. But he had less luck at the Hôpital de Saint-Denis where SS guards warned him off while herding their prisoners to a railway siding. Himmler had personally ordered the train's departure. Many of these prisoners died *en route* to Germany, but Nordling had done all he could. He would soon play his greatest role yet.[56]

Occupied Paris

Pierre Taittinger, Head of the Paris Municipal Council in which he represented the exclusive Vendôme district. Like Boineburg-Lengsfeld, Abetz and Nordling, Taittinger pleaded fulsomely with von Choltitz not to destroy the city he loved but was, nevertheless, arrested as a collaborator and barred from public life after the war. (Photo: *Roger-Viollet/ The Image Works.*)

Otto Abetz, Nazi Ambassador to Occupied France. An avowed Francophile married to a French woman, also an art thief and despoiler of his wife's country. When Henriot was killed, Abetz negotiated Georges Mandel's return to France, which weighed against Abetz at his postwar trial. He advised von Choltitz against destroying Paris and von Choltitz's statement helped save Abetz from the death penalty. (Photo: *Roger-Viollet/The Image Works.*)

Vichy Prime Minister Pierre Laval thought collaboration was the most realistic way to mitigate Nazi demands upon his defeated country, even saying he hoped Germany would defeat the Soviet Union. Yet, when Mandel was murdered, Laval cried, "I cannot cover up these horrors any longer." His attempts to form an interim government were scuppered by the Germans and he was forcibly taken into custody on 17 August. Departing from the Matignon, knowing his guards would switch to de Gaulle, Laval said, "I envy you." De Gaulle, however, would never forgive Laval's weathercock politics and he died a traitor's death in late 1945. (Photo: *Roger-Viollet/The Image Works.*)

Vichy propaganda minister Philippe Henriot hectored many young Frenchmen into joining the anti-resistance *Milice* from 1943 onwards. When he was assassinated at his Rue Solferino apartment on 28 June posters appeared saying, "He told the truth—They killed him." To de Gaulle's disgust Henriot was given a state funeral in Notre Dame. (Photo: *Roger-Viollet/The Image Works.*)

In vengeance for Henriot, French politician Georges Mandel was returned to France from Buchenwald during early July 1944 simply so the *Milice* could murder him. Mandel's assassin, *Milicien* Jean Mansuy, was captured at the Liberation posing as a *résistant*. (Photo: *Roger-Viollet/The Image Works.*)

Georges Bidault who replaced Jean Moulin. Bidault greeted Dronne, Granell and Michard to the Hotel de Ville on the evening of 24 August with the words, "*Bien joué.*"—"Well played." (Photo: *Memorial du Maréchal Leclerc et de la Libération de Paris, Musée Jean Moulin, Ville de Paris.*)

Liberators

Captain Alain de Boissieu. Sent by Leclerc to see de Gaulle in December 1943 to ascertain that Leclerc's division would be chosen to join in the Normandy campaign, Boissieu returned with a letter from de Gaulle appointing Leclerc "interim" military governor of Paris, signifying that Leclerc's division was chosen to liberate the French capital and re-establish the French state. (Photo: *Memorial du Maréchal Leclerc et de la Libération de Paris, Musée Jean Moulin, Ville de Paris.*)

Colonel—later General—Pierre Billotte. After escaping from German captivity via Russia, Billotte served as de Gaulle's ADC from 1942 to 1944 when he replaced Colonel Malaguti as Leclerc's third battle-group commander. Billotte led the 2e DB's southern advance into the city which took the liberation. After the war Billotte befriended General von Choltitz. (Photo: *Memorial du Maréchal Leclerc et de la Libération de Paris, Musée Jean Moulin, Ville de Paris.*)

A former WW1 fighter pilot and cavalry officer, Colonel Paul de Langlade brought enough personnel into Leclerc's 2e DB to form two tank regiments, including valuable officers like André Gribius. Langlade's battlegroup helped close the Falaise Gap and liberated western Paris. (Photo: *Memorial du Maréchal Leclerc et de la Libération de Paris, Musée Jean Moulin, Ville de Paris.*)

Cavalry to the rescue. Shermans of 2 Squadron, 12 *Régiment des Chasseurs d'Afrique* assemble at Vesly after disembarking at Utah Beach on 1 August 1944. (Photo: *akg-images/The Image Works.*)

The Memorial to the 2e DB's fallen at Alençon during 9–11 August 1944. (Photo: *John Bate-Williams.*)

Résistants

De Gaulle's military delegate to the Resistance in northern France, Jacques Chaban-Delmas was among the French Army's youngest brigadier generals. Unobtrusive, highly intelligent and a fast runner, Chaban-Delmas took easily to the discipline required for clandestine life. (Photo: *Memorial du Maréchal Leclerc et de la Libération de Paris, Musée Jean Moulin, Ville de Paris.*)

The FTP's Henri Rol-Tanguy was a disciplined Left-winger. Wrongfully accused of saying that Paris was worth 200,000 dead, Rol-Tanguy sent two envoys to the Allies and by the time Leclerc's men arrived Rol-Tanguy's men had confined the German garrison to a few central strongpoints. Here he wears the uniform of an infantry colonel in Billotte's 10th (Paris) Division during the last months of the war. (Photo: *Memorial du Maréchal Leclerc et de la Libération de Paris, Musée Jean Moulin, Ville de Paris.*)

"The Gentleman of Paris,"—Swedish Consul General Raoul Nordling who saved over two thousand *résistants* from transportation to Germany during the last days of the Occupation and pleaded successfully with General von Choltitz for a truce to save both lives and heritage sites like Notre Dame and the Sainte-Chapelle. He also helped the 2e DB negotiate the last hours of fighting in Paris. (Photo: *Roger-Viollet/The Image Works*.)

The degradation of a *boulevardier*, Sacha Guitry interrogated by *Comité Parisien de la Libération* officials following his arrest as a *collabo*. In fact he had not collaborated with the Nazis at all but, since his Théatre Madeleine was frequented by off-duty German officers, Guitry *looked* like a *collabo*. After a few deeply unpleasant months in prison, including mock executions, Guitry was released without charge. (Photo: *Henri Cartier-Bresson, Magnum Agency*.)

Famous among the expats who lived in Paris during the interwar years, war correspondent and novelist Ernest Hemingway loved the city as much as any Frenchman. Appointing himself a *de facto* resistance leader, Hemingway gathered useful information on German positions between Rambouillet and Paris. But, following a personality clash with General Leclerc, Hemingway followed Langlade's men into the city from the west, departing from the Champs Élysées to call on Picasso and Sylvia Beach before liberating the Ritz. (Photo: *akg-images/The Image Works.*)

Massu and his driver Georges Hipp. Massu followed Leclerc for seven years beginning in Africa. He was disappointed when Langlade prevented him from advancing beyond the Pont de Sevres on the night of 24 August. Entry into central Paris was reserved for Pierre Billotte's battle group. (Photo: *Memorial du Maréchal Leclerc et de la Libération de Paris, Musée Jean Moulin, Ville de Paris.*)

While Paris suffered little devastation compared to other cities during World War 2, there was plenty of repair work after the Liberation. Here Cartier-Bresson records damage to a mansard room at the Quai d'Orsay, where small arms fire smashed through slates, battens and inner walls to evict its German defenders. (Photo: *Henri Cartier-Bresson, Magnum Agency.*)

Après l'Ondée. The Place de la Concorde, Autumn 1944. The leaves have fallen, the ground is wet. While lanterns shimmer like tiny pearls, only torn-up cobbles testify to the summer's excitement. The lights are back on in the City of Light. (Photo: *Henri Cartier-Bresson, Magnum Agency.*)

Chapter 5

Marianne Rises, 18–21 August

18 August 1944 (continued …)

AT 11PM, ON A NIGHT AS DARK AS INK, Paul de Langlade arrived at Leclerc's CP at Fleuré. Gaffey's attack, Gribius told him, was on again, albeit in a revised form. Langlade's men would act as flank guard for US 90th Infantry Division's push towards Chambois, Sainte-Eugénie and Aubry-en-Exmès. GT Langlade would advance towards Omméel east of Chambois, and prevent German traffic from using the D13 and D16 highways to reach Rouen's Seine crossings.

"What about Paris?" asked Langlade.

"It's very much on the General's mind," replied Gribius.

Before Langlade visited the US 90th ID, Gribius warned him against any "real intervention" before receiving "particularly important instructions". Arriving at the 90th's CP in pitch dark, Langlade bumped into General Leclerc who arrived simultaneously, accompanied by Commandant Weil.

"We'll meet the 90th Infantry's CO together," said Leclerc, placing his hand on Langlade's shoulder. "You will listen to their orders. You will simply say, 'I have understood'—you won't ask for any explanations and you leave. Then wait for me at your Jeep."

The plan had changed, insofar as GT Langlade was now to advance on Omméel, Mont Omméel and then Trun. Langlade listened attentively and said the words Leclerc told him.

"I have understood," followed by a cheery "Good-bye Sir."

Outside Leclerc spoke directly into Langlade's ear.

"Now listen," began Leclerc. "We've got to set off for Paris in forty-eight hours or we're never going to get there. I am going to go to Bradley to get this decision stopped. When I have that, we're going to turn about and go like hell for Paris. It is therefore essential that you do not get yourself involved in a scrap that you can't pull out of, certainly not one causing losses. I need everyone. Do what you would do anyway, but with the *caveat* that you come back to me as soon as I call you and you don't incur losses. Understand?"

"*Oui, mon Général,*" replied Langlade.

"*Alors, au revoir,*" said Leclerc before disappearing into the night.

At 2am on 19 August, at his Médavy CP, Langlade explained Leclerc's thinking to Massu and Minjonnet, telling them to start straight away. By dawn they had bypassed the Forêt de Petite Gouffern and taken positions at Omméel, overlooking the Dives.[1]

The US 90th ID's artillery destroyed designated objectives and targets of opportunity on the roads north and south of the Dives even as General Maczek's 1st Polish Armoured Division, operating with Canadian First Army, reached the northern side of Chambois. At Exmès, from his new CP on an abrupt hill with dominating views, Langlade watched Minjonnet's men patrol into the pocket, which pivoted between GT Langlade's position and Polish positions a few kilometres north, while the Germans guarded the roads with anti-tank guns and Panther tanks.[2]

Maczek's position on Mont Ormel was almost a mini Monte Cassino, giving excellent fields of fire over the Dives valley. However, the Poles were not blocking an advancing army, but a retreating one desperately escaping a charnel house. For two days Maczek's division fought grimly to confirm the Germans' encirclement, getting badly chewed up; exactly what Leclerc wanted to avoid.

IN PARIS, WHILE LECLERC BRIEFED LANGLADE, the Resistance meeting chaired by Alexandre Parodi on the Rue de Grenelle ended.

As the delegates surreptitiously departed, a *Tricolore* was fluttering above a nearby police station.[3]

On hearing from Parodi that there would be a big meeting to decide the Insurrection's timetable, Yves Bayet decided the police should take the initiative and Charles Luizet and Henri Rol-Tanguy should co-operate. Since both men were uncontactable except by bicycle, Bayet decided to mobilise the police resistance groups himself, sending written orders to Sergeant Armand Fournet, head of *Honneur de la Police*, to assemble as many policemen as possible outside the Préfecture at 7am the following morning.[4]

To deliver Bayet's messages before curfew, Bayet's young liaison agent, Suzanne, pedalled her old bicycle as fast as she could. Then a slow puncture released her front tyre's last cubic centimetres of air. As she angrily pumped away at the roadside, a BMW halted beside her and, in excellent French, a Wehrmacht officer offered help. After both failed to coax any air into the perished tyre, the German offered her a lift, dropping her near the café where she had to deliver Yves Bayet's messages.[5]

At the Jardin des Plantes Sergeant Armand Fournet met the other two members of the *Comité de Libération de la Police*. While their *collabo* seniors slept, Fournet presented a *fait accompli* to Charles Lamboley and Léon Pierre. Both thought seizing the Préfecture was premature. Fournet, however, believed that once begun the Insurrection must keep rolling. His frustration at the Herriot operation's cancellation kicked in. "We must wait for instructions?" he said sarcastically. "When I prepared the snatching of Herriot, I waited for them, *these* instructions. I received a counter-order and had to send it to my men. If it then restarts, I will look a fool. I won't let that happen twice. You do what you like. Me, I'm in."[6]

They were not the only ones taking action before dawn. Police General Hary took control of the *Garde Republicaine*, the *Garde Mobile*, the *Gendarmerie* and the city's fire fighters. Accompanied by Marcel Flouret, de Gaulle's new Prefect of the Department of the Seine, Hary seized the large *Gendarmerie* building at 53 Boulevard de Latour

Maubourg, west of Les Invalides. All personnel with *collabo* sympathies were confined to barracks. The remainder, by agreement with Parodi (and subsequently with Rol-Tanguy)* protected government buildings until the Resistance and GPRF arrived. An undersung character in 1944's Paris drama, General Hary paid lip service to Vichy while maintaining links to the Resistance. He controlled the guards of the Matignon, where the departing Laval recognised their underlying sympathies.[7]

19 August 1944

SHORTLY AFTER DAWN, Fournet, Lamboley and Pierre arrived by bicycle on the *Parvis* of Notre Dame. Policemen queued as rifles and submachine-guns were handed down from a lorry. Then they banged on the Préfecture's big east gate.

"What's all this?" asked Georges Valette, opening the heavy arched gate before his comrades.

"Don't you understand? It's the Resistance," replied a policeman, pushing past, letting his colleagues into the courtyard. A large, freshly laundered *Tricolore* was run up the flagpole as Fournet's men belted out the *Marseillaise*. Informed by Godard de Donville that *Gaulliste* policemen were massed outside, Amedée Bussière—still in his pyjamas—looked out from his window and said, "But it's a revolution." Recovering his self-possession, Bussière asked Fournet to send him a delegation. But Fournet's followers intended something more assertive; breezing into Bussière's apartment, they told him they controlled the Préfecture.

"One must be reasonable, *my children*," said Bussière.

---

* Pierre Bourget says that Rol-Tanguy was aware of this at the outset. But at the 1994 *Colloque* to commemorate the 50th anniversary of the liberation of Paris (attended by survivors and academics), Rol-Tanguy said this only happened on 22 August.

Though widely reckoned a *bon bougre* (decent man) Bussière was overtaken by events.

"Consider," continued Bussière, "the Germans could be here within a quarter of an hour. I would happily negotiate with them and do whatever I can, but this is folly."

Bussière and other senior police officers were placed under house arrest. Fournet's men were delighted to arrest Commissioner Rotté, director of police intelligence, who collaborated with the Gestapo; he would later be shot. But Commissioner Hennequin—another *collabo*, dismissed by Bussière five days before—escaped.

When Yves Bayet arrived in the courtyard, he mounted a box before hundreds of policemen wearing FFI armbands instead of uniforms, and announced, "In the name of General de Gaulle and the provisional government of the Republic of France, I take possession of the Préfecture of Police."

Bayet joined Fournet in Bussière's suite, introducing himself by his *nom de guerre*, "Jean-Marie Boucher, secretary general of the Préfecture de Police."

"What?" asked Bussière.

"There it is," replied Bayet.

Not being devoid of patriotism, Bussière offered to man the telephone in case the Germans called.

"Excellent idea!" replied Bayet.[8]

Bayet then bicycled towards the Latin Quarter. After convoluted precautions familiar to *clandestins*, Bayet approached the corner of the Rue du Dragon and nodded at André Godin who waited in a dark limousine bearing a discreet *Tricolore* cockade, then cycled on towards Danton's statue at the Odeon crossroads, to meet Charles Luizet.

"*Monsieur le Préfet*," Bayet said. "The Prefecture has been taken and at your command."

Luizet smiled.

"Your car is waiting," said Bayet, nodding towards Godin's limousine which was now guarded by armed policemen in a second vehicle.

At the Préfecture, Luizet went straight to Bussière's office. Fournet, Pierre and Lamboley addressed Luizet as *"Monsieur le Patron"*.[9] Luizet was soon joined by his deputy designate, Edgard Pisani, a brilliant *grande école* student. Pisani believed that the Delegation had no wish to provoke the German garrison yet, but such considerations were superseded by events. Again Bussière offered to man the telephone but Pisani told him firmly not to communicate with anyone; the Préfecture's switchboard was temporarily left unmanned.[10]

One caller unable to get through was Raoul Nordling, returning Bussière's call from the previous evening. Driving between his consulate, Romainville and the Hôtel Meurice, Nordling thought little had changed that sunny Saturday morning. But, seeing policemen milling around outside the Préfecture, Nordling asked what was happening.

"The Germans will be going soon. So I will be able to resume my job under the Marshal," said the policeman, clearly unaware of Bayet's declaration.

Inside, Nordling saw frenetic activity in the courtyard.

"What are you doing here, Monsieur le Consul?" asked a policeman.

"I would like to see the Prefect," said Nordling.

Approaching Luizet's office, Nordling was made *au courant* with the morning's events. Nordling told Luizet that he was still trying to get political prisoners released.

"You can see Monsieur Bussière, without any problem, if you wish, Monsieur Nordling," said Luizet.

Unfortunately for Nordling, Bussière's Gaullist replacement was unlikely to win favours from the Germans. Nevertheless, Nordling briefly visited Bussière.[11]

AFTER PERSISTENT WARNINGS AGAINST PREMATURE ACTION, it was with some concern that Colonel Henri Rol-Tanguy heard the *Marseillaise* emanating from the Préfecture as he bicycled past Notre Dame towards the Rue de Meaux—especially since he carried orders prohibiting attacks on German patrols until public buildings were secured.[12]

After propping up his bicycle, Rol-Tanguy tried to gain entrance, but the *Gardien* on the gate barred him. Rol-Tanguy departed to a quiet place nearby and donned the military tunic he carried in his panier. Returning to the Préfecture, Rol-Tanguy found the policemen more amenable. The Préfecture courtyard was an extraordinary scene as *Gardiens de la Paix*, some uniformed, others in mufti, but all wearing FFI brassards, ran hither and thither fetching arms and painting vehicles with the letters FFI, sometimes accompanied by a V for Vercors, in honour of the premature rising in Isère during July.[13]

No one forwarned Rol-Tanguy of this development and he felt they should have. But he marvelled that the police rank and file had finally aligned themselves firmly alongside the Resistance; it was wonderful. Nevertheless, he thought them woefully unprepared for German retaliation.[14] Refered by Bayet to Commissioner Chassagnette to discuss military matters, Rol-Tanguy said two thousand men was too many to defend the Préfecture and keep supplied with food and ammunition. They should disperse around police sub-stations. In any case, at best, their armouries only held a few dozen rifles and a handful of machine-guns, which was not enough, though more might be found in abandoned *collabo* arsenals. The Préfecture's supply of sandbags, previously stockpiled to defend the building against 1930s rioters, should, said Rol-Tanguy, be used to defend windows, especially at corners, where their best marksmen should be.[15] As he spoke Rol-Tanguy noticed a door open slightly and saw Bussière's face. Hearing that Bussière was under arrest, Rol-Tanguy nodded, then saw another face, "Who's that?" he asked.

"Nordling, the Swedish Consul," replied Chassagnette.

Knowing nothing of Nordling's efforts to release political prisoners, Rol-Tanguy said, "Well, he has no business here."[16]

Moments later Nordling returned to Luizet's office. "In any case," said Nordling, taking his leave, "If you need anything, don't hesitate to give me a call as I am one of the more senior consuls in the city."

By now the streets around the Prefecture were deserted. Getting into his car, Nordling looked up at the *Tricolore* fluttering in the sunlight. It was good to see.[17]

AT 9AM HENRI CULMANN ENTERED the Ministry of Industrial Production on the Rue de Grenelle. Since French industry notoriously collaborated with Germany, Culmann was nervous. On reaching his office he learnt that fifty FFI would soon take over the building; their pickets were already in the courtyard, warning that the Minister would soon be arrested. Now worried, Culmann asked if any FFIs had mentioned him and was relieved to hear that he was not on their hit list. After conferring with Secretary-General Jarillot, Culmann thought, "having reflected for a few moments on how to reconcile my duty and my preference to stay alive, I decided to remain in my office but that if the building was invaded by large numbers of armed FFIs so that I was directly threatened, I would escape through the gardens and jump the wall into the hotel garden next door".[18] As rifle reports intensified around the Prefecture, Culmann ran to a window. A large black Citroen 11CV carrying armed policemen and emblazoned with the letters FFI flew along the Rue de Grenelle.[19]

SETTING OFF FROM THE HÔTEL CRILLON on his usual rounds, Sonderführer Robert Wallraf visited the Chamber of Deputies whose building, the Palais Bourbon, was designated a *Stützpunkt* (strong-point). Its garrison displayed typical Wehrmacht pugnacity while its courtyard was choked with vehicles. "When ordered to evacuate we didn't want to find ourselves without transport," wrote Wallraf. "We had no desire to walk five hundred kilometres to reach the German frontier." Yet the Palais Bourbon's defenders seemed sad; most German soldiers remembered good times in Paris and hated to see the population turn on them. Conversely, angry hoteliers complained that when their German clients left they had no immediate likelihood of re-letting their rooms.

"They've really gone?" asked Wallraf.

"Yes," came the reply. "No one's there. They have even left weapons and ammunition for the Resistance."[20]

Witnessing the morning's events unfold, Wallraf took no pleasure in seeing well-trained German soldiers returning fire, sewing panic on the streets below. When an FFI prisoner was brought in, instead of executing him, he was sent to the Hôtel Meurice under guard. Some FFIs were firing into the Palais Bourbon's courtyards from nearby apartment buildings on the Rue Aristide Briand, which Wallraf thought recklessly unprofessional. A rifle-grenade fired by a trained soldier could easily set such buildings alight.[21]

STILL HOLDING THE POCKET'S SOUTHERN JAWLINE at Écouche, *la Nueve*'s day began when a shot-down RAF pilot was guided into their lines by a French farmer. The previous night was sufficiently uneventful for Dronne's Spaniards to catch up on personal washing, cleaning weapons and food. There was also a roll call; *la Nueve* lost seven killed in Normandy, including two useful section commanders; ten badly injured and two with light injuries who refused to leave the company. Two destroyed half-tracks were replaced by the Americans, while lightly damaged vehicles were repaired by the men themselves.

Surveying the area around Écouché, Dronne lost count of the burnt and blackened German vehicles. Then there were the dead; hideously posed, ballooning in the summer heat, whose stench could be smelt hundreds of metres away. The pocket was now collapsing and British troops from Dempsey's Second Army were threading their way through the wreckage of the German defeat with the sensible, experienced caution of veterans.[22]

At Leclerc's CP Christian Girard studied the map. With US V Corps south of Chambois, he wondered why Langlade's men had not taken the town.[23] But Langlade knew that if he entered the gap he might find himself in a costly tank battle contrary to Leclerc's orders. Nevertheless he ordered sub-group commanders Minjonnet and Massu to maintain pressure on the enemy with tank and artillery fire without being drawn into anything larger. Langlade knew that Massu needed keeping on the leash.[24]

Commandant Weil was sent to V Corps to ascertain Gerow's plans for Paris. American thinking remained that Paris would be bypassed north and south, thereby avoiding costly street fighting and the burden of feeding the city, estimated to need 3,000 tons a day from Allied stocks landed in Normandy. "Too kind," Girard wrote sarcastically in his diary after taking Weil's report. "Always seen through the same lens. It's the big omelette that counts."[25]

Leclerc and Girard gamefully speculated which Allied generals were most sympathetic about Paris. Horrocks—Leclerc's former commander in Tunisia? "*Surement pas!*" Montgomery? Impossible to say. Patton? "Possibly sympathetic, but he would put it to one side until after the fighting was over." Leclerc then said urbanely that unless something happened soon he would, "re-run his march on Tripoli" on his own initiative. Girard nodded in agreement. "But it would be a pity," wrote Girard, "to be obliged to arrive at such a position."[26]

Naturally the 2e DB preferred to advance on Paris with American support, though some were claiming more petrol and ammunition than they had used from American stores. More replacement tanks and half-tracks arrived than were lost. Notwithstanding that Uncle Sam's dollar paid for everything, Leclerc criticised Allied strategy. Considering the Allies' vast material advantage, he reckoned they could have passed Paris by mid August, even as far as Champagne. "But there wasn't a plan," wrote Girard. "Improvisation had reigned and confusion was the result; it showed itself particularly in the *affaire* of the Falaise pocket."[27] France's only armoured division in Normandy liked criticising its American backers and vice versa. While far from being a perfect Stalingrad-style encirclement, Falaise was far more than an *affaire*—it was the decisive victory that opened the road to Paris.

CONFINED TO HIS APARTMENT with his family, Amedée Bussière could only watch events unfold. Allowed back into his office to collect personal effects, he found Edgard Pisani sitting at his desk and Pétain's bust—a *de luxe* version of Cogné's sculpture—shoved into a cupboard. While senior police *résistants* rifled through files, looking for evidence against *collabo* colleagues, the younger ones positioned sandbags around windows.[28]

In the Prefecture's wine cellar policemen uncorked bottles, regretfully pouring their contents down the drain and refilling them with a dangerous mix of petrol and sulphuric acid. Once recorked the bottle was wrapped in paper soaked in potassium chlorate which would react with the sulphuric acid when the bottle hit its target. Most Molotov cocktails consist of a bottle filled with petrol and bunged with a rag which is lit shortly before being thrown. The Prefecture's version was devised by Frederic Joliot-Curie, a career chemist who, with his wife, had won the 1935 Nobel chemistry prize for discovering artificial radioactivity. After *la Chute* Joliot-Curie and his team automatically drew Nazi interest. But, although paid by Germany via the Wehrmacht's science directorate, Joliot-Curie played the *double-jeu*, joining the communist affiliated *Front National* in 1941. Seeing the *Tricolore* above the Préfecture that morning, Joliot-Curie immediately offered his services.

Having taken positions with good fields of fire over the surrounding roads, the police began shooting at any Wehrmacht personnel or vehicles coming within range of the Préfecture. "Already one could hear gunfire from the windows," Bussière wrote. "And there was plenty of commotion down on the Jean Chiappe Courtyard."[29]

When Germans fell either on the Rue de la Cité or along the Quai Saint-Michel, they shrieked with delight, savouring the aroma of cordite coming off their weapons. Younger policemen found the Insurrection's first two hours utterly exhilarating, though older heads knew the Germans would soon retaliate, sending tanks against them. When a call came from the Hôtel Meurice, Bussière's offer was accepted.

"There is an officer from the Meurice on the line," said one of Luizet's men.

Bussière grabbed the receiver. "I am the Prefect of Police. I would like to speak to General von Choltitz; it is both urgent and important."

"He's not here, *Monsieur le Préfet*," replied a German officer. "But I will repeat your words to him exactly."

"Tell him that everything is fine at the Préfecture but tell him also that if, as it has been rumoured to me, there is an intention to enforce a curfew beginning at 2pm, then I ask him most seriously to do no such thing. This would be a catastrophe for public order. Parisians, whether they are aware or not, will be on the city's streets in large numbers. In any case 2pm is the time when many of them return to work. Your repression could only have bloody consequences. The general certainly would not want that. He will understand why I have called him. I meant it as warmly as possible."

"Understood, *Monsieur le Préfet*," replied the Meurice officer. "I will pass on what you have said to the general. I will call you back should it be necessary."

"That officer never called me back," wrote Bussière. "And the curfew was never set for 2pm."[30]

But Germans were returning fire at the Préfecture and police casualties were mounting. Bussière's son Jacques, a junior doctor at the nearby Hôpital Hôtel-Dieu, offered his services to Charles Luizet. Many wounded policemen were faces Jacques Bussière knew. With a pass signed by Luizet, Dr. J. Bussière tended the wounded throughout the Insurrection.[31]

AS A PRELIMINARY GERMAN REACTION the area around the Rue de Rivoli was cordoned off, creating a no-go area as Maurice Goudeket found to his cost. Cabin-crazy at the benign house-arrest imposed by Colette in their Palais Royale apartment, Goudeket ventured into the Tuileries Gardens to see what was happening. While he was there the barriers were put in place; civilians could not pass without showing their papers. Being a Jew in hiding, Goudeket had no papers. Suddenly finding himself in a dire predicament, Goudeket hid in an air-raid shelter scooped out during the *drôle de guerre* (the Phoney War) and now used for storage by the gardeners. When Goudeket failed to return, Colette frantically telephoned their friends.[32]

Most Parisians warned or reassured each other by telephone. Although besotted by Françoise Gilot, when Picasso's ex-mistress Marie-Thérèse Walter telephoned from the Ile Saint-Louis saying that she and their daughter could hear gunfire nearby, the artist decided that Marie-Thérèse and Maya most needed his protection.[33] Hence Picasso spent the Insurrection at Marie-Thérèse's apartment on Boulevard Henri IV, painting portraits of Maya and a series of sketches based on Poussin's *The Triumph of Pan*.[34]

AT RADIO PARIS ALL THE RESISTANCE needed to do to control the airwaves was expel Vichy's director. Once this happened, Pierre Schaeffer placed Radio Paris under the Préfecture and broadcast for the Resistance, ending "*Radio Paris ment, Radio Paris est allemand*"— "Radio Paris lies, Radio Paris is German."[35] But Jean Guignebert advised against over-stepping a very limited brief until Paris was firmly in French hands, directions which came from Alexandre Parodi.

Following longstanding preparations, resistance groups began seizing newpaper premises the previous day. The Rue de Rivoli offices of the *collabo* daily *Je suis partout* were swiftly taken by lightly armed *résistants*. Also within swastika-draped central Paris, the Rue des Pyramides offices of Alphonse de Châteaubriant's *La Gerbe* suffered similarly with worse to come when *résistants* sacked the premises two days later, throwing papers into the street.[36]

Events at *Paris Soir* were more complex. When Paris fell in 1940, the newspaper's owner, Jean Prouvost, the editorial staff and print workers fled to the Free Zone rather than publish a bastard journal controlled by the Nazis' *Propaganda Abteilung*. The janitor, Jean Schiessle, was ordered to resume production with dredged up hacks foisted upon him as editorial staff. Thus a great Paris newspaper was irrevocably tainted by the Occupation.[37] When liberation became imminent, several of the original staff returned to Paris hoping to reinstate *Paris Soir* to its former glory, reinstalling themselves in their Rue de Louvre offices on 18 August. At 8.30 on the 19th Lieutenant Guirche (*nom de guerre*: Marceau) accompanied by Aspirant Claude Brézillon and Police Cadet

Broyau, with one pistol between them, arrived at *Paris Soir*'s offices supported by journalists and print-workers determined to reclaim their lost jobs. If matters were not already complicated enough, a motley selection of *résistants* linked to *Libération-Nord* and the police also arrived and began arresting the anti-*collabo* prewar staff.[38]

The *résistants* in the *Paris Soir* building now split into two groups. The first seized the premises of the right-wing evening journal *L'Intransigeant* (from where the German *Pariser Zeitung* was also published), while the other repossessed the great Quartier du Croissant print works. Later that evening the *Pariser Zeitung* placard, bolted to the facade of the *Intransigeant* building, was hacked down with sledgehammers. When the Germans heard of this, lorries were sent to collect as many papers as possible. Someone in the German-held hotels foresaw that *Pariser Zeitung*'s offices would contain compromising information.[39]

But formerly great Paris newspapers could not be reinstated by simply "liberating" premises; *Paris Soir*'s owner Jean Prouvost, never having taken any side convincingly, made himself detested by *Vichystes* and *résistants* alike and fled Paris to avoid arrest, though in fact he had little to fear. Even so *Paris Soir* had to become *France Soir* to reinvent itself. But right wing dailies *L'Intransigeant* and *Petit Parisien* never appeared again. Soon three new newspapers appeared from the *Paris Soir* building: *Ce Soir*, the *Front National* and *Libération*. From *L'Intransigeant*'s former premises came *Combat*, the *Franc-Tireur*, and *Défense de Paris*. From the red house which published *Le Matin* came *Populaire* and *Libération Soir*. The communist *L'Humanité* also reappeared, from the *Petit Parisien* premises on the Rue d'Enghien.[40]

In Prouvost's armchair now sat Gaullist academic Jacques Debu-Bridel, exclaiming with brio, "The proof that the revolution is a fact is that I am sitting here." But Paris still had an armed German garrison to eject, a reality recognised by Albert Bayet, another academic co-opted into the Resistance to re-found France's media, "The Resistance has only won the battle of liberation in the domain of the press."[41] But the Resistance could hardly retake Paris without the press there to report its deeds. There was, however, such a thing as jumping the gun. As with Radio Paris, Alexandre Parodi intervened.[42]

ARRIVING AT ALGIERS' MAISON BLANCHE AIRFIELD to begin his second journey to France since D-Day, de Gaulle was advised to travel in the Flying Fortress the Americans had allocated to him. For his own reasons, probably because his personal pilot, Lionel de Marmier, was a *Gaulliste de la première heure*, de Gaulle decided to fly in his usual Lockheed Hudson while his chief of staff, General Alphonse Juin, followed in the Flying Fortress. Accompanied by the tall, personable Captain Claude Guy who joined him after an accident ended his flying career, the Constable took his seat for the flight that would carry him on the final stage of the journey that began in 1940.

While refuelling at Casablanca, de Gaulle visted local officials and was struck by the crowd gathered around the aerodrome. "The tension on every face showed that they had guessed the reason for my journey, even though it was left unsaid; hardly *bravos* and acclamations, but doffed hats, waving and concerned looks. Such a salute, ardent yet silent was like being witnessed by a multitude at a decisive moment. I was moved," de Gaulle wrote.

"What a destiny you have," said the resident general, Gabriel Puaux.[43]

After a delay caused by technical problems on the Flying Fortress, they continued to Gibraltar, where de Gaulle dined with the governor. But the Flying Fortress's problems persisted. Although advised that the Lockheed Hudson was unsuitable for flying through potentially hostile airspace, whereas a Flying Fortress bristled with machine-guns, de Gaulle decided to continue his journey.

IN RETURN FOR THE EXPERTISE OFFERED THAT MORNING, the police allocated Rol-Tanguy a Citroen and bodyguard to resume his journey to the Rue de Meaux. As experienced *clandestins* Rol-Tanguy's staff knew that security required frequent movement, and relocated their HQ to the waterworks building on Rue Victor Schoelcher, near the Place Denfert-Rochereau. The decision made, Rol-Tanguy returned to the Préfecture via the Faubourg Saint-Michel. Luckily the German garrison still thought police vehicles were *hors de combat*; they swept along boulevards clogged with retreating Wehrmacht vehicles without mishap and were waved through the *Feldgendarmerie* checkpoint at the Porte Saint-Martin.[44]

At 1pm Henri Rol-Tanguy met Charles Luizet for the first time. Luizet confirmed that Alexandre Parodi had ordered the Insurrection to begin, a fact which made little difference now. Luizet, however, wanted to pull Rol-Tanguy properly under de Gaulle's authority and, as Rol-Tanguy was about to depart, Luizet invited him to meet Parodi on Avenue Lowendal.[45]

"Put on some civilian clothing," ordered Luizet, glancing at Rol-Tanguy's hybrid uniform, a beret, his Spanish tunic with colonel's *galons* roughly stitched to the cuffs, worn jodhpurs and riding boots.

"I would appear lacking in guts," replied Rol-Tanguy.

"You can't wear a uniform into a building frequented by members of the Delegation," Luizet emphasised. "You would risk having them all arrested."[46]

Reluctantly Rol-Tanguy co-operated. On meeting Parodi, Rol-Tanguy gave him a quick resumé before demanding that all FFI forces in Paris should be placed under his command. Parodi conferred briefly with the Delegation before agreeing. Reflecting on this event with Roger Bourderon, Rol-Tanguy said that Parodi was wise to agree; any other reply would have divided the Paris Resistance at its crucial moment.[47] At Rol-Tanguy's insistence, a declaration was drafted placing all FFI forces in the Paris region under Rol-Tanguy's authority with Parodi as his superior, responsible to General de Gaulle:[48]

> République Française.
> Liberté Égalité Fraternité
>
> 1. The Commissioner Delegate of the Provisional Government of the French Republic (GPRF), in agreement with the *Comité Parisien de la Libération* orders that all organised formations or movements of the Resistance, or otherwise outside these movements, forming an integral part of the FFI, as well as all police forces, including *Gendarmerie* are, for the departments of the Seine,

Seine et Oise, Seine et Marne and Oise, under the orders of regional chief, Colonel Rol.

2. All men between the ages of 18 and 50, capable of bearing arms, must be mobilised. They must, either through their businesses, *quartiers*, locality and arrondissements, form themselves into combat groups of 8 men directed by sergeant-chiefs into detachments. (Equivalent to infantry sections and platoons.) They must make contact with the nearest FFI formation to direct their use in action; combat missions, or protection of public services, works and water services.

3. All arms stocked or held by individuals must be handed over to combatants. Attack plans, whether individual or collective, must be developed for seizing arms from both the Germans and from Darnand's *Miliciens*. "We need to arm ourselves by disarming the enemy."

4. Actions must be directed generally against all enemy targets; transport, communications, radio masts and isolated enemy forces, by using whatever means are available, knives, anti tyre nail-beds, petrol bombs and cutting down trees.

FRENCHMEN—ALL MUST FIGHT!

OPEN THE ROADS TO PARIS TO THE VICTORIOUS ALLIED ARMIES!

VIVE DE GAULLE!

VIVE LA RÉPUBLIQUE!

VIVE LA FRANCE![49]

DECIDING NOT TO RETURN TO THE PREFECTURE, Luizet sent Edgard Pisani to deputise for him, knowing the dark, romantic looking law student was trustworthy. Pisani spent the Insurrection's first afternoon by the Prefecture's switchboard while incidents accumulated.

Provoked by the sight of the freshly laundered *Tricolore* flying over the Préfecture, the crew of a *Kübelwagen* on the Boulevard du Palais opened fire at their windows, quickly finding themselves fired on in return. A section of German infantry attempting to approach the building via the Petit Pont also came under fire. With no available cover except the quay wall, they were easily gunned down, dancing like rag dolls until their bloodied bodies collapsed motionless. On the opposite side of the Seine two Wehrmacht lorries, abandoned by their owners amid a hail of bullets, were quickly wheeled into position to form a barricade, while a third lorry, burning fiercely, was searched for arms.[50]

Not a single German lorry passed along the Quai Saint-Michel that afternoon. From Notre Dame's presbytery, Monsignor Brot watched doctors and nurses draped in white with Red Cross armbands dashing everywhere with stretchers to tend casualties of both sides. Germans who surrendered had good chances of surviving while their wounded were taken to the Ile de la Cité's Hôpital Hôtel-Dieu, the oldest hospital in France.[51]

By 3pm the German reaction had became more purposeful; three tanks pushed their way onto the *Parvis* of Notre Dame via the Petit Pont. Two of these tanks were Panthers armed with powerful 75mm PAK guns, while the third was a pre-war French type. A Panther fired at the Préfecture's gates, its armour-piercing shell shearing the left-side gate off its hinges but otherwise causing little damage. Other shots, also armour-piercing, hit the Préfecture's east wall, causing panic more than anything else. When a shell struck the tower above the isolation block, policemen in the courtyard ran towards the tunnel joining the Préfecture to the nearby Cité Metro station. But Sergeant Fournet stopped them at pistol point.

"Our only chance of survival is to win," said Fournet.

CLP members inside the Préfecture called for calm. Standing on a cart, Leo Hamon said, "The people of Paris have often struggled against you. Today, you are on their side. They won't forget this. It's the beginning of a lasting alliance."[52]

Outside the Préfecture's front gate the commander of one of the Panthers imprudently peered out of his turret cupola and was quickly shot. According to reports, this was the moment a Panther was struck by a Joliot-Curie cocktail. In any case they suddenly withdrew. Next the Préfecture's defenders were assailed via the west entrance, when a convoy of German lorries advanced along the Boulevard du Palais.[53]

Directed by Maitre Blanc, a left-wing barrister, *résistants* in the Palais de Justice sighted their guns on the approaching convoy, firing only when Maitre Blanc gave the word. They were carrying arms, ammunition and jerry cans of petrol. Once their crews were eliminated the trucks were pushed through the Prefecture's west gate and the weapons distributed.[54]

No one concerned for medieval gems such as Notre Dame, the Sainte-Chapelle and the Conciergerie could have imagined a worse place for the Insurreection to start.

EXCEPT FOR THE SOUND OF GUNFIRE a few blocks away, Henri Culmann found the Rue de Grenelle comparatively quiet. But a new face appeared in the ground floor lobby; a pleasant looking youth wearing a Lacoste sport shirt now sat behind the entrance desk. When challenged he declared uncompromisingly, "FFI."

Culmann noticed a Sten gun leaning against the wall behind him and two magazines of 9mm bullets lay on the desk.

"We expected you this morning," said Culmann.

The young FFI told Culmann that the Ministry of Industrial Production was scheduled for occupation on Monday morning and that he and two comrades were merely an advance guard.

"Come back on Monday," said the young FFI. "If nothing else you will meet your new boss."[55]

At 5pm another attack materialised outside the Préfecture. This was less purposeful than two hours earlier and amounted to an attempted infantry infiltration from the Pont Saint-Michel, along the quayside and up the stairs by the Quai des Orfèvres. The leading soldiers were quickly shot from the Préfecture windows and the rest withdrew.[56]

This small victory was down to a group of FFI who installed themselves around the Place Saint-Michel from mid-day onwards, covering the Metro station, and a machine-gun nest was installed at the Café de Départ, ready to confound approaching Germans. The Wehrmacht was slow to warn transport staff of the escalating situation around the Préfecture, and several convoys of retreating troops were using these riverside roads. The first lorry had an exhausted soldier draped on its cabin roof when the *résistants* opened fire. He was hit and, while frantically trying to save himself, fell into the road. The driver stopped to help him and with that the FFI emerged from cover to hose the lorry with Sten guns. When the next lorry arrived, its driver was quickly killed and it crashed into the Rôtisserie Périgourdine, a restaurant on the corner of the Place Saint-Michel and the Quai des Grands Augustins. Another twenty-five German vehicles were shot up in a similar fashion. The Préfecture courtyard soon resembled a scrapyard as damaged German lorries were pushed inside and their cargoes rifled. Some lorries were re-used, while others were pretty charred, including their crews. The corpses of fallen Germans were gathered discreetly out of sight by the river bank while *résistants* sat nonchalantly at street-side cafés, keeping their weapons hidden, ready for the next lot to arrive.[57] A few exhausted Normandy veterans were taken prisoner. "*Messieurs*," said one unfortunate, "I did not know that it was not allowed to cross Paris."

On the Quai des Grands Augustins a smart staff car was shot up, injuring its driver who crashed into the river wall. The FFIs took him to Alexandre de Saint-Phalle's home on the Rue Séguier which Roland Pré used as his CP. Interrogating their prisoner, they found he carried a LVF ID card; he was a Frenchman who had fought for Hitler in Russia. The FFIs pistol-whipped the wretched youth bloody in Saint-Phalle's dining room, until Saint-Phalle stopped them. Later that evening, he was shot and thrown in the Seine.[58]

Further along the *rive gauche*, when another car was shot up, three German soldiers ran for the Quai Saint-Michel's river wall hoping to dive into the Seine but landed fatally on the lower quay thirty feet below. South of the Place Saint-Michel, a captured German being led along the narrow, restaurant-filled Rue de Saint-André des Arts had food waste tipped over him from first-floor kitchen windows. This torment ended once he passed the École Maternelle and turned up Rue Séguier. At Saint Phalle's house, Roland Pré's intelligence team categorised him mercifully: "He's just a German doing his duty, we don't want him." They wanted *collabos* irrespective of gender. In the courtyard, behind the high doors separating *chez* Saint-Phalle from the ancient street beyond, the barbers of vengeance were shaving the heads of women who had slept with *les Boches*.[59] The mother of one unfortunate complained that since her daughter was merely seventeen and would also sleep with Americans if asked, such punishment was too extreme.[60]

AFTER HE LEFT THE PRÉFECTURE, newly erected barricades forced Nordling to take a meandering route back to his Consulate. He noticed many contrasts; checkpoints manned by German soldiers adjacent to government buildings flying the *Tricolore*; streets made impassable by gunfire while Parisians queued for food only a block away; the Rue de Rivoli checkpoints, while opposite them children played in the Tuileries gardens. At around noon Nordling visited the Hôtel Meurice to thank von Choltitz for his help over Romainville, finding him on the balcony with sporadic gunfire audible from all directions.[61]

So far von Choltitz's reaction had been restrained, as demonstrated by his Day order: "Civilian life must be as little troubled as possible during the day. Our troops must be ordered to avoid useless firefights. Order and calm should be maintained by all means."[62] To Field Marshal Model, von Choltitz gave an understated report that, "Terrorists are shooting around the centre of the city (Concorde, Madeleine, Tuileries, *Quartier* around the German embassy). The terrorists apparently intend to take the Chamber of Deputies (Palais Bourbon)." Model agreed to send him the much depleted 352nd Infantry Division as reinforcement.[63]

"These louts have even been loosing off rounds under my windows," von Choltitz told Nordling. "The men intervened and then pulled back."

Without being drawn into matters involving the Insurrection, Nordling thanked von Choltitz for Romainville and left. But when he learnt that another train of political prisoners had just left Pantin,

Nordling returned to the Meurice. On his second arrival von Choltitz rose from his bureau and crossed the room to greet him; then, hearing why Nordling had returned so quickly, von Choltitz became visibly angry.

"I've been releasing prisoners," he yelled. "And now terrorists have taken over the Préfecture of Police, there is gunfire under my windows, they kill my soldiers. I have responsibilities. I have orders which I have to obey. I will destroy the Préfecture. I will kill these louts."

Nordling watched von Choltitz's face redden.

"I could blow up Paris. I have the means and the experience," said von Choltitz. "After Stalingrad I made a fighting retreat, destroying towns along the way."

"If you destroy the Préfecture," said Nordling, "you will also, at the same time, destroy Notre Dame, the Sainte-Chapelle, and many architectural treasures of Paris."

"I must protect the security of my troops," insisted von Choltitz. "Order must be restored. Who are the responsible authorities to whom I can address myself?"

"There are no other authorities besides the Resistance," replied Nordling.

"Never," said von Choltitz. "I am not having any dealings with such terrorists, those louts and communists." Von Choltitz remarked to an aide that the Allies should be fighting the Russians.

Nordling reassured von Choltitz that several senior *résistants* were "gentlemen", particularly those sent from Algiers. "You ought to have more respect for them ... If you were French, you would be among them."

"It's just a gathering of rubbish," said von Choltitz irritably. "Now, we're speaking all the time about the 'Resistance' or the 'French Forces of the Interior' as if one's dealing with organised and disciplined troops where there is real authority, and they're just snipers who incessantly shoot at my soldiers. If this continues I shall have to resort to tougher measures. I have been ordered to defend Paris and to destroy the city before evacuating it."

"It is not the rubbish that you're dealing with," replied Nordling. "Behind de Gaulle and the Resistance are the French people. France was defeated but she has not submitted. It's the élite of this country who have raised the flag of revolt. And this revolt is not only against the Germans but against the detested government of Vichy."

"But *it is not* a French civil insurrection. It's *us* they're firing at. Look!" said von Choltitz, gesturing towards the Tuileries gardens. "There are men who take pot-shots at the German sentries on the Rue de Rivoli and, if we retaliate, we risk killing women and children. Is this what you call an insurrection against the Vichy government?"

Suddenly von Choltitz softened. Looking outside, Nordling understood immediately. Oblivious of the gunfire, a pretty *Parisienne* was bicycling past the Hôtel Meurice. Nordling observed von Choltitz's expression as he watched the summer breeze lift her cotton frock revealing shapely legs.

"Well, we don't want to shoot anyone like that," chuckled von Choltitz. Then, changing the subject, he remarked, "Paris *is* a pretty town."[64]

"Yes," agreed Nordling.

Emboldened, Nordling virtually paraphrased Taittinger's words as he explained the choice von Choltitz faced. Von Choltitz explained the difficulty of allowing attacks on German troops without resorting to reprisals.

"Why get involved?" asked Nordling. "Don't hit out. Negotiate!"

"If only there was a chief on the other side, with whom it was possible to negotiate, one could perhaps find a *modus vivendi*," said von Choltitz. "But who can I negotiate with?"

Nordling assured von Choltitz that there were senior *résistants* with whom sensible negotiations could be made.[65]

THE WATERWORKS ON RUE VICTOR SCHOELCHER were marked down as militarily useful during 1939–1940. Twenty-six metres below ground there was a generator to pump fresh air and provide electric light, and metal staircases and dingy corridors branched off in all directions. One corridor lead to the Place Denfert-Rochereau Metro station from where resistance groups unreachable via the main telephone system could be contacted. Having taken up residence, Rol-Tanguy sent two aides to Montrouge to fetch Cécile. Without being stopped at checkpoints, Cécile Tanguy reached 9 Rue Victor Schoelcher with her typewriter and all Rol-Tanguy's files.[66]

As the Insurrection gathered momentum, Rol-Tanguy's *résistants* found other groups, of whom they were utterly unaware, performing different operations nearby. These were usually Colonel Lizé's people taking over district town halls, banks, factories and print works; essential springboards for re-installing the state.[67] Unified command might have prevented the duplication of missions. However, the FTP's essentially left-leaning nature meant that they could not resist taking over *mairies,* notably at Montreuil and Bondy, in competition with less ideological rivals. Sometimes the FTP arrived first, sometimes Lizé's men.[68]

As FFI attacks multiplied, so did their arsenals. Attacks on Wehrmacht depots and service garages often furnished small arms and usable vehicles. Lorries retreating from the front might break down, as at Levallois where the FFI attacked two lorries, killing their crews and seizing four MG42s, twelve Schmeisser submachine-guns and two hundred and fifty rifles along with abundant ammunition. Another useful haul came when two Wehrmacht lorries collided at the junction of Boulevard Victor-Hugo and Boulevard Jean-Jaures, revealing nine MG42s, fifteen Schmeisser submachine-guns and eight Mauser rifles. Nor did French armaments production cease after 1940, though its sole customer became Germany. The Hotchkiss factory was seized, providing machine-guns and hand-grenades.[69]

Despite German troops remaining in Paris, General de Gaulle's new order arrived at their ministries. André Mutter installed himself at the colonial ministry's Rue Oudinot premises. At the Ministry of Justice on the Place Vendôme the newly appointed under-secretary, Marcel Willard, arrived with his new staff, astride bicycles, to prepare *l'épuration* (the purge). They were welcomed by a *résistant* already *in situ* who left the door ajar at the arranged moment. Former *collabo* staff discreetly disappeared, except one who was locked up. Armed with pistols and a Sten, Willard's team secured the building under the noses of German officers still residing at the adjacent Ritz.[70]

With the *Gendarmerie* of La Tour-Maubourg secured by General Hary, the previous evening, Parodi sent the capable young Felix Gaillard to take possession of government buildings along the Rue de Grenelle, whose *Garde* garrisons expected him. As Pierre Laval knew well, the Matignon's staff and garrison had quietly turned *Gaulliste* even while serving him. Felix Gaillard bicycled up to the main gate, immediately finding himself facing the building's "chief of interior services".

"We are waiting for General de Gaulle," he told Gaillard.

Gaillard wandered the magisterial building which, for a few hours, he controlled. Entering the cabinet room where, three days before, Laval received Abetz and Nordling, Gaillard sat behind the desk. The captain of the guard arrived; a big fellow wearing shiny black kneeboots.

"Monsieur le Ministre," said the captain. "We are waiting to place ourselves under General de Gaulle. What are your orders?"

After telling him to send reinforcements to the Préfecture, Gaillard took a bicycle ride around other nearby government buildings, coming under fire from the Palais Bourbon's south facade as he passed Les Invalides.[71]

THE TAKEOVER OF GOVERNMENT BUILDINGS was only partially successful. In the 1st and 20th Arrondissements the Germans chased the FFI away from the *mairies* and re-established control. Then there was Neuilly-sur-Seine. Always an upmarket, placid northwestern *banlieue*, housing numerous *Vichystes* and *collabos*, the Germans expected to recover Neuilly fairly easily. The nearest FFI group avoided attacking Neuilly's *mairie* because a thousand German soldiers were barracked nearby. Instead a motley group around sixty strong, led by a greying factory worker called André Caillette, breezed in and took over. As soon as local FFI leader, de Laage, heard of Caillette's move he telephoned Colonel Lizé, who advised him to stay out of it.

Predictably a lorry of German soldiers arrived whose officer stood with his hands on his hips and yelled, "Surrender and come out!"

"Surrender yourselves," replied Caillette from a first floor window. "We are the army of the liberation."

The German officer then unholstered his pistol, immediately provoking return fire which killed him instantly along with several of his men.

Morale among Caillette's band briefly soared. But then a German armoured car and six tanks arrived. At this point Max Roger, Neuilly's Vichy mayor, intervened, promising Caillette's men that their lives would be spared if they surrendered. They refused, so the tanks opened fire and German infantry assaulted the building. Predictably the *résistants* were soon prisoners lined up in the *mairie*'s courtyard with their hands on their heads.

When a FFI tried to escape, he was quickly gunned down. Once again Max Roger intervened, insisting to the senior German officer that several prisoners were merely state functionaries involved with the Red Cross and civil defence who never shot at the German garrison.

"They don't have any papers," said a German soldier guarding the captives.

"Your men have taken them," said one of the FFI disingenuously.

"Well," said the head German officer, pretending to be taken in. "They had better have their papers tomorrow."

Several FFI were allowed to leave. As they left, a youth approached Roger's assistant saying, "*Monsieur*, I was never with the Red Cross ..."

"Shut up and get out of here, you little fool," he replied.

Only twenty of Caillette's men were taken to Mont Valérien. One man captured with a pistol was shot that afternoon, but the rest were later exchanged for German prisoners.[72]

AT ALEXANDRE DE SAINT-PHALLE'S HOUSE, Roland Pré took stock of the Insurrection's first day. There were undoubtedly successes, but Resistance casualties seemed high, as often happens when civilians fight trained soldiers. Alexandre Parodi was visited at his Avenue Lowendal HQ by Colonel Jean Arnould (aka Ollivier), chief of the *réseau Jade Amicol*. Arnould let rip furiously, "You've gone off far too soon. You're at the mercy of the Germans. Many of their divisions must still make a fighting retreat to cross the Seine in Paris or in the Paris area. You have nothing to fight them with. The Americans certainly won't arrive before next Wednesday and between now and then you could be annihilated. I have sent a message to speed up their advance."

But the Insurrection had started and could not easily be stopped. Leo Hamon informed Parodi about Neuilly amid reports that ammunition was running low at the Préfecture. Predictably Jacques Chaban-Delmas said that starting an insurrection under such conditions was utter foolishness since the Allies were not planning to enter Paris but preparing a long envelopment instead. They should have waited for General Koenig's orders.

"I take full responsibility for this and everything else," said Parodi gravely. "If a catastrophe is the result, I will have the rest of my life to regret it. In the meantime, there are measures to be taken."

Chaban's advice, supported by Paul Ély, was that the disparity of forces left little chance for the Paris FFI to fight a successful battle from fixed strongpoints. If enemy pressure around strongholds like the Préfecture became too strong they would have to be abandoned. But now that Henri Rol-Tanguy commanded the Paris FFI, such orders could not be given without his consent. What if he refused? General Dassault, a career air force officer who acted as technical adviser to the FTP, could perhaps influence Rol-Tanguy; Dassault reached Avenue Lowendal by late afternoon. After consulting Parodi, Dassault agreed that the FFI should adopt hit-and-run attacks. The buildings already taken should be held as long as possible, only given up when local commanders could hold out no longer. Parodi and Dassault returned to the room where the Delegation was gathered.

"There is nothing else to do but evacuate the Préfecture," said Parodi.

"The FTP are under your orders," said Leo Hamon glancing at Dassault. "Are you authorising (us) to say that this is your decision?"

"Yes," said Dassault, undertaking to confer with Rol-Tanguy as soon as he could.

In the meantime Parodi sent out urgent messages that all *résistants* holding public buildings must do so as discreetly and unprovocatively as possible. The orders to evacuate the Préfecture were given by telephone as coming from Hamon, Pré, Ribière and Parodi—and addressed to Lamboley, Pisani, Pierre and Fournet.

"The situation is bad. You must not let yourselves be massacred. You must leave."

But retreating is sometimes the most dangerous military undertaking. How were they meant to leave the Préfecture? Someone suggested they jump from windows onto the river bank which could be padded with mattresses brought from the Rue Séguier. But there is no sheer drop onto river banks beneath the Préfecture's walls, and the idea that German troops would allow *résistants* to position mattresses and benignly watch their foes escape was plainly ridiculous.

"It is practically impossible," came the Préfecture's reply. "If we leave we will lose most of our people. It is also morally impossible. We're here and it's best to stay here."

The situation inside the Préfecture was grave. As afternoon became evening the *Comité de Libération de la Police* ordered their men only to fire in self-defence to conserve ammunition. South of the Seine, German troops hosed the Boulevard Saint-Germain with machine-gun fire, causing serious casualties among non-combatants. Only an hour earlier, after beating off an attack on the Préfecture from the Pont Saint-Michel, Edgard Pisani anxiously telephoned his young family.

"Things are going badly," he told his wife. "We will probably never return."

Requests for reinforcements went out at 3.15pm, 5.20pm and 8pm. In response Colonel Lizé sent twenty men armed with machine-guns to create a diversion, but they could not get inside. The *résistants'* pessimism was founded on their belief that, even without artillery, von Choltitz could easily retake the Préfecture with two companies of infantry and a troop of tanks.[73]

ALTHOUGH VON CHOLTITZ seemed willing to negotiate, accumulating reports of FFI attacks forced him to act against the Resistance. But the weakness of his garrison meant that tough orders had to be qualified by advising his men to avoid fruitless gun battles.[74] About the late afternoon on 19 August, Sonderführer Robert Wallraf wrote, "Little by little the situation became uncomfortable. The main network of central buildings, our 'strongpoints', was not seriously defended and an attack by the Resistance could have, supposing it was made with some guts, every chance of success, given the small numbers, desperate for reinforcement, of our defenders. We placed lookouts everywhere to warn us of the slightest thing."[75] Both sides were weak and feared the options available to their adversary.

"One could hear machine-guns not far away," wrote the Resistance's Dr. Victor Veau. "There was an atmosphere of revolution; sometimes ghostly silences during which any conversation could be heard, then dogs barking and whistles."[76]

Émil Bender first told Nordling that German forces were preparing a serious attack on the Préfecture. But at around 7pm, Nordling's nephew, Édouard Fiévet, took a call from the Préfecture claiming that the Germans were preparing a larger assault than before, that the police would be unable to defend themselves successfully, and someone should arrange some kind of ceasefire. There is considerable controversy over who made this plea for quarter from the Prefecture, but made it was.

In 1949 André Bussière, one of Amédée Bussière's sons, said his father called the Swedish Consulate, while Édouard Fiévet believed it was possibly Edgard Pisani's voice. In 1989 Henri Rol-Tanguy said he knew who it was but could not say, nor did he inform his biographer, Roger Bourderon.[77] Whoever it was, Nordling heard words like "The situation is very serious. Do something!" So Nordling asked Émil Bender to visit the Meurice and inform General von Choltitz that the Préfecture wanted a truce, reiterating that fighting around the Préfecture risked collateral damage to heritage sites like Notre Dame. Furthermore, if this opportunity was missed it might become impossible to control the Insurrection or arrange a truce again. Nordling then telephoned the

Préfecture to ask Resistance leaders if they would agree to a ceasefire if it could be negotiated.[78]

Blackouts and barricades made it impossible to cross Paris by car. There were eventually around six hundred barricades whose locations, once charted, bore an unsurprising resemblance to the "poor maps" drawn up in the late nineteenth century to identify localities vulnerable to TB.[79] Without electricity Paris felt even darker. Sporadic gunfire occurred whenever German and FFI patrols came across each other. By keeping to roads patrolled by the Wehrmacht, Émil Bender reached the Hôtel Meurice.[80]

Nordling periodically telephoned the Préfecture to update them on the negotiations' progress. On one occasion Charles Luizet himself answered and held up the telephone receiver for Nordling to hear the gunfire outside.[81]

The first draft of an agreement with von Choltitz was available by 8pm. In the first paragraph the German garrison undertook to recognise the new French authorities installed by de Gaulle's provisional government. Second, von Choltitz agreed to negotiate with these authorities provided that all shooting at German soldiers ceased forthwith, in return for which the German garrison would agree not to fire upon buildings controlled by nominees of de Gaulle's provisional goverment. All reprisals against the French would cease and no hostages would be shot. But none of this would work unless each side could control its men. To this end von Choltitz allowed the French thirty-five minutes between 9.05 and 9.40pm to prove they could put a ceasefire order into effect. If that was successful the ceasefire would begin at 10pm.[82]

Nordling telephoned these terms to the Préfecture at around 8.30pm. Edgard Pisani took the call. At first Pisani insisted that the truce should only apply to the vicinity of the Préfecture, which was not enough for von Choltitz. More telephone calls were exchanged and Luizet's men ceased firing shortly after 9pm. Satisfied that the *résistants* could be controlled, von Choltitz extended the truce until 6am the following morning.

After the war General von Choltitz denied having formal dealings with the "enemy", claiming to have agreed only to a "local" *modus vivendi* so retreating German troops could cross the Seine peacefully. But the Swiss Consul, René Naville, who also saw von Choltitz on 19 August, described him as "imperturbable", merely doing his duty while warmly admitting that his "only desire was to return to an intact Paris, as a tourist, after the war".[83]

Von Choltitz subsequently claimed that he knew about Major Émil Bender's role only from documents furnished by Raoul Nordling after the war, and that Bender "played a vague role in the Consul's entourage". Von Choltitz claims a senior intelligence officer told him that "a certain Bender was an officer in the counter-espionage service who, towards the end, thought it useful to furnish information to the enemy". More equivocation follows: "Personally I do not remember him [Bender], I only know that the Consul-General came on two occasions, accompanied by men unknown to me and that one of these was von Posch-Pastor. According to my staff and my secretary, who had run the desk there for several years, Bender never came without Raoul Nordling." He then continues, saying that Bender was never even an officer and that any maps that Bender furnished to others indicating areas held by the Resistance which would not be attacked by the Germans, or thoroughfares where the Germans would be allowed to pass unimpeded, never came from the Hôtel Meurice with his authority.[84] Why should von Choltitz say this? Writing in West Germany during the early Cold War period, neither a full member of the anti-Hitler resistance, nor an unapologetic Nazi, von Choltitz was clearly troubled by his war record. Meantime, Bender's role is fully acknowledged in Nordling's memoirs and reputable histories.

Leo Hamon called Nordling from the Préfecture to agree on precise, practical details of the truce agreement which were communicated to all buildings occupied by the Resistance. All prisoners were to be treated according to the rules of war. Neither side would inpede the Paris fire brigade in preventing the destruction of property. With respect to violations of the truce, General von Choltitz would distinguish between isolated incidents and concerted attacks. Resistance leaders Alexandre Parodi, Roland Pré, Paul Ribière, Charles Luizet, Leo Hamon and Yves Bayet approved the truce while refusing to negotiate directly with von Choltitz, a role they left to Nordling.

Nordling's telephone rang incessantly with reports that German troops were not respecting the truce. One call complained that German troops were attempting to infiltrate the Préfecture from the Metro. Nordling immediately rang von Choltitz, who was in bed.

"If I wanted to take the Préfecture, I wouldn't take it via the Metro," replied an exasperated von Choltitz. "I would send tanks and aircraft and in five minutes everything would be destroyed."

Nor were sins against Nordling's truce entirely on the German side. Henri Buisson witnessed the arrival at the Préfecture of a lorry containing five tons of weapons and ammunition, which certainly went against the *spirit* of the truce.[85] Several Resistance strongholds used those precious hours to replenish their armouries.

As incidents continued, the Swedish Consulate became, in Nordling's words, a *"véritable plaque tournante"*. When a message arrived that the Germans had arrested policemen wearing FFI brassards, a call from Nordling's Consulate secured their release.[86]

At 11pm Nordling heard from one of de Gaulle's delegates saying that de Gaulle's provisional government had not yet decided its position on the truce but, until they had, Nordling could be their foreign minister. Nordling's priority was to gain time. It would have been impossible to negotiate with von Choltitz without knowing Resistance intentions, what they would accept and what they would reject. Nordling needed to meet the CNR to do this, asking them, "Are you really speaking in the name of *all* the Resistance or only for a few groups of isolated *résistants*?"

"The majority of the *Conseil de la Résistance* and the delegates of the government in Algiers support this mission which it prays you will accept," came the reply.

Until the liberation, Nordling and his collaborators lived in the Swedish Consulate, their evenings lit by oil lamps and candles. When lucky their meals came from the canteen of a bank in the same block, otherwise they ate their way through the consulate's tinned stores. They barely slept and when they did the telephone would wake them, the pleading and negotiating would resume, and so on throughout that momentous week.[87]

DOCTOR VICTOR VEAU ONLY HEARD ABOUT Nordling's truce at 10.30pm. The version he heard came from the International Red Cross, that if the fighting did not cease by the following morning the Germans would bomb central Paris, which was something of a *canard*.[88]

In the meantime another resistance doctor, Liebovici, noticed how corpses were filling the city mortuaries. Despite the comparatively high casualties among the Resistance, they had made fifteen clearly defined attacks around the city while the Germans had made only six *ripostes*. "That night," wrote Commandant Dufresne (aka Raymond Massiet), "the FFIs had full control of forty-three out of forty-eight *quartiers*, and our patrols, wearing FFI armbands, were patrolling the streets of the capital and exchanging shots with the Germans. Soon a member of one of my *groupe-franc*, the one commanded by Lieutenant Barat de Sars, was killed near the Quai de Conti. Fred Palacio was our group's first victim." Returning to Colonel Lizé's Rue Guénégaud HQ, Dufresne was drawn into the effort to deflate the situation following the ceasefire.[89]

Colonel Lizé, being both an old-school professional artillery officer and a longstanding *résistant*, thought the truce smacked of *la Chute* and the Armistice of 1940, which revolted him. Notwithstanding his traditional antecedants, for the liberation of France, Lizé was content to march with men of the Left.

But Lizé's traditionalism made his group an obvious target for *Pétainistes* to approach. The former Inspector General of Cavalry, General Charles Brécard, who marked down Lieutenant Philippe de Hauteclocque (*devenu* Leclerc) as a high-flyer during the 1920s, was Grand Chancellor of the *Légion d'Honneur*, known for spending the Occupation at the races and sufficiently sucked into Vichy's nomenklatura to represent Pétain at Henriot's funeral. In what was widely interpreted as Pétain's last attempt to seize the initiative in Paris, Brécard sent two emissaries to Commandant Dufresne with an extraordinary proposal. From the balcony of the Hôtel de Ville, Brécard would ceremoniously entrust the flag of the *Legion d'Honneur* to the people of Paris ready for General de Gaulle's arrival. The Resistance treated this suggestion with contempt. In fact Brécard was a decent, albeit unintellectual man, always anti-German, whose loyalty to Pétain was founded on them both belonging to the *génération de feu*—the Great War generation. After sending Brécard's emissaries packing, Dufresne placed Brécard under house arrest in a comfortable hotel. Having promised Dufresne's men that he would make no telephone calls, Brécard tried to pull a telephone into the lavatory. Dufresne's guard cut the line. "They stripped me of everything!" protested Brécard.[90]

At the Hôtel de Ville, Pierre Taittinger and Victor Constant passed this time drafting and redrafting an *affiche* asking Parisians to remain calm and disciplined. But Taittinger's first *affiche* claimed falsely that Paris had been declared an open city. The Resistance made him redraft it as an appeal for calm and discipline, which typified the behaviour of most non-combatant Parisians anyway.[91]

Despite their political differences, Rol-Tanguy and Lizé were pleased that sizeable portions of Paris were now under FFI control. Their main concerns, however, were first, that weapons stocks remained too low; second, that the *Quartier Latin* was the epicentre of conflict with the Germans. The Boulevard and Place Saint-Michel, the Place de l'Odéon, the Boulevard Saint-Germain and the Rue Saint Jacques experienced serious gun battles. This quarter now represented an obvious point for German retaliation.[92]

Hence Nordling's truce promised to be patchy at best. On the Ourcq Canal the Germans blew up a barge full of explosives, wrecking Pantin's dockside warehouses. Watching the smoke column mingle with a summer storm in the night sky, Henri Rol-Tanguy did not feel much like compromising with anyone.[93]

20 August 1944

AT DAWN ON 20 AUGUST at Vichy's Hôtel du Parc, the ever-attentive Dr. Bernard Ménétrel prepared Marshal Philippe Pétain for his journey into captivity. When first told that he would be moved to Belfort, Pétain frantically considered alternatives, even throwing himself on the mercy of the *Maquis*.[94] To test feasibility, Ménétrel sent envoys to contact the FFI in the Auvergne and enquire what sort of reception Pétain could expect if he surrendered to them. To Pétain's surprise the FFI's command structure was more hierarchical than he expected; he would be held under house arrest until his former subaltern, General de Gaulle, decided what to do with him. Pétain quickly dropped that idea.[95]

As a second option, now that Paris was uncontactable by telephone, Pétain sent Commandant Féat to consult Laval at the Hôtel Matignon. But when Féat reached Paris, Laval had already been removed. Féat saw Pierre Taittinger instead. Amazed that Pétain was still at Vichy, Taittinger told Féat about the Insurrection. Pétain now recognised that his only choice was to co-operate with the Germans, who threatened to bomb Vichy if he was not ready to leave for Belfort at 6am on 20 August.[96]

Walter Stucki, the Swiss Ambassador in Vichy, was the fullest observer of Pétain's final hours at the Hôtel du Parc. At 6.45am Stucki found the hotel surrounded by SS soldiers, with a tank in reserve. Stucki's diplomatic pass got him through the cordon to the hotel's entrance. Once inside he found that the brass grille gates to the upper floor stairs were locked and guarded by men from the *1e Régiment de la France*. On the fourth floor he was greeted by Pétain's staff, assembled and ready to say their *adieux*.

The SS now forced their way into the hotel, sweeping up the stairs until they were blocked by the closed grilles. Through these, an SS major asked the French guard commander for directions to Pétain's suite.

"I am sorry," said the officer. "The Marshal is resting. No one is allowed to disturb him."

The SS major withdrew but returned fifteen minutes later with General von Neubronn who politely asked Pétain's guards to open the grilles. When they refused the grilles were kicked open by a jack-booted SS sergeant. Neubronn went straight to Pétain's suite. Pétain asked to be allowed to finish dressing and Neubronn waited.

"Are you aware of the Marshal's age?" Dr Ménétrel asked Neubronn's adjutant. "He has been brusquely awoken. He is facing a long and tiring journey. Don't you think he should be allowed to take some breakfast?"

While Pétain and Nini took their time over coffee and croissants, Ménétrel took Stucki and Valeri into his office to show them the latest conditions imposed on Pétain, drafted by Cecil von Renthe-Fink; namely that Charles Rochat, Général Bridoux and Admiral Bléhaut should be included in the Belfort convoy. By now Pétain was ready and, according to Stucki, "looking as composed and calm as I have ever known him". He handed some letters to Stucki and Papal Nuncio Valerio Valeri—protests against his treatment and declarations of his patriotism. Pétain wanted the whole *Corps Diplomatique* to know what was happening, hoping they could prevent him being taken to Germany. But his fate was decided.

Walking down a line-up of his staff, Pétain shook their hands before entering the lift. In the foyer he was saluted by a guard of honour from the *1e Régiment de la France*, each man's eyes welling with tears. Dressed like a country gentleman, Pétain muttered, "Anyone who did not know what was going on, seeing me in this outfit on such a morning, would probably think I was going for a walk in the country." Then Pétain told his staff, "Carry on as normal. Continue to work just as if I was there, better than before, if possible." As he turned away towards the cars, the little daughter of one of the staff who always greeted him ran up to kiss him good-bye. Even Stucki cried.

By now a considerable crowd had gathered to see him off, breaking into the *Marseillaise* as Pétain got into one of several large, dark limousines.[97] They remembered the hero of Verdun, not the shameful years of *collaboration* and *Milice* excesses.

At 1pm, Admiral Auphan, Pétain's personal representative in Paris, received a radio message from the Hôtel du Parc. He was ordered to publish Pétain's final proclamation. Few copies ever saw daylight, but those that did made Pétain's excuses: he tried to save France from the worst, and that even if he was not France's sword, he tried to be her shield. He now prayed that the French would "gather around those who will guarantee to take you along the road to honour and the paths of order".[98]

AT HIS HÔTEL DE VILLE SUITE Pierre Taittinger was woken at 3am by a telephone call warning him that the Hôtel de Ville would face a Resistance assault at 6am.

"What on earth?" thought Taittinger. "An *assault!*"

It seemed ridiculous considering that Colonel Lizé's deputy, Commandant Dufresne, had spent several hours there the previous day.

An hour later Taittinger received another call.

"There's something you don't know which is that, contrary to anything else that may have been agreed, you are going to be arrested, and it is so that you can avoid this unpleasantness that I am warning you."

Gulping with emotion, Taittinger thanked his caller for the warning and asked his name; no answer. The caller admitted that although he was now with the FTP, Taittinger once helped him.[99]

At 6am, washed, shaved and wearing a fresh shirt, Taittinger felt ready for whatever came his way. Across the building's frontage the windows were open and he saw Resistance sentries taking position and sections of FFI patrolling the square.

The assault party included FFI, Delegation bodyguards, police and female auxiliaries, and was led by Roland Pré and Leo Hamon.[100]

Suddenly a Panther tank appeared from the Rue de Rivoli, its massive tracks grinding the cobbles, while its turret and powerful cannon turned menacingly from side to side. The FFIs took cover in doorways, front areas and the Metro station staircase. Once the Panther had passed, the FFIs continued their so-called assault.[101]

Sixty FFIs armed with assorted weapons took over the Hôtel de Ville. Then a car arrived pulling a small trailer loaded with more arms and ammunition. Contemplating their youth, Taittinger felt he was watching a cadets' wargame. Nevertheless, they took themselves seriously and soon informed Taittinger they were arresting Périer de Féral, despite several protests from municipal officials, including Taittinger, that Féral was a longstanding member of the *Armée Secrète*.[102]

Leo Hamon found René Bouffet, Prefect of the Department of the Seine, in his office.

"In the name of the *Comité Parisien de Libération* and on behalf of the provisional government of the Republic, I am taking possession of the Hôtel de Ville," said Hamon.

"You will have to account for everything that you do," said Bouffet, struggling to remain composed. "I have been trying to save Paris. You are committing a youthful prank which might have appalling consequences."[103]

In the meantime, in an unassuming diplomatic way, FFI Lieutenant Roger Stéphane established control. Inside the Hôtel de Ville, FFI numbers increased to four hundred. Political arrests began. Those detained considered escaping via the same underground passages suggested to Édouard Herriot three days before. But Taittinger decided to face whatever music came his way, along with Romazotti, Marcel Cornillat—who had negotiated the city's food provision throughout the preceding weeks—and André Ruegger, the Municipal Council's secretary, none of whom believed they had acted shamefully.[104]

Now a prisoner, Taittinger was led along corridors where previously he had met only deference. Although his chauffeur Léon remained loyally beside him, it hurt. First he was taken to Bouffet's office, now occupied by Lieutenant Stéphane, its magnificent furnishings submerged by weapons and boxes of ammunition as purposeful looking young men and women wearing blue clothing and FFI armbands came and went. Cradling an arm injured outside the Préfecture the previous day, Stéphane appeared exhausted. Attempting conversation with Stéphane, Taittinger mentioned his time at Verdun.

"I wasn't there," replied Stéphane. "That's something that distinguishes us."

There was a burst of machine-gun fire outside and Taittinger threw himself under the table.

"I did not do Verdun," said Stéphane tersely. "And I am not under the table either."

Stéphane told Taittinger that he was a prisoner, albeit for his own protection.

"We are in a revolutionary period," said Stéphane. "And it would be best from all points of view if you allowed yourself to be taken into protective custody until there is freedom on the streets again."[105]

After allowing Taittinger to telephone his wife, Stéphane told his prisoners they would eventually be going to "the Depot"—the cells connected to the Palais de Justice. But first stop was the Préfecture. Accompanied by Romazzotti, Cornillat and Ruegger, Taittinger descended the Hôtel de Ville's red-carpeted staircase. This time there were no *Gardes Républicaines* in resplendent cavalry uniforms to raise their swords to their chins in salute, merely young men toting rifles and Sten guns.

A passing German armoured car noticed the FFI emblazoned Citroen parked outside the Hôtel de Ville and opened fire. Again Taittinger threw himself down, breaking the gold watch in his waistcoat pocket. A few bursts of fire shooed the armoured car away but Stéphane's men were unsettled. It seemed unwise to approach the Préfecture by the obvious route across the Pont d'Arcole. With his virtually unparalleled knowledge of central Paris, Taittinger suggested the underground passage to the Assistance Publique building on the opposite side of the Place de l'Hôtel de Ville. Exiting on the Avenue Victoria, they encountered Taittinger's friend, Dr. Durand, who guided them to the Secretariat General where suitable rooms for holding prisoners were available.[106]

Held in a room overlooking the Place de l'Hôtel de Ville, Taittinger, his colleagues and their guards found dead corners in which to avoid stray bullets whistling through the open windows as the gunfire increased. With his captors' permission Taittinger made some telephone calls, including to Raoul Nordling, but no one could prevent such incidents. In the distance FFIs could be seen firing from the Hôtel de Ville at German vehicles and any Parisian not wearing a *Tricolore* armband. Taittinger watched as a German staff car crossed the Place de l'Hôtel de Ville unscathed while a *Parisienne* and an elderly gentleman were shot dead. A young man *sans* armband emerging onto the Place de l'Hôtel de Ville from the Pont d'Arcole swiftly retraced his steps. "Do they have commemorative plaques, these Parisians pointlessly gunned down by our own?" Taittinger asks bitterly in his memoirs.[107]

When an ambulance arrived to collect the injured and dying, a white-clad nurse waved a Red Cross flag while saying curtly "You will not kill," rather than the more plaintive "Don't shoot." Momentarily the shooting ceased while the injured were gathered up. But when a German lorry passed a few hundred metres away, firing recommenced, sending the ambulance driver diving for cover. The nurse waved her Red Cross flag and continued. After delivering these casualties to the Hôpital Hôtel-Dieu they returned within moments. Taittinger saw around a dozen people wantonly gunned down, all French.[108]

WHILE STÉPHANE'S MEN INVESTED THE HÔTEL DE VILLE, Alexandre Parodi held a meeting of senior *resistants* on Avenue de Lowendal. In the first place Roland Pré brought them up to date regarding Nordling's truce, which, they acknowledged, had saved the Préfecture. They subsequently agreed to send representatives to Nordling's consulate, including Roland Pré, Alexandre de Saint Phalle and Leo Hamon, who came across from the Hôtel de Ville.[109]

They reached Nordling later than expected and went straight into a long, detailed discussion of the truce's minutiae.

"May I introduce two German officers," said Nordling. "Austrians in fact." Both Bobby Bender and Erich von Posch-Pastor were present along with Swiss Consul René Naville.

"I can't see the point," replied Leo Hamon.

"Regarding the capabilities of the German Army," said Nordling, looking at Hamon, "you can discuss all that with them."[110]

Nordling explained that von Choltitz had no wish to fight in Paris unless absolutely forced to. On the other hand Nordling understood the Resistance's desire to actively eject the Germans. He believed, however, that, if the Resistance continued down this path, there would be terrible damage to Paris and dreadful loss of life.

Leo Hamon responded that Parisians had taken up arms, not to make truces, but to give France her capital city, liberated by her own people. But Hamon recognised that the Resistance was not strong enough to withstand determined German retaliation, either at the Préfecture nor the Hôtel de Ville. The number of armed *résistants* in Paris remained puny. Whatever their standpoint, everyone present accepted that Nordling had gained time and agreed for his truce to be prolonged.

"Are there any Communists among you?" asked Nordling.

Raising his hand, Roger Besse admitted to representing the Union of Syndicates on the *Comité Parisien de Libération*. He was entrusted with a message for the Resistance at the Préfecture that contained the following text: "Due to undertakings made by the German Command not to attack public buildings occupied by French forces, and to treat all French prisoners in accordance with the laws of war, the Provisional Government of the French Republic and the *Conseil National de la Résistance* order you to cease fire against the occupying forces until the total evacuation of Paris. The greatest calm is recommended to the population and they are requested to stay indoors."

The *Conseil National de la Résistance* accepted this wording, while General von Choltitz—on reading the document later that morning—disliked the insinuation that the Wehrmacht was collapsing and thought that clauses concerning *résistants*' conduct should be altered to: "The population is requested to control itself, not to create incidents nor to walk in the streets." Nordling later wrote, "I never had the impression that the Resistance wished to avoid an armed conflict with the occupiers. I thought that they only desired to delay hostilities until a more propitious moment suited them. When I remarked to these gentlemen that, practically speaking, they had already achieved an important victory over the Germans by forcing the garrison commander of Paris to recognise *de facto* the Resistance as an authority with which they could enter negotiations, it seemed that, all the same, they accepted my point of view."[111]

Immediately afterwards Parodi visited 41 Rue de Bellechasse to meet the *Conseil National de la Résistance*, including Georges Bidault, and explain the truce. Jacques Chaban-Delmas supported it, insisting that their wisest choice was to await the Allies. But the counter-argument, that the Resistance needed to show they could fight, was deeply rooted. COMAC's Pierre Villon and André Tollet regarded negotiation as treasonous in itself, insisting that hostilities must be resumed and more barricades erected. When the vote was held, however, to Villon and Tollet's disgust, the motion was carried in favour of Nordling's truce. Georges Bidault maintained that the truce helped preserve Paris.[112] Shortly afterwards Chaban-Delmas, Leo Hamon and Roland Pré visited Nordling saying that the CNR approved the text and wanted it published as soon as possible "in all the *quartiers* of Paris".[113]

Von Choltitz's reservations mirrored those of Villon and Tollet. While he recognised the truce's practical benefit for his garrison, it involved negotiations with the enemy when Nazi thinking towards irregular forces was uncompromising. If the agreement was broadcast by radio, it could embarrass him and endanger his family. To secure French discretion, he offered to release Wehrmacht food reserves from cold storage.[114]

AT AROUND 11AM PIERRE TAITTINGER heard that Nordling's truce was official. Cars with loudspeakers announced the ceasefire in French and German while, at the Hôtel de Ville, a *Garde Republicaine* sounded the recall with a bugle.

At the Secrétariat Général building Madame Miret, an official's wife, arranged lunch for both the internees and their guards, setting up a well laid table in the vestibule. Everyone was surprisingly hungry and the food, though plentiful, disappeared quickly. *Résistant* Fournier telephoned the Hôtel de Ville to ask Lieutenant Stéphane if he might release Taittinger and his colleagues, but Stéphane insisted that the truce changed nothing. Surprised by Stéphane's intransigence, Fournier advised Taittinger to plead his case with the *Commissaires du Peuple* (People's Commissars) who had set up a tribunal at the Hôtel de Ville.[115]

Outside once again, Taittinger recognised the report of Mausers exchanging fire with the FFIs' diverse weaponry. Not all Resistance factions would willingly cease combat.[116]

THE PREVIOUS EVENING'S CEASEFIRE ORDER reached Henri Rol-Tanguy only at 7am on 20 August, after taking a circuitous route via Chaban-Delmas to Colonel Lizé's chief of staff, Commandant Dufresne, who was preoccupied with taking the Hôtel de Ville. Despite lack of sleep, Rol-Tanguy reacted vigourously, first warning COMAC who were unaware of it. Next, he told Colonel Lizé that he intended to continue with the Insurrection. Uninterested in the motives behind Nordling's efforts, Rol-Tanguy insisted that "The order for the Insurrection was given in accordance with the 'delegate Commissar' of the Provisional Government of the French Republic, in agreement with the Committee for the Liberation of Paris, and *must* be carried out."[117]

Around 8am, Rol-Tanguy heard that Colonel Lizé believed the Germans were again preparing an "*offensive brutale*" on the Préfecture. He advised Lizé to create a diversion elsewhere, then told Dufresne emphatically, "I am a soldier. All negotiation with the enemy in time of war is a crime against the Nation." Rol-Tanguy and Lizé issued the following directive: "The formal order [from headquarters] is to attack *à l'outrance* the enemy wherever he is to be found. This order annuls any other orders given which may contradict this prescription." From mid-morning on 20 August the commander of the Paris FFI declared Nordling's truce over.[118]

Henri Rol-Tanguy's biographer, Roger Bourderon, emphasises that since Rol-Tanguy had not attended the meetings held either by Parodi or Nordling, the mixed messages regarding the truce were attributable to communication failures. While Parodi always insisted that, since he was senior, he should have been obeyed, it seems extraordinary that, having appointed Rol-Tanguy as FFI commander on 19 August, no communication about Nordling's negotiations reached his HQ on Rue Victor Schoelcher, which is not far from Avenue de Lowendal.[119]

In any case, Rol-Tanguy insisted on fighting, and it was the renewed gunfire following his decision to disregard Nordling's truce that Taittinger heard during luncheon at the Secrétariat Général.

ACCOMPANIED BY *RÉSISTANT* FOURNIER, Taittinger returned along the subterranean corridor towards the Hôtel de Ville to plead with the Commissars of the People who now sat in one of the grand committee rooms. There were five of them, four quite young and a fifth, more senior, who seemed to be in charge. They introduced themselves to Taittinger by their *noms de guerre*—"fantasy names", Taittinger called them. Expecting to be released along with his colleagues, Taittinger explained that neither he nor the Conseil Municipal had done anything shameful during the Occupation.

The chief Commissar—Valin—brandished his left-wing credentials, emphasising that they came from "different sides of the barricade". He accused Taittinger of playing a "harmful" role under the Germans, even saying Taittinger acted treasonously by negotiating with Boineburg-Lengsfeld for the lives of hostages. When Valin said that saving factories from destruction went against "the revolutionary mystique", Taittinger was stupefied.

"It is," declared Valin, "only on the smoking ruins of Paris that the Commune can be installed. In a Paris that is protected, with its houses still standing, we would never be able to plant the red flag!"[120]

Between the wars Taittinger had been a notable member of France's anti-democratic Right. But these details from his opinionated, snobby memoirs—which were praised by the Academie Française—make extraordinary reading and are probably true. In the next line he calls Valin an *énergumène* (oddball) before writing that Valin's accomplices seemed disappointed that Paris was not becoming another Warsaw. Irrespective of his several years as a *clandestin*, Valin did not strike Taittinger as someone who had risked much. Their exchange ended when Lieutenant Stéphane arrived, saying that Yves Bayet wanted Taittinger at the Préfecture.[121]

This time Taittinger was led to the Cité Metro station and the staircase up to the Préfecture. At the top they encountered three policemen in mufti sitting behind sandbags, armed with revolvers, a rifle and some freshly made sandwiches. The main courtyard, the Cour Jean-Chiappe, named after a 1930s police chief notable for suppressing the Left, was now clogged with vehicles of diverse provenance. Taittinger joined other deposed officials, including René Bouffet and Périer de Féral. Bussière's son André welcomed them, but André-Jean Godin, whom Taittinger had known many years, without suspecting that he was head of *Ajax Nord*, cut him dead.

"At the Préfecture," Taittinger wrote, "there reigned an atmosphere of civil war and revolution. One heard shouts, orders and gunfire. Every so often the arrival of new arrestees elicited frenzied clamours. Blows rained down on them producing cries of sorrow and pain. We were in the centre of a great drama, beginning there and which, *quartier* by *quartier*, was taking over Paris, a drama called *épuration*." Taittinger, Bouffet, Bussière and the deposed officials of Occupied Paris were relieved to be together, but having to lie on bare flagstones amid the cries of *collabos* being beaten up was nerve-racking. One of Luizet's deputies told Taittinger that they were "considered hostages, destined to be shot if any captured *résistants* were executed either by *Miliciens* or the Germans".[122]

AT 8AM DE GAULLE LANDED AT MAUPERTUIS in Normandy. Though aware that the flight from Gibraltar was pushing the limits of his Lockheed Hudson's range, de Gaulle "never for a moment seemed worried about the risks we were running. He didn't look out of the window until France was under our wheels," remembered Lionel de Marmier. The Constable was more worried about the communists among the Paris Resistance and whether the Americans would finesse France towards a transitional assembly led by Laval and Herriot, delaying the Republic's restoration. "Why do you think," de Gaulle later asked his son Philippe, "that I struggled so much in London and Algiers in 1943 to see your unit take part in the landings if it wasn't to be sure of seeing Paris liberated by ourselves, whatever the Allies wanted?"[123]

Welcomed at Maupertuis by General Koenig, de Gaulle was anxious for news of Paris and Leclerc. Koenig told him Laval had been taken to Belfort, alleviating one of the Constable's worries. Of von Choltitz's role de Gaulle wrote in his memoirs that "the enemy, busying himself with the withdrawal of his *services*, had not, so far, reacted very harshly, but with more of his columns passing through Paris, he could, at any time, have inflicted reprisals".[124]

Perusing the campaign map at Shellburst, de Gaulle complimented Eisenhower on the Allied Expeditionary Force's stunning successes. But he noticed that Patton had two corps near the Seine at Mantes and Melun while Hodges' First Army, which controlled Leclerc's division, merely mopped up around Falaise. Given that First Army's General Courtney Hodges had earmarked the 2e DB for Paris as early as 15 August when American corps were being reorganised, de Gaulle could have been more trusting.[125]

"From the strategic point of view," began de Gaulle, "I cannot understand why, since you cross the Seine at Melun, at Mantes and at Rouen, it is only at Paris that you do not cross. If it were the question of an ordinary place and not the capital of France, my opinion would not be binding on you, because normally the conduct of operations is your concern. But the fate of Paris is of essential consequence to the French government. For this reason I think myself obliged to intervene and to urge you to send my troops. It goes without saying that it is the French 2nd Armoured Division that must be selected to take first place."[126]

De Gaulle claimed that Eisenhower was embarrassed. But Eisenhower's reply, that he prefered to avoid fighting in large cities which would involve horrific damage and casualties, was legitimate. But what about the Insurrection? Eisenhower replied that it had kicked off too soon.

"Why too soon?" asked de Gaulle. "At this very moment, your forces are on the Seine."

Without giving precise dates, Eisenhower reassured de Gaulle that when he ordered an advance on Paris Leclerc would have the honour of entering the city first. De Gaulle nevertheless impressed upon the Americans in slow, precise French that "*l'affaire*" was one of "*une telle importance nationale*" and that he would send the 2e DB to Paris himself if necessary. Describing this interview with Eisenhower, de Gaulle omits to mention his concerns over the communists in Paris.[127] However, de Gaulle's American biographer Don Cook quotes Eisenhower's summary of this meeting: "He made no bones about it; he said there was a serious menace from the communists in the city, and that if we delayed moving in we would risk finding a disastrous political situation, one that might be disruptive to the Allied war effort."[128]

De Gaulle seems to have believed that Roosevelt wanted to prevent him from reaching Paris and that Laval's proposed transitional government (based on André Enfière's tenuous OSS connections) was part of this. During the years of solitary struggle to maintain his ideals of French greatness, perhaps the Constable had developed a form of paranoia which discounted the myriad concerns affecting both Churchill and Roosevelt.[129] That Leclerc should be held back with Hodges' First Army reinforced a terrible fear that the Americans wanted to reach the Eiffel Tower first.

"But," de Gaulle later wrote, "*renconfort*—reassurance—was not far away. A great wave of enthusiasm and popular emotion greeted me when I entered Cherbourg and followed me all the way to Rennes, through Coutances, Avranches and Fougères. In the ruins of destroyed towns and wrecked villages the population massed by the roadside to hail my passing. Whatever remained of windows was decorated with flags and bunting. Bells sounded. Roads pocked with shell-holes seemed joyful under the flowers. Mayors gave martial addresses with sobbing voices. I then said a few words, not of pity that would not have been wanted, but of hope and pride, finishing with *la Marseillaise* which the crowd sang with me."[130]

Hoping to expedite matters, Leclerc visited V Corps' General Leonard Gerow accompanied by Weil. Gerow conceded: "You are not only a divisional commander, you represent the French Army." But when Leclerc sought a more substantial commitment, Gerow replied, "That does not depend upon me. You'll have to go higher."

Gerow's "puritan sense of discipline" got Leclerc down. "There were things they simply didn't understand," wrote Girard, "and the General was right to go and explain things to them, but I doubt that it will make them see the reasons for his attitude any more clearly. They will continue to take for indiscipline what is in fact his conscientiousness in having to carry out an extra-military mission."[131]

Next Leclerc took a Piper Cub to Hodges' HQ. According to First Army's war diary, Leclerc argued incessantly that his division should march on Paris, first claiming to have sufficient supplies, then admitting that he needed more. French pride kept colliding with "poor relation" status. "The General [Hodges] was not impressed with him or his arguments, and let him understand that he [Leclerc] was to stay put until he gave orders otherwise."[132]

For the French the oft-used American arguments about regrouping were wearing thin.[133]

OSS COLONEL DAVID BRUCE and his entourage of well-travelled, multi-lingual patricians were anxious to lead the Americans into Paris. After witnessing the first phases of *l'épuration* in newly liberated Chartres, they had spent the previous night in a field near US 5th Infantry Division's CP. Eschewing K rations, Bruce's party sustained themselves on omelettes washed down with wine or instant coffee depending on the time of day. Visiting châteaux could be disappointing; one had been used as a German HQ and left filthy, with weapons strewn about and "the usual heaps of empty wine bottles". They also found packs of booby traps which the Germans had not had time to set.[134]

The roads in 5th Infantry's area were littered with blackened corpses, mostly German but some Americans as well. While Bruce chatted to General Irwin and 5th ID's chief of staff, Colonel Thackeray, John Mowinckel arrived requesting supplies from an abandoned Wehrmacht warehouse to furnish a Special Intelligence HQ. Bruce found enough stock to furnish "all the hotels on the Riviera", as he colourfully described it.[135]

It was at Irwin's CP that Bruce hooked up with writer Ernest Hemingway and his driver, Red Pelkey. Hemingway had installed himself at Rambouillet following two days of "unofficial reconnaissance work" which suited his partisan spirit. Hemingway also wanted to be the first American into Paris and was accompanied by two truckloads of FFIs he had met near Rambouillet; an ill-clothed little group, commanded by an exhausted looking Frenchman called Tahon Marceau. Although armed only with a few captured pistols and a couple of Sten guns, their patrolling was competent enough to ascertain that the Germans had abandoned Rambouillet that morning. Patrolling the town's southern approaches with them, Hemingway found a deserted roadblock which had earlier accounted for an American patrol. The locals had kindly buried the dead Americans, but their equipment remained with their vehicles and Marceau's FFIs helped themselves.[136]

As they patrolled Rambouillet, the inhabitants told them that a German battlegroup including tanks remained east of the town. Hemingway advised an American sapper party to leave all mines *in situ* and requested heavy machine-guns from Irwin. Irwin refused, but felt unable to leave a great American writer in danger and sent a reconnaissance detachment to reinforce him.[137]

Hence it was on the morning of 20 August, when Hemingway visited Irwin's CP the second time, that he met David Bruce and they agreed to meet at Rambouillet later that day. It would be exaggerating to say "Papa liberated Paris" but, aided by Marceau's FFIs, he certainly "liberated" Rambouillet which became an essential springboard for liberating Paris.[138]

IT WAS BECOMING A HOT DAY. The air of Paris was fetid from uncollected refuse. On those streets that avoided becoming shooting galleries, housewives queued outside bakers' shops and the faithful still attended Mass. Bathers still swam in the Seine by the Pont Royal or sunbathed on the artificial beach near the Pont Iena. There remained moments of humanity between occupiers and occupied; guards manning the barriers around the Rue de Rivoli apologised before hand-searching anyone wishing to pass. At the checkpoint on the Boulevard de la Madeleine, seeing an old man visibly distressed when tipping out his shopping basket to be searched, a German soldier helped him repack it. There were similar barriers on the Boulevard Saint-Germain, the Rue du Bac, the Rue de Luynes and the Rue Gribeauval. When an elderly *Parisienne* approached German sentries on the Place des Pyramides asking if she could search for her cat in the Tuileries gardens, the sentries accompanied her, calling the cat's name among the shrubs.[139]

Not far away, Maurice Goudeket skulked in the air-raid shelter, wondering if he dared show his Semitic face while briskly returning to the Palais Royale apartment he shared with Colette. "Comrade, comrade," said the gardener, "the gates are open and there are people walking in the gardens." Furtively peeping outside, his heart racing, Goudeket made a brisk dash for the Palais Royale. Approaching the building, Goudeket recognised the comely frame of France's greatest erotic authoress outside their home, visibly distressed. Just as he expected, Colette had sent many friends searching for him. Whenever they drew a blank, she despaired that he might have been deported. Then she saw him. At first she was cross at being caused such worry and his explanation was unimpressive. She berated him over her efforts to protect him during the previous four years. Goudeket listened, tears coursing down his unshaven cheeks, and then they embraced and went inside.[140]

At this late stage of the Occupation, German theft lacked the methodology of Kurt von Behr's *M-Aktion*. On the Boulevard de la Madeleine, a lorry, loaded with bedding, skidded while turning out of a sidestreet, throwing a smart mattress into the road. Good bedding was much sought after and the mattress was quickly picked up by two Parisians and pulled into a doorway. The lorry reversed and its German crew made the Parisians surrender the mattress at gunpoint.[141]

There were more German patrols than previously, sometimes mounted on ubiquitous *Kübelwagens* carrying a MG42 machine-gun or a similarly armed motorcycle-sidecar. These patrolled the streets checking for anything that might impede retreating German columns. A Panther and various smaller tanks attached to the Luxembourg *Stützpunkt*, laagered along the Rue Crébillon, would sally forth to show Parisians that the Germans had not yet departed.

But, where the Wehrmacht were thinner on the ground, the FFI took advantage. The FTP's aggressive patrolling caused lively engagements in the 13th Arrondissement around the Place d'Italie, Avenue des Gobelins and Place de l'Hôpital. In the 10th Arrondissement, home of the great railway stations Gare du Nord and Gare de l'Est, the Germans remained in possession until the end. Being in strength at the Clignancourt barracks meant the German garrison was difficult to dislodge from the 18th Arrondissement; northern Paris would be liberated last.[142]

In the Latin Quarter's Rue de Buci, the FFI expelled some Japanese from a small hotel, pushing the hapless Orientals into the street for debagging and degradation. While on the Place Saint-Michel the FFI laid out planks with nails sticking up. When Wehrmacht trucks drove over them, puncturing their tyres, Rol-Tanguy's men opened up with machine-guns. A bus pressed into German service was also immobilised.

Stepping outside his home in the university area, Jean Galtier-Boissière noticed the FFI machine-gun set up on the pavement watching over the Pont Saint-Michel and the young men in shirt sleeves and armbands toting rifles and small pistols, using all their brute

274 • Paris '44

strength to push disabled vehicles into position to form a barricade.[143] Nordling's truce made time for more *impromptu* fortifications to be erected. Entire neighbourhoods cooperated to build them, not just working-class militants as in 1871. A barricade could be made from anything; a wrecked vehicle, or an overturned cart or trailer was often a good start, followed by pieces of furniture, household junk, hacked up cobblestones, felled trees, the circular grids covering tree roots, paving stones or macadam (that could sometimes be lifted like thick vinyl). If situated near a park, soil provided useful aggregate. Barricades came in all sizes, whether blocking off an entire street or merely protecting a machine-gun nest. Often of questionable military value, barricades undoubtedly offered some protection to those behind them. But their effectiveness hugely depended on where they were and what hostile forces they had to face.

Galtier-Boissière watched fascinated as the Boulevard Saint-Michel barricade took shape, supported by around fifty FFIs. But being untrained they scurried for cover in doorways when a *Kübelwagen* appeared. The *Kübelwagen* waited. A few moments later a bus used as an ambulance needed to be let through. When the FFIs lifted the spiked planks to let the bus pass, the *Kübelwagen* rushed through behind. Inexperienced FFIs fired from all sides, forgetting the risk of hitting each other in the crossfire. Luckily only one was injured.

"Well, what's the situation?" Galtier-Boissière asked a young FFI.

"Confused," admitted the lad. "We're supporting our comrades at the Palais de Justice and the Préfecture. Yesterday we made a great job of shooting up a convoy. Didn't you see?"[144]

Relieved to be past military age, Galtier-Boissière thought 1944's street fighters more akin to the Parisians who defended Clichy for Napoleon in 1814 than Great War veterans like himself. "One could go home at lunchtime with one's rifle; everyone was at the windows watching you and cheering, from the milkman to the grocer and the bistro owner offering a glass of white wine."

More unreal to Galtier-Boissière were the *badauds* (onlookers) who were sometimes desperately naïve, understanding the risks only when someone fell down dead. Galtier-Boissière explained the rankings among the *badauderie héroïque,* or heroic onlookers. *Les risques-tout,* the risk alls, were happy to mill around behind combatants where they had good chances of being hit, while *les autres,* the others, observed from street corners, like Galtier-Boissière himself. Less *chic* but more sensible were *les moins braves,* the less brave, who stood considerably further back.[145]

The Latin Quarter had quickly become a no-go area for the Wehrmacht. Once its narrow streets were barricaded, *résistants* could move around freely. Their only uniform was an armband. Whether adorned with the letters FFI or FTP, these easily made armbands usually bore the *Tricolore's* blue, white and red, and the Cross of Lorraine. Simply wearing one made its wearer a combatant, especially if he had a weapon.[146]

RAOUL NORDLING WAS ANXIOUS lest the precious truce he negotiated fell to pieces. But General von Choltitz's good faith was confirmed when an officer at the Meurice telephoned Nordling to discuss arrangements for loudspeaker cars to circulate the city. Similar suggestions came from the Préfecture. However, the FFI had problems providing loudspeaker cars because those obedient to Rol-Tanguy and Lizé refused to recognise the truce, barricades increasingly restricted circulation, and FFI vehicles were mostly garaged at Denfert-Rochereau south of Montparnasse. But an arrangement was made for German and French loudspeaker teams to meet at the Place Vendôme at 2.30pm where Raoul Nordling, assisted by Émil Bender, would issue guidelines.[147]

On the way, Nordling was gratified to see the Place de l'Opéra filled with Parisians taking their Sunday stroll, discussing his truce and the huge concession made by von Choltitz. *Tricolores* were unfurling from windows and rooftops, in a way not seen since 1940.[148]

Reaching the Place Vendôme, Nordling and Bender found German *Feldgendarmerie* and French police wearing Resistance armbands awaiting them. But they soon discovered that neither team had any formal orders beyond translated copies of the morning's agreement. Furthermore, the German envoy was being more cooperative than the French, who had not sent anyone of significant rank. On his own authority, Nordling gave Bender orders for the Germans; then, turning towards the French policemen, he explained that the German authorities had agreed to suspend hostilities, which would also save Paris from destruction, though he believed that danger had receded. Switching between speaking German and French, Nordling gave both groups orders to tour Paris reading out the ceasefire proclamation with loud speakers.[149]

"What are you lot doing down there?" yelled the Gaullist Marcel Willard from the balcony of the Ministry of Justice.

Nordling explained that he was giving orders to announce the truce.

"What truce?" scoffed Willard. "There isn't a truce!"

Shaking his head, Nordling went up to Willard's office.

"Would you please telephone the Préfecture of Police," said Nordling wearily.

After doing as Nordling asked, Willard accepted that a truce was in force. Nordling returned outside and sent both loudspeaker teams on their way. Unbeknown to him, something had happened which became the day's highlight.[150]

ALEXANDRE PARODI BELIEVED THAT MEETING Resistance leaders personally would be more effective in getting the truce honoured on the French side. Accompanied by his sister, Roland Pré, Émile Laffond and a young female driver wearing a blue Red Cross uniform, Parodi left Rue Séguier at around 2.30pm. Perhaps the truce made Parodi's staff over-confident and sloppy about security. Their car contained several Resistance documents which would make compromising reading if they fell into German hands. Emerging from the Boulevard Saint-Germain opposite the War Minstry, they were halted at a checkpoint which included two 75mm PAK guns, and twenty well armed German soldiers. Speaking bad French, a sergeant said, "Terrorists to kill our comrades." Then he gesticulated, saying,

"To visit car." After finding documents and a FFI armband on the car's floor they arrested everyone. With their hands in the air, Parodi's party were searched. A German intelligence colonel perused the seized papers and artefacts. "Very serious," he said.

"We are important people in the Resistance," said Parodi. "A truce has been concluded with the general commanding Gross-Paris, negotiated by Monsieur Nordling, the Swedish Consul, and we were circulating to see that it was applied. We have been arrested during the truce. You should set us free immediately." The colonel decided to take them to von Choltitz to clarify the situation. They departed for the Hôtel Meurice in two cars.[151]

AT AROUND 3PM CHARLES LUIZET EMERGED from the Préfecture's main gate to announce the ceasefire. According to Notre Dame's Monsignor Brot, who watched from the opposite end of the *Parvis*, Luizet was wearing dress uniform including a sword, though few other accounts confirm this. "I descended from my lodgings and went to look outside, accompanied by a curate and one of the Cathedral's workmen," wrote Brot. "The front of the basilica had received a few good hits from German tanks. While we were taking stock of the damaged sculptures, thankfully not too serious, a car full of German soldiers arrived, letting rip all around with their machine-guns. We only just had time to take cover, running as fast as we could and throwing ourselves on the ground. It was a close one and, looking about us, there were plenty of dead and dying lying on the ground. Once again, we learnt not to trust German promises." Notre Dame remained closed that Sunday.[152]

Luizet's appearance outside the Préfecture was the culmination of several events; at 2.20pm he advised all departmental *commissariats* in Paris that the ceasefire must be respected. Then, at 3.18pm he gave the formal ceasefire order to all police stations in the name of the *Comité de la Liberation de la Préfecture de Police*. All shooting at German personnel was to cease until they had left Paris.[153]

AROUND 4PM, STEPPING OUT FOR A STROLL amid sporadic gunfire, Henri Culmann reached the Boulevard Saint-Michel's junction with the Rue Monsieur le Prince where he saw a police car with an attached loudspeaker, followed by a Wehrmacht vehicle on whose roof sat a Paris policeman. "Every fifty metres these vehicles would stop and the loudspeaker informed the population that the Germans had consented to regard the FFIs as combatants and therefore to treat as prisoners of war rather than *francs-tireurs* any FFI who fell into their hands. A truce had been agreed whereby both the FFI and the Germans ceased firing at one another."

On the Place Edmond Rostand, beyond the pretty, *art nouveau* fountain, Culmann saw five Panther tanks hovering around the Rue Gay-Lussac, their commander chatting to a French fireman officer, before departing in opposite directions. Suddenly machine-gun fire raked the Boulevard Saint-Michel. Fearing for his life, Culmann retreated along the Rue Soufflot where a concièrge gave him a glass of water. When the firing ceased he rejoined the Boulevard Saint-Michel from the Rue Le Goff. Four of the Panthers were still around and, when firing broke out again, Culmann watched in horror as a Panther's turret turned towards an assumed target and fired a long burst from its coaxial machine-gun. "I will remember all my life the sight of that turret cranking jerkily round and then the thin blue plume of smoke drifting up from that weapon," Culmann wrote. "Everyone fled screaming and falling about. I stumbled and found myself on top of someone, while nearby five fallen bodies lay on the cobbles bleeding and trying to get up. These unfortunates were moved to an aid post in the foyer of a hotel on the Rue Le Goff where, thanks to the angle of the road, they could not be hit by that tank's machine-gun. Remembering their injuries, they were mostly legs and lower body, since the burst had been aimed low. I used my neck-tie to tourniquet the leg of a young woman who was bleeding profusely and went to telephone for help. Following my pleas, the first stretcher bearers arrived with a speed and courage I will always admire. The worst injury was a man with a hideously broken thigh, visible through his ripped trousers. He was taken into a nearby house. I later learnt that he lost his leg and that two others died."[154]

If Nordling's truce held, even patchily, most Parisians welcomed it as a saviour from death, injury and damage. But many FFI regarded cars with loudspeakers announcing the truce as an absurdity, a German ruse to divert attention from their suppression of important centres of resistance. If the SS violated the truce, some FFI denied its existence.[155]

Sonderführer Robert Wallraf thought French ceasefire initiatives were worth no more than Monsignor Brot thought German ones were. "They fired from all sides at any location where German soldiers expected to feel safe. Resistance vehicles drove at breakneck speeds along all avenues; inoffensive in appearance, they fired with machine-guns at any German vehicle they encountered. The Resistance turned the streets of Paris into an environment full of dangers."[156]

IRRESPECTIVE OF NORDLING'S TRUCE, the Resistance continued seizing government buildings. Having got inside the Ministry of the Interior on the Place Baveau, senior *résistants* Gus, Chevrier and others headed for the minister's apartment. Brushing past the entrance hall's famous renaissance tapestry of God the Father—onto which someone wittily pinned Pétain's image over a prostrate man—they reached the minister's luxurious bathroom where they showered before sitting naked in the *salon*'s armchairs smoking. Surveying the minister's luxurious apartment, Roger Chevrier remarked, "If I ever return to being an ordinary soldier, I reckon that after today living like a proconsul, I will have paid for it."

They then returned to Saint-Phalle's house where, amid the comings and goings of armed *résistants*, someone played the *Marseillaise* and Chopin's *Tristesse* on the grand piano.[157]

"We're playing with them with this talk of an armistice, but if they take it for the real thing that would be boring," Saint-Phalle told a young *résistant*. "Tell them [the Allies] that they can come, that the Germans are not numerous and that, for them, it will be nothing."[158]

AT THE HÔTEL MEURICE, PARODI'S PARTY waited in the lobby for nearly an hour. Parodi felt convinced that once they explained themselves to von Choltitz they would be released immediately. Then a red-faced Gestapo officer appeared. "Follow me," he said contemptuously. "I have a few little questions to ask you." Parodi protested that their arrest contravened the agreement agreed with von Choltitz. Outside, except for his sister and the chauffeuse, Parodi and the men were driven to a Gestapo sub-office at 64 Avenue Henri-Martin in the 16th Arrondissement.[159]

Albeit writing twenty years apart, both Adrien Dansette and Raymond Dronne produced very similar accounts of the afternoon's events. The interrogation began in a roguish tone, but turned nasty once Parodi announced that he was the "Head of the Resistance".

"You are terrorists, spies, best to shoot you," came the menacing reply.

Parodi, Pré and Laffond watched their papers being sorted into official Gestapo envelopes while their hands were cuffed behind their backs. Armed soldiers bundled them into the car for a journey across the Bois de Boulogne, over the Pont de Saint-Cloud, ending up outside a large, bourgeois house signposted "Military Tribunal".[160]

"*Ach, schön!*" ("Wonderful!") exclaimed the officer who welcomed them.

"What's your resistance name?" asked another Gestapo officer.

"Cerat," replied Parodi.

"*Cerat!*" exclaimed the German. "Now tell me your real name."

Telephones had been ringing across Paris since Parodi's arrest. They were seen entering 64 Avenue Henri-Martin by Madamoiselle Jaqueline de Champeau, who happened to be Émile Laffond's fiancée. She telephoned Philippe Clément who alerted Alexandre de Saint-Phalle, who telephoned Nordling, who telephoned the Hôtel Meurice. The Meurice called the military tribunal, where the interrogation was halted. Their handcuffs removed, Parodi, Pré and Laffond were bundled back into the cars and returned to the Meurice where they began two hours earlier.[161]

Von Choltitz received them in his office, sitting behind the flat-top bureau with officers at smaller desks on each side. Von Choltitz claimed to know little about the Resistance, but he knew that if he washed his hands of them, the Gestapo would shoot them before dusk.[162]

"Do you take my soldiers for Boy Scouts?" asked von Choltitz, pointing at their compromising documents which were now piled on his desk.[163]

Nordling wrote that it was due to a gloating German telephoning his consulate, rather than Saint-Phalle, that he learnt of Parodi's arrest. Accompanied by Bender, he hastened to the Meurice and breezed up the stairs.[164]

Entering von Choltitz's office, Nordling immediately recognised Parodi and his companions. He was relieved to see Erich von Posch-Pastor acting as interpreter.

"Are these *messieurs* the 'gentlemen' with whom you suggested I should negotiate the other day?" asked von Choltitz.[165]

Nordling acknowledged that they were.

"You are well aware, Monsieur Consul Général," interjected Parodi, "that I am the only Minister representing the French Government in Paris."[166]

"We have taken these three men," said von Choltitz, "Here is their paperwork. Do you know whether they are terrorists or *messieurs*?"

"I don't know their names, but I have met them," replied Nordling. "These are the men with whom you can discuss the truce."

"I am," admitted Parodi, "the only Minister of the Algiers government working here."

"They were arrested before the truce could be applied through being announced by [loudspeaker] cars," von Choltitz told Nordling. "They represent the highest risk to the German authorities by virtue of the papers relating to the resistance and espionage which they were carrying with them. They ought to be shot outside immediately."

An officer produced a draft *affiche* found among Parodi's papers and read out the headline, "The German Army abandons Paris ..."

"This has nothing to do with the truce," said von Choltitz.

"That proclamation was written before the truce," replied Parodi, who sat between Pré and Laffond opposite von Choltitz.

"I struggle to accept your explanation," said von Choltitz.

"I am a minister of the French government," replied Parodi, "and I can't accept that you should doubt my word."

"Your ministerial ranking does not hold any value for us," said von Choltitz. "We don't know General de Gaulle. There are, however, Communists among you."

"The Communists are part of the Resistance," said Parodi coolly. "We have all formed a *bloc*."[167]

"I have no wish to see this incident take a tragic turn," said von Choltitz. "The essential thing is to preserve Paris. Its fate is in your hands. If the truce is not respected, the insurrection will be crushed."

Parodi recognised very well that, had he been captured a day earlier, he would have been shot at one of the Gestapo's well-used execution sites. But now the situation was different.[168]

Struggling with angina and the irritation of using a slow interpretor, von Choltitz asked, "I want to know if you're going to respect this truce. Are you capable of communicating your orders to your men? Will they obey you?"[169]

"You must understand," said Parodi in a fearless voice, "that a population in arms is not controllable in the same way as regular troops, especially in the *banlieues*. You are a general commanding an army. You give orders. You are obeyed. I lead a number of groups of differing political hues. I do not control them all. The Resistance is spontaneous."[170]

Von Choltitz listened. Parodi then asked, "Will you respect the Resistance's occupation of the ministries? Will you leave our newspapers alone?"

"Your occupation of ministerial buildings is *political*," replied von Choltitz. "Your newspapers are also political. It is essential to maintain the suspension of hostilities. I will give the order not to fire at buildings. But you must not fire at my troops, and no more barricades."

"If you want such incidents to cease," replied Parodi, "your troops should keep to designated areas and stop patrolling."

"I have to place men at barriers," said von Choltitz, "so that they can indicate the routes to be taken, avoiding the centre where possible. Inevitably some vehicles will pass through the centre. Then you shoot at them. You must accept that there are soldiers in Paris. If *authority* is going to be maintained there have to be patrols."

"The authority of the Germans—not the authority of the French?"

"For *order* to be maintained," von Choltitz replied, "you must prevent anything that provokes *disorder*. Your police can keep their *Tricolores*, but get back to work."[171]

Nordling interjected an observation. "It can't be easy for Parisians to respect the truce if they have nothing to put in their mouths."

"We have the means to produce what they need to eat," said von Choltitz. "When the electricity is cut, it will all go off anyway," he remarked.

Parodi stood impassively while Posch-Pastor translated.

"Parisians have been hungry for four years," replied Parodi brusquely. "They can endure another four days."[172]

"Don't you want to avoid riots and famine?" asked von Choltitz.

"I can only undertake that the truce will be respected," said Parodi. "Paris is not worried about riots and famine."[173]

Von Choltitz told Nordling that he would place food supplies under the authority of the Swedish and Swiss consulates for public distribution. "But these supplies must not fall into the hands of the Resistance," he insisted, trying to lower tensions while holding to his position.[174]

"Monsieur le Consul," von Choltitz told Nordling, "these three men no longer concern me. Take them under your protection. The fate of Paris has been decided."

With that Parodi, Pré and Laffond were safe.

"Are you an officer?" von Choltitz asked.

"Officer of reserve," replied Parodi.

"From one officer to another," said von Choltitz offering his hand.[175]
But Parodi refused the gesture.

"A French *minister*," said Parodi stiffly, "cannot, in the present circumstances, shake the hand of a German general."

Nordling sensed German hackles rising. A security officer advised that Parodi, Pré and Laffond should be held as hostages, but von Choltitz had made his decision.[176]

"I've been courteous all along," said von Choltitz. "I am handing these men over to you along with their papers. You will decide if international law allows you to release them."

Under the protection of Nordling, Parodi, Pré and Laffond were led to the main foyer by Bobby Bender. Seeing them reappear, the SD officer who arrested them stood incredulous. "What!" he exclaimed to an orderly. "That was the best arrest of my career. It's absolutely crazy to release those men!" As they exited the front door, Bender heard him mutter, "I'll see to them!"[177]

Outside Bender noticed a large, black Packard, its engine idling. A trilby-wearing plain-clothes Gestapo man sat beside the driver, cradling a submachine-gun. The Frenchmen got into Nordling's Citroen.

"I'll follow but don't wait if I get held up," said Bender.

Nordling nodded.

As Nordling's car pulled away towards the Rue de Rivoli's security barrier, the Packard followed, but Bender's torpedo Citroen cut in between them, screeched to a halt and stalled, preventing the Packard from passing. Hearing Bender's screeching brakes, von Choltitz went to his window just as his guards allowed Nordling's car onto the Place de la Concorde, its Swedish pennant fluttering in the sunshine, while at the checkpoint the Gestapo gunman gesticulated angrily at Bender.[178]

In his car Nordling returned Parodi's papers, but Parodi bade the Swede keep some for form's sake. Then Nordling dropped them at the corner of the Rue d'Anjou and Rue Saint-Lazare.

Parodi subsequently admitted to Francis Crémieux that von Choltitz was nowhere near as harsh as he could have been. French historian Pierre Bourget wrote, "Choltitz affected to be a 'harsh' general for the sake of appearances. But, in reality, he showed that he was relatively conciliatory, particularly when dealing with Nordling."[179]

GIVEN THE ILL-ASSORTED VEHICLES pressed into service as loudspeaker cars to announce the truce, it was not always easy to tell which cars were official. Implacably, Rol-Tanguy pronounced that "white flags are for troops who are surrendering". If, Rol-Tanguy insisted, anyone asked for a truce, it would be the Germans, and his troops would be informed in due course by senior *résistants*. When, at 4.45pm, Raymond Massiet found Rol-Tanguy, still at Rue Schoelcher, to lay to rest the rumour that Rol-Tanguy had agreed to the ceasefire, Rol-Tanguy said he had received "no *official* superior order". At that particular moment the only man capable of giving an authoritative order, Alexandre Parodi, was being passed between German offices following his arrest. Unaware of this, Massiet passed Rol-Tanguy's information to Colonel Lizé who, at 5.40pm, published a fresh order, "The orders recently transmitted by superior authorities impose on all fighting troops the imperative mission to continue combat according to previous instructions. All orders contrary to this do not emanate from military authorities, who have not been advised, and are therefore without value."[180]

At about the same time Rol-Tanguy ordered that *all* loudspeaker cars found announcing the truce should be seized. Not even Charles Luizet was immune from having his car stopped, but neither Rol-Tanguy's nor Lizé's powers entitled them to interfere with the Delegation.[181]

THAT THE SS AND SD CARED NOTHING for Nordling's truce was demonstrated by their seizure of the Rue de Lyon police station. Once taken prisoner, Commissioners Silvestri, Dubret and their *Gardiens* stood little chance. While they stood against a wall, their station was searched, yielding one FFI armband and three standard issue Lebel revolvers. For this, they were taken to Vincennes. "It's too late today," said an SS NCO. "We'll shoot them in the morning." After a sleepless night followed by the gunfire of dawn executions, Silvestri and his men were lead into the courtyard and lined up facing eleven freshly shot corpses. There was, however, no firing squad. Instead a lorry reversed up with its tailgate dropped to reveal a tripod mounted MG42 machine-gun with a belt of ammunition fed to the breach. Rather than executing them immediately, the SS forced Silvestri's men to carry the eleven corpses to a patch of open ground. As they lifted the corpses, Silvestri's men recognised them as fellow policemen. After a couple of hundred metres they laid down the bodies and were given shovels and picks with which to dig a burial pit while SS men kicked them around.[182]

Despite their situation, Commissioner Dubret kept their spirits up. So the SS picked on him. When the ditch was dug, they made Dubret stand in it.

"Well, who's going to perform the last rites?" Dubret joked.

The SS then turned on Silvestri. Though never a *résistant*, to save the younger men's lives, Silvestri claimed responsibility for the FFI brassard found at their police station. The SS made him lift a large stone with his arms stretched out in front of him and run with it while they kicked him. For further amusement, Silvestri was forced to carry a large beam while being mocked as Christ carrying his cross. Being middle-aged, wearing full uniform, Silvestri soon became exhausted.

Eventually, Silvestri was stood at the edge of the fresh mass grave. Knowing what was about to happen, he tried to smarten himself. Standing to attention, he shouted "Vive la France!" Machine-gun bullets ripped into his chest and he fell into the pit.

The other policemen also expected to die. But instead the SS NCO decided to make them fill in the grave. Dronne's information is that these SS came from the notorious 2nd SS Panzer Division *Das Reich* which had pitched up in Paris having lost their officers. This division had committed the massacre at Oradour Sur Glane, and the NCO who fed his cruelty on Silvestri's *Gardiens* bragged that he had nailed an infant to Oradour's church door with a bayonet. Perhaps the unexpected arrival of a Wehrmacht officer made him reconsider his conduct. But three recently executed FFIs were placed alongside Silvestri before the grave was filled in.[183]

REJOINING *LES BADAUDS* around mid-afternoon, Jean Galtier-Boissière found solid sand-bag defences a metre high around the Place Saint-Michel with FFIs in organised sections behind them. *Les badauds autres* huddled in doorways and pretty girls flaunted FFI armbands. When a whistle blew loudly, everyone turned. A German lorry was advancing along the Boulevard Saint-Michel. All but *les risques tout* scurried for shelter. Pausing at the barricade checkpoint, its crew faced gesticulative FFIs whose chief parleyed with the driver and the armed soldier beside him. Though inaudible to Galtier-Boissière, the FFIs must have been persuasive. The co-driver jumped out, surrendered his Schmeisser to one FFI, his pistol to another, gave his ammunition belt to a third, and put his hands up. The rest surrendered except the one on the roof. But a young FFI pointed out the guns trained on him and talked him down. Next came a lorry carrying female auxiliaries wearing looted furs and handbags. Similarly intimidated, they surrendered amicably. The FFIs gathered around their captives, asking if they were glad their war was over. Then they were marched towards the Préfecture while FFIs shared out their weapons and juggled with potato-masher hand-grenades.[184]

When a third lorry appeared at the end of the road, it reversed towards the Luxembourg and tried another route. With the excitement over, Galtier-Boissière continued towards the news kiosk on the corner of the Boulevard Saint-Germain. The seller had vanished and two day-old journals—*collabo* rags *Revolution Nationale* and *Au Pilori*—lay unsold. Leaving some coins, Galtier-Boissière grabbed a few. As he browsed, his veteran's eye noticed something bloody on the sidewalk: human brains.[185]

WHEN COLONEL DAVID BRUCE REACHED RAMBOUILLET, neither the Resistance nor Hemingway's group had entered its famous château, the French president's country home. Situated on the town's west side with its parkland, elaborate *bassins* and long, north-facing avenue, this impressive castle had witnessed many great moments in French history.

Hemingway's CP was two rooms inside the bijou Hôtel du Grand Veneur, located on the bending road towards Épernon, southwest of Rambouillet. Its well-stocked kitchens enabled Hemingway's party to live well, and Bruce's group were "enchanted to see him".[186]

"Agents and patrols kept rushing in with reports, some of them contradictory," wrote Bruce, "but all indicating that the Germans were laying mines down the road towards us about eight miles away, with a force of approximately 150 men. As there were no American troops in Rambouillet, Hemingway and the French were more or less convinced the Germans would retake the town tonight. We grilled the only Boche prisoner we could find. He either knew nothing or was a good actor, so we turned him back to the French, whom he was firmly convinced intended to execute him."[187]

David Bruce automatically became the senior American officer in Rambouillet. Situation reports went to Irwin's US 5th Infantry Division along with further requests for weapons and ammo. But all its nearest regiment could spare was boxes of captured German grenades. The Resistance in Maintenon promised, however, to send thirty men as reinforcements. Meanwhile Bruce wrote, "Agents were nipping in and out and everyone, including a stray American woman resident in France, was buttonholing me, asking questions and giving the answers at the same time. Newspaper correspondents had sprouted out of the ground, and the world and his wife were eating and uncorking champagne."[188]

Although Bruce's force numbered merely thirty Americans, ten FFI and fourteen *gendarmes*, large numbers of journalists now converged on Rambouillet. They knew liberating Paris was the campaign's big event and were already spreading the word that the honour of entering the city was reserved for the 2e DB. Even if America's greatest war correspondent, Ernie Pyle, had not arrived yet, he soon would.

Since the Geneva Convention clearly states that, like medical personnel, journalists are *hors de combat*, Hemingway's pride in his group of irregulars provoked angry questions from some reporters. This provoked the bully in Hemingway's nature, which he reserved for those he regarded as lesser mortals. Recognising that he had crossed the line towards being a combatant, Hemingway persuaded David Bruce to pen a note confirming his combatant role due to the extraordinary situation at Rambouillet. But Bruce Grant, a hefty reporter representing the *Chicago Daily News*, said that "General Hemingway and his Maquis" were taking too much space within the now cramped Hôtel du Grand Veneur. Fisticuffs followed, but they were quickly pulled apart. Hemingway had higher concerns than professional demarcation lines. He wanted to gather all the intelligence he could to help the Allies liberate the city he loved as much as any Frenchman.[189]

THE SAME AFTERNOON THAT NORDLING'S TRUCE half lived and half died, Henri Rol-Tanguy moved his HQ from Rue Schoelcher to the cellars beneath the Department of Roads and Transport on Place Denfert-Rochereau. These catacombs are accessed via the eighteenth-century Barrière d'Enfer,* a tax collection pavilion dating from the *ancien régime*.

"We installed ourselves twenty-six metres below ground in a vast complex of rooms, offices and underground corridors remarkably arranged since before the war by the *défense passive* should they need to shelter several official services in the case of the capital being bombarded," Rol-Tanguy told Roger Bourderon. "A very important factor is that they are very well ventilated. I was already aware of this since 1936 because the ventilation was installed by Nessi in Montrouge

---

* While this location might have been mentioned in Victor Hugo's *Les Miserables* and its name, Enfer, means "Hell", the Place Denfert-Rochereau is actually named after the Colonel Pierre Denfert-Rochereau who successfully defended the town of Belfort in eastern France against the Prussians in 1870. The Lion of Belfort statue at its centre is a smaller version of the sculpture in Belfort crafted by Frederic Bartholdi, who also created the Statue of Liberty.

where I had worked and been a Syndicalist delegate. It ran on diesel motors with a bicycle style dynamo in case it broke down. Thank God we never had to use it. How did this all happen? General Bloch-Dassault, who was on the committee of the *Front National*, personally put it at my disposal at the beginning of August. He [Bloch-Dassault] was in contact with Avia and the engineer Taves, thanks to whom we were able to go to Rue Schoelcher, and who organised our move underground with his own men."[190]

Rol-Tanguy's staff evacuated the Rue Schoelcher building via a network of tunnels connecting both the Place Denfert-Rochereau and the Gare Denfert-Rochereau. During the remainder of the Insurrection, Rol-Tanguy rarely left his new CP. When he did he used the large, dark Citroen loaned by the Préfecture on the 19th along with a driver, Roger Barrat, and a policeman called Dubarry who, alternating with FTP *résistant* Vacek, acted as Rol-Tanguy's bodyguard.[191]

Within this subterranean world Cécile Tanguy controlled the secretariat and loose ends of liaison aided by Mademoiselle Nicolas, whose services came with the premises to keep the complex going, particularly the switchboard, electricity and ventilation machinery. Their spartan meals consisted of boiled potatoes with dripping, tinned fish, white bread and water to drink, albeit finished with a tot of Benedictine while the bottle lasted. "I always kept in mind the restrictions imposed on other Parisians," Rol-Tanguy told Bourderon.[192]

The Germans knew about the Barrière d'Enfer complex, but their attention was limited by insufficient manpower. A telephone call at around 10am would be fobbed off by Mademoiselle Nicolas' switchboard staff. Since the complex was guarded by the usual municipal workers, nothing attracted suspicion. Access was strictly on an essential basis; not even Rol-Tanguy's chauffeur or bodyguards went down there. Important *résistants* like Raymond Massiet or Police General Hary visited under Rol-Tanguy's personal supervision. For those practised in *la vie clandestine,* such measures were perfectly normal. "As for liaison officers," Rol-Tanguy told Bourderon, "they arrived via the Gare de Sceaux, were received by an officer of my staff, and departed via the Rue Schoelcher."[193]

Thanks to the railwaymen's union the Metro's telephone system was placed at the FFIs' disposal, offering over two hundred telephone outlets across Paris. Again, declining German manpower meant that, although they knew these facilities existed, they were unable to control them. "Through these multiple sources, telephones, correspondents, liaison officers, a mass of information converged on my staff," said Rol-Tanguy. "Reports of combats in process, enemy dispositions, building of barricades, and requests for reinforcements. We followed the movements of German tanks very precisely; this allowed us to alert FFI units and send combat groups to harass them and put them out of action." Naturally some information reaching Rol-Tanguy's CP was unreliable, but the intact telephone system meant that reports about the approaching Allies also reached the Barrière d'Enfer from further afield.[194]

For all the accusations that Rol-Tanguy was a bolshy left-winger with his own agenda, he was increasingly concerned not to have heard anything from André Trutié de Varreux (*Brécy*), whom he had sent to the Allied lines with a message requesting them to march on Paris immediately. Rol-Tanguy had to assume that Varreux was dead, which he was. To replace Brécy Rol-Tanguy needed someone *au courant* with the situation in Paris, sufficiently senior to command respect from other resistance cells, and who spoke excellent English. The obvious candidate was reserve Commandant Roger Cocteau (codename *Gallois*). An industrialist in civilian life, Gallois acted as Rol-Tanguy's chief of staff, often liaising with Colonel Lizé. "I had total confidence in my chief of staff," Rol-Tanguy told the 1994 *Colloque*, "not only for his loyalty, but also for his diplomatic sense, way with words, for the certainty that he would make the Americans aware of the problems in supporting the Paris insurrection, regarding its armaments as well as sending a marching force, the 2e DB in particular. Chaban-Delmas had already told me, as early as July, that it would be the 2e DB who would be directed first towards the capital."[195]

"Nothing in the manner by which Colonel Rol managed the Insurrection permits one to think that he had any other object than to fight the Germans. For my part, I never had—during the seven days of the Insurrection—any serious worries in this regard, knowing that shortly afterwards France would be united behind General de Gaulle," said Alexandre Parodi many years afterwards.[196]

"IN THE COMPANY OF ANDRÉ LE TROQUER, minister delegate to the liberated territories, the generals Juin and Koenig and Gaston Palewski," de Gaulle wrote, "I arrived at the Préfecture of Rennes." His machinery for re-installing French sovereignty was working "invincibly". At Rennes' Hôtel de Ville the new *maire* (mayor) Yves Millon, "surrounded by his council, *résistants* and notables", asked de Gaulle to reopen the "golden book" of the Breton capital, thereby renewing its civic life. Afterwards, in torrential rain, de Gaulle addressed a large crowd.[197]

While Rennes was undoubtedly an improvement on his staged arrival in Bayeux, de Gaulle's thoughts were naturally on Paris. As soon as a solitary moment could be found he wrote to General Eisenhower, airing the anxieties accumulated since their meeting earlier in the day.

My dear General,

The information I have received from Paris today makes me think that, in view of the almost complete disappearance of the Police, and of the German forces in Paris, and the extreme shortage of food there, serious trouble is to be expected in the capital very shortly. I believe it is necessary to have Paris occupied by the French and Allied forces as soon as possible, even if it means a certain amount of fighting and a certain amount of damage within the city. If a disorderly situation were now to arise in Paris, it would be difficult to take things in hand without serious incidents, and this might even hinder subsequent military operations. I am sending you General Koenig who has now been appointed military governor of Paris.

As for the city's interim military governor appointed the previous December, after two days of being courteously slapped down by the Americans, Leclerc was considering unilateral action, and ordered Jacques de Guillebon to assemble an advance guard.[198]

Chapter 6

Rol-Tanguy Takes the Initiative

20 August 1944 (continued)

DOCTOR ROBERT MONOD had been covered in blood all day, beginning with his morning drive to the Laennec Hospital. A *Parisienne* had been shot while bicycling along the Boulevard Saint-Germain. Losing the struggle with her internal injuries, Monod only wished *badauds* and cyclists would be more careful on streets that had become battlefields.

Monod assumed that nothing had come of his efforts the previous day to connect the FFI with the Americans through his tenuous connections. But around 3pm, Dr. Jean-Claude Duchène, a *résistant* from Versailles, visited Monod with a message from Dominic Roumajou, his sector chief, saying that the Americans were reachable near Montfort l'Amaury. Impressed that the Allies seemed so close, Monod contacted a comrade in *Ceux de la Résistance* asking for Rol-Tanguy to be informed.[1]

This synchronised perfectly with Rol-Tanguy's recognition that *Brécy's* mission had failed. Within an hour Monod was visited by another *résistant* demanding precise details of how he knew about Americans at Montfort l'Amaury. Monod refused to tell anyone but Rol-Tanguy or a significant member of his staff.[2]

According to Dronne, Monod's visitor came from Colonel Lizé rather than Rol-Tanguy. But Gallois' version is that Rol-Tanguy recognised that "it was necessary that a relief column arrive to support our effort and to exploit without delay the results that we had achieved. From this originated the decision by Colonel Rol to send one of his officers to request the necessary support as soon as possible."[3]

Rol-Tanguy's view, shared with Bourderon, was that the proximity of the Allies represented an unmissable opportunity. "There remained the problem of finding a way for Gallois to cross the German lines. Examining this problem at our HQ, we thought it best to contact the FFI responsible for the Corbeil sector, Commandant 'Georges', whose real name was Georges Desnoues."[4]

Around 6pm Monod took a call from his linkman Guillaume; Monod's offer to help contact the Americans had been accepted; an envoy would soon arrive. Monod recognised Roger Cocteau/Gallois immediately from the *Armée Secrète*; "Such coincidences were frequent in the double lives of *clandestins*." Gallois admitted to Monod that the FFI had barely enough ammunition for an hour's fighting.[5]

YET, AT A COMAC MEETING ON Avenue du Parc Montsouris, Rol-Tanguy and other so-called *extrémistes* drew up a communiqué protesting their exclusion from the truce negotiations. Rejecting one of Nordling's key justifications, they claimed that the city's monuments were just as vulnerable from air attack as destruction by ground forces. The possibility of reprisals against the Parisian population was also rejected, since Germany held enough French prisoners to use as hostages if they wished. Chaban-Delmas was criticised for over-estimating German forces in Paris. COMAC also considered how to harass the three depleted German divisions guarding the southwestern approaches to the city, calling in Allied air support if they needed to.[6]

"As far as the urban guerilla war was concerned, we began by holding the enemy by the throat so that we could not let him go," Rol-Tanguy told Bourderon. "He needed to play for time, which he did. The remarkable thing in the development of the Insurrection during the 20 and 21 August was that, in spite of the losses among the FFI caused by surprise attacks from an enemy taking advantage of the confusion which accompanied the proclamation of the 'truce', the balance of forces had definitely turned in favour of the Paris insurgents."[7]

Von Choltitz's garrison could hardly be expected to respect an agreement flouted by the FFIs. Ordinary Parisians who, merely hours earlier thought the war might be over, had their hopes dashed as loudspeakers denounced the FFI as "Criminal elements bent on terrorising the city". Once again the Germans warned that any captured FFI would be treated as *francs tireurs* and shot. A poster appeared evoking an execution pit, showing a blindfolded man and the caption, "We warn you! Think of Paris!"[8]

On the Place Saint-Michel, the FFI fought so ferociously that a tank and four lorries were destroyed and many Germans either killed or taken prisoner. The telephone exchange at 103 Rue de Grenelle was seized by fifty FFI. When von Choltitz's garrison finally recognised their oversight in not controlling this utility, they sent infantry supported by a tank to seize the exchange on the Rue du Louvre, but were repulsed by determined FFI.[9]

On the south side of the city, furthest from embattled central areas and least likely to see loudspeaker cars, 20 August was punctuated by several brutal incidents. Wehrmacht soldiers guarding the generator at Villejuif were sent packing and replaced by FFI, while on the east side more district *mairies* were taken over: Les Lilas, Bagnolet, Bondy, Drancy, Noisy-le-Sec, Pantin, Romainville, Montreuil and Pavillon-sous-Bois. But when FFI went to take over the fort at Vincennes they were repulsed by tanks.[10]

WAVED THROUGH THE PORTE D'ORLÉANS CHECKPOINT by FFI, Monod turned towards Versailles. By the time they got through German checkpoints around Versailles and Saint-Cyr, it was 7pm. All around them German tanks, artillery and soldiers prepared to face the Allies. A few kilometres further on, approaching a checkpoint, they found themselves behind a *Kübelwagen*. Surprised to see a civilian vehicle behind them, two officers got out and approached Monod's car. Roumajou calmly explained that Monod was a doctor and they needed to evacuate women and children from a holiday camp before the area became a battlefield. Roumajou claimed to be Monod's assistant and that Gallois was a paramedic.

"I've got all our papers," said Monod.

Declining to inspect their documents, an officer said the roads ahead were mined and showed them a map marking minefields between Versailles and Trappes. They would have to retrace their steps.

They turned towards Clayes but were blocked by felled trees guarded by truculent looking Germans. Roumajou asked to speak to someone senior and was led away while Monod and Gallois waited apprehensively. Unable to bear it any longer, Monod went to look for Roumajou who was chatting in a garden with an officer who calmly explained that the roads ahead were either blocked or mined, while bridges would have been blown.

"You should make a detour," the officer said.

"Yes, we will," said Roumajou, departing.

Deciding to make a final effort to reach Montfort l'Amaury from the north, instead of following German advice, they headed for Villepreux where they learnt that only one road-block separated them from no man's land and the American lines. It was merely a pair of obstructively positioned bollards guarded by two German soldiers. Unfortunately, while one was happy to let them pass, the other was more obstinate.

"*Nichts! Nichts! Kein! Kein!*" said the obstinate soldier.

Noticing camouflaged troop positions nearby, the Frenchmen recognised that forcing their way across would get them shot. Monod made a U-turn and they set off to find another route via Saint-Nom-la-Bretèche. But it was nearly 9pm. The streets were empty and windows shuttered. Some houses were still inhabited by anxious villagers praying their homes would survive the clash of armies. As Monod drove at a crawl, they noticed two lovers walking arm in arm. They told Roumajou that the mayor lived on a farm two kilometres outside the village. Even in 1944 mayors were often Vichy supporters, but Roumajou knocked on a cottage door whose elderly owner assured them the mayor was, "Certainly not for them."

Past curfew, they set off to find the mayor but found another German checkpoint supported by a machine-gun beside the farm's entrance. Worse, they were quickly surrounded by well-armed Waffen SS. Again they moaned about children marooned at a nearby holiday camp, Monod keeping the Germans talking while Roumajou and Gallois knocked up the mayor. One of the SS told Monod that he too should visit the farm to find the children rather that chatting to his men.

The mayor said it was impossible to reach Neauphle-le-Château that night, since the area was crawling with German troops, and local farmers were banned from working their fields. The mayor agreed, however, that one of his farmhands would guide them to Neauphle at daybreak. Otherwise he advised Monod to get his car under cover since the Germans would requisition even the humblest barrow.

Returning to the village, they knocked on a door hoping to find somewhere to spend the night. To their surprise it was opened by friends of Gallois who told them that Saint-Nom-la-Bretèche had been liberated by an American patrol, but that no positions were established before the SS returned and prepared their defence line. Monod, Roumajou and Gallois crashed out in the living room. Torrential rain rattled the shutters. Unable to sleep, Monod woke Gallois to discuss what they were going to do at sunrise.

"We arrived too late," Monod told Gallois. "The route which was passable yesterday wasn't today."

In such conditions, Monod believed their best option was to approach the American lines from Dourdan-Étampes where he had Resistance contacts. When Gallois told him that Rol-Tanguy merely wanted information and an air-drop of weapons and ammunition, Monod argued instead that "A few tanks arriving as reinforcements, to reduce their redoubts with cannonfire, would be sufficient to secure their surrender. To abandon Paris at such a moment would, perhaps, be to expose her to worse, when it looks easy to save the city by occupying it without delay. Not to do this would be seen in the eyes of the world a gross dereliction. Would the Americans remain indifferent to the possibility of their prestige being debased in the eyes of Parisians? Their methodical advance appears somewhat over-cautious in the eyes of the French."

What if these arguments did not persuade the Americans to enter Paris? In that case Gallois should ask to see Leclerc, if only to shake his hand.[11]

21 August 1944

AT 7AM, PIERRE TAITTINGER, Ruegger and Cornillat were led by gloating guards to the Préfecture's Room 22 which, they were warned, was their last stop before the firing squad. There was a long table, chairs and a high barred window. Among his captors Taittinger recognised various *Gardiens* but also noticed several new men. Taittinger noticed how many senior *résistants* were not Parisians; Luizet was Lyonnais while several had Breton accents. It was less humiliating than being imprisoned by fellow Parisians. Then a policeman Taittinger recognised said menacingly, "We know who you are," while another mentioned more convivially that his parents lived in a Girondin village where Taittinger had connections. "Why bother guarding them?" asked a third. "Shoot them in the back and throw them in the ditch with the others!"[12]

Expecting to die, Taittinger and his friends spent the day in Room 22, remembering how many famous Frenchmen had been imprisoned there. Looking down into the courtyard, Taittinger noticed that the Préfecture's defenders included a *Martiniquais* sergeant whose runner was merely a boy. This lad became adept at using Joliot-Curie's special Molotov cocktails to destroy German vehicles. "His tactic was simple," wrote Taittinger. "Holding the petrol bomb behind his back, he approached a German vehicle, whose crew believed him harmless. When close enough he threw the bottle, which exploded, then threw himself on the ground to see what happened next. When the Germans left the vehicle they were gunned down by other *résistants*. This youth destroyed several lorries and a half-track in this fashion; he was the main, if not the only, true combatant inside the Prefecture. One of our guards assured us that almost all the wrecked vehicles gathered in the courtyard were this young man's handiwork!"[13]

MONOD, ROUMAJOU AND GALLOIS left Saint-Nom-La-Bretèche at first light. The lanes seemed deserted. Threading their way back through the villages of Villepreux, Trou-Moreau and Bois d'Arcy, eventually they reached the crossroads with the GC 104. Again truculent Germans appeared from nowhere. One forced Monod to slow down by throwing a bicycle on the car's roof. Then a tall officer appeared, angrily pointing towards Pontchartrain.

"If you value your lives," said the officer, "turn left immediately." Then, gesturing northeastwards, he said firmly, "Paris is that way."

Arguing was clearly pointless. They turned back past Villacoublay and called at the hospital in Perray-Vaucluse where Monod knew Doctor Bonnaud. He guided them to Villiers where they learnt that Captain Georges, the FFI commander around Corbeil, had encountered Americans near La Ferte-Alais.

Captain Georges agreed to help and transfered them to a camionette which would hopefully draw less attention. Despite the urgency, extraordinarily they stopped for lunch at the Patte d'Oie, a restaurant in Mennecy, whose owner arranged a private dining room where they could talk. Gallois now intended to ask the Americans for nothing less than a significant tank force, preferably Leclerc's, to march on Paris immediately. After a substantial meal, they toasted Gallois with champagne. Outside, the local FFI arranged a little parade to cheer Gallois on his way.

Afterwards Gallois was taken in hand by Captain Georges' group. Shaking Monod's hand, Gallois promised that he would ask for Leclerc to be sent to Paris.[14]

DURING 20–21 AUGUST, von Choltitz understood that, with Nordling's truce in force, the police would resume their normal role. He also thought the arrangement sufficiently useful to Army Group B to be able to tell Field Marshal Model's emissary, "On this matter the situation on the ground is decisive; there remains no other guarantee that can be made to prevent German troops from being fired upon."[15]

The usually intransigent Field Marshal Model, knowing he had nothing to reinforce Paris, tolerated these compromises but nevertheless wanted preparations made to blow the city's bridges. When General Blumentritt raised this matter on Model's behalf, von Choltitz insisted that the Wehrmacht still needed the bridges, though only around 15% of retreating German traffic passed through Paris. Between Army Group B and von Choltitz's HQ at the Hôtel Meurice, several officers, such as General Speidel, played for time while appearing assiduous in their duties.[16]

When Hitler complained that demolitions had not begun, Model replied that the existing twenty-thousand-man garrison was insufficient to suppress a significant uprising, and that preparing fallback positions northeast of Paris was a higher priority. Hence, while Hitler wanted to destroy Paris, neither Model nor Kitzinger attached much importance to his orders. When von Choltitz sent a communiqué saying that "the Ile de la Cité has been taken over by terrorists and turned into a defensive strongpoint; given the lack of artillery no appropriate countermeasures can be taken"; he then covered himself by demanding artillery and a contingent of *Feldgendarmerie*, the traditional sign of a general keeping a grip on his command. Army Group B offered him artillery and an engineer battalion—even though von Choltitz already had sappers twiddling their thumbs doing nothing—but wanted to swap elements of the 48th Infantry Division for 88mm guns which were already in position. A combination of von Choltitz's obfuscations and Allied pressure turned Paris into a low priority.[17]

As disenchanted as he was, an incident which singularly disaffected von Choltitz was the arrival in his office that morning of two SS officers wanting to requisition the medieval Bayeux Tapestry—which depicts the Norman invasion of Saxon England—from the Louvre.

"The Louvre is in the hands of the Resistance," said von Choltitz impatiently, pointing eastwards along the Rue de Rivoli from his balcony. "Ask them for the tapestry."[18]

ONCE PROSCRIBED NEWSPAPERS and new Resistance journals like *Franc-Tireur*, *Le Parisien Libéré* and *Combat*, became available to anyone prepared to venture onto the streets. Strikes and the breakdown of utilities meant that this was the first time in four days that Parisians could obtain printed news. *Franc-Tireur* announced in a six-column article, "The two glorious days of August 1944. Paris fights! Paris frees herself! The people of Paris rise up! An epic saga continues at the Préfecture de Police! The Germans are leaving the capital. The flag of the Resistance flies over the Hôtel de Ville." Another article reported General de Gaulle's arrival at Cherbourg and how eight French departments had been liberated through "joint effort" between the Allies and the FFI. A third article crowed that Pétainists "will not escape popular vengeance".[19]

Even though the Resistance was too weak to conclude its Insurrection unaided, *Franc-Tireur* bumptiously slanted their articles. "After violent combat lasting forty-eight hours, the German authorities asked for a truce, recognising that they would otherwise be unable to evacuate their troops, and in order to avoid unnecessary bloodshed and be able to destroy documents. This temporary truce was agreed and the order to cease fire was given by represenatives of the Provisional Government."

Historian Pierre Bourget later wrote, "It would be difficult to be more inexact in so few words! The Germans never demanded anything; a form of ceasefire had been proposed by Nordling who, with diplomatic subtlety, allowed the Resistance to believe that it resulted from a German initiative (rather than) Choltitz, whom representatives of General de Gaulle in Paris had solicited. But it was only partially observed and never at any time did the Germans consider this pause in the fighting, to which they had agreed, as anything other than a means to facilitate their evacuation of the capital."[20]

"MORE QUESTION OF A TRUCE?" wrote Jean Galtier-Boissière. "*Au contraire.* I witnessed the construction of a large barricade across the Boulevard Saint-Michel on the rise of the Boulevard Saint-Germain. They were piling on benches from public squares, old bedsteads, coffee plants, tree grilles, a little of everything really. On the Rue Saint Jacques there was another barricade, but more regularly constructed using paving stones and sandbags taken from the Metro."[21]

Barricades effectively sealed off all routes onto the Ile de la Cité. When some Germans commandeered an ambulance to trick their way across the Pont Saint-Michel, every French gun turned on them. None survived their trickery. "It was impossible to spare the ambulance," Monsignor Brot wrote regretfully.[22]

To save the collapsing truce, Alexandre Parodi arranged to meet Colonel Henri Rol-Tanguy. "On this occasion the meeting took place at the Hôtel de Ville," Rol-Tanguy told Bourderon. "Parodi asked me to agree with the Germans on specific routes for their retreating forces. The relevant departments of the Préfecture of the Seine had already advised which routes were suitable for large armoured vehicles. Parodi justified his demands on the basis of very alarming intelligence reported by Chaban, in particular the number of heavy tanks in Paris in case the truce failed. Parodi would say later that he was very concerned by this information, which was in fact inaccurate, having been passed on by Nordling. This could only have been a bluff by Choltitz who was risking everything. No worthwhile intelligence that we had received at the Denfert CP allowed us to give this any credence; in fact the opposite, it confirmed that the enemy was pulling back towards specific strongpoints. This was not the time to allow him freedom of manoeuvre. Besides, we knew that it was the enemy's intention to retreat, avoiding the capital, in order to regroup further east. In short I refused to agree to play traffic policeman along their lines of retreat and replied drily to Parodi, '*C'est joué!*'"[23]

LECLERC'S ADJUTANT, JACQUES WEIL, visited Bradley's HQ hoping to get the 2e DB transferred to a corps nearer Paris. While waiting for Weil's return, Leclerc wondered if the Americans were retaliating for his refusal to obey General Gaffey a few days before. In the meantime he wrote to de Gaulle explaining his decision to send Guillebon's patrol towards Paris. "I cannot sadly do the same with the bulk of the division owing to considerations of fuel supply and also not wanting to overtly violate the rules of military subordination."[24]

Since this advance guard was being sent on Leclerc's own initiative, their mission had to be kept secret from the division's US liaison officers, the charming Major Robert Loumiansky and Captain Plutschak. Who could keep them out of the way? Captain Alain de Boissieu knew better than most what was at stake. Since he was recovering from an injury sustained helping comrades escape a brewed-up Sherman, entertaining these Americans was perfect light duty for him.

"Take them on a little sightseeing trip," said Leclerc.[25]

"Where?" Boissieu wondered. The idea that Plutschak and Loumiansky were suddenly interested in medieval architecture seemed weird. So he guided them around the 2e DB's first battlefields, following Jacques Branet's route detouring the Foret d'Écouves via Sées on 12 August, following the trail of burnt-out trucks and tanks. Burial parties had yet to reach the corpses inside these charred hulks, stinking in the summer heat.[26]

La Patrouille (the patrol), as Guillebon's force became known, consisted of half a squadron of RMSM M8 armoured cars under Captain Alfred Bergamin, and a squadron of Stuart light tanks under Captain Martin-Siegfried, supported by Captain Parceval's slightly depleted company from the Chad regiment. Guillebon also had with him *Chef d'Escadrons** Morel-Deville and the RMSM's colour party, so that if they got into central Paris they could raise one of the division's regimental flags.[27]

"There is nothing important keeping us in Normandy," Leclerc told Guillebon before waving him off. "I am doing everything I can and,

---

* *Chef d'Escadrons* is a French cavalry rank equivalent to major, which literally means squadron leader. The RAF rank is derived from it.

after your departure, I will continue to push incessantly to be allowed to go to Paris. You realise that the Allies shouldn't enter Paris without the French Army. That would diminish the national and international importance of the event. So go as fast as possible. If some Allied unit is entering Paris, then I would want you to go in alongside them. I will join you, but in the meantime you will act in my place both towards the Allies as towards the French, with the functions of military governor."

Guillebon saluted.

"However," continued Leclerc, "if you can go in alone, don't hesitate, go in!"[28]

AROUND 4PM JEAN GALTIER-BOISSIÈRE'S BOOKSHOP was rattled by an explosion. German tanks from the Palais Luxembourg *Stützpunkt* had fired at the Boulevard Saint-Michel barricade. Galtier-Boissière watched speechless as two Renault tanks, repainted in Wehrmacht sand yellow, rumbled past his window, fired and withdrew. A little later he saw a large plume of black smoke. The noise of engines came closer again. This time five Renault tanks passed Galtier-Boissière as they withdrew towards the Luxembourg. Stepping outside to close the shutters, Galtier-Boissière noticed white-clad stretcher bearers running frantically. They returned moments later carrying an elegant, agonisingly wounded youth. "His face had a green tone which reminded me of the mortally wounded of the *other* war," he wrote.[29]

Despite Nordling's truce stipulating that FFIs were to be regarded as combatants under the laws of war and vice versa, many Germans dreaded falling into FFI hands. Sonderführer Robert Wallraf describes the ordeal of a Wehrmacht lieutenant and two of his men captured by FFI on the south bank late on 21 August.

"Do you know how to swim, *Sales Boches*?" asked one of the *résistants*, dragging the three Germans to the river's edge.

At the bridge's mid-span they made them stand on the parapet. The lieutenant managed to keep steady but both his men lost balance and fell into the Seine. When their heads broke the surface the FFIs shot at them until they disappeared. Then they took the lieutenant to a nearby apartment and fed him after which they forced him to drink several *coups* of Cognac, shouting "*Vive de Gaulle*" with each gulp. After an exchange of prisoners, the lieutenant returned to a German strongpoint where he told his comrades that he would rather die than endure such torment again. "Many such stories circulated among us," wrote Wallraf. "Naturally they reinforced our determination to defend ourselves against the Resistance and only to give up the fight once disciplined regular troops attacked out strongpoints." However, Wallraf recognised that FFI excesses were a reaction to SS misdeeds. Von Choltitz's garrison believed that FFI policy was to shoot captured SS immediately.[30]

Yet there were simultaneous examples of restraint. On the Rue des Saussaies, a narrow street within the government area, made infamous by the Gestapo depot, when some *résistants* taking over a ministerial annexe encountered a German patrol, they pocketed their pistols and claimed to be concièrges maintaining a presence. They were left alone.[31]

HENRI CULMANN SPENT THAT MONDAY in his office, justifying his salary by shuffling papers. Around a hundred FFI now guarded this building while, among the ministry's employees, several *fonctionnaires* who, unknown to Culmann, were longstanding *résistants*, now proudly sported FFI brassards. The only weapons between them, however, were three shotguns, two Stens and a few revolvers. Towards the afternoon's end, having seen Marshal Pétain's portrait replaced by one of President Raymond Poincaré, Culmann was interviewed by the interim minister, Robert Lacoste, a militant syndicalist. "The new minister exposed to us the psychology of our new governors, divided between the needs of justice which tested men who, for four years, watched while their comrades were arrested, tortured, killed or were denounced, to have their parents shot, their homes burnt—while they lived happily at home—with no reaction to injustice after injustice." For Culmann this tirade indicated what *épuration* would really mean; knee-jerk justice administered by rabble, bypassing France's well-trained lawyers and handsome courthouses.[32] Culmann listened as Lacoste explained, "The great disappointment with which he [de Gaulle] views the passivity of the French *bourgeoisie* and the higher sense he has of French greatness."[33]

Around 6pm the fighting in the Latin Quarter calmed down, and Galtier-Boissière ventured out for news. A German fuel tanker had been blown up by a *résistant*'s petrol bomb, and an elderly veteran's apartment was raked with machine-gun fire, even grazing his nose. But the Boulevard Saint-Michel barricade remained intact because, a *badaud* explained, it was erected in a slight dip, beneath the trajectory of a Renault 35's puny cannon.[34]

LATER THAT AFTERNOON, the CNR went into plenary session in the salon of a gracious apartment opposite the Gare Denfert-Rochereau, the details of which were reproduced by French journalist Adrien Dansette shortly after the war. On arrival, Alexandre Parodi offered his hand to Roger Ginsburger, COMAC's Villon, which was refused.

"*Eh bien*, Villon," said Parodi. "You won't say 'hello'?"

"It is not possible to launch, then put a halt to an insurrection," replied Villon. "You're ruining it. Haven't you any pride?"

While Parodi, Bidault, Chaban-Delmas and COMAC's three Vs sat on Louis Seize chairs, others stood. Combined with August heat, the need to close windows to keep their discussions inaudible from the street, and everyone in shirt sleeves, made for a tense atmosphere. Villon questioned the validity of Nordling's truce since the decision was taken by a majority rather than a unanimous vote as required by CNR rules, and those who drafted it had no right to do so.[35]

Chaban-Delmas explained that, given the urgency and the impossibility of contacting COMAC's members, the Delegation approved Nordling's truce. After all, Chaban continued, the FFI possessed hardly any weapons and, according to his information from senior Allied generals, the Allies would not reach Paris for another week, which meant they needed to buy time. For these reasons, said Chaban, the Delegation requested the Allies to parachute weapons into Paris and come as soon as possible. (Even then, the most significant efforts to reach the Allies to request intervention were made by Rol-Tanguy.)[36]

Georges Bidault declared the truce valid, even though, owing to the difficulties of *la vie clandestine*, not everyone could attend the vote. The decision needed to be taken quickly and Nordling had a deadline to meet with General von Choltitz. Bidault said he took responsibility for what happened, while Parodi insisted that the welfare of Parisians was a paramount concern. In spite of this, Louis Saillant asked Bidault to read aloud the *appel* voted upon that morning by the CPL—*Comité Parisien de Libération,*—which criticised the truce as "an enemy manoeuvre intended to stab in the back those Parisians who, for forty-eight hours, have been heroically fighting the *Boches* to liberate their capital". The CPL wanted to circulate it as an *affiche*.

"Are you going to publish that declaration as it stands?" asked Parodi, appalled.

"The posters have already been ordered," replied Villon.

"In that case," said Parodi, "the truce is totally finished!"

"No," replied Jacquis Debu-Bridel. "Until the Americans arrive in Paris, the unity of the Resistance must be maintained more than ever. But the CNR must tell us exactly under what circumstances they have entertained this truce and what they have agreed to."[37]

Until this moment the atmosphere was immensely confrontational. Then, over thirty-five minutes, Chaban-Delmas gave a well-informed, objective *resumé* of the situation. First, without interruptions, he explained the practical problems facing the Resistance in Paris; the fine balance between political objectives and the slender military means for pursuing them. He explained Nordling's contribution, and the German High Command's need to maintain order in a city through which they still needed to withdraw battle-worn divisions. He explained the negotiations immediately before the meeting at Nordling's consulate; pointing out that von Choltitz made an enormous concession by accepting that the Resistance controlled certain areas and recognising them as regular forces. But when Chaban used the English phrase "gentleman's agreement", disapproving groans rose from COMAC's three Vs and FTP members.

"You don't make 'gentleman's agreements' with murderers," said an FTP member.

"And you," retorted Chaban, "you want to massacre 150,000 people for nothing?"[38]

"He speaks a lot of *technique*," said another, alluding to Chaban's *grande école* education. "*Eh bien!* Well, this *technique* of his, it is not the *technique militaire*, it's the *technique financière!*"

Several found Chaban's notions of fair play somewhat trite.

COMAC's Kriegel-Valrimont said, "There is among certain factions of the Resistance, particularly those *résistants* who have come from London, a manifestation of a deliberate desire to prevent the people from seizing by force of arms a tangible victory which might gave them a say in government."

Irrespective of the risks to the people and fabric of Paris, Kriegel-Valrimont declared that by disregarding Nordling's truce, "I place myself on the *sentimental* plan." Though pale and exhausted after days of unceasing activity, Valrimont continued, "We will not stop fighting in open battle. It is unthinkable to deprive the people of Paris of a battle they've wanted for four years. I left combatants behind in order to come here and I am going back to be with them. There is where I feel at ease. One's duty is clear. I am speaking as a French officer who, for four years, has waited for this battle."

Villon, staring at Chaban with hard eyes, said icily, "He would do better to stick to his previous job."

Then, as the squabbling escalated, Villon said loudly, "That's the first time I've seen a French general so cowardly."

As Chaban smiled wrily, Parodi remarked on the courage required of anyone living *la vie clandestine*, and told Villon to withdraw his insult.

"I was not accusing him of cowardice," said Villon, "simply saying that he was conducting himself like a coward."

"That's insupportable and disgraceful," said another member of the Delegation. "He wants to rupture the truce."

"I'm leaving," said Parodi.[39]

At that moment there was a smash of breaking glass. The journalist Debu-Bridel, using a gesture familiar among the French Revolution's political clubs, startled the room to order.

But Villon had not finished. After apologising to Chaban, he explained that, while there might only be six hundred men at the Préfecture and a few thousand FFI, the *Milice Patriotique* and the people at large offered "enormous possibilities". Since FFI actions elsewhere in France had achieved great successes since D-Day, "Why shouldn't there be similar successes in the capital which is the best place in the world for guerrilla warfare? It's *in* Paris that we should be doing this. The [Paris] FFI are not mobile. They are attached to their homes. They can hardly go and fight the Germans *outside* Paris. Apart from anything else the 'military delegate' has not said whether the Allied governments agree with this truce. It can hardly have been agreed among them given their policy of leaving the enemy no respite until they capitulate unconditionally."

Remembering his discussions with General Ismay and General Koenig, Chaban replied confidently that they agreed with him. "We are not talking about an armistice, but the *neutralisation* of a portion of French territory."[40]

Villon claimed that the threat of German reprisals was not worth worrying about because the Resistance could retaliate against thousands of German wounded presently in Paris hospitals, along with German prisoners taken earlier during the Insurrection. Villon claimed the truce was a con since the numbers provided by the FFI medical service were not available until either Sunday evening or Monday morning; ninety-nine killed and two hundred and forty-four wounded on the French side against five hundred and thirty-four on the German side. "Unless these are fantasy figures bearing no relation to reality, one can hardly see that the truce has had a *sensible* influence on our losses," said Villon.[41]

Parodi, the Delegation and moderate members of the CNR such as Georges Bidault felt the argument slipping away from them.

Exhausted by arguing their case to ears that refused to listen, and uncomfortable owing to the heat, they were being ground down. Briefly Chaban thought he was pulling COMAC and the FTP around to his way of thinking, but then he hit the hard reality that continuing the truce meant dividing the Resistance. Both Villon and Vaillant—the populist Count Jean de Vogüé—insisted that a proclamation should end the truce.

Though haunted by the possibility of a Warsaw-style catastrophe, Parodi consoled himself with the thought that the Insurrection was only two days old and the Allies knew the situation in Paris. Every passing hour brought liberation closer. His arguments having failed, Chaban remained aware that, if the Allies did not arrive soon, the Insurrectionists might share the fate of their comrades at Vercors. But the Resistance wanted and needed this battle. There was also the fear that Paris might come under AMGOT unless she was seen to liberate herself.[42]

With a heavy heart, Parodi agreed to the resumption of hostilities. "He did not have the sense of certainty of a revolutionary," wrote Adrien Dansette, "nor of a man of iron who, having given himself a goal, would march towards it, crossing everything without having any care for the victims harmed along the way. He had the scruples of a politician who worried profoundly for those men and things he had to do his best for." Before agreeing to end the truce, however, Parodi had a condition of his own: that fighting would not resume until 4pm on the afternoon of 22 August. The CPL's poster was not to appear.[43]

"Until now," said Chaban, "my role was to put the brakes on. Today I am committed to fighting."

"Console yourself," replied Count Jean de Vogüé. "You have not put the brakes on anything *that* big."[44]

Though present at the meeting, Henri Rol-Tanguy said very little. Following his discussions with Parodi earlier at the Hôtel de Ville, he foresaw much of this, although he felt for Chaban's predicament. After Rol-Tanguy left, Parodi spoke to Colonel Lizé. Afterwards Lizé prepared an order telling his men to respect the truce for the time being, attached to which were notes detailing the routes to be permitted to German troops retreating through the city. Given Lizé's previous hostility to the truce, Rol-Tanguy wondered what Parodi said to him. Had Lizé submitted to Parodi, whose place in the chain of command led straight to de Gaulle? Given that Lizé was his immediate deputy, Rol-Tanguy gave him an order of his own; that hostilities must resume. In effect, Lizé obeyed both.[45]

"WEIL RETURNED," WROTE GIRARD. "His mission seemed not really to have been to report the sending of Guillbon's detachment, but to explain to Bradley that we were under-employed, that our troops were not advancing, that—apart from Haislip—the Corps generals were hopeless and the general commanding the army should be sacked." Naturally this was not what Weil said; Girard was simply venting his frustration in his diary. "I exaggerate," he continued. "But it was a bit like that. Bradley received him very graciously and told him that everything was going very well, that we needed to have a little patience and that we would go to Paris just as he said we would go and be the first."

On debriefing Weil, Leclerc was disappointed that Bradley had said nothing more tangible.

"If you send a simple cavalry major with such a message to a general commanding a whole army group, what do you expect?" said Weil.[46]

Almost concurrently, General Eisenhower welcomed de Gaulle's chief of staff, General Alphonse Juin, to Shellburst. Juin told Eisenhower, "De Gaulle was my classmate at Saint-Cyr. I know his determination. Give the order to march on Paris to the 2e DB yourself, because they are going to go anyway."

Eisenhower *apparently* replied, "Stop nagging! I know what I'm going to do. I shall send a telegram to Marshall to persuade Roosevelt. I have decided to send Gerow's Corps. And, if the boss [Roosevelt] doesn't agree, I'll do it anyway."[47]

Meanwhile, Gerow's staff kept a firm eye on Leclerc's division, and air reconnaissance patrols reported American vehicles around

Sénonches, beyond the 2e DB's authorised axis of advance. Who were they? Leclerc's operations officer, André Gribius—presumably because he was not a *gaulliste de la première heure*—had not been informed of Guillebon's *Patrouille*. Hence Gribius denied knowledge of Guillebon's force in good faith.

"You're sure?" asked V Corps.

"I'm quite sure," replied Gribius.

"*Really* sure?"

"Absolutely sure," replied Gribius.[48]

WHEN A LOCAL DELEGATION, including an archbishop, presented Colonel David Bruce with a gold-fringed French *Tricolore* and a signed certificate confirming his role in liberating Rambouillet, he recognised the deep emotion and hope with which the French awaited their Liberation. Many of his compatriots, however, seemed to be disbanding. US XX Corps' push south of Paris, and the 7th Armoured Division's arrival in Fontainebleau suggested that Rambouillet was *not* the Allies' route into Paris. Hence many journalists left, leaving Hemingway to await his big moment at the Hôtel du Grand Veneur. "Hemingway and I are holding this position," wrote Bruce, "and sending out small patrols along all the roads. It is maddening to be only thirty miles from Paris, to interrogate every hour some Frenchman who has just come from there and who reports that even a very small task force could easily move in, and to know that our Army is being forced to wait, and for what reason?"[49]

Other interviews yielded some useful local knowledge. "One man knew the exact location of a minefield he had seen the Germans lay last night. Another had taken part in *yesterday's insurrection* in Paris. Another had spent the preceeding night at Trappes and so on."[50]

While boastfully claiming that his scouting operations were akin to those of the Confederate cavalry raider John S. Mosby, in fact when it came to intelligence gathering, Hemingway was a real expert.[51] Bruce and "Mouthard"—a local reistance leader—listened as Hemingway performed skilful interrogations in fluent French, building up a picture of German troop dispositions between Rambouillet and southwest Paris. The positions of roadblocks, minefields, tanks and artillery were plotted with corrections being updated every hour.[52]

Sometimes there were moments of immense humour, as when a French husband and wife arrived in Rambouillet with three German prisoners in the back of their car guarded by a youth toting a Sten gun. Two Alsatian women were accused of *collaboration horizontale*, a hotel worker accused of being the mistress of a Gestapo officer in Paris, and a woman with a family to support was vilified for working for Vichy. All the FFIs present at the Hôtel du Grand Veneur were convinced that she had also committed *collaboration horizontale*, openly speculating whether her husband looked like a cuckold, "the sort of conversation in which the French delight and excel", wrote Bruce. More usefully, "a very young Pole deserted from the German tank unit ahead of us", wrote Hemingway. "He buried his uniform and his submachine-gun and filtered through the lines in his underwear and a pair of trousers he found in a shelled house. He brought good information and was put to work in the kitchen of the hotel." Then an old man was picked up on the road north of Rambouillet who furnished complete information on minefields and anti-tank guns beyond Trappes. "He joined the Polish child in protective custody," Hemingway wrote, but only after interrogation.[53]

Gene Currivan of *The New York Times* had joined them. Unaware that Bruce and Co. had already arranged their dining, Currivan cut himself badly opening a K-ration tin and "pretty damn near bled to death" before Hemingway applied his renowned first aid skills. Dinner compensated for this little drama. The Hôtel du Grand Veneur's owner hailed from Périgord and served them "pate de foie gras stuffed abundantly with truffles".[54]

As they dined, news arrived that weapons would be dropped to the FFI around Rambouillet that night. "So," wrote Bruce, "we decided we ought to warn any American patrols, and to place Frenchmen with them to identify any friendly transport that might have to pass through in this connection. Ernest, Mouthard, Gravey (Graveson), Red (Pelkey) and the Resistance Adjutant sallied forth with us into the blackness for this purpose." Gathering in Uncle Sam's parachuted largesse was, Bruce wrote, "a comedy of errors". The cannisters contained dismantled bazookas, rifles, grenades and ammunition, which found their way into Hemingway's arsenal. When Mac returned from Le Mans with cash, Papa could both arm and pay his irregulars.[55] Hemingway's men loved him, all wondering when they were going to *Paname*—to Paris!

MUCH TO TAITTINGER'S SURPRISE after the morning's menacing treatment, he and his colleagues were served a decent tea including jam and biscuits. Shortly afterwards they learnt they were finally going to the Depot. Once again they were taken through the Préfecture's great courtyard, now even more crammed with seized German vehicles, including open-top cars with bloody seats. Taittinger also noticed captured *Miliciens*—who had missed Bassompierre's buses on the 17th—being roughly herded towards the cells, their womenfolk pulled along by their hair. From every direction firearms could be heard.[56]

With Taittinger and René Bouffet in front, *résistants* herded the deposed dignitaries of Occupied Paris through the Préfecture's west gate into the relatively calm Boulevard du Palais. "Those are toffs," remarked an FFI. But there was little degradation at this stage. Taittinger and his friends were marched past the Palais de Justice, near the exquisite medieval Sainte-Chapelle. As they walked, Taittinger remembered a saying from the "Great Revolution": "Whoever salutes the King will be hung. Whoever insults him will suffer the same fate." Neither saluted nor injured, he had survived so far. Now in the cells of the Depot, whose usual occupants were petty criminals, tarts and low-lifes, Taittinger noticed René Bouffet's morale beginning to collapse. "There's a little sunlight still. There are balconies with geraniums," said Taittinger comfortingly. The Depot's warders were professionals; recognising the extraordinary situation they promised to treat Taittinger and his colleagues according to the rules. It was now forty hours since the FFIs had seized the Hôtel de Ville. Taittinger thought their impertinence breathtaking, presuming to liberate Paris and only making matters worse.[57]

Their cell was in *Quartiers des Soeurs*, that part of the Depot normally reserved for female prisoners, now filling up with the *épuration*'s first victims.

"If there isn't enough room you could always put us in the Concièrgerie, where the Royal Family were held during the Revolution," Taittinger quipped to a wardress.

Smiling slightly, she replied that those cells were now a museum, as he well knew. Instead Taittinger and his colleagues were allocated the cell once occupied by Monsignor Darboy, the Archbishop of Paris executed by the Communards in 1871.

"I hope this doesn't mean that history is going to repeat itself," Taittinger remarked.

"Show me a cell that doesn't have a history," the wardress replied.

At least they could see daylight, but in the lower cells women accused of collaboration, horizontal and otherwise, wailed piteously. Unlike Bouffet, Taittinger noticed that Cornillat and Ruegger kept their spirits up well.[58]

AT 11PM, AS THE ELECTRICITY CAME BACK ON, and news-hungry Jean Galtier-Boissière frantically tuned his radio to any frequency offering hope, Bobby Bender arrived at Nordling's consulate. Nordling's truce was in tatters, but von Choltitz had a proposal for resurrecting it.

The previous evening von Choltitz was visited by Otto Abetz, who had briefly returned to Paris to tie up various loose ends. Abetz claimed that von Choltitz wanted to discuss political matters, and they reaffirmed to each other that Hitler's destruction order should be disobeyed. But the path von Choltitz was following, with the danger it posed for his family under *Sippenhaft*, was tearing him apart. Sympathising with von Choltitz's position, Abetz promised that when he returned to Berlin he would protest against Wehrmacht conduct, thereby making von Choltitz appear over-zealous rather than the opposite. Later that night

Abetz sent two telegrams to OKW emphasising how conscientiously von Choltitz was behaving.[59]

Perhaps power cuts exacerbated the misunderstandings between Joachim von Ribbentrop's *Auswärtigesamt* (Foreign Office) in Berlin and Abetz, placing the latter incommunicado for several hours. Given the paranoia among senior Nazis after 20 July, it was unsurprising that Ribbentrop considered whether Abetz would defect to the Allies, launching investigations to find him. Abetz was probably incapable of a complete *volte face*, but he undoubtedly began laying down moral capital intended to save his skin when Hitler's Germany collapsed.[60]

Even while holding Pétain's government captive, Hitler's inner circle never thought them *collabo* enough. Goebbels farcically regarded Jacques Doriot as "more suited to our needs", to be Vichy's Prime Minister "in exile" than Laval. But, preferring Laval's sophisticated wit to the bully-boy Doriot, Abetz scuppered this idea. Hence Goebbels regarded both Laval and Abetz as disastrous for Germany's cause, writing, "What could have been accomplished, if instead of Abetz we had had a real National Socialist managing German politics in Paris!"[61]

But Abetz had bought von Choltitz some time, during which he set about devising a new accommodation with the Resistance. First von Choltitz wanted French *patriots*, as he described the FFI, to keep within a zone of central Paris which German forces would undertake not to enter. This area, an irregular rectangle of around fifteen hundred metres by eight hundred, would include the Ile de la Cité and Ile Saint-Louis, and two bands of territory, one on the right bank up to the Rue de Rivoli, and the other on the left bank as far as the Boulevard Saint-Germain.

Second, *les patriotes françaises* would only be allowed out of these areas if they were travelling either from west to east, or east to west, since that was the same direction as German forces retreating through Paris.

Third, German forces entering Paris would keep to predetermined routes through the city in order to reduce violent incidents.

Fourth, *les patriotes françaises* must agree not to erect further barricades except within the area described above.[62]

Although he recognised how difficult von Choltitz's position had become, Nordling saw immediately that it was pointless offering the Resistance such terms. First they would have to evacuate the area between the Hôtel de Ville and the Préfecture. Second, senior *résistants* would regard "ghettoization" as a potential trap, whereby FFI-controlled areas could subsequently be destoyed Warsaw-style. Shaking his head, Nordling showed von Choltitz's proposals to Saint-Phalle, who confirmed the Resistance would never consider such terms.[63]

But later that night von Choltitz telephoned Nordling, wanting a response. Nordling immediately explained why von Choltitz's terms would be unacceptable to the Resistance and not worth presenting. Amazingly, von Choltitz offered to send a tank to fetch Nordling from his consulate so they could discuss the matter face to face. Nordling refused, saying that it would be unsuitable for a neutral consul to ride in a German combat vehicle. Then, in a moment of wishful thinking, Nordling claimed that the truce was still "*en vigueur*" and the Germans had no good reason to recommence hostilities.[64]

CAPTAIN GEORGES DROVE GALLOIS through La Ferte Alais and along quiet backroads, avoiding German checkpoints which had sprung up in the area. On reaching the Chalmette valley they saw American troops on the far side, at the edge of a wood. Taking a potentially lethal calculated risk that a camouflaged German machine-gun nest beside a hayrick would not dare disclose its position by shooting at them, Captain Georges' driver manoeuvred the camionette so that it remained unnoticed until they were almost upon the American lines, and then put his foot down. Moments later they were surrounded by GIs. It was now early evening. After handing Gallois over to an American officer, Captain Georges bid him an emotional farewell.[65]

Following a brief interview with a battalion intelligence officer, Gallois was taken to the US Third Army HQ at Courville, arriving after dark. There he was questioned by Third Army's Resistance expert, Lieutenant Colonel Powell, who decided the occasion justified waking Patton. Gallois was taken to the tent of *un monsieur* who appeared with unbrushed hair and his shirt open, the collar of which bore the three stars of a US lieutenant general.

"*Je vous écoute*"—"I am listening," said Patton.

Gallois gave Patton a *resumé* of the situation in Paris, the arguments for intervention rehearsed with Robert Monod, and what they needed from the Allies.

"You should consider," said Patton, "that such vast operations as we are undertaking are not conceived lightly nor without deeply thought-through plans which we must follow to the letter. Nothing else that might happen, whether anticipated or unexpected, can change these plans, certainly if such events are not of extraordinary importance.

"Our objective is Berlin and our wish is to end the war as quickly as possible. The immediate taking of Paris is not in our planning and we are not going to Paris, because the capital is not a military objective and its taking is not important for us. On the contrary, taking Paris would be a burden because we would have to ensure the supplying of a large population and the immediate repair of lots of things destroyed by the Germans. We are trying to destroy German armies, not take cities. You should have waited for orders from the Allied High Command before launching your insurrection and not taken the initiative yourselves."[66]

"All right, General," said a crestfallen Gallois. "So it's a 'No.' So, what do I do now?"

"It's for you to answer that question, not for me," Patton replied crisply.

"I think the only thing that I can do is return to Paris to advise my superiors of this *refus* from the American Army."

"That sounds like the best solution," said Patton.

"Before I return, can I ask a great favour of you?" said Gallois. Patton nodded.

"I am a Frenchman and you have been very honest with me," continued Gallois. "But before returning to Paris with the disappointing news that I must bear, I would like to see a French uniform. I would like to speak to a *French* general. I would very much like to see Leclerc."

"Leclerc is not under my orders," said Patton. "I don't know where he is but I will go and see what I can do."

In fact, Leclerc's men had hardly moved since Haislip's XV Corps relinquished the 2e DB to Gerow's V Corps under Hodges. Patton decided to send Gallois straight to Bradley's Eagletac HQ. He also sent an orderly to find a bottle of champagne and two glasses.

"Not too exhausted to make a long journey?" asked Patton, uncorking the champagne.

"Absolutely not," replied Gallois.

Patton filled the glasses.

"*À la France et la victoire!*" said Patton, his eyes twinkling.

Gallois gulped back the golden liquid. Then he began the long drive to General Bradley's Eagletac HQ at Laval. Gallois looked at his watch. It was 3.30am on 22 August; his information about Paris was nearly three days old.[67]

22 August 1944

AT EXACTLY 8AM ALEXANDRE DE SAINT PHALLE visited Nordling. The truce's disintegration profoundly worried Saint Phalle, and the terms for its reinstatement offered by von Choltitz the previous evening made him fearful. Unprompted, Saint-Phalle concluded that the Americans should come as soon as possible. Nordling agreed.[68]

Meanwhile, events at the Hôtel Meurice demonstrated how justified Saint-Phalle's concerns were. Von Choltitz had received renewed orders to destroy Paris. "The preliminary text," von Choltitz later wrote, "alluded to the gravity of the situation on the Western front, exhorting the soldiers to oppose the unremitting onslaught, and not to give way but to redouble their energy. The order then continued, expressing the intention of the Supreme Command to hold the line Pontarlier-Plateau de Langres-Troyes, using Seine-Paris as a pivot. It is particularly recommended to the General commanding Gross-Paris, to take account of the decisive importance of the city as the hinge of this new front." Then von Choltitz quotes, "*Paris is to be transformed into a pile of ruins. The General commanding should defend the city to the last man and perish, if necessary, in the rubble.*" On reading these last two sentences von Choltitz felt ashamed. What struck von Choltitz most was the tone of "*Paris is to be transformed into a pile of ruins*", which contrasted so absurdly with the unemotive language in which General staff officers were trained to write orders.[69]

"Look at this," he told his adjutant, Colonel Hans Jay.

They shook their heads. Von Choltitz telephoned Lieutenant General Hans Speidel, a friend of the injured Field Marshal Rommel, now chief of staff at Army Group West HQ at Cambrai.

"Thank you for the lovely order," said von Choltitz sarcastically.

"Which order is that, General?" Speidel replied.

"Well, the demolition order," said von Choltitz. "Here is what I am to do. I must lay three tons of explosives in Notre Dame, two tons in Les Invalides, a ton in the Chamber of Deputies. I must blow up the Arc de Triomphe because it obstructs my line of fire ..."

Speidel breathed deeply at the other end.

"I am acting with your knowledge and agreement, yes, dear Speidel?"

Speidel hesitated. "Yes, General."

"So it's you who have given this order?"

"No, it isn't us," replied Speidel. "It's the Führer who must have given that order."

"Listen," said von Choltitz. "It's you who have transmitted this order and you who will answer to History." Gathering steam, von Choltitz continued. "I will tell you what I have stopped; the Madeleine and the Opera, we were going to annihilate those. Then, when it comes to the Eiffel Tower, I am to blow it up in such a way that it makes a tank trap behind the blown bridges."

At that point, Speidel, a decent man, connected to the 20 July conspirators who would soon face Gestapo investigation, spotted the irony in von Choltitz's voice.

"General," said Speidel as he signed off. "How lucky we are to have you in Paris."[70]

Von Choltitz spoke several times with Speidel during the following week; it was some comfort that another general understood his unenviable position. Von Aulock was holding the Paris perimeter as best he could. "But," von Choltitz wrote, "the defence force was only observing. Logistics troops were beginning to leave."[71]

Later that morning Nordling thought von Choltitz appeared stressed. Nordling was not feeling particularly well himself. Both were chubby, middle-aged men. Neither would get through the week's events with his health unaffected.[72]

"Do you see any way of reasoning with the Resistance?" asked von Choltitz.

Nordling said General de Gaulle was the only man the FFIs might obey.

Von Choltitz wrote that he "*thought* that someone should try to contact him".[73]

This was another key moment when von Choltitz's deep disillusionment over Hitler's war amazed Nordling. In his memoirs von Choltitz clings to practical motives: "I decided to influence the opposing chief in person in a last effort to calm the Resistance. As always, the interests of different parties were converging towards the same point: I wanted to save my soldiers from further losses and the French interest was to preserve their capital."[74]

Nordling asked von Choltitz if he would authorise someone to cross the lines to negotiate with the Allies.

"Why not?" replied von Choltitz.[75]

Nordling later said, "A chance offered itself to von Choltitz to give Germany a more humanitarian face, which he seized."[76]

AT THE PRÉFECTURE, Saint-Phalle met Alexandre Parodi, Roland Pré and Charles Luizet in the latter's office. They were joined by Henri Rol-Tanguy and Maurice Kriegel-Valrimont representing COMAC. When Parodi put forward von Choltitz's proposals, Kriegel-Valrimont and Rol-Tanguy rejected them immediately, as Nordling predicted. They were glad Nordling's truce was terminated following the CNR's decision, and that *affiches* were being printed proclaiming "*aux barricades*". Saint-Phalle thought Kriegel-Valrimont and Rol-Tanguy were raising the spectre of another Commune, when Paris fell under mob rule following Napoleon III's defeat by Bismarck's Prussians. But for the moment, Saint-Phalle wanted their agreement for Nordling to cross the German lines and beg Eisenhower to march on Paris.[77]

"Nordling will tell the Germans that he is presenting himself to the Allied generalissimo in order to negotiate the [German] retreat," said Saint-Phalle.

The *résistants* agreed that Saint-Phalle should go but refused to change their own plans.

That afternoon Parodi held a meeting at the Matignon for provisional ministers who had taken control of government buildings since the 19th. He told them the truce was over and that they should leave their ministries in the hands of a "*local clandestin*" where possible or else abandon them. Everyone was aghast.

"Is that an order?" asked Courtin, the caretaker minister at the Treasury.

"I am the Delegate General of the Government," replied Parodi, slapping the table. "It's a formal order."

But Parodi's order was unenforceable; most government buildings remained in Resistance hands. The Treasury building was occupied by one hundred and fifty *résistants* with only ten rifles, six pistols and a case of grenades between them. With fourteen kilometres of corridors, Courtin's *résistants* estimated that not even the SS would fight for the Treasury room by room. They stayed put.[78]

The final declaration was different from Parodi's order:

> Council of Ministers 22 August.
>
> Information received from the Allies remains imprecise. The Allied High Command has received different accounts of the situation in Paris. Combat continues.
>
> I appeal for attention to be paid to the danger presented by the retreat of German troops *on* Paris. We must reduce the risk of reprisals being made

against public buildings occupied by the Resistance. It is recommended that general secretaries take security precautions appropriate to their circumstances and which vary according to local dispositions and protection forces available to them.[79]

BEFORE THE TRUCE ENDED things appeared calm around German strongpoints. Their vehicle park near the Madeleine remained undisturbed, though Resistance officials still using the truce's white flag might be searched, *les Fridolins* being friendlier towards those who spoke German. However, on the Place Saint-Augustin tanks circled menacingly accompanied by trucks carrying German sailors who, like the SS, believed the Wehrmacht needed stiffening after 20 July. "Depending where they were, the Germans did not systematically open fire on civilian vehicles," wrote Pierre Bourget. "It is one of the most striking contrasts of the Insurrection; there were zones where the Germans remained totally passive and others where they displayed more aggression, witnessing extraordinary cruelty."[80]

Troops retreating through Paris could not understand what all the fuss was about, until they reached central hotspots.

"What devilry!" said a German officer on reaching a fuel depot.

"What happened?" asked Robert Wallraf.

"Well may you ask," replied the officer. "Don't you see? All these bullet holes in my car! One grazed my leg. The swines! We were driving calmly along beside the Seine when suddenly we got this from all sides. You can't see anyone. They fire from windows and roofs. Where are my vehicles? These swines won't even have their skins! We should have gone round. What's happened to the others?"

"There are strongpoints where you will always be safe," said Wallraf.

"Strong points! *Schiesse* upon your strong points," said the convoy officer. "I want to regroup my men and vehicles and get them safely to the Gare d'Orsay."[81]

Although von Choltitz claimed the necessity of keeping the roads open, the number of troops retreating through Paris was diminishing, the available routes were being closed, and those that remained passable were easily blocked by damaged vehicles. Yet on this matter von Choltitz apparently remained stern, telling junior officers to "follow orders without discussion. I will shoot with my own pistol any officer, clerk or simple soldier who tries to flee Paris." Yet, that same day, after discussions with Swiss Consul René Naville, von Choltitz sent a hundred and forty lorries to Verneuil l'Étang to collect flour for Parisian bakeries. "Early afternoon," wrote Naville, "I arrived with Dr. Morsier to see General von Choltitz. He made no objection to the proposed action. He himself immediately gave the orders to make this possible, promising us that no lorry carrying a Wehrmacht pass would be obstructed by German troops."[82]

FOLLOWING ROL'S "*AUX BARRICADES!*" these impromptu defences multiplied. "Along the avenues with large trees, wood cutters, some certainly novices lifting an axe for the first time, cut through their trunks," wrote Parisian commentator Charles Lacretelle. "The trees would crash down, their green mass falling across the road and blocking it while ... assistants in this handiwork shouted appreciatively, 'They can come now, *Les Fritzs*, they won't pass.'"[83] Some barricades, like the images in Victor Hugo's *Les Miserables*, rose as high as first floor balconies, their size almost becoming pointless. After a priest from St Germain des Prés admirably directed the construction of his local barricade he was asked to supervise others.[84]

Commandant Dufresne (aka Raymond Massiet) wrote, "Across the scope of the capital, except in the western arrondissements, the battle continued throughout the 22 August." This observation was supported by Pierre Sonneville: "In the rich *quartiers* where it was possible to minimise the consequences of rationing and live a life close to normal, the general desire was to get through it all with the minimum of damage." After Rol-Tanguy eased him off P1's staff, Sonneville's role became liaison, cycling around Paris with paniers stuffed with banknotes.[85]

Alongside mushrooming barricades, FFI numbers increased from around three thousand five hundred on 19 August to more like five thousand. Weapons remained inadequate, hence anything captured from the Germans constituted a modest victory. But not all captured weapons were suitable for untrained hands; when a PAK 75mm anti-tank gun was captured along with its limber at the bottom of the Boulevard Saint-Michel, *Gardiens* from the Préfecture sensibly removed it.[86] Lack of training among the FFI became a serious problem. That same morning three *Gardiens*, patrolling near the Préfecture in a requisitioned taxi, suffered "friendly fire" which killed *Gardien* Avriac. They diverted their mission to the overspill mortuary at the little convent on Rue Charles Divry.[87]

For most FFI, local leaders were their only recognised authority figures, so whether they recognised Nordling's truce depended on whose command they followed: Rol-Tanguy, Lizé or the Préfecture. Around mid-day Charles Luizet ordered fifteen *Gardiens* to announce via loudspeakers that combat would be resumed.[88]

Many FFI had fought continuously since 19 August. A *groupe-franc* chief from the 1st Arrondissement began on the 18th, jumping on a German motorcycle-sidecar and seizing its MG42 from its mount. On the 19th, he killed a German naval officer, captured a Waffen SS soldier and "recovered" a French car. Adrien Dansette omits to say whether this man killed anyone on the 20th, if not perhaps Nordling's truce deprived him of the opportunity. But on the 21st, with the truce *en vigueur* across swathes of Paris, he destroyed a German vehicle, killing an officer and two soldiers. Meanwhile at Neuilly, another plucky *resistant*, in a scene resembling a *Godfather* film, was chased into a house by a German patrol. He then escaped over the roof, regained the street from another building and captured the Germans pursuing him from behind. Then there was the Gabonais negro Georges Dukson* who prowled the 17th Arrondissement armed with a Colt 45. Once, seeing a German patrol car, Dukson lay doggo on the pavement, then

---

* A sergeant in a colonial regiment, Georges Dukson was captured in 1940. In 1943 he escaped back to Paris, earning his living as a small-time trader in the Batignolles until the Insurrection's outbreak offered an opportunity to distinguish himself, taking part in the seizure of the 17th Arronndissement's *mairie* on 19 August and the fighting on the Rue Boursault.

leapt up and shot the Germans dead. Nicknamed the *lion noir*, "the black lion", he was elected an officer.[89]

Roger Bourderon writes that with "the final burying of the truce, the 22 August saw the lifting of heavy uncertainties". Writing of this day, Colonel Villate, one of Rol-Tanguy's deputies, emphasises Rol-Tanguy's professionalism. "The CP functioned normally, like a real organ of command. Several times during the day, the Colonel [Rol-Tanguy] and his adjutants went out, accomplishing the various tasks of liaison in the different *quartiers* of Paris, the Préfecture, Rue Guénégaud—the CP of the FFI of the Seine—to the *organs* of the Resistance around the arrondissments and *quartiers* of Paris. Often there were only two officers left at the main CP beneath the Barrière d'Enfer. A direct telephone line from the Préfecture permitted the receiving of numerous messages through which it was possible to pass on information to district police stations from where other sources of information reverted to the Préfecture, thereby making it the symbol of the Resistance. This information, often exaggerated, was analysed at the Barrière d'Enfer, checked by workers from either the water department or the Metro, who were easily contacted from the CP at Denfert-Rochereau and usually *au courant* with the real battle situation, and able to take a well-advised view of what should be done. It should be remembered that while the CP was at Denfert-Rochereau there were 285 calls from the Préfecture, which represents fifty per day."[90]

Interviewed by Francis Crémieux during the 1960s, Alexandre Parodi said that while he understood the reasons for ending the truce, it bought Paris two precious days during which most Parisians recognised what was happening under their noses. "When on Tuesday 22 August we resumed combat, I think I can honestly say that, on that day, there was a total difference in the situation because the Resistance now had behind them, not only *episodiques* movements partial to uprisings, like those I have alluded to, but truly all the people of Paris."[91]

Though Parodi's last clause needs qualifying, a real spirit of *fraternité* reigned behind the barricades from the FFI and their supporters down to the most retiring *badauds*. Most FFI simply wanted to kill a *Boche* and cared little for the distinct groupings within the Resistance. In the 17th Arrondissement, a youth approaching an FTP CP seeking food was told "There's nothing for you here" by a FTP veteran. But the commander interjected, "Here there are only Frenchmen."[92]

THAT NOT ALL PARISIANS WERE INVOLVED is proved by maps which demonstrate that barricades, while plentiful in some areas, were virtually non-existent in others. Generally speaking there were noticeable differences between smart areas, *les quartiers aisés*, and those working-class areas usually reckoned *traditonellement révolutionaires*. Where the proletarian and the aristocrat worked together on local barricades, these would usually be in older *quartiers* like the Latin Quarter where aristocratic homes exist behind high walls alongside buildings comprising modest apartments, the Rue Séguier being a good example. Barricades occurred where there was something to barricade *against*, such as a German-occupied barracks or an established strongpoint.[93] As Pierre Bourget said, "Let us not forget the presence, throughout the *combats*, of fishermen beside the Seine, and bathers taking the sun on the beach created after the *Exposition International* of 1937 near the *debouche* of the Pont d'Iena on the *rive droite*, without forgetting also those who chose the Square du Vert-Galant (patch of garden on the west end of the Ile de la Cité behind the Statue of Henri of Navarre) to bask in the Sun before plunging their heads in the river."[94]

Among the Haussman-style *quartiers* of western Paris, the *haute bourgeoisie* observed the *résistants'* arrival at ungarrisoned *mairies* with measured concern. Most wealthy Parisians never suffered the vindictiveness inflicted on *collabo* suspects like Pierre Taittinger. Usually they were relieved to witness the Insurrection's nationalist character, finding themselves smiling at *résistants'* apparent contempt for military tradition. "This is not serious," remarked a retired officer on seeing a young FFI standing in an open car; an excellent target for German snipers. For such veterans, being serious meant joining either de Lattre's First Army or Leclerc's 2e DB.[95]

BEFORE SENDING REPITON-PRÉNEUF TO V CORPS, General Leclerc emphasised that Gribius was unaware of Guillebon's detachment, and that fact must be clarified to Gerow's staff, hoping the Americans would understand. French thinking—sending Guillebon's *Patrouille*—spoke for itself. "But," wrote Girard, "difficulties *were* inevitable." And when Weil piped up that Bradley intended to envelop Paris from north and south, where forces were already taking position, Leclerc was furious.

"What!" he exclaimed. "There's going to be a battle north of Paris and we aren't going to be there?"

When Repiton-Préneuf returned it was found that General Gerow's response was predictable: the 2e DB was under his corps' command and was not allowed to go anywhere without his orders. Regarding Guillebon's *Patrouille*, Gerow was emphatic: "If your general has sent this detachment then he had better recall them." Leclerc decided immediately that his only option was to board a Piper Cub and fly to Bradley's 12th Army Group HQ at Laval.[96]

Roger Gallois reached Bradley's HQ at 9am. Set in verdant woodland, the HQ was the Château du Bois Gamats, built in a mix of styles whose overall impact was nineteenth-century Gothic. A village of olive-green tents guarded by armoured vehicles covered its lawns. Gallois waited around thirty minutes until Bradley's French liaison officer, Colonel Lebel, appeared. "*Venez*," said Lebel. First stop was the mess for breakfast, during which Lebel took details from Gallois. Then Lebel spoke to Bradley's chief of staff, General Edwin Sibert, who gathered around forty staff officers in a large *salon* to hear Gallois' resumé. Entering the room, tired, scruffy and unshaven, Gallois noticed that Lebel looked almost as nervous as he was.

"We are listening, *Monsieur*," said Sibert.

For half an hour Sibert questioned Gallois. Gallois repeated what he had told General Patton, that while the Resistance was under-equipped, the Germans were sufficiently weak to countenance compromise as evidenced by Nordling's truce, and that Paris was there for the taking. "The people of Paris wanted to liberate their capital themselves and present it to the Allies," he said emotionally. "But they cannot finish what they have started. You must come to our help or there is going to be a terrible slaughter. Hundreds of thousands of Frenchmen are going to be killed."[97]

Afterwards Lebel informed Gallois that General Bradley would shortly attend an important conference at Eisenhower's HQ where Paris would be discussed. Gallois also learnt that General Leclerc was arriving soon. Recognising that they would be pitching for a major change in Allied plans following Gallois' plea, Sibert took him aside before departing for Shellburst.

"I want your word as an officer that everything you have told me is true," said Sibert.

"I give you my word," replied Gallois.

For good measure Lebel inserted his own personal note with Sibert's papers: "If the American Army, seeing Paris in a state of insurrection, does not come to its aid, it will be an omission the people of France will be unable to forget."

As Sibert left he tugged Lebel's arm. "Your impatient lion Leclerc is coming today. Take care of him. We may have news for him tonight."[98]

Several Eagletac officers shook Gallois' hand. Then Lebel approached him. "My dear friend, you cannot imagine how you have arrived just at the right time. For two days," said Lebel, "everyone has been coming here asking whether we're going to take Paris. When Leclerc arrives, we'll go and find him."[99]

As soon as Leclerc's Piper Cub landed on Eagletac's airstrip Lebel introduced Gallois.

"Come at once, *mon garçon*," called Leclerc. "We need to talk."

Seeing Leclerc's *divisionnaire* stars, carrying his ubiquitous cane, representing France in the massive Allied machine, Gallois was in tears.

"*Mon garçon*," said Leclerc. "No emotion, no emotion. We have serious work to do."

Between Lebel, Gallois, Leclerc and Repiton-Préneuf, the conversation flowed easily. After Gallois had described conditions in Paris, Leclerc explained the difficulties he had dealing with the American High

Command. "I would very much like to march on Paris but I am being prevented and I haven't the supplies."

"But *Mon Général*," said Gallois. "Can't your division reach Paris in forty-eight hours?"

"You're really somewhat naïve to be an officer," scoffed Leclerc. "Do you really think that a whole armoured division can move around like a company of infantry? I depend on the Americans for my supplies and I can't do it just like that."

But Gallois soon realised that liberating Paris was the 2e DB's *raison d'être*. After lunch an American officer told them, "General Bradley is in conference with General Eisenhower. He will return at 1600 hours and then examine modifications to the plans."[100]

Eisenhower had considered the question of entering Paris the previous evening and wrote to General Bedell-Smith.[101] Now, on 22 August, the choice was clear. Either the Allies could stick with their original plan or else, recognising the thin German defences and the compounding humanitarian situation inside the city, go in. "It is important to note," Gallois later wrote, "that before my arrival the Allied High Command had no idea of the importance, nor the scale of the achievement by the Resistance, of the Seine."[102]

"NOBODY CAN UNDERSTAND THE PRESENT ALLIED STRATEGY," wrote David Bruce. "General Patton's Third American Army has been in a position for several days to take Paris. Two of his divisions are across the Seine and have moved north. There are no German forces of consequence between us and the capital. Rumours have been prevalent for some days here that the failure to allow Third Army to press forward and fully realise its capabilities is due to high politics. Some even say the delay is to permit President Roosevelt to arrive and enter the city himself. Most, however, claim that the Americans are being forced to await the entry of General Montgomery and the British, who, unable to clear a way through the territory assigned to them, are now to swing through the American Sector and thus get ahead. Whatever the reason may be, it does not seem to make much sense to sit around here as if there was serious opposition in front of us, thus allowing the Germans to lay mines, disengage troops, and withdraw supplies that otherwise we could mop up with ease."[103]

Several of Bruce's speculations fell wide. Roosevelt had little interest in France beyond ensuring that the French contributed to their own liberation, thereby saving American lives. And although he had welcomed Leclerc to Tripoli in January 1943 and praised Force L's conduct in Tunisia, Montgomery was no Francophile, as his treatment of de Gaulle over Bayeux demonstrated. Unaware that Leclerc was still awaiting his marching orders, Bruce wrote of the 2e DB, "Like the Scarlet Pimpernel, it is said to be here, there and everywhere."

"This morning, a Frenchman wearing the red képi and the American uniform characteristic of a portion of that division appeared outside our hotel," wrote Bruce, describing a Spahi officer. "He was promptly pounced upon and induced to lead Gravey, Mouthard and myself to an advance element of Leclerc's." This was Guillebon's CP pitched in a wheatfield at Nogent le Roy. "We gave the colonel [Guillebon] a fill on the situation to the North, East and West of Rambouillet, and, while we were having lunch, his tanks and retainers lurched off, with the intention of going as far as Sceaux."[104]

Several correspondents also arrived, asking the 2e DB's plans for Paris, but the taciturn Guillebon could not answer.[105] Even with tanks fighting just up the road, the cream of the American press corps—including William Randolph Hearst, Jr.—descended on Rambouillet that afternoon. But when a dejected German soldier was brought to the Grand Veneur in triumph, Hemingway invited John Mowinckel, freshly returned from Le Mans, to join in the interrogation over a few beers.

"I'll make him talk," said Hemingway, signalling Mowinckel to dump the petrified youth on the bed, saying, "Take his boots off. We'll grill his toes with a candle."

"Go to hell," said Mowinckel.

The young German, who clearly knew very little, was released.[106]

Another arrival at Rambouillet was Major Airey Neave. Captured in 1940, Neave was the first man to escape from Colditz Castle, and subsequently joined MI9, organising escape lines. Neave was pursuing British traitor Harry Cole who wreaked havoc with his venal betrayals, thereby helping the Gestapo arrest hundreds of evading servicemen along with the *résistants* who hid them. A third were executed, making MI9 keen for Cole to face British justice.[107]

EVEN WITH THE TRUCE OVER, General von Choltitz's restraint was self-evident. Far from being blown apart in a storm of fire and blood like Warsaw, no Stukas screamed down on Resistance strongpoints; nor did 88mm guns blast barricades apart with a single high-explosive shell, which is all it would have taken. Von Choltitz played patball. His garrison dominated central Paris and much of the west, principally around the Étoile and the area north of the Tuileries-Louvre network of streets, especially the west end of the Rue de Rivoli, including the Hôtel Meurice, stretching along to the classical columned buildings of the Hôtel Crillon and the Naval Ministry on the north side of the Place de la Concorde. South of the river the Palais Bourbon, Quai d'Orsay buildings and the École Militaire were held with considerable garrisons. Von Choltitz kept his tanks at junctions like the Place Saint-Augustin, the Villiers crossroads and the Place Malesherbes, from where they could fire along several avenues as envisaged when nineteenth-century Paris was laid out. The Germans had abandoned several of the hotels requisitioned in 1940, along with garages and depots involved in Wehrmacht logistics. Outside central areas a few redoubts remained, principally the Luxembourg Palace and the Jardin de Luxembourg, and the oft renamed barracks on the Place de la République from which they patrolled unbarricaded thoroughfares.

German forces retreating through Paris could still use outer boulevards and roads along the Seine's north bank, such as the Avenue de la Grande Armée which leads up to the Étoile from the west, from which they could then turn northeast along the Avenue de Friedland, then Boulevard Haussmann, branching northeast along the Rue La Fayette, under the grey, functional looking railway bridge at the Rond-Point de la Villette—now the Place de la Bataille de Stalingrad—and veer northeast again along the Avenue Jean Jaurés. From there outwards retreating Germans were safe from being shot at by *résistants*.[108]

Despite the Insurrection's second wind, western *quartiers* like Auteuil saw no fighting at all; shops remained open, the leisured classes sat outside at cafés. In central Paris streets were largely empty. The Champs Élysées stood in sun-drenched, apprehensive silence broken periodically by a German tank or armoured car, or the panicked running of an office worker or woman pushing a perambulator. Offices, including government premises, mostly remained open. For the non-partisan silent majority the insurrection experience was simply something to get through. "Can one pass here?" Parisians asked both *résistants* and German soldiers. "Yes, but watch out over *there*," might come the reply. In more embattled *quartiers* a *résistant* might announce himself by calling out "FFI!" whereas an *infirmière* (nurse) escorted by a *brancardier* (stretcher bearer) both draped in white, would announce themselves at the top of their voices as "Croix Rouges".[109]

While Gallois confered with Leclerc, Rol-Tanguy remained optimistic while nevertheless recognising the FFIs' precarious position. "We had to achieve the paralysis of the enemy, to prevent him from using thoroughfares, to stop him from employing his tanks. We knew they [the Germans] were not particularly numerous, but we also knew that he could call in some very persuasive assets if he could move them from one end of the city to the other. This remained a great danger, even if the enemy had been pushed onto the defensive since the early days of the Insurrection. The barricades were intended to reduce this danger," he told Bourderon. Then, possibly exaggerating, Rol-Tanguy said, "They [the barricades] were effectively real tank traps, possibly more effective against enemy vehicles in general ... They produced negligible military gains but had disastrous psychological effects on vehicle crews whose morale was already low, who found themselves confronted by barricades, gunmen and petrol bombs."[110]

Rol-Tanguy continued: "[Our] anti-tank capabilities were not limited to petrol bombs. Before the Insurrection, the staff gave essential descriptions of German tanks, explaining how best to attack them with specially grouped grenades and explosive packages, in a manner similar to *dynamiteros* during the Spanish Civil War. We also demonstrated that it was possible to obstruct tanks with chains placed across their path which would entangle their tracks, otherwise to puncture with bullets the tyres of armoured cars and place in front of barricades deposits charged with explosives serving as anti-tank mines."[111]

Even if FFIs fought tanks less frequently than their Warsaw counterparts, the fighting could be merciless. German outposts, pinpointed during the truce, became targets for the FFI. Easily taken, their occupants were either killed or taken prisoner, the second outcome often involving degradation, and the "blue fear" of being murdered. Yet, to qualify this, while some Parisians vented their resentments by injuring or killing prisoners, Raymond Dronne insists such incidents were rare. "Nearly all wounded Germans were gathered up by Red Cross teams, correctly treated and well cared for," he wrote. "One of these, taken to a hospital where there was lots of coming and going and noise, expected to be shot in the head and closed his eyes. When he opened them again he found a Frenchman leaning over him, offering a cigarette and saying, 'For you, *Fridolin*, the war is over.'"[112]

It is also believed that German troops used the truce to infiltrate the Ile de la Cité. Monsignor Brot, archdeacon of Notre Dame, was surprised when FFIs patrolling the Pont-au-Double complained of being fired at by snipers inside Notre Dame; either behind the main roof parapet or from the towers. It was certainly possible for snipers to hide there. Infiltration merely involved tagging along with workmen who frequent such a building: "Germans or *mauvais Français*—'bad Frenchmen' or '*Miliciens*'—could mix among them and take positions in the towers or among the rafters," wrote Brot. Following calls to the Préfecture, patrols of *gardiens* searched Notre Dame's empty spaces but found no one. "Often during the course of the day," Brot continued, "people on the barricades fired at the Cathedral, each time believing they had seen someone behind the statues or the buttresses. The glasswork, luckily not the most valuable, suffered. Even the lodgings of both the treasurer and the archdeacon received a few hits." The spectre of gunmen hiding out in Notre Dame continued until the liberation.[113]

JUST WHEN NORDLING NEEDED HIS HEALTH, his *bon-viveur* years exacted their vengeance. His chest tightened, and he became breathless and barely conscious. This inconvenient heart attack rendered him unfit to travel across the lines of two opposing armies. Instead his brother, Rolf Nordling, would accompany Saint-Phalle to Allied Headquarters.[114]

Nordling asked his nephew, Édouard Fievet, to collect Saint-Phalle from the Rue Séguier and, supposing Sweden's pennant was insufficient to satisfy German checkpoints, Nordling advised Fievet to take Bender with him. After an edgy exchange with German guards on the Place Saint-Augustin, they reached the Place de la Concorde before experiencing more difficulties at the Pont de la Concorde, where SS men insisted they got out of the car with their hands up. After words with Bender, they were allowed to pass. Once Saint-Phalle had been collected and they came back the other way, the SS troops on the Pont de la Concorde cheered.[115]

While resting in his study, Nordling was disturbed by three German *Feldgendarmes* asking him to release one of their men then incarcerated among the Santé's political prisoners. No one could be returned to German custody without Nordling's authority. It became clear that this man was wanted for treason, a capital offence. Nordling chose to be difficult.

"He's my prisoner," insisted Nordling.

"He ought to be shot," said a *Feldgendarme.*

"Then I categorically refuse to release him," said Nordling.

Dissatisfied, the *Feldgendarmes* departed, but returned later bearing a *Feldgendarmerie* certificate claiming the prisoner was an agent who must not fall into Resistance hands. Nordling telephoned the Santé's director and had him interrogate the prisoner, who asked to remain at the Santé. Feeling for a pretext to obstruct the *Feldgendarmes*, Nordling noticed their certificate was unstamped and so refused to act upon it. They returned with the required stamp. So Nordling said there were not enough stamps. Thanks to Nordling the prisoner survived.[116]

IT WAS LATE AFTERNOON BEFORE Rolf Nordling's two-car convoy finally left Paris. In the first car, a *torpedo* Citroen decorated with Swedish and white pennants, Alexandre de Saint-Phalle drove while Erich Posch-Pastor sat beside him and Rolf Nordling, Jean Laurent and the French colonel Ollivier sat behind. Bender followed in a German car. According to Dronne's account, von Choltitz placed Bender at Nordling's disposal, which Nordling confirms. Nordling and Dronne also wrote that Bender had no precise written orders from von Choltitz, who would not have wanted a document bearing his signature to fall into the wrong hands.[117] Although he subsequently denied knowing Bender, von Choltitz agreed that, if they were stopped at a German checkpoint, he could be telephoned and would give verbal authority for the party to pass.[118]

Unlike Bender, Erich von Posch-Pastor carried documents confirming his service to the Resistance, intended to ensure his favourable treatment in Allied hands. Jean Laurent was included because, as a director of the Banque de l'Indochine, he had met de Gaulle during 1940 when France was falling. While Laurent probably over-egged his closeness to de Gaulle, his role in financing the Resistance was important. Dronne wrote that Colonel Ollivier (aka Jean Arnould or "Jade Amicol") urgently needed to leave Paris. The Jade Amicol *réseau* was virtually the last British-backed cell remaining in northeast France. It ran hundreds of agents from the Couvent de la Sainte-Agonie in the 13th Arrondissement where its radio was hidden.[119]

Saint-Phalle approached the first checkpoint nervously. Luckily Bender's confident authority got them through that post, and several other posts around Versailles and Saint-Cyr. Past Trappes they speeded along tree-lined, sun-dappled roads until, inevitably, they were stopped by a Waffen SS officer wearing a *Feldgendarmerie* gorget plate. As the officer and two soldiers inspected the two multi-flagged cars, a senior officer appeared, red with anger.

"What's going on here?" he asked furiously.

Bender explained.

"Since July 20th, we don't listen much to Wehrmacht generals," said the officer.

Bender eventually got him to agree to drive back to Versailles with him from where von Choltitz could be telephoned. "It will only take half an hour," Bender said.

Surprisingly the SS officer agreed. Leaving the others under the watchful guard of four Waffen SS troopers, Bender and the SS officer returned to Versailles.

"We're all going to get shot in that ditch," said Arnould, mumbling his rosary. The five emissaries waited nervously for Bender's return. Bender got through to von Choltitz easily, but their return was obstructed by a newly arrived artillery unit. With immense relief they were permitted to cross the lines and continue on their way. Bender returned to Paris.

But combat engineers were laying landmines in no-man's land. An officer showed Saint-Phalle a map before courteously offering to walk ahead of their car. After a hundred metres, the sapper officer announced, "The American lines are five hundred metres ahead." Angry shouts of "Traitor!" were audible from nearby foxholes, but the sapper officer muttered, "Orders are orders." Saint-Phalle edged the Citroen gently forward into a darkening countryside that seemed familiar. Turning towards Neauphle le Vieux, he recognised his grandmother's house. Then an American ordered him to halt. Saint-Phalle explained his mission in English, mentioning that his wife was American.[120]

Chapter 7

Paris Saved, 22–25 August

22 August 1944 (continued)

WANDERING AMONG THE RBFM'S PARKED TANK-DESTROYERS, Raymond Maggiar knew where everyone wanted to go. For him the whole rotten mess of conflicted French loyalties, which particularly affected the French Navy, would finally make sense if the 2e DB could liberate Paris. Nearby two Rochambelles knelt by an ambulance praying aloud, "Saint Geneviève, please let us return to Paris!"

"Poor little girls," said a passing captain.

"They would do better to plead with Eisenhower," replied Maggiar.[1]

At Shellburst, Eisenhower's head was full. Around four million souls lived in Paris and its environs who needed four thousand tons of food daily; supplies the Allied Expeditionary Force simply did not have. De Gaulle's hand-written letter, delivered by General Juin two days earlier, increased the pressure. In the margin Eisenhower wrote, "We might be obliged to go into Paris." All intelligence reports pointed that way. And, while Eisenhower knew nothing of men like Raoul Nordling and Bobby Bender, the fact that the Paris Resistance had negotiated a local truce suggested that von Choltitz wanted a way out. Writing to General George Marshall, Eisenhower acknowledged that it was preferable from the logistical viewpoint to bypass Paris, delaying its liberation until the German Fifteenth Army in the Pas de Calais was also destroyed. Alternatively, Paris was France's largest city and Ike recognised that if

Hitler made a stand there it could impede Allied progress eastwards, obliging his forces to go in before they could do anything else. There was also a third possibility: that the Germans might generously allow Paris to fall into Allied hands like a ripe plum. "That would please us, wouldn't it?" Eisenhower suggested to Marshall.[2]

The information Gallois gave Sibert that morning resulted in Eisenhower famously saying, "Well, what the hell, Brad. I guess we'll have to go in." Bradley later wrote contemptuously that "emissaries of the Resistance sneaked out of Paris into our lines with frantic pleas for help" and that, "Reluctantly, I delegated the task to Gee Gerow's Vth Corps and asked him to send Leclerc's French 2nd Armoured Division."[3] Other narratives indicate that Bradley's attitude was more amenable on the day.

Bradley's Piper Cub returned to Laval at around 7pm to find Colonel Lebel, Gallois, Leclerc and Repiton-Préneuf waiting impatiently beside the grass landing strip. Bradley got out and gestured for Leclerc to come to him.

"Well, you win," said Bradley. "They've decided to send you to Paris."

In simple, emphatic sentences the US 12th Army Group commander said, "An important decision has been taken and the three of us carry a very great responsibility, heavy with consequence; me, because I have given the order to take Paris. General Leclerc because he has the task of seizing the capital, and Commandant Gallois because it was due to information that he brought us that we are acting and due to his insistence."

Hearing this, Gallois felt such relief that he simply wanted to sleep. As Leclerc turned towards his own aircraft Bradley called him back. "We're not having a big battle," Bradley told Leclerc "I want you to remember one thing above all: I don't want any fighting in Paris itself. It's the only order I have for you—at no cost is there to be heavy fighting in Paris."

Leclerc saluted.[4]

And so the decision was taken.

"*Au revoir, Monsieur*," Bradley told Gallois.

Serenely twirling his cane, Leclerc walked towards his Piper Cub. "I've absolutely got to get back to my HQ before nightfall," he told Gallois. "I will send you instructions tonight."[5]

At Fleuré Leclerc's staff strained their eyes against the lowering sun, sighing with relief as his aircraft approached the landing strip and bounced along the grass. Pumped with adrenalin, Leclerc jumped youthfully to the ground. "*Direction Paris*," he said, mounting the Jeep *Koufra* to ride the last few metres to the apple orchard where his CP was sited. Bearing "the smile of great moments", approaching his command tent Leclerc called out sonorously, "Gribius, *mouvement immediat sur Paris!*"[6]

While Leclerc was at Eagletac a letter arrived from de Gaulle regarding Guillebon's advance guard.

> I saw Trevoux and read your letter. I approve your intention. One needs a unit at least in contact with Paris without delay.
>
> I saw Eisenhower on the 20th. He promised me that you would be sent to Paris. General Koenig is, at the moment, with Eisenhower, so is General Juin. He is *au courant*.
>
> I will sleep tonight at Le Mans and try to meet up with you tomorrow.
>
> (Signed: Charles de Gaulle)

An order soon arrived from General Gerow demanding that the 2e DB set off within the hour. Since it was now dark and Paris was two hundred and fifty kilometres away, the division's logisticians, Lantenois and Compagnon, had quite a task. Petrol tankers would have to leave first, through countryside still infested with German stragglers, to provide refuelling points in the Chartres-Tourville area. However one looked at it, US General Gerow's new goal, that the 2e DB reach Paris by the 24th, was unrealistic unless they reached Rambouillet in strength by the evening of the 23rd. If that was not possible, if there was serious resistance, they would seize the bridges at Gennevilliers northwest of Paris which control the loop of the Seine between Billancourt and Nanterre.[7]

FOR GUILLEBON'S ADVANCE GUARD, getting into Paris on the 23rd seemed feasible. The 2/RMT's Maurice Jourdan wrote, "After a night sleeping on hay, we found ourselves at Arpajon. There I received the order warning our sections to look our best since we might have the honour of being first into Paris, which was said to be free of Germans. We rummaged in our packs for the last clean shirt, and polished up our faces as well as our vehicles. We wanted to be ready to meet those Parisian girls. Many of us had never seen Paris where those lovely girls were certain to be. The end of the journey was close."[8]

But Guillebon was disappointed that several western arteries into Paris were barred, certainly to his small force. Beginning the day patrolling the west and northwest approaches cost the Spahis Marocains one killed and two wounded. They strapped the slain Spahi to a Jeep's bonnet and continued.[9] The road into Dampierre was mined, but Lieutenant Marson claimed the local château uneventfully, circled the front esplanade and reported back before finding a clear northerly route. Meanwhile Guillebon's infantry hooked up with local FFIs and began lifting mines.[10]

Around Port-Royal-des-Champs, Guillebon's Spahis met more German resistance. An armoured car was badly shot up entering Voisins, and at Guyancourt the Germans fought hard to hold a defunct airfield, costing the RMT its brave Chief-Sergeant Vourc'h and other casualties.[11]

23 August 1944

FOR MOST OF THE 2e DB EVERYTHING BEGAN AT MIDNIGHT. Amid a flurry of intense activity, campfires were extinguished, tents dismantled, rolled up and stowed, and baggage organised and strapped to the sides of tanks, half-tracks, lorries and Jeeps.[12] Massu heard the news at 2am amid an intense rainstorm. His men were "drunk with happiness".[13] Captain Charles d'Orgeix of the 12e Cuirassiers, from an old Parisian family, had defended the city's northern approaches against insuperable odds in 1940.[14] When Leclerc's order came d'Orgeix was close to tears; he commanded a squadron of Shermans; his own was called *Paris*.[15] Their new mission burnished a desire for smartness. Three weeks' worth of grime was wiped away and razors appeared. Those who had never seen Paris were teased by those who had; many had family there while others had been colonials their whole lives.[16]

All night Gribius prepared plans; GTs Dio and Langlade would advance via Sées, Mortagne, Châteauneuf-en-Thymerais, Maintenon, Rambouillet; while GT Billotte would make the main push from Mamers, Nogent-le-Rotrou, Chartres, Ablis and Limours. That Billotte's battlegroup would be first into Paris had long been decided. Billotte's Gaullist credentials were impeccable. He also thoroughly understood the politics of the situation. After the difficulties with the Americans Billotte was amazed they were on their way at last.[17]

To accompany the 2e DB into Paris, General Hodges designated the US 4th Infantry Division which was recuperating in a rest area nearby. The 4th had landed on Utah Beach on D-Day, took Cherbourg, helped repulse the Mortain counterattack, and was part of the final operation to close the Falaise pocket. Its commander, General Raymond "Tubby" Barton, was loved by his men and a friend of Hemingway. As Hodges saw it, it was not Leclerc's division that would liberate Paris but Gerow's V Corps.[18]

Gerow's HQ received orders for Paris from Shellburst as soon as they were drafted. Particularly emphasised was that heavy fighting should be avoided. However, this only applied to central Paris, the area within its traditional boundaries. Outside that area artillery and air support could be used. Attached was a situation report, numbering the FFI, including the police, at twenty-five thousand, saying they controlled substantial areas of the city. Based on their intelligence, Eisenhower and Gerow believed the Germans would withdraw once the Allies arrived in force.[19]

GT LANGLADE WAS ON ITS WAY BY 6AM, their day's target being Rambouillet. Colonel Peschaud's route teams marked the way as dark clouds promised more rain.[20] Grim, burnt-out vehicles from the previous week reminded them that more fighting lay ahead.

After backtracking through Alençon, Dronne's Spaniards were glad to leave Normandy's dangerous, undulating valleys behind them and enter Beauce's less complex landscape. Dronne thought *les Beaucerons'* welcome cooler than in Normandy, which he attributed to cooler blood.[21]

Passing through villages developed a particular routine; the rumble of engines sent villagers into their houses, fearing they were German. Doors and shutters closed. Once the tanks entered the village, curious kids saw green vehicles with their white stars and yelled, "*Les Americains! Les Americains!*" Doors opened, everyone came out, even more overjoyed on discovering that they were French.

"Where are you from?" villagers would ask.

"From Chad," replied RMT members.[22]

Such scenes made General Bradley write, "Concerned that Leclerc's forces might be engulfed by champagne-bearing well-wishers and thus diverted and delayed in their mission, I also asked Gerow to send Ray Barton's battle-hardened 4th Infantry Division to help. Goaded by that threat, Leclerc's men, nearly overwhelmed with wine and women, rolled and reeled into Paris."[23]

Since it was unthinkable to send an armoured division into a major engagement without infantry support, it seems surprising that Bradley should write things which would inevitably offend French sensibilities. Billotte later wrote that Bradley, "in a book of memoirs under his name, referring to the conduct of the 2e DB *en route* for Paris, mentioned things that he had neither seen nor verified; namely that the column dawdled along and that its men were drunk all along the route, partying with the population. Allegations utterly without foundation and unworthy of such a great military leader. As if the Free French, who were returning after four years to liberate Paris, were going to waste a single second on the way to accomplishing the ambition of their lives!"[24] Paul de Langlade also protested against Bradley's criticisms in his memoirs.[25] Most of the 2e DB, including Leclerc, had not seen their homes and families for longer than nearly any Allied soldiers except the Poles. Their imaginations raced with joy or horror at what they might find, feelings common to all ranks without exception.

The route to Rambouillet passed near Chartres. "My parents were there," wrote Alain de Boissieu, "but in what condition would I find them? Could they perhaps have been deported due to me? Or killed in an air-raid?" Boissieu handed command of his squadron to Lieutenant Duplay and drove his Jeep as though on auto-pilot along lanes he knew since childhood. He found his sister, Chantal, at Chartres' préfecture. She told him their parents were safe, but their home was wrecked when a nearby bridge was destroyed. Finding them in temporary accommodations, Boissieu embraced his parents for the first time since 1940. "Tomorrow we're going to liberate Paris," he said. His parents proudly told him how many of his relations were in the Resistance. The Boissieu family mostly saw the Occupation the same way. It was like that sometimes.[26]

BREAKFASTING AT THE HÔTEL DE VILLE'S CANTEEN, Marie-Hélène Lefaucheux witnessed *résistants'* rising confidence; thirty German prisoners and two young *Miliciens* sat under guard at a nearby table. Although worried sick over her husband's fate, Marie-Hélène knew that *Miliciens* were usually misguided boys. "They will be shot tomorrow," said a FFI guard. Marie-Hélène was chilled to her spine.[27]

Having been up all night tending casualties, Dr. Victor Veau was amazed by the euphoric atmosphere at his local library, where he went to read the latest newspapers, and roundly disabused fellow readers of thinking everything was over. Earlier, from his surgery room window, Veau saw an old couple selling *Libération* having their papers confiscated at pistol point by a German officer yelling guttural obscenities. Once this officer disappeared the couple were resupplied with more copies. Even now some Germans still behaved ruthlessly; a young *cheminot* was shot for obstructing the requisition of a locomotive at the Gare de l'Est. With bullets in the chest and head, Veau hardly needed a long autopsy to deduce cause of death.[28]

Although the situation was intensifying, Nordling was disconcerted when von Choltitz placed sentries outside his Consulate. Claiming the Swedish flag was sufficient protection, Nordling persuaded von Choltitz to remove his men. Representing the GPRF required Nordling to receive one Colonel Lelorrain to liaise with the 2e DB when they arrived. Lelorrain, aka Lorrain Cruze, was a tough, stocky man whose glasses made him look intellectual. Like Chaban-Delmas, Lelorrain was another political appointee sent to witness Nordling's conversations with Bender and representatives of the Occupation authorities.[29]

THE FIRST BIG INCIDENT OF AUGUST 23 occurred around 9am when a column of thirty vehicles, including armoured cars, light tanks and a Tiger, arrived on the Champs Élysées heading for the Seine quays. Little happened until it reached the junction with the little tree-lined Avenue de Selves. Now used for parking, this slip road accesses the service area of the Grand Palais' exhibition halls. The cellars of this great *belle époque* edifice were used as an overspill lock-up for *collabos* and German prisoners. But, in the main halls above, Swedish impresario Jean Houcke's Circus Honcha was preparing the liberation's first great show; an extravaganza of acrobatics and wild animals, from which he anticipated making a fortune. Unfortunately, from the Commissariat office, *Gardien* Chastagnier, who probably could not see the full extent of the column descending the Champs Élysées, shot and killed a German soldier. The German convoy reacted quickly; fifty infantrymen took position to suppress the gunfire from the Grand Palais.

Once the gunfire began, Jean Houcke feared the worst while, from the cells, German prisoner Captain von Zigesar-Beines saw two small contraptions resembling miniature tanks chugging towards the building. These were remote-controlled explosives called Goliaths. Sadly *Gardien* Chastagnier had fired upon a German convoy which included combat engineers. As Parisians butchered one of Houcke's circus horses which was caught in the crossfire, the two Goliaths rattled ever closer to the Grand Palais. Zigesar called out a belated warning just as a Goliath exploded, rattling windows across western Paris. German infantry then threw hand-grenades while one of their tanks fired explosive shells. As fire engulfed the Grand Palais, the policemen had no option but to release prisoners from the basement; Germans, *collabos* and low-lifes. Despite the gun-battle going on, brave Paris firemen attempted to control the fire. Since the German convoy on the Champs Élysées was not under General von Choltitz's authority, they even shot the fire-hoses, chuckling when the water pressure became a dribble. Eventually, to avoid further destruction, the Police *résistants* asked Zigesar to arrange the Grand Palais' surrender. Jean Houcke wept in the street. "Don't worry, the Allies will be here in a few days, you'll see," said an elderly *Parisienne*. But Houcke was inconsolable.[30]

When Lieutenant von Arnim called Nordling about the Grand Palais incident he confusingly called the building the *"Palais Royal"* — the apartment building where Colette lived—causing some delay before the confusion was rectified.[31] Several police *résistants* captured at the Grand Palais were taken to the Hôtel Meurice, arriving just as Nordling's deputy, Gustav Forssius, and Swiss Consul René Naville were negotiating the release of Wehrmacht food supplies. Since the city's authorities were now virtually indistinguishable from the Resistance leadership, German demands that these foodstuffs should be withheld from the Resistance became impossible to enforce. Nevertheless von Choltitz agreed for more French lorries to pass German checkpoints to collect flour. That business over, von Choltitz led Forssius to the balcony. To the west smoke rose above the Grand Palais. "They've smashed the glass," sighed von Choltitz, pointing at his window. Forssius warned that reprisals would simply aggravate the situation. "It's like a pretty girl," said von Choltitz. "When she gives you a slap, you don't return it."[32]

At Nordling's behest the *Gardiens* captured at the Grand Palais were exchanged for German personnel held by the Resistance. The destruction of the Grand Palais, which was restored soon after the war, demonstrates just how lightly General von Choltitz dealt with the Insurrection. He played a double game with Field Marshal Model, sending communiqués that Paris was in full revolt, that he had no artillery and that the garrison's food—which he was giving away—was running out.[33]

IN THE DEPOT'S *QUARTIER DES SOEURS* Taittinger witnessed several distinguished Parisians arriving as prisoners. Since smart, traditional General Herbillon was too old to serve Vichy or de Gaulle, Taittinger could not understand why he was there. His concièrge denounced him for warning (realistically) that the Torch landings would curtail food shipments from French North Africa, causing his arrest twenty months later.[34]

Another important arrival was the famous actor, playwright and impresario, Sacha Guitry. Despite his abiding faith in Allied victory, by continuing his *boulevardier* lifestyle under the Occupation Guitry laid himself open to envy and copious denunciations. A late riser, like many thespians, Guitry was still in bed when the FFIs came, though apparently he had taken a telephone call from the distraught Arletty shortly before. Determined to degrade him as much as possible, the FFIs only allowed Guitry to put a dressing gown over his pyjamas, slip on some jade green mules and place a panama on his distinguished head. Without his wallet, he had no cash for paying the warders to get him sundries. Luckily, since Guitry was famously generous, other prisoners chipped in to find what was necessary.[35]

However, former naval officer and right-wing writer Paul Chack deserved arrest. Though, not originally anti-semitic, Chack was seduced by fascism and embraced *collaboration* wholeheartedly. After chatting amicably about the 1930s, Taittinger thought Chack seemed "marked by death". Chack recognised that he would become a marked man at the liberation and slumped into a deep melancholy. He was shot the following year.

When *haut monde* financiers and bankers arrived, Taittinger thought all his *Quartier Vendôme* friends had come to see him. Monsieur

Miret, Secretary General of Assistance Publique, who unlike Guitry was allowed to dress properly, arrived looking so smart that Taittinger thought he was negotiating their release.

When Taittinger and friends visited the exercise yard, Madame Marie Goublet, one of France's first female barristers, dropped a note to René Bouffet. Goublet's crime was to include General Karl-Heinrich von Stulpnagel in a dinner party. In fact, for distinguished prisoners—rather than low-life *collabos*—the FFIs respected due process. But Guitry remained a target for spite. In a macabre practical joke, FFIs called on him every two hours, saying the firing squad was ready. Each time he calmly smartened himself, ready to meet his end. After ten minutes they told him to wait. And so on all night. At daybreak Guitry admitted that he had not slept well.[36]

"PARIS WAS IN THE PROCESS OF BECOMING A KIND OF REFUGEE CAMP, in the interior of which freedom of circulation was only for the FFI," Rol-Tanguy told Bourderon. "This objective was achieved by the evening of 22 August. The enemy continued to give ground; seventy *quartiers* were now free, or abandoned. The Germans were only able to move on certain routes. On the 23rd a column coming down the Champs Élysées was the cause of the violent incident which led to the fire at the Grand Palais. Nevertheless, the essential objective was achieved; the enemy had retreated to various strongpoints where they reinforced the exterior defences, notably multiplying the barbed-wire barriers, and in which they waited until Leclerc's tanks arrived. My 2e *bureau* had these pinpointed since the 22 August; the Hôtel Majestic, Luxembourg, République, the Foreign Ministry, Chamber of Deputies and the Hôtel Meurice."[37]

More sobering than Rol-Tanguy's ebullient reminiscences was a document presented at the Préfecture to Georges Maurice, the new director-general of the Municipal Police, containing casualty figures for the Insurrection's first four days. Police casualties were 62 killed and 172 wounded; Resistance 483 killed and 1,197 wounded, while the German garrison, whose figures are possibly suspect, lost merely

68 killed and 82 wounded. There is a limit to what conclusions should be drawn from such figures. They did not include captured *résistants* who were summarily executed, whose corpses were discovered weeks later. It must also be recognised that, towards the war's end, German propaganda often minimised bad news.[38]

And German generals, sickened by Hitler's war, sometimes played their own game. Pierre Billotte wrote that General Speidel and others ensured that reinforcements were diverted from Paris to arguably more important sectors on the lower Seine, while claiming that retreating Wehrmacht units needed secure bridges in Paris.[39] This conflicted with the destruction orders von Choltitz continually received from Rastenburg, of which he candidly informed Nordling at their afternoon meeting.[40] As for the sappers sent to blow the bridges; following the extraordinary welcome that von Choltitz gave them, nothing had happened. At luncheon inside the Meurice, one of von Choltitz's officers asked whether the bridges would be blown.

"If I execute that," replied von Choltitz, "there will be nothing left to do on the seventieth bridge than leave a monument to the dead."

"It would be best to put it on the one where there is already a statue," said the officer.

"What statue?" asked von Choltitz.

"Sainte Geneviève."

"That one," agreed von Choltitz. "With a virgin, we will go straight to Heaven." Then, turning to the officers dining with him, von Choltitz said, "Gentlemen, since our enemies won't listen to our *Führer* any more, this whole war is going to pot."

News of this exchange reinforced Nordling's opinion that von Choltitz would only make a token resistance when the Allies arrived. It was reported to Jacques Chaban-Delmas and reached Leclerc within twenty-four hours.[41]

Going through the motions of taking the offensive, von Choltitz threatened to attack all Resistance-held buildings with heavy weapons. But either through conscience or pragmatism, this never happened. The journalist, lawyer and future politician, Raymond Dronne, later wrote, "They only needed to launch their tanks; a few shells to blow the doors off, some high explosive shells through the windows, and all positions could have been quickly retaken." Dronne continues, "The Resistance did not have the means to prevent the destruction of Paris, let alone pursue a desperate struggle like in Warsaw. Whether aerial bombardments, cannonades by tanks or artillery, systematic demolitions or simply allowing fires to burn their way through, if not all of Paris, then a significant area, von Choltitz did not do any of it. Whatever the reasons behind this may have been, it is to his credit."[42]

During his meeting with Nordling, von Choltitz was called from his office. On returning he told Nordling, "That's too bad. I am going to get a visit from the chief of staff of the Grossdeutschland Panzer Division which is cantoned around Beauvais. He proposes to offer me a hundred and fifty heavy tanks from his unit, the ones that destroyed Kovel. He assures me that in forty-eight hours all Parisians will be dead or so terrorised that I could walk through Paris with a cigar between my lips and a walking stick. I told him I didn't need any of them and that I was in control of the situation." Explaining this, Dronne says von Choltitz was bluffing. The Grossdeutschland Division was fighting on the Eastern Front; nor did German units escaping Normandy have many serviceable tanks left.[43] If true, perhaps it resolves where rumours of German reinforcements came from.

AFTER SPAHI LIEUTENANT BERGAMIN met Mouthard at a crossroads outside Trappes, Mouthard gave the *Patrouille* Hemingway's painstakingly accumulated details on German positions west of Paris. Bergamin was ordered to maintain contact with the enemy in order to gauge German strength. From his Jeep, Bergamin directed three M8 armoured cars and a Stuart-mounted 75mm howitzer (*lance-patates*) towards German lines, soon coming under intense fire. A German 88 destroyed the Stuart, killing two Spahis and wounding two other crewmen. After physically removing his casualties, Bergamin's uniform was drenched in blood. Sickened, Bergamin slumped down in one of Rambouillet's bars and downed a bottle of champagne, watched by

Hemingway and Bruce. Mistaking the blood on Bergamin's uniform for his own, Bruce wrote, "He was, however, in wonderful spirits."[44]

Given that GT Langlade completed the march to Rambouillet in ten hours, it becomes obvious that, Bradley's criticisms aside, the 2e DB made good time.[45] Leclerc's HQ convoy trundled along in front led by Captain Savelli's Jeep. Every so often Leclerc and Girard stood like Colonel Peschaud's route guides watching the 2e DB make the march they were born for.

"While we were talking to him [Bergamin]," wrote Bruce, "General Leclerc arrived in a three-star Jeep. He is tall, spare, handsome, stern-visaged, and a striking figure."[46]

Journalists' cameras clicked away; one snapped Leclerc looking irritable in his Jeep. Although Leclerc's attitude towards journalists had softened since his time in Africa, he muttered, "Buzz off you unspeakables!" in something above a whisper, audible to Bruce and Hemingway. "A rude general is a nervous general," Hemingway wrote, thereafter calling one of France's greatest wartime heroes, "That jerk Leclerc!"[47]

"All his [Leclerc's] people were in light vehicles and went into the park of Rambouillet," wrote Bruce. The 2e DB's CP pitched its tent beside the château's broad, tree-lined avenue and Gribius began drafting the order entitled "*S'emparer de Paris*"—"To seize Paris." At least Leclerc appreciated Bruce and Hemingway's reconnaissance activities, asking them to pass their information to Repiton-Préneuf's *2ème Bureau*. "This, with the assistance of Hemingway, Mouthard and Mowinckel, I did," wrote Bruce.[48]

"The correspondents are furious with Leclerc because he will not tell them his plans," Bruce continued. "He in turn is angry with them for they are looking for a story and he is trying to make plans to capture Paris. Apparently the pressure from the resistance people in Paris, who are being chopped up by the Germans, was finally too great for the High Command, and they belatedly decided to capture the capital."[49]

After finding the capital's western approaches blocked, but less resistance around Arpajon, Guillebon radioed Leclerc asking permission to enter Paris via Arpajon. Unfortunately the message did not get through. Guillebon sent out two more patrols, one to Versailles which quickly met opposition, and another towards Chevreuse which reported frail German defences; hence a potential opportunity. But, deciding discretion was the wiser option, Guillebon turned back towards Limours-Rambouillet, leaving disappointed bystanders.

"What? Are you going again?" they asked. "You're abandoning us? What about Paris?"[50]

Turning back was disappointing, but Guillebon's force was too small. GT Billotte, designated to enter Paris from the south, would not reach Rambouillet until evening. Guillebon also reported that when French civilians asked American patrols why they had not taken Paris, they replied, "That mission is reserved for the 2e DB." "They said that three days ago," wrote Girard, "three days during which we had bridled with impatience and, above all, the Americans had wasted for nothing. *Le Général* has been right all along."[51]

Leclerc sent Captain Janney to de Gaulle with a situation report. "I have received Captain Janney and your note," replied the Constable. "I should like to see you today. I expect to be at Rambouillet this evening and to see you there. I embrace you."[52]

UNDOUBTEDLY THE RESISTANCE'S MAIN FEAT on 23 August was capturing a German train between Place Gambetta and Les Buttes-Chaumont. During the early morning, medical student Madeleine Riffaud, a member of the FTP's Saint-Just company, who had been captured by the Gestapo a few days before and released thanks to Nordling, received a telephone call. "*Attention!*" said a voice she knew. "There is an armoured train [not armoured in fact], we do not know how many Germans there are inside but, in any case, it's on its way from Ménilmontant to Belleville-Villette. It is evident that they are coming to take us by surprise."

Accompanied by a nineteen-year-old metalworker called Guy, a middle-class student called Max and a third carrying between them two Sten guns, several hand-grenades, some light rockets and some fuse cable, Madeleine set off for the Pont de Belleville-Villette, which overlooks the track from Les Buttes-Chaumont.

"We combined the hand-grenades as we had been told that this is what *dynamiteros* had done in Spain during the Civil War," wrote Madeleine. "When the train emerged from the tunnel, as well as firing machine-gun bursts we began to throw grenades and rockets on the track, and at the locomotive. We threw and fired so much that the Germans, being startled by the noise, could only think that there were a hundred of us. The train withdrew back inside the tunnel."

While this happened more FTP from the Saint-Just company and other Resistance groups sent by the CPL, following fast liaison work, arrived on the scene.

"It was here that an elderly *cheminot* committed an act of great courage," wrote Madeleine. "We had already lost a *copain* killed because he got too close to the opening of the tunnel. The *cheminot*, who had retired from the railways, courageously entered the tunnel, mounted the engine and detached it. Then, bottled up in the tunnel and not knowing what to do, the Germans surrendered. There were eighty of them, with weapons and baggage, plenty of fuel, lots of food and cigarettes, which were all very welcome."[53]

According to Georges Maurice, the whole Ménilmontant incident lasted five hours. On the French side three *résistants* were killed. André Tollet, the President of the CPL, noted that *résistants* from the 19th and 20th Arrondissements were most enthusiastic in attacking the Germans, particularly those guarding supplies and logistics.[54]

In the meantime, with no refuse collection for several days, parts of Paris became untidy; stale waste odours being worsened by summer sunshine. *Affiches* advised Parisians to burn their rubbish. Then Rol-Tanguy's HQ advised that refuse lorries and tipper trucks, filled with earth, could make excellent battering rams or low-level wrecking balls for use against German pill-boxes. The obvious question of how the driver escaped was circumvented by reversing the vehicle towards its target. Luckily for whoever cleaned up once Paris returned to normal, this idea was rarely used, not that Paris lorries were safe from requisition.

To avoid leaving their vehicles unattended, many food haulers sold their wares in the street.

Where food was concerned, demand far outstripped supply, leading to brief but acute price hikes. Salad stuffs, an important part of French summer diet, rose to thirty francs a bag, while seasonal fruit reached fifty francs a kilo. To prevent flagrant profiteering, *Gardiens* were sent from the Préfecture to order traders to lower prices and prevent customers from buying large amounts to hoard. Water was stored in baths in case the water mains were destroyed, although von Choltitz never intended any such action. On the contrary, that morning he supplied Red Cross officials with detailed lists of Wehrmacht stores to facilitate distribution.[55]

EVEN IF VON CHOLTITZ HAD BLUFFED NORDLING that a hundred and fifty tanks would reinforce him, the sight of Panthers circling the Préfecture and the Hôtel de Ville was intimidating to *résistants*. After four days, most were becoming exhausted. But, despite the burning of the Grand Palais and the train at Ménilmontant, that Wednesday was less eventful than others.[56]

Thanks to the Red Cross and Raoul Nordling, prisoners were exchanged in quantities of between one and two hundred per day at the Préfecture and the Hôtel de Ville in central Paris, or at Clichy, Saint-Denis and Parreux in the *banlieues*. While some Wehrmacht officers still expected to exchange one Frenchmen for two or more Germans, few still insisted on such a bias. Most Germans captured by the Resistance expected to be shot; one officer immediately requested a pencil and paper to write to his family before anyone even mentioned shooting him. Wounded Germans captured by the Resistance sometimes refused medication, fearing they might be poisoned. However, once they realised that most insurrectionists were observing the Geneva Convention, several German prisoners avoided being exchanged and having to continue the war. Several Germans held at the Préfecture tried to hide when FFIs searched the cells for prisoners to exchange.[57] As Lieutenant Harvai observed in the 19th Arrondissement, many

Germans happily surrendered to any FFIs who appeared "official". From his post on Rue Jourdain, Harvai reported Germans in civilian clothes roaming the 19th Arrondissement looking for someone to take them prisoner. Some Germans, sickened by Nazi crimes, actively turned traitor. In Folie-Méricourt a German joined the Resistance under a pseudonym, helped them raid a German armoury, and then trained them to use German weapons.[58]

As von Choltitz well knew, belief in the war was receding among ordinary German soldiers just as much as among the officer corps. "Certainly some soldiers submerged themselves by wearing civilian clothes, and human weakness appeared in all its most hideous forms. I was obliged to send out patrols commanded by officers to combat disorder."[59]

By 1944, the German military executed on average fifteen men per day for offences ranging from cowardice and desertion to sleeping on guard duty, and the number reprimanded for writing home criticising the Nazi war effort exceeded 10%. The temptation to escape a train hurtling to *Götterdämmerung* and melt away into *la France profonde* became enormous. At the Hôtel Crillon, Sonderführer Robert Wallraf was packing. Looking around his room, its 1930s tourist pictures targeting Americans, and then at his well-tailored clothes, Wallraf was tempted to slip out of *feldgrau* and become a dapper civilian. But the moment passed and he pushed his valise under the bed. That evening he shared his last bottle of Cognac with friends, acknowledging Germany's imminent collapse.[60]

AFTER ESCORTING ROLF NORDLING'S PARTY across the German lines, Bobby Bender returned to Paris. He spoke in depth with Colonel Lelorrain, Chaban-Delmas' representative, about the value of the truce insofar as it existed. More importantly, following von Choltitz's extravagant boast that reinforcements were *en route*, Bender tried to coax out of von Choltitz which Panzer divisions were coming, and what the German commander's personal concerns were.[61]

Later that evening von Choltitz informed Army Group B that General Blumentritt was unable to reach the Meurice due to more barricades. He also reported that the police were loyal but powerless—a downright lie—that German strongpoints were unable to hold out much longer, nor was it possible to carry out public executions to deter the Resistance. Regarding Paris's bridges, von Choltitz warned Model's staff that while the bridges were needed, he could not blow them; if he blew them he could not blow them all; and blowing them would ensure that more of the population joined the Resistance. Finally von Choltitz said that OKW should be informed of the gravity of the situation immediately.[62]

On receiving von Choltitz's report, Army Group B offered a small armoured force and elements of the 7th Infantry Division, to reach Paris by 25 August. Model asked OKW's chief of staff General Jodl for clear instructions. When Jodl replied "Hold Paris", Model angrily wired back, "I am not asking for provisional orders, but clear and precise instructions addressing the possibility that we can not control the situation in Paris." When Jodl replied that Army Group B was already sending reinforcements, Model replied, "A unit of self-propelled guns, or any other small corps, is far from sufficient to defend either the exterior or interior of a city of over a million souls." This appreciation was presented to Hitler by nightfall. To defend Paris convincingly required a greater effort than Stalingrad; with the Allies taking position to envelop the city, Army Group B had insufficient means to do that.[63]

SHORTLY BEFORE LEAVING LE MANS the Constable was updated on Parodi's arrest, the barricades and the failing truce while the Germans kept to main routes through the city. He was particularly fascinated by von Choltitz's restraint. "These considerations, weren't they inspired by his fear of the future, this concern to spare Paris, or through the agreement he made with the Allies whose agents appeared at his HQ rather than that of Oberg and the Gestapo who by then had left the capital?" His view was not far off the mark.[64]

De Gaulle's *homme tout faire*, Commandant de Lignières, arrived at Rambouillet ahead of him and began making arrangements. The Wehrmacht had left the château mostly intact, but without electricity. Luckily a local electrician repaired the generator.[65] In their tents alongside the drive, Leclerc's staff prepared the following day's plans and by 4pm were ready to hold a briefing.[66]

De Gaulle's aircraft landed on Rambouillet's long avenue. At first he waited in the château library, briefly distracting himself with an exquisite edition of Moliere's *Le Bourgeois Gentilhomme*. After hastily consuming cold rations he went into conference with Leclerc. Not all of the 2e DB had reached their start lines ready for the morning's operation. Where contact had been made with the enemy west of Paris, resistance was "entrenched and resolute", de Gaulle wrote in his memoirs. "It is necessary to pierce these positions," said Leclerc. GT Langlade would advance towards Toussus le Noble and Clamart while a sub-group under Morel-Deville created a diversion around Versailles. However, GT Billotte would make the main effort into southern Paris via Antony with GT Dio in reserve.

Although these plans revised US V Corps' orders to head for Versailles, the Constable approved everything. But he advised Leclerc that after entering Paris via the Porte d'Orléans he should make the Gare Montparnasse his HQ; its communications were perfect. Then, looking at Leclerc who had served him unfailingly for four years, de Gaulle said, "How lucky you are!" Next, he told Leclerc, "Go quickly, we cannot have another commune!"[67]

Did de Gaulle honestly believe a repeat of the 1871 Commune was possible? Decades afterwards his son Philippe told journalist Michel Tauriac, "I remember that, returning to this proposition following the publication of his memoirs, he was inclined to moderate it somewhat. According to him the resistance in Paris was greatly exaggerated for political reasons—which more or less continues today—and this resistance was not only composed of communists, and those were only ever around twelve hundred men under arms. He wanted, above all, to re-establish French sovereignty and impose his authority in the face of the Americans."[68]

That night, however, when Commandant de Lignières told him that the President of the Republic's bedroom was ready, de Gaulle thought, "No." Preferring not to appear presumptuous, he asked Lignières to prepare a less important bedroom.[69]

"ATTENTION! ATTENTION! PARIS EST LIBÉRÉ!" came a BBC announcement at 10pm, repeated in many languages. Pastor Marc Boegner did not believe it. The reappearance of his favourite newspaper, *Le Figaro*, was joy enough for one day. But, after seeing lightly armed *résistants* holding government buildings while German anti-aircraft batteries fired at Allied aircraft above the city, Boegner thought premature announcements dangerous.[70]

The BBC's error happened as the electricity was reconnected for the evening's thirty-minute session, permitting cooking, light and radio. Parisians heard Londoners joyfully singing the *Marseillaise* and thumping out *Sambre et Meuse*. When that half hour's electricity ended, plunging everyone back into darkness, they wondered how the normally reliable BBC got it wrong.[71]

The muddle began when Free French journalist Georges Boris announced on air that the liberation of Paris was "anticipated" and someone composed a premature announcement that "Yesterday, after four days of fighting, the enemy has been defeated. Patriots have occupied all public buildings. Representatives of Vichy have either been arrested or fled. The people of Paris have therefore played a determinant part in the liberation of the capital." This was mostly true but hardly justified the headline "Paris is free!" It was repeated on "The Voice of America", becoming worldwide headline news within hours. King George VI sent de Gaulle a premature telegram of congratulation.[72]

Convinced of his right to regard himself as *de facto* head of the French state, de Gaulle pondered how to enter Paris. He sent Dr. Favreau back into the city with his reply to a message received earlier from Luizet. "My intention had been to go first, not to the Hôtel de Ville where the Council of the Resistance and the Parisian Committee of Liberation were sitting, but to 'the centre'. As I saw it, that meant the Ministry of War, the obvious place for the French government and High Command. It was not that I did not urgently wish to get into contact with the leaders of the Paris rising. But I wanted it to be established that the State, after trials that had been unable to destroy or subjugate it, was in the first place simply returning to its own dwelling. As I read the papers, *Combat*, *Défense de la France* and *Franc-Tireur*, I was both happy to see the fighting spirit that they expressed and strengthened in my determination not to accept any sort of investiture for my authority other than that directly given to me by the voice of the crowd."[73]

De Gaulle finished the evening by receiving Saint-Phalle's party, whose main purpose was pre-empted by Roger Gallois. Otherwise de Gaulle was fascinated by Nordling's group: Rolf Nordling, brother of "the Gentleman of Paris", and Baron von Posch-Pastor, whom de Gaulle misunderstood to be von Choltitz's ADC. Although Jean Laurent performed an important role supporting the Resistance, de Gaulle was unimpressed that Laurent had not committed himself earlier, especially since they both served Reynaud in 1940.[74]

AS THE 2e DB ASSEMBLED around the Forest of Rambouillet, the nearest formations to Paris were GT Langlade's sub-group under Massu, and Morel-Deville's Spahi recce squadron at Dampierre, being welcomed by the locals with delirious enthusiasm. Langlade's CP welcomed several civilians describing flimsy German defences, begging him to enter the city. "The civilians were at a loss to understand why roads that were passable to them and where they had hardly seen any serious activity, could not, without serious fighting, be passable for an army." But Langlade knew it would be a different story once his Shermans advanced down those roads.[75]

GT Billotte was only just arriving. Irrespective of General Bradley's criticisms, de Gaulle thought his former ADC's battlegroup made excellent time, covering two hundred kilometres in a day along difficult roads. After Chartres, dusk and rain combined to reduce visibility forcing vehicles to follow bumper to bumper. "At last we halted," wrote Dronne on reaching Limours. "We settled down for the night under driving rain that both diluted and made runny the coating or fine dust and film of engine oil inside our clothes so that it ran all over our skin." But one of Dronne's platoons fell behind when a half-track threw a track. *La Nueve* would regain full strength only at dawn.

At 9.30pm, Billotte received the orders drafted four hours earlier and briefed his men. Having been driving for twenty-three hours, many of his officers could barely keep awake. Although chosen for the most important role, GT Billotte was without relevant maps, except for a blood-spattered German map, captured when Spahi armoured cars surprised a German patrol. "Rarely have I had to give orders in such fluid conditions," wrote Billotte.[76]

Sleeping in whatever dryness they could find, under tents and bivouac sheets propped against the sides of vehicles, their orders, "*S'emparer de Paris*" ("To seize Paris") reverberated in their heads. For Parisians among the troops, anxiety over their families dominated their thoughts. Comparatively speaking, Paul de Langlade was lucky. Although his mother lived in Paris, his family were *seigneurs* in the Loire, now liberated.[77] Having already found his family in Chartres, Alain de Boissieu's worries were also relieved, but Christian Girard's parents lived in central Paris, and André Gribius' family lived in Versailles. Massu, another Parisian, worried for his brothers.[78]

24 August 1944

"THE ADVANCE CP LEFT RAMBOUILLET IN THE SMALL HOURS," began Christian Girard's diary entry for 24 August. "The General was with me in the Jeep. It was a horrid day." Leclerc was impatient. Inspecting final preparations in pouring rain, his trench coat and trousers became soaked through. Girard offered his American raincoat sporting his new captain's *galons* on the cuffs. "Are you demoting me?" asked Leclerc.[79]

Pierre Billotte was only too aware of the gravity of the moment as the final move toward Paris got under way. "Never before had a Frenchman received such an order," he wrote. "I knew about commanding armoured units in 1940 and the question one asked before such a mission was undoubtedly one was entitled to have answered. What strength were the enemy and where were they?" Billotte was veteran enough to expect the unexpected. At least he could see the Eiffel Tower; his battlegroup had to keep it to their west as they advanced into the city.[80]

GT Billotte was divided into two sub-groups. Joseph Putz, with two companies of the 501e RCC (Gavardie and Witasse), two companies of the RMT (Dronne and Wagner), a section of engineers (Cancel) and a battery of artillery (Touyeras), would lead the battlegroup into action with the balance in reserve under Cantarel. Contrary to intelligence reports, they found German defences well organised.[81]

Jacques Branet, leading sub-group Putz's advance, writes little other than that the 24th was "a tough day". Dronne, once he received his orders, gathered his platoon commanders, all of whom were very experienced, and marked out the likeliest points of German resistance. He did not like simply advancing up a main road which was inevitably defended with anti-tank guns issuing enfilading fire from side streets. Once in contact with the enemy, Dronne's way, learnt in Africa, was to bypass opposition and attack from the side and rear.

GT Billotte passed through Arpajon and Montlhéry uneventfully, reaching Longjumeau by 8am. The local population came out of their houses shrieking with delight and were quickly all over Putz's entire sub-group, singing the *Marseillaise* and opening bottles saved specially. Then, reaching more built up areas, sub-group Putz came under accurate gunfire from industrial hangars at Ballainvilliers, east of their axis. From *la Nueve* Elias' platoon dismounted their half-tracks and, supported by Shermans, closed with the German opposition, setting hangar roofs on fire with incendiary bullets. This opposition was crushed with the cost of a man wounded; Juan Vega was hit by friendly machine-gun fire from a Sherman, causing him many months in hospital.[82]

La Nueve's remaining platoons were involved in small skirmishes; swift, brutal exchanges as German troops fought delaying actions from several linked positions. Dronne wrote that his Spaniards took forty prisoners "but did not have time to count the German dead".[83]

Captain Buis' Shermans dealt with more opposition from Massy and Wissous, but these hold-ups meant that sub-group Warabiot, held in reserve, was sent to deal with heavy opposition around Morangis, losing two tanks.[84] If an armoured battlegroup must advance along a limited axis it only took a well sited 88mm gun to hold it up. 20mm heavy machine-guns could also inflict costly damage.[85]

De Gaulle's chief of staff, General Juin, took a close interest, particularly since Billotte had been appointed partly for political reasons and his battlegroup faced a testing day.

"Do you think you can get into Paris today?" asked Juin.

"Everything depends on the seriousness and duration of engagements," replied Billotte. "There is also the problem of keeping us supplied with fuel and ammunition, given that we're using those faster than we previously expected."

Juin was nodding appreciatively when a lieutenant arrived asking for artillery support and tank reinforcements. As he spoke a German shell exploded nearby, giving the young officer a light shrapnel wound on his cheek, which Juin helped bandage.[86]

Model's HQ learnt of GT Billotte's progress when a telephone call from the Meurice complained that, "The forces in this sector, tasked with defending both the exterior and the interior from terrorists, are insufficient."[87]

HENRI ROL-TANGUY WAS INFORMED of GT Billotte's arrival at Arpajon via both the 2e DB's *2ème bureau* and his own information lines. The Sceaux railway line's unbroken telephone connection north to the Barrière d'Enfer ensured that Rol-Tanguy received hourly updates. Sub-group Putz's progress was followed with passionate interest. By 10.15am Rol-Tanguy knew they were at Longjumeau. By 11.30am Rol-Tanguy knew they had reached the Juvisy roundabout.[88]

Across Paris the German pull-out accelerated and they made less effort to contest embattled *quartiers* compared to the previous day, although combat remained very violent around the large barracks on the Place de la République which the Wehrmacht called their Prinz Eugen barracks. Built around a courtyard like the Préfecture on Ile de la Cité, it was to these barracks that the German garrison's remnants retreated from *rive droite* Paris.[89]

Again, Dr. Victor Veau found his fellow Parisians talking hopefully. But this time he refrained from squelching anyone. Two cars appeared and took off again towards the Arc de Triomphe almost like tourists. "Would one see any more Germans?" Veau wondered. At the corner of Avenue de Messine and Boulevard Haussmann, German traffic signs had been removed, and when a *Gardien* bicycled past, Parisians clapped enthusiastically. Reaching the Champs Élysées amid drizzle, Veau sheltered in a doorway while watching a German column roll westwards. "One asked oneself if that was in order to surrender to regular forces rather than the FFI," he wrote.[90]

After queueing for the morning's edition of *Combat*, Charles Lacretelle found no mention of the BBC's premature announcement, just a bulletin from the Préfecture: "According to information appearing at 6pm yesterday ... an Allied column composed of 30,000 men and 300 tanks has occupied Arpajon and is moving towards Paris. Therefore three divisions are at our gates." The same article continued, "We are awaiting more information. We would like to be more precise and to know above all when they will arrive, but all this depends on a great number of factors to which we can not fix a timetable."[91]

Stepping out with his dog, Jean Galtier-Boissière found the Saint-Jacques barricade decorated with portraits of Hitler, Goering and Mussolini taken from the Italian library on the Boulevard Saint-Germain. The Germans contesting the Latin Quarter had withdrawn to the Palais Luxembourg. Miraculously a butchers' shop on the narrow Rue Mouffetard had acquired meat and opened its doors to jubiant customers. From a selection of the day's newspapers, Galtier-Boissière read articles preaching *résistance à l'outrance* (resistance to the death) and repeating the slogan, "*À chacun son boche*"—"to each a Hun." Instructions for making a Molotov cocktail were written like a recipe. Both *Franc-Tireur* and *la Parisien Libéré* carried premature announcements that *collabo* writer Pierre Drieu-la-Rochelle had killed himself. In fact, after overdosing on sleeping tablets, Drieu-la-Rochelle was found by his maid Gabrielle and rushed to Neuilly's American Hospital to have his innards pumped. Their political disagreements aside, Galtier-Boissière always respected Drieu's talent and found the premature obituaries denouncing him distasteful. In any case the Drieu-La-Rochelle story, like several others, was days old.[92]

THE FFI'S OPTIMISM ON THE INSURRECTION'S SIXTH DAY was reflected in Alexandre Parodi's declaration, "Paris is freeing herself by her own efforts," signed *Cerat*. Rol-Tanguy also released an upbeat communiqué:

> During the night of the 23 to 24 and during the day of 24 August, our offensive continued without respite. In all *quartiers* of Paris, the enthusiastic population has joined in the construction of barricades, and the effectiveness of these measures is resoundingly confirmed; the enemy, obliged to give up light patrols with lorries and armoured cars, now confines his activities to armoured reconnaissance missions which vainly fire their cannons at a certain number of buildings and public offices occupied by the FFI.
>
> Generally, our victorious offensive has now achieved the effective liberation of the greater part of Paris. German-controlled areas now consist of a few islands of isolated resistance.

Discounting von Choltitz's restraint, the situation could be seen like that. But Rol-Tanguy finished up by mentioning the previous day's success at Belleville-Villette, the captured equipment and prisoners, in an exultant tone. Naturally leaders must maintain morale, but

Rol-Tanguy's biographer Roger Bourderon comments that, "These [propositions] were without doubt somewhat excessive, particularly in the matter of armaments which were always uncertain." Rol-Tanguy's exuberance reflects how the Resistance needed to see itself, "opening the road to Paris for Allied armies ... liaising with the Leclerc division for a shared victory. ... To conquer and give our country back, in the words of General de Gaulle, her independence, her freedom and her greatness."[93]

Now Rol-Tanguy wanted the Insurrection to go up a gear; to prevent *all* German passage through Paris, to hold every bridge and isolate German strongpoints. Commanding such activities from beneath the Barrière d'Enfer became more challenging. So far Paris had avoided large-scale destruction, so Rol-Tanguy issued a directive that no heritage or official buildings could be used to house prisoners, or by FFI. This meant that venues like the Vélodrome d'Hiver, the cycling arena used to round up Jews during 1942 and subsequently for *collabo* rallies, would be used to imprison *collabos*. Rol-Tanguy also ordered the suppression of looting, including summary execution for anyone caught red-handed.[94]

FFI were now firing upon von Choltitz's compound on the Rue de Rivoli. His garrison no longer controlled the Champs Élysées west of the Rond-Point. From dawn until dusk on the 24th there were twenty-nine individual FFI attacks compared with ten counterattacks by the Germans, mainly directed against the barricades on the *rive gauche* and around the Hôtel de Ville. Appearing content to intimidate rather than press attacks home, where the Germans took tough action, such as destroying the barricade on the Rue de Bourgogne, it was usually to maintain access to their strongpoints. Unless the FFI could attack strongpoints there were few manageable targets left for them. An FFI report said, "*Coups de main* were now rendered extremely difficult by the fact that isolated Germans no longer circulated, not even in cars. Their movements now took the form of convoys and columns." But smaller convoys still offered tempting targets, like the one near the Observatory which rendered eight prisoners.[95]

LIEUTENANT SORRET'S PLATOON, supported by 12e RCA Shermans, was chosen by Massu to be GT Langlade's advance guard. The sky appeared wrung out, though grey clouds still billowed past sprinkling fine drizzle.

"Right! Let's get going. Let's move!"

Sorret's men moved out, the 12e RCA's Shermans leaving dust and blue exhaust smoke as they ground along roads that had already taken a beating.[96] Passing through Dampierre, Sorret's column met cheering locals sheltering under umbrellas by the roadside.

"*Allez-y les gars!*"—"Go, boys!" they said.

"And what were you doing in 1940?" asked one of Sorret's newest recruits; he only joined in Normandy.

Advancing along the D58 into Chevreuse, a bend in the road, around a small hill with copses and fruit groves, looked perfect for laying an ambush. Sure enough, machine-gun fire began cutting up the macadam. Sorret's men alighted from their half-tracks, running to outflank and flush out the Germans. There were only four, who fled immediately after firing. Sorret's men remounted their vehicles while watching the woods on each side of them. Sorret's radioman passed him the headset.

"Don't let yourself be held up by small incidents," came the order.

"Understood," replied Sorret.[97]

Even today Chevreuse's bucolic atmosphere belies its proximity to Paris. Its citizens cheered while sheltering from the drizzle in shop doorways. But Sorret's men soon encountered more sniper-fire, craning their necks to spot their adversaries amid green August foliage. Once again a handful of Germans withdrew after a few shots. Past Chevreuse, advancing towards the plateau of Toussus-le-Noble, the wind carried the report of gunfire. From their Sherman turrets, the Chasseurs saw the recently vacated airfield. More gunfire, and Sorret's men began patrolling along the roadside hedgerows.[98]

Now reinforced by Lieutenant Batiment's platoon, they entered Toussus-le-Noble where the locals were either hiding or else had fled their houses. Sorret's and Batiment's men fanned out ahead of the tanks, moving nimbly between buildings until they reached the northern exit where the Germans had blocked the road with debris; this was intended to force the Shermans and half-tracks into the fields which were covered by anti-tank guns hidden in hedgerows. Turning into the sodden fields the Shermans struggled to avoid getting bogged, the rain-soaked mud sticking glutinously to their tracks, forcing drivers to lower gears and accelerate. Followed by Sorret's infantry, the Shermans screeched up the slopes towards the crest hedgerows. Then the Germans opened fire. Sorret's infantry desperately buried themselves in whatever cover there was as MG42s scythed the air, bullets rattling on the Shermans' hulls. Next came explosions as 88mm shells found their mark. The Sherman *Ardennes* burst into flames, seeming to stop dead for a moment before slumping in the mud. The sub-group's 105mm SP guns opened fire while Quillichini's support section put down smoke. Sorret's and Batiment's infantry began moving again.[99]

Massu watched grimly through binoculars. Intelligence reports claiming the 2e DB could simply walk into Paris were wrong. Langlade ordered sub-group Minjonnet to outflank enemy positions from Massu's right towards Jouy-en-Josas. If this persuaded the Germans to withdraw, GT Langlade might still be first into Paris.

Once Captain Hargous' 4th squadron 12e RCA had refuelled they pushed forward shouting "Our turn to play!" Lieutenant Jean Zagrodski's troop joined forces with two keen platoons from Captain Fonde's 7th Company 2/RMT led by Lieutenants Guigon Miscault and Maret. Jean Zagrodski, eager to avenge his brother Michel, killed at Alençon, had renamed his tank *Zagrodski II*. Supported by Commandant Mirambeau's artillery, these men led GT Langlade towards Christ de Saclay.[100]

Bruce and Co., along with Hemingway's irregulars, were following GT Langlade—"one of Leclerc's columns," as Bruce described them. Past military age, Bruce repaired to a farmhouse. "In no time we were snugly ensconced in a warm kitchen, eating an omelette and drinking a bottle of wine that had been given to us along the road. When we emerged we found that Hemingway and the Private Army, including

Mouthard, had been engaged in a battle between French tanks and two Boche 88 guns. The latter were demolished and prisoners taken."[101] According to Raymond Dronne, Leclerc banned Hemingway from following GT Billotte's main effort because of his drunkenness.[102]

Spaciously arranged, Jouy en Josas is a satellite village southwest of Paris, built around a railway track which joins the capital's dormitory towns. Its buildings are mainly nineteenth-century and its principal streets are named after Jean Jaurés and Louis Pasteur. To its north lies a belt of forest now dominated by the rumbling six-lane N12. Though normally tranquil and leafy, on 24 August 1944 Jouy en Josas saw a spasm of intense fighting.

Supported by Guigon's infantry, Zagrodski's troop crossed a beet field to reach the Saclay canal, which was shallow enough for them to drive down one bank and up the other. On the far side they found both a crossroads and a bridge left undefended, enabling them to push on, Zagrodski and Guigon on the right and Miscault and Marct on the left. Zagrodski was energised, leading his Shermans forward like stampeding bison, firing at anything that might conceal the enemy, sending geysers of earth into the air.[103] Then a German MG42 opened up, its torrent of bullets mauling the asphalt. They had reached von Aulock's southwest defence line. *Zagrodski II* took up the machine-gun duel. A harvest-filled barn caught fire, burning like a lighthouse. More Chad infantry pushed forward, returning German gunfire from beyond the Paris-Versailles railway track. In the village itself Guichard's *sergent-chef* ran forward to the first road junction. Seeing Germans pulling back, he signalled that the road was clear. Sub-group Massu pushed through Jouy en Josas amid further gunfire. Past the village more Germans were blocking the Versailles-Petit Clamart road from woods to the north.[104]

It now fell to Guichard's platoon to lead the advance, but as soon as they moved three men were hit by German machine-gun fire, Guichard being hit in the chest. Far from demoralising the platoon, these casualties spurred them on. Even so, amid fire from all directions, it was impossible to continue without support from 12e RCA Shermans, which would become vulnerable to German anti-tank guns. These were under camouflage, five hundred metres away, ready to engage the first Sherman they saw. The *Gascoigne* was hit, immediately bursting into flames, while the rest of the troop withdrew to the dead ground of a railway cutting. With casualties mounting, Lieutenant Guigon decided this route out of Jouy en Josas was impassable.

"Return to Jouy," said Captain Fonde. "We will try to force our way through the Forêt de l'Homme Mort."

In Jouy en Josas villagers were congregating enthusiastically around Fonde's Jeep. But Fonde was only thinking about entering western Paris.

"Anyone know anything about the Germans' positions?" Fonde asked.

A villager stepped forward, the fireman.

"The Germans are positioning their anti-tank guns on the high ground in the forest, at the crossroads of l'Homme Mort."

"'*Positioning*' or '*have positioned*'?" Fonde asked urgently. There was no time to withdraw Guigon's platoon. Supported by two of Zagrodski's Shermans, Fonde set off.

"The Germans have not yet finished digging in," said the fireman.

Armed only with a Garand rifle, Fonde set off in a Jeep to see for himself, taking the fireman to act as guide. Back on the open road, driving towards Versailles, Fonde now had l'Homme Mort woods on his right.

"They're there," said the fireman, pointing towards a wooded bend a hundred metres ahead. Then he jumped from the Jeep and ran away.

"Stop," yelled Fonde.

An 88mm gun's muzzle was just visible among the foliage. From a bend in the road, alerted by the fleeing fireman, Zagrodski also noticed it. The *Zagrodski II* fired, rattling the 88's crew. It fired back, missing *Zagrodski II*, probably because the gun-aimer was under-trained. Fonde approached *Zagrodski II* to give directions just as a second shell, clearly aimed at the tank's front hull, ploughed into the road's surface sending a shard of shrapnel into Fonde's thigh. While being evacuated, Fonde told Lieutenant Maret precisely where the 88 was.

Maret sent his infantry through the woods to outflank the 88, finding its crew huddled behind the gun's shield just as a well-aimed shell from *Zagrodski II* smashed its barrel.[105]

The sub-group pushed on towards the crossroads where they encountered more sustained fire, this time from 20mm machine-guns whose heavy bullets could gouge a Sherman's armour without penetrating. While tank crews were reasonably safe from such weapons, infantry were pinned down in ditches on each side of the road. Inside his tank Lieutenant Zagrodski strained to spot the 20mm guns through his periscope. Exasperated, he opened *Zagrodski II*'s turret and scanned the woods with binoculars. Immediately a 20mm gun opened up on *Zagrodski II*, hitting Zagrodski fatally in the head, extinguishing his hopes of avenging his brother's death.[106]

The situation required extraordinary leadership. *Adjutant-Chef* Rolland, armed with an M1 Carbine and as many grenades as he could carry, crawled along roadside ditches to where the 20mm guns were situated. When close enough, Rolland peeped above the ditch's edge and spotted the 20mm gun. The crews' camouflage jackets and black collar patches indicated that they were Waffen SS. Leaning his carbine in the fork of a shrub's trunk, Rolland took steady aim and fired. The gunner fell dead, followed by the loader. The rest fled.

"We're expected for tea!" said Captain Ivanoff, glad to get his company moving again.[107]

The Shermans continued towards the Petit-Clamart crossroads, warily checking the roadsides. To their right Villacoublay's great military aerodrome was still as a graveyard. Von Aulock's defensive line had been pierced.

"Faster, faster," said Ivanoff. On reaching Petit-Clamart he ordered them to "Stop!"

"Why?" they wondered.

Pointing to a column of tanks following from Villacoublay, Ivanoff said, "Massu has got to catch up."

"That's just great," railed Guigon. "We bust ourselves to secure the route and others get to use it."

Soon crowds gathered around the Petit-Clamart crossroads, singing the *Marseillaise* and clambering over their vehicles. To any German gunner such scenes made inviting targets. A shell exploded, followed quickly by another.

"There's an 88 in that thicket," someone shouted.

Sergeant Duc dismounted from his half-track and ordered *Tiraileur* Schmidt to follow him with a bazooka. They climbed a wooded embankment, seeking cover under which to advance on the 88. Duc eventually stopped, pointing out the gun to Schmidt.

"Load," said Duc.

As they approached the gun it fired a shell past their legs. A few metres in front of the 88, Duc stopped, put the bazooka to his shoulder, aiming at the gun shield. The bazooka shell slammed into the gun's breach area, buckling its shield and killing several of its crew. The rest bolted for the gun tractor standing nearby. Schmidt reloaded the bazooka and destroyed the tractor as well. Rejoining the main force, Duc noticed that his trousers were badly ripped exposing burnt skin. Realising that the 88's last shell had passed between his legs, Duc said, "*Les vaches!* Any higher and I could have said 'good-bye' to my descendants!"

Once the Petit-Clamart crowds had been shed from their vehicles, GT Langlade could move again. While sub-group Minjonnet held the road, sub-group Massu moved through to lead them towards Sèvres. Three weeks' continuous action had made their vehicles look fit for the scrapyard.[108]

IN WESTERN PARIS Dr. Nussbaum saw German vehicles heading for the Porte Maillot from which to join the northern boulevards and effect their retreat.[109] The fact that, at noon on 24 August, Rol-Tanguy's FFI could not prevent this, demonstrated that the FFI had reached the limits of what it could do. They would never be strong enough to take the Prinz-Eugen barracks on the Place de la République or the Palais de Luxembourg until the 2e DB arrived. Indeed the Palais de Luxembourg could still attack the Latin Quarter and pressure the Ile de la Cité.

"I need a hundred men if I am going to recover the barricades in this sector," Raymond Massiet (aka Dufresne) told Parodi's chief of staff. "Give me the *Gardes Republicains*!"

"I have had no such orders from the FFI command," came the reply.

"That's a pity, because we need bird scarers!" said Massiet sarcastically.[110]

But Massiet returned to his position with around fifty young FTP who helped beat back the attack on this sector.[111]

Massiet's report for 24 August indicates pessimism. The Palais de Luxembourg *Stützpunkt* still had twelve tanks. Admittedly eight were pre-war French tanks whose machine-guns were probably more dangerous than their cannons. The Rue de Bougogne barricade needed twelve hits from a Somua's 47mm gun to dismantle it. Luckily, no one was killed. Once the Somua moved on, the FFIs began rebuilding it. Elsewhere, irrespective of von Choltitz's orders, frustration made the Germans use 75mm PAK guns; while from the rooftops, much harassing fire came from desperate *Miliciens*. Another concern was that petrol needed for Molotov cocktails was running low. Used sump and cooking oil caught fire easily but had little explosive value. Coal oil was effective, however, and could be obtained from the Boulevard Ney gas works.[112]

Massiet's superior, Colonel Lizé, insisted that the offensive should be maintained. Believing that too many FFIs were engaged in defence, he ordered fighting patrols plentifully armed with petrol bombs. "If you don't yet know the formula for bottle bombs, ask at once from the 3e Bureau at my HQ," finished Lizé's mid-day order.[113]

ON THE RUE D'ANJOU, RAOUL NORDLING was horrified by the sound of fifty German railwaymen running for their lives from the Gare Saint-Lazare. Trying to reach one of the main Wehrmacht routes eastwards, they strayed into FFI controlled side streets before a German patrol rescued them. They were scared witless by a refuse tipper truck which they suspected had been converted into something more dangerous.[114]

Negotiations to keep retreat routes open now involved Bobby Bender. While undoubtedly motivated by salvaging Germany's conscience, Bender's intrigues became significant acts of treason now that the Paris garrison was engaging the 2e DB. Why should Bender inform Nordling and Colonel Lelorrain that the German garrison was ordered to resist? Concerned for ordinary German soldiers, Bender asked, "What will become of them? Must more soldiers die uselessly? What do we do? Will it be possible to spare them, whatever their orders?"[115]

Neither Nordling nor Lelorrain could answer him.

"General von Choltitz cannot surrender without some clash of sabres," declared Bender. "His family is threatened; held hostage by Hitler. He himself is a soldier tied to traditions of military honour. He can not surrender without a fight." Bender continued, shaking his head, his eyes welling up, "Yes, he has to fight, but bloodshed for nothing must be avoided. What's the point of attacking them [the German strongpoints] from all sides? The key to the defence is the Hôtel Meurice where the general is based. One attack is all that is necessary. The general will defend himself. A military leader cannot surrender without fighting first. When he goes, the other strongpoints will surrender with him."[116]

Hence Bender believed that saving German lives, along with Paris, depended upon von Choltitz surrendering quickly. Colonel Lelorrain decided that General Leclerc should be informed of Bender's viewpoint via one of Jacques Chaban-Delmas' liaison officers, Lieutenant Jacques Petit-Leroy.[117]

Behind von Choltitz, OKW still insisted that Paris should be held to the last man and the Insurrection squashed uncompromisingly. Locally, however, General Blumentritt recognised that a small tank force could punch its way into Paris and once that happened, its liberation would be unpreventable. Only the Panzer Lehr Division was close enough to reinforce Paris, though it now amounted to little more than a mixed brigade. The 47th Infantry Division was ordered to Paris but held up at Amiens because Allied air strikes had wrecked the required rolling stock.[118]

WATCHING GT LANGLADE PASS THROUGH PETIT CLAMART, Lieutenant Sorret noticed Lieutenant Guigon's glum expression.

"Cheer up," said Sorret. "I'll save you a place at Fouquet's."

That superb Champs Élysées restaurant beloved of France's bright young things was an obvious goal for Langlade's officers.

"You aren't there yet," replied Guigon, smiling.

Shermans from Lieutenant Rives-Henry's troop rumbled past with Lieutenant Batiment's platoon riding shotgun. They reckoned their next stop was the Pont de Sèvres; provided that felled trees along Avenue Trivaux did not delay them.[119]

Parisians were beginning to kiss and hug *Les Leclercs*. For cooler souls like Sorret, however, it got a bit much. "Leave it out," he said. Others, less familiar with Parisian charms, were more impressed.

"Look!" exclaimed *Caporal-chef* Bernadicou, pointing towards the dome of Sacré-Coeur, bathed in early evening sunshine.

"And there's the Eiffel Tower!"

"It isn't true!"[120]

Southwest Paris has changed enormously since 1944. Roads and flyovers have often been completely rebuilt to accomodate modern transport. Surrounded by his staff officers—Langlois de Bazillac, Vigneux and his gypsy driver Georges Hipp—Massu was pleased with his sub-group's progress. Seeing waving *Tricolores* as they passed through Meudon gave them all a lift. But the Germans still arranged little ambushes from higher ground overlooking Sèvres. From the Ile Saint-Germain a German machine-gun firing along a side street inflicted several casualties among jubilant civilians. "Yet again," Massu wrote, "we witnessed the foolish temerity of those whose joy and enthusiasm pushed them towards us while the battle was still raging." But by 8.30pm his infantry had reached the Seine.[121]

Dating from the 1960s, today's Pont de Sèvres is a mighty steel and concrete affair supporting six lanes of traffic. However, the bridge representing GT Langlade's finish line on 24 August 1944 was a stone multi-arched design, with spans barely wide enough for an old fashioned barge to pass easily. It was fitted with mining pans so that it could be blown up if military exigencies required it.

"Sorret here," came a voice over Massu's radio. "I am at the Pont de Sèvres."

Driven by Georges Hipp, the *Tricolore* with *Croix de Lorraine* fluttering from his Jeep's radio mast, Massu rushed to the Seine's west bank. Despite his toughness, Massu was deeply emotional. He knew what Sorret would ask him.

"Our orders were to reach the Pont de Sèvres. We're there," said Sorret. "So? Do we cross or not?"

So long as the bridge was not mined it was possible. Lieutenant Batiment was ready with his platoon and Rives-Henry's Shermans. Some FFIs offered assistance. Scouring the bridge's opposite end with binoculars, Massu saw little to oppose them. "Should they continue?" He radioed Paul de Langlade who was already concerned that huge crowds were restricting his battlegroup's movements. The built-up sprawl of Paris impeded radio contact with those battlegroups approaching from the south. Langlade hesitated. He had reached the limit of his orders and his supplies were running low.

"Continue? That's impossible," Langlade declared firmly. "Fuel supplies have not caught up with us and we've only got an hour left of *autonomie*."[122]

Massu assured Langlade that he had enough fuel to reach the Place de la Concorde.

"That is not your mission," Langlade said firmly.[123]

Massu sent his men cautiously across the Pont de Sèvres, wondering with each step if somewhere a German sapper's hand was pushing down on a detonator's plunger ready to send them sky high. "*Non!*" wrote Massu. "Thank God!"[124]

Lieutenant Batiment established a bridgehead while others checked the bridge itself for explosives; there were none. Darkness was descending, making further progress unrealistic. Sorret radioed Guigon, "Fouquet's is off for tonight, the Germans are saying their *Adieux*!"[125]

AT MID-DAY *LA NUEVE* REACHED ANTONY, a satellite industrial
town south of Paris. Covered by its 57mm anti-tank gun, Montoya's
platoon advanced up the main street and found the local butcher had
placed a trestle table outside his shop to serve them snacks. Then an
88 shell exploded, wounding Montoya and sending his platoon diving
for cover. The 88 was firing from the Croix de Berny crossroads further
north, which would remain an obstacle for several hours.[126]

La Nueve's other platoons were luckier, outflanking and capturing
a set of four German 20mm machine-guns. But the order which
superseded all others was to keep advancing and bypass opposition.
Dronne kept pushing northwards along the Route Nationale. He would
have preferred to outflank that 88 rather than comtinue advancing as
though it was not there. So Putz altered his orders, allowing Dronne
to act independently, sending Campos' platoon along Antony's eastern
arteries up to the railway in a flanking manoeuvre. They captured
twenty-four Germans and killed many others for the loss of one from
la Nueve.[127]

With GT Billotte blocked at Antony, Leclerc visited the forward CP.

"Why have you stopped?" Leclerc asked. "Don't you want to do
any more?"

Putz's officers expected a Leclerc tongue-lashing.

"It's all in hand, *Mon Général*," replied Putz, pointing north. "Branet
and Sarazac are in front of Massy."

"Well, that's all right," replied Leclerc. "But tell Branet firmly not
to let himself get held up. Manoeuvre, right? Manoeuvre!"[128]

Soon afterwards these elements were targeted by German artillery
whose shells passed over their heads but damaged Lieutenant Teddy-
Rasson's troop of Shermans following behind. The crowd prevented the
Shermans from firing back. While most of Antony's citizens ignored
the danger of obstructing the 2e DB's progress, some understood
perfectly. From upper-storey windows, they squinted through
binoculars and telescopes looking for German positions, relaying
information back along the road. 88s were waiting up ahead. Maurice
Sarazac's 10th Company 3/RMT was ordered to hunt them down.

As they began advancing to contact, they were pestered by boys eager to carry their gear.

"How bizarre," remarked Lieutenant Granell, watching the 10th Company advance through *la Nueve*'s positions. "I'm beginning to miss Normandy. At least there one only had the Germans to worry about!"[129]

Again, only German methods could clear the roads; several high-explosive shells scattered shrapnel and macadam in all directions. Screaming, terrified civilians vanished into buildings or sought whatever safety they could find, leaving Antony's main road littered with all types of personal items and whimpering casualties both civil and military.[130]

To the right of the main road, Sarazac's men slowly manoeuvred towards Wissous and Orly. When contact was made with the enemy, the ensuing action was fast and savage. Their opponents were often Eastern Front veterans.[131] They fought hard. No sooner had Warabiot outflanked German positions at Morangis, where a strongpoint incorporated the local orphanage, than he faced an 88 which turned ninety degrees, re-sighted and knocked out three 501e RCC Shermans.

Standing beside Putz, Leclerc called forward Tank Destrroyers and Captain Buis' squadron of Shermans, "Move up on the left towards Massy. Perhaps you can bypass the obstacle." Buis' Shermans infiltrated through side roads until they reached the railway viaduct from whose cover a 75mm PAK and some 20mm heavy machine-guns were causing the problem. Buis decided upon a two-pronged tank charge; the *Elchingen* destroying the 75mm PAK and sending its crew scurrying for cover, while other Shermans attacked the German positions from further along the railway, shooting up every gun crew they saw under cover of the viaduct's embankment.

"Faster, faster," said Leclerc.[132]

No sooner was this obstacle dealt with than Buis ran into another at Rungis; there was more confused fighting amid the built-up areas north of Orly airport. Another two hours.

"Keep pushing, keep pushing," Putz told his officers.

GT Billotte's entrance into southern Paris was degenerating into time-consuming street fighting. Bradley had forbidden heavy artillery only in central Paris; this was *les banlieues*. 2e DB 105mm artillery shells began hammering German strongpoints, suspect crossroads and anywhere a 20mm heavy machine-gun was reported.[133]

None of this was helped by the crowds, congregating then receding in waves, depending on the fighting's intensity. Oblivious of the dangers, they sang, passed bottles around and accepted Camel cigarettes from Leclerc's men. For everyone who witnessed it, the march up the National 20 was unforgettable; one moment could be intensely tragic and the next utterly bizarre. Second Mate Meté, commanding the Tank-Destroyer *Audacieux*, saw his machine-gunner Manet suddenly collapse backwards. He had simply recoiled under a bouquet of flowers thrown from a fourth-storey window.[134]

Again a German 88 halted the jollity, sending the crowds inside their houses, leaving only an injured child in the street who was gathered up by senior Rochambelle Suzanne Torres.[135] By the time the 501e RCC passed Rungis it was 4pm.

"Get yourself to Croix de Berny," Billotte ordered Warabiot. "Putz is in trouble."

The Germans' defence system was quite elaborate. Witasse's 2nd Company 501e RCC and Sarazac's 10th Company RMT were held up by anti-tank and mortar fire.[136] *La Nueve*, along with Dupont's 11th Company RMT, was now directed towards the Fresnes prison. After Nordling released the political prisoners a few days before, the remaining inmates were German personnel held on disciplinary charges. As GT Billotte pushed north, Wehrmacht warders trawled the cells for men fit enough to fight. Incentivised by hopes of a reduced sentence, these men fought hard. Captain Dupont was mortally wounded; a tragic loss of a man who had followed de Gaulle since 1940.[137]

Yet, after hearing Dupont had fallen, Dronne recognised that once this strongpoint was defeated the road ahead would be clear and they could outflank the Croix de Berny. Even so, the German punishment unit fought desperately, held to their task by an officer who shot one of them dead in plain view of Dronne's men. Seeing this, a Spaniard shot the officer dead from one hundred metres. *La Nueve* cheered and pushed forward, forcing the punishment unit's survivors back inside Fresnes. "Take care," shouted a TD commander. "There are French people in these buildings!"[138]

Shortly afterwards Dronne was ordered to return to the main axis of advance, the National 20, which was still obstructed by an 88 at the Croix de Berny. Dronne was furious but the voice on the radio was insistent. It made little sense. There was another factor. "The crowd, an immense crowd, invaded pavements and roads, surrounding all our vehicles, stopping them, submerging them, embracing the men, giving them preserves and bottles which had been carefully set aside for this day." Nor did the Germans refrain from firing long bursts of machine-gun fire into the crowds. Dronne saw "a beautiful young girl, her torso sodden with blood, sliding down the side of a tank, her arms stretched out trying to grab hold of the steel turret".[139]

With support weapons held up by the crowd, Putz wanted the Croix de Berny's 88 eliminated. The National 20 was essential to GT Billotte's advance. Always, it seemed to Dronne, such tasks fell to men who had already given a lot.[140]

Supported by a Sherman from Witasse's 2nd Company and a section of combat engineers, Moreno's platoon set out to outflank the 88 from the railway station. Everywhere the crowd made movement virtually impossible. It took a bemedalled Great War veteran to persuade ecstatic civilians to let Moreno's men through. From there the veteran guided them to a road behind the 88's position and the Sherman fired at its breech mechanism, immediately disabling it. Six Germans were killed and eight taken prisoner. The Croix de Berny flooded with ecstatic civilians. Putz personally thanked *la Nueve*.[141]

The day, however, was disappearing. Had he known of GT Langlade's excellent progress in western Paris, Leclerc might have been happier. But Leclerc heard little from GT Langlade after Massu reached Massy. Turning to Boissieu, Leclerc said, "Your friend Billotte doesn't know how to manoeuvre." Though respectful of Billotte's tank experience,

Leclerc regarded him as a political appointee who had been foisted on his division by de Gaulle.

Frustrated by the 2e DB's apparently slow progress up the National 20, US V Corps commander Leonard Gerow considered ordering the US 4th Infantry Division to outflank the 2e DB's axis and assume the liberation, but Bradley vetoed this idea. American criticisms, while possibly tinged with "frog-bashing", discount the 2e DB's two-day route march.[142]

CHABAN-DELMAS' MESSENGER, Lieutenant Petit-Leroy, had reached the 2e DB's positions and showed Billotte Chaban's message. "It is important that you come quickly or very quickly, especially because we lack arms and ammunition and we can not be sure of being able to continue, without excessive losses, a resistance so under-armed. But also because we believe information that two German divisions are due to arrive from north of Paris to aid General von Choltitz. If these arrive before yourselves, you will not be able to liberate Paris without numerous victims and considerable destruction. As it is the Germans have all this time been able to prepare mines which are now in place. Chaban-Delmas wants you to know in any case that Choltitz does not appear to have decided to fight to the bitter end, since he appears to have been persuaded that such combat would be in vain, but he is being menaced by the SS. Hence it is equally necessary to come quickly in order to negotiate with him rather than a Hitlerian extremist who might replace him. His CP is at the Hôtel Meurice." Billotte knew about Chaban-Delmas and that his missive should be given utmost priority.[143]

Witnessed by Alain de Boissieu, Petit-Leroy gave Leclerc a fulsome exposé of the latest situation in Paris, describing personalities like Rol-Tanguy and the traditional but equally uncompromising Colonel Lizé. When Leclerc asked about the police's role, Petit-Leroy explained that the police had been on strike since 15 August and that General Hary now controlled all Parisian security organisations, including the fire brigade.[144]

Petit-Leroy continued, "Certain factions have their eyes on power. Vichy has collapsed. The GPRF is only present as 'the Delegation', whose leader Alexandre Parodi ranks as a government minister, but he has to deal with the most audacious and determined members of the CNR who would pass themselves off as the government while seeing the role of General de Gaulle as consultative." Nor did Petit-Leroy hide his concern that communists among the Resistance wanted a new Paris Commune and to present de Gaulle with a *fait accompli*. That evening Boissieu entered all this in his squadron's diary.[145]

At Rambouillet, de Gaulle had warned Leclerc of the dangers of a new Commune. Now, a second warning had come from Chaban. For immediate delivery by air to the Préfecture, Leclerc had his artillery chief, Jean Crépin, draft the unforgettable note, "*Le general Leclerc me charge de vous dire: 'Tenez bon. Nous arrivons.'—Lieutenant Colonel Crépin.*"[146] "Hold on. We're coming."

Divisional pilots Captain Callet and Lieutenant Mantoux listened in awed silence as Crépin explained their mission. Callet warned Crépin that the Piper Cub is a slow aircraft vulnerable to even small levels of hostile fire. But Crépin insisted their mission was vital. Flying over southern Paris they saw eerily empty streets as they steered towards Notre Dame. Looking down into the Préfecture's courtyard, strewn with wrecked trucks and a crowd waving from the Quai du Marché-Neuf, they lobbed out the weighted canvas bag containing Leclerc's message and pulled away, as bullets pierced the fuselage's light fabric.[147]

After discussing the barricades and street fighting with Petit-Leroy, Leclerc decided to write personally to General von Choltitz, saying he would be held personally responsible for damage to Paris. This was translated into German by Captain Betz, who strengthened the text with references to war crimes. But how could this message be delivered? Boissieu suggested using a *Kübelwagen* captured at Arpajon, but Leclerc dismissed the idea of using captured vehicles in favour of a Jeep. *Adjutant-chef* Dericbourg from Boissieu's squadron volunteered to drive Petit-Leroy back through the lines. It would be the last thing Dericbourg and Petit-Leroy did. Their Jeep was shot up by a Waffen

SS patrol. But these SS were professional enough to search Petit-Leroy's body, and Leclerc's letter reached von Choltitz's desk later that evening. Many years later von Choltitz told Alain de Boissieu that this was the *first* time he truly feared being treated as a war criminal.[148]

Through the afternoon von Choltitz kept Army Group B and OB West informed of the increasing pressures he faced. Eventually, around 6.45pm, he spoke to General Blumentritt. "The situation in Paris never ceases to deteriorate hourly," said von Choltitz. "It is foreseeable that we will not be able to hold Paris in the face of violent attacks from both the west and south and actions by the Resistance." But Model's orders remained that Paris should be defended at all costs.[149]

THE FAILURE OF ESSENTIAL PETROL SUPPLIES to reach GTs Billotte and Dio forced Billotte's decision at 7pm that his men had done all they could that day. Seeing Leclerc's disappointment, Billotte suggested that he order Dronne—"the captain nearest to us at the time"—to enter Paris. "Otherwise," wrote Billotte, "there was nothing else to be done than take positions for the night and get going as fast as possible in the early morning."[150]

Walking along Antony's main road, Leclerc recognised *la Nueve*'s Germán Arrúe, who had given him a haircut in Yorkshire but refused payment.

"Where's Dronne?" Leclerc asked.

Arrúe pointed towards fellow Spaniards returning to the National 20.

"Where's your chief?" Leclerc asked Lieutenant Amado Granell.

"*El Capitan?*—Just back there," said Granell.

Dronne found Leclerc leaning on his cane.

"Dronne, what are you doing there?" asked Leclerc.

"*Mon Général*," replied Dronne, "I am carrying out the orders I was given. I am returning to the main axis, at which point we now are."

"One should never obey stupid orders," said Leclerc.

Dronne explained events at Fresnes. Smiling at the unshaven captain in his battered képi and sweat-soaked uniform, Leclerc put a hand on his arm.

"Dronne, march on Paris," said Leclerc pointing northwards with his cane. "Get *into* Paris."

"*Tout de suite, mon Général*," replied Dronne. "But I've only got two platoons of infantry left after Montoya was sent over to reinforce the 11th Company and I am going to need more than that."

"Take what you can find and do it quickly," said Leclerc.

La Horie and other divisional officers gathered around Leclerc. Dronne needed clarification.

"If I am to understand you correctly, *mon Général*, I am to avoid resistance and not concern myself with whatever may be happening in my rear?"

"That's it exactly, right into Paris," said Leclerc, now smiling generously. "Get in any way you like. We must get in. You tell them that the whole division will arrive in Paris in the morning."[151]

So a Catholic aristocrat descended from crusaders gave a middle-class intellectual commanding a company of Spanish Republican atheists the most important mission of the whole Paris operation. Its motive was to bolster the Resistance and reassure Parisians that their anxieties would soon be over. "It was to show them, to prove to them, that the division was coming," Dronne later wrote. He looked at his watch; it was 7.30pm.[152]

Needing support for *la Nueve*, Dronne noticed three Shermans commanded by Lieutenant Michard, a monk from the White Fathers.

"I'm going into Paris," said Dronne. "You are coming with me; orders of General Leclerc."

Michard's troop was originally five tanks but two had succumbed to mechanical failure during the march. The remaining three were named after battles during Napoleon's 1814 campaign; *Montmirail*, *Champaubert* and *Romilly*. Dronne described Michard as "one of the very best".[153]

Once Dronne collared a section of engineers under *Adjutant-Chef* Gérard Cancel, they were ready to go. At that point an eighteen-year-old civilian called Georges Chevallier, who saw Dronne being briefed by Leclerc, offered himself as a guide.

"I know these *banlieues* like the back of my hand," said Chevallier in a freshly broken, deep voice.

"Very good, you *can* be our guide," said Dronne.[154]

At 8pm, in fading light, '*la Colonne Dronne*' set off. Dronne led the way in his Jeep, *Mort aux Cons*, followed by Michard's Shermans and fifteen White half-tracks. Passing freshly liberated Fresnes they were cheered by other tank crews. From there Chevallier guided them past l'Hay-les-Roses, Cachan, Arcueil, and Kremlin-Bicêtre, using small, unobvious roads he knew were clear. Despite the gathering darkness, the crowd remained an enormous factor. Warned by Chevallier that Germans still held the Fort de Bicêtre; *la Colonne Dronne* headed for the Porte d'Italie.

At the Porte d'Italie a crowd assembled, expecting Allied troops to arrive along the National 6. Seeing Dronne's column emerge from a secondary road, they worried that they were German, scattering amid cries of "*Barrez-vous! Voila les Boches!*" But once they saw Michard's olive-green Shermans the cries of "*les Boches! Les Chleus!*" were quickly replaced by "*Les Américains! Ce sont les Américains!*" The crowd filled the street. *La Colonne Dronne* could barely move.[155]

"Welcome! Long live America," said an old man.

"I'm from the Rue de Tolbiac," said one of Michard's drivers. "Long live the 13th Arrondissement!"

Another elderly gentleman approached *Montmirail* carrying a brandy glass and a finely cut decanter. He explained how he had kept some Cognac *d'un age très respectable*, to offer the first Allied soldier he met.

"But I am French, Sir," said Michard.

The old man appeared deeply moved. "French!" he mumbled, his voice beginning to crack. "They are French!"

"That's not all," said Dronne. "We've got to get on."[156]

Dronne had little idea where he should be heading. Then it occurred to him that he should head for the Hôtel de Ville, focus of the rights and liberties of all Parisians. But he needed to bypass German strongpoints and barricades. Again a young civilian offered to guide them. Resembling an Albert Dubout cartoon character,

Lorenian Dikran was an Armenian and rode a moped cycle for which he somehow acquired petrol.

"Do you know a route bypassing German resistance and without any barricades by which we can quickly reach the Hôtel de Ville?"

Dikran nodded affirmatively, but other youths called him a bluffer.

"Shut up," said Dikran commandingly. "I know the way and I will show them."

Meanwhile Jeanne Borchert, a curvaceous blond in Alsatian costume, had seated herself on the folded down windscreen of Dronne's Jeep, cracking the glass. Her demeanour clearly indicated that she would remain there.[157]

Dronne's cosmopolitan force followed Dikran along the Rue de Vistule, then the Rue Baudricourt, the Rue Esquirol, and the Boulevard de l'Hôpital. Where Parisians encountered Dronne's column, they usually took cover until someone shouted, "They're French!" Crossing the Seine at the Pont d'Austerlitz, they rumbled along the *rive droite*'s quays; the Quai de la Rapée, the Quai Henry IV, and Quai des Célestins—then the Quai de l'Hôtel de Ville. Finally La Place Hôtel de Ville.[158]

Arriving via a slightly different route, Amado Granell's half-track *Guadalajara* arrived on La Place Hôtel de Ville a few moments earlier, parking on the north side outside those famous shops, *Les Ciseaux d'Argent* and *Chaussures Mansfield*. After ordering his Spaniards into all-round defence, Granell entered the Hôtel de Ville, becoming the first officer of the 2e DB to meet the *Conseil Nationale de la Resistance*, whose leaders greeted him generously, quickly calling for someone to photograph him with Georges Bidault. For pre-empting Dronne's arrival, Granell was nominated "the man who liberated Paris" by *la Nueve*'s legend builders.[159]

The three Shermans took positions supporting the Spaniards and Michard joined Dronne. Dismounting from Dronne's Jeep, Jeanne Borchert appointed herself *la Nueve*'s Marianne. Dronne looked up at the Hôtel de Ville's great clock; it was 9.22pm.[160]

For Michard's tankers, who were mostly *Gaullistes de la première heure*, for the Spaniards of *la Nueve* and the sprinkling of Armenians also among them, and for Dronne himself, their arrival outside the Hôtel de Ville "constituted the supreme recompense", wrote Dronne, "the realisation of a beautiful dream that wiser heads might well have judged unreasonable". *Aspirant* Bacave radioed to Leclerc that they had reached the Hôtel de Ville without loss.[161]

For the time being the Place de l'Hôtel de Ville remained empty. Little by little, as Parisians realised that Dronne's column were not *les Fridolins*, joyful crowds overwhelmed them, everyone singing the *Marseillaise*.[162] Ecstatic at discovering that *la Colonne Dronne* was Leclerc's advance guard, Parisians were even more amazed to discover half-tracks "*Conduit par les Espagnols!*"—news which soon reached the Spanish Republican refugee, Victoia Kent. In her shabby lodgings, knowing she no longer lived under Fascism, she wept.[163]

UNKNOWN TO DRONNE, his progress through southern Paris to the Place de l'Hôtel de Ville was telephoned to the Barrière d'Enfer. Resistance historian Henri Noguères later wrote, "On the one side was the Insurrection, without doubt a little brawling though spontaneous and generous; (almost) a revolution, the people, the nation. While on the other hand in strict format, or perhaps a grubby uniform, order was being restored, hierarchy, the return of calm, it is already the new power, and it is always the state."[164] One can only conclude that the Insurrection's leaders recognised how things must be. Why else did Rol-Tanguy send two envoys to the Allies? Why else did his wife, Cécile, and the women running the Barrière d'Enfer command centre "dance the *Java*" and celebrate Dronne's arrival with a pillow fight?[165]

Dronne could only savour the moment. Entering the Hôtel de Ville's ornate entrance lobby with its Pierre Puvis de Chavannes paintings, Dronne caught Granell's eye, smiled and told him to take charge of the men outside. Then, escorted by Pirlian Krikor and Michard, he ascended the marble staircase. Entering the brilliantly lit, gold-leaf-encrusted *grand salon* Dronne saw faces he would encounter again as a post-war politician. Looking pale and skinny, but very moved, was

Georges Bidault who succeeded Jean Moulin as head of the CNR. Then there was Joseph Laniel, Daniel Mayer, Georges Marannes and several others, all shaking hands with Dronne and Michard, saying "*Bien joué!*" Georges Bidault began a speech but was overcome with emotion. Dronne replied by "proclaiming the joy of *résistants de l'exterieur* at this junction with the élite of the *résistance de l'interieur*", and prematurely called General de Gaulle "President de Gaulle!" No one contradicted him.[166]

Surveying these élite Frenchmen who, despite the Occupation's privations, remained clean and presentable, Dronne became painfully aware that he was filthy and smelled.[167]

Seeing the lights glowing inside the Hôtel de Ville, some Germans decided to shoot out the chandeliers' light bulbs. Next came a long, horizontal burst of machine-gun fire, luckily too high to hit anyone. No one knew where the light switches were. Worrying about a German counterattack, Dronne returned outside where the crowd had dispersed.[168]

The news of *la Colonne Dronne*'s arrival spread quickly via the city's traditional messengers, the clergy. Churches began ringing their bells; the din becoming more vibrant as belfries were pulled into action, sloughing off four years' of cobwebs, their strikers swinging free for a languid moment before smashing into ancient bell-metal with a resounding "dong!" Soon the greatest bells of all, high up in Notre Dame, added their voice to the cacophony.

Chastened by Leclerc's threatening letter, von Choltitz was dining with his officers at the Meurice.

"Why are they ringing?" asked a young secretary.

"They are ringing for us, my little girl," replied von Choltitz paternally. "They are ringing because the Allies are coming into Paris. Why else do you suppose they would be ringing?"[169]

Seeing his staff's glum faces, von Choltitz said, "What else did you expect? You've been sitting here in your little dream world for years. You haven't seen what's happening to Germany in Russia and Normandy. Germany has lost this war, and we have lost it with her."

Von Choltitz retired to his office, opened the balcony window and telephoned General Speidel.

"Listen," said von Choltitz, holding the receiver up to the open window. "The bells of Paris ringing to tell the city the Allies are here." Then von Choltitz asked Speidel to look after his family.[170]

THE NEWS REACHED COLONEL LIZÉ'S HQ on Rue Guénégard as they began dinner. The housekeeper's simpleton lodger Henri was whistling annoyingly like a wound-up doll. Just as he was asked to leave the room, multi-coloured rockets shot into the sky above the Préfecture. "Was it possible?" wondered Raymond Massiet. When Notre Dame's great bells began ringing, they knew it was true. "*Les Français! Les Français!* They're at the Hôtel de Ville!" Every eye moistened. An exhausted-looking Colonel Lizé shook hands with everyone before donning his uniform to present himself at the Hôtel de Ville.[171] Alone in his office, Massiet savoured these moments in virtual darkness while, outside, Parisians sang the *Marseillaise* heartily. "Was it really over?" he wondered. "Thank God!"[172]

Henri Rol-Tanguy ordered his driver to take him to the Hôtel de Ville via the Rue Saint-Jacques, avoiding the Boulevard Saint-Michel which was still endangered by the Palais Luxembourg strongpoint. As Rol-Tanguy arrived two uniformed *Gardiens* demanded to escort Dronne to the Préfecture. Escorted by Pirlian Krikor, Dronne crossed the Pont Notre Dame. In the Préfecture's *grand salon*, albeit less ornate than the Hôtel de Ville's, Dronne met Jacques Chaban-Delmas—"a very young general, svelte and elegant in a beautiful, brand new khaki uniform"—and Charles Luizet.[173]

Dronne told them the whole 2e DB would enter Paris at dawn, in a few hours. Luizet asked Dronne if he wanted anything.

"A bath," replied Dronne.

Luizet nodded. Felix Gaillard led Dronne to the Prefect's bathroom while Krikor returned to his Jeep to fetch a fresh shirt and clean socks from his pack. "Washed, refreshed, changed and made presentable, I felt a new man," Dronne wrote.[174]

Escorting Dronne back to the Place de l'Hôtel de Ville, the two *Gardiens* said the Paris Resistance was very weak and the Germans could easily have taken the Préfecture. Dronne saw how the German garrison had not really been trying, but he had yet to learn how war-weary von Choltitz was.[175]

On the Place de l'Hôtel de Ville a rota was organised for Dronne's men to take baths in nearby houses, and FFIs helped guard the square while they rested.[176] Michard's Shermans covered the main thoroughfares, *Romilly*'s cannon pointing down the Rue de Rivoli. After dissuading over-excited FFIs from drawing his men into ill-conceived night attacks, Dronne laid out his bedroll on the pavement. As *la Nueve* sang *El paso del Ebro*, a song of resistance from the Napoleonic Wars, the exhausted captain fell asleep.[177]

ON HEARING OF DRONNE'S SUCCESS Leclerc considered entering Paris immediately, but darkness, the fact that they needed resupply, and that his men needed rest made him reconsider. Girard had found him a bedroom in a private house, but Leclerc slept on the ground with a bedroll and djellabah. Before turning in Leclerc chatted with his nephew Bernard, a veteran of the cadets' heroic stand at Saumur in 1940. His father's Pétainiste sympathies prevented Bernard from joining de Gaulle, but he had enlisted in his uncle's division a few days earlier. After talking *en famille*, Leclerc tried to sleep before the most momentous day of his life.[178]

At his CP in western Paris, Paul de Langlade ceased worrying about GT Billotte's progress when the church bells started ringing. Supported by RBFM Tank Destroyers, Massu's men were holding defence positions east of the Pont de Sèvres. 5th Company RMT held the Avenue Bellevue and surrounding road junctions while the 6th bathed in the crowd's acclamation. The local German garrison retreated to the Renault factory and the Ile Saint-Germain. But the Germans would not remain passive for long. Shortly after 1am Lieutenant Postaire heard German vehicles approaching Avenue Bellevue, and German infantry had crept even closer, pulling up an anti-tank gun by hand. They were virtually on top of 5th Company's positions when a Moroccan soldier attacked the anti-tank gunners with his bare hands, raising the alarm before being cut down by machine-gun fire. Another Moroccan, *Sergeant-Chef* Broukseaux, drove off several Germans with hand-grenades, but thirty successfully penetrated French positions, bringing up dreaded 20mm machine-guns which set a half-track alight. After thirty minutes' fierce fighting the Germans withdrew, leaving behind them forty dead and twenty prisoners, three abandoned *Kübelwagens*, three 20mm machine-guns and several bicycles.[179]

25 August 1944

TO PREVENT FURTHER GERMAN SURPRISES, GT Langlade sent out patrols. Dawn found them unshaven, wandering southwest Paris. In the meantime, FFIs warned Langlade that German forces were regrouping around the Bois de Boulogne and the Porte Saint-Cloud, preparing to reopen a route eastwards. A lorry tried making a dash from the Renault factory but was destroyed by a Stuart special's howitzer. More lorries tried escaping through the smoke; these too were destroyed. Their crews mostly surrendered but others threw themselves in the Seine; they were fished out by divisional engineers. 6th Company RMT captured two hundred prisoners, fifteen light vehicles and twenty lorries full of supplies.

Approaching 10am, the petrol tanker convoy finally reached GT Langlade.

"*Mais enfin, bon Dieu!*" exclaimed Paul de Langlade. "Where on Earth have you been?"

"We got lost in Sèvres," replied the convoy commander. "So we thought it best to wait until day."

After exchanging empty jerry cans for full ones, GT Langlade was ready to enter central Paris.[180]

PIERRE BILLOTTE WAS WOKEN AROUND 1AM when Commandant Weil brought fresh orders. "Get yourself to the Ile de la Cité at dawn, as prearranged, but disengage from the routes around the Croix de Berny because Dio will be coming along those advancing level with you. Go via Villejuif and the Porte Gentilly."

"I hope," said Billotte, "there's no change concerning the dispositions previously agreed with General Leclerc yesterday afternoon regarding manoeuvres *within* Paris."

"I don't know about those dispositions," replied Weil.[181]

During the small hours reports reached Leclerc's CP from reconnaissance units and the Resistance that the routes into Paris via the Porte d'Orléans were free of German forces and the Gare Montparnasse had been abandoned. General von Aulock had been ordered to pull his men back *behind* the Seine. Meanwhile von Choltitz lied to OKW that southern Paris was held "to the last man".[182] He also lied when he claimed that he had ordered the bridges of eastern Paris to be blown.[183]

After a brief absence during which he had himself professionally shaved by a barber in Antony, Leclerc told Alain de Boissieu that the Gare Montparnasse was suitable for the divisional CP. "Go on ahead of me with the protection squadron," said Leclerc. Boissieu ordered Lieutenant de la Fouchardière's troop to the Lion de Belfort and next, depending on German reaction, to secure the Gare Montparnasse. Duplay's troop would follow behind.[184]

Knowing this was the day they would enter Paris as liberators, the 501e RCC made an extra effort to be smart. But Billotte thought getting started was more important.

"Stay calm," said Sergeant Laigle, climbing into his Sherman *Villers-Cotterets*. "I'm sure General von Choltitz is having an easy morning."

Ignoring Laigle's impudence, Billotte discussed details with Warabiot before giving Jacques Branet command of the battlegroup's lead elements.

"Have you fully understood?" Billotte asked him. "Porte de Gentilly, Rue Saint-Jacques, and then right on to Notre Dame."

"Understood, *mon Colonel*," nodded Branet. "*En route.*"

He saluted Billotte and mounted his Jeep. Behind him Debout stood by the Jeep's 0.5" Browning, one hand on the firing grips while waving to tanks and armoured cars behind.[185]

Soon after moving off Branet allowed Spahi Lieutenant Vézy's M8 armoured cars to lead the way, guided by FFI. The crowd were filling the streets, only parting to let vehicles pass at the last moment.

"It's like Moses parting the Red Sea," Sergeant Laigle told his gunner. Like most of the 501e RCC, Laigle had swapped his tanker's helmet for his black beret.[186]

At 7.45am GT Billotte found the Porte Gentilly *noir de monde*—"thick with people"—all shouting with joy, singing the *Marseillaise* and throwing flowers. Standing in his Scout Car, Billotte saw a magnificent apple flying straight at him and caught it with both hands.[187] Agile young women climbed aboard every vehicle, smothering the 2e DB's freshly shaved cheeks with lipstick.

On his Sherman *Douaumont,* Sergeant Bizien took a beautiful brunette in his arms. He had not hugged a French girl in years. Suddenly gunfire sent the crowd scattering for shelter while French soldiers scoured windows and rooftops for snipers. The girl in Bizien's arms slumped heavily; her eyes rolling as she died. She had taken three bullets in the back and was covered with blood. Recognising that he had been the intended target, Bizien was horrified. "She saved my life!" he murmured.[188]

The crowd backed off, enabling Vézy's Spahis to push on, zigzagging along the Rue Saint-Jacques, their M8s devouring the road until they saw the towers of Notre Dame and an enormous crowd greeted them on the *Parvis*.[189]

"LECLERC'S TANKS ARE MARCHING ALONG THE RUE SAINT JACQUES," exclaimed Lucienne, Jean Galtier-Boissière's assistant as she arrived for work. Galtier-Boissière's wife threw a dressing gown over her night-dress and they ran along the Rue de la Sorbonne to see shrieking crowds surrounding 2e DB vehicles. "On every tank, on every armoured car, beside their khaki clad crews wearing their red caps, the grasping arms of young girls, of women, of kids and *fifis* wearing armbands, the whole throng applauded them, blowing kisses, shaking their hands as they passed, crying to these conquerors their joy at being liberated. These French soldiers, Spahis in fact, were smart, charming, good kids. Without any showing off, they took the gratitude of the people in their stride, smiling with white teeth and suntanned, exhausted faces." They followed them northwards past the Saint-Jacques barricade, on to the Ile de la Cité where Spahi M8s fanned out along the quays. There, as cameras filmed them, *Parisiennes* draped themselves over these gods who peered out from green machinery, offered babies to be kissed and flower after flower. "Amid this charming crowd," wrote Galtier-Boissière, "this march-past was a hundred times more moving than the solemn victory march of 1919."[190]

HOSTILE GUNFIRE CAME from the *rive gauche*; a watchtower on the Rue Saint-Jacques had clear fields of fire towards the *Parvis*. Billotte's party retreated into the Préfecture while *Villers-Cotterets*' machine-gun gutted the watchtower. It was now 8am. Billotte ascended the Préfecture's grand staircase to meet Charles Luizet, Alexandre Parodi and Jacques Chaban-Delmas. GT Billotte's CP was installed in the billiard room.[191]

Chaban-Delmas spent the night by the Préfecture's switchboard. At dawn he took a brief walk by the Seine, contemplating four years of *la vie clandestine* and the luck which saved his life while others, most cruelly in those last few days, made the ultimate sacrifice. Being familiar with politico-military appointments, Billotte avoided remarking on Chaban's youth and the smart uniform which outranked his own.[192]

Outside the Hôtel de Ville the crowd thickened, becoming even more curious about Dronne's eclectic force than the previous evening. While Dronne shaved, a young "collector" stole the pennant from his Jeep's radio antenna and various FFI oddballs tried again to persuade him to join in hair-brained missions against German strongpoints which would probably fall during the day. Dronne duly sent them *au diable*.[193]

However, when two officials arrived from the Préfecture complaining that German sappers were mining the Central Telephone Exchange on the Rue des Archives, Dronne recognised this had to be stopped. Immediately he sent Michard's tanks, Elias' platoon and Cancel's engineers to attack the Telephone Exchange from front and rear. A reporter with a camionette-mounted cine-camera tried to join in but, at the risk of *la Nueve*'s deeds going unrecorded, Dronne excluded him for safety reasons.

Attacking from the Rue de Temple, Elias' platoon found themselves facing determined German resistance. Both Elias and Sergeant Cortes were severely, though not mortally, wounded before the Exchange was taken. On the German side a dozen sappers were killed and thirty captured including the burly lieutenant commanding them. Dronne asked this officer to remove the explosives since his men knew where they were. In passable French the officer replied that such an action was contrary to the rules of war. Dronne replied in German that such rules did not apply to non-military installations. The officer remained unyielding until Dronne's men resorted to physical menaces. Only then did these German sappers remove their explosives and booby traps. They were everywhere: under tables, chairs, cupboard doors as well as among the main machinery. If anyone else had cleared them casualties would have been inevitable.[194]

WHEN GT DIO HALTED AT CHAMPLAN the previous evening the availability of working telephone lines meant that men with families in Paris could contact their loved ones.

"We're coming," they yelled enthusiastically into the mouthpiece.

Leclerc tasked Louis Dio with investing western Paris south of the Seine, thereby linking GT Billotte and GT Langlade. Dio's staff subsequently telephoned local residents for information on German positions. First they would cordon off the Chamber of Deputies and the Quai d'Orsay in a block which included several important buildings between the Rue de l'Université and the Seine's south bank. A second sub-group under Colonel Noiret would fan out westwards taking in the Champ de Mars with the École Militaire and link up with GT Langlade.[195]

At 8.30am GT Dio marched northwards into Paris. Reaching the Porte d'Orléans they split balletically in two; Rouvillois' tanks rumbling along the tree-lined Avenue de Maine while Noiret's veered leftwards along the Boulevard Brune, advancing in small detachments of tanks and infantry, halting at notable junctions and squares, going into all-round defence. 12e Cuirassiers' Shermans and Spahi armoured cars took possession of the Champ de Mars, drawing up under the Eiffel Tower. To their south a swastika flag flew over the École Militaire.

"It would only take a 37mm shell to knock that down," said a Spahi, patting his M8's cannon.

"Go on, then!" said an officer.

The shot went wide, drawing German fire from the building, forcing the crowd to take cover among the Champ de Mars' hedge-lined edges. Captain Perceval saw a man approaching from the Pont d'Iena.

"A German pillbox is preparing to fire at you," he said. "It is situated at the bottom of the Pont d'Iena, exactly between the Trocadero's colonnades."

Perceval sent Lieutenant Jourdan and four men armed with a bazooka and rifle grenades. The Place Trocadero was empty, but beyond the pavillions Jourdan discovered a pillbox at the south corner of Avenue Kléber, one of several ugly concrete pillboxes defending the German HQ area, in which a MG42 would be sited.[196]

The German machine-gunners soon spotted Jourdan but there were mature, wide-trunked trees behind which he could take cover as he approached, followed by a *Tirailleur* toting the section's bazooka. Their first bazooka shell narrowly missed the pillbox, setting a camionette alight instead. The pillbox machine-gun fired furiously, its bullets passing perilously close to Jourdan. Just then a civilian crossed the road, apparently oblivious to the danger, holding an unopened bottle of champagne. "Come back to my place where you could be far more peaceful than out here. I would like to introduce you to my wife," said the man.

"Not at the moment," replied Jourdan, smiling. "Excuse us, but we've got to destroy a pillbox over there, do you see?"

Adding to the farcically risky situation, civilians were coming from the nearby Rue Boissière to greet Jourdan's men, ignoring the fire coming from the pillbox.

"You don't need to do that," a civilian advised Jourdan. "The main bunch are inside the Hôtel Baltimore."

Jourdan withdrew towards the civilian.

"I speak German," said the man. "I will be your interpreter."

The two men advanced northwards up Avenue Kléber and entered the Hôtel Baltimore's lobby, facing plenty of armed German soldiers.

"Surrender!" called Jourdan.

"*Hände hoch!*" said the civilian.

Cowed by Jourdan's confidence the Germans surrendered and marched out in a large column, their hands in the air, soon joined by the machine-gunners from the pillbox. As Jourdan's men herded them towards the Champ de Mars, they had to protect them from the crowd's abuse, much to the amusement of *Tirailleur* Naouri, an Algerian Jew.[197]

On the Champs de Mars, Perceval's company still faced hostile fire from the École Militaire, whose defenders included *Miliciens*. The sandbags packed into window openings suggested that these Germans would put up a fight. The 12e Cuirassiers' Shermans hosed the façade with machine-gun fire. Although Louis XV's defeat in the Seven Years War prevented the École Militaire from becoming the great edifice Ange-Jacques Gabriel envisaged, it remains a fine building. Nevertheless its German occupants could not be ignored, so a platoon of 2e DB sappers, supported by Shermans, blew the main gate off its hinges and entered the courtyard. Some of Lieutenant Borrewater's sappers climbed through first-storey windows to outflank German snipers, sending them fleeing down great staircases to where prisoners were being gathered up. Sometimes white flags appeared, but some ornate rooms were cleared using grenades, submachine-guns and, to avoid structural damage, knives. Two hundred German and *Milice* prisoners were taken at the École Militaire. The *Tricolore* was re-hung in the Hall of Honour. From his command tank beneath the Eiffel Tower, Colonel Noiret radioed, "We have taken all our objectives."[198]

DRESSED IN A US TANKER'S JACKET, topped off with a khaki képi onto which he had recently pinned his *divisionnaire*'s third star, General Leclerc entered Paris in a White Scout Car accompanied by Christian Girard. At the Place Denfert Rochereau, amid screaming crowds, they were joined by Jacques Chaban-Delmas. Further along the Boulevard Montparnasse they halted outside the Brasserie Dumesnil[199] where, over long lunches, de Gaulle discussed the mechanisation of the French Army with Colonel Émile Mayer during the 1930s. Using a recently updated map, Chaban explained the latest developements while photographers, including Magnum's Robert Capa, created some of the day's most memorable images.[200]

The Gare Montparnasse now became Leclerc's HQ. A powerful antenna placed on the roof connected to the radio van. Its waiting rooms, still bearing German names, were draped with *Tricolores*. But, as local politician François Corbel and station secretary Monsieur Thomas fetched tables and chairs from the deserted Wehrmacht canteen, a stray bullet whistled down the main platform.

"Anyone harmed?" asked Leclerc.

"No," came the answer.

"Bad shot!" said Leclerc.[201]

A map table was arranged on the main esplanade.

"Now let's see where we are," said André Gribius. "It's ten o'clock. Rouvillois has reached Les Invalides and Noiret is securing the main quays."

"What about Billotte?" asked Repiton-Préneuf.[202]

To Francois Courbel's "wishes of welcome in the name of the SNCF", Leclerc replied matter of factly, "I still have several points of resistance to quash, that around the Place de la Concorde being the most serious. It will take us some time, but tomorrow the war should be finished in Paris."[203]

Once contact was established with the Préfecture and the Hôtel de Ville, several officers begged permission to use the station switchboard for personal calls. Leclerc nodded urbanely. "You're *liberated*. My family is in [the department of] the Somme and we're not there yet," he told Courbel.[204]

Was it possible, Girard wondered, to dial a number kept in his heart so long? But four years of silence held him back. He asked the station's operator to transfer a call to a kiosk in the main hall. But when he heard his mother's voice, Girard's emotions paralysed him. His mother, however, guessed.

"Paul, Paul," Madame Girard called to her husband. "It's Christian."

Unable to speak, Girard replaced the receiver. After a few moments anxiously wandering the station he asked for twenty minutes' leave. Leclerc offered his driver. Apart from a white-shrouded nurse outside the Laennec Hospital, the Rue de Sèvres was deserted. Along the Rue du Bac the crowd grew. The Rue de Varenne turning soon appeared and, seconds later, they halted at Number 19 where Madame Girard was waiting outside the high, arched front door, wearing a black day-dress.

"*Te voila, mon fils.*"—"There you are, my son," she said, opening her arms.[205]

HAVING INFORMATION THAT GENERAL VON CHOLTITZ would capitulate once Allied forces arrived, Pierre Billotte wrote him a letter. "I would invite the *Commandant* of *Gross-Paris* to cease all combat rendered pointless by the inequality of available forces," was the key sentence. Billotte elaborates in his memoirs: "So as not to make it worse for his men, if Choltitz surrendered to my *present* invitation, and in any case since he would be in our hands, we would demand of him that he sign the capitulation of troops under his command throughout the sector of *Gross-Paris* and will organise with him the surrender as quickly as possible of the isolated packets of resistance. ... So I rapidly dictated these terms to La Horie, assisted by Felix Gaillard, who kept the draft under plate glass on his desk until his death," wrote Billotte. He then signed it, "General Billotte, commanding the First French

Armoured Brigade", to impress von Choltitz, even though he was merely a colonel and his battlegroup was never an independent entity.[206]

Then, believing von Choltitz might prefer being offered terms by a Frenchman of equivalent social rank, Billotte sent La Horie, escorted by two Spahi M8s, to Nordling's Rue d'Anjou consulate. Despite his diminutive physique, La Horie was a fine horseman and brave as a lion, something he concealed behind a laid-back manner. Nordling was standing in the road with Bender when the Spahi M8s arrived via the Rue Saint-Lazare. As local residents poured into the street, La Horie introduced himself and, having established Bender's *bona fides*, directed the more threatening aspects of Billotte's terms towards Bender. There was only one possible solution, both humane and honourable: capitulation. Bender warned La Horie that, while von Choltitz was no Nazi, he cared about military honour.[207]

"*Il pria*," wrote Nordling. "*He* [La Horie] *begged* the consulate to kindly pass on the ultimatum to von Choltitz." While Nordling was willing to plead with von Choltitz for Paris within days of suffering a heart attack, he suddenly had staff problems. With gun battles raging around the Place de la Concorde, Nordling's chauffeur refused to drive him. During the previous week the poor man had been under fire several times; he had his family to think of. Bender offered his services.[208]

They reached the Madeleine without incident, but thereafter found themselves amid intense gunfire, forcing them to wait on the corner of the Rue Royale. They continued on foot to the Rue Saint-Honoré where German sailors manned a checkpoint. Seeing Nordling and Bender approach in smart suits, the sailors ordered them to stop. Waving a white handkerchief Bender advanced slowly, offering his papers to a Kriegsmarine officer. From outside the Café Weber, Nordling saw that Bender was having difficulties; the Kriegsmarine were frequently as uncompromising as the SS. Bender explained that they were trying to negotiate the German garrison's surrender to the French.

"In the Kriegsmarine we don't know what a white flag looks like," replied the naval officer disdainfully. Eventually Bender was allowed into the Hôtel Crillon to telephone the Hôtel Meurice. Merely a hundred metres separates these two hotels but, with Germans on the Rue de Rivoli exchanging gunfire with *résistants* on the Champs Élysées, it required a brave man to make that walk. Lieutenant Dankwart von Arnim met Bender at the junction of the Rue Royale. "General von Choltitz has got your measure," said von Arnim loudly. "He won't accept it." Then, in a low voice, Arnim gave Bender off the record information regarding von Choltitz's true position, admitting that if von Choltitz was taken prisoner he would co-operate with Billotte's demands. "In effect," wrote Nordling, "von Choltitz was ready to lay down his weapons at the very moment that French regular forces penetrated the Hôtel."[209]

After rejoining Nordling outside the Café Weber, they returned to the Swedish Consulate where Bender told La Horie that von Choltitz could not surrender without a fight.

"You've just got to make a lot of noise," said Bender.

"So it's a *baroud d'honneur*,"* La Horie remarked.

"*Absolument!*" said Bender.

"We will attack around 3pm," replied La Horie.[210]

ADVANCING INTO CENTRAL PARIS from the Pont de Sèvres, Sub-group Massu was quickly overwhelmed by the crowd, slowing their progress virtually to a standstill.[211] Atop the Sherman *Champagne*, Lieutenant Berne had a good view over the thickening crowd. But those following behind could barely see what was happening. Reaching the Porte Saint-Cloud, Massu was amused by thirty *Gardiens* arriving on bicycles from the Bois de Boulogne to control the crowd.[212]

Reduced to a crawl, they witnessed all the joy and, in some instances, downright ugliness of liberation. Sorret's platoon saw FFIs pushing along a naked and degraded girl with head shaven and breasts daubed with black tar swastikas for *collaboration horizontale*.

---

* *Baroud d'honneur*= a token resistance.

"'My heart is French, but my cunt is international!' That's what they say," someone explained.

"What a pity, *mon lieutenant*," said Sergeant Picquet. "She's quite a looker, that little one."

Much had happened since Sorret last dined at Fouquet's.[213]

Colonel Paul de Langlade now ordered Massu's sub-group to halt. Though Massu's men were unlikely to be fazed by 20mm machingun fire from German remnants holding out around Garches, Langlade recognised the potential panic and civilian casualties. Having located the offending guns, GT Langlade's artillery rained 105mm shells on them so that, for a few minutes, western Paris reverberated with explosions.[214]

Massu visited Langlade's CP.

"*Mon vieux* Massu, you really should look at yourself in a mirror," said Langlade, laughing heartily. "You're covered in lipstick. One would think a Red Indian had enlisted."

"You would know, *mon colonel*," replied Massu. "My face could hardly be worse than yours."

Langlade inspected his own face in a Jeep's wing mirror and frantically rubbed rouge from his jawline.[215]

"It was a triumphal march amid cries of '*bravo!*'," wrote Massu. "Carried by popular enthusiasm we arrived within sight of the Étoile. Now it had become serious; we had exact information on the positions of German pillboxes and knew that the area around the Hôtel Majestic would be well defended."[216]

A call of "*Attention!*" soon came as FFI emerged from a crossroads. "There are plenty of Germans up ahead."

Moments later a GMC lorry was badly shot up by machine-gun fire from a first floor apartment. At once Sergeant Mesnier, a Thompson in one hand and a grenade in the other, entered the building and ran up the stairs. After killing two German soldiers he found two teenage lads wearing *Tricolore* brassards and a Frenchman in Wehrmacht uniform claiming that a German had stolen his clothes at gunpoint and forced him to wear his discarded uniform. Outside the two lads begged forgiveness from the FFIs, but no one knew what to make of the Frenchman in Wehrmacht uniform.[217]

CHRISTIAN GIRARD REGAINED THE GARE MONT PARNASSE in time to escort General Leclerc to the Préfecture. Neither Leclerc nor Billotte were surprised when La Horie reported that von Choltitz would fight. The attack would go ahead.[218]

US 4th Infantry Division's General Barton arrived for the big luncheon prepared in the Préfecture's dining room. "He did not seem very happy," wrote Girard. "I think our situation seemed strange to him." Leclerc summoned Girard outside, needing to confide his impatience that von Choltitz remained inside the Meurice with de Gaulle arriving that afternoon. After Leclerc returned to the dining room, Girard found Commandant Bagneux dining downstairs with several FFI. "I joined them," wrote Girard, "and enjoyed an excellent lunch in an atmosphere of extraordinary festivity. To this day it seems so unreal when considering what was happening only a few hundred metres away."[219]

While others dined, Billotte finished his plan. Jacques Branet would lead a group of tanks and infantry along the Rue de Rivoli up to the Place de la Concorde, while Lieutenant Bricard took a similar force along the *rive droite* quays, to take on any Panther tanks supposedly in the Tuileries gardens. Sammarcelli would take the Rue Saint-Honoré, covering the Rue de l'Opéra and the Rue Royale, while Putz took a southerly axis from the Place Saint-Michel towards the Jardins du Luxembourg. Billotte hoped the Germans would surrender honourably when faced with overwhelming forces and therefore ordered his men not to fire first; chivalrous considerations he later regretted.[220]

"La Horie came to find me," wrote Branet. "We're going to attack the Hôtel Meurice, the centre of German resistance. The German general was there and, opposite, Panthers in the Tuileries. Probably they would surrender. [We're] not to fire first."[221] Branet's tanks would be supported by two platoons from 3/RMT's 11th Company commanded by lieutenants Franjoux and Karcher. La Horie mentioned a *baroud d'honneur*.

"A *baroud d'honneur*?" said Branet. "And what, I wonder, is their conception of 'honour'?" he thought.

La Horie arranged an advanced CP beneath the arches of the Théatre Française whose young actresses set up a First Aid post using nurses' uniforms from the costume store.

"It's the best part they've ever played," quipped Branet, smiling indulgently as he mounted his Jeep.

"I would like to be just lightly wounded," said Lieutenant Franjoux, "enough to come and get one of your autographs."[222]

THE BRASS-HELMETED FIREMEN rehanging the *Tricolore* above the *Soldat Inconnu* had escaped German gunfire.[223] But when 2/RMT's 5th Company reached the Étoile a MG42 opened up from a pillbox on the Rue de Presbourg. The 12e RCA's Sherman, *Bourgogne*, promptly turned towards the pillbox followed by Lieutenant Gauffre's platoon. For a moment silence was absolute.

"It's like going to an execution, isn't it?" piped up *Tirailleur* Murcia, as the *Bourgogne*'s crew cranked down its 75mm gun. A high-explosive shell was fired straight into the pillbox's gun slit which shattered the plate window of an adjacent novelty shop, showering broken glass all over the street. The pillbox's occupants were undoubtedly dead.[224]

Once Sub-group Massu arrived in force on the Place de l'Étoile, at 2.30pm, Shermans and Tank-Destroyers sealed off every junction. Massu breathed a deep sigh of relief. Paul de Langlade arrived and, together with Commandant Mirambeau, they approached the Arc de Triomphe and introduced themselves to the firemen. Standing soberly to attention before the *Soldat Inconnu*'s bronze-plated covering, no sooner had they saluted than a shell fired from the Champs-Élysées, clearly aimed at the newly hung *Tricolore*, whistled over their heads. A second shot hit the Arc de Triomphe itself, damaging one of the four high relief sculptures which decorate its uprights—François Rude's *Le*

Départ des Volontaires de 1792. Stone fragments littered the pavement where the officers were standing.[225]

"*MOTEURS EN ROUTE*," shouted La Horie. Policemen blew whistles and Branet watched the crowd evaporate, leaving the Rue de Rivoli utterly empty and looking enormous.[226] At the opposite end, from her beloved Jeu de Paume, Rose Valland watched nervous Wehrmacht soldiers crouching behind sandbags in the museum courtyard.[227]

Franjoux's platoon began advancing, crossing the Rue de Rivoli and taking positions alongside the Finance Ministry, while Karcher's platoon threaded their way forward between the elegant arches outside the smartest shops in the world. Behind them followed Shermans *Mort-Homme*, *Villers-Cotterets* and *Douaumant* like enormous olive-green snails.[228]

Branet followed behind, walking alongside his idling Jeep holding a radio microphone. Ahead of them the road remained eerily empty. Behind them, once they passed, Parisians re-emerged from buildings, silent and fascinated. Franjoux eventually reached the Louvre's northwest corner on the Place des Pyramides with Emmanuel Frémiet's golden statue of Joan of Arc to his right and the Louvre's open courtyard on his left. In the Jardins des Tuileries, tank engines were audible. Franjoux continued to the Rue de Castiglione junction. Then the obvious happened. A German machine-gun opened up from a hotel balcony, knocking down four of Franjoux's men. Immediately Franjoux ordered the rest of his platoon under the shelter of the archways on the north side.

"If I had known that I was expected to play 'moving targets', I would have refused," Franjoux said afterwards.

Karcher's platoon threw grenades at windows and balconies where machine-guns had been identified, climbing up building facades to neutralise them.[229]

Branet decided to send his Shermans a few metres ahead of his infantry. The *Mort-Homme* took the lead, advancing towards the Hôtel Meurice where Germans were firing from windows and the roof.

Sergeant Bénard was standing in *Mort-Homme*'s turret with the hatch open when hand-grenades began showering down from the Meurice's roof. Most glanced off the armour before exploding harmlessly a few metres away, but one fell inside Bénard's hatch before exploding. Bénard and his gunners managed to escape, burnt and bleeding. The Meurice's defenders refrained from gunning them down as they walked away, leaving *Mort-Homme* smoking outside the Meurice.[230]

Villers-Cotterets pushed past *Mort-Homme* just as a Hotchkiss tank emerged from the Jardins des Tuileries. Seeing this pre-1940 French tank, painted with a black *Balkenkreuz*, *Villers-Cotterets*' gunner loaded an armour-piercing shell and knocked it out. Moments later *Villers-Cotterets*' commander, Sergeant Laigle, standing in his turret's open hatch, was killed by machine-gun fire from the Ministry of Marine.[231]

There was now fighting at both ends of the Champs Élysées. The Panther whose fire had disturbed Langlade, Massu and Mirambeau as they saluted the *Soldat Inconnu* was firing from the Obelisk* on the Place de la Concorde.

AFTER THE PANTHER'S SECOND SHELL smashed into the Arc de Triomphe's northeast upright, Massu called forward RBFM Tank-Destroyers, *Simoun* and *Sirocco*. From his Jeep, Naval Lieutenant Durville surveyed the Champs Élysées through binoculars. All along its length it appeared deserted, its occupants keeping back from windows, and the pavements free of *les badauds*. Durville directed *Simoun* to the Étoile's north side while *Sirocco* took up position beside him. German machine-gun bullets scythed the trees above them, bringing foliage down onto *Sirocco*'s open turret. Sensing the unfolding danger, the Panther switched its machine-gun fire to the north side, wrecking a street lantern near *Simoun*. The Panther's nervous crew now fired three

---

* Standing on an axis running due west from the centre of the Louvre, up to the Étoile and beyond, the rose granite Obelisk stands in memory of Francois Champolion, the first European to read hieroglyphs, and as a thumb to France's rivals in Egyptology, the British.

shells, each missing *Simoun* and arching towards the Bois de Boulogne. Second Mate Quiniou ordered *Simoun* and *Sirocco* slowly forward.[232]

Post-war enquiry confirms that only one Panther emerged from the Jardins des Tuileries, hence Robert Wallraf, watching from the Crillon, wrote accurately when he called it "the last tank in the defence of Paris". Sergeant Bizien's *Douaumont* was hurtling along the Rue de Rivoli past the *Mort-Homme*, obscured from the Panther's view by the Jardins des Tuileries' sumptuous greenery and the Jeu de Paume, while simultaneously, from the Arc de Triomphe, Lieutenant Durville ordered his Tank-Destroyers to engage the Panther. Quiniou ordered his gunner Robert Mady to load an armour-piercing shell and set the gunsight for fifteen hundred metres. But Mady, being a Parisian, knew from boyhood that the Champs Élysées was eighteen hundred metres long and set the sight to the correct distance.

Wallraf's testimony suggests that the shot which disabled the Panther came from Bizien's *Douaumont* as it approached from the Rue de Rivoli. But during these hectic seconds Bizien decided that *Douaumont*'s best chance at such close range was to ram the Panther. Whether it was *Simoun*'s shot, or a shell fired by the 12e RCA's Lieutenant Nouveau, whose Sherman *Champagne* arrived on the Champs Élysées at the Rond Point, remains a small historical mystery; both tanks carried the 76mm gun capable of disabling a Panther.[233]

Either way, the Panther's crew debouched and escaped into the Jardins des Tuileries, just as Sergeant Bizien was dismounting from the *Douaumont* to take them prisoner. The sight of Bizien, triumphant in that city's greatest square, would have drawn any sniper's eye. During the morning a *Parisienne* had died taking bullets meant for him; this time they found their mark. Marcel Bizien was a *Gaulliste de la première heure* and an original member of the squadron Branet forged in England.[234]

With Bizien down and *Douaumont* slammed into the Panther by the Obelisk, Lieutenant Bricard's troop of Shermans reached the Place de la Concorde from the *rive droite*, immediately raking the Crillon's frontage with machine-gun fire and sending its occupants, Robert

Wallraf included, scurrying for cover. When a young SS soldier fired a *Panzerfaust* through a broken window, hitting one of Bricard's Shermans, another Sherman fired back, destroying the Crillon's fifth column.[235]

The attack on von Choltitz's lair was becoming costly. But Franjoux and Karcher's platoons had reached the Meurice's front entrance with Branet close behind. Looking up at that world-class hotel, Branet was on the verge of triumph. Then a grenade fell from above injuring two Chad infantrymen, soon followed by another which exploded near Branet. His ears singing, he stumbled through the Rivoli arches and collapsed under the covered way, oozing blood from shrapnel injuries down his back and side.[236]

While Branet's driver organised his evacuation, Lieutenants Franjoux and Karcher took over.

"Not so clever are you, captain?" Franjoux quipped cheekily as Branet was lifted onto a stretcher.

Followed by their men, the two lieutenants rushed the Meurice's front door, firing anywhere a German hesitated to raise his hands. An official portrait of Hitler, hosed by machine-gun fire, clattered to the floor.

"Where is the general?" Karcher demanded.

"He is upstairs," replied a German officer raising his hands.

Von Choltitz later wrote, "Combat was raging, the enemy army mounted its assault on my Headquarters. ... Colonel Jay told me the situation in an urgent manner. After a short discussion with my chief of staff, Colonel von Unger, I agreed to end the combat. Colonel Jay asked his orderly to find an enemy officer."[237]

Von Choltitz was unimpressed by American uniform combined with French insignia, and described Karcher as "a haggard and excited looking *civilian*"; he frequently criticises those lacking "self-possession" in his memoirs. Behind von Choltitz stood Colonels Unger and Jay and Dr. Eckelmann."The *civil* pointed his weapon at me and asked after several attempts, '*Sprechen deutsch?*'"

"Undoubtedly better than you!" von Choltitz replied.[238]

Von Choltitz then describes Commandant La Horie's arrival, wearing a képi.

"*Mon general*, are you ready to cease combat?" asked La Horie in French.

"Yes, I am ready," von Choltitz replied.

La Horie told von Choltitz to follow him out of the Meurice via a service staircase. "We arrived at my car which was parked not far away, but the key had been left behind. We continued on foot."[239]

French accounts describe a more contemptuous exchange: "You refused the ultimatum which was sent to you this morning," began La Horie. "You fought and now you're beaten. There are pockets of resistance still holding out. I require that you give orders to all officers commanding these centres of resistance to cease fire."

"Yes," replied von Choltitz. "But I would wish my men to be treated as soldiers."

"Follow me," La Horie ordered.

At around 3pm La Horie led von Choltitz towards the staircase accessing the Rue du Mont-Thabor, a narrow back street servicing business premises along the Rue de Rivoli's west end, where a Jeep waited, surrounded by a growing crowd. Meanwhile von Choltitz's staff were gathered up by Karcher's and Franjoux's men.[240]

Under La Horie's supervision von Choltitz was relatively safe, although someone deprived him of his valise which was wrenched open. He last saw his spare pair of general's breeches, with their distinctive scarlet *lampassen* down the outside seams, being waved enthusiastically by a Paris crone. As von Choltitz's staff were led out of the Meurice's front entrance, Lieutenant von Arnim recognised immediately that Nazi atrocities could make them a target of vengeance. Moments later a rabid Frenchman stepped forward from the crowd and shot one of Arnim's comrades dead.[241]

Anticipating problems, Billotte arrived behind the Hôtel Meurice with his White Scout Car, which was more suitable for transporting a high-profile prisoner. Despite the protective arm of a uniformed nurse, von Choltitz seemed relieved to be transferred to the larger vehicle.[242]

Billotte was fascinated by von Choltitz: "He was a large man, around fifty years old, with as sportive and soldierly a demeanour as one could have; although obviously suffering from the heat. ... So this was the devil who had fought so vigourously in Normandy. Awkwardly he seated himself in one of the two seats in my Scout Car, facing the small map table, then, very politely, he asked if we could take his chief of staff with us. I agreed, though remarking that his colonel would have to sit on the floor under the table, which was the only place available and probably uncomfortable. Both accepted gratefully. It was in this chaotic fashion that we departed for the Préfecture, with von Choltitz's feet and my own resting on the torso of his unhappy chief of staff."

"I quite understand," Billotte said to von Choltitz, "the reasons why you would have refused my ultimatum. I suppose that you were threatened by the SS. I imagine equally, from what I've heard, that your family in Baden-Baden is in a hostage situation and that they would be treated savagely by Hitler if you had not given combat. That said, I quite understand that you could only carry out a *baroud d'honneur*. On the other hand, and without yet knowing the number, I know I've lost too many of my men. We are therefore placed in the situation envisaged in the second part of my ultimatum, continuing combat until the total destruction of your forces. What can you propose to me to prevent my pursuing this course?"[243]

"*Monsieur le Général*," began von Choltitz, red-faced and breathing deeply, "what you say to me is not fair. I have done a lot for Paris. If you knew the orders I had from the Führer ..."

"Right," replied Billotte brusquely. "Well, if you think you've done so much for Paris, you had best continue in that role and complete your good work by accepting the surrender conditions which will be imposed upon you and by *collaborating*—it is now your turn—with our officers in seeing that the remaining centres of resistance cease fire immediately. Those are the terms for avoiding further destruction and human losses for which, ultimately, you will be held responsible."

Von Choltitz sat silently, his eyes betraying his discomfiture.

"Do you have any news," continued Billotte, "of the two divisions that were being sent to you from the north?"

Von Choltitz remained silent.

"Choltitz had *de la tradition*," Billotte wrote.[244]

REDUCED TO A CRAWL BY THE CROWD, Billotte's Scout Car took its time reaching the Préfecture. Waiting with Leclerc was US General Raymond Barton, whose 4th Infantry Division was ranging freely over east central Paris, receiving the same rapturous welcome as the 2e DB. "You should be alone here in Paris," Barton told Leclerc.[245]

Following a slow drive along the Rue de Rivoli during which von Choltitz saw his soldiers being disarmed and gathered into rows of prisoners, Billotte's Scout Car crossed onto the Ile de la Cité and pulled into the Préfecture's truck-choked courtyard. Billotte led his prisoner up the grand staircase to the billiard room where Leclerc waited impatiently.

"*Le voila*," said Billotte, presenting von Choltitz.

Choltitz later wrote, "I found myself in a *salle* in front of a large number of officers." Entering the billiard room with Billotte, von Choltitz would have looked across the table's green baize to a large ornate window looking over the Boulevard du Palais. Standing between the chimney piece and the window were Guillebon, Girard and Lieutenant de Dampierre. Leclerc stood at the room's north end behind a bureau table with Captain Betz to act as interpreter. As the meeting began Henri Rol-Tanguy and Maurice Kriegel-Valrimont, believing they should be included, opened the door.

"*Pas de civils ici!*" shouted Leclerc.[246]

Kriegel-Valrimont pointed out his FFI armband.

"Some of them are members of the liberation committee," remarked Girard. "They insist on being present."

Chaban-Delmas and Luizet nodded their agreement.

"All right," said Leclerc. "Let them stay."[247]

Billotte wrote, "The surrender ceremony began; Choltitz comported himself with dignity, Leclerc with grandeur."

Von Choltitz wrote, "A general came towards me and said with all the courtesy of a true soldier, '*Sind Sie General von Choltitz? Ich bin General Leclerc.*'" Then apparently Leclerc asked, "Why have you opposed *un fin* and not replied to my letter?" referring to Billotte's proposal sent via Nordling and Bender during the morning. Von Choltitz does not report his reply.[248] Other versions say that von Choltitz offered Leclerc his hand but that this was refused.

Leclerc bade von Choltitz sit before confronting him with the freshly typed surrender document.

"*Lisez!*" Leclerc ordered Captain Betz.

Betz read the document aloud, first in French, then in German.

At this point, French versions describe von Choltitz becoming visibly uncomfortable, with laboured breathing. But his memoirs say, "We followed the paragraphs one after the other. Such a document was not, in my view, necessary. It was not as though there would be a capitulation before the end of combat; my headquarters had been taken by the enemy and I was a prisoner along with my staff. This verbiage changed nothing, nor the real situation in so far as it affected myself and my aides. On the other hand the document did address those strongpoints still holding out."[249]

Through Captain Betz, von Choltitz explained that, while he could order troops under his command to surrender, there were others either outside his command or who were uncontactable. Recognising these practical difficulties, Leclerc explained that his Gare Montparnasse CP was better equipped for communicating the surrender to all interested parties. Von Choltitz signed the surrender document.[250]

EVEN AS VON CHOLTITZ SIGNED, his garrison continued fighting in the roads around the Étoile. GT Langlade's tanks and infantry left a trail of *feldgrau*-clad corpses and burning vehicles on elegant avenues. As 2/RMT's 5th Company infiltrated deserted streets, reports arrived that the Germans in the Hôtel Majestic would continue fighting and that its Rue la Pérouse entrance was protected by a concrete pillbox.[251]

But from the ground floor, Lieutenant Holz heard that the Majestic's defenders might surrender to someone of significant rank. Almost simultaneously Massu was approached by a German carrying a white flag from Rue la Pérouse. After reporting to Langlade's CP—a former car showroom on the Avenue de la Grande Armée—Massu decided to approach the Majestic personally. Yet, and proving how disjointed the German command chain had become, as Massu approached the Majestic accompanied by *Sergent-Chef* Dannic, a sniper on the Majestic's roof shot Dannic in the chest, killing him instantly. Demonstrating considerable cool, Massu continued, entering the Majestic from Rue la Pérouse, soon finding himself facing armed Germans in the east foyer. "*Heraus!*" Massu yelled.

At first Massu faced some protests.

"*Heraus! Schnell!*" he insisted.

His confidence prevailed, and soon three hundred soldiers along with two colonels and fifty officers were herded towards the Étoile and handed over to Commandant Mirambeau to feed into the Allied POW system.[252]

Next, Lieutenant Sorret reported that 24 Avenue Kléber, premises of an insurance company called L'Abeile, was a nest of Waffen SS. Anxious to regroup his men around the Étoile, Massu sent Lieutenant Berne's platoon to parley with them. Preceded by a white flag, Berne entered L'Abeile's main hallway, quickly finding a Schmeisser's barrel pressed to his chest.

"I am a regular army officer," said Berne. "I would like to speak to your *chef.*"

An SS major approached.

"All resistance is futile," said Berne. "In any case, you have one minute to surrender. Don't waste time. I am giving you one minute. After that, I will attack."

For a moment the SS men appeared truculent. Then their commander surrendered his pistol, followed by several others. His arms full of guns, Berne led a hundred and fifty Waffen SS out of 24 Avenue Kléber.

"You look like a Mexican pistolero," joked Sorret.

"I would like to have seen how you handled these *guignols* all armed to the teeth," replied Berne.[253]

Within minutes of knowing that the German strongholds around the Étoile had surrendered, the 16th Arrondissement's inhabitants invaded the streets in a human wave. As disarmed Germans were gathered near the Arc de Triomphe, Parisians yelled abuse, and one woman even attempted to gouge out a German officer's eyes with a knitting needle until Mirambeau's men stopped her. Prisoners belched with fear while Parisians shrieked filth at them and FFIs shot at shadows on rooftops. Small wonder that one German prisoner, unbalanced by apprehension, pulled out a hidden phosphorous grenade and threw it at Mirambeau's guards. Corporal Néri caught most of the flash, his uniform burning brightly until his comrades smothered the flames; one of his arms was subsequently amputated. Commandant Mirambeau was also wounded.[254]

IN MID-AFTERNOON, AFTER ROBERT MADY, Lieutenant Nouveau and Sergeant Marcel Bizien put France back in control of the Champs Élysées, David Bruce's party parked their Jeeps on Avenue Foch and approached the Arc de Triomphe where six Great War veterans, one of whom was wheelchair bound, stood vigil around the *Soldat Inconnu*. Their officer permitted Bruce and Co. to visit the Arc's roof where Bruce met the same firemen who had greeted Langlade earlier, all standing to attention. One of them gave Bruce his medal and saluted. After this surprising little ceremony Bruce savoured the view of a city he loved as much as any in America, and to which he would return as his country's ambassador.[255]

Returning to their Jeeps they saw liberation's grim reality: seven dead Germans lying in a heap. A gunfight between Langlade's infantry and German personnel still inside the Gestapo building forced them to shelter behind a French tank, where an elegant Parisian invited them for champagne *chez lui*. This was Robert Lalou, who lived with his beautiful wife in a sumptuously decorated apartment nearby. To the music of gunfire they drank three bottles of champagne, while outside a retired French officer offered champagne to Hemingway's irregulars. "We dallied there for a while and decided to push on," wrote Bruce.[256]

Did Hemingway personally liberate the Travellers' Club? "What actually happened," wrote the author's biographer, Carlos Baker, "was that Hemingway, Bruce and Pelkey, finding the Champs Élysées completely bare of traffic, drove at breakneck speed down the broad avenue and pulled up at the Club door. All the rooms were closed except the bar, where the Club president, an elderly Frenchman, was stationed with a number of the Old Guard. Since the Americans were the first outsiders to reach the Club, a testimonial bottle of champagne was quickly opened and toasts offered. As they drank, a sniper began to fire from an adjoining roof. Pelkey shouldered his rifle and made for the roof, but was balked in his attempt to deal with the sniper."[257]

Bruce and Hemingway did not stay long at the Travellers' Club and separated after briefly visiting the Café de la Paix. Among Hemingway's first calls was Picasso's home on the Rue des Grands Augustins. Picasso was still protecting Marie-Thérèse Walter and their daughter Maya on the Ile Saint-Louis, so Hemingway was greeted by the concierge who, according to Françoise Gilot, was timid but not bashful, with an eye to the main chance. Since Picasso often shared his food with her, she asked Hemingway if he could leave a gift. Hemingway collected a wooden case of hand-grenades from his Jeep and plonked them down in her *loge* with a note saying "To Picasso from Hemingway!" When the concierge discovered what the box contained she fled the building, refusing to return until Papa's gift was removed.[258]

In her Rue de l'Odéon lodgings, Sylvia Beach, the American former owner of the bookshop Shakespeare and Company, was relieved when "a string of Jeeps came up the street". Then she heard "a deep voice calling 'Sylvia!' Everyone in the street took up the cry 'Sylvia!' 'It's Hemingway!' cried Adrienne. I flew downstairs. We met with a crash. He picked me up and swung me around and kissed me while people on the street and in the windows cheered."[259]

Beach took Hemingway upstairs and gave him her last piece of soap to wash with. "He wanted to know if there was anything he could do for us. We asked him if he could do something about the Nazi snipers on the rooftops in our street, particularly on Adrienne's rooftop. He got his company out of the Jeeps and took them up to the roof. We heard firing for the last time in the Rue de l'Odéon. Hemingway and his men came down again and rode off in their Jeeps—'to liberate the cellar at the Ritz'."²⁶⁰

Hemingway breezed through the Ritz's Rue Cambon entrance, his gun flapping against his thigh, shouting "*Raus*" at various British people already there. Papa reportedly liberated the cellars and checked the roof for snipers, shooting down a clothesline. "It was breathtaking to see him behave as if the hotel was his home," said Lucienne Elmiger. "He had presence," she continued. "But no chic."²⁶¹

LECLERC LED VON CHOLTITZ FROM THE PRÉFECTURE, pausing briefly to congratulate Raymond Dronne for the previous evening. Billotte then told Dronne to organise security at the Hôtel de Ville for the important visitor due shortly.²⁶²

Von Choltitz mounted Leclerc's Scout Car followed by Chaban-Delmas, Rol-Tanguy, Kriegel-Valrimont, Girard and Leclerc. Outside the Préfecture and around the Pont Notre Dame, crowds were gathering, determined to yell at von Choltitz. But, elegantly waving his cane, Leclerc emphasised that his prisoner was subject to the rules of war. In the rear of the Scout Car, Henri Rol-Tanguy pondered the Insurrection's extraordinary outcome as they drove through the screaming crowd. Gunfire from rooftops continued, though its targets were hard to guess.²⁶³

At the Gare Montparnasse, von Choltitz seemed to deteriorate. Stumbling out of the Scout Car, he wrapped his arm around the gun-rail and swung himself lumberingly to the ground, inadvertently catching his backside on Maurice Kriegel-Valrimont's boot.²⁶⁴ The Préfecture proceedings struck Kriegel-Valrimont as lacking an important element: Rol-Tanguy's signature on the surrender document. Valrimont raised this issue with Chaban-Delmas, who supported the idea.

"So long as everyone is happy," said Leclerc, who had also registered von Choltitz's discomfiture. Turning to Commandant Weil, Leclerc said, "You speak German. Take him for a walk."

Ambling along the platform under the Gare Montparnasse's enormous skylights, von Choltitz gaspingly asked Weil for water to wash down a pill. Weil worried that von Choltitz intended suicide, but it was merely a hypertension remedy. After swallowing the pill and gulping back the water, von Choltitz turned to Weil: "If I might give you some advice," he said. "When you get into Germany and meet up with the Russians, don't stop, march on to Moscow."[265]

After rewording the surrender document to satisfy FFI sensibilities—Leclerc was more interested in post-war French unity than fussing over such details—Rol-Tanguy signed above Leclerc.[266] During this second signing, von Choltitz heaved with pain and humiliation. Also to be signed were surrender orders to be taken by French and German officers to those German strongpoints still holding out. Before the 2e DB finished with Dietrich von Choltitz, Leclerc's chief engineer asked whether Wehrmacht sappers had mined the city's bridges. Von Choltitz assured him they had not, a fact confirmed by public works officials who checked the bridges twice every twenty-four hours.[267] While most might regard this as further evidence of von Choltitz's restraint, Maurice Kriegel-Valrimont later argued that, since von Choltitz lacked the means to destroy bridges and monuments, Paris owed him nothing.[268] But, seeing von Choltitz in the flesh, Raymond Massiet asked why, even with the modest means at his disposal, he did *so little* to suppress the Insurrection.

"I couldn't destroy Paris, whatever Hitler's orders," said von Choltitz, his voice cracking. "*Your reprisals* would have been too horrible."[269]

When, at Alain de Boissieu's request, the intelligence officer Cossé-Brissac asked von Choltitz whether Leclerc's threatening letter drafted by Captain Betz the previous day reached him and if it had any effect, von Choltitz replied, "And how!"[270]

Room 32 already contained prisoners from the Meurice. They stood smartly when von Choltitz entered, then offered him a centrally positioned chair. Lastly von Choltitz mentioned losing his valise outside the Meurice. Betz sent Lieutenant Braun, another Alsatian officer, to take details. The Gare Montparnasse was now awash with photographers, one of whom snapped Lieutenant Braun taking down von Choltitz's plea for his valise; a photograph believed, for many years, to depict the surrender itself.[271]

Chapter 8

The Man of 18 June Arrives

25 August 1944 (continued)

AT RAMBOUILLET, CHARLES DE GAULLE SPENT the early part of that day of days pacing the château's great terrace. As hourly bulletins of Leclerc's progress arrived, the Constable reflected that, while only a colonel, he lobbied France's patrons for seven modern armoured divisions. It took the Americans, persuaded partly by General Giraud, to provide three. Now one of those divisions had liberated France's capital.[1]

For his triumphal entry into Paris, Commandant de Lignières acquired a smart black Hotchkiss chauffeured by a Rambouillet fireman and escorted by two M8 armoured cars. The rest of de Gaulle's entourage would travel in two requisitioned *gazogene*-fuelled buses, hurriedly sprayed light green and decorated with the Cross of Lorraine.[2] Mounting the Hotchkiss, de Gaulle felt "gripped by emotion and filled with serenity". Dressed in his dark blue French air force uniform and improbably crushed cap, Claude Guy took the front seat beside the Rambouillet fireman.[3]

Driving from Rambouillet into central Paris normally takes under an hour. Even compared to Rennes, de Gaulle was amazed by the cheering crowds and fluttering *Tricolores*. At Longjumeau the numbers multiplied. At Bourg-la-Reine they doubled again. Then came the "exulting tide" at the Porte d'Orléans.[4]

Philippe de Gaulle had been ordered to the Gare Montparnasse to meet his father. After witnessing von Choltitz's surrender, Philippe was one of those chosen to deliver surrender orders to the remaining German strongpoints. By 4.30pm, either in Jeeps, M8 armoured cars, or Stuart light tanks, these teams were ready to leave. Getting through the crowds would be difficult, especially if accompanied by a German officer. Some of these '*homologues allemands*' even suffered abuse from the 2e DB before leaving the Gare Montparnasse; one German officer was clonked on the head with a helmet as he mounted a Jeep, an act caught on film. But French officers usually behaved correctly.[5] Philippe's *homologue allemand* was a despondent major whose health had been broken on the Eastern Front. But, before setting off to parley with the Waffen SS holding the Chamber of Deputies, Philippe was permitted to await his father.[6]

A cacophony of cheering accompanied de Gaulle's entry inside the Gare Montparnasse where Leclerc recounted the afternoon's events. Introduced to Henri Rol-Tanguy, de Gaulle looked over the young Resistance colonel appreciatively, recognising that such men had saved France's honour. Moving on to Chaban-Delmas, whom he had met briefly, de Gaulle muttered, "Well I'll be damned!" before shaking hands. "*C'est bien, Chaban.*"[7] Then de Gaulle saw his son. Claude Guy had just told Philippe how anxious his father was to see him.

"Come with us," the Constable said.

"*Mon Général,*" said Leclerc. "*Enseigne de vaisseau* de Gaulle has a mission which he must go and fulfil."

The Constable's expression changed to disappointment, "even disarray". "Without a word he embraced me, something he didn't usually do," wrote Philippe. "He was probably aware of the new danger that I had to confront and worried perhaps whether I would return."[8]

After Philippe's departure the Constable inspected the second surrender document signed before his arrival. "You allowed Rol-Tanguy to sign!" he exclaimed to Leclerc. "Why do you think that I nominated you interim governor of Paris back in Algiers, if it wasn't to take command of all forces in Paris until the arrival of General Koenig?"

"But Chaban agreed," replied Leclerc.

"Even so it is not correct," ruled the Constable. "In this matter you are the higher ranking officer and consequently solely responsible. Anyway, the plea that led you to accept this wording comes from those with unacceptable views."[9]

But de Gaulle recognised that Leclerc acted in good faith.

"You have done well," said de Gaulle. "I will nominate Rol-Tanguy a *Companion of the Liberation*." Nevertheless he showed Leclerc a proclamation published that morning by the CNR which he believed demonstrated his point.[10]

De Gaulle's next stop was the Ministry of War on the Rue Saint-Dominique. As they turned into Rue Eblé, a burst of machine-gun fire came from the tower of Saint Francis Xavier. De Gaulle stood in the road defiantly smoking a cigarette, while General Juin dismounted the Hotchkiss bearing a submachine-gun to protect his former *petit-co*. After a short detour, at around 5pm de Gaulle re-entered the building he had left as a junior minister in 1940.[11]

"Immediately I was seized by the impression that nothing had changed inside these venerated offices," he wrote. "Gigantic events had upturned the Universe. Our army had been destroyed. France had been darkened. But at the old Ministry of War, the *aspect* of things remained immutable. In the courtyard a troop from the *Garde Republicaine* did the honours, as before. The vestibule, the stairs, the decoration; all remained as they were. There, in person, were the staff who formerly ran the place. I entered the minister's office which Paul Reynaud and I left together on the night of 10 June 1940. Not a stick of furniture, not a carpet, not a curtain had been moved. On the table remained the telephone exactly where I had left it, with exactly the same names written by the buttons. Then I realised that there were other buildings particular to the Republic. All that was missing was the state. It fell to me to reinstate it."[12]

Le Troquer and Parodi came to find him; public order and food provision required his attention. The exhausted Parodi insisted that de Gaulle visit both the Préfecture and the Hôtel de Ville. "We'll go tomorrow," de Gaulle replied, arguing that as national leader there was no need to present himself to a municipal authority. But Parodi knew this would not do and called Charles Luizet across from the Préfecture. Then Pierre Billotte arrived in person to report mission accomplished. No sooner had Billotte finished speaking than a large explosion came from the direction of the Palais Luxembourg.

"And you tell me it's over," mocked de Gaulle. "Go fast! There's still a racket that needs sorting out."

Billotte turned on his heel.

"Go," said de Gaulle. "And should you feel daring enough to make an appearance at the Hôtel de Ville, there will be [the sort of] music which might cheer you up."

Luizet told France's new leader that the police were mounting a parade for him and that enormous crowds gathering outside the Hôtel de Ville would be disappointed if he did not come.

"Then if one must go, we'd better go," said de Gaulle.[13]

At the Préfecture a smart parade of *Gardiens de la Paix* belied its hasty preparation. Their band played the *Marseillaise* and the *Marche Lorraine*. Whatever evils the Paris police collaborated with during the Occupation, the Insurrection saved their honour. Nearly eight hundred of them fought like lions for seven days; many were killed, some murdered. When de Gaulle thanked them they cheered him loudly. Their role is commemmorated by the red lanyards they still wear. Before leaving the Préfecture, de Gaulle and other senior *résistants* decided upon the great march down the Champs Élysées for the following day; something France needed. More good news reached de Gaulle from General Koenig: in order to regularise the Allies' relationship with France's administration, General Eisenhower had recognised him as *de facto* French head of state.[14]

AT THE JEU DE PAUME, Rose Valland knew the Occupation was over when she saw German soldiers shot dead as Chad infantry took possession of the Place de la Concorde. A museum porter seen on the roof was suspected of being a German sniper until Rose volubly intervened. Immediately after being liberated, the Jeu de Paume was used to store surrendered weapons and German helmets.[15]

It was only when a negotiating party arrived bearing von Choltitz's surrender order that Germans inside the Hôtel Crillon gathered on the ground floor. "So the road into captivity was beginning," wrote Robert Wallraf. "Outside the Hôtel entrance stood two soldiers from Leclerc's division. They took each man's pistol and threw it in a basket. With my left hand I gave one of them my pistol."

"And your watch, and your ring," said a French soldier, pointing to Wallraf's bracelet watch and signet ring. "Damn!" he thought, regretting not putting them in his pockets.

"Can't I keep the ring?" asked Wallraf. "It came from my father."

"Do you value your skin?" replied the French soldier.

Wallraf surrendered them before being led past crowds of angry Parisians.

"Murderers! Thieves! *Sales Boches*! Hitler *kaput*!" they screamed.

Then a Parisian called out, "These bandits don't need their baggage! Take it all away!"

"*Sans baggages!*"—"Without baggage!" went up the cry.

Wallraf's carefully packed rucksack was wrenched away. Along with others, he was pushed onto a lorry. Crowded together under the dark canvas canopy, they became unbearably hot. More prisoners were pushed aboard, one having his arm broken as the tail flap was bolted. Wallraf and his comrades were relieved when the canopy's tail curtain was pulled down and the truck departed.[16]

DRIVING WITH HIS *HOMOLOGUE ALLEMAND* along the liberated Rue de Rivoli, Philippe de Gaulle was pleased to see Chad infantry controlling the Hôtel Meurice, but uncollected corpses, French and German, testified to the cost. It seemed perverse seeing central Paris decorated with war debris yet surprisingly undamaged. Past the Place de la Concorde, 2e DB vehicles were parking garrison-style, guarded by patrolling Shermans. The commander of *Uskub* agreed to escort Philippe to the Chamber of Deputies and a few FFI volunteered their support. Unfortunately an untrained FFI fired some shots towards the Seine, provoking a needless firefight, which took Philippe fifteen minutes to control.[17]

Around the Tuileries Philippe met Lieutenant Étienne Mantoux, Captain Robert Caillet's co-pilot, who had dropped Leclerc's message to the Préfecture the previous day. Having performed a similar mission, Mantoux advised Philippe that the Palais Bourbon's defenders should see his German major waving the white flag in the first instance, especially since the rising camber of the Pont de la Concorde meant they would be approaching as though over a horizon. So Philippe's unhappy prisoner had to sit on *Uskub*'s turret with his Wehrmacht tunic and cap fully visible while he waved a white flag. Faced with this extraordinary sight lumbering towards them against the backdrop of the Obelisk and the Crillon, the Palais Bourbon's SS defenders held their fire, allowing *Uskub* to approach the railings and chain barriers. While his pale German major sweated, Philippe grappled with the barriers. "The SS won't obey the Wehrmacht," said the German major in halting French. "They will kill me, and you as well." Keeping his cool, Philippe ordered Le Coz, his Jeep driver, to push the barrier enough for him to squeeze through. Recognising that his German major was frightened to the point of uselessness, Philippe called to Le Coz, "If you don't see me come back out within a quarter of an hour, give the alarm," and advanced alone towards the Palais Bourbon's imposing frontage. Nearby, several FFI corpses underlined the danger of his mission.[18]

Entering through the great front door, Philippe met a tall, fair SS officer who said in slowly enunciated English, "We very much prefer to surrender to the Americans. We will fire at any civilians who approach. We only wish to negotiate with regular forces and will have nothing to do with partisans or terrorists."

Philippe understood perfectly but, as his father would have done, he replied in French.

"There are no Americans in [this part of] Paris," said Philippe, unaware of Hemingway boozing in the Ritz, a few blocks away. "You will surrender to French troops commanded by General Leclerc. Here is the surrender order from your General von Choltitz."

Noticing the SS officer eyeing his naval ensign's cap and the red pom-pommed *bachi* worn by Le Coz, Philippe wondered whether the garrison would accept his *bona fides*. All around France's beautiful parliament building, Philippe saw the Waffen SS's defensive measures; sandbags piled around windows, racks of stick grenades and *Panzerfausts* readily to hand. He had never been inside before, not even on a school outing during the 1930s. Led into an immense *salon* overlooking the Quai d'Orsay gardens, Philippe faced several SS officers eyeing him cautiously from behind a large, ornate table which was being ruined by German kit. The miserable Wehrmacht major mumbled indecipherably before going to stand alongside them. Philippe laid the surrender order before them.

"Here is the order of your general," Philippe said in slow, deliberate French. "You must surrender to General Leclerc's *Deuxième Division Blindée* of which I am the emissary."

The SS officers exchanged worried glances.

"We will consider this and decide what to do," said their senior officer.

"Leave your weapons," said Philippe. "Gather up your personal belongings and assemble at the foot of the steps of the entrance on the Rue de l'Université, officers and men separately."

"Who will collect us?" asked the large young SS officer. "We only want military lorries."

Philippe assured them that they would not be harmed. Lieutenant Mantoux arrived with FFI to take all four hundred into custody. As soon as the Palais Bourbon returned to French control its Rue de Lille gates were opened enabling a fire engine to reach a burning Sherman, brewed up by FFIs mishandling captured weapons. Securing abandoned weapons became a priority.[19]

THE DEPOT WAS FULL, and few cells remained to accommodate new arrivals. Deciding to move prominent *collabos* to the Manège

Huyghens assembly hall, the FFI posted a list in the exercise yard. Pierre Taittinger and his associates were dismayed to find their names on it, but that was a mistake. Following Rol-Tanguy's directive to avoid using heritage buildings for FFI purposes, prominent *collabos* were being assembled at the Vélodrome d'Hiver, the winter cycling track made infamous by the *grande rafle* and *collabo* rallies. "Our names were read out by an armed FFI walking past the cells," wrote Taittinger. "We hastily swallowed a little hot water, baptised 'soup', and awaited a *panier de salade* [basket of salad, French slang for a police van]. ... We were then confined in these tiny, stiflingly hot sheet metal cages in which one could neither stand nor sit, and to reach them we were making our first walk since being imprisoned."[20]

Following a twenty-minute drive, with shrieking crowds banging on the van's sides, "Eventually we arrived in front of the Vélodrome d'Hiver, where everything had been prepared to give us a welcome which would remain in the memory as a symbol, to the shame of those who devised it, of these *revolutionary* days," continued Taittinger. They waited in the van for around ten minutes as their guards added their own voices to the insults.

"You are about to see a band of *collaborateurs*, of men who sold out to the *Boches*, of traitors," an FFI told the baying crowd.

Like a tumbril beside the guillotine, the police van discharged its prisoners singly while a senior *résistant* named and maligned each prisoner. "I present the dirty *collaborateur* Sacha Guitry," he said as the great *boulevardier* stumbled from the van (the guards refused to fold down the van's metal steps), struggling to keep his balance. Someone raised a foot to trip him, but Guitry sidestepped. Receiving truncheon blows to his neck and kidneys, Guitry recoiled but, turning round, he saw former Vichy education minister Jérôme Carcapino, beaten to a bloody mess. Seeing Carcapino tottering dizzily, Guitry caught him as he collapsed.[21]

Next came the former Prefect of the Department of the Seine, René Bouffet. Once out of the van, Bouffet was so badly beaten that he died a few days later. With Bouffet lying severely injured, it was the turn of Taittinger's friend Romazzotti, who was also beaten up but not fatally. When his turn came, being a former rugby player, Taittinger wrapped his arms around his head, bent down and ran the gauntlet, suffering a few bruises.

Taittinger complained vigorously to an official. This turned out to be the Vélodrome d'Hiver's concièrge who had previously organised rallies for both Doriot and Déat. Recognising him, several imprisoned *collabos* called out "*Vive le Maréchal*", only to receive more beatings from this wretched man, desperately dissociating himself from Vichy.[22] By evening Taittinger and Judge Dinthilac were organising first aid and food for those who chose *le mauvais camp*—the wrong camp.

ALAIN DE BOISSIEU'S SQUADRON had taken the La Tour-Maubourg barracks near Les Invalides. When its German garrison refused to surrender, Boissieu's men fired machine-gun bursts at the windows. White flags appeared and Boissieu watched fascinated as fanatical Germans were pushed into the courtyard at gunpoint by wiser comrades. André Gribius transfered the divisional HQ from the Gare Montparnasse to La Tour-Mauborg.[23]

Returning from the Palais Bourbon via the Place de la Concorde, Philippe de Gaulle noticed people gathered around the "liberated" Navy Ministry. Inside, a French Navy cover-up operation was under way. Various officers were searching filing cabinets and throwing papers down into the courtyard where an incinerator burnt vigorously. "We're destroying papers which could compromise those of our comrades who merely obeyed orders," said a naval officer. Philippe was told to mind his own business. Admiral Darlan's intrigues would embarrass France for decades to come.[24]

Returning to the Gare Montparnasse, Philippe found little left of the 2e DB's presence that day but a First Aid post staffed by white-clad nurses. Setting out to find his unit, he was astonished to see a *petit voyou* (little thug) holding a dozen Germans at gunpoint while rifling through their personal effects. Philippe drew his 45 automatic on the youngster, forcing him to drop both his pistol and his swag.

He ran away yelling obscenities in a low Parisian brogue. Shortly after rejoining his troop Philippe was approached by a terrified girl who recognised him from schooldays and needed help rescuing her brother, another Stanislas alumnus. With a few sailors for back-up, Philippe visited her apartment where her brother sat collapsed on a chair, surrounded by thugs in remnants of *franciste* uniform, attempting to cover their *collabo* tracks by purporting to "arrest" an introverted youth. After securing the apartment's keys, Philippe sent the *francistes* packing but advised the vulnerable youth to *prendre le large*—get out more.[25]

OF THOSE TAKING THE SURRENDER of German strongpoints, Colonel Jean Crépin's task was among the hardest, at the Palais du Luxembourg where Panzers manned by SS remained in the gardens. During the morning they destroyed a Sherman from Captain Witasse's 2e Compagnie 501e RCC and inflicted losses on both 3/RMT and Colonel Fabien's FFIs. Sub-group Putz had the Luxembourg surrounded, but hopes of evicting the SS without destruction seemed slim. Crépin approached from the Rue de Vaugirard brandishing a white flag.[26]

Once Putz's men ceased firing, Crépin and his *homologue allemand* entered the Senate courtyard, quickly finding several guns trained on them. Crépin's German received several slurs about 20 July. They were led to the office of a Standartenführer, a full colonel, who perused von Choltitz's surrender order in stony silence for several minutes.

"This order seems genuine," he said. "We will lay down our weapons at 1830hrs."

But his men continued shooting to the very last moment. Many were in tears; one shot himself. The rest assembled smartly behind their colonel and marched out along the Rue de Tournon where Allied flags fluttered from the windows.[27]

The Place de la République's Prinz Eugen barracks and its supporting network of pillboxes also held out all week. The FFIs' final attack was supported by former tank Lieutenant Aubry in a captured German armoured car. Unfortunately its machine-gun lacked the punch to knock out pillboxes.[28]

Supported by his *homologue allemand, Lieutenant de vaisseau* Vivier radioed the garrison inviting them to surrender. But thanks to undisciplined FFIs it took several attempts for a ceasefire to hold so that Vivier and his captured interpreter could enter. After an hour's negotiation they requested medical provision for the German wounded. Reassured by the arrival of a French doctor with battle trauma experience, the five-hundred-man garrison surrendered.[29]

At 8pm GT Langlade's Captain Hargous approached the Kriegsmarine barracks on Boulevard Lannes. The German sailors soon surrendered, marching docilely enough along the Avenue Victor-Hugo towards the Étoile until FFI machine-gun bursts forced them to lie prostrate on the cobbles, praying for their lives. Some Parisians dipped their handkerchiefs in the blood of the few who were killed.[30]

At the eastern *banlieue* of Fontenay sous Bois, von Choltitz's former information officer, Dr. Eckelmann, accompanied by a French officer and a *resistant*, approached the Wehrmacht-controlled *mairie* requesting their surrender. They refused, saying that von Choltitz had signed the order under enemy duress. At Army Group B, Model issued an order that von Choltitz's surrender was "false" and that German resistance should continue "to the last man". At this stage OKW believed that the situation in Paris needed "clarification".[31]

Near the Place Chatelet a Parisian lunged at a column of German prisoners with a knife screaming, "I've got to kill one!" After their FFI guards disarmed him, he turned out to be a known Les Halles meat dealer who survived the Occupation by trading with the Germans.[32]

At Palaiseau, two thousand Germans surrendered uneventfully except for a captain who left the column and blew himself up with a hidden hand-grenade. At Champigny a *homologue allemand* was gunned down amid cries of "*Verater!*"—"Traitor!" And at Vincennes the Germans took a French emissary prisoner because "he had seen too much". He was released to the American lines from Metz later that autumn.[33]

WHILE TWO PLATOONS OF *LA NUEVE* STOOD GUARD outside the Hôtel de Ville, Roger Stéphane arranged his blue-clad FFIs smartly up the main staircase. "I know he's General de Gaulle," muttered Georges Bidault. "But he doesn't have to keep us waiting half the day!"[34]

All the dignitaries of the *Résistance Interieure* were waiting, including Georges Marrane of the CPL, Marcel Flouret, the new Prefect of the Seine, Henri Rol-Tanguy and Raymond Massiet, to hear de Gaulle's first speech in Paris.

"There are more people here than yesterday," quipped Georges Marrane.

"It's easier today," said Rol-Tanguy, smiling after finally meeting Raymond Dronne.[35]

At 7.15pm de Gaulle arrived, walking through a multitude of ecstatic Parisians followed by Parodi, Le Troquer, Juin and Charles Luizet. The FFI honour guard smartly presented arms. At the foot of the stairs de Gaulle was welcomed by Georges Bidault as FFIs and Dronne's Spaniards stood to attention, their eyes moistening with pride. To Roger Stéphane, de Gaulle resembled a returning king. "Under a thunder of cheers" the Constable was escorted to the main salon where Resistance leaders awaited him. The first speech of salutation came from Georges Marrane. Next came Georges Bidault who included a moving tribute to Jean Moulin. Then it was de Gaulle's turn, giving one of his finest speeches with no draft or rehearsal whatsoever:

"Why should we hide the feelings that fill us all, we men and women who are here in our own city, in Paris that has risen to free itself and that has succeeded in doing so with its own hands? No! Let us not hide this deep and sacred emotion. There are moments that go beyond each of our poor little lives. Paris! Paris outraged! Paris broken! Paris martyred! But Paris liberated! Liberated by itself, liberated by its people with the help of the armies of France, with the support and help of the whole of France, of fighting France, of eternal France."[36]

The Constable finished off by appealing for national unity during the war's last months. Then Georges Bidault said, "*Mon Général*, here, all around you are the *Conseil Nationale de la Résistance* and the *Comité Parisien de la Libération*. We ask you to solemnly proclaim the Republic in front of the assembled people."

"The Republic has never ceased to exist," replied de Gaulle. "Free France, Fighting France, the French Committee for National Liberation, have, in their turn, been part of it. Vichy always was and remains nul and void. I myself am the President of the Government of the Republic. Why should I have to proclaim it?"

"Perhaps he was right, but it would have given us such pleasure," wrote Edgard Pisani.

De Gaulle approached the window to bathe in the crowd's acclamation: "*Vive de Gaulle!*" and—even if he refused to say it— "*Vive la République!*" Then, somewhat recklessly, he clambered onto the balcony seat to stand full height, showing his compatriots his immense, khaki-clad frame. Seeing that the railing was well below de Gaulle's centre of gravity, Claude Guy prised two fingers under his belt, eliciting a flash of princely irritation. Fists clenched, de Gaulle raised his immense arms in a great V sign. The crowd roared.[37]

PARISIANS WITH RELATIONS IN THE 2e DB were now out looking for them. On the Champs Élysées Jean Massu asked a member of 2/RMT if he knew of his brother, Jacques.

"Are you kidding?" replied the soldier. "He's our battalion commander, the King of Noses!"

Jean Massu found his brother near the Arc de Triomphe, manning his Jeep's command radio. The brothers Massu were inseparable for hours. However, their family would remain incomplete until André and Henri were repatriated from imprisonment and STO in Germany.[38]

In many instances members of the 2e DB with Parisian relations had alerted them by telephone of where they would be. But one family found their son crashed out asleep in his US uniform in a café's backyard. Nudged awake by his little sister, he blearily rose to his feet and embraced his family. Siblings were reunited, young fathers rediscovered pretty but austerely dressed wives who had been left to raise young children under the Nazi boot. Most families understood why these young men had to get away to de Gaulle, but not all.

There were also tragedies. The same telephone system that reunited loved ones also intensified pain. Around midday the 12e Cuirassiers' Lieutenant Bureau telephoned his family to let them know he would soon be home. Later that afternoon they discovered he had been killed when his Sherman, *Quimper*, was knocked out as it approached the Quai d'Orsay shortly after his telephone call.[39]

One of the saddest occurrences was in western Paris where the 12e RCA's Arthur Kaiser witnessed the following heart-breaking incident: "The crew of *Bordelais II* dismounted onto the pavement to stretch our legs. No sooner were we on our feet than a lady, elegant, wearing a black dress and visibly anguished, took me to one side and asked me somewhat shyly and discreetly: 'Young man, you appear to be with the *Chasseurs d'Afrique*?'"

"Yes, Madame," Kaiser replied.

"Do you know Lieutenant Zagrodski and an *aspirant* of the same name?"

"I was taken back and extremely embarrassed by this question," Kaiser wrote, "because I knew at once that I was talking to the mother of the brothers *Zagro*. The eldest had been killed during out first engagement at Mézières, and the younger one had met his end at Jouy en Josas, on entering Paris. Very moved by this elderly mother, I directed her to the *commandant* so as not to have to tell her such terrible news."[40]

AS THAT MOMENTOUS DAY BECAME AN EVENING OF CARNIVAL, Leclerc arrived at the Ministry of War, bringing de Gaulle early casualty figures. The 2e DB had lost twenty-eight officers and six hundred other ranks killed and wounded. FFI casualties, according to Louis Vallery-Radot's early estimate, stood in the region of two thousand five hundred killed and wounded with about a thousand civilian casualties.[41]

Paris was still endangered, said Leclerc. German forces around Saint-Denis and La Villette were refusing to surrender since they had never came under von Choltitz's authority. Elements of the German 47th Infantry Division were taking positions around Le Bourget airport and Montmorency. US V Corps commander, General Gerow, was already ordering the 2e DB to keep the Germans on the run.[42]

"Tomorrow I will walk down the Champs Élysées," de Gaulle told Leclerc. "You will position your tanks along the route." While it was entirely understandable that France's liberation leader would want this, fighting continued. That same evening the SS massacred twenty-seven *résistants* at Chatou. General Gerow could be forgiven for regarding this parade as premature.[43]

Roumiantzoff's Spahis were sent northeast to provide a screen. In the meantime the bulk of the 2e DB laagered for the night. GT Langlade parked their vehicles around the Étoile. Billotte positioned his battlegroup from the Place de la Concorde to Chatelet, while GT Dio cantoned themselves along the quais eastwards from Notre Dame.[44]

Les Invalides was also back in French hands, and General Koenig arranged a great dinner in the governor's dining room to which those senior officers not dining with de Gaulle were invited. Arriving at the gates with Alain de Boissieu, a radiantly smiling Leclerc exclaimed, "Look, Boissieu! It's extraordinary to have liberated Paris without any destruction of her treasures; all the bridges, all the buildings, all the artistic treasures of the capital are intact. Look at Les Invalides! What luck we have had!" Then Leclerc pulled from his wallet a piece of well-fingered writing paper. "Do you remember the day you brought me this letter from de Gaulle awarding me the mission of liberating Paris and appointing me interim military governor?" Boissieu nodded. "Well," continued Leclerc, "that document, which I keep with me all the time in my wallet, along with another letter from de Gaulle, whenever I felt down or in doubt, I always re-read them."[45]

Broadly smiling, Koenig greeted Leclerc, Jacques Chaban-Delmas, Colonel Lizé, Colonel Paul de Langlade and Navy Commissioner Rolin along with their ADCs. As they took their places at the beautifully laid table there was a rumpus in the rooms above where *Gardes Républicaines* had caught German stragglers. After being guided past undismantled barricades by his brother Jean, Jacques Massu arrived slightly late, but cheerfully pointed out that his men took the Pont de Sèvres before *la Colonne Dronne* reached the Hôtel de Ville. As he sat down, Massu noticed oil on his combat trousers and draped a knapkin over his chair's embroidered seat. Chaban-Delmas explained how Nordling's truce bought time for the Préfecture and demonstrated that von Choltitz could be trusted. On the other hand many FFI, both FTP and Gaullist, including those under Colonel Lizé's command, had not respected it. Irrespective of their sensibilities, General Marie-Pierre Koenig declared, "We have narrowly avoided a new Paris Commune!"[46]

LIEUTENANTS SORRET AND GUIGON FINALLY MADE IT TO FOUQUET'S where, for one evening, that great eatery allowed their liberators to dine free. Also dining, while his friend Sacha Guitry languished in the Vélodrome d'Hiver, was the great actor Jules Auguste Muraire, aka Raimu. "Enjoy it while you can," Raimu told the young officers. "It won't last long."[47]

Around the Étoile, many of GT Langlade's rankers entertained *Parisiennes* under groundsheets and tarpaulins. Jacques Massu was no prude but wrote in his memoirs that he had "to throw a *voile pudique* (discreet veil) over what happened near the *Soldat Inconnu*".[48]

While sleeping beside his Tank-Destroyers, Philippe de Gaulle was woken around 10pm. A friend needed help to find a senior officer who was "making scandal in a disreputable place". On a night when many threw conventional morality aside, this officer needed saving from himself. Four RBFM lieutenants joined the search, which ended up at 122 Rue de Provence, a famous upmarket brothel. Fascinated, Philippe took in the quasi top-drawer décor, reproductions of suggestive paintings by Boucher and Fragonard, and the respectable looking couple who owned the place. It was all very gracious until *la patronne* remarked that the 2e DB's practical American uniforms were less *chic* than German ones. Having found the missing officer in an ornate *salon*, his pistol on the table—with which he had fired a few shots at the ceiling, watched by a handful of well-presented tarts—Philippe and his comrades drank champagne for a while before heaving him away to the Hôtel Claridge.[49]

Jacques Branet also found Parisians commenting on his American uniform. Unable to believe that he was a captain, someone asked if having all ranks similarly dressed undermined discipline. After being patched up at the Comédie Française aid post, Branet acquired walking wounded status and spent the evening with his men around the Rue de Rivoli, admiring pretty girls, drinking wine, answering silly questions and telling FFIs not to injure German prisoners. Towards midnight he booked himself into the nearby Hôtel Sainte-Marie. "We've taken Paris," Branet murmured as his head hit the pillow. "Tomorrow I will sleep in my own bedroom on the Avenue Hoche."[50]

Raymond Dronne was collared by his old student friend Gérard, with whom he dined at Polidor's on the Quartier Latin's Rue Monsieur le Prince, owned by Albert Bony, another old friend. The well-respected Bony kept his restaurant running for his usual intelligentsia clientele without using the black market throughout the Occupation. After they finished eating Bony locked his doors and told Dronne what had happened to their old crowd during the Occupation. *Avocat* Bouin, a barrister he knew well, was among over a million French soldiers captured in 1940 and died in Germany. The Penet brothers, both doctors, were arrested by the Gestapo. Other friends had fled to *la France profonde*. As Bony spoke, young FFIs banged on the doors, hoping for a liberators' free meal. Bony gestured that he was closed and would remain so. Besides, with *El Kapitan* in there, no one would give him trouble.[51] The last thing Dronne mentions in his *Carnets* for that extraordinary day is seeing Hemingway carousing with his irregulars. Dronne considered introducing himself, then decided he would prefer to do that when the great Ernest was sober enough to remember.[52]

Captains Gribius, Compagnon and Gachet manned the 2e DB's CP through the night. Jean Compagnon, a future general and historian, told the 1994 *Colloque*, "It was quite a disturbed night because, by

8pm only the southern half of Paris had been liberated, up to a line level with the Opera and the great boulevards. The north was still not free. Hence, throughout the night Gribius, Gachet and myself received telephone calls from the northwest suburbs of Paris who weren't yet liberated, on behalf of FFIs and FTPs wanting to know when we were coming to help. We could do nothing because everything was positioned (for the night). We knew that towards the northwest sub-group Rémy was around Neuilly, but that was all. So one had to calm them and say, 'Wait until tomorrow'."[53]

SINCE IT WAS PROTOCOL THAT A GENERAL entered captivity via the HQ of an officer of equivalent rank, General von Choltitz was handed over to US V Corps commander General Leonard Gerow. Gerow questioned him at length, discovering that von Choltitz had no intention and probably insufficient means to destroy Paris; information which contributed to American beliefs that Paris was never really endangered at all. Gerow subsequently insisted that von Choltitz surrender to US V Corps, and he set up his CP in an office at Les Invalides formerly used by Marshal Pétain.[54]

As Paris was being liberated, Pétain was being held by German *Feldgendarmerie* at Château Morvillars near Belfort. A stone and red-brick renaissance style affair, Château Morvillars was owned by Louis Vieillard who, like many patrician members of the Resistance, had fled the country, in his case to Switzerland, leaving his intrepid wife to hold the fort. But with Paris liberated, Madame Vieillard saw little danger in admitting to Pétain that not only was her husband a *résistant* but herself as well. "You?" said Pétain, astonished that a chatelaine could be *Gaulliste*. "It isn't possible."

"Why, *Monsieur le Maréchal*, do you think there are only terrorists in the Resistance?"

"I haven't heard anything," insisted Pétain before inviting his host to dine with him.

Madame Vieillard replied that she could dine with him provided no Vichy ministers were present. Petain agreed.

On 25 August Pétain finally recognised that his position as French head of state no longer existed. He paid off his personal staff with whatever monies were available and refused any more deference than was due to a retired marshal. He became visibly uncooperative towards the Germans, forcing them to deal instead with Fernand de Brinon. Acknowledging the success of his former subaltern, Pétain told a friend, "I thought the French nation incapable of serious effort; these hundreds of thousands of men who have risked their lives for the liberation have given proof of a heroism in which I no longer dared to believe. I knew that de Gaulle was intelligent, but I never thought he could succeed in so splendid an undertaking."[55]

26 August 1944

MOST OF THE 2e DB SPENT THAT NIGHT in central Paris, either bivouacked, bringing in what eventually amounted to twelve thousand German prisoners, or fighting around Vincennes and La Villette. Nevertheless, de Gaulle stood by his decision to hold a celebratory march down the Champs Élysées, capped with a special Mass in Notre Dame. However, it was a decision fraught with difficulties. First it was inconceivable to run such an event without the guardianship of Leclerc's troops. But General Gerow held the equally understandable viewpoint that the 2e DB should be engaging enemy forces north and east of Paris.

In the second place the use of France's premier cathedral necessarily involved the clergy, especially the Archbishop of Paris, Cardinal Emmanuel Suhard. While undoubtedly a decent man, the fact that Suhard apparently permitted, though Heaven knows how he could have prevented it, Henriot's state funeral remained an enormous point against him in Resistance eyes. Against this, Suhard's humanitarian efforts during the Occupation counted for little.

Leclerc recognised early on that more than Boissieu's HQ protection squadron was necessary to guarantee de Gaulle's safety. If trouble erupted on the Champs Élysées the Spahis' M8 armoured cars would have to take and hold the Seine bridges. Infantry would have to protect de Gaulle himself, and his most experienced street fighters were Raymond Dronne's Spaniards. At midday Joseph Putz ordered Dronne to present *la Nueve* and their half-tracks immediately at the Étoile. Even though Dronne's men were largely Atheists, de Gaulle knew how to make his pleasure felt.[56]

Through the morning the disagreement between Leclerc and General Gerow rumbled on. Something of this nature had been inevitable ever since de Gaulle appointed Leclerc interim military governor of Paris nine months before. On 24 August, as US V Corps commander, General Gerow ordered the 2e DB to pursue the Germans out of the city. Even though Paris was mostly back in Allied hands, Gerow expected this order to be carried out. On discovering that Leclerc was obeying his political master rather than himself, at around 10am Gerow sent a liaison officer to La Tour-Maubourg barracks to remind Leclerc that the 2e DB should be engaging the enemy northeast of Paris. Predictably Leclerc pointed out that, since General de Gaulle was now France's head of state, he had to obey de Gaulle's orders. Hearing this, Gerow put his order in writing and sent it to Leclerc's adjutant, Commandant Weil. Knowing neither Leclerc nor de Gaulle would change their plans for anyone, Weil left the note in his pocket, but the matter did not rest there.[57]

CARDINAL SUHARD'S HUMILIATION BEGAN EARLY. At 9.30am Bishop Lancrenon, a longstanding member of the Resistance who owed his freedom to Suhard's intervention in 1942, arrived at 30 Rue Barbet de Jouy to inform Suhard of the *Conseil National de la Résistance*'s decision regarding the service in Notre Dame that afternoon. "Given their attitude under the Vichy government, neither Monsignor Beaussart nor the Cardinal should be present in Notre Dame." De Gaulle knew how to make his displeasure felt.[58]

Seeing Suhard's despair at such disrespectful treatment, Père Le Sourd telephoned the Préfecture for confirmation.

"We apologise for not keeping you informed," said one of Luizet's staff. "There has been a lot to organise. Yes, there will be a *Te Deum* at Notre Dame. It has been fixed for 4.30pm."

The fact that Notre Dame fell under the authority of the Archbishop of Paris was utterly disregarded. With disrespect engulfing Suhard, Notre Dame's Deacon, Monsignor Brot, tried to soothe him.

"There you are, Eminence! They've fixed the time for the *Te Deum* and I haven't even been told. Please Sir, don't be too concerned with protocol. They haven't had time to address matters of etiquette. Don't expect too much."

Once again Cardinal Suhard believed he had a right to officiate in his own church.[59]

But when Parodi's staff explained the situation, de Gaulle simply said, "If the Cardinal's safety is in danger then he must not come."

Next, after confering with Père Bruckberger, the priest who, with Suhard's blessing, offered himself as chaplain to the Préfecture when the Insurrection began, Francis-Louis Closon and Monsieur Segala came to inform Suhard of de Gaulle's decision.

"By what right," retorted Suhard, "does the government deny me access to my own Cathedral?"

"The government can not guarantee your safety. Paris has largely liberated itself through insurrection. There are still outbreaks of violence."

"I can not accept that reason," replied Suhard. "I have every intention of presiding over the prayers for the liberation of Paris. In any case, who has sent you on this errand?"

"The Government of the Republic," said Segala.

"You mean General de Gaulle?"

"The General has approved the decision of the provisional government," said Segala.

"Well that's dreadful for me," said Suhard, visibly moved. "Infinitely sad! But if that is what General de Gaulle really wants then I will have to go along with it, but not without protesting."

As Parodi's emissaries left, Closon turned around to say, "Eminence, I am sure you would be glad to know that the General's first visit to Paris is to Notre Dame."[60]

DE GAULLE WAS LUNCHING WITH LECLERC and other 2e DB officers at Chez Chauland, a popular restaurant in the military quarter, when Gerow's liaison officer made his second attempt to cancel the parade. General Juin later remarked, "That Gerow certainly had no equal when it came to meddling inappropriately in French affairs."[61] Fuming, Gerow drafted another order:

"Since you are operating under my direct command you are not to take orders coming from any other sources. I am told you have been instructed by General de Gaulle to cause your troops to take part in a parade this afternoon at 2pm. You will pay no attention to this order. The troops under your command will not take part in the parade either this afternoon or any other time except on orders signed by me personally."

As veteran French correspondent Jean Lacouture wrote, "Of course, both de Gaulle and Leclerc would have had to be shot to make them give up a plan whose symbolic significance seemed to them wholly irreplaceable. Gerow gained nothing but humiliation."[62]

Gerow's emissary asked Leclerc if he was refusing a direct order, warning him that, if he was, the US Army would regard it as a court martial offence. Leclerc is believed to have replied, "Precisely because these orders were given by idiots means I don't have to carry them out!"[63]

Leclerc directed the American to de Gaulle, who was observing their exchange with interest from his table.

"I *lent* you General Leclerc," de Gaulle declared firmly. "Surely I can *borrow* him back for a little while."[64]

The American departed but, shortly before the parade, he reappeared at La Tour Maubourg barracks, collared Commandant Weil and demanded that Leclerc report immediately to Gerow at Les Invalides. Considering the dangers, Gerow's concerns were justified.

De Gaulle's planned parade involved over a million people with only one regiment of the US 4th Infantry Division and Roumiantzoff's small battle group between Paris and the German front line. Small bands of Wehrmacht soldiers and disgruntled *Miliciens* remained at large. But it was too late to cancel the parade. Jean Guignebert and Pierre Crénesse at Radio Paris, and other liberated radio stations, had announced it for over twelve hours. *Tricolores* adorned with the Cross of Lorraine were already fluttering from windows and lampposts. Printing presses had worked all night producing posters proclaiming "*Vive de Gaulle!*" Thousands of Parisians were massed all the way from the Étoile, down the Champs Élysées and along all routes to Notre Dame.

AT 30 RUE BARBET-DE-JOUY, lunch passed quickly, though Cardinal Suhard could barely eat. Two policemen now guarded his residence; he was under house arrest. When the front door was opened to Monsignor Courbe, gunfire was audible nearby.

"We should be available to everybody," insisted Suhard.

"Eminence," said Courbe, "this won't last. If the General returns to Notre Dame without you he risks the fate of Heliodorus."

"Père Bruckberger has just telephoned me," said Brot. "He told me in an unrepeatable tone '*General* de Gaulle is coming to Notre Dame. He will be accompanied by Père Houchet, Chaplain of the Leclerc division and myself. Cardinal Suhard should not be there. It is you who will receive the General and me who will speak!' The tone was dry and military."

"We've been thinking of a protest," said Père Le Sourd. "Here is a statement of the Cardinal's position."

Brot read quickly.

"Held under house arrest in my residence by order of the Prefect of Police and the President of the Council, I can only accept their decision. But I must protest against any measure that prevents the Archbishop of Paris from entering his Cathedral. I would be grateful if you would make my protest known to General de Gaulle. And I pray that you pass on, dear Archdeacon, the expression of my pain in the midst of such national rejoicing and my deep affection."

"Tell his Eminence that I will do this," Monsignor Brot told Le Sourd.

Later Alexandre Parodi told Père Bruckberger, "I've had a protest from the Archbishop, but I have not replied."[65]

PASCALE MOISSON AND HER FRIEND MARCELLE intended to watch the parade from the Place de l'Hôtel de Ville, but the crowd coming from Montmartre swept them towards the Place de la Concorde. On the way, Pascale saw two young women climb aboard a US 4th ID M8 armoured car to be hugged and kissed. Pascale stretched out her arms to an American sergeant who embraced her gently. Reaching the Place de la Concorde around which several RBFM Tank-Destroyers were parked, Pascale realised she would be unable to see de Gaulle unless she climbed onto a Tank-Destroyer, but a smart *Gardien de la Paix* with white gloves shouted abruptly, "Civilians are not allowed to climb on tanks! Your safety!" Then the *Gardien* led Pascale towards the front of the crowd, between the police cordon and the Tank-Destroyer, whose commander was scanning the Champs Élysées with binoculars. "When something starts happening, I will tell you," he said, smiling down at Pascale. "There's an enormous *Tricolore* unfurled inside the Arc de Triomphe."[66]

At the Étoile the Stuart tanks of Boissieu's protection squadron were ready to lead the parade; their names redolent of *la France profonde—Lauraguais, Limagne, Limousin,* and *Verdelon.* Then came *la Nueve*'s half-tracks, *Brunete, Ebro* and *Don Quichotte.* Paris' Spanish refugee community turned out to cheer them, carrying a twenty-metre-long red, yellow and purple Spanish Republican flag. But it was France's day and *la Nueve*'s supporters were quietly asked to roll up their flag, though each half-track bore a discreet Spanish Republican pennant.[67]

Roger Gallois caught up with Leclerc at the Arc de Triomphe. "Well, that wasn't too bad!" said Leclerc cheerily.[68]

Photographs of Leclerc taken before the parade show him looking exhausted but serene as he spoke with Louis Dio, Paul de Langlade and Jacques de Guillebon, his comrades of the previous four years. At 3.10pm, de Gaulle arrived. An honour guard of the Régiment de Marche du Tchad presented arms. He rekindled the eternal flame and laid a Cross of Lorraine-shaped wreath of gladioli on the tomb of the *Soldat Inconnu* while Leclerc, Koenig, Juin and officers of the 2e DB saluted. Their dream had come true.[69]

Just then a throng of around three hundred men and women broke onto the Champs Élysées dressed in 1830s costume, some women bare-breasted, dressed in *Tricolores* and Phrygian bonnets, re-enacting Delacroix's painting, *La Liberté guidant le peuple* (Liberty guiding the people). Langlade wrote that no one was impressed and their caper fell flat.[70]

Turning away from the Arc de Triomphe, de Gaulle looked down the eighteen hundred metres of the Champs Élysées, where the crowd grew every second. His entourage, senior officers and members of the Paris Resistance were waiting for the march to begin. Also prominent from his black skin and white shirt was Georges Dukson, the Lion of the 17th Arrondissement, who appointed himself to de Gaulle's entourage following a bet.[71] Claude Guy was shorter than de Gaulle but still pretty tall, making the Gabonais Dukson appear diminutive.* Seeing a young man smoking, de Gaulle told him to extinguish his cigarette. Then he told COMAC leaders Jean de Vogüé and Maurice Kriegel-Valrimont to keep in line. "This made little sense and was of no importance, but the naval officer [de Vogüé] was deeply affected," wrote Kriegel-Valrimont.[72]

But that afternoon was about more than a few thousand Insurrectionists. Hundreds of thousands of Parisians were making a

---

* Following the Liberation, Georges Dukson found it difficult to reintegrate into civilian life, falling into petty crime. Shot in the leg while trying to escape from jail, he died on the operating table. The photographer Henri Cartier Bresson made a particular point of ensuring that his photograph including Dukson was published as widely as possible.

spontaneous display of popular emotion. They came to see the most popular man in France, Charles de Gaulle; to put a face to the strong, deep voice that had upheld their sense of patriotism since 1940.

"It was a sea!" de Gaulle wrote. "An immense crowd was massed from one side to the other of the great avenue. Perhaps there were two million souls. The rooftops were also covered with people. In every window groups mingled with curtains. Others were clustered around signposts and street lamps. As far as the eye could see, it was a living mass, under sunshine, under the *Tricolore*."[73]

As a loudspeaker van declared, "*Le général de Gaulle confie sa sécurité au peuple de* Paris!"—"General de Gaulle entrusts his safety to the people of Paris!"—Raymond Dronne's half-track *Guadalajara* began rolling steadily along the avenue's south side. Wearing his battered képi, arms folded against the gun-rail, Dronne marvelled at the "ocean of heads" acclaiming de Gaulle. "To undertake a march like that was utterly crazy," he wrote. "It only needed a fanatic or someone unbalanced out of that immense crowd, where so many ordinary people had guns" for de Gaulle to be endangered.[74]

On this day de Gaulle trusted Fortune to watch over him. Emotional yet calm, he looked straight ahead as he marched "through the midst of the indecipherable exultation of the crowd, under a tempest of voices proclaiming my name". The crowd swirled and eddied, making a gap for his entourage while they waved and shouted, "*Vive de Gaulle!*" and "*Vive la France!*" "It was happening at that very moment," de Gaulle wrote, "one of those miracles of the national conscience, one of those gestures from France, which, from time to time, throughout the centuries, arrive to brighten our history." Only someone fiercely patriotic with a romanticised idea of his nation's character could write such a thing. "In such a community," he continued, "there was but one thought, one spirit, one cry; differences faded, individuals disappeared." From the Étoile down to the Rond-Point and thence to the Place de la Concorde children shrieked freely, women made dowdy by the Occupation's shortages cried with forgotten joy, men cried with happiness and rediscovered pride in their country. "*Merci, merci*," they said as de Gaulle passed. With a restrained smile, he acknowledged their gratitude. It had been his proudest duty to be the instrument of France's destiny.[75] Marching behind de Gaulle, Maurice Kriegel-Valrimont turned round to see Jean de Vogüé with tears streaming down his cheeks. "*C'était une spectacle splendide*"—"It was a splendid sight" Kriegel-Valrimont wrote many years later.[76]

Paris was liberated but much of France remained under German control; more than at the height of the First World War. More men would die before German boots left French soil. With each pace de Gaulle remembered how the 1919 victory parade trod that same macadam. Passing the statue of Georges Clemenceau, who guided France through that great conflict, de Gaulle turned to salute. Here his memoirs include a cinematic flight of fancy, imagining Clemenceau climbing down from his plinth to walk alongside them.

"What a triumph, *Mon Général!*" exclaimed Georges Bidault.

"Yes, but what a crowd!" de Gaulle replied.

Looking up, he savoured the great chestnut trees with their enormous green leaves, remembering how Napoleon's son, the hapless *Aiglon*, dreamt of them while imprisoned in Austria. Ahead of him, beyond the Obelisk, lay the Tuileries gardens and the great north and south wings of the Louvre. On his right, beyond the Seine bridges, he could see Les Invalides, whose church housed the tombs of France's greatest soldiers. A thousand years of French history flooded through his mind.[77]

At last, from the Place de la Concorde, Pascale Moisson saw de Gaulle. "He was there, so close to us, surrounded by glory; very tall, thin and dignified, marching at quite a fast pace. I could not keep my eyes off him. His face was energetic yet immobile, letting no smile respond to the *vivats* of this multitude which had gathered to applaud him, but also honest, inspiring trust and sympathy. It was the face of a hero," she wrote. Then, slightly behind, followed Leclerc, the soldier who had kept de Gaulle in the game. Next came the FFIs, then white-clad nurses and nuns who had tended the Insurrection's wounded and dying, and public workers whose strikes helped make the Germans' grip on the city untenable.[78]

At the Place de la Concorde de Gaulle remounted the black open-top Hotchkiss. Raymond Dronne's Spaniards were now relieved by Colonel Peretti's security team. But, just as Peretti took over de Gaulle's protection, gunfire broke out. "It was in front of us, stretching along the Rue de Rivoli, reaching the Place de la Concorde and up the Champs Élysées," wrote Dronne. "Gun shots seemed to be coming from everywhere. Panic-stricken people were running in all directions, falling in the gutters, lying down in dried-out fountains, huddling behind trees, flower-troughs and even behind our vehicles."[79]

In her memoirs, Pascale Moisson writes unequivocally that *Miliciens* were behind the gunfire. Dronne believed that isolated pockets of gunmen, probably very few, shot into the crowd, possibly aiming at de Gaulle. Some were perhaps suicidally fanatical Germans as well as *Miliciens*, possibly both. "The Place de la Concorde was rapidly transformed into a battlefield," wrote Pascale. "Having earlier that afternoon wished my parents were there, now I was glad they were far away. Pushed by several others, I found myself pressed underneath one of the tanks. What a noise! Everyone, albeit without *that* much panic, was hitting the deck." Then, just for long enough for people to think it safe to move, the gunfire ceased. Pascale and others got up, just as tanks and soldiers began firing back. Again the crowd threw themselves to the ground. "Like everyone else," wrote Pascale, "I pressed my nose into the dirt, my ear against someone's leg; not quite what a young woman would choose." Lifting her head, Pascale saw white-clad *brancardiers* running with stretchers. Eventually Pascale and Marcelle found shelter in a building off the Place de la Concorde. Although German stragglers and *Miliciens* were the obvious suspects, abandoned weapons had undoubtedly fallen into irresponsible hands. The French fired back anywhere they perceived or misperceived a threat.[80]

AT 2.30PM A 2e DB JEEP PULLED UP OUTSIDE 30 Rue Barbet-de-Jouy carrying Bishop Rodhain, now wearing a military chaplain's uniform, accompanied by Leclerc's head chaplain, Père Houchet.

Both priests were concerned over who should act as celebrant for the Liberation *Te Deum*.

"Eminence, we've come to find you," Rodhain told Cardinal Suhard. "We're going to drive you by Jeep to Notre Dame. We'll brush past any barricades we have to."

Cardinal Suhard looked visibly pained.

"Thank you, dear child," he said. "But we can't go to Notre Dame because I am under house arrest."

Rodhain's next words must have refreshed Suhard's hopes of taking the service, because he began robing up. Next the new Commissioner of Police, Monsieur Pinault, arrived, accompanied by two inspectors and his secretary.

"The General's secretary has rebuked us for appearing to go back on this," Pinault told Père Le Sourd. "What is decided is decided."

"Wait a moment," said Le Sourd, departing briefly and returning, accompanied by Pères Delouvrier and Bohan and Monsignor Chappoulie. "His Eminence still has every intention of going to Notre Dame for the *Te Deum* at 4.30pm."

But Commissioner Pinault was adamant that Cardinal Suhard was barred from taking any part in the Liberation *Te Deum* that afternoon. With that, Le Sourd presented Pinault with Cardinal Suhard's formal protest on paper bearing the coat of arms of the Archbishop of Paris. It read as follows: "The Cardinal Suhard, Archbishop of Paris, protests the measure preventing him from appearing in his own Cathedral. He does not accept the given pretext relating to his security. [Signed] H. Le Sourd. Personal Secretary."

After Pinault left, Suhard asked Le Sourd to call Père Depierre.

DESPITE HER SIZE AND SERENITY, as August sunshine bounced off her flying buttresses, chaos reigned in Notre Dame's Sacristy. Resistance chaplain Père Bruckberger arrived to enrobe for what he believed was his big moment, assisting at the Liberation *Te Deum*, a role that would normally go to a higher ranking priest. But Monsignor Beaussart, who was involved in Henriot's funeral, was already there.

"*Mon Père*," began Beaussart. "I am sure your friends in the [provisional] government would permit you to tell me. Why has the Cardinal been placed under house arrest?"

"The government does not want the General to be received by someone who has welcomed the German governor of Paris into Notre Dame. The government would prefer that you resigned."

"That's an abuse of power," replied Beaussart. "The Cardinal is appointed by the Pope, not the government."

"He [the General] is well aware," said Bruckberger. "As soon as the Nuncio arrives in Paris he will be asked to advise the Vatican of this wish."

"The government is taking on its shoulders a heavy responsibility in taking such an anti-religious attitude."

"Monsignor," said Bruckberger, "you are wrong. There isn't one member of the government who entertains anti-clerical sentiments. It's a question of personalities."[81]

Fascinated by this conversation, other priests were listening from the corridors. About then Monsignor Brot arrived in the Sacristy. Bruckberger reminded Beaussart how he edited the film *Les Anges du Péché* to satisfy the Occupation authorities.

"I couldn't have done otherwise," said Beaussart.

"Well, there you are then," said Bruckberger. "If you had *des rapports* with the Occupation authorities, the Cardinal, him even more so, couldn't have done otherwise and over far more serious matters."

"I've had enough," said Beaussart. "My political role is over. I am going to become a padre with the *Division Leclerc*."

This remark was heard by the 2e DB's Père Houchet, who said, "To become one of our padres you've got to get past me and I strongly advise you not to try."[82]

Their arguments were curtailed by the sound of gunfire outside. Furthermore it became clear that gunfire was coming from inside the Cathedral, from the King's Gallery and other places.

Of the Suhard affair de Gaulle wrote, "At 4.30pm I went, as planned, to Notre Dame. At the appointed time, on the Rue de Rivoli, I got into a car and, after a short stop-off at the steps of the Hôtel de Ville I arrived at the esplanade (of Notre Dame). The Cardinal-Archbishop would not be welcoming me at the threshold of the basilica. Not because he did not want to but because the new authorities asked him to abstain from doing so. In fact, *Monsignor* Suhard had thought it his duty, four months previously, to solemnly receive there Marshal Pétain during his visit to German-occupied Paris, then, the next month, presided over the funeral service that Vichy wanted to mark the death of Philippe Henriot. Due to this, several among the Resistance were indignant at the idea that this priest should be present to introduce General de Gaulle [he often wrote of himself in the third person] into the Cathedral. For my own part, knowing that the Church considers itself obliged to accept 'the established order', not ignoring that in the Cardinal's mind charity and piety are so eminent that they leave little room in his soul for the appreciation of temporal matters, I would have been willing to consider otherwise. But the state of tension among a large number of combatants the day following the battle and my wish to avoid any disagreeable consequences for Cardinal Suhard drove me to approve of the decision by my Delegation to bar the Archbishop during the ceremony. Subsequent events showed that this decision was correct."[83]

GENERAL DE GAULLE ARRIVED AT NOTRE DAME several minutes before the *Te Deum* service was due to begin. With the gathering congregation talking energetically, Monsignor Brot shouted for silence.[84]

Outside it remained uncertain whether Germans or *Miliciens* were taking potshots at de Gaulle, the 2e DB and the crowd.

"Your men aren't used to street fighting, are they?" said Colonel Rol-Tanguy.

"*Mon cher colonel,*" replied Guillebon. "They will learn."[85]

From the choir, Monsignor Brot saw de Gaulle entering the cathedral as shots rattled around the massive carved stone ceiling. The congregation, now about two thousand, grovelled in their pews as much in fright as in prayer. Brot swiftly walked the length of the nave and introduced himself to France's new leader.

"*Mon général*," Brot began. "His Eminence has asked me to welcome you to Notre Dame de Paris. I should not have had this honour since it is the Cardinal Archbishop himself who should be welcoming you into his cathedral. His Eminence has asked me to protest to you regarding the treatment of which he has been a victim. Given what he has done for France during these last difficult years, he certainly did not deserve such an insult."

Appearing unmoved, de Gaulle replied, "*Monsieur l'Archiprêtre*, have you noticed the gunfire going on around us? Surely it is best that the Cardinal is not here?"

"But, *mon général*, it doesn't seem that the shooting is aimed at the Cardinal."

"That may be true," de Gaulle replied.

"*Mon général*," continued Brot. "May I pass on your regrets to the Cardinal over what has happened?"

"Yes," de Gaulle replied quietly.

"You're giving me permission to pass on your regrets to His Eminence?"

"Yes, *Monsieur l'Archiprêtre*," repeated de Gaulle. "Tell His Eminence that I regret what has happened."[86]

Among the congregation sat British Intelligence officer Malcolm Muggeridge. "The Cathedral was packed tight," Muggeridge wrote. On Monsignor Brot's signal the *Magnificat* began. "The choir sang melodiously," Muggeridge continued. "And, up in front the heads of the General and his associates could just be seen. It was at this point that someone fired a pistol; as was subsequently discovered, by mistake. The effect was fantastic; the huge congregation who had all been standing suddenly fell flat on their faces, supposing that some plot—Communist, Pétainist, Nazi, maybe even Gaullist—was about to be put into operation. There was a single exception, one solitary figure still standing, like a lonely giant. It was, of course, de Gaulle. Thenceforth, that was how I always saw him—towering and alone; the rest, prostrate."[87]

"One could see more bottoms than faces," observed André Le Troquer. With a sharp tap from his cane, General Leclerc prevented one of his soldiers from returning fire towards the ceiling's medieval stonework, while Claude Hettier de Boislambert disarmed someone with similar intentions, saving a stained-glass window.[88] In the meantime shots continued, hitting three members of the congregation, one fatally. Determined not to be intimidated, Brot tried to restart the service. But continuing gunfire made this impossible. Père Bruckberger asked to take the microphone but Brot told him tersely to be quiet. As Bruckberger retook his place, de Gaulle walked insouciantly towards the door. Considering what a wonderful target he made at that moment, several eyes welled in admiration of his bravery.[89]

Enquiries into the shooting inside Notre Dame elicited that, an hour before de Gaulle's arrival, three men armed with submachine-guns—purporting to be FFI—asked to go up to the King's Gallery to raise a *Tricolore* with a Cross of Lorraine on behalf of the Préfecture. That these men should also bar the main organist from reaching his perch suggests that flag-waving was not all they intended. But did they initiate the gunfire inside Notre Dame or simply draw the fire of other zealous and suspicious FFIs among the congregation?[90] When the police pulled them down they claimed they were firing at "indistinct enemies". As de Gaulle wrote, "Who could imagine that enemies would make targets of chimneys while I myself was walking around in the open?"[91]

After the war, Alain de Boissieu discussed the shooting inside Notre Dame with Prefect Charles Luizet. "He [Luizet] interrogated them personally and believed they had no other motive than committing an *attentat* (assassination) against General de Gaulle. For whose gain? Vichy, the *Milice*, agents of foreign powers, opponents of the CNR? I owe it to historical truth to write that Luizet inclined towards the last possibility and he had solid grounds for this; I leave to him the responsibility for this grave judgement, not having myself any appreciation of this matter."[92]

De Gaulle taking power benefited neither the Left nor the *collabo* Right. But he was not the only target. Vengeance, paranoia and suspicion were as much a part of the Liberation as joy and relief. In one apartment building, after their concièrge assured them a sniper was on their roof, student Bernard Pierquin and his father ventured out over the leadwork and slates armed only with an old service revolver. "*Pas de salopards!*"—"No bastards!"—but their appearance drew fire from other roofs. Prudently they returned inside.[93]

Isolated Germans were sometimes responsible; so too were *Miliciens* who stayed behind to make trouble, rather than decamping to remuster in the new SS Charlemagne Division. One of the men pulled out of the Hôtel de Ville's attic was the same *Milicien* Mansuy who had murdered Georges Mandel in the Forest of Fontainebleau a few weeks before.[94] Wearing an FFI brassard, Mansuy claimed to be defending the Hôtel de Ville. But when a *résistant*, a veteran of run-ins with the *Milice*, recognised Mansuy, the game was up. He was shot in true *Milice* style "while trying to escape".[95]

WITH LECLERC'S PERMISSION, André Gribius missed the march down the Champs Élysées. After 1940 his parents moved to an apartment on Versailles' elegant but modest Rue Sainte-Victoire. Gribius had never seen their new home, but towards the end of the Vichy period in French North Africa, their letters included diagrams and vivid descriptions which made him feel Rue Sainte-Victoire was the last place he saw them. Expecting them to be under-nourished, Gribius loaded his Jeep with "tinned foods, particularly *beans*, cheese, jam and biscuits".

Arriving at his parents' building, he took the stairs two at a time and rang their bell. "It was my father who opened the door. In the shadow behind him, my mother stood frail and barely recognisable. My father also appeared terribly thin, and, while taking them tenderly in my arms, with sadness for all they had endured, I was unable to speak a word."

But, as with Christian Girard, the initial silence passed.

"They told me how they had lived during those four years, speaking of our relations and our friends. I looked around their apartment, recognising all our old furniture. I admired the taste with which my mother had arranged them.[96] I asked my parents all sorts of questions about their lives, their difficult subsistence, knowing they would never have bought anything that looked 'black market'. ... If my father remained, by tradition, more trusting in Marshal Pétain, although happy, despite his worries, to have a son in the opposite camp, my mother had never ceased to listen to London, both from conviction and in the hope of obtaining, between two *emissions*, some news of myself. ... I knew my parents well enough to know that, like so many French, they were attached to order and recognised a place for authority. And I knew at what point certain dramas would have appeared to them hard to bear. More than the lack of food, I discovered, the fear and trepidation had been the most wearing."[97]

In her west Paris apartment, Greek diplomat's widow Princess Henriette Petrocochino was also visited by a tall officer. The husband of one of her nieces, an officer with Dempsey's British Second Army, came to check up on her welfare, bringing tea and butter, both of which had been a rarity for four years. In his honour she pulled out a bottle of good Cognac she had saved especially for the liberation.[98] Even with four Jewish grandparents this splendid old woman had survived.

Between the Allied armies, American rations were more likely to be welcomed by Parisians, most of whom were not starving but had lost weight fast that last summer when the city's food supplies were at their most erratic. Most Parisians remembered excellent French produce. They were grateful when GIs pulled oranges from their packs, but only a toddler would never have seen one before. The "compo" rations issued to British troops were nutritious, but less pleasant to eat with their hard biscuits and tinned bread with raisins.

While General Montgomery refrained from sending British combat troops into Paris, supply and logistics personnel became involved immediately, formally putting a British shoulder to the city's food needs. One of these officers had a charming encounter with the erotic novelist Colette.

"I cannot believe, I cannot believe it, it isn't over," Colette moaned when Maurice Goudeket assured her that Paris was now full of French and Allied troops.

"I shan't believe it till you've brought a Scottish major here."

"In a kilt?" asked Goudeket, dumbfounded.

"In a kilt," insisted Colette.

"I'll go at once," replied Goudeket.

"I crossed the garden," wrote Goudeket. "As it happened some British troops were stationed on the Place du Palais Royal, and I ran straight off into the most Scottish of majors, with a kilt and a little tooth-brush moustache. I fell into conversation and he told me his job was to re-victual Paris."

"Good man," said Goudeket. "We rather need you."

"Yes," replied the Scottish major. "But in the meantime, I've eaten nothing for twenty-four hours."

Goudeket invited the Scot to their Palais Royal apartment where, over corned beef sandwiches, he explained that his wife was the novelist Colette.

"Have you heard of her?" asked Goudeket.

"My wife reads a lot," he replied. "I expect she'll know."[99]

THE 2e DB'S QUAKER STRETCHER BEARERS were probably the first British troops to enter Paris.

"Paris was absolutely fantastic," Dennis Woodcock told Henry Maule. "Men of the 2e DB could have anything they wanted, absolutely anything. Whatever shops they went into, or restaurants, or cafés, or wherever they went, the people would insist they had anything it was humanly possible to provide. The great affection and admiration the people had for the British was tremendously apparent. If they were prepared to give everything in their power to the French soldiers then it would be true to say this was doubly so as far as the British were concerned."[100]

Part of GT Langlade, after the German surrender, Woodcock's ambulance unit parked along the Avenue Victor Hugo, immediately being given champagne and bottles of scent from a nearby beauty salon. "We were continually called out to deal with casualties. ... We took large numbers of Germans to hospital because there was a great deal of shooting and beating up to pay off scores. ... It was important to find out routes to the hospitals quickly so we were given guides and I did very well, mine being a very charming girl."

"One particularly happy incident," Woodcock continued, "was when a delightful and exceedingly well-spoken man ... came across from some flats nearby and, after introducing himself, asked, 'If you are not otherwise engaged tonight I should be most honoured if you would come and have dinner with me.' When I, and another of the fellows, were able to accept his invitation, he said, 'I would very much like you to meet my two daughters. I have not let them go out of the house since the Germans arrived.' And this was quite true; these two absolutely charming girls—as we found out—had actually been incarcerated ever since the Germans entered Paris."[101]

AMONG THE BRITISH OFFICERS arriving in Paris was Lieutenant Colonel Victor Rothschild, a British member of the Jewish international banking family. Being a bomb disposal expert, Rothschild's primary concern was explosives and booby traps. Another pressing concern was taking possession of his family's substantial property in the leafy Avenue de Marigny before anyone else requisitioned the building.[102]

Not wishing to rattle around alone inside No. 3 Avenue de Marigny, Rothschild offered temporary lodgings to Malcolm Muggeridge, who struck up a fascinating rapport with the Rothschilds' superb butler, Félix Pacaut. "It astonished me, when we first moved into the house, to find its contents intact and undamaged," wrote Muggeridge. "As belonging to one of the most famous Jewish families in Europe, one would have expected it to have suffered. During the German occupation, it was taken over by a Luftwaffe general [Hanesse] who, according to Monsieur Félix—he continued to function as a matter of course—behaved impeccably; not only refraining from tampering with the house and its contents himself, but also preventing others from doing so. When I got to know Monsieur Félix better, I asked him how he accounted for the general's good behaviour, he being, after all, a Nazi. His reply was interesting; Hitlers come and go, he said, but Rothschilds go on forever. He said it with a droll smile; not a man, I concluded correctly, to tell me that he had hidden RAF officers in the cellar along with the Mouton Rothschild. Someone clearly with his wits about him. We often had chats together after that."[103] In truth, General Hanesse was as greedy and corrupt as any other senior Luftwaffe officer close to Goering, but Pacaut was wise to him, discreetly removing family treasures and either hiding them in the building or elsewhere in Paris.[104]

Following a roundabout route into Paris via Chartres came four young officers from the second (armoured) battalion of the Grenadier Guards, one of the Guards Armoured Division's three tank regiments. Allowed a brief period of relaxation after the Wehrmacht's Normandy débacle, Lieutenant David Fraser—a future general, Captain the Lord Carrington—a future Foreign Secretary, and two others called Teddy Denny and Neville Berry decided to check out freshly liberated Paris. Fraser, though the most junior, was elected their guide since his father had been British military attaché during the 1930s. Reaching the Champs Élysées around early evening, passing GT Langlade's Shermans parked under the trees, they found immense, joyful crowds everywhere.

"Where shall we go now?" they wondered as they passed the knocked-out Panther on the Place de la Concorde.

"To the Ritz," said Fraser.

"We were travel-stained and certainly had no easily negotiable funds," wrote Fraser, "but Neville Berry was put in charge of that side of life and persuaded us (and indeed the Ritz) that any shortfall would be made good by Kemsley newspapers."[105]

Although the Ritz was full of foreign journalists, the four officers took a suite. Exploring the hotel's *salons* and bars where they drank several glasses of Perrier Jouet champagne, they saw Ernest Hemingway and noticed "perched at bar stools, long rows of very chic *Parisiennes* who looked as if they had been there every evening since the war began, and probably had". After meeting up with a Welsh Guards officer who arrived at the Ritz accompanied by several *résistants* and a rifle slung over his shoulder, the four Grenadiers ordered dinner. In perfect English the head waiter apologised for the limitations of the menu and took their orders.

"Did you speak English when the Germans were here?" Carrington asked.

"I spoke German when the Germans were here," replied the head waiter.[106]

AMERICAN JOURNALIST MARY WELSH caught up with Hemingway at the Ritz, being greeted in his suite with "a welcoming merry-go-round bear hug", like the one he had given Sylvia Beach the previous afternoon. He introduced his latest love to four of the irregulars who had followed him from Rambouillet. Looking around, Welsh noticed a K-ration stove set up in the fireplace and Hemingway's newly acquired combat jacket bearing the US 4th Infantry Division's four-leaf ivy insignia.

Hemingway's mob now consisted of three committed *résistants* and Marcel Duhamel, who acted as his secretary. Thanks to Duhamel, Hemingway was soon visited by André Malraux, whose adventures almost matched his own. While Ernest and his little band, whom he jokily called "worthless characters", cleaned their weapons, sitting on "nice delicate old furniture", Malraux breezed into Hemingway's room dressed in a French colonel's smart khaki tunic and polished high boots.[107]

"*Bonjour,* André," said Hemingway.

"*Bonjour,* Ernest," Malraux replied. "How many have you commanded?"

"Ten or twelve," Hemingway replied, modestly on this occasion. "At the most two hundred."

"Me, two thousand," replied Malraux, contorting his face.

"What a shame then that we didn't have your help when we were taking this little town of Paris." Hemingway replied.[108]

Hemingway's biographer Carlos Baker develops this scene, quoting one of Hemingway's sidekicks offering "to shoot the fool". Olivier Todd, Malraux's biographer, although maintaining an affectionate yet unimpressed attitude to Malraux, knew his claims could be "pretty preposterous". Both Hemingway and Malraux enjoyed bragging. Nevertheless de Gaulle respected Malraux enough to appoint him Minister for Cultural Affairs.[109]

AT 11.30PM, JOYFUL PARISIANS were shaken back to reality by loud explosions. In vengeance for losing the French capital, the Germans were bombing Paris. At first the aircraft engines sounded like Allied bombers heading for Germany. Then air-raid sirens sounded and destruction fell from the sky. Those capable of counting aircraft from engine noise reckoned there were one hundred and fifty, representing a considerable Luftwaffe effort at that time.[110]

Les Invalides was not only a veteran's hospital and Napoleon's final resting place, but also the residence of the military governor of Paris. After spending much of the evening discussing the Gerow affair, interim governor General Leclerc and General Marie-Pierre Koenig turned in for the night. Hearing the first explosions, semi-undressed, de Gaulle's two most loyal generals ran barefooted from their rooms to the balcony overlooking the front esplanade, from where they witnessed explosions to the north and east. It was the hardest the Germans had hit the city since their use of "the Paris Gun"—sometimes mistakenly called "Big Bertha"—during the First World War.

"*Les salauds! Les salauds!*" said Leclerc. "The swines! The swines!"[111]

The aircraft came over in several waves, mainly dropping incendiary bombs.

"The Ack-Ack was very feeble," wrote David Bruce. When it began Bruce sallied forth into the streets, noticing that "people were shooting at the airplanes with pistols, rifles and machine-guns. In a few minutes, the sky back of Morgan's Bank was glowing brightly. An alcohol dump was on fire there."[112]

Checking on the damage, Prefect Charles Luizet called at the Halles des Vins, whose stocks of alcohol challenged the city's firefighters, illuminating central Paris "like a Bengal fire". Driving further eastwards, Luizet was stopped by 2e DB soldiers, "It's the front line!" Luizet could not believe that they had marched down the Champs Élysées with the enemy so near. Not only were the remaining German forces never under von Choltitz's command, but more troops were arriving on bicycles to reinforce them.[113] Recognising that the air-raid was his priority, Luizet turned back.

At the Préfecture, a curious *bonne bouche* ended Luizet's evening; his predecessor, Amedée Bussière, pushed a neatly scripted rectangle of paper into Luizet's hand. During the previous week's excitement Bussière had forgotten to hand over a cheque for fifty thousand francs that he had been given for the Police social fund.[114]

With little water to douse the fires, over five hundred buildings were destroyed. The human cost was one hundred and twenty three dead in central Paris, including members of the *Garde Republicaine* at the Caserne Schomburg and two American soldiers, and four hundred and sixty-six injured. In the north and eastern *banlieues* there were eighty dead and four hundred and twenty-two injured.[115]

27 August 1944

AT 6AM, WITH ALL DOORS LOCKED, arch-deacon Monsignor Brot and Canon Lenoble performed the sacrament of reconciliation to cleanse Notre Dame of any evil that might have tainted her during that turbulent week. The last time this ritual had been performed was fifteen years before, when someone committed suicide within her confines. Fully robed, and with no congregation, the priests toured the nave and transcepts, inside and outside, saying prayers of cleansing and sprinkling *eau grégorienne* (St Gregory's water), a mixture of water, salt, ashes and wine, on the grey medieval carved stone. Thereby, as Pierre Bourget wrote, "The Church, Catholic and Apostolic, of Rome symbolically effaced all traces of human misdeeds which have no place within consecrated walls."[116]

AS DUST FROM THE NIGHT'S AIR RAID SETTLED, Paris awoke to her first Sunday of freedom. David Bruce could congratulate himself on saving the retired General Aldebert de Chambrun from arrest for being too loyal for too long to Pétain. Bruce also prevented JP Morgan's Paris premises from being shelled by a 2e DB Sherman; all "between two courses at dinner". On Sunday morning, Bruce's eventful life did not let up. "The most unusual requests are made of one here," he wrote. "As I was talking to someone on the street outside the Ritz, a young Frenchman came up to me and introduced quite a nice-looking young man in civilian clothes whom he said was a German soldier who wanted to surrender to the American authorities. The German had formerly enabled the Frenchman to escape when the latter was a prisoner in Germany, and now wanted a favour in return. The story was very complicated; technically, the soldier had once been an American citizen. I finally arranged something about his disposition which was almost as complicated as the story."[117]

The four Grenadier Guards officers' first visit was the British Embassy at 35 Rue du Faubourg Saint-Honoré, which was protected by a custodian of enemy property throughout the Occupation, though an elderly servant playfully told the young officers that he had personally shooed Goering away. David Fraser was happy to find that possessions from his family's former apartment had been brought inside the Embassy. When, the following month, Sir Alfred Duff Cooper arrived as first British Ambassador to liberated France, he found that 35 Rue du Faubourg Saint-Honoré had become a furniture depository for over thirty British households.[118]

After liberating his country's embassy, Lord Carrington was returning to the Ritz when he was hailed by an elderly lady.

"Young man, are you from the *Times*?" asked Lady Westmacott, the elegant widow of a British Indian Army general.

"No, as a matter of fact I'm in the Grenadiers," replied Carrington.[119]

Lady Westmacott, a known Francophile and collector of Rodin sculptures, was another elderly *grande dame* whose comfortable survival in wartime Paris seems incongruous.

Checking on his family's apartment on the Rue Cognacq-Jay,* David Fraser found the same concièrge, albeit more careworn than when he previously saw her. She politely asked after his mother while, in her office, a dark-haired, plump looking girl eyed Fraser nervously.

"Are you Jewish?" asked the girl.

"No," he replied, hoping not to sound curt.

"I am," said the girl.

At last she could say this to someone in uniform without being afraid. "There must have been a mighty pressure of relief, of escaping fears, behind that exchange," Fraser wrote.[120]

For these British officers their Paris visit was necessarily fleeting. The 4th/7th Dragoon Guards had crossed the lower Seine. British Second Army was gobbling up northeastern France. Guards Armoured Division would soon have their own great city to liberate, Brussels. In any case the Ritz, along with other hotels, had run out of food.

Also leaving Paris was Madame Marie-Hélene Lefaucheux. Though bursting with pride as she watched de Gaulle march down the Champs Élysées on the 26th, she was dressed in black, just in case she was already a widow. She too had a faith to keep; to find out what had become of her husband, Pierre.[121]

WHILE JACQUES BRANET SPENT THE NIGHT of 26–27 August at his family's Avenue Hoche apartment, the remnants of his squadron bivouacked in the Bois de Boulogne, watching the rich, who had kept their horses safe throughout the Occupation, take their early morning rides as though nothing had changed. As for Branet's wounds, the 2e DB doctors advised a few days' light duty.[122]

With GT Dio fighting east of Paris, Leclerc set up his advance CP in a *café-tabac* at the Porte de la Chapelle. His first choice had been

---

* This street was named after the founders of the La Samaritaine department store.

a café owned by a Breton lady. But on learning that her parents had died during the bombardment of Fougères, he chose somewhere else.[123] "We were finishing operations in order to disengage from Paris," wrote Girard. "There were still numerous islets of resistance, notably at Le Bourget. It is unbelievable to be making war in such familiar places and in an atmosphere of Bastille Day! I was obliged to contain the crowd while the general read a message from a liaison officer, consulted a map and decided which orders to give. How does one explain to these brave people that we're doing something serious?"[124]

The stakes remained quite high. The German 47th Infantry Division was arriving in strength from the Pas de Calais and making its presence felt aound Saint-Denis, Vincennes and Le Bourget airport.[125] In some northeastern districts the Germans regained a few *mairies*, took hostages, and there were even summary executions.

Attacking towards Saint-Denis, Écouen and Montmorency, GT Dio quickly ran into trouble at Le Bourget where, once again, German 88s and 20mm machine-guns took a heavy toll of men and vehicles. "We watched the Nazis coming back at us across virtually flat terrain," wrote Philippe de Gaulle. "They showed yet again that their infantry are the best in the world." But the 12e Cuirassiers' Shermans pushed their way onto Le Bourget supported by Chad infantry. No sooner was one objective taken than more Germans fired on them from the airfield's many drainage ditches. Captain Gaudet's tanks hosed the area liberally with machine-gun fire.[126]

"It was a serious business," wrote Alain de Boissieu. "Commandant Corlu, Lieutenant de Waziers, a cousin of General Leclerc, and Lieutenant Pity, Gaudet's deputy, were killed before General Leclerc's eyes while other brave men, such as Captain Samarcelli and Lieutenant Kirsch were seriously wounded."[127] The German 47th Infantry Division left hundreds of dead at Le Bourget.

Writing to de Gaulle, Leclerc mentioned painful losses like Jean-Marie Corlu, who had made a long camel trek from Niger in late 1940 to join the Free French. Leclerc also said that, after three weeks in action, the 2e DB needed a rest.

DE GAULLE DISMISSED THE WILDCAT GUNFIRE in Notre Dame as "a vulgar piece of showing off". Nor was he impressed by the untrained *résistants* wandering around Paris. "Many are walking about with weapons, excited by the fighting of these last days, always ready to fire at the roofs. The first shot starts a wild fusillade. We shall stop this too."[128]

General Eisenhower was due to visit, his first time in Paris since serving with the War Graves Commission. He smiled serenely as Kay Summersby drove his armoured Cadillac through villages decorated with Allied flags. After hooking up with General Gerow in a side street, Ike's convoy was greeted at the Porte d'Orléans by General Koenig and led to de Gaulle at the Préfecture.[129]

"I went to call on de Gaulle promptly, and I did this very deliberately as a kind of *de facto* recognition of him as the provisional President of France," Eisenhower told Don Cook after the war. "He was very grateful, he never forgot that. After all, I was commanding everything on the Continent, all the troops, all that de Gaulle could count on, everything supplied by America was under my orders. So he looked upon it as what it was, and that was a very definite recognition of his high political position and his place. That was of course what he wanted and that Roosevelt had never given him."[130]

The Champs Élysées was filled with cheering Parisians shouting, "Eisenhower! Eisenhower!" Military police cleared a passage through the crowds for Ike's Cadillac to reach the Étoile. Getting out of his car, Eisenhower had both cheeks wetly kissed by a large Frenchman. "The crowd squealed with delight," said Bradley, "as Ike reddened and fought free." Bradley tried to escape by running to a Jeep but a heavily rouged *Parisienne* caught him.[131]

Now the serious business of Ike's visit began; with liberation, de Gaulle faced new worries. Paris needed food and fuel. Knowing his own supplies would barely last a few days, Eisenhower authorised a relief operation; exactly the kind of demand he foresaw would delay his armies' principal task of destroying the Wehrmacht. The US official history states, "More than a month and a half after the liberation of Paris, French relief was still a consequential Allied military responsibility."[132]

ANOTHER PROBLEM FACING DE GAULLE was the useful employment of Resistance personnel. While Henri Rol-Tanguy had nobler instincts than de Gaulle credited, his regular officer's distaste for partisans remained. Although the FFI were essential for rebuilding French self-respect, de Gaulle knew that irregular units attracted lawless elements; a view Leclerc shared. Dividing the FFI into three categories, Leclerc called the top ten percent "very good, brave and real fighters", twenty to twenty-five percent were "acceptable but needed leading", while the remainder, over sixty percent, he dismissed as "*racaille et fumisterie*"—"rabble and con-artists". "This isn't really my affair, being only a soldier, but having witnessed some unforgettable scenes, I thought it needed pointing out."[133]

The FFIs' titular commander, General Koenig, supported Leclerc's viewpoint saying, "The FFI represents the worst of dangers for Paris." But to formally enroll the best *résistants* in the French Army, de Gaulle needed more uniforms and equipment than the Pentagon envisaged in their French rearmament programme. But Uncle Sam's coffers were not bottomless and de Gaulle's new divisions had to use up pre-1940 French uniform stocks the Germans disdained to requisition and bolts of *feldgrau* cloth they left behind. Equipping them meant using pre-war and captured weapons.

De Gaulle's most extraordinary request that day, and one which he subsequently denied,[134] was that American troops should march through Paris not just as an Allied victory march but to support his authority and warn the French Left who was in charge. Considering that the previous year in French North Africa, French officials eschewed seeking Allied help to maintain order (Leclerc's freshly equipped division undertook a small police operation in Morocco), Eisenhower was amazed. "Here there seemed a touch of the sardonic in the picture of France's symbol of liberation having to ask for Allied forces to establish and maintain a similar position in the heart of the freed capital."[135] But liberated France was not French North Africa, and Paris was the largest city the Allies had liberated. If it became politically unstable it could undermine subsequent operations. "I understood de Gaulle's problem," Eisenhower wrote, and he personally ordered two infantry divisions to parade through Paris on their way to the front.[136]

Maurice Kriegel-Valrimont was surprised by de Gaulle's attitude to the Resistance after 1944. "Was he really worried by the *menace* of subversion? Were we really dangerous in his eyes?" COMAC and the Resistance's command structure remained in place for months after the Liberation. With the Germans gone the Resistance could only become a kind of Home Guard. Valrimont states unequivocally that they never intended to challenge de Gaulle's authority. "Ah, but you don't understand that he [de Gaulle] was afraid of you," Philippe Ragueneau told Valrimont.[137] De Gaulle recognised that paranoia is sometimes the price of survival.

General Bradley wrote scathingly of the affair, "By this time Leclerc's men had disappeared into back alleys, brothels and bistros. I worked out a plan with Gerow whereby we could redeploy Norman Cota's 28th Infantry Division through the streets of Paris to its jump-off point east of the city without loss of time. In this way, on 29 August, de Gaulle got his 'parade' down the Champs Élysées and I got the 28th Division tactically poised for pursuit of the German Army."[138]

28 August 1944

OFFERING NEW CASUALTY FIGURES of twenty-five killed and eighty wounded, post-Liberation newspapers not only blamed *Miliciens* for the wildcat shootings of the 26th, but extravagantly claimed that *Miliciens* launched rocket flares to guide the Luftwaffe air raid that evening. To Jean Galtier-Boissière's intense pleasure, formerly sidelined, anti-Vichy writers like Claude Mauriac and Georges Duhamel made their comebacks almost immediately.[139]

"*Eh bien, mon cher,*" said Petiet, a stamp seller on the Rue de Tournon, who knew Galtier-Boissière laid down his pen in 1940, "you were right all along."

Sharing the inter-class camaraderie of those who chose "the right camp", Petiet introduced Galtier-Boissière to a cobbler who was tortured by the Gestapo following a neighbour's denunciation.

"I suppose now that you're going to sort this creep out?" suggested Petiet.

"That would be difficult," replied the cobbler."He is now a full member of the Resistance and denouncing *collabos* for all he's worth!"

Having seen *un vieux plaisantin* (an old joker) poncing around in an old naval uniform, whom he remembered sporting a Nazi buttonhole in 1941, Galtier-Boissière knew such conduct was widespread.[140]

There were also tragic mistakes immediately after the Liberation, such as when the Louvre's Jean Jaujard was arrested at gunpoint and an elderly couple was arrested and lynched after their Japanese servant showed himself at a window on the Rue de Rivoli.[141]

Some former *Vichystes* were more tragic than contemptible. Placed under house arrest on 19 August, General Charles Brécard, Vichy's Chancellor of the Légion d'Honneur, was visited by his friend Pastor Marc Boegner. Before being allowed to see Brécard, Boegner was interviewed by interim Chancellor of the Legion d'Honneur, the Resistance General Bloch-Dassault, who remembered Boegner from his time as a Protestant chaplain to the French Vth Corps during the First World War, reeling off names of mutual acquaintances. Bloch-Dassault then told Boegner that, as a former Vichy official, Brécard would face a tribunal. But recognising that Brécard was, at worst, a borderline *collabo*, Bloch-Dassault wanted to know if Brécard would agree to talk to him. Boegner found it infinitely sad seeing Brécard treated as a traitor when he should have spent his retirement as a decent, uncomplicated old general, fond of horses and racing. After chatting with Boegner, Brécard chose to face the music and speak frankly with Bloch-Dassault.[142]

CAMPED IN THE BOIS DE BOULOGNE, the Spaniards of *la Nueve* were totally uninterested in the *épuration* (purge) or Laval's last political manoeuvres. "For us, de Gaulle, Free France, the Resistance, now in triumph; those were the only things that counted," wrote Dronne.[143]

The Bois was invaded by Parisians wishing to meet them, and *Parisiennes* looking for men whose *Gaulliste* record hopefully fitted the freedom-loving years that lay ahead. One member of *la Nueve*, picked up by an elegant *Parisienne* of a certain age, after making love, slept on her bedroom floor using his boots as a pillow; too used to the hard life.[144]

Leclerc's warriors were also bemused by aspects of emerging youth culture; *Zazous* sported whatever extravagant clothes, usually retro, they could find along with long, quaintly arranged hair. While completely uninterested in the war, *Zazous* liked Jazz and could be friendly and kind unless begging for Camel cigarettes which were included in US ration packs. To one who asked too insistently, one of Dronne's Spaniards replied, "If you want cigarettes, blondie, join up and you will get them in your rations." The *Zazou's* face turned so sour that three Spaniards dragged him and two others into a half-track and gave them each a military haircut. Released a few minutes later with buzzed hair, they looked mortified.[145]

During the 2e DB's rest period, Raymond Dronne drove a Jeep back to the Sarthe where he came from. He wanted to hug his mother for the first time since 1937 and catch up on family news. He also discovered that when Vichy condemned him to death *in absentia*, a notice was placed outside the *mairie* in Le Mans. More fascinating was reading the "blue paper" requiring his family to pay the court costs, and discovering that the officer who chaired the tribunal was none other than General Jean de Lattre de Tassigny, who now commanded the French First Army.[146]

29 August 1944

PREMISES USED BY THE OCCUPATION AUTHORITIES were targeted by the US Army. The *Soldatenkino* (Soldiers' Cinema), formerly the Cinema Marignan at 27 Avenue des Champs Élysées, was soon under American supervision. The Avenue Kléber's Hôtel Majestic was soon fitted with an American radio mast to service the US High Command. The city's excellent hospitals, La Pitié, Lariboisière and Beaujon, quickly became military hospitals. There was also the American Hospital in Neuilly, surrendered to the 2e DB on the 25th.[147]

Unlike the departing Germans, American GIs were unlikely to speak a second language and were easily impressed. While many happily gave their K-rations, others sold their food expensively. They gambled in the streets, chatted up French girls, chewed gum, drank too much, laughed too loudly and seemed strangers to old world notions of respect and deference. With demand outstripping supply in bars and cafés, and one dollar buying fifty francs, the temptation to raise prices or rip off *les boys* was understandable.[148] Despite witnessing the liberated city's outpouring of joy merely days before, such practices—mixed with the bitter lees of collaboration—led Ernie Pyle to write cynically, "I am glad you share my rather low opinion of Paris. When I was there I felt as though I were living in a whorehouse, not physically but spiritually."[149] But some Americans would always visit Paris for the same things Hemingway came for.

While GIs drank in cafés around the Champs Élysées, Parisians gathered to watch General Norman Cota's 28th US Infantry Division march from Neuilly to the Place de la Concorde. "Enthused by the power of all this new equipment and by the sporty and practical uniforms of the men, these spectators did not shrink from making the comparison between them and the fatigued soldiers and clapped vehicles of the retreating Wehrmacht that they had seen during the last few weeks in the same place," wrote Charles Lacretelle.

Accompanied by Girard, Leclerc lunched again at Chez Chauland before joining General de Gaulle on the dais erected on the Place de la Concorde. From there, accompanied by US Generals Bradley, Hodges and Gerow, they would watch the 28th Infantry Division march past.[150] With a red keystone emblem as its shoulder patch, the 28th Infantry Division was largely composed of National Guard regiments, some of which pre-dated the American Revolution. Unlike General Barton's 4th Infantry Division, Norman Cota's 28th ID had taken no part in D-Day but landed in France on the 22 July. By the time the 2e DB reached Paris the 28th had fought solidly for over four weeks, earning from the Germans the nickname "bloody bucket division" for their doughty conduct.

Their parade from Neuilly to the Arc de Triomphe and then down the Champs Élysées began with Jeeps rolling slowly along in low gear carrying General Norman Cota and his staff. Cota had only been with the 28th ID since 14 August, but on D-Day he became a hero; hence it was fitting that he should lead his men through Paris and be saluted by his friend General Gerow. Behind them were M8 armoured cars from the division's reconnaissance regiment. Reaching the Place de la Concorde the parade split, half turning north along the Rue de Rivoli while the other half turned south along the Seine's quayside, reuniting east of the Louvre. Next came the infantrymen of the 110th and 112th Infantry Regiments, marching twenty-four abreast so that their phalanxes stretched the width of the Champs Élysées; the fit, well-fed young men of the New World rescuing the Old.

De Gaulle subsequently insisted that this parade had nothing to do with his régime needing a show of Allied support. While Norman Cota's men basked in the cheers of Parisians, they were blissfully unaware of the politics behind the piece of theatre in which they were taking part. From there they rejoined the battlefield and cleared the forest of Compiègne. Americans would liberate the Réthondes' forest clearing where that luxurious *wagon-lit* had stood, where Marshal Foch humiliated the Germans in 1918 and where Hitler humiliated the French in 1940.

IT TOOK THREE DAYS FOR FIELD MARSHAL MODEL to recognise that Dietrich von Choltitz's performance fell considerably short of the "last man" defence expected by Hitler. But, when he did, Model demanded an OKW enquiry into von Choltitz's conduct.[151] Otto Abetz helped to mitigate the effects for von Choltitz's family. "He helped me to his utmost," von Choltitz testified at Abetz's post-war trial.[152]

Provided his family was safe, von Choltitz was philosophical about captivity, writing in his memoirs of the fortitude of German soldiers who became prisoners. After passing through French and American hands he was flown to England and held at Trent Park, an attractive Regency mansion in the Essex countryside once owned by the Sassoon family. Since 1940 it had accommodated important German prisoners of war in considerable comfort. They ate in a formal dining room, and there were well laid out salons where they could sit and converse freely. They were allowed alcoholic drinks, to listen to the radio, and to read newspapers and books. The books had previously belonged to the German Embassy in London and included all genres, beautifully bound. They were waited on, could send out for sundries, and have their uniforms repaired while they lasted, after which, like other POWs in British hands, they wore a chocolate-coloured version of Battledress. "But," wrote von Choltitz, "in each room they [the British] had installed a microphone."[153]

German Jews employed by British Intelligence listened to their conversations on headsets below stairs. When a conversation took an interesting turn it was recorded onto black disc records and transcribed for analysis. The captive "house party" began during 1942 and its first guests were senior officers from Rommel's Afrika Korps. Hence several inmates already had two years during which to discover microphones before von Choltitz's arrival, always supposing they ever entertained more than a suspicion.[154]

By mid-1944 Trent Park's inmates had separated into cliques, with a distinct anti-Nazi circle established around aristocratic panzer generals like General Wilhelm Ritter von Thoma, captured at Alamein, and

General Friedrich Freiherr von Broich, captured in Tunisia, who had been Claus von Stauffenberg's CO when he was seriously wounded. Among such men Dietrich von Choltitz could speak candidly.

On 29 August, four days after Lieutenant Karcher rushed up the stairs of the Hôtel Meurice, recordings show von Choltitz describing his interview with Hitler on 7 August: "I saw Hitler four weeks ago when he nabbed me for Paris. ... It was shortly after the assassination attempt and he was still rather jaded. ... Hitler made me a speech for three quarters of an hour, as though I were a public meeting. ... I was almost sorry for him because he looked so horrible."[155]

Ritter von Thoma urbanely drew him out.

"I have witnessed some *dreadful* things," von Choltitz continued, describing various SS atrocities in Paris which he was unable to control, particularly the murdered French women left naked in one of the city's prisons, to which he was alerted by the Swiss Consul René Naville.

"Yes," replied von Thoma. "That is known here. The only consolation for the Army is that the papers here always lay stress on the SS and Gestapo."[156]

Then von Choltitz updated von Thoma, von Schlieben and von Sponeck on the fate of their friends following 20 July, estimating that three or four hundred Germans had been executed both officially and otherwise following the failed coup.[157]

Under von Thoma's spell, von Choltitz soon admitted involvement in events that undoubtedly marked him down as a potential war criminal.

"The worst job I ever carried out," said von Choltitz, "which I carried out with great consistency, was the liquidation of the Jews. I carried out this order *down to the very last detail.*"

"The whole thing is done on Hitler's orders," replied von Thoma.[158]

At the 1994 *Colloque* about the Liberation of Paris the elderly Henri Rol-Tanguy said, "On the 16 and 21 August [1944] the BBC announced that General von Choltitz' name was on a list of War Criminals. This is an event of great importance which could not have failed to affect the attitude of the Commander of *Gross-Paris*."[159] For all

his bullishness, here Rol-Tanguy effectively admits facing an opponent
hobbled by conscience and remorse.

30–31 August 1944

ON THE MORNING OF 30 AUGUST Leclerc visited General
Leonard Gerow to set the record straight over the parade on the
26th. On hearing something of French priorities, presented with that
patrician charm which Leclerc could manage when required, translated
by Girard, Gerow seemed mollified.

"If I had known I could have organised air cover," said Gerow, now
smiling. "If you had come and seen me as I asked, I could have let you
use your whole division for the ceremony."

Leclerc listened with a bored expression that Girard knew
well. Outside Gerow's office Leclerc told Girard, "It doesn't make
any difference. One can't discuss matters which have diplomatic
implications. General de Gaulle didn't want the Americans involving
themselves. One could hardly tell them that. In such conditions it's
obviously difficult to speak out."[160]

Their next stop was the Hospital Val de Grace to visit the 2e DB's
wounded.

"*Ah, Girard*," groaned Leclerc, seeing the rows of his wounded
soldiers. "Can we really go further? Into Germany?"

Liberating Paris was something of an anti-climax for Leclerc. "The
General is going through a period of pessimism," wrote Girard. "He
is disappointed by the French among whom he finds neither verve
nor national pride."

"They have done nothing, prepared nothing, only thought about
getting by," said Leclerc in one of his flowing discourses.[161]

Compromise with former Vichy supporters was something Leclerc
found exceedingly difficult. As a *Gaulliste de la première heure* he was
always convinced that France's route to freedom lay in fighting alongside
the Allies, even if he did not particularly like *les Anglo-Saxons*. But if

there was anyone Leclerc seriously disliked, it was a "*Vichyssois*"—said with a deliberate nod to the well-known potato-based soup, *Vichyssoise*. Yet there were exceptions, like when he was approached by his former comrade from 1930s North African policing operations, Henri Lecomte. Though once they were great friends, enquiries suggested that, since 1940, Lecomte had merely been a wine merchant and, while not actively *Vichyssois*, he had leant that way. At first Leclerc inclined to send Lecomte packing. But Lecomte pleaded, begging for a chance to expiate his previous indolence by bringing his organisational skills to the 2e DB's staff. Leclerc agreed.[162]

Yet, on another issue, Leclerc seems to have taken an opposite standpoint. Visited by Jacques Branet at the La Tour-Maubourg barracks, Leclerc agreed that the 501e RCC should replace its colonel, Louis Warabiot, who was not a *Gaulliste de la première heure*, with Colonel Émile Cantarel who, while not one either, had joined de Gaulle much earlier, and was also younger and more likely to be respected by a regiment whose character was always *Gaulliste*. Having failed to get this change from Billotte during early August, Branet wrote with satisfaction, "My walking stick indicated that I had been wounded, and perhaps my wounds giving weight to my requests, I obtained from the General the head of our colonel, and his replacement by Cantarel."[163]

PHILIPPE DE GAULLE WAS INVITED TO DINE with his father at the War Ministry on the Rue Saint-Dominique. After the Liberation, black-out curtains and gaffer tape crosses had disappeared. Dust-sheets had been lifted from the impressive Empire furniture. As on the evening before D-Day, it was a Spartan meal "based on American military rations, curiously completed by beef *en gelée*, called 'monkey' and sardines in oil. ... A reasonable wine and freshly baked bread were the only luxuries enjoyed by a small committee of men; an ADC, a member of Leclerc's staff, a member of the Resistance and someone from 'outside'."[164]

"In liberating Paris, we have redressed the scuttling of the fleet at Toulon!" de Gaulle told Philippe.[165] He struggled to forgive the French

Navy for mostly remaining under Vichy's authority until November 1942, and wasting the expensive ships they received during the 1930s. When, that same August, Pétain sent Admiral Auphan to Paris to negotiate a gracious transfer of power, de Gaulle ignored Auphan's feelers. Albeit a footnote, this detail indicates de Gaulle's anger towards the French Navy over the Vichy period.

But what had the Liberation of Paris cost the 2e DB? "My father regretted that the French, particularly Parisians, ignored the human cost of this battle. He would say, 'They only remember the *image* of a day of jubilation and acclamation,'" Philippe de Gaulle told journalist Michel Tauriac. "They did not know that in Paris, and in the Paris region, the 2e DB lost more people than during the rest of the campaign in France. Effectively we sustained losses of ninety-six killed and two hundred and eighty-three wounded out of twelve thousand men *intra muros*—within the walls—of Paris and two times as many within the environs of Paris, making a little less than fourteen per cent of our strength out of action after eight days in combat."[166]

On the German side, during the last actions at Le Bourget, their 47th Infantry Division is believed to have left seven hundred dead on the ground. Other figures for German losses around Paris run at between three and four thousand dead and up to fourteen thousand prisoners while casualties among the FFI and French civilians were nine hundred and six hundred dead, respectively, and many more wounded. Civilian casualties were difficult to attribute; if someone living alone was shot while looking out of their window they might not have been found for weeks.

At one hundred and seven hectares, the cemetery at Pantin, which opened in 1886, is the largest in Paris. It was here that the 2e DB brought the *Tricolore*-draped coffins of their dead. Watched over by General Leclerc, their souls prayed for by the divisional chaplain Père Houchet of the White Fathers, they were interred. "Sadly moving," wrote Girard in a diary entry that also mentions departed comrades he knew well.[167]

AS PIERRE TAITTINGER AND SACHA GUITRY languished, first in the Vélodrome d'Hiver, then the Drancy housing estate internment camp, others, who either collaborated or avoided taking sides, testified to the art of surviving well. Although Coco Chanel's affair with German attaché Baron von Dincklage was well known, the famous couturier got off lightly compared to other Frenchwomen accused of *collaboration horizontale*. Arrested at the Ritz early one morning, she told her maid Germaine Domenger that if she did not return reasonably soon Domenger should contact "*Monsieur* Churchill". Domenger waited anxiously, then went to her mistress's home on the adjacent Rue Cambon to search for useful telephone numbers. Released after a brief interrogation, Chanel was already at her home when Domenger arrived.[168]

Chanel's survival undoubtedly had everything to do with the fact that, whoever she slept with, she was a world brand. "She just put an announcement in the window of her emporium that scent was free for GIs, who thereupon queued up to get their bottles of Chanel No. 5, and would have been outraged if the French police had touched a hair on her head. Having thus gained a breathing space, she proceeded to look for help *à gauche et à droite*, and not in vain, thereby managing to avoid making even a token appearance among the gilded company— Maurice Chevalier, Jean Cocteau, Sacha Guitry, on a collaborationist charge," wrote Malcolm Muggeridge in amused, worldly tones.[169]

For Picasso, being a world brand also undoubtedly saved him from an ugly fate during the Occupation. He was a Spaniard who hated Franco, who claimed impishly to be a communist despite the stashes of cash secreted around his home, a trail-blazer of exactly the kind of degenerate art the Nazis officially despised—and Hitler barely touched him. Intellectuals among the occupiers, notably Ernst Junger, befriended him, albeit not in a particularly meaningful way, and acquired some of his paintings. But when a man has painted *Guernica*, the greatest anti-Fascist statement committed to canvas, accusations of *collaboration* could never have stuck. "It is not that I behaved well, but others behaved worse," he said afterwards.[170]

According to his biographer, Arianna Stasinopoulos-Huffington, Picasso became a "Symbol of the victory over oppression, of survival and of the glory of old Europe. He was a celebrity they could co-opt to add more glamour to their triumph. Having always had a preference for symbols over reality, he accepted. There were thousands of anonymous heroes in the Resistance, but Picasso, although certainly no hero, was a monument, as well known as the Eiffel Tower and almost as accessible."[171]

Shortly after the Liberation, Françoise Gilot found around twenty American soldiers snoozing in the *atelier* she shared with her elderly lover on the Rue des Grands Augustins. They had come to see Picasso.[172]

The lights were back on in the City of Light.

Epilogue

SEEN FROM THE AIR, WARLUS, IN THE DEPARTMENT OF THE SOMME, is an agricultural village of modest size, built in red brick and *torchis*—a mix of clay and straw. The village green, bracketed by pollarded trees, lies slightly to the west of the main road through the village. The honey-coloured stone church to which Madame Philippe de Hauteclocque was taking her children on Assumption Day stands on the green's northeast side. To the north, among irregularly shaped rectangles of woodland, at the end of an oval-shaped gravel drive, the manor house Tailly stands like a squadron of dragoons. By early September, Montgomery's British 21st Army Group had taken Amiens, placing General Leclerc's home behind Allied lines.

On the morning of 6 September a 2e DB Piper Cub landed in a pasture west of the woods behind Tailly. To Leclerc's immense relief the first people he saw cycling along the track towards the aircraft were his eldest sons, Henri and Hubert, now substantially larger than when he left them in 1940. In the meantime, young estate worker Léopold Doualle cycled to the main house to tell Madame Thérèse de Hauteclocque of her husband's return.

"Give me your bicycle," said Thérèse.

Seeing his wife cycling out of the woods, Leclerc grabbed Hubert's bicycle and pedalled towards her. Each astride the standard transport of the Occupation they were reunited. Later that day, with his wife's approval, Leclerc gave his elder sons permission to join the 2e DB.[1]

ANOTHER JOYFUL HOMECOMING THAT SEPTEMBER was had by Pierre Lefaucheux, whose arrest in June had enabled Henri Rol-Tanguy to step further up the hierarchy of the P1 FFI. After leaving Paris on 27 August, Marie-Hélène Lefaucheux made her way into German-held territory in her relentless quest to find and, if possible, rescue her husband. Field Marshal Model had yet to reconsolidate the Wehrmacht's western front, and Marie-Hélène managed to get through with the help of an Italian haulage contractor from Nancy who had a friend in Buchenwald. Miraculously, Molinari put Marie-Hélène in contact with a Gestapo official in Nancy, another Nazi anxious to demonstrate that Germans could be humane; a young, thin man called von Else. Von Else discovered that the prison train of 16 August took Pierre Lefaucheux to Buchenwald. Von Else also had sufficient rank to order both the release of Lefaucheux and Molinari's friend back to the Gestapo in Nancy. Even better, von Else drove Molinari and Marie-Hélène Lefaucheux to Buchenwald to ensure that his order was carried out. While Marie-Hélène waited anxiously at the camp's gates, von Else spent several hours negotiating her husband's release, eventually returning to the gate with a dishevelled, thin looking individual who was indeed Pierre Lefaucheux. Like a classical legend, Marie-Hélène ventured to the gates of Hades to save the man she loved. Thrilled by her success, Marie-Hélène telephoned Claire Girard, whom she met during mid-August when Claire was trying to save her brother, only to discover from her mother that Claire was among the last people the Germans shot before withdrawing from Courdimanche northwest of Paris.[2]

NOW THAT THE *PÉRIODE INSURRECTIONELLE* WAS OVER, Henri Rol-Tanguy had to consider his future. Although some former *résistants* felt that de Gaulle had acted both brutally and ungratefully towards the Resistance, returning France to the rule of law was a priority. Most Parisians wanted this above all, even telling Leclerc's boys that, while they were grateful for the liberation, it was time they moved on. Liberated France had massive re-organising to do, particularly rebuilding its armed forces. To this end Rol-Tanguy gave the French Army full information on the most useful members of his former command, who mostly joined the new 10th Infantry Division, largely composed of Parisians, and whose badge was the ship and *lys* of Paris. Rol-Tanguy's clandestine rank of colonel was confirmed and he was given a regiment.

Soon after leaving Paris the 2e DB was in action again as part of General Patton's drive into the Vosges. After liberating Vittel the 2e DB fought two classic armoured battles at Dompaire and Baccarat where Leclerc demonstrated that, even if Paris was set up for him, he was an excellent armoured division commander. Much of the damage to the counterattacking Panzer forces at Dompaire was inflicted by the RBFM's Tank-Destroyers. Leclerc rewarded them by reinstating their red lanyards. The dying of course did not stop. Shortly after becoming a sub-group commander, Jean Fanneau de la Horie was killed by shrapnel at Badonvilliers.

But the 2e DB was not big enough for both Leclerc and Pierre Billotte. There were insinuations that Billotte could have entered Paris quicker. As de Gaulle's former ADC, Billotte had become used to the diplomatic aspect of soldiering and the benefits that went with it. Matters finally boiled over when Billotte used von Choltitz's Mercedes to get around the units in his battlegroup while Leclerc merely used a Jeep. Luckily de Gaulle had another plan for Billotte: command of the newly formed 10th Infantry Division. His departure enabled Leclerc to give Jacques de Guillebon a battlegroup command, something Guillebon had long deserved.

ON 13 SEPTEMBER FORTY-EIGHT SPITFIRES escorted Alfred Duff Cooper to take up his new appointment as British ambassador to France. "It was a perfect morning and we enjoyed the flight," wrote Duff Cooper. "It was interesting to see the traces of war as we went along. We flew quite slowly over Paris and saw all the familiar buildings. The streets looked very empty but I do not think they are really emptier than the London streets, and there are many more bicycles and horse carriages. We were met by the staff, Holman, Reilly, etc., and also by representatives of General de Gaulle and the Ministry of Foreign Affairs. We were attended on our way from Le Bourget by French police motorcyclists, and everywhere as we passed the people seemed pleased to see us, saluting and waving. We went to the Arc de Triomphe where I had to lay a wreath on the grave of the Unknown Soldier, and then to the Berkeley Hotel, where we always used to stay, and which Freddie [Fane] has requisitioned complete for us and the staff. There we had an excellent lunch, and then went round to the embassy."[3]

At 35 Rue de Faubourg Saint-Honoré, Duff Cooper saw virtually the same spectacle of expatriate possessions as Lord Carrington and his comrades three weeks earlier; although a start had been made sorting out the belongings of those who had fled in 1940. Otherwise there was little damage and the only obstacles to immediate habitation were lack of utilities.

The following day Duff Cooper met Georges Bidault, now de Gaulle's Foreign Minister, who admitted being over-promoted. Difficulties continued over de Gaulle's status as a *de facto* but unelected head of state, something Duff Cooper knew remained a sensitive issue for the proud Frenchman. When Major Desmond Morton said that Churchill wanted to visit Paris as soon as possible, Duff Cooper replied that the British should recognise de Gaulle's government first. "Nothing could do more harm," Duff Cooper wrote in his diary, "than if he [Churchill] came as part of SHAEF and lived outside Paris with them at Versailles."[4]

Socially, Duff Cooper and his wife, Lady Diana, were in their element. In the words of Malcolm Muggeridge, the Coopers "raised the banner of pre-war smartness and many flocked to it, some of whom for various reasons had been lying low since the liberation".[5] Duff Cooper's diary acquires a whiff of Proust as he describes these gatherings. "Nelly de Vogüé was there, and also her husband, whom I had not met before. He has been a leading light in the Resistance movement, and was wearing the FFI armlet."[6]

There were plenty of people in Paris anxious to tell Duff Cooper everything that had happened during the Occupation. Prefect of Police Charles Luizet, whom Duff Cooper knew from Algiers, gave him a guided tour of Nazi torture chambers. A few weeks later, Luizet was the catalyst of a lighter moment when he ordered the arrest of British comic novelist P.G. Wodehouse, who was living quietly at the Hotel Bristol after his release from internment in Germany where he unwisely made light-hearted broadcasts. Once Luizet recognised that Wodehouse's sins were caused by unworldliness rather than treachery, a face-saving fudge was arranged whereby Wodehouse was released via a short stay in hospital. Discussing the Wodehouse affair at the British Embassy, Duff Cooper began falling asleep, until Muggeridge more amusingly pointed out that, "Though so dyed in the wool a noncombatant, Wodehouse had, all unconsciously, made at least one useful contribution to the war effort. The Germans, in their literal way, took his works as a guide to English manners, and used them when briefing their agents for a mission across the Channel. Thus it happened that an agent they dropped in the Fen country was wearing spats—an unaccustomed article of attire that led to his speedy apprehension. Duff Cooper agreed that this was a notable service deserving of an OBE, but did not feel that, in the circumstances, he could recommend Wodehouse for one."[7]

Sacha Guitry received less understanding. Asked by an examining magistrate why he agreed to meet Goering, Guitry replied "*par curiosité*".[8] Merely meeting a senior Nazi amounted to a smoking gun for those administering the *épuration* (purge). Perhaps, like Wodehouse, Guitry's real crime was to continue his career, apparently indifferent to the suffering around him. Towards the end of his Paris appointment Duff Cooper wrote, "He [Guitry] was a notorious collaborator and was in prison for a long time, but everything appears now to be forgiven. He told some funny stories and told them beautifully."[9]

COMPARED TO OTHERS, Guitry's *collaboration* was comparatively minor. Liberation courts were far more concerned with active displays of common cause with the Nazis and Vichy. Drieu la Rochelle, having already attempted suicide during the liberation and been revived by his housekeeper's intervention, avoided liberation justice by taking a second overdose but carefully left a note, "This time, Gabrielle, let me sleep." She did.[10]

Robert Brasillach's trial happened fairly quickly. He made the mistake of giving a great speech, declaring that he was prepared to pay for what he had done. Had he been content to let his counsel do the talking he might have lived. The jury condemned him by a majority rather than unanimously. Brasillach accepted his death sentence with the words, "*C'est un honneur.*"[11]

But de Gaulle's government really wanted those who wisely left the Metropole in the slipstream of *la grande fuites des Fritzs*; men like *Milice* leader Joseph Darnand, and his henchmen Max Knipping and Jean Bassompierre, Vichy's plenipotentiary in Paris, Fernand de Brinon, who even Laval called a "pig"; men with French blood dripping from their hands. They also wanted Pétain and Laval themselves, and everyone who, by following Vichy's line, promoted Nazi Germany's interests. Although Pétain and Laval detested each other, both honestly believed they were serving France's interests, regarding their forcible abduction to Germany that August as a form of martyrdom.

For young Frenchmen like Christian de la Mazière who took *collaboration* to its logical conclusion and re-mustered in the SS Charlemagne Division that autumn, their choice might still mean something if Pétain gave them his blessing. But when La Mazière and a brother officer, in new SS uniforms, arrived at Sigmaringen hoping Pétain would see them, they were disappointed. "The Marshal cannot receive you," they were told by an official. "He can't receive us though we're going to get ourselves killed?" protested La Mazière. "What about Laval?" But he also refused to see them. "We walked back into Sigmaringen where there were several *Gasthause* where the French congregated," wrote La Mazière. "Feeding time for us is a sacred hour, but it was first come, first served. We saw Rebatet, Céline with his wife, and Vigan pass in the street. I wanted to speak to them, but La Buharaye, who had not got over his anger, told me to forget it."[12]

DE GAULLE WAS ANXIOUS that France finish the war not only with her liberty restored but with her rank in the world reinstated as well. "Coming home" was not enough. And even if Paris was French again, neither Roosevelt nor Churchill seemed willing to take France seriously. One reason for this was obvious: France's coffers were empty. The Americans were unenthusiastic about financing any more units for France's renascent armed forces. Once de Lattre de Tassigny's First Army got past its initial burst up the Rhone valley, its divisions were used to hold the line rather than conduct major thrusts into Germany. Leclerc, who hated de Lattre anyway, believed that his treasured 2e DB would finish the war better if they remained under US command. For their part, American generals Patton, Haislip and Patch were glad to have Leclerc. But when Leclerc asked for the RBFM to be re-equipped with the new Tank-Destroyer, he was told such items were not included in the French rearmament programme.

Shortly before the liberation of Paris, de Gaulle was angered when Churchill visited the newly liberated island of Corsica without first consulting the GPRF in Algiers. De Gaulle, supported by several British MPs, thought it perverse that Churchill's government should recognise Italy's first post-Mussolini government before that of France.[13] When, in late October, de Gaulle learnt that Churchill was intending to visit Paris, de Gaulle sent the following message to the Quai d'Orsay and all relevant ministries: "If Mr Churchill happens to pass through Paris, no arrangements, no demonstrations, no presence of any kind must be organised on the French side without my agreement. Inform everybody that I attach the greatest possible importance to this."[14]

It took the combined efforts of Georges Bidault and Duff Cooper to get the relationship between the French and *les Anglo-Saxons* onto a more gracious footing. Armistice Day, 11 November, was suggested as a good opportunity for an official visit by Churchill. At first de Gaulle objected that this celebration was not exclusively French, but

Georges Bidault pulled the Constable around. On the British side, despite Lord Beaverbrook's petty frog-bashing behind the scenes, Churchill was also persuaded to put on a show with his former protégé in Paris.[15] De Gaulle issued the invitation on 30 October. Roosevelt was also invited but declined, possibly because he was involved in his fourth election for the US presidency. Churchill, accompanied by his family as well as Anthony Eden and General Ismay, arrived in Paris on 10 November. "We received them as best we could," wrote de Gaulle. "Paris, to acclaim them, gave all its voice. With Bidault and several ministers, I went to Orly to welcome them and conducted the British Prime Minister to the Quai d'Orsay where we were accommodating them."[16]

Armistice Day 1944 was chilly. After collecting Churchill, who wore an RAF uniform and greatcoat, from the Quai d'Orsay, de Gaulle took him across the Seine to the Place de la Concorde, escorted by the *Garde Republicaine* on horseback. Parisians turned out in force to see Great Britain's war leader who, in 1940, picked out de Gaulle as *l'homme du destin*. "The Champs Élysées was crowded with Parisians and lined with troops. Every window was filled with spectators and decorated with flags," wrote Churchill.[17] Duff Cooper had never seen anything like it either. "Never have I heard such a sustained roar of cheering as heralded their approach," wrote General Ismay.[18] Standing in an open car, Churchill made his famous two-fingered V sign as Parisians yelled, "*Vive de Gaulle! Vive Churchill!*" Eventually they reached the Étoile where both men laid wreaths of poppies on the tomb of the *Soldat Inconnu*. "After this ceremony was over," wrote Churchill, "the General and I walked together, followed by a concourse of the leading figures of French public life, for half a mile down the highway I knew so well."[19]

When they reached Georges Clémenceau's statue, Churchill laid another wreath. Then, prearranged by de Gaulle, the band played *Le Père la Victoire*, the patriotic song made famous by Jean-Paul Habans, aka Paulus, during the *belle époque*. "For you!" said de Gaulle in English. "That was fitting," wrote de Gaulle. "Since, remembering how at Chequers, at the end of a very bad day, he sang to me* that old song of Paulus without forgetting a single word."[20]

Their next stop was Les Invalides to visit the tomb of Marshal Foch. While there, Churchill looked over the marble balustrade at Napoleon's red quartzite sarcophagus as Hitler had done fifty-three months before. "*Dans le monde*," growled Churchill, "*il n'y a rien de plus grand*."— "There was no-one greater in the world."[21] Had Churchill's ancestor been Wellington rather than Marlborough, he might not have said that. But on this occasion he was being generous, and de Gaulle was the perfect host. Arriving at the Ministry of War for lunch, Churchill was confronted by a bust of Marlborough, placed there on Gaston Palewski's orders. "It's too much," murmured Churchill.[22]

Turning to business, de Gaulle asked Churchill for weapons. Churchill's response was sensible but pragmatic. If the war was only going to last a few more months then it made sense to concentrate new equipment on proven units. If, on the other hand, matters dragged on, then the Allies would call for more French forces who would be equipped. "Without the French Army, there can be no European settlement," said Churchill. Bidault replied that it was crucially important for the French to participate as fully as possible, "They have to revenge themselves for the past."[23]

TO THIS END GENERAL LECLERC was doing his utmost. He also had a sympathetic US Corps commander in General Wade Haislip who knew about the oath Leclerc and his men had sworn at Kufra, that they would never lay down their arms until the *Tricolore* flew again over Strasbourg Cathedral. Haislip arranged things so that it was the 2e DB who swept into the city after a brilliant campaign of feint and

---

* *Le Père la Victoire* is a long and complex song written during the 1880s when the spirit of *révanche* imbued French life. The voice of a centenarian calls on younger men to win the glory he can no longer do himself. By 1918 the song was synonymous with Clémenceau. For Churchill to have sung it word perfect to de Gaulle takes some doing. He must have practised at some stage with a gramophone and sheet music.

manoeuvre at Saverne. Among the division's tragic losses was their senior chaplain, Père Houchet.[24]

For de Gaulle, the impoverishment of French life after the Occupation, the disappointing return of pre-war politicians to old quarrels, and France's continuing poor relation status rankled. It made him impish, capable of behaving naughtily among the other powers. Visiting the Soviet Union, de Gaulle was taken to see Stalingrad. According to legend de Gaulle said to Molotov, "What a great people, the Germans I mean," apparently admiring the Wehrmacht's military achievement in making such enormous inroads into European Russia. This Patton-like gaffe went down very badly with the Soviets and was vehemently denied on the French government's behalf by the diplomat Jean Laloy. Yet Laloy admitted that the previous day de Gaulle had expressed admiration for Germany's war effort.[25]

For Christmas, de Gaulle took refuge among the 2e DB. The renascent French Army was in turmoil. De Lattre's First Army was incapable of keeping order in those areas of France it had liberated, allowing resistance factions to impose rule of the gun behind his front line. Leclerc contemptuously named these areas "*zones contaminées*", which provided him with a useful pretext for refusing to serve under de Lattre. When eventually prevailed upon to co-operate with First Army to reduce the Colmar pocket, Leclerc criticised de Lattre all the way; their rows becoming the talk of Parisian society. US 6th Army Group commander, General Jacob Devers, had no option but to allow Leclerc's return to American command.

For indulging Leclerc's conduct towards de Lattre, the French chief of staff, General Alphonse Juin, felt Leclerc owed him a favour. While two-thirds of the 2e DB was allowed a period of rest, GT Langlade was sent to reinforce the taking of the Atlantic town of Royan, one of the so-called "Atlantic pockets" still held by the Germans. Knowing these redoubts would fall in good time, Leclerc was furious, calling the mission a "*coûteuse* inutilité"—a "costly waste of time," which it was. It cost the division several good men and the brilliant planner André Gribius was seriously wounded. Furthermore, with Hitler's Reich now collapsing, the Royan operation risked preventing the 2e DB from being on German soil for the final Allied victory.

Thanks to both Leclerc's lobbying and the resourcefulness of his logistics team, the 2e DB soon re-joined Devers' 6th Army Group for the push into southern Germany. When the US 12th Armored Division entered Munich to take up garrison and occupation duties, the only armoured force available to push on to Hitler's mountain retreat at Berchtesgaden was the 2e DB. There is much controversy over which Allied unit reached Hitler's Eagle's Nest first, or which part, but the 2e DB was certainly prominent.* When Jacques Massu visited Dachau's French political prisoners, Abbé Hénocque, a former chaplain at Saint-Cyr military academy, fell into his arms, and Gaullist *résistant* Edmond Michelet gave Massu a guided tour.[26]

Around Berchtesgaden the 2e DB found stashes of looted French artefacts including cases of vintage wines, and packed them up for return to France, causing a serious altercation with a staff officer from US XXI Corps under whose authority Leclerc's division now came. This time Christian Girard prevented a re-run of the Gerow affair and the matter ended amicably.[27]

On the whole Leclerc got through the war with a string of successes and little controversy, but he would not escape forever. When the Americans delivered a dozen veterans of the French SS Charlemagne Division, which had been virtually destroyed fighting the Russians in Pomerania and Berlin, controversy arrived with knobs on. The 2e DB's staff eyed Hitler's Frenchmen with interest.

"Aren't you ashamed to serve in this [German] uniform?" Leclerc asked an officer.

"You look very fine in an American one," he replied.

Recoiling, Leclerc muttered, *"Débarrassez moi de ces gens-la."*—"Get rid of those people."[28] It is uncertain whether Leclerc intended these

---

* According to Leclerc's granddaughter, Madame Bénédicte Coste, there was no doubt among the 2e DB that they were first to the Eagle's Nest and that 2e DB tanks subsequently blocked the road.

words to be taken as a death sentence, but they were shot by a firing squad from the Chad Regiment the following day. Perhaps seeing Dachau influenced Leclerc's snap decision; according to French military law it was an open and shut case. But the extent of *collaboration*, especially when Nazi conquest was at its height, forced de Gaulle's government to invent new punishments like a "period of national indignity" for those who chose *le mauvais camp*. With hindsight this episode, which blights Leclerc's reputation to this day, could have been avoided if he had simply fed these young men into the *épuration's* justice system.

Towards the end of May 1945, with the war in Europe over, the 2e DB retured to France. On 18 June, the fifth anniversary of de Gaulle's *Appel* from London, there was a big parade in Paris led by Leclerc in his command tank, *Tailly*. De Gaulle had new tasks for Leclerc, in the Far East. On 22 June he said good-bye to the 2e DB at a private parade at Fontainebleau.

"Why, nearly two years ago, did we not hesitate to take into this division men of the most varied origins and beliefs?" Leclerc asked his men. "Because we knew that France could only revive itself through a great union of all Frenchmen. Why did we demand and obtain the right to land in Normandy with the other Allied troops? Because we knew that it was indispensable that the Ile de France, the heart of our country, should be liberated in part by French troops. Why did we march on Paris? Because the Division understood the moral importance for our country."[29]

WITH GERMANY'S DEFEAT, IMPORTANT *COLLABOS* now fell into the hands of de Gaulle's government. Senior *Miliciens* Joseph Darnand, Max Knipping and Jean Bassompierre would never receive the Constable's mercy; after trials whose verdicts were forgone conclusions, they were shot.

But could the Constable consign his first colonel to such a fate? Marshal Pétain returned voluntarily to French soil via Switzerland in April 1945. He was met at the border by General Koenig who told the guards neither to salute nor acknowledge the marshal. When Pétain offered Koenig his hand, Koenig refused it. In Gaullist eyes Vichy had much to answer for: the suspension of French freedoms, the political trials at Riom, which condemned pre-war politicians like Leon Blum and Georges Mandel to imprisonment in Germany, a two-year undeclared war with the British and, concurrently, a civil war with the Free French, not to mention the *Milice* and co-operation with the Nazis' anti-Jewish programme. The conspiracy theorist Albert Bayet put it about that Pétain had been against his fellow Frenchmen since 1918 and had longed to see France stumble so that the extreme Right could take over the country.[30]

Obviously Bayet's ideas were nonsense. But, although a very old man, Pétain was neither senile nor devoid of moral compass and clearly knew what was happening under Vichy. Predictably, he claimed to have been as much a prisoner of the Germans as anyone else. "Each day, with a dagger at my throat, I struggled against the enemy's demands," he said.[31] A central tenet of his defence was that he was merely a figurehead while Laval prostrated France before her Teutonic conquerors. Jacques Isorni, an immensely talented barrister, undoubtedly did his best for Pétain and became fond of him during the trial.* Some of the prosecution's case was undoubtedly unreasonable; for example, accusing Pétain of agreeing to a treasonous armistice in 1940 when the Wehrmacht had totally defeated France's army. But the new government required a guilty verdict and got it.

When it came to sentencing, the court faced a difficult situation. The obvious punishment for treason in wartime is death; otherwise the French penal code allowed a punishment of prison with hard labour. Since Pétain was clearly too old for hard labour he was sentenced to death. But Pétain was also the hero of Verdun. Could de Gaulle see his

---

* In November 1951, four months after Marshal Petain's death, Maitre Isorni joined several prominent former members of the Vichy establishment, including Pierre Taittinger and General Brécard, in forming a committee dedicated to rehabilitating Pétain's reputation.

former colonel shot? He commuted the sentence to life imprisonment on the Ile d'Yeu off the Atlantic coast.

At his trial Laval seemed not to fully recognise that his life was at stake, expecting his *esprit* and fluency to protect him. When he was condemned to death he could not believe it. Laval's lawyers pleaded unsuccessfully with de Gaulle to commute Laval's sentence to life imprisonment. "If Laval is executed, after everything that's happened, would it really be an execution?" asked Pastor Marc Boegner. But de Gaulle listened impassively. In that case the law of his *épuration* had to take its course.[32]

Shortly before his execution Laval took poison, but he was found before it took effect. After his stomach was pumped, Laval groggily admitted getting the poison from the writer Louis-Ferdinand Céline in Germany the previous winter. Perhaps Céline was defrauded; it merely made Laval ill.[33]

In a fabulous display of scruple, Prefect Luizet referred to de Gaulle, wondering if Laval should be executed before he had recovered. The Constable listened with a pained expression, his eyes half closed, then said, "Pierre Laval no longer belongs to us. Let the officer commanding the firing party perform his duty."[34]

Outside Fresnes prison the firing squad was kept waiting, being given second servings of rum to steady their nerves. When Laval was finally presented to them, their volley was un-uniform and messy, though not quite botched. Other *collabos* inside the jail shouted and banged on their cell doors, "*Bandits! Salauds! Assassins!*"[35]

FROM THE AUTUMN OF 1944, PARISIANS clamoured for memorials to those who were killed during the Liberation. The Bailly family requested a memorial for their son who died on the corner of the Rue de Rivoli and the Place de la Concorde on the 25 August. Then the *Comité de Libération de L'Hay-les Roses* requested that Sergeant Marcel Bizien, who was killed on the Place de la Concorde as he dismounted his Sherman that same afternoon, should also have a commemorative plaque. Marie-Hélène Lefaucheux, now vice-president of the post-liberation Municipal Council, became involved and the idea mushroomed. The inscriptions are not uniform; some plaques carry the Cross of Lorraine, others crossed *Tricolores* or emblems important to the person commemorated.[36] Bizien's plaque reads, "*ICI TOMBA HÉROIQUEMENT LE 25 AOUT 1944 MARCEL BIZIEN CHEF DE CHAR 2EME DIVISION BLINDÉE DU GÉNÉRAL LECLERC APRES AVOIR ATTAQUÉ ET DÉTRUIT UN CHAR TIGRE ALLEMAND.*" ("Here fell heroically on 25 August 1944, Marcel Bizien tank commander of the 2e DB after having attacked and destroyed a German Tiger tank.") The fact that the German tank was in fact a Panther is unimportant; the plaque, set into a sandstone wall above an alcove with a stone plant stand, provides a dignified tribute to a fine young man cut off in his prime.* So too does the plaque near the Place de la République where twenty-two-year-old Michel Tagrine fell when, after the Germans had raised a white flag, he went to help a wounded comrade and was shot by a Waffen SS soldier.[37]

All these plaques which discretely adorn Paris are immensely moving, but particularly so are those to several people, like that commemorating Maurice Violeau and ten of his comrades in the *Garde Républicaine* who died of smoke asphyxiation when the Caserne Schomberg was hit by incendiary bombs during the air-raid on the evening of 26 August.[38]

Usually these plaques are uncontroversial and the facts described on them are un-contestable. But at 65 Rue Chardon-Lagache a plaque was put up to commemorate the forty-two victims of the Captain Jack sting who were shot by the waterfall in the Bois de Boulogne. It read, "*ICI, DANS CE GARAGE, ONT ÉTÉ TROUVÉ LE 17 AOUT 1944, LES CORPS DE QUARANTE-DEUX PATRIOTES, JEUNES CATHOLIQUES COMBATTANTS, ORGANISATIONS CIVILE ET MILITAIRE, FTP, FFI, FUSILLÉS PAR ORDRE DU GÉNÉRAL ALLEMAND VON CHOLTITZ.*" ("Here, in this garage, were found

---

* Bailly's and Bizien's memorial plaques and niches are within a row of ten set into the wall of the Jardin des Tuileries, outside the Jeu de Paume, facing onto the west end of the Rue de Rivoli.

on 17 August 1944, the bodies of forty-two patriots, *Jeunes Catholiques Combattantes*, *Organisation Civile et Militaire*, FTP, FFI, shot by order of the German General von Choltitz.") Two details on this plaque were incorrect. First, the bodies were only taken to the garage on Rue Chardon-Lagache *after* being found beside the waterfall in the *bois*. Second, they were not shot on the orders of General von Choltitz, who was immensely frustrated at being unable to control SS and Gestapo personnel during the Occupation's last days. These inaccuracies would have probably remained uncorrected if von Choltitz had not heard about it and visited Paris privately during 1963. "I never ordered any Parisian to be shot," von Choltitz told French libel barrister, Maitre Louis Guitard. After three years of legalities involving witness reports, including Jacques Chaban-Delmas and Alexandre Parodi, by then senior French politicians, the Prefect of the Department of the Seine, Haas-Picard, ordered the wording altered to "shot by order of the Gestapo".[39]

AFTER HIS SOJOURN AT TRENT PARK, General von Choltitz was transferred to a POW camp in America. In 1947, while a French military attaché at the UN, Pierre Billotte obtained from General Eisenhower a release date for von Choltitz. "His colleagues, the other German generals, could not help but accentuate their disapproval of him, which they had already shown, for an astonishing perversion of their ideals in disobeying the monstrous orders of the Führer," wrote Billotte.[40]

When Otto Abetz was put on trial in 1949, von Choltitz appeared as a defence witness. Lawyers were now well familiarised with the *épuration*'s tribunals in Nanterre. But in Abetz's case the facets of French life in which he involved himself were so numerous, creating voluminous paperwork, that the tribunal was swamped. Thus, despite the fact that Abetz had been held in French prisons for three years, the case against him was ill-prepared. As the post-war French economy revived, ambitious French lawyers became less interested in state prosecution work, especially if it was complex. Abetz's prosecutor was a young captain from the army's legal service, who was out of his depth and tried to hide his inexperience behind an air of dilettantism. Contrastingly, Abetz had an experienced and sophisticated barrister who relished fighting a difficult case.[41] His role in the deportation of Jews and the cynical negotiations to return Georges Mandel to France so the *Milice* could murder him were hugely to Abetz's detriment. To counter this problem, his counsel played the Paris card for all it was worth.

In his statement, von Choltitz claimed that Abetz vehemently advised him against carrying out Hitler's destruction order. Once von Choltitz began disobeying Hitler, Abetz protected him by raising fake protests against the brutal conduct of Wehrmacht forces commanded by von Choltitz, saying that he personally ordered the torching of the Grand Palais to punish the French police, thereby giving the impression that von Choltitz was a *ganzharter*, in order to save his family from repercussions under *Sippenhaft*. This bought time for von Choltitz, enabling him to delay carrying out Hitler's destruction order until it was too late anyway.[42] Spared the death penalty, Abetz was sentenced to twenty years' imprisonment. Further depositions reduced this to fifteen years' hard labour, but a petition, whose signatures included von Choltitz and Ernst Junger, effected Abetz's release in 1954.[43]

On the afternoon of 25 August 1944, something about von Choltitz impressed Billotte, making him write, "Choltitz had *de la tradition*." Writing in the early 1970s, Billotte continued, "If Paris was not destroyed it is also thanks to decisions taken by enemy personnel such as Dietrich von Choltitz, without forgetting the philosopher General Hans Speidel, Rommel's former chief of staff. By chance, Speidel was then chief of staff to Field Marshal Model. He reassured von Choltitz in his conduct and it seems that he detoured to the lower Seine all or some of the divisions that the Wehrmacht sent to reinforce Paris. In doing this, this German patriot in no way betrayed the interests of his country. The actions of these divisions on the lower Seine were just as obstructive to the Allied offensive as if they had been in Paris. But even if it has never been sworn to me, I remain convinced that this civilised man, choosing between two manoeuvres of equal military value, chose the one that spared 'the City of Light'."[44]

Billotte later claims that his efforts to get von Choltitz released in 1947 contributed to his social ostracism when he returned to West Germany and his inability to get more than a modest job in recruitment.[45] Since many German gentlefolk, whose family property fell behind the Iron Curtain in 1945, struggled to regain their former status in West Germany, von Choltitz's post-war misfortunes were unremarkable. Billotte continues, "This professional soldier of the Reichswehr respected military tradition, the rules of war, and the natural rights of men and women subjected to conflict. Nor was he without culture, and his sensitivity to Paris, which he regarded as a treasure of humanity and masterpiece created over centuries, was real. This soldier put the principles of morality which he had forged within himself above the duty to obey orders he regarded as immoral. Before he was a soldier, von Choltitz was a man. It is truly sad that more of Hitler's generals did not practice the same ethics; Nuremberg would not have had to deal with the criminals among them."[46] It is clear from these words that Billotte liked von Choltitz. Nevertheless Billotte qualifies this viewpoint, rejecting von Choltitz's attempt to establish that Paris' survival was entirely attributable to him. "Contrary to certain excessive passages in his memoirs, Paris does not owe him everything, but it owes him a lot."[47] Billotte ended the war with enough prestige to give a "serene judgement" of von Choltitz, which was to regard him as an honourable soldier.[48] From the Vichy side, Pierre Taittinger, who was banned from taking part in post-war public life, wrote, "Von Choltitz made me a promise. He kept it."[49]

"QUI EST DONC LE HÉROS?"—"Who, then, is the hero?" French civic society takes this question immensely seriously. Street names are changed with greater frequency than in most countries, depending on which new great ones require honouring. The Second World War naturally provided a new, complicated and fascinating generation of men and women needing recognition. Though which type of heroes

received a road, avenue or town square named after them would depend on which political party controlled a town. Among the Resistance, men like Jean Moulin and Alexandre Parodi do well. Fittingly, as a keen rugby player, Jacques Chaban-Delmas has a stadium named for him. The "Gentleman of Paris", Raoul Nordling, has his Avenue du Consul Général Nordling. But FTP leaders like Charles Tillon and Henri Rol-Tanguy are less lucky. For the Free French, Charles de Gaulle comes out on top with the Étoile and even an aircraft carrier named after him.

But if one wants to see who the French, and Parisians in particular, really regard as the heroes of 1944, among the pale stone plaques and street names the 2e DB seem to do best. The Avenue de la Libération is named after GT Billotte's route into the city. While around the old Gare Montparnasse—which has become the long-named Mémorial du Maréchal Leclerc et de la Libération de Paris, Musée Jean Moulin, Ville de Paris—several 2e DB officers, including Jacques de Guillebon and Raymond Dronne, have small roads named after them.

After the European war ended, General Leclerc was sent out to the Far East, firstly to represent France at the Japanese surrender aboard the USS *Missouri* in Tokyo Bay, then to reassert French authority in Indo-China after the Japanese Occupation. Although successful in the southern half of the country, Leclerc began to recognise over the next two years that only a negotiated political settlement could bring peace to the region. "Negotiate, negotiate at all costs," he told Émile Bollaert during early 1947.

Leclerc's next appointment was as Inspector General of French Forces in French North Africa, an appointment first created for Marshal Lyautey. Leclerc's rank now entitled him to a personal aircraft. Surplus American machines were plentiful in Western Europe and the Mediterranean in 1945, and a B-25 Mitchell medium bomber was converted for his use, given the name *Tailly II*, and painted with the divisional badge of the 2e DB. But *Tailly II* had not been converted according to its North American manufacturer's guidelines. It had also taken quite a beating during Leclerc's last fact-finding mission to

Indo-China for Leon Blum, sustaining several bullet holes, and, by November 1947, needed a comprehensive service.

The winter of 1947–1948 was one of the coldest on record, and when Leclerc arrived at Villacoublay for his last trip to French North Africa, his take-off was delayed until midday because the engine lubricants had been congealed by the frost. Once airborne, Leclerc's flight was uneventful. His inspections went well, many *colons* proudly turning out to meet the Liberator of Paris. But on his flight inland to Colomb-Béchar, amid a thickening sandstorm, tragedy struck. While local dignitaries gathered on Colomb-Béchar's camel square to welcome him, there was a crisis aboard *Tailly II*. Her pilot, Francois Delluc, clearly tried to make a crash-landing alongside the Mediterranean-Niger railway but, as he tried to put her down, *Tailly II* exploded, killing everyone aboard instantly, throwing aircraft parts and human remains over a wide area.

France came to an immediate halt. For the comparatively new president, Vincent Auriol, trying to keep his government on track in the face of frequent resignations, Leclerc's death was the last thing he needed. De Gaulle was deeply upset, quickly visiting Thérèse and the children. As he left the Leclerc apartment on Avenue Kléber, the Constable was so overcome with grief that he needed his wife to help him down the stairs. The bodies of Leclerc and everyone else aboard *Tailly II* were brought back across the Mediterranean aboard the *Émile Bertin* and greeted at Toulon by a RBFM honour guard commanded by Philippe de Gaulle and sombrely escorted to Paris.

As de Gaulle predicted, Auriol's government honoured Leclerc with a state funeral in Notre Dame, finally allowing Cardinal Suhard the opportunity to conduct such an event for someone who deserved it. "All Leclerc's boys are pouring into town," wrote English novelist Nancy Mitford. Before the funeral the crash victims, all draped with *Tricolores*, and Leclerc's coffin aboard the self-propelled 105mm gun *Alsace*, lay in state at the Étoile for Parisians to pay their respects. Men of the 2e DB formed up in immense phalanxes around veteran officers like Jacques Branet to honour their leader and condole with

Thérèse and her children. Modern France has seen few occasions to match it.

Films and photographs show that, during Leclerc's obsequies, scaffolding stood around much of the Arc de Triomphe. As part of this repair programme François Rude's *Le Départ des Volontaires 1792* was restored. Looking at that magnificent sculpture today one would need an expert mason's eye to spot where the Panther's armour piercing shell made its mark. The repairs have had seventy years to weather in. The scars the Occupation inflicted on France's psyche have taken as long to fade.

Acknowledgements

It seems ages since my first book, a biography of General Leclerc, first came out, written in part as preparation for this, my second book. Paris during the last months of Occupation and the Liberation has been a source of fascination for me since first reading *Is Paris Burning?* by Larry Collins and Dominique Lapierre during my late teens. Ever since then I have wanted to know more, to have a fuller, more detailed picture which gave background to names and to understand the emotions and motivations behind the liberation of the most important city in western Europe to be occupied by the Nazis. I hope this book achieves the task I set myself even though various other books on this subject have also appeared recently.

In the first place I should thank both Giles MacDonogh and Martin Windrow for the kind endorsements they have both offered after reading the manuscript. Among my relations my mother, Bea Mortimer-Moore, to whom this book is dedicated,—has been a kindly rock throughout. My first cousin Rachel Dowding-Roberts read through the manuscript. My accountant and cousin Bertie Garforth-Bles has kept me out of trouble while I wrote. Another cousin, John Bate-Williams, gave me his excellent photograph of the 2e DB memorial at Alençon and, with his son Rory, found me various source books on French AMAZON and Mark Whitcombe, himself an experienced writer, was also helpful. I also owe immense gratitude to Lord Hotham,—whose home served as Leclerc's divisional HQ before they embarked for France,—who read through the first draft. Madame Benedicte Coste, Leclerc's excellent grand-daughter, corrected my French and sometimes, worryingly, my English as well and Dr Kate Culley helped me with photograph layout and captions.

At Casemate, who seem to be getting used to me, I would like to thank Steve Smith, Tara Lichtermann and Libby Braden in New York; while in Oxford I would also thank Clare Litt and Mette Bundgaard. Once again Dr Christine Levisse-Touzé and her assistant Cécile Cousseau at the Memorial du Maréchal Leclerc et de la Libération de Paris, Musée Jean Moulin, Ville de Paris were very helpful regarding photographs. Ruth Hoffmann at the Magnum Agency was also helpful; it is not every day that one negotiates to use photographs taken by Robert Capa and Henri Cartier-Bresson. Lastly and mostly I would like to thank my agent Robert Dudley for his patience in putting up with me and guiding this book to its present home.

WIlliam Mortimer-Moore.

Source Notes

Preface

1 De Boissieu, Alain. *Pour Combattre avec de Gaulle.* Plon 1981. Page 214.
2 Ibid. Pages 214–215.
3 Boissieu. Interview with Jean-Christophe Notin shortly before Boissieu's death. Notin. Page 227.
4 Boissieu. Page 216.
5 Ibid. Page 217.
6 Lacouture, Jean. *De Gaulle. The Rebel: 1890–1944.* Collins Harvill. 1990. Pages 514–515. This conversation was taken down at once by de Gaulle's staff and appears in the appendices to his *Memoires de Guerre. Vol II.*

Chapter 1

1 Lottman, Herbert. *The Fall of Paris. June 1940.* Sinclair-Stevenson. 1992. Page 162.
2 Lacouture. Page 187.
3 Guy, Claude. *En écoutant de Gaulle.* Grasset. 1996. Page 91.
4 Ibid. Page 89.
5 De Gaulle, Charles. *Mémoires de Guerre.* Plon 1999 Edn. Pages 60–61.
6 Kersaudy, Francois. *Churchill and de Gaulle.* Fontana 1990. Page 66. & Spears. Vol 2, Page 162.
7 De Gaulle's ADC, Geoffroy Chaudron de Courcel was standing with de Gaulle at that moment and told French historian Francois Kersaudy that he never heard Churchill say this. De Gaulle himself dismissed the anecdote with "Churchill is a romantic type." Kersaudy, *Churchill and de Gaulle.* Page 66.
8 Spears, General Sir Edward. *Assignment to Catastrophe.* 1954 Vol 2. Pages 218–219.
9 Lottman. *The Fall of Paris. June 1940.* Page 286.
10 Spears. Vol 2. Page 136.
11 Lottman. *The Fall of Paris. June 1940.* Pages 297–298.
12 Lottman. Pages 299–300.
13 Lottman. Pages 300–301 & Bullitt, William C. *For the President.* Vol 2.
14 Lottman. Pages 335–340.
15 Lehrer, Steven. *Wartime Sites in Paris.* SFTafel. 2013. Page 28.

16 Kersaudy, François. *Churchill and de Gaulle.* Fontana 1990. Pages 71–76. & Lacouture, Page 204. Lacouture says that the source of Ybarnegaray's quote was Sir Edward Spears and that it was hearsay.

17 De Gaulle, Charles. *Mémoires de Guerre.* Plon 1999 Edn. Page 73.

18 Ibid.

19 Amouroux, Henri. *Le Peuple du Désastre.* Laffont 1976. Page 353.

20 De Gaulle, Charles. *Mémoires de Guerre.* Page 75. Lacouture, Jean. *De Gaulle. The Rebel.* Pages 211–212. & De Gaulle/Tauriac. *De Gaulle, Mon Père.* Vol 1. Pages 115–120.

21 Lacouture, Jean. *De Gaulle. The Rebel.* Page 212. Quotes from Lacouture's interviews with Courcel and Malraux.

22 Lacouture. Pages 221–222.

23 CAB 65/7, WM 171 (40) 11, 18/6/40

24 Lacouture. Page 223.

25 Moisson, Pascale. *Anecdotes sous la botte.* L'Harmattan 1998. Page 14.

26 Boissieu, Alain de. *Pour Combattre avec de Gaulle.* Plon 1999. Page 56.

27 Branet, Jacques. *L'Escadron.* Flammarion 1968. Page 56.

28 Gribius, André. *La vie d'un officier.* Éditions France Empire 1971. Page 47.

29 For fuller information on this aspect see *Free France's Lion* by William Mortimer-Moore.

30 Guitry, Sacha. *Quatre Ans d'Occupations.* Éditions de l'Élan. 1947. Pages 103 and 255–256.

31 Taittinger, Pierre. *... et Paris ne fut pas détruit* Nouvelles Éditions Latines. 1956. Pages 23–26.

32 Gilles, Christian. *Arletty ou la liberté d'être.* L'Harmattan. 1988. (Re-issued 2000). Pages 38–39.

33 Pryce-Jones. David. *Paris in the Third Reich.* Collins. 1981. Pages 69–70.

34 Jackson, Julian. *France—The Dark Years.* Oxford UP. 2001. Page 275.

35 Ousby, Ian. *Occupation. The Ordeal of France. 1940–1944.* John Murray 1997. Pages 208–209.

36 Bourderon, Roger. *Rol-Tanguy.* Tallandier. Paris. 2004. Pages 151–154.

37 Ibid. Pages 172–173.

38 Mortimer-Moore, William. *Free France's Lion.* Casemate 2011. Pages 72–94.

39 Bourderon. Page 175.

40 Kupferman, Fred. *Laval 1883–1945.* Flammarion 1988. Pages 306–307.

41 Gildea, Robert. *Marianne in Chains.* Macmillan. 2002. Page 257.

42 Bourderon. Page 187.

43 Ibid. Pages 190–191.

44 Ibid. Pages 192–197.

45 Ibid. Pages 198–201.

46 Ibid. Page 202.

47 Ibid. Pages 203–206.

48 Webster, Paul. *Pétain's Crime.* Macmillan. 1990. Page 149.

49 Whitcombe, Mrs G.M.V. née Elisabeth Bles. Conversation with author—October 1992.

50 Feliciano, Hector. *The Lost Museum*. Basic Books. New York 1995. Pages 49–50.

51 Valland, Rose. *Les Carnets de Rose Valland*. Fage Éditions 2011. Page 43. & Edsell, Robert. *Monuments Men*. Preface Publishing 2009. Pages 193–196.

52 Kupferman, Fred. *Laval. 1883–1945*. Flammarion 1988. Page 327.

53 Ibid. Pages 337–338.

54 Billotte. Pierre. *Le Temps des Armes*. Plon. 1972. Page 237.

55 Billotte. Page 239.

56 For a full account of this episode, read Colin Smith's excellent *Fighting Vichy—England's Last War with France*. Weidenfeld 2010.

57 Levisse-Touzé, Christine. *L'Afrique du Nord dans la guerre*. Albin Michel. 1998. Pages 276–277. & Beevor, Antony. *The Second World War*. Weidenfeld 2012. Pages 394–395. & Atkinson, Rick. *An Army at Dawn*. Little Brown. 2003. Pages 251–253. There is even a story that Darlan was murdered by a British agent sent by Ian Fleming!

58 Ibid.

59 Kersaudy. *De Gaulle et Roosevelt* Tempus 2006. Page 141.

60 Guy, Claude. *En écoutant de Gaulle*. Grasset. 1996. Page 418.

61 Girard, Christian. *Journal de Guerre*. L'Harmattan. 2000. Pages 55–56.

62 Maule, Henry. *Out of the Sand*. Odhams 1964. Page 160.

63 Levisse-Touzé, Dr. Christine. Pages 340–341.

64 Langlade, Paul de. *En Suivant Leclerc*. Au fil d'Ariane. 1964. Pages 15–18.

65 Notin, Jean-Christophe. *Leclerc*. 2005. Page 214.

66 Compagnon, General Jean. *Leclerc*. Flammarion 1994. Pages 322–325.

67 Beevor, Antony. *The Second World War*. Weidenfeld and Nicolson. 2012. Pages 428–429.

68 Cobb. Matthew. *The Resistance*. Simon and Schuster. 2010. Pages 150–151.

69 Cobb. Pages 152–153 & Beevor, Pages 429–430.

70 Lacouture, Jean. *De Gaulle—The Rebel*. Collins Harvill. 1990. Pages 467–468 & 481–482.

71 Cobb. *The Resistance*. Pages 164–169.

72 Tillon, Charles. *FTP.* Julliard 1962. Pages 256–257.

73 Chaban-Delmas, Jacques. *L'Ardeur.* Stock. 1975. Pages 67–93.

74 Kriegel-Valrimont, Maurice. *Mémoires Rebelles*. Éditions Odile Jacob. 1999. Page 56.

75 Levisse-Touzé, Christine. *Le Comité Parisien de Libération*. Essay for *Paris 1944*. Albin Michel. 1994. Page 202.

76 Levisse-Touzé. Page 204.

77 Levisse-Touzé & Archives de Paris, CPL, Series 1027W and 1520W. Page 206.

78 Levisse-Touzé. Page 206.

79 Levisse-Touzé. Pages 207–208.

80 Levisse-Touzé. Page 208.

81 Levisse-Touzé. Pages 208–209.

82 Dronne, Raymond. *La Liberation de Paris.* Éditions France-Empire. 1970. Pages 139–141.

83 Taittinger. Pages 52–53.

84 Ibid. Page 55.

85 Ibid. Page 57.

86 Ibid.

87 Ibid. Page 56.

88 Taittinger. Page 129.

89 Ibid. Pages 58–60.

90 Callil, Carmen. *Bad Faith.* Jonathan Cape 2006. Pages 330–331.

91 Muller, Klaus Jurgen. *Witzleben, Stulpnagel and Speidel.* Essay for *Hitler's Generals.* 1998. Weidenfeld. Pages 56–60. & Junger, Ernst. *Journal Parisien.* Vol III. 31/5/44. Christian Bourgeois 1995.

92 Lambauer, Barbara. *Otto Abetz et les Français.* Fayard 2001. Pages 607–610.

93 Nordling, Raoul. *Sauver Paris.* Éditions Complexe. 2002. Pages 11–34.

94 Nordling. Pages 61–76.

95 Jackson, Julian. *France. The Dark Years. 1940–1944.* OUP. 2001. Page 319.

96 Pryce-Jones. Page 184.

97 Guitry. Pages 185–192.

98 Girard, Christian. *Journal de Guerre. 1939–1945.* L'Harmattan. 2000. Pages 63–64.

99 Pryce-Jones. Pages 52–53. & Beevor and Cooper. Page 37.

100 Beevor and Cooper. Page 155.

101 Gilot, Françoise. *Vivre avec Picasso.* Éditions 10/18. Pages 39–41 & McGraw Hill. 1964. Page 47.

102 Jackson. Page 106. & Huffington, Ariana Stasinopoulos. *Picasso—Creator and Destroyer.* Simon and Schuster. 1988. Pages 282–283.

103 Gilot. Éditons 10/18. Pages 33–34.

104 Huffington. Page 256.

105 Edsell, Robert. *Monuments Men.* Preface Publishing 2009. Page 126.

106 Lambauer, Barbara. *Otto Abetz et les Français.* Fayard 2001. Page 162.

107 Valland, Rose. *Les Carnets de Rose Valland.* Fage Éditions 2011. Page 120.

108 Mesquida, Evelyn. *La Nueve.* Cherche Midi 2011. Pages 47–58.

109 Vézinet, Général. *Le Général Leclerc.* France Empire. 1997. Page 124.

110 Churchill. 26/1/1944. (PRO) FO 371 40361.

111 Fenby, Jonathan. *The General.* Simon and Schuster. 2010. Page 233 & Girard, Christian. *Journal de Guerre.* L'Harmattan. 2000. Page 153.

112 Fenby, Jonathan. *The General.* Simon and Schuster. 2010. Pages 233–234.

113 Norwich, John Julius. *The Duff Cooper Diaries.* Weidenfeld 2005. Pages 297–300.

114 Johnson, Professor Douglas. *La Grande Bretagne et la Libération de Paris.* Essay for *Paris 1944.* (& FO 371 40361.) Albin Michel 1994. Pages 53–54.

115 *The Duff Cooper Diaries.* Page 287.

116 Johnson (& FO 371 41863).
117 *The Duff Cooper Diaries.* Page 299.
118 *The Duff Cooper Diaries.* Page 300.
119 Girard. Pages 172–173.
120 Taittinger. Pages 68–69. Pétain's visit is also briefly covered on pages 462–464 of Charles Williams' new biography, *Pétain*, published May 2005 by Little Brown. But Taittinger's account of the day is better, livelier and firsthand.
121 Ibid. Page 70.
122 Ibid. Pages 70–71.
123 Ibid. Page 72.
124 Ibid.
125 Ibid. Page 73.
126 Girard, Christian. *Journal de Guerre.* L'Harmattan. 2000. Page 182.
127 Mesquida Pages 128–131 & Dronne CdeR Page 249.
128 Dronne. *Carnets de Route.* Pages 249–250. Hereafter I refer to Dronne's *Carnets de Route* as CdeR in the source notes as distinct from his other book *La Libération de Paris*—LdeP.
129 Dronne. CdeR. Pages 251–253.
130 Massu. Page 103.
131 Billotte. Pages 286–287.
132 *The Duff Cooper Diaries.* John Julius Norwich. Page 307.
133 *The Duff Cooper Diaries.* Page 308 & Billotte. Page 287.
134 *The Duff Cooper Diaries.* Page 308.
135 Billotte. Page 288.
136 Lacouture. Pages 520–521.
137 Billotte. Page 289.
138 De Gaulle. Vol II. Page 223.
139 Béthouart, General Émile. *Cinq années d'ésperance.* Plon 1968. Pages 240–243. & Lacouture. Pages 521–522.
140 Lacouture. Pages 522–523.
141 Lacouture. Page 523.
142 Lacouture. Page 524. Quoting memoir note by Pierre Viénot.
143 De Gaulle, Philippe. & Tauriac *De Gaulle Mon Père.* Vol 1. Pages 330–332.
144 De Gaulle. Philippe. Page 299.

Chapter 2

1   Pierquin, Bernard. *Journal d'un étudiant parisien sous l'occupation.* 1983. Page 125.
2   Cazaux, Yves. *Journal secret de la Libération.* Albin Michel. 1975. Page 14.
3   Taittinger. Pages 117–118.
4   Tournoux. Page 301 & Barthelémy Page 397. (Bourget).
5   Notin. Page 240.
6   Bourderon. Pages 261–262.

7   Bourderon. Pages 262–264.
8   Histoire de la Résistance. Noguères. Page 147.
9   Mousseau, Jacques. *Chaban-Delmas*. Perrin. 2000. Page 98.
10   Bourderon. Page 307.
11   Mousseau. Pages 98–99.
12   Bourget. Pages 68–70.
13   Bourderon. Pages 334–335.
14   Wallraf. Pages 114–115. (Bourget).
15   Archives Nationales. W III 141.
16   Guérin, Alain. *La Résistance*. Le Livre Club Diderot. Paris 1976. Vol V. Page 303.
17   Noguères, Henri. *L'histoire de la Résistance en France*. Robert Laffont. 1981. Vol V. Pages 187–190.
18   Girard. Pages 212–213.
19   Girard. Pages 213–214.
20   Girard. Page 214.
21   Girard. Page 214.
22   De Gaulle. MdeG. Page 501.
23   De Gaulle. MdeG. Page 501 and Robert Aron. Pages 67–68.
24   Aron. Page 68.
25   Aron. Pages 68–69.
26   Aron. Page 69.
27   Fenby, Jonathan. *The General*. Simon and Schuster 2010. Page 242.
28   Rémy. *Les Mains Jointes*. Page 147.
29   De Gaulle. MdeG. Page 502.
30   Aron. Pages 70–71.
31   Aron. Page 72.
32   Aron. Pages 72–74.
33   Aron. Page 74. & Hamilton, Nigel. *Monty*. Vol 2. Page 653. & Fenby, Johnathan. *The General*. Simon and Schuster 2010. Pages 252–253.
34   This stirring speech has been translated and quoted in full from General Jean Compagnon's *Leclerc, Maréchal de France*. Flammarion 1994. Pages 360–363.
35   Girard. Pages 219–220.
36   Noguères. But there is a second, sanitised version also told by "Morlot" in which he claims he tried to arrest Henriot before shooting him.
37   Braibant, Charles. *La guerre à Paris*. Corrêa. 1945 Page 501.
38   Bussière. Page 273.
39   Vinatier, Jean. *Le Cardinal Suhard*. Le Centurion. 1983. Page 194.
40   Vinatier. Pages 194–195.
41   Lacouture, Jean. *De Gaulle*. Vol 1. Collins 1990. Page 537.
42   Kersaudy, Francois. *Churchill and de Gaulle*. Fontana 1990. Page 364 Quoting Stimson, Henry. *On Active Service*. Pages 546–551.
43   Lacouture. Page 538.

44 Lacouture. Page 539. Quoting Hervé Alphand. *L'Étonnement d'être*. Page 179.

45 Fenby, Jonathan. *The General*. Simon and Schuster 2010. Page 244.

46 Quoted by Lacouture. Page 539.

47 Fenby. Page 244.

48 Kersaudy, Francois. *De Gaulle et Roosevelt*. Perrin 2004. Page 415.

49 Fenby. Page 244.

50 Fenby. Page 244.

51 Morgan, Ted. *FDR: A Biography.*Grafton. 1985. Pages 723–724.

52 De Gaulle. *Memoires de Guerre*. Vol II Plon. 1999 Edn. Page 511. And quoted by Kersaudy, *De Gaulle et Roosevelt*. Perrin 2004. Page 419.

53 Lacouture. Pages 540–541. Quoting De Gaulle's *Memoires de Guerre*.

54 Lacouture. Page 541 & Fenby Page 245.

55 Fenby. Page 245. Quoting Aglion Pages 205–210.

56 Kersaudy, Francois. *De Gaulle et Roosevelt*. Pages 420–421.

57 Fenby. Page 245.

58 Kersaudy. *Churchill and De Gaulle*. Fontana 1990. Pages 364–365.

59 Girard. Pages 226–227.

60 Girard. Page 227.

61 Massu. Page 109.

62 Girard. Page 228.

63 Girard. Page 228.

64 Favreau, Bertrand. *Georges Mandel, ou la passion de la République*. Éditions Fayard 1996. Pages 400–401.

65 Favreau. Pages 472–473.

66 Lambauer. Page 611.

67 Favreau. Pages 474–475.

68 Favreau. Pages 475–476.

69 Favreau. Page 476.

70 Favreau. Page 476.

71 Favreau. Pages 477–478. Using trial records of Boéro, Néroni and Lambert. (AN 334AP8)

72 Favreau. Page 478.

73 Favreau. Pages 478–479.

74 Lambauer. Page 612.

75 Favreau. Pages 479–481.

76 Philippe de Gaulle. Pages 300–301.

77 Girard, Christian. *Journal de Guerre*. L'Harmattan. 2000. Page 197. & Martel, André. *Leclerc. Le Soldat et la Politique*. Albin Michel. 1998. Page 254.

78 Compagnon, General Jean. *Leclerc. Maréchal de France*. Flammarion 1994. Page 364.

79 Cobb, Matthew. *Eleven Days in August*. Simon and Schuster 2013. Pages 18–19. & Debu-Bridel, Jacques. *De Gaulle et le CNR*. 1978. Paris France-Empire. Pages 269–271.

80 Cobb. Pages 19–20.

81 Cobb. Page 20.

82 Bourget. Page 145.

83 Bourget. Pages 146–148.

84 Bourget. Pages 148–150.

85 Bourget. Pages 150–151.

86 Bourget. Pages 152–153.

87 Bourget. Page 153.

88 Bourget. Pages 154–156. & Giolitto, Pierre. *Histoire de la Milice*. Perrin. 1997. Page 417.

89 Giolitto. Page 417.

90 Bourget. Pages 156–158.

91 Bourget. Pages 158–159.

92 Bourget. Pages 161–165.

93 Bourget. Pages 252–253. & Jackson. Pages 181–182.

94 Bourget. Pages 254–255 & Aziz, Philippe. *Tu trahiras sans vergogne*. Fayard. 1973. Page 27.

95 Bouard. Article *Revue d'histoire de la Deuxieme Guerre Mondiale*. No 54. 1964.

96 Bussière. Statement and Muracciole Page 133.

97 Bourget. Page 255.

98 Bourget. Page 256 & Lefranc, Serge. *Les Policiers français dans la Résistance*. op cit. Page 71.

99 Bourget. Pages 256–257.

100 Bourget. Pages 258–259 & Monniot. Pages 54–58.

101 Bourget. Page 259.

102 Bourget. Page 260.

103 Bourget. Page 260 and Muracciole Page 146.

104 Gribius, André. *La Vie d'Une Officier*. Éditions France-Empire. 1971. Page 110.

105 Compagnon. Page 365.

106 Langlade. Pages 117–118.

107 Compagnon. Page 365.

108 Girard. Page 233.

109 Langlade. Page 119.

110 Boineburg-Lengsfeld and Kraewel. Statements quoted by Pierre Bourget.

111 Kraewel Statement.

112 Boineberg-Lengsfeld. Statement.

113 Schramm Wilhelm von. *Conspiracy among the Generals*. Allen and Unwin. 1956. Pages 57–65.

114 Schramm. Pages 66–80.

115 Kraewel. Statement.

116 Schramm. Pages 80–95.

117 Kraewel. Statement.

118 Boineburg. Statement.

119 Boineburg Statement.

120 Kraewel. Statement.

121 Abetz, Otto. *Histoire d'un politique franco-allemande*. Stock. Paris 1953. Pages 319–321.

122 Schramm. Pages 96–113.

123 Boineburg and Kraewel. Statements.

124 Lottman. Page 511.

125 Taittinger. Pages 115–116.

126 Girard. Page 237.

127 Schramm. Pages 120–121.

128 Junger. Vol 3. Pages 306–307.

129 Schramm. Pages 125–128.

130 Boineburg. Statement. Another explanation, offered by Randall Hansen in his 2014 book, *Disobeying Hitler*, is that the SS and SD were further embarrassed at being arrested with no resistance by Kraewel's Security Regiment who were far from "the cream of the German Army".

131 Cobb, Matthew. *Eleven Days in August*. Simon and Schuster 2013. Pages 26–27.

132 Conversation with author, September 2004.

133 Girard. Page 234.

134 Girard. Pages 234–235.

135 Bourdan, Pierre. *Carnet de Retour avec la Division Leclerc.* Édition Pierre Trémois 1945. Page 22.

136 Massu, Suzanne. *Quand j'étais Rochambelle*. Grasset 1969. Page 120.

137 Langlade. Page 120.

138 De Gaulle, Philippe. Page 307.

139 Bouderon. Page 340.

140 Bouderon. Page 340.

141 Bourderon. Pages 340–342.

142 Bourderon. Pages 344–345.

143 Bourderon. Pages 346–347.

144 Cobb. Pages 26 & 408–409.

145 Bourderon. Pages 296–297.

146 Bourderon. Pages 319–320.

147 Wieviorka, Olivier. *La Résistance Intérieure et la Libération de Paris*. Essay for *Paris 1944*. (& AN 72 AJ 3). Albin Michel 1994. Page 146

148 Valland, Rose. *Les Carnets de Rose Valland*. Fage Éditions 2011. Pages 94–95.

149 Valland. Pages 95–96.

150 Valland. Page 96.

151 Notin, Jean Christophe. *Leclerc*. Perrin 2005. (& SHAT 11K239(7). Page 243 using Leclerc's letter to Koenig dated 28/7/1944.

152 Compagnon, General Jean. *Leclerc. Maréchal de France*. Flammarion 1994. Page 364.

153 Girard, Christian. *Journal de Guerre*. L'Harmattan. 2000. Pages 243–244.

Chapter 3

1 Girard. *Journal de Guerre*. L'Harmattan. 2000. Page 244.
2 Ibid. Page 245.
3 Langlade. *En suivant Leclerc*. Au File d'Ariane. 1964. Page 124.
4 Langlade. Page 127.
5 De Gaulle, Philippe. *Mémoires accessoires 1921–1946*. Plon 1997. Page 309.
6 De Gaulle, Ph. Page 310.
7 Vézy. Édith. *Gargamelle*. L'Harmattan. 1994. Pages 46–47.
8 Massu, Jacques. *Sept Ans Avec Leclerc*. Éditons Rocher. 1997. Page 114.
9 Maggiar, Raymond. *Les Fusiliers Marins de Leclerc. Route difficile vers de Gaulle.* Éditions France Empire. 1954 Page 165.
10 Warlimont, Walter. *Inside Hitler's Headquarters* 1939–1945. Page 445.
11 Beevor. *D-Day* Pages 398–399. Hastings *Overlord*. Pages 328–329. Neillands *The Battle of Normandy* Pages 334–339. Blumenson. *The Duel for France 1944*. Pages 200–201. D'Este. *Decision in Normandy*. Page 409.
12 D'Este. *Patton—A Genius for War*. Page 631.
13 Dronne CdeR. Pages 271–272.
14 Dronne CdeR. Page 273.
15 Dronne. CdeR Page 274.
16 Mousseau, Jacques. *Chaban-Delmas*. Perrin 2000. Pages 100–102.
17 Neitzel, Professor Sonke. *Tapping Hitler's Generals*. Frontline 2007. Page 286.
18 Evans. Richard J. *The Third Reich at War* Penguin 2008. Page 751.
19 Melvin, General Mungo. *Manstein*. W&N 2010. Pages 227–228 see also Benoit Le May, & Marcel Stein.
20 Burleigh, Michael. *Moral Combat*. Collins. 2010. Page 252.
21 Gilbert, Sir Martin. *The Holocaust*. Collins 1986. Page 322.
22 Dronne LdeP. Page 98.
23 Choltitz, Dietrich von. *De Sebastopol à Paris*. J'ai Lu (Flammarion) 1969. Page 130.
24 Choltitz. Page 203.
25 Ibid. Pages 96–97.
26 Ibid. Page 94.
27 Ibid. Pages 94–95.
28 Choltitz. Pages 201–205
29 Neitzel. Page 258.
30 Choltitz. Pages 201–205.
31 Neitzel. Page 258.
32 Confirmed by testimony from Timo von Choltitz, the general's son.
33 Choltitz. Pages 205–209.
34 Dronne CdeR. Page 276.
35 Dronne. CdeR. Page 276.
36 Beevor, Antony. *D-Day*. Penguiin. 2009. Pages 398–421. Beevor's account of the Mortain counterattack is one of the liveliest anywhere.

37 Beevor. Pages 419–421.
38 Dronne. Pages 61 and 69.
39 Dronne. Page 69.
40 Dronne. Page 70.
41 Dronne Page 70.
42 Dronne. Page 70.
43 Muracciole, Jean-Francois. *La Libération de Paris.* Tallandier 2013. Page 42.
44 Choltitz Page 210 and P44EDLL Page 335.
45 Muller, KJ. *Le Développement des Opérations du groupe d'armées B fin Juillet-fin Aout 1944.* Essay for *Paris 1944.* Albin Michel 1994. Page 102.
46 Choltitz. Page 211 & Dronne Page 100.
47 Wallraf. Pages 162–163.
48 Choltitz. Page 211. & *Disobeying Hitler* by Randall Hansen. Faber and Faber 2014. Page 78, referring to Dankwart von Arnim's memoir in the possession of the Mémorial de Caen.
49 Dronne. Page 100.
50 Muracciole. Page 33.
51 Wallraf. Pages 167–169.
52 Bradley, Gen Omar. *A General's Life.* Simon and Schuster 1983. Page 295.
53 Bradley. Page 296. & Hansen's diary entry for 8/10/44.
54 Bradley, quoting his earlier *Soldier's Story.* Pages 375–376.
55 Bradley. Page 294 & D'Este *Decision in Normandy* 1983. Page 426.
56 Bradley. Page 296.
57 Langlade. Pages 137–138.
58 Girard. Page 250 & Boissieu. Page 235.
59 Billotte. Page 306.
60 Billotte. Pages 306–307.
61 Branet. Page 172, & Billotte. Page 308.
62 Nordling. Pages 79–80.
63 Nordling. Page 80.
64 Nordling. Pages 80–81.
65 Nordling. Pages 81–82.
66 Nordling. Page 82.
67 Nordling. Page 84.
68 Repiton-Préneuf. *2e DB La Campagne de France.* Imprimerie Nationale. Pages 5–6.
69 Girard. Pages 250–251.
70 Massu. Pages 120–121.
71 Boissieu. Page 236.
72 Girard. Page 251.
73 Girard. Page 251.
74 Nordling. Page 85.
75 Dronne. Pages 61–63.
76 Nordling. Pages 87–88.

77 Nordling. Pages 88–89.
78 Nordling. Page 89.
79 Nordling. Page 90.
80 Nordling. Page 90. (I have reconstructed some of this exchange from the narrative in Nordling's memoirs.)
81 Nordling. Pages 90–91.
82 Nordling. Page 91.
83 Girard. Pages 251–252.
84 Beevor. Page 435.
85 Girard. Page 252. & Forget, Dominique *Le Général Leclerc et la 2e DB.* Heimdal 2009. Pages 98–99.
86 Girard Page 252 and Forget Page 102.
87 Dronne. Pages 70–71.
88 Girard. Pages 252–253.
89 Girard. Page 253 & Boissieu. Pages 239–240.
90 Gaudet. *Alamanach du Combattant.*
91 Compagnon. Page 376 & Forget. Pages 122–126.
92 Notin. Page 255.
93 Branet. Pages 172–173.
94 Branet. Page 173. & Bergot. Erwan. *La 2ème DB.* Presses de la Cité. 1999. Pages 82–83.
95 Dronne. CdeR. Page 282.
96 Dronne CdeR. Pages 282–283, & Mesquida. Page 146.
97 Branet. Pages 173–174.
98 Branet. Pages 174–175.
99 Branet. Page 175. & Bergot. Page 84.
100 Blumenson. *The Battle of the Generals.* Page 204.
101 Blumenson. Page 205.
102 Bradley. Pages 297–298.
103 Blumenson. Page 206 and D'Este Page 429.
104 Bumenson. Pages 206–207. D'Este Page 430, & Bradley. *A Soldier's Story.* Page 377.
105 Dronne Pages 72–73.
106 Dronne Pages 73–74.
107 Dronne Page 72.
108 Branet. Pages 175–177.
109 Dronne. CdeR. Pages 284–285.
110 Mesquida. Pages 147–148.
111 Forget. Page 166.
112 Boissieu. Pages 242–243. & Girard. Page 255.
113 Langlade. Pages 161–163.
114 Bergot. Pages 95–96.
115 Dronne. CdeR. Pages 288–289.
116 Dronne CdeR. Page 290.

117 Nordling. Pages 91–92.
118 Nordling. Page 92.
119 Dronne. Page 74.
120 Dronne. Page 74.
121 Patton Papers. Pages 509–511.
122 Bradley. Page 300.
123 Patton Papers. Page 510.
124 Beevor. Page 442. Quoting captured German information FMS A-922.
125 Hastings. *Overlord.* Page 290. & Beevor. Page 442.
126 Langlade. Page 169.
127 Bergot. Pages 97–99.
128 Bergot. Page 99.
129 Dronne. CdeR. Pages 292–294.
130 Dronne CdeR. Page 294.
131 Dronne CdeR Pages 299–300
132 Blumenson. Pages 221–222.
133 Bradley. Pages 302–303.
134 Lamb, Richard. Essay on Kluge in *Hitler's Generals.* Weidenfeld. 1989. Page 407, quoting David Irving and Lamb.
135 Bergot. Page 100.
136 Forget. Page 182.
137 In rural parts of France where a sense of feudalism still exists it is usual for most women of a titled family to be acknowledged by that title. Leclerc's family are Papal counts.
138 This incident is included in *Is Paris Burning?* by Larry Collins and Dominique Lapierre. Since there are several mistakes in that book, I asked Leclerc's granddaughter, Madame Bénédicte Coste, if it was true. She questioned her father, Hubert Leclerc de Hauteclocque, on my behalf, who said that it was.
139 Girard. Pages 255–256.
140 Notin. Jean Christophe. *Leclerc.* Perrin. 2005. Page 259. In this instance Notin is quoting Alain de Boissieu who may actually have been present.
141 Notin, Page 258. Quoting Leclerc's letter to Patton, a copy of which is held by the Service Historique d'Armée de Terre. (SHAT 1K239(7)).
142 Notin. Pages 258–259.
143 Patton Papers. Page 511.
144 Repiton-Préneuf. Pages 20–21.
145 Notin. Page 259. From an interview with Wallerand de Hauteclocque.
146 Bourderon. Page 365.
147 Bussière. Statement.
148 Bourget. Pages 261–262,
149 Bourderon. Page 365.
150 Bourget. Page 262.
151 Bourget. Page 262.
152 Bussière. Statement.

153 Bussière. Statement.
154 Bussière. Statement.
155 Dronne. Page 75.
156 Dronne. Page 75.
157 Nordling. Pages 92–93.
158 Mousseau. Pages 102–103 & Dronne Pages 15–16.
159 Mousseau Page 103. Dronne Pages 17–18.
160 Nordling. Page 93.
161 Nordling Page 94.
162 Nordling 94 and Interview in *Franc-Tireur* October 1949.
163 Nordling. Pages 94–95.
164 Dansette. Page 115.
165 Blumenson. Pages 224–227.
166 Blumenson. Pages 227–228. Hastings. Page 355, & Beevor. Pages 459–460.
167 D'Este, Carlo. *Hitler's Generals*. Biographical essays. Weidenfeld 1989. Page 325.
168 Patton Papers. Pages 513–514.
169 Beevor. Page 456.
170 Girard. Page 256.
171 Beevor. Pages 456–457.
172 Girard. Pages 256–257.
173 Billotte. Pages 309–310.
174 Patton Papers. Page 514.
175 Dronne Page 76.
176 Dronne. Pages 76–77.
177 Nordling. Pages 95–96.
178 Nordling. Page 96.
179 Nordling. Page 97.
180 Edsel, Robert M. *Monuments Men.* Arrow. 2010. Pages 181–182.
181 Valland, Rose. *Les Carnets de Rose Valland.* Éditions Fage. 2011. Pages 97–99.
182 Valland. Page 99.
183 Valland. Page 99.
184 Bourget, Pierre. *Paris '44.* Plon 1984. Pages 281–282, & Archives Nationales 334 AP 29 & CJ 736/5481 containing statements of Marcel Bernard, and details of the *réseau* Marco Polo respectively.
185 Bourget. Pages 282–283, & Archives Nationales 334 AP 29.
186 Bourget. Pages 283–284, & Archives Nationales 334 AP 29.
187 Bourget. Page 285.
188 Bourget. Page 285, & Statement of Michelle Bourssier Archives Nationales 334 AP 29.
189 Ibid. Bourget's account of this episode is probably the best.
190 Rayski, Adam. *Le Massacre de la Cascade du Bois de Boulogne.* Online article 2007.
191 Bourget. Pages 286–291.
192 Bourget. Page 292, & Archives Nationales CJ 736/5481.

193 Bourget. Page 297.
194 Bourget. Page 297, & Archives Nationales CJ 736/5481.
195 Neitzel, Sonke. *Tapping Hitler's Generals*. Frontline Books 2007. Pages 190–191. The quoted transcript shows von Choltitz telling fellow prisoners at Trent Park that "the highest SS official arrived". But names are avoided, possibly due to the suspicion of bugging. The senior SS official in Occupied France at this time was Karl Oberg.

Chapter 4

1 Nordling. Page 99.
2 Nordling. Pages 99–100.
3 Nordling. Page 100, & Dansette. Page 116.
4 Nordling. Pages 100–101.
5 Nordling Interview. *Franc-Tireur* 1949.
6 Nordling Page 102.
7 Nordling. Pages 103–104.
8 Nordling. Page 104.
9 Nordling. Pages 104–105.
10 Nordling. Pages 105–106.
11 Nordling. Pages 106–107, & Nordling Interview *Franc-Tireur* 1949.
12 Nordling. Pages 107–108.
13 Bourget. Pages 216–217.
14 La Mazière. Pages 15–30.
15 Bourget. Pages 217–218.
16 Kaplan. Page 64.
17 Callil. Pages 371–380.
18 Choltitz. Page 221.
19 Choltitz. Page 222. After reading Professor Sonke Neitzel's research in *Tapping Hitler's Generals* it is easy to smile when reading von Choltitz's memoirs.
20 Girard. Page 258, & Langlade Page 174.
21 Patton Papers. Pages 514–515.
22 Bradley. Pages 303–304.
23 Dronne, Page 79, quoting the last interview between Laval and Herriot reported by André-Jean Fauré in *Le Monde* 19/8/1969.
24 Dronne. Page 79.
25 Dronne. Page 79.
26 Chambrun, René de. *Pierre Laval. Traitor or Patriot*. Scribners. 1984. Page 195.
27 The historian of Westminster Cathedral, Patrick Rogers, informed the author that the Cathedral suffered only light damage during the war, mainly due to an unexploded anti-aircraft shell. The main incident was a high explosive bomb landing on the Choir School playing field, which was then used as an allotment.
28 Taittinger. Pages 164–174.

29 Glass, Charles. *Americans in Paris. Life and Death under the Nazi Occupation 1940–1944.* Pages 381–382.
30 Dronne Pages 81–82. & Glass Page 382. & Collins Page 101.
31 Taittinger. Page 163.
32 Dronne. Page 82, & Glass Pages 382–383.
33 Dronne. Pages 79–80, & Chambrun Page 195.
34 Dansette. Page 126.
35 Dansette. Page 127, & Bourget Page 249.
36 Bourget. Page 249, & Bourderon. Page 375.
37 Tillon. Page 285.
38 Bourget. Page 249.
39 Dansette. Page 127.
40 Dansette. Page 128.
41 Crémieux. Pages 17–18.
42 Bourget. Page 250.
43 Crémieux. Page 50.
44 Bourget. Page 250 & Crémieux Pages 21–22.
45 Bourderon. Pages 377–378.
46 *Paris 1944—Les Enjeux de la Libération.* Débats. Albin Michel 1994. Page 79.
47 Bourderon. Page 378.
48 Levisse-Touzé. Page 213.
49 Levisse-Touzé. Pages 213–214.
50 Dansette. Pages 129–130.
51 Quoted by both Dansette. Page 130, & Bourget. Page 251.
52 Bourget. Page 251.
53 Nordling. Page 108.
54 Nordling. Page 108.
55 Bourget. Page 247.
56 Nordling. Pages 108–109.

Chapter 5

1   Langlade. Pages 178–179.
2   Langlade. Pages 179–180.
3   Dansette. Page 133.
4   Dansette. Page 133.
5   Collins/Lapierre. Pages 107–109.
6   Dansette. Page 134.
7   Bourget, Pierre. *Paris '44.* Plon 1984. Page 266, & *Paris 44 Les Enjeux de la Libération.* Albin Michel 1994. Page 169.
8   Dansette. Pages 134–135, & Dronne.LdeP. Pages 188–189.
9   Dansette. Pages 136–137, & Dronne LdeP. Pages 189–190.
10 Pisani, Edgard. *Persiste et Signe.* Éditons Odile Jacob. 1992. Pages 49–50.

11   Nordling. Pages 111–112.
12   Dronne. LdeP Page 183.
13   Bourderon, Roger. *Rol-Tanguy.* Tallandier. 2004. Page 384.
14   Bourderon. Page 384.
15   Dansette. Page 136.
16   Bourderon. Page 386.
17   Nordling. Pages 112–113.
18   Culmann. Statement.
19   Culmann. Statement.
20   Wallraf. Statement.
21   Wallraf and Massiet. Page 132.
22   Dronne. CdeR. Pages 310–311.
23   Girard. Page 260.
24   Langlade. Pages 180–181.
25   Girard. Pages 260–261.
26   Girard. Page 261.
27   Girard. Page 261.
28   Bussière. Statement.
29   Bussière. Statement.
30   Bussière Statement.
31   Bourget. Page 315.
32   Goudeket, Maurice. *Close to Colette.* Secker and Warburg. 1957. Pages 164–165.
33   Gilot, Françoise. *Life with Picasso.* McGraw-Hill 1964. Pages 60–61.
34   Penrose, Roland. *Picasso: His Life and Work.* New York, Schocken 1962. Page 313.
35   Pryce-Jones. Page 36.
36   Dansette. Page 147.
37   Pryce-Jones. Page 47.
38   Dansette. Page 147.
39   Dansette. Page 148.
40   Dansette. Page 148.
41   Dansette. Page 148 & Dronne LdeP Page 196.
42   Dansette. Page 148–149 & Dronne. LdeP
43   De Gaulle. MDG Page 566. Plon. 1999.
44   Bourderon, Page 386.
45   Bourderon. Page 387.
46   Dansette. Page 137.
47   Bourderon. Page 387.
48   Bourderon. Page 388.
49   Bourderon. 100 docs.
50   Monsignor Brot. Statement. & Dansette. Page 138.
51   Monsignor Brot. Statement.
52   Dansette. Page 139. Monsignor Brot. Statement & Collins/Lapierre. Page 129.
53   Dronne. LdeP Page 191, & Collins/Lapierre, Page 130.
54   Dronne. LdeP Page 191, & Dansette. Page 139.

55 Culmann. Statement.
56 Dronne. Pages 191–192, & Dansette. Page 139.
57 Dronne. Page 192, & Dansette Page 139.
58 Dronne. Page 192.
59 Dronne. Page 193.
60 Galtier-Boissière, Jean. *Mon Journal de l'Occupation*. La Jeune Parque. 1944. Pages 269–270.
61 Nordling, Raoul. *Sauver Paris*. Éditions Complexe. 2002. Pages 113–114.
62 Dansette. Page 156.
63 Muller, Prof KJ. *Paris 1944. Les Enjeux de la Libération*. Albin Michel 1994. Pages 103–104. Quoting Gorlitz Page 200, RH 19/IX/88 Page 67 & Choltitz Page 248.
64 I prefer Nordling's version of this anecdote since it is his own and the most detailed.
65 Nordling, Raoul. *Sauver Paris*. Éditions Complexe. 2002. Pages 114–116.
66 Bourderon. Page 392.
67 Dansette. Page 140.
68 Dronne. Pages 193–194.
69 Dansette. Page 141.
70 Dronne LdeP Page 194, & Dansette. Page 146.
71 Dronne. LdeP. Page 195.
72 Dronne LdeP Pages 197–198 & Dansette. Pages 143–144.
73 Dansette. Pages 149–153, & Dronne LdeP Pages 200–201.
74 Bourget. Quoting an order from Choltitz. Pages 317–318.
75 Wallraf. Statement.
76 Dr. Victor Veau. Statement.
77 *Paris 1944. Les Enjeux de la Libération*. Albin Michel. 1994. Page 246. Extrraordinarily, however, in his interview with Philippe Ragueneau, Jacques Chaban-Delmas says that the truce was initiated by Nordling who telephoned the Préfecture at around 7pm. Pisani apparently answered and Nordling asked if they would agree to an hour's ceasefire. Ragueneau/Florentin. Pages 189–190.
78 Nordling makes clear that this is what he remembers though others may deny it.
79 Tollet, André. Conversation with Philippe Ragueneau. Page 127.
80 Nordling. Pages 117–118.
81 Nordling. Page 118.
82 Nordling. Page 118.
83 Bourget, Pierre. Essay. *Paris 1944, Les Enjeux de la Libération*. Albin Michel 1994. Page 244. Also on pages 277–278 Bourget questions whether Bender even existed, appearing to support von Choltitz on this matter. However, Nordling's memoirs only came out in 2002.
84 Choltitz. Page 232.
85 Rol-Tanguy, Henri and Roger Bourderon. *Libération de Paris. Les Cents documents*. Hachette 1994. Page 219.

86 This section has been pieced togther from Adrien Dansette, Raymond Dronne and the memoirs of both von Choltitz and Raoul Nordling.
87 Nordling. Pages 113–120.
88 Bourget. Page 323.
89 Massiet. Page 134.
90 Massiet. Vautrain 1952. Page 94.
91 Taittinger. Pages 190–191.
92 Bourderon. Pages 393–394.
93 Bourderon. Page 392.
94 Williams. Page 470.
95 Michèle Cointet. *Les ultimes manoeuvres de Vichy.* Essay for—*Paris 1944. Les Enjeux de la Libération.* Albin Michel 1994. Pages 129–130.
96 Dronne. Pages 56–57.
97 Lottmann. Pétain. Pages 521–523.
98 Lottmann. Pétain. Pages 523–524.
99 Taittinger. Pages 197–198.
100 Dronne. Pages 207–208.
101 Taittinger. Page 198.
102 Taittinger. Pages 198–199.
103 Dronne. Page 208.
104 Taittinger. Page 199.
105 Taittinger. Pages 214–216. & Ragueneau/Florentin Pages 109–110.
106 Taittinger. Pages 217–218.
107 Taittinger. Pages 218–219.
108 Taittinger. Pages 219–220.
109 Dronne Page 210.
110 Ragueneau/Florentin. Page 148.
111 Nordling. Pages 121–124.
112 Dronne. Page 210–211.
113 Nordling. Page 124.
114 Ibid.
115 Taittinger. Page 220.
116 Taittinger. Page 220–221.
117 Bourderon. R-T. Tallandier 2004. Pages 399–400.
118 Bourderon. Page 400, & Massiet. Page 135.
119 Bourderon. Pages 402–404.
120 Taittinger. Pages 221–222.
121 Taittinger. Page 223.
122 Taittinger. Pages 224–225.
123 De Gaulle, P. *De Gaulle Mon Père.* With Maurice Tauriac. Pages 347–348.
124 Ibid. and De Gaulle MdeG. Page 567.
125 D'Este. *Eisenhower* Page 575. DeGaulle MdeG Page 567, & Hodges Papers.
126 DeGaulle. MdeG. Page 568.

127 DeGaulle. MdeG. Pages 568–569.

128 Cook, Don. *Charles de Gaulle.* Page 238.

129 Fenby. Page 250, & DeGaulle. MdeG. Page 569.

130 DeGaulle. MdeG. Page 569.

131 Girard. Pages 261–262.

132 Hodges. War Diary. Page 102.

133 Girard. Page 262.

134 Bruce. Pages 156–159.

135 Bruce. Pages 159–160.

136 Bruce. Page 160, & Carlos Baker. Pages 621–622.

137 Baker. Pages 622–623.

138 Baker. Page 623.

139 Dansette. Page 172–173.

140 Goudeket, Maurice. *Close to Colette.* Secker and Warburg. 1957. Page 166, & Thurman, Judith. *A Life of Colette.* Bloomsbury. 1999. Page 466.

141 Dansette. Page 173.

142 Dansette. Pages 173–174.

143 Dansette. Page 174. JG-B. Page 259.

144 Galtier-Boissière. Pages 259–260.

145 Ibid Page 261.

146 Dronne. Pages 211–212.

147 Nordling. Page 126.

148 Ibid.

149 Nordling. Page 127.

150 Ibid.

151 Dansette. Pages 177–178. The arrest of Alexandre Parodi on the afternoon of Sunday 20 August 1944 was one of that day's key incidents. Adrien Dansette's account has not been improved upon.

152 Brot. Statement.

153 Report. Prefecture de Police. Quoted by Bourget.

154 Culmann. Statement.

155 Dansette. Page 176–177.

156 Wallraf. Statement.

157 Gus. Statement.

158 Bourget. Page 330.

159 Dansette. Page 178.

160 Dansette. Page 178.

161 Dansette. Pages 178–179.

162 Dansette. Page 179.

163 CollinsLapierre. Page 161.

164 Nordling. Page 129.

165 Nordling. Page 129.

166 Nordling. Page 129.

167 Dansette. Page 180.

168 Dronne. Pages 214–215.
169 Dansette. Page 181.
170 Dansette. Page 181.
171 Dansette. Page 182.
172 Nordling. Page 130.
173 Dronne. Pages 215–216.
174 Nordling. Pages 130–131.
175 Dronne Page 216, & Dansette Page 182.
176 Nordling. Page 131.
177 Dronne. Page 216.
178 Dronne Page 216. Dansette. Pages 182–183. Collins & Lapierre. Pages 162–163.
179 Bourget. Pages 333–334.
180 Bourderon. Page 406.
181 Dronne.LdeP. Page 217.
182 Dronne. Pages 222–223.
183 Dronne. Page 224.
184 JGaltier-Boissière. Pages 262–263.
185 Ibid. Pages 263–264.
186 Baker. Page 623, & Bruce. Page 160.
187 Bruce. Pages 160–161.
188 Bruce. Page 161.
189 Bruce. Page 161, & Baker Pages 624–625.
190 Bourderon. Pages 421–422.
191 Bourderon. Pages 422–423.
192 Bourderon. Page 423.
193 Bouderon. Pages 423–424.
194 Bourderon. Pages 424–425.
195 Bourderon. Pages 428–430, & *Paris 1944. Les Enjeux de la Libération*. Débats. Albin Michel 1994. Page 79.
196 Bourderon. Page 404.
197 DeGaulle. MdeG. Page 570.
198 Lacouture. Pages 563–564.

Chapter 6

1   Monod, Dr Robert. *Les heures décisives de la Libération de Paris.* Éditions Gilbert. Paris 1947. Pages 47–48.
2   Monod. Page 48.
3   Bourderon. Pages 430–431.
4   Bourderon. Page 431.
5   Monod. Page 49, & Dronne. Pages 239–240.
6   Bourderon. Pages 407–408.
7   Bourderon. Page 416.

8   Bourderon. Page 409.

9   Rol-Tanguy & Bourderon. *Les Cents Documents*. Page 238.

10   Ibid. Page 238.

11   Monod. Pages 49–59.

12   Taittinger. Page 226.

13   Taittinger. Pages 226–227.

14   Monod. Pages 59–62.

15   Muller, Professor KJ. *Le développement des opérations du groupe d'armées B fin juillet-fin aout 1944*. Essay for *Paris 1944. Les Enjeux de la Libération*. Albin Michel 1994. Page 105, & using RH 19/IX/88. Page 49.

16   Muller, KJ Essay. Pages 105–106, & using RH 19/10/88. Pages 67–72.

17   Muller. Pages 106–107.

18   Edsel, Robert M. *Monuments Men*. Arrow. 2010. Page 133, & Choltitz article, *Pourqoui en 1944 je n'ai pas detruit Paris*.

19   Bourget. Page 336.

20   Bourget. Pages 336–337.

21   Galtier-Boissière. Page 265.

22   Brot. Statement.

23   Bourderon. Pages 410–411.

24   Notin. Page 263.

25   Boissieu. Pages 244–245, & Collins Lapierre. Pages 166–167. Extraordinarily Collins and Lapierre give the US liaison officers' names as Dick Rifkind and Bob Hoye.

26   Boissieu. Page 245.

27   Boissieu. Pages 245–246.

28   Notin. Pages 263–264. Quoting from articles by Guillebon in the *Revue Historique de l'Armée*.

29   Galtier-Boissière. Pages 265–266.

30   Wallraf. Statement.

31   Bourget. Page 340.

32   Culmann. Statement.

33   Culmann. Statement.

34   Galtier-Boissière. Pages 266–267.

35   Dansette. Pages 188–189.

36   Dansette. Pages 190–191.

37   Dansette. Pages 189–190.

38   Dansette. Page 190, & Collins/Lapierre. Pages 186–187.

39   Dansette. Pages 191–192.

40   Danestte. Page 193. This exchange is described in Dansette but not written as a conversation.

41   Dansette. Pages 193–194.

42   Dansette. Page 194.

43   Dansette. Page 195.

44   Kriegel-Valrimont. Memoirs.

45 Bourderon. Pages 412–414.
46 Girard. Pages 264–265.
47 Notin. Page 265. This extraordinary exchange was reported to Jean Christophe Notin by General Alain de Boissieu shortly before the latter's death. Boissieu told Notin that Bradley told him this in 1970 and that he had heard it from Eisenhower himself. Notin's narrative in his biography of Leclerc places the conversation on the evening of 21 August.
48 Girard. Page 265.
49 Bruce. Pages 162–164.
50 Bruce. Pages 164–165.
51 Baker. Pages 625–626.
52 Baker. Pages 626.
53 Baker. Page 627, & Bruce. Pages 165–166.
54 Baker. Page 627, & Bruce. Page 166.
55 Baker. Page 627, & Bruce. Page 166.
56 Taittinger. Pages 228–229.
57 Taittinger. Pages 230–231.
58 Taittinger. Pages 242–243.
59 Lambauer. Page 640. Although this is not mentioned by von Choltitz in his memoirs, it is mentioned in his testimony at Otto Abetz's trial.
60 Lambauer. Page 640. Barbara Lambauer states that while it is proven that Ribbentrop sent telegrams there is nothing to say they arrived.
61 Lambauer. Page 641.
62 Dansette. Page 203.
63 Nordling. Pages 136–137.
64 Nordling. Page 137.
65 Captain Georges and his two FFIs had an eventful return trip to Paris where only their experience and *sang froid* saved them from being shot at yet another roadblock.
66 Monod. Pages 77–78, & Dansette. Pages 240–241.
67 Crémieux. Pages 111–112, Monod. Pages 77–78, & Dansette. Pages 240–241.
68 Dansette. Page 202.
69 Choltitz. Pages 238–240.
70 Choltitz. Pages 240–241.
71 Choltitz. Pages. 242–243.
72 Dronne. Pages 225–226.
73 Choltitz. Page 244.
74 Choltitz. Pages 244–245.
75 Collins/Lapierre. Page 203.
76 Dronne. Page 226.
77 Dronne. Page 226.
78 Dansette. Pages 202–203, & Dronne Page 227.
79 Veau. Statement.
80 Bourget. Page 347.

81 Wallraf. Statement.
82 Wallraf. Choltitz. Page 272, & Naville. Page 19.
83 Lacretelle, Charles. Memoirs.
84 Dansette. Page 214.
85 Massiet. Page 165, & Sonneville. Pages 343 and 348.
86 Bourget. Page 345, & Crémieux. Page 111.
87 Bourget. Page 345.
88 Bourget. Page 345.
89 Dansette. Page 215.
90 Bourderon. Pages 432–433.
91 Crémieux. Page 81.
92 Dansette. Pages 215–216.
93 Bourget. Pages 350–351.
94 Bourget. Pages 351–352.
95 Dansette. Page 216.
96 Girard. Page 265.
97 Monod. Page 78. Dronne Page 246. Collins/Lapierre. Page 196, & *Paris 1944. Les Enjeux de la Libération.* Albin Michel. 1994. Pages 80–81.
98 Collins/Lapierre. Page 196.
99 Crémieux. Pages 113–114.
100 Crémieux. Pages 114–115.
101 Eisenhower Papers. See also in *Paris 1944. Les Enjeux de la Libération.* Page 229.
102 Monod. Page 79.
103 Bruce. Pages 166–167.
104 Bruce. Page 167.
105 Baker. Pages 628–629. Baker says it was Leclerc on 22nd at Rambouillet, but it could only have been Guillebon since Leclerc was waiting for Bradley at Eagletac.
106 Beevor and Cooper. Page 46. AB conversation with Mowinckel during 1992.
107 Beevor and Cooper. Page 47, & Murphy. Page 206.
108 Dansette. Pages 216–217.
109 Dansette. Page 217.
110 Bourderon. Pages 435–436.
111 Bourderon. Page 436.
112 Dronne. LdeP. Page 221.
113 Brot. Statement.
114 Nordling. Page 137.
115 Nordling. Page 138.
116 Nordling. Pages 138–139.
117 Dronne. Page 248.
118 Nordling. Pages 143–144.
119 Dronne. Page 248, & Funk, Professor Arthur. *Les services secrets alliés et la libération de Paris renseignement et action.* Essay for *Paris 44. Les Enjeux de la Libération.* Albin Michel 1994. Page 227.
120 Dronne. Pages 249–250.

Chapter 7

1   Maggiar. Page 199.
2   Kaspi. Professor André. *Les États Unis et la libération de Paris.* Essay for *Paris 1944 Les Enjeux de la Libération.* Albin Michel, 1994. Pages 44–45, & Kaspi. *La Libération de la France.* Tempus 2004. Pages 120–122.
3   Bradley. *A General's Life.* Simon and Schuster, 1983. Page 309.
4   Monod. Pages 79–80, & Collins/Lapierre. Pages 210–211.
5   Crémieux. Page 115.
6   Boissieu. Page 246. Gribius Page 126. *Paris 1944.* Page 366. General Jean Compagnon says that Leclerc simply said "Direction Paris," rather than "Gribius, mouvement immediat sur Paris." Perhaps he said both, but the second version is caught on film and shows Leclerc's Jeep pulling up and calling to Gribius.
7   Dansette. Pages 258–259, & Compagnon's interview in *Paris 1944.* Pages 366–367. Albin Michel 1994.
8   Boissieu. Page 246.
9   Dronne. LdeP. Page 264, & Boissieu. Pages 246–247.
10   Dronne. LdeP. Page 265.
11   Dronne. LdeP. Page 265.
12   Bergot. Page 108.
13   Girard Page 269, & Massu Page 134.
14   Collins and Lapierre. Page 266.
15   Ibid. There is more about d'Orgeix in Christine Levisse-Touzé's *Paris 1944. Les Enjeux de la Libération.* Albin Michel 1994. Page 311.
16   Dronne, Raymond. *La Libération de Paris.* Presses de la Cité 1970. Page 267.
17   Billotte. Page 12.
18   Blumenson. Essay. *Paris 1944. Les Enjeux de la Libération* Albin Michel 1994. Page 320.
19   Blumenson. Essay. *Paris 1944.* EDLL. Page 321.
20   Bergot. Page 109.
21   Dronne. CdeR. Page 321.
22   Bergot. Pages 109.
23   Bradley. Page 309.
24   Billotte. Page 312.
25   Langlade. Pages 193–194.
26   Boissieu. Page 247.
27   Bourget. Page 361.
28   Dr. Victor Veau Statement (Bourget. Page 360.), & Galtier-Boissière. Page 271.
29   Nordling. Pages 139–140.
30   Dansette. Page 220, & Collins/Lapierre. Pages 220–222.
31   Nordling. Pages 139–140.
32   Nordling. Pages 141–142.

33 Muller, KJ. *Le dévelloppement des operations du groupe d'armées B fin Juillet-fin Aout 1944*. Essay for *Paris 1944* Albin Michel 1994. Pages 108–109, & RH 19/IX/88. Page 90. RH 19/IX/9. Page 95.

34 Taittinger. Pages 243–244.

35 Taittinger. Page 244.

36 Taittinger. Page 245.

37 Bourderon. Pages 439–440.

38 Bourget. Pages 352–353. Quoting documents formerly belonging to Georges Maurice.

39 Billotte, Pierre. *Le Temps des Armes*. Plon 1972. Page 330.

40 Dronne wrote of a meeting between Nordling and von Choltitz during the early afternnon of 23 August which is not refered to in Nordling's memoir. In respect of Dronne's sources, René Masson and René Dunan, I have included these details.

41 Dronne. LdeP. Pages 234–235.

42 Dronne. LdeP. Pages 227–229.

43 Dronne. LdeP. Pages 232–234.

44 Dronne. LdeP. Pages 265–266, & Bruce. Page 168. It is possibly taking a liberty to say that Bergamin, Bruce and Hemingway drank together but, given that Dronne refers to Bergamin speaking with "Pasteau" (Mouthard) who was in Bruce and Hemingway's party, it is hard to see who else the "attractive lieutenant" Bruce refers to could be.

45 Bergot. Page 110.

46 Girard. Page 269, & Bruce. Page 168.

47 Baker, Carlos. *Ernest Hemingway*. Penguin 1972. Page 629.

48 Bruce. Page 168, & Gribius. Pages 127–128.

49 Bruce. Page 169.

50 Dansette. Page 261.

51 Girard. Page 269.

52 Lacouture, Jean. *De Gaulle. The Rebel, 1890–1944*. Collins Harvill, 1990. Page 568.

53 Récit de Madeleine Riffaud. *Humanités Dimanche*. August 1974. (Bourget.)

54 Tollet. Page 265, & Georges Maurice. Documents.

55 Bourget. Pages 356–357.

56 Dansette. Pages 220–221.

57 Dansette. Page 221.

58 Georges Maurice. (Bourget.)

59 Choltitz. Page 275.

60 Wallraf. Statement.

61 Dansette. Page 235.

62 Muller, KJ. *Le dévelloppement des operations du groupe d'armées B fin Juiller-fin Aout 1944*. Essay for *Paris 1944*. Albin Michel. 1994. Page 109. Quoting von Choltitz communiqué to Army Group B.

63 Muller. Pages 109–110, & RH 19/IX/9b, RH 19/IX/88, & RH 19/IX/18.

64 De Gaulle. Pages 573–574.

65 Aron. Page 305.
66 Dronne. Pages 267–268.
67 De Gaulle. Page 574.
68 Tauriac. Pages 347–348.
69 Aron Pages 305–306, & De Gaulle. Pages 574–575.
70 Boegner, Philippe. *Carnets du Pasteur (Marc) Boegner, 1940–1945.* Fayard. 1992. Pages 290–291.
71 Bourget. Pages 363–364.
72 Bourget. Page 364, & Crémieux-Brilhac, Jean-Louis. *Ici Londres. L'arme radiophonique et l'insurrection nationale.* Essay for *Paris 44. Les Enjeux de la Libération.* Albin Michel, 1994. Page 162. Dansette. Page 255.
73 De Gaulle. Page 575.
74 De Gaulle. Pages 575–576, & Lacouture. Pages 569–570.
75 Massu. Page 134, & Langlade Page 196.
76 Billotte. Pages 312–313, & Dronne CdeR. Pages 322–323.
77 Langlade. Pages 195–196.
78 Bergot. Page 114.
79 Girard. Page 270, & Dronne. LdeP Page 278.
80 Billotte. Pages 313–314.
81 Billotte. Pages 314–315.
82 Dronne CdeR. Pages 323–324.
83 Dronne. CdeR. Page 324.
84 Dronne. LdeP. Page 276.
85 Girard. Page 270.
86 Billotte. Page 315.
87 Muller, KJ. *Le développement des operations du groupe d'armées B fin-Juillet-fin Aout 1944.* Essay for *Paris 1944. Les Enjeux de la Libération.* Albin Michel, 1994. Page 110, & RH 19/IX/88 Page 144.
88 Bourderon. Pages 445–446.
89 Bourderon. Page 446.
90 Veau Statement. (Bourget.)
91 Lacretelle. (Bourget.)
92 Galtier-Boissière, Jean. Page 274.
93 Bourderon. Pages 446–448, & Massiet.
94 Bourderon. Pages 448–449.
95 Bourget. Page 366.
96 Bergot. Pages 114–115.
97 Bergot. Page 115.
98 Bergot. Page 115.
99 Bergot. Page 117.
100 Bergot. Page 117, & Massu. Pages 136–137.
101 Bruce. Page 170.
102 Dronne, Raymond. CdeR. Page 326.
103 Bergot. Pages 117–118.

104 Bergot. Page 118.
105 Bergot. Pages 118–120.
106 Bergot. Pages 120–121, & Forget. Pages 200–201.
107 Bergot. Page 121.
108 Bergot. Pages 121–123.
109 Boegner. Page 292.
110 Massiet. Page 96.
111 Massiet, Raymond. *La Préparation de l'Insurrection et la bataille de Paris.* Payot,1945. Page 184.
112 Massiet. PIBP. Pages 184–186.
113 Massiet. PIBP. Page 187.
114 Nordling. Page 150.
115 Dansette. Pages 235–236.
116 Dansette. Page 236.
117 Dansette. Page 236.
118 Muller, KJ. *Le développement des operations du groupe d'armées B fin Juillet-fin Aout 1944.* Essay for *Paris 1944.* Albin Michel, 1994. Pages 111–112, using KTB der OKW 1944–1945. Vol VI. Munich, 1982. Pages 101–117.
119 Bergot. Pages 124–125.
120 Bergot. Page 125.
121 Massu. Pages 137–138.
122 Bergot. Pages 125–126.
123 Notin. Pages 268–269.
124 Bergot. Page 126, & Massu Page 139.
125 Bergot. Page 126.
126 Dronne. CdeR. Pages 324–325.
127 Dronne. CdeR. Page 325.
128 Bergot. Page 130.
129 Bergot. Page 130.
130 Bergot. Page 131.
131 Bergot. Page 131.
132 Bergot. Page 131.
133 Bergot. Page 132.
134 Bergot. Page 132.
135 Suzanne Massu. Pages 146–148.
136 Bergot. Page 133.
137 Dronne CdeR. Pages 326–327.
138 Dronne. CdeR. Page 327 & Bergot. Page 133.
139 Dronne Cde R. Pages 327–328.
140 Dronne. CdeR. Page 328.
141 Dronne. CdeR. Page 328.
142 Martel. Page 283.
143 Billotte. Pages 316–317.
144 Boissieu. Pages 250–251.

145 Boissieu. Pages 251–252.
146 Dronne. LdeP. Page 279.
147 Dronne. LdeP. Pages 279, & Bergot. Page 134.
148 Boissieu. Page 252.
149 Muller, KJ. *Le developpement des operations du groupe d'armées B fin Juillet-fin Aout 1944.* Essay for *Paris 1944.* Albin Michel, 1994. Page 114 using RH 19/IX/88. Pages 113–123.
150 Billotte. Page 316.
151 Bergot. Pages 134–135, & Mesquida. Page 189, & Dronne. CdeR. Page 329.
152 Dronne. CdeR. Pages 329–330.
153 Dronne. CdeR. Page 330.
154 Dronne. CdeR. Page 330, & Bergot. Page 135.
155 Dronne. CdeR. Page 331.
156 Bergot. Pages 135–136.
157 Dronne. CdeR. Pages 331–332.
158 Dronne. CdeR. Pages 332–333.
159 Mesquida. Pages 159–160.
160 Dronne. CdeR. Page 333.
161 Dronne. CdeR. Page 334.
162 Dronne. CdeR. Pages 334–335.
163 Mesquida. Page 158.
164 Nogueères. Vol5. Page 544.
165 Bourderon. Page 450.
166 Dronne. CdeR. Page 335.
167 Dronne. CdeR. Pages 335–336.
168 Dronne. CdeR. Page 336.
169 Collins/Lapierre. Page 280.
170 Collins/Lapierre. Pages 280–281.
171 Massiet. PIBP. Pages 191–192.
172 Massiet. Page 192.
173 Bourderon. Pages 451–452, & Dronne. CdeR. Page 336.
174 Dronne. CdeR. Page 337.
175 Dronne. CdeR. Page 337.
176 Dronne. CdeR. Pages 337–338.
177 Dronne. CdeR. Page 338.
178 Notin. Page 271, & Girard. Page 270.
179 Massu. Pages 139–140.
180 Bergot. Page 147, & Massu. Pages 140–141.
181 Billotte. Pages 320–321.
182 Girard. Pages 270–271, & Boissieu. Page 253, & Muller, KJ. *Le développement des operations du groupe d'armées B fin juillet-fin aout 1944.* Essay for *Paris 1944.* Albin Michel, 1994. Page 112.
183 Muller, KJ. Essay. Pages 115 and 124, & Choltitz memoirs. Page 229.
184 Girard. Pages 270–271, & Boissieu. Page 253.

185 Branet. Page 179, & Bergot. Pages 138–139.
186 Branet. Page 179, & Bergot. Page 139.
187 Billotte, Page 321.
188 Bergot. Page 139.
189 Bergot. Page 139.
190 Galtier-Boissière. Pages 275–276.
191 Billotte. Page 322, & Branet. Page 179.
192 Mousseau. Page 113.
193 Dronne. CdeR. Page 338.
194 Dronne. CdeR. Pages 339–340.
195 Bergot. Pages 139–140.
196 Bergot. Pages 140–141.
197 Bergot. Pages 141–142.
198 Bergot. Pages 142–143.
199 Now the site of the Cinema Bretagne.
200 Dronne. LdeP. Page 287.
201 SNCF PC de Montparnasse. Journal of 24–26 August 1944. Notes of F Courbel. Page 2.
202 Bergot. Page 155.
203 Courbel. (Bourget.)
204 Courbel.
205 Girard. Page 271.
206 Billotte. Pages 322–323.
207 Nordling. Page 152, & Dronne. Page 300.
208 Nordling. Page 152.
209 Nordling. Page 153, & Dronne, LdeP, Pages 300–301.
210 Nordling. Page 153, & Dronne, LdeP, Page 301.
211 Massu. Page 141.
212 Massu. Page 142, & Bergot. Page 148.
213 Bergot. Page 148.
214 Massu. Page 142, & Bergot. Page 148.
215 Bergot. Page 149.
216 Massu. Page 142.
217 Bergot. Pages 149–150.
218 Girard, Page 273. Billotte. Page 323. Bergot Page 157, & Dansette. Page 287.
219 Girard. Page 273.
220 Billotte. Pages 323–324.
221 Branet. Page 181.
222 Bergot. Page 157.
223 Massu. Page 142, & Bergot. Page 150.
224 Massu. Page 142, & Bergot. Page 150.
225 Bergot. Page 150, & Pérouse de Montclos. Page 534. The scaffolding for the repair of this sculpture was still standing at the time of Leclerc's funeral during December 1947.

226 Branet. Page 181.

227 Valland, Rose. *Le Front de l'Art.* Plon 1961.

228 Bergot. Page 158, & Dronne. LdeP. Pages 301–302.

229 Bergot. Page 158, & Branet. Page 181.

230 Bergot. Page 158.

231 Bergot Page 158, & Dronne. LdeP. Page 302.

232 Maggiar. Page 214.

233 Wallraf Testimony, & *Paris 1944.* Page 303, & Bergot. Page 153.

234 Bergot Pages 158–159, & *Paris 1944. Les Enjeux de la Libération.* Pages 303–304.

235 Wallraf Testimony.

236 Branet. Page 182.

237 Choltitz. Page 253.

238 Choltitz. Page 254.

239 Choltitz. Page 254.

240 Dronne. LdeP. Page 304.

241 Collins/Lapierre. Page 341. Larry Collins and Dominique Lapierre claimed to have done hundreds of interviews for *Is Paris Burning?* But in their account of the taking of the Hôtel Meurice even the tank names of Branet's squadron are wrong.

242 Billotte. Page 325.

243 Billotte. Page 326.

244 Billotte. Pages 326–327.

245 Dronne. LdeP. Page 305, & Kriegel-Valrimont. Page 66.

246 Choltitz. Page 254, & Notin. Page 273.

247 Bergot. Page 160.

248 Choltitz. Pages 254–255.

249 Choltitz. Page 255.

250 Bourderon. Testimony of Rol-Tanguy. Page 454.

251 Bergot Page 151, & Massu. Page 143.

252 Massu. Page 143, & Bergot. Page 152.

253 Bergot. Page 151, & Massu. Pages 143–144.

254 Massu. Page 144.

255 Bruce. Pages 171–173.

256 Bruce. Pages 173–174.

257 Baker. Page 634.

258 Gilot, Francoise. *Vivre avec Picasso.* McGraw Hill, 1964. Pages 60–61, & Éditions 10/18. Pages 55–56, & Huffington, Arianna Stasinopoulos. *Picasso.* Simon and Schuster, 1988. Page 286. Quoting an article by John Pudsey in the *New Statesman* from September 1944. I have inserted this incident here because it fits with the geography of Hemingway's visit to Sylvia Beach a few streets away.

259 Beach. Pages 219–220.

260 Beach. Page 220.

261 John Follain, Reuters. 25 August 1944. Published Deseret News on line.

262 Dronne. CdeR. Page 341.

263 Choltitz. Pages 255–256, & Bourderon. Page 454.
264 Kriegel-Valrimont. Page 67.
265 Notin. Page 274.
266 Bourderon. Page 454.
267 Article. *Le Monde.* 9e November 1966.
268 Kriegel-Valrimont. Page 65.
269 Massiet. Raymond. *Le Carnaval des libérés ou la drame de ceux qui se disaient français.* Vautrain. Page 105.
270 Boissieu, Alain de. Addressing the Colloque of February 1994. *Paris 1944. Les Enjeux de la Libération.* Albin Michel, 1994. Débats. Page 510.
271 Betz. Statement.

Chapter 8

1 De Gaulle. Page 576, & Lacouture. Page 572.
2 Aron. Page 305.
3 De Gaulle. Page 576.
4 De Gaulle. Page 577, & Lacouture. Page 572.
5 Dronne. LdeP. Pages 308–309.
6 De Gaulle, Philippe. Pages 319–320.
7 Lacouture. Page 572, & De Gaulle. Page 577, & De Gaulle, Philippe. Page 320.
8 De Gaulle. Philippe. Page 320, & De Gaulle, MdeG. Page 577. I have inserted the incident involving de Gaulle's son in the order that de Gaulle himself describes the incidents at the Gare Montparnasse in his *Memoirs de Guerre.*
9 Notin. Page 275, & De Gaulle, Page 578, & Boissieu. Pages 255–256.
10 Notin. Page 275, & De Gaulle. Page 578.
11 De Gaulle. Page 578, & Dansette. Page 307.
12 De Gaulle. Page 578.
13 Dronne. LdeP. Page 314, & De Gaulle. Page 578, & Dansette. Pages 309–310, & Billotte. Page 328.
14 Dronne. LdeP Pages 314–315. & Massiet Page 83 & De Gaulle Pages 578–579.
15 Valland, Rose. *Le Front de l'Art.* Plon 1961. Quoted by Robert M. Edsel. *Monuments Men.* Preface Publishing, 2009. Pages 203–204.
16 Wallraf. Statement.
17 De Gaulle, Philippe. Pages 320–322.
18 De Gaulle, Philippe. Pages 322–323.
19 De Gaulle, Philippe. Pages 323–324.
20 Taittinger. Pages 247–248.
21 Taittinger. Pages 248–249.
22 Taittinger. Page 249.
23 Boissieu. Page 256.
24 De Gaulle, Philippe. Pages 324–325.

25 De Gaulle, Philippe. Pages 325–326.

26 Bergot. Page 161–162.

27 Bergot. Page 162, & Dronne. LdeP. Pages 308–309.

28 Bergot. Page 162, & Dronne. LdeP. Page 309.

29 Bergot. Page 162, & Dronne. LdeP. Page 310.

30 Bergot. Page 162, & Dronne. LdeP. Page 310.

31 Muller, KJ. *Le développement des operations du groupe d'armées B fin-Juillet-fin Aout 1944.* Essay for *Paris 1944.* Albin Michel, 1994. Pages 115–116.

32 Dronne. LdeP. Page 311.

33 Bergot. Pages 162–163, & Dronne. LdeP. Pages 310–311.

34 Ragueneau. Page 112. Interview with Roger Stéphane.

35 Massiet. Page 99.

36 Lacouture. Pages 547–575, & De Gaulle. Page 580, & Ragueneau. Page 112.

37 Lacouture Page 575, & De Gaulle. Page 580.

38 Massu, Jacques. *Sept ans avec Leclerc.* Plon 1974. Pages 147–148.

39 Courdesses, Colonel Maurice. *Les combats de la 2e Division Blindée dans Paris.* Essay for *Paris 1944.* Albin Michel, 1994. Page 311.

40 Kaiser, Arthur. *Un artisan Alsacien dans la Division Leclerc.* Éditons Muller. 2001. Page 149.

41 De Gaulle. Page 580–581.

42 De Gaulle. Page 581.

43 Dansette. Pages 319–320.

44 Bergot. Page 163, & Jaufret, Professor Jean-Charles. *Les combats de la 2e DB au nord de Paris.* Essay for *Paris 1944, Les Enjeux de la Libération.* Albin Michel, 1994. Page 345.

45 Boissieu. Page 257.

46 Boissieu. Pages 257–258, & Massu. Pages 148–149.

47 Bergot. Page 164.

48 Massu. Page 149.

49 De Gaulle, Philippe. Pages 326–327.

50 Branet. Pages 182–183.

51 Dronne. CdeR. Pages 342–343.

52 Dronne. CdeR. Page 343.

53 Compagnon, General Jean. *Débats* for the 1994 *Colloque.* Quoted in *Paris 1944, Les Enjeux de la Libération.* Albin Michel, 1994. Page 364.

54 Beevor. Pages 510–511, using NA II 407/427/24235, & Hodges Diaries.

55 Lottman. Pages 522–524, & Aron. Page 306.

56 Dronne. Pages 343–344.

57 Dansette. Pages 319–320.

58 Vinatier, Jean. *Le Cardinal Suhard.* Le Centurion. 1983, Page 199.

59 Vinatier. Pages 199–200.

60 Vinatier. Pages 200–201.

61 Juin, Maréchal Alphonse. *Mémoires.* Fayard. 1959.

62 Lacouture. Page 577.

63 This somewhat fruity version can be found in Arthur Kaiser's book on page 153. Since he is a close friend of Leclerc's eldest surviving son, Hubert, this anecdote seems likely to be true. A slightly cleaned up version also exists in Paul de Langlade's *En Suivant Leclerc* on Page 226.

64 Dansette. Page 320.

65 Vinatier. Page 201.

66 Moisson. Pages 126–127.

67 Dansette. Pages 326–327, & Mesquida. Pages 166 & 212.

68 Gallois statement. AN 72AJ/61/1/17. Page 42.

69 De Gaulle. Pages 582–583.

70 Langlade, Paul de. *En suivant Leclerc.* Au fil d'Ariane, 1964. Pages 224–225.

71 Article by Francois Audigier. *La Media et la Liberation.* Christian Delporte, 2006. Page 393.

72 Kriegel-Valrimont. Pages 68–69.

73 De Gaulle. Page 583.

74 Dronne. CdeR. Page 344.

75 De Gaulle. Pages 583–584.

76 Kriegel-Valrimont. Page 69.

77 De Gaulle. Pages 584–585.

78 Moisson. Page 128.

79 Dronne. CdeR. Page 344.

80 Dronne. CdeR. Page 345, & Moisson. Page 129.

81 Vinatier. Pages 202–203.

82 Bourget. Page 384, quoting testimony by Monsignor Brot.

83 De Gaulle, Charles. *Mémoires de Guerre.* Plon, 1999. Page 586.

84 Brot. Témoignage.

85 Guillebon. Témoignage.

86 Brot. Témoignage.

87 Muggeridge, Malcolm. *Chronicles of Wasted Time.* Volume 2. *The Infernal Grove.* Page 211.

88 Lacouture, Vol 2. Page 3.

89 Brot. Témoignage.

90 Brot. Témoignage.

91 De Gaulle. Page 587.

92 Boissieu. Page 259.

93 Pierquin. Page 134.

94 Bourget. Page 387.

95 Giolitto. Page 358. *Milicien* Mansuy's fate remains a point of controversy. One version, told by Adrien Dansette, has it that he was recognised at the Hôtel de Ville on the afternoon of the 25th shortly before de Gaulle's arrival and then interrogated through the night, before being shot, presumably on the 26th. But Pierre Giolitto, the historian of the *Milice,* says Mansuy was arrested on the 26th at the Hôtel de Ville, and killed the *following* day, i.e. the 27th.

96 Gribius. Page 139.
97 Gribius. Page 140.
98 Whitcombe, Elisabeth. *Never a Dull Moment*. Ashmole Books, 1994. Page 71.
99 Goudeket. Pages 167–168.
100 Maule. Pages 227–228.
101 Maule. Page 228.
102 Beevor and Cooper. Pages 79–80.
103 Muggeridge. Vol 2. Page 221.
104 Feliciano, Hector. *The Lost Museum*. Basic Books. New York, 1995. Pages 49–50.
105 Fraser, General Sir David. *Wars and Shadows*. Penguin Allen Lane, 2002. Pages 215–216.
106 Fraser. Page 217.
107 Baker. Pages 637–638.
108 Quoted from Carlos Baker's biography of Hemingway, Page 638.
109 Baker. Pages 638–639, & Todd. Pages 288–299.
110 Dansette. Page 334.
111 Collins/Lapierre. Page 374.
112 Bruce. Page 177.
113 Dansette. Page 334.
114 Bourget. Page 390.
115 Bourget, Page 390.
116 Bourget. Page 399.
117 Bruce. Pages 177–178.
118 Fraser. Page 218, & Duff Cooper. Page 337.
119 Carrington. *Reflect On Things Past*. Collins, 1988. Pages 55–56.
120 Fraser. Pages 217–218.
121 Cobb, Matthew. *Eleven Days in August*. Simon and Schuster, 2013. Page 358.
122 Branet. Pages 185.
123 Boissieu. Page 260.
124 Girard. Page 275.
125 Compagnon. Pages 414–415.
126 De Gaulle. Philippe Page 330, & Boissieu. Page 260.
127 Boissieu. Page 260.
128 Cook. Page 251.
129 D'Este. *Eisenhower*. Page 576.
130 Cook. Page 251.
131 D'Este. *Eisenhower*. Pages 576–577.
132 D'Este. Page 577, & Blumenson. Page 627.
133 Notin. Pages 279–280, using Leclerc letter 27/8/44. SHAT 1K239(8).
134 Lacouture, Vol 2. Page 8.
135 Eisenhower. *Crusade in Europe*. Op cit.
136 D'Este. Page 577.
137 Kriegel-Valrimont. Page 70.

138 Bradley Page. 309.

139 Galtier-Boissière. Pages 286–287.

140 Ibid. Pages 287–288.

141 Ibid. Pages 288–289.

142 Boegner. Pages 300–301.

143 Dronne. CdeR. Pages 346–347.

144 Dronne. CdeR. Page 347.

145 Dronne. CdeR. Pages 347–348.

146 Dronne. CdeR. Page 348.

147 Bourget. Page 402, & Glass. Page 401.

148 Bourget. Page 403.

149 Miller Papers. 3/1/45 Letter to Reed Switzer. EPSHS.

150 Girard. Page 276.

151 Muller, KJ. *Le développement des operations du groupe d'armées B fin Juillet-fin-Aout 1944.* Essay for *Paris 1944.* Albin Michel, 1994. Page 120, & OKW/WFst 28/8/1944. 12.45pm. /Ia No 770/44 sec.

152 Limbauer, Barbara. *Otto Abetz et les Français.* Fayard 2001. Page 683, quoting JB Derosne *D'une prison.* Page 32.

153 Choltitz. Pages 261–263.

154 Neitzel. Pages 17–20.

155 Neitzel. Page 94.

156 Neitzel. Pages 190–191.

157 Neitzel. Pages 257–259.

158 Neitzel. Page 192. On page 75 of his 2014 book *Disobeying Hitler*, Randall Hansen casts some doubt on whether von Choltitz actually said this since, while transcripts survive, the original recordings do not, nor is there any corroborating evidence that von Choltitz was involved in any massacres of Jews in Russia.

159 *Paris 1944. Les Enjeux de la Libération.* Débats. Albin Michel, 1994. Page 179.

160 Girard. Page 277.

161 Girard. Page 277.

162 Notin. Pages 280–281.

163 Branet. Page 185.

164 De Gaulle, Philippe. Pages 331–332.

165 De Gaulle, Philippe, & Tauriac. Page 352.

166 De Gaulle & Tauriac. Pages 352–353.

167 Girard. Page 277.

168 Picardy, Justine. *Coco Chanel. The Legend and the Life.* Harper Collins, 2010. Pages 262–263.

169 Muggeridge, Vol 2. Pages 241–242.

170 Huffington. Pages 283–284.

171 Huffington. Page 285.

172 Huffington. Page 286.

Epilogue

1   Notin, Jean Christophe. *Leclerc*. Perrin, 2005. Page 281.
2   Cobb, Matthew. *Eleven Days in August*. Simon and Schuster, 2013. Pages 358–359. Cobb is very strong on the human and compassionate side of the Paris story.
3   Norwich, John Julius. *The Duff Cooper Diaries*. Weidenfeld, 2005. Page 320.
4   Ibid. Page 321.
5   Muggeridge, Malcolm. *Chronicles of Wasted Time. The Infernal Grove*. Collins. 1973. Page 234.
6   *The Duff-Cooper Diaries*. Page 321.
7   Muggeridge. Pages 235–236.
8   Beevor, Antony & Cooper, Artemis. *Paris after the Liberation*. Hamish Hamilton, 1994. Page 153.
9   *The Duff Cooper Diaries*. Page 476.
10 Lottmann, Herbert R. *The People's Anger*. Hutchinson, 1986, & Pryce-Jones, David. *Paris and the Third Reich*. Collins 1981. Page 196.
11 Beevor & Cooper. Pages 159–161, & Kaplan, Alice. *The Collaborator*. Chicago, 2000. Pages 186–187.
12 La Mazière, Christian de. *Ashes of Honour*. Wingate, 1975. Page 97.
13 Lacouture, Jean. *De Gaulle The Ruler*. Collins Harvill, 1990. Vol 2, Page 41, & Kersaudy, Francois. *Churchill and de Gaulle*. Fontana, 1990. Pages 370–371.
14 Lacouture. Page 41, & De Gaulle. *Lettres*. Vol V, Page 349.
15 Lacouture. Page 42, & *The Duff Cooper Diaries*. Pages 331–333.
16 De Gaulle, Charles. *Memoires de Guerre*. Vol 3. Plon, 1999. Page 645.
17 Churchill, WS. *The Second World War*. Cassell, 1954. Vol 6, Page 218.
18 Ismay, Hastings. *Memoirs*. Heinemann, 1960. Page 381.
19 Churchill. Vol 6. Page 281. Kersaudy. Page 377.
20 De Gaulle. *Mémoires de Guerre*. Plon, 1999. Page 645.
21 Ibid.
22 Lacouture. Page 42.
23 Lacouture. Page 43.
24 Mortimer-Moore, William. *Free France's Lion*. Casemate, 2011. Pages 346–360.
25 Lacouture. Page 47.
26 Massu, Jacques. *Sept ans avec Leclerc*. Éditions du Rocher, 1997. Pages 219–220.
27 Girard, Christian. *Journal de Guerre*. L'Harmattan, 1975. Page 369.
28 Notin, Jean-Christophe. *Leclerc*. Perrin, 2005. Pages 330–331.
29 For a full translation of this speech, see *Free France's Lion* by William Mortimer-Moore. Pages 402–403.
30 Lottman, Herbert. *Pétain*. Seuil, 1984. Pages 537–539.
31 Isorni, Jacques. *Philippe Pétain*. La Table Ronde, 1973. Page 476, & Beevor and Cooper. Page 191.
32 Beevor and Cooper. Page 194, & Boegner. Pages 352–353.

33 Kupferman, Fred. *Laval 1883–1945*. Champs Flammarion, 1988. Pages 512–513.

34 Lacouture. Pages 82–83.

35 Beevor and Cooper. Page 195.

36 Veillon, Dominique. *Lieux de Mémoire et Commémoration*. Essay for *Paris 1944*. Albin Michel, 1994. Page 491.

37 Castetbon, Philippe. *Ici est tombé*. Éditions Tirésias, 2004. Pages 36–41 and Pages 188–193.

38 Castetbon. Pages 219–225.

39 Bourget, Pierre. *Paris '44*. Plon, 1984. Page 303.

40 Billotte, Pierre. *Le Temps des Armes*. Plon, 1972. Page 331.

41 Lambauer, Barbara. *Otto Abetz et les Français*. Fayard, 2001. Page 688.

42 Lambauer. Page 640.

43 Lambauer. Page 689.

44 Billotte. Page 330.

45 Billotte. Page 331.

46 Billotte. Pages 331–332.

47 Ibid.

48 Billotte. Page 332.

49 Taittinger, Pierre. *Et Paris ne fut pas détruit*. Nouvelles Éditions Latines, 1956. Page 174.

Select Bibliography

The following list contains those source books which have been used directly in my own account of events in and involving Paris during 1944. This list does not pretend to be exhaustive or to represent the full extent of my reading. It is simply intended to serve as an indicator of the wells where I have sipped, hoping that those readers who wish to know more can then acquire some of these books and develop a deeper knowledge of this fascinating chapter of Second World War history for themselves.

Amouroux, Henri. *Le Peuple du Désastre*. Laffont 1976.
Aron, Robert. *De Gaulle before Paris*. Putnam 1962.
Atkinson, Rick. *An Army at Dawn*. Little Brown 2003.
Atkinson, Rick. *The Guns at Last Light*. Little Brown 2013.
Aziz, Pierre. *Tu trahiras sans vergogne*. Fayard 1973.
Baker, Carlos. *Ernest Hemingway*. Scribners 1969.
Barnet, Correlli. Editor. *Hitler's Generals*. Weidenfeld and Nicolson 1989.
Beach, Sylvia. *Shakespeare and Company*. Bison 1991.
Beevor, Antony. *D-Day*. Penguin Viking 2009.
Beevor, Antony, with Artemis Cooper. *Paris after the Liberation. 1944–1949*.
    Hamish Hamilton 1994.
Beevor, Antony. *The Battle for Spain*. Weidenfeld and Nicolson 2006.
Beevor, Antony. *The Second World War*. Weidenfeld and Nicolson 2012.
Bergot, Erwan. *La 2ème DB*. Presses de la Cité 1980.
Berthon, Simon. *Allies at War*. Harper Collins 2001.
Béthouart, General Émile. *Cinq Années d'Ésperance*. Plon 1968.
Billotte, Pierre. *Le Temps des Armes*. Plon 1972.
Blumenson, Martin. *The Battle of the Generals*. Morrow 1993.
Blumenson, Martin. Editor. *The Patton Papers*. Da Capo 1974.
Blumenson, Martin. *The Duel for France, 1944*. Da Capo 2000.

Boegner, Philippe. Editor. *Carnets du Pasteur Boegner, 1940–1945.* Fayard 1992.

Boissieu, Alain de. *Pour Combattre avec de Gaulle.* Plon 1981.

Boterf, Herve le. *La Vie Parisienne sous l'Occupation.* 2 vols. Éditons France Empire 1975.

Bourderon, Roger. *Rol-Tanguy.* Tallandier 2004.

Bourdan, Pierre. *Carnet de Retour avec la Division Leclerc.* Trémois 1945.

Bourget, Pierre. *Paris 44.* Plon 1984.

Bradley, General Omar. *A General's Life.* Simon and Schuster 1983.

Braibant, Charles. *La guerre à Paris.* Corrêa 1945.

Branet, Jacques. *L'Escadron.* Flammarion 1968.

Bruce, Colonel David. Edited Nelson Lankford. *OSS against the Reich.* Kent State UP 1991.

Burleigh, Michael. *Moral Combat.* Collins 2010.

Callil, Carmen. *Bad Faith.* Jonathan Cape 2006.

Carrington, Lord. *Reflect on Things Past.* Collins 1988.

Castetbon, Philippe. *Ici est tombé.* Éditions Tirésias 2004.

Cazaux, Yves. *Journal secret de la Libération.* Albin Michel 1975.

Chaban-Delmas, Jacques. *L'Ardeur.* Stock 1975.

Chambrun, René de. *Pierre Laval. Traitor or Patriot.* Scribners 1984.

Choltitz, Dietrich von. *De Sébastopol à Paris.* Éditons J'ai lu 1969.

Cobb, Matthew. *The Resistance.* Simon and Schuster 2010.

Cobb, Matthew. *Eleven Days in August.* Simon and Schuster 2013.

Collins, Larry & Dominique Lapierre. *Is Paris Burning?* Gollancz 1965.

Compagnon, General Jean. *Leclerc.* Flammarion 1994.

Cook, Don. *Charles de Gaulle, A Biography.* Putnam 1983.

Crémieux, Francis. *La vérité sur la Libération de Paris.* Belfond 1971.

Crémieux-Brilhac, Jean-Louis. *La France Libre.* 2 vols. Gallimard 1996.

Curtis, Michael. *Verdict on Vichy.* Weidenfeld and Nicolson 2002.

Dansette, Adrien. *Histoire de la Libération de Paris.* Fayard 1966.

Debu-Bridel, Jacques. *De Gaulle et le CNR.* Paris France Empire 1978.

D'Este, Carlo. *Decision in Normandy.* Collins 1983.

D'Este, Carlo. *Patton—A Genius for War.* Harper Collins 1995.

D'Este, Carlo. *Eisenhower, Allied Supreme Commander.* Weidenfeld and Nicolson 2003.

Dronne, Raymond. *La Libération de Paris.* Éditions France Empire 1970.

Dronne, Raymond. *Carnets de Route.* Éditons France Empire 1984.

Duff-Cooper, Alfred. *Old Men Forget.* Hart-Davis 1953.

Edsell, Robert. *Monuments Men.* Preface Publishing 2009.

Egremont, Max. *Under Two Flags: The Life of Major-General Sir Edward Spears.* Weidenfeld and Nicolson 1997.

Favreau, Bertrand. *Georges Mandel—ou la passion de la République.* Fayard 1996.

Feliciano, Hector. *The Lost Museum.* Basic Books. New York. 1995.

Fenby, Jonathan. *The General.* Simon and Schuster 2010.

Fest, Joachim. *Plotting Hitler's Death.* Weidenfeld and Nicolson 1996.

Forget, Dominique. *Le Général Leclerc et la 2è DB.* Heimdal 2008.

Fraser, General Sir David. *War and Shadows.* Penguin Allen Lane 2002.

Galante, Pierre. *Hitler Lives and the Generals Die.* Sidgwick and Jackson 1982.

Galtier-Boissière, Jean. *Mon Journal pendant l'Occupation.* La Jeune Parque 1944.

Gaulle, Charles de. *Mémoires de Guerre.* Plon 1999 edn.

Gaulle, Philippe de. *Mémoires Accessoires, 1921–1946.* Plon 1997.

Gaulle, Philippe de & Michel Tauriac. *De Gaulle Mon Père.* vols 1&2. Plon 2003.

Gildea, Robert. *Marianne in Chains.* Macmillan 2002.

Gilles, Christian. *Arletty ou la liberté d'être.* L'Harmattan 1988.

Gilot, Françoise. *Vivre avec Picasso.* Éditions 10/18. 1964.

Giolitto, Pierre. *L'histoire de la Milice.* Perrin 1997.

Girard, Christian. *Journal de Guerre.* L'Harmattan 2000.

Goudeket, Maurice. *Close to Colette.* Secker and Warburg 1957.

Gribius, André. *La vie d'un officier.* Éditons France Empire 1971.

Guérin, Alain. *La Résistance.* Le Livre Club Diderot 1976.

Guitry, Sacha. *Quatre Ans d'Occupation.* Éditions de l'Élan 1947.

Guy, Claude. *En écoutant de Gaulle.* Grasset 1996.

Hamilton, Nigel. *Monty.* 3 vols. Hamish Hamilton 1984.

Hansen, Randall. *Disobeying Hitler.* Faber and Faber 2014.

Harding, James. *Sacha Guitry: The Last Boulevardier.* Methuen 1968.

Hastings, Max. *Overlord.* Michael Joseph 1984.

Hoffmann, Peter. *The History of the German Resistance, 1939–1945.* MIT Press 1977.

Horne, Alistair. *To Lose a Battle.* Macmillan 1969.

Horne, Alistair. *Seven Ages of Paris*. Macmillan 2002.

Hostache, René. *De Gaulle 1944: Victoire de la Legitimité*. Plon 1978.

Huffington, Ariana Stasinopoulos. *Picasso—Creator and Destroyer*. Simon and Schuster 1988.

Ismay, General Lord. *Memoirs*. Heinemann 1960.

Isorni, Jacques. *Philippe Pétain*. Éditions La Table Ronde 1973.

Jackson, Julian. *France—The Dark Years*. Oxford UP 2001.

Junger, Ernst. *Second Journal Parisien*. Christian Bourgeois 1995.

Kaiser, Arthur. *Un artisan Alsacien dans la Division Leclerc*. Éditon Muller 2001.

Kaplan, Alice. *The Collaborator: The Trial and Execution of Robert Brasillach*. Chicago UP 2000.

Kaspi, André. *La Liberation de la France. Juin 1944–Janvier 1946*. Perrin 1995.

Keegan, John. *Six Armies in Normandy*. Jonathan Cape 1982.

Kersaudy, François. *Churchill and de Gaulle*. Fontana 1990.

Kersaudy, François. *De Gaulle et Roosevelt*. Tempus 2006.

Kriegel-Valrimont, Maurice. *Mémoires Rebelles*. Éditons Odile Jacob 1999.

Kupferman, Fred. *Laval, 1883–1945*. Flammarion 1988.

Lacouture, Jean. *De Gaulle: The Rebel, 1890–1944*. Collins Harvill 1990.

Lacouture, Jean. *De Gaulle: The Ruler, 1944–1980*. Collins Harvill 1990.

Lambauer, Barbara. *Otto Abetz et les français*. Fayard 2001.

Langlade, Paul de. *En suivant Leclerc*. Au fil d'Ariane 1964.

Lehrer, Stephen. *Wartime Sites in Paris*. SF Tafel 2013.

Levisee-Touzé, Christine. *L'Afrique du Nord dans la guerre*. Albin Michel 1998.

Levisse-Touzé, Christine. Editor. *Du Capitaine de Hauteclocque au Général Leclerc*. Éditons Complexe 2000.

Levisse-Touzé, Christine. Editor. *Paris 1944. Les Enjeux de la Libération*. Albin Michel 1994.

Lormier, Dominique. *La Libération de la France, jour après jour*. Cherche Midi 2012.

Lottmann, Herbert. *Pétain*. Seuil 1984.

Lottmann, Herbert. *The People's Anger*. Hutchinson 1986.

Lottmann, Herbert. *The Fall of Paris, June 1940*. Sinclair-Stevenson 1992.

Luck, Hans von. *Panzer Commander*. Cassell 1989.

Maggiar, Raymond. *Les Fusiliers Marins de Leclerc*. Éditions France Empire 1984.

Mangold, Peter. *Britain and the Defeated French*. IB Tauris 2012.

Martel, André. *Leclerc: Le soldat et le politique*. Albin Michel 1998.

Massiet, Raymond. *La préparation de l'insurrection et la bataille de Paris*. Payot 1945.

Massu, Jacques. *Sept ans avec Leclerc*. Éditons de Rocher 1997.

Massu, Suzanne. *Quand j'étais Rochambelle*. Grasset 1969.

Maule, Henry. *Out of the Sand*. Odhams 1964.

La Mazière, Christian de. *Ashes of Honour*. Wingate 1974.

Mesquida, Evelyn. *La Nueve*. Cherche-Midi 2011.

Michel, Henri. *Paris Allemand*. Albin Michel 1982.

Moisson, Pascale. *Anecdotes sous la botte*. L'Harmattan 1998.

Monod, Dr Robert. *Les Heures Décisives de la Libération de Paris*. Éditions Gilbert 1947.

Morgan, Ted. *FDR—A Biography*. Grafton 1985.

Mortimer-Moore, William. *Free France's Lion*. Casemate 2011.

Mousseau, Jacques. *Chaban-Delmas*. Perrin 2000.

Muggeridge, Malcolm. *Chronicles of Wasted Time*, vol. 2: *The Infernal Grove*. Collins 1973.

Muracciole, Jean-François. *La Libération de Paris*. Tallandier 2013.

Neiberg, Michael. *The Blood of Free Men*. Basic Books 2012.

Neillands, Robin. *The Battle of Normandy—1944*. Cassell 2002.

Neitzel, Sönke. *Tapping Hitler's Generals*. Frontline 2007.

Noguères, Henri. *L'histoire de la Résistance en France*. Robert Lafont 1981.

Nordling, Raoul. *Sauver Paris*. Éditions Complexe 2002.

Norwich, John Julius. *The Duff Cooper Diaries*. Weidenfeld and Nicolson 2005.

Notin, Jean-Christophe. *Leclerc*. Perrin 2005.

Ousby, Ian. *Occupation—The Ordeal of France 1940–1944*. John Murray 1997.

Patton, General George S. *War As I Knew It*. Houghton Mifflin 1995.

Paxton, Robert O. *Vichy France—Old Guard and New Order, 1940–1944*. Knopf 1972.

Picardy, Justine. *Coco Chanel—The Legend and the Life*. Harper Collins 2010.

Pierquin, Bernard. *Journal d'un étudiant parisien sous l'occupation*. Chez l'auteur. 1983.

Pisani, Edgard. *Persiste et Signe*. Éditions Odile Jacob 1991.

Pryce-Jones, David. *Paris in the Third Reich*. Collins 1981.

Pyle, Ernie. *Ernie's War*. Random House 1986.

Ragueneau, Philippe & Eddy Florentin. *Paris Libéré. Ils étaient là!* France Empire 2011.

Repiton-Preneuf, Paul. *2e DB—La Campagne de France*. Imprimerie Nationale 1994.

Schramm, Wilhelm von. *Conspiracy among Generals*. Allen and Unwin 1956.

Smith, Colin. *Fighting Vichy—England's Last War with France*. Weidenfeld and Nicolson 2010.

Souhami, Diana. *Gertrude and Alice*. Harper Collins 1991.

Spears, General Sir Edward. *Assignment to Catastrophe*. 1954.

Taittinger, Pierre. *... et Paris ne fut pas detruit*. Nouvelles Éditions Latines 1956.

Thomas, Jean-Marie. *Un Marin dans La 2e DB*. Éditon Muller 2000.

Thurman, Judith. *Secrets of the Flesh—A Life of Colette*. Bloomsbury 1999.

Tillon, Charles. *FTP*. Julliard 1962.

Tobin, James. *Ernie Pyle's War*. Free Press 1997.

Todd, Olivier. *Malraux*. Knopf 2005.

Valland, Rose. *Les Carnets de Rose Valland*. Fage Éditons 2011.

Vézinet, General Adolphe. *Le général Leclerc*. Éditions France Empire 1997.

Vézy, Édith. *"Gargamelle", mon ambulance guerrière 2è DB*. L'Harmattan 1994.

Vigneras, Marcel. *Rearming the French*. Office of the Chief of Military History, Department of the Army, Washington 1957.

Vinatier, Jean. *Le Cardinal Suhard*. Le Centurion 1983.

Weber, Eugen. *Action Française*. Stanford UP 1962.

Webster, Paul. *Pétain's Crime*. Macmillan 1990.

Whitcombe, Elizabeth. *Never a Dull Moment*. Ashmole Books 1994.

Williams, Charles. *Pétain*. Little Brown 2005.

Index